Making the Modern American Fiscal State

Law, Politics, and the Rise of Progressive Taxation, 1877–1929

At the turn of the twentieth century, the U.S. system of public finance underwent a dramatic transformation. The late nineteenth-century regime of indirect, hidden, partisan, and regressive taxes was eclipsed in the early twentieth century by a direct, transparent, professionally administered, and progressive tax system. This book uncovers the contested roots and paradoxical consequences of this fundamental shift in American tax law and policy. It argues that the move toward a regime of direct and graduated taxation marked the emergence of a new fiscal polity – a new form of statecraft that was guided not simply by the functional need for greater revenue but by broader social concerns about economic justice, civic identity, bureaucratic capacity, and public power. Between the end of Reconstruction and the onset of the Great Depression, the intellectual, legal, and administrative foundations of the modern fiscal state first took shape. This book explains how and why this new fiscal polity came to be.

Ajay K. Mehrotra teaches law and history at the Maurer School of Law at Indiana University, Bloomington. He is co-editor of *The New Fiscal Sociology: Comparative and Historical Approaches to Taxation* (Cambridge, 2009). Research for this book was supported by the American Academy of Arts & Sciences, the National Endowment for the Humanities, and the William Nelson Cromwell Foundation.

Cambridge Historical Studies in American Law and Society

Series Editor

Christopher Tomlins, *University of California, Irvine*

Making the Modern American Fiscal State

Law, Politics, and the Rise of Progressive Taxation, 1877–1929

AJAY K. MEHROTRA
Indiana University, Bloomington

CAMBRIDGE
UNIVERSITY PRESS

CAMBRIDGE
UNIVERSITY PRESS

University Printing House, Cambridge CB2 8BS, United Kingdom

One Liberty Plaza, 20th Floor, New York, NY 10006, USA

477 Williamstown Road, Port Melbourne, VIC 3207, Australia

314-321, 3rd Floor, Plot 3, Splendor Forum, Jasola District Centre, New Delhi - 110025, India

79 Anson Road, #06-04/06, Singapore 079906

Cambridge University Press is part of the University of Cambridge.

It furthers the University's mission by disseminating knowledge in the pursuit of education, learning and research at the highest international levels of excellence.

www.cambridge.org
Information on this title: www.cambridge.org/9781107043923

First published 2013
First paperback edition 2014

A catalogue record for this publication is available from the British Library

Library of Congress Cataloging in Publication data
Mehrotra, Ajay K., 1969–
Making the modern American fiscal state : law, politics, and the rise of progressive taxation, 1877–1929 / Ajay K. Mehrotra, Indiana University.
pages cm
Includes index.
ISBN 978-1-107-04392-3 (hard covers : alk. paper)
1. Taxation – United States – History. 2. Fiscal policy – United States – History. 3. Taxation – Law and legislation – United States – History. I. Title.
HJ2373.M44 2014
336.200973–dc23 2013013590

ISBN 978-1-107-04392-3 Hardback
ISBN 978-1-107-61973-9 Paperback

For my parents, Neena and Vishnu

Contents

Tables, Charts, and Illustrations

Tables

Charts

Illustrations

Acknowledgments

It is only fitting that a book about the importance of social obligations and collective responsibilities – as embodied in changing conceptions of taxation – should begin by acknowledging the many people and institutions that helped make this book possible. This book began, more years ago than I care to recall, as a doctoral thesis in the history department at the University of Chicago. There a committee of dedicated historians consisting of Bill Novak, Kathy Conzen, and Amy Stanley helped guide my initial interests in taxation and American state building. At U of C, I also benefited from an interdisciplinary intellectual environment developed by scholars such as Andy Abbott, David Galenson, and Gary Herrigel, and sustained by fellow graduate students Amy Amoon, Doug Bradburn, Cathleen Cahill, Joanna Grisinger, Scott Lien, Matt Lindsay, Rebecca Mergenthal, Kim Reilly, Andrew Sandoval-Strausz, Tracy Steffes, and Mark Wilson.

Before graduate school, my interests in taxation and legal history began at the Georgetown University Law Center. There, Dan Halperin first demonstrated to me how tax law and policy affected nearly every aspect of daily life. Indeed, my interest in taxation can be traced back to the many lessons I learned working with Dan. Similarly, Dan Ernst, Mark Tushnet, and Norman Birnbaum cultivated my interests in American legal history and encouraged me to pursue that interest in graduate school. Dan Ernst in particular has been instrumental in shaping this book and my development as a scholar and teacher.

The process of transforming the dissertation into this book took place at Indiana University, Bloomington. At IU, I have been fortunate to have a generous and thoughtful group of colleagues – at the Maurer School of Law and elsewhere – who have encouraged, critiqued, and supported my scholarship. Many of these colleagues read early draft portions of this book, often multiple times, and provided me with outstanding comments: thanks to Jeannine Bell, Dan Conkle, Ken Dau-Schmidt, Charlie Geyh,

Alex Lichtenstein, Leandra Lederman, Mike McGerr, John Mikesell, Carl Weinberg, Susan and David Williams, Elisabeth Zoller, and especially Mike Grossberg and Bill Popkin who have been consistent and generous mentors throughout my career. The students in my legal history seminar and my many research assistants over the years read and discussed a great deal about the rise of the American fiscal state. I am indebted to many of these students, particularly Charles Persons, Collin McCready, James Motter, Ryan Guillory, Joel Koerner, Dustin Plummer, Lisa Fahey, Ken Burleson, Charles Gray, Scott Ritter, and especially Megan McMahon who more than any other research assistant helped see this book to completion. Deans Lauren Robel and Hannah Buxbaum provided a valuable sabbatical and summer funding to complete this project. The staff and librarians at the law library, especially Keith Buckley, Jennifer Bryan Morgan, and Rebecca Bertoloni-Meli, provided critical research assistance. And my friends and colleagues Luis Fuentes-Rohwer, Jay Krishnan, Ethan Michelson, Christy Ochoa, and Tim Waters have read and commented on more of my scholarship than they care to admit, and in the process they've reminded me of the true meaning of a scholarly community of friends.

Many other scholars and friends also took on the social obligation to review and provide comments on various portions of this book and in many cases the entire manuscript. I am grateful to Mark Aldrich, Reuven Avi-Yonah, Steve Bank, Gerry Berk, Michael Bernstein, Cheryl Block, Dorothy Brown, Richard Bensel, Andrea Campbell, Chris Capazolla, Lawrence Friedman, David Galenson, Dan Halperin, Richard John, Marianne Johnson, Robert Johnston, Carolyn Jones, Marjorie Kornhauser, Mark Leff, Shu-Yi Oei, Julia Ott, Sheldon Pollack, Gautham Rao, Adam Rosenzweig, Bruce Schulman, Steve Sheffrin, David Tannenhaus, Jon Teaford, Mark Tushnet, Dennis Ventry, Jr., Michael Willrich, Vicky Woeste, and Julian Zelizer. A special group of friends and colleagues read the entire manuscript, provided trenchant comments, and have been discussing our mutual interest in fiscal history for many years: I am deeply indebted for all that I have learned from Elliot Brownlee, Robin Einhorn, Isaac Martin, Monica Prasad, and Joe Thorndike.

Numerous institutions and the individuals associated with them have also assisted me with this project. Generous funding support from the William Nelson Cromwell Foundation, the National Endowment for the Humanities, and the American Academy of Arts & Sciences helped launch the writing of this book. In fact, the first draft of the book began when I was a Visiting Scholar at the American Academy. There Leslie Berlowitz and Patricia Spacks created a welcoming environment for junior scholars, and an energetic group of fellow visiting scholars consisting of Victoria Cain, Taylor Fravel, Tony Mora, Bethany Moreton, Laura Scales, and Anne Stiles made the year in Cambridge productive and enjoyable.

After a brief hiatus to work on other research, I was able to return to this project during a sabbatical semester at the IU Institute for Advanced Study, where John Bodnar and Ivona Hedin provided me with the space and time to re-engage with the manuscript. During that time and afterwards, I had the opportunity to present portions of the book at the annual meetings of the Law & Society Association, the Social Science History Association, the Midwest Political Science Association, and the American Society for Legal History, as well as at workshops at Emory University, Washington University in St. Louis, Tulane University, and the IU Ostrom Workshop in Political Theory and Policy Analysis. I am grateful for the comments I received at these venues. All of the above individuals helped me clarify my arguments and avoid mistakes. Any remaining errors are, of course, my own.

Much of the research contained in this book would not have been possible without the assistance of librarians, archivists, and staff at numerous libraries. Among the many libraries and archives that I consulted, I am especially thankful for the assistance I received at the Library of Congress, the National Archives and Record Administration (both in Washington, D.C., and in College Park, Md.), Columbia University's Butler Library, the University of Michigan's Bentley Library, the University of Chicago's Regenstein Library, the Harvard University Libraries, the Hebert Hoover Presidential Library, the Newberry Library, the Wisconsin State Historical Society, and the Yale University Libraries.

Back when this book was merely an idea, Chris Tomlins believed in this project and its author. His patience and assistance as an editor, mentor, and friend have been invaluable. The two anonymous referees also provided useful guidance. One of them (Brian Balogh) disclosed his identity and generously provided continued assistance. Indeed, Brian, like Chris, has been molding my research and scholarship from the start of my career. I am deeply indebted to both of them. Debbie Gershenowitz and her colleagues at Cambridge University Press have skillfully managed the production process. Debbie inherited this project at a late date, but her support has been unwavering.

Certain portions of this book were previously published in journals. Parts of Chapter 1 appeared as "'More Mighty than the Waves of the Sea': Toilers, Tariffs, and the Income Tax Movement, 1880–1913," *Labor*

History 45:2 (May 2004), 165–98. Portions of Chapter 4 appeared as "Forging Fiscal Reform: Constitutional Change, Public Policy, and the Creation of Administrative Capacity in Wisconsin, 1880–1920," *Journal of Policy History* 20:1 (Winter 2008), 94–112. And an extended version of Chapter 6 appeared as "Lawyers, Guns & Public Monies: The U.S. Treasury, World War One, and the Administration of the Modern Fiscal State," *Law & History Review* 28:1 (February 2010), 173–225. I thank these journals for allowing me to reprint portions of my work.

My most significant gratitude is to my family. My parents, Neena and Vishnu, to whom this book is dedicated, have always supported my dreams and ambitions, even when they didn't always agree with them. My uncle Biren has always been among the first to ask about and spur my writing, as he has shared his own work with me. My brother Amit and his wife Parul have welcomed me on many a research trip to New York and have continued to encourage my research and writing. And most important of all, my wife Yamini and our two boys, Nikesh and Siddhartha, have given me the emotional sustenance to complete this project. Nik and Sid have literally grown up with this book, and together with Yamini they've reminded me of the collective obligations and responsibilities worth having in life.

Introduction

"The taxation system is unjust in the United States," New York City tailor Conrad Carl boldly informed national lawmakers in the summer of 1883. "It is only indirect taxes, which fall back upon the workingman.... He is the last one that they can fall back upon, and they get the taxes out of him. It is only the workingman that is the taxpayer, in my opinion, in the United States." Testifying before the U.S. Senate Committee investigating the relations between labor and capital, Carl described how the existing system of import duties and excise taxes exacerbated the already dismal daily living conditions of ordinary American workers. He explained how these indirect taxes imposed a greater financial burden on the poor than on the rich, taking more from those who had less.[1]

A tailor for nearly thirty years, Carl had witnessed firsthand how a new industrial and technological revolution (exhibited in his case with the advent of the sewing machine) had radically transformed the production process and lowered wages. He described how his meager earnings were often not enough to provide for his family, how the grueling intensity of the work day "from sunrise to sunset" left him "no time to eat dinner," how workers like him lived with their families in the squalor of "a tenement house four or five stories high," how they were able to save close to nothing from their paltry wages, and how he and other tailors could only afford "the clothing that they make – the cheapest of it."[2]

For the lawmakers gathered in New York during those late summer inquiries, Carl's testimony corroborated what they had being hearing

[1] "Testimony of Conrad Carl, New York, August 20, 1883" in U.S. Senate Committee on Education and Labor, *Report of the Committee of the Senate upon the Relations Between Labor and Capital, Vol. I* (Washington, D.C.: Government Printing Office, 1885), 413–21.

[2] Ibid., 419, 413–16.

across the country from other ordinary workers, union leaders, and social reformers. The ravages of modern urban-industrial life were taking a devastating toll on nearly all parts of American society. Although the recent upturn in the economy had quelled an earlier wave of violent and bitter industrial conflicts, the "labor question" remained on the minds of most Americans. Charged with finding ways to improve social relations between labor and capital, the Senate committee asked Carl what Congress might do to help American workers. "So long as legislation is unjust to the poor," he replied, "to tax the poor who have nothing but their daily earnings, to tax them by indirect taxes, there is no way to better the condition of the workingman."[3]

The injustice of the existing fiscal system was not limited, however, to the economic implications. Carl and others also stressed how the party politics of taxation permitted wealthy citizens to shirk their social and civic responsibilities. Carl referred obliquely to how indirect taxes in the form of import duties protected certain domestic industries from foreign competition. "The rich," he claimed, "receive donations from the State by legislation." These partisan "donations," Carl implied, were purchased by "the millionaire [who] corrupts the courts and legislation." Wealthy Americans routinely turned to the rule of law to protect their private interests, but they had little concern for the public good. As a result, they had no sense of the ethical obligation to support the commonweal. The millionaire "does not care for the law or the Constitution. He has neither a duty nor a love for the country," Carl concluded. "No wonder the rich become proud and brutal and say 'Damn the public.'"[4]

Some legislators seemed to absorb Carl's central message that "labor is the pack-horse that carries all the burden." But the moderate tone of their laconic questions suggested they were incapable – or perhaps unwilling – to change industrial conditions. Carl warned the senators that if they ignored the existing fiscal imbalances, it would be at the nation's peril. "The indirect taxes are a fraud and a crime against the workingmen, and society will have its punishment sooner or later for it," Carl admonished his audience. "When there lies so great a wrong on the bottom of society as to tax the laboring man by indirect taxes, there grows wrong after

[3] Ibid., 419. On the origins of the U.S. Senate Committee investigating industrial relations at this time, see Melvyn Dubofsky, *The State & Labor in Modern America* (Chapel Hill: University of North Carolina Press, 1994), 12–13.

[4] "Testimony of Conrad Carl," 419.

wrong, and it will grow as high as Babylon's tower if we do not go against it."[5]

The national tax system that Carl and others railed against consisted mainly of customs duties and excise taxes on alcohol and tobacco – the two dominant sources of late-nineteenth-century federal revenue. Economic experts at the time were uncertain who ultimately paid these indirect taxes, but popular perception held that ordinary consumers generally bore the brunt of these levies. The import duties that made up the tariff were identified, in particular, as unduly increasing the cost of living, or what contemporaries referred to as the "necessaries of daily life." Merchants who sold imported finished goods directly to consumers, it was believed, simply tacked the costs of customs duties on to their final prices. Meanwhile, manufacturers who used raw materials from the duty list tabulated the tariff as an additional cost of production. Regardless of what the experts might have thought, most late-nineteenth-century Americans believed that the tariff insidiously fell upon end users, that it was a hidden levy passed along to the quotidian consumers of most ordinary products.[6]

The breadth of goods that fell under the late-nineteenth-century tariff's duty list was indeed astonishing. The Tariff Act of 1883, for instance,

[5] Ibid. For more on working-class struggles in the late nineteenth century, see Rosanne Currarino, *The Labor Question in America: Economic Democracy in the Gilded Age* (Urbana: University of Illinois Press, 2011); David Montgomery, *Citizen Worker: The Experience of Workers in the United States with Democracy and the Free Market in the Nineteenth Century* (New York: Cambridge University Press, 1995).

[6] Economic and political historians have aptly demonstrated how the tariff operated to protect selected industries and how it at times raised the cost of living. Paul Wolman, *Most Favored Nation: The Republican Revisionists and U.S. Tariff Policy, 1897–1912* (Chapel Hill: University of North Carolina Press, 1992); Joanne Reitano, *The Tariff Question in the Gilded Age: The Great Debate of 1888* (University Park: Pennsylvania State University Press, 1994); John Mark Hansen, "Taxation and the Political Economy of the Tariff," *International Organization* 44:4 (autumn 1990), 527–51; Mark Bils, "Tariff Protection and Production in the Early U.S. Cotton Textile Industry," *Journal of Economic History* 44:4 (December 1984), 1033–45; Brad J. DeLong, "Trade Policy and America's Standard of Living: An Historical Perspective," in *Imports, Exports, and the American Worker*, ed. Susan Collins (Washington, D.C.: Brookings Institution, 1998); Douglas A. Irwin, "Tariff Incidence in America's Gilded Age," *Journal of Economic History* 67:3 (September 2007), 582–607; Mark Aldrich, "Tariffs and Trusts, Profiteers and Middlemen: Popular Explanations for the High Cost of Living, 1897–1920," *History of Political Economy* (forthcoming). On how the tariff was one of the many hidden powers of the national government during this period, see Brian Balogh, *A Government Out of Sight: The Mystery of National Authority in Nineteenth-Century America* (New York: Cambridge University Press, 2009), 129–32.

placed a levy on eleven different categories of products, including "Chemicals," "Earthenware and Glassware," "Metals," "Wood and Wooden Wares," "Sugar," "Cotton and Cotton Goods," "Hemp, Jute, and Flax Goods," "Wool and Woolens," "Silk and Silk Goods," "Books and Papers," and the catch-all category of "Sundries." The schedule for "Provisions" listed in the 1883 law alone consisted of such everyday necessities as "Beef and pork; Hams and bacon; Cheese; Butter; and substitutes thereof; Lard; Wheat; Rye and barley; Oats; Corn-meal; Oat-meal; Rye-flour; Potato or corn starch; Potatoes; Rice; Hay; Honey; Hops; Milk; Salmon and other fish; Pickles and sources, of all kinds; Vegetables; Vinegar; Chocolate; Dates, plums and prunes; Oranges; Lemons; Raisins," and a large assortment of nuts. Though the duty charges, or rates, were relatively low, ranging from "one cent per pound of beef and pork" to "four cents per pound of cheese," they had a significant impact on the daily cost of living.[7]

While the national tax system may have adversely affected most ordinary Americans as consumers, the state and local property tax regime took a similar toll on producers such as rural farmers and other small property holders. The general property tax that dominated nineteenth-century subnational government revenues was also a highly politicized and polarizing levy. Like the tariff, it too undermined public faith in the rule of law and the promise of social solidarity. Aimed, in theory, at taxing all property uniformly, the general property tax was extremely arbitrary in practice. Not only were wealthy property holders able to conceal and evade property tax liabilities, politically appointed or locally elected tax officials often capriciously determined property tax assessments. Illinois, for example, formally levied a general property tax in 1883 on "all real and personal property in the state," which specifically included "the value of agricultural tools, implements, and machinery." Although the law also required that all "personal property" including "all moneys, credits, bonds or stocks and other investments" be assessed at "fair cash value," such intangible assets frequently escaped assessment either because taxpayers failed to disclose their holdings or because assessors frequently looked the other way.[8]

[7] Schedules A–N, Section 2502, Chapter 121, Tariff Act of March 3, 1883, *The Statutes at Large of the United States of America, Vol. XXII* (Washington, D.C.: Government Printing Office, 1883).

[8] *Revised Statutes of the State of Illinois*, Chapter 120, Sections 1, 3, 25 (Chicago: Chicago Legal News Co., 1883); Clifton K. Yearley, *The Money Machines: The Breakdown and Reform of Party Finance in the North, 1860–1920* (Albany: State University of

The practical defects of the property tax had serious consequences. Farm families such as the Arnos of Oshkosh, Wisconsin, experienced first-hand how the haphazard and politically driven assessment process affected their everyday lives. As Mary Arno recounted to her mother, Augusta Hurd, in 1887, the Arnos barely had enough money from their farm earnings to pay their periodic property tax payments. Like other neighbors, they had no choice but to sell portions of their small holdings to fulfill their tax obligations. By contrast, Augusta Hurd admitted to her daughter that she had not been paying property taxes on her small rental properties because her name had somehow "slipped off" the Oshkosh assessment rolls. Similar tales throughout the country illustrated the pernicious implications of the prevailing tax system.[9]

Even during leisure activities, ordinary Americans were confronted by the taxing powers of government. When machinists or farmers sought to relax with their favorite drink or by lighting a pipe after a long day of work, they were reminded yet again of their financial obligations to the state. The tobacco they smoked, the alcohol they consumed, and even the playing cards that brought fleeting moments of enjoyment to an otherwise dreary day of toil were all subject to national taxation.[10]

By contrast, more affluent members of American society had a dramatically different experience with the existing tax system. As consumers and property holders, they too were subject to the economic obligations presented by the tariff, excise taxes, and the property tax. But because of their enhanced wealth and earning power, well-to-do Americans did not feel the same pinch of daily taxation. Unlike Carl and the Arnos, the wealthy could easily afford the indirect taxes on everyday consumption items and the direct tax on property, and still have plenty of resources available for luxury goods and contributions to savings and investments. For the truly wealthy, those who were prospering enormously from the late-nineteenth-century industrial and technological revolution, taxation was a negligible nuisance. The Rockefellers and Vanderbilts barely noticed

New York Press, 1970); Morton Keller, *Affairs of State: Public Life in Nineteenth Century America* (Cambridge, Mass.: Harvard University Press, 1977), 322–4.

9 Mary Arno to Augusta Hurd, January 3, 1887; May 14, 1894, Hurd-Arno Papers, Folder No. 21, Box 1, American Manuscript Collections, Newberry Library, Chicago, IL. See also Helen Hazen Cooperman, ed., *The Letters of Ann Augusta Jaquins Hurd and Mary Olivia Hurd Arno, 1858–1897* (Chicago: H. H. Cooperman, 1988).

10 Revenue Act of 1894, 28 Stat. 509, 522 (Schedule F, Tobacco and Manufactures of), 525–6 (Schedule H, Spirits, Wines and Other Beverages), 533 (Playing Cards).

their tax burdens, though they did everything they could to limit their national as well as state and local tax liabilities.[11]

Indeed, in some cases, wealthy Americans were practically immune to certain taxes. Because the rich held much of their wealth at the turn of the century not only in real property but also in intangible, personal property – namely, bonds, stocks, and other financial assets – they benefited from the ineffective administration of state and local property taxes. They paid few or no taxes on their concealed personal property and thus frequently dismissed public debates about fiscal problems. At the municipal level, moreover, the prevalent use of "special assessments" meant that private citizens could pay directly for "public" improvements that benefited their individual property more than the community at large.[12] With little at stake in how the public sector generated its revenue, wealthy citizens thus became increasingly disconnected from the broader political and social community of which they were ostensibly a part. They were fast becoming part of what contemporary social theorists referred to as a new "leisure class" that privileged private ambitions and consumption over public responsibilities and obligations.[13]

Within five decades, the American fiscal landscape was radically transformed. By the end of the 1920s, the late-nineteenth-century national regime of indirect, hidden, disaggregated, and partisan import duties and regressive excise taxes was eclipsed by a direct, transparent, centralized, and professionally administered, graduated tax system that dramatically altered fiscal burdens and profoundly revolutionized federal government finances. Although the 1913 federal income tax, which initiated the permanent national taxation of incomes, had high exemption levels and relatively modest rates, it soon surpassed all other levies as the main source

[11] "New York City The Paradise of Rich Men; Millions Escape Taxation at Home," *New York Herald*, February 5, 1899, 21; Ron Chernow, *Titan: The Life of John D. Rockefeller, Sr.* (New York: Random House, 2004), 107–8, 566–7; Michael McGerr, *"The Public Be Damned": The Kingdom and the Dream of the Vanderbilts*, Ch. 16 (forthcoming). On the many ways in which wealthy Americans evaded import duties, see Andrew Wender Cohen, "Smuggling, Globalization, and America's Outward State, 1870–1909," *Journal of American History* 97:2 (2010), 371–98.

[12] Robin L. Einhorn, *Property Rules: Political Economy in Chicago, 1833–1872* (Chicago: University of Chicago Press, 1991), 16–17; Stephen Diamond, "The Death and Transfiguration of Benefit Taxation: Special Assessments in Nineteenth-Century America," *Journal of Legal Studies* 12 (1983), 201–40.

[13] Thorstein Veblen, *The Theory of the Leisure Class* (New York: Macmillan Co., 1899); Richard T. Ely, *Taxation in American States and Cities* (New York: Thomas Y. Crowell & Co. Publishers, 1888), 288.

TABLE I.1. *Federal Government Receipts by Source, 1880–1930, as Percentage of Total*

	1880	1890	1900	1910	1917	1920	1930
Customs Duties	56%	57%	41%	49%	21%	5%	14%
Alcohol and Tobacco Excise Taxes	34%	35%	43%	39%	35%	7%	11%
Income Taxes	–	–	–	–	33%	66%	59%
Other*	10%	8%	16%	12%	11%	22%	16%
Total	100%	100%	100%	100%	100%	100%	100%

* Includes receipts from sales of public lands, estate and gifts taxes, stamp taxes, and "manufactures and products taxes."

Sources: Historical Statistics of the United States, Millennial Edition, ed. Susan B. Carter et al. (New York: Cambridge University Press, 2006), Table Ea588–593; *Statistical Appendix to Annual Report of the Secretary of the Treasury on the State of the Finances for the Fiscal Year Ended June 30, 1971* (Washington, D.C.: Government Printing Office, 1971), 12.

of national receipts.[14] Whereas customs duties and excise taxes together raised roughly 90 percent of federal receipts in 1880, by 1930 they generated only a quarter of total national revenue. Over the same period, taxes on individual and corporate income skyrocketed from a nonexistent source to nearly 60 percent of total federal government receipts (see Table I.1).[15]

A similar, albeit much less pronounced, shift occurred at the state and local level. There the taxation of incomes, profits, and inheritances came to challenge the dominant reliance on antiquated general property taxes. These new forms of direct and progressive taxation did not have the same overwhelming and enduring impact at the subnational level as they did at the federal. Still, these levies created an opening for state and local governments to consider other forms of taxation besides the general

[14] The 1913 income tax levied a "normal" tax of 1 percent on incomes above $3,000 for single persons ($4,000 for married couples) and had a maximum "surtax" rate of 6 percent for incomes over $5,000. Pub. L. No. 63, Statute I – 1913, Chapter 16, Sections II-A, II-C, *Statutes at Large of the United States of America from March 1911 to March 1913*, Vol. XXXVIII, Part 1 (Washington, D.C.: Government Printing Office, 1913). With these high exemption levels, the income tax in its early years touched roughly 2 percent of American households. John F. Witte, *The Politics and Development of the Federal Income Tax* (Madison: University of Wisconsin Press, 1985), 78; W. Elliot Brownlee, *Federal Taxation in America: A Short History*, 2nd ed. (New York: Cambridge University Press, 2004), 57.

[15] Susan B. Carter et al., eds., *Historical Statistics of the United States: Millennial Edition* (New York: Cambridge University Press, 2006), Table Ea588–593.

property tax. As Northern industrial states began to experiment with both new levies and innovative forms of tax administration, others took notice. Soon, these fiscal innovations spread to neighboring commonwealths and gradually influenced the national tax reform movement.

Ultimately, the turn of the century fiscal revolution was a watershed in the development of modern American public finance. The move from taxing goods toward taxing people and processes – through levies on individual incomes, business profits, and intergenerational wealth transfers – underscored the radical nature of this sea change. Despite modest beginnings, the early-twentieth-century tax laws were, as legal historian Lawrence Friedman has observed, "the opening wedge for a major transformation in American society."[16] In short, the late-nineteenth-century tax structure, which inordinately burdened everyday Americans while only marginally affecting the wealthy, was dramatically remade at the turn of the twentieth century.

The move toward a national regime of direct and progressive taxation marked the emergence of a new fiscal polity – a new form of statecraft that was guided not simply by the functional need for greater revenue but by broader social concerns about economic justice, civic identity, administrative capacity, and public power. More specifically, this new fiscal state was concerned about reallocating tax burdens across both class and geographical region, promoting a new social democratic sense of citizenship, creating a more centralized and professionally administered structure of fiscal governance, and laying the groundwork for more robust forms of government action. These objectives variously animated the different reform groups that sought to build the modern American fiscal state. Some of these aims would not be fully realized, if at all, until much later. Nonetheless, between the end of Reconstruction and the onset of the Great Depression, the central foundations of the modern American fiscal state first took shape. The aim of this book is to uncover the contested

[16] Lawrence Friedman, *History of American Law*, 3rd ed. (New York: Simon & Schuster, 2005), 430. Other economic and legal historians have recognized the significance of taxation to American state-society relations. Harry Scheiber, for instance, has included taxation, along with eminent domain and the police power, as part of the state's "trinity of powers." Scheiber, "The Road to Munn: Eminent Domain and the Concept of Public Purpose in the State Courts" *Perspectives in American History* V (1971), 329–402, 400. Likewise, J. Willard Hurst noted that the government's "powers to tax and to spend" and to control public lands were the "two principal means to affect the directions of domestic investment" and hence create a favorable environment for the release of energy. Hurst, *Law and the Conditions of Freedom in the Nineteenth-Century United States* (Madison: University of Wisconsin Press, 1956), 61–2.

roots and paradoxical consequences of this fundamental transformation in tax law and policy and to explain how and why this new fiscal polity came to be.

This great transformation in American public finance was led by a conceptual revolution. A new generation of professionally trained intellectuals, drawing on the raw social experiences of the modern industrial age and responding to the massive material inequalities of the time, changed the way that educated Americans and policymakers thought about and imagined the financial basis of government programs.[17] At the heart of this seismic shift was the idea that citizens owed a debt to society in relation to their "ability to pay." This curt yet crucial phrase encapsulated the idea that individuals who had greater economic power also had a greater social obligation to contribute to the public good – to contribute not only proportionally more but progressively more. Influential thinkers and political leaders used the keywords "ability to pay" as a cognitive map, as a type of mental frame, to illustrate the widening circle of modern associational duties and social responsibilities.

They also used "ability to pay" and similar keywords as political tools to galvanize support for the progressive tax reform movement during critical periods of crisis. "Each word has its practical cash value," pragmatist philosopher William James noted. We do things with words. And what these progressive activists sought to do with their words, as well as their actions, was to convince lawmakers, government administrators, and ordinary Americans that a new fiscal system based on the notion of taxing a citizen's "ability to pay" could transform American state and society. Ideas, in this sense, were critical weapons and blueprints for building powerful political coalitions.[18] Revenue reformers understood

[17] As Stephen Skowronek has observed, a new generation of intellectuals during this period became "America's state-building vanguard." Skowronek, *Building a New American State: The Expansion of National Administrative Capacities, 1877–1920* (New York: Cambridge University Press, 1982), 42–5. On the growing awareness of late nineteenth-century economic inequality, see James L. Huston, *Securing the Fruits of Labor: The American Concept of Wealth Distribution, 1765–1900* (Baton Rouge: Louisiana State University Press, 1998).

[18] Daniel T. Rodgers, *Contested Truths: Keywords in American Politics since Independence* (New York: Basic Books, 1987); William James, *Pragmatism: A New Name for Some Old Ways of Thinking* (1907). On the importance of economic ideas to institutional change, see Mark Blyth, *Great Transformations: Economic Ideas and Institutional Change in the Twentieth Century* (New York: Cambridge University Press, 2002); John L. Campbell, "Institutional Analysis and the Role of Ideas in Political Economy," *Theory and Society* 27 (1998), 377–409.

that "fairness" and "ability to pay" were protean concepts with multiple meanings. Their goal was to mold these words and ideas to energize a social and political movement that reflected the growing antagonism toward the prevailing fiscal order.[19]

These new notions of taxation were, of course, a product of their times. The reform-minded political economists who led the intellectual campaign for a new fiscal order harnessed increasing social frustrations to challenge the fundamental assumptions of an earlier age. Recognizing how the forces of modernity had recreated a more interdependent society, these thinkers stressed the need for greater cooperation and bureaucratic authority.[20] They sought to discredit the Victorian theories of atomistic individualism and laissez-faire political economy and constitutionalism that underpinned the existing late-nineteenth-century tax system. Chief among these outdated theories was the principle that an individual's economic obligations to the state were limited to the benefits that such individual received from the polity. Progressive tax experts targeted "benefits theory" as an obsolete principle of modern fiscal relations. They played a pivotal role in supplanting the prevailing "benefits theory" of taxation, and its attendant vision of the state as a passive protector of private property, with a more equitable principle of taxation based on one's "faculty" or "ability to pay" – a principle that promoted an active role for the positive state in the reallocation of fiscal burdens, the reconfiguration of civic identity, and the rise of administrative authority. For these reformers, the state was, as University of Wisconsin political economist and labor activist Richard T. Ely once noted, "an ethical agency whose positive aid is an indispensable condition of human progress."[21]

[19] The ability-to-pay rationale has been severely criticized by legal theorists and philosophers who have neglected to see how this principle operated historically as a political instrument rather than a coherent, air-tight political theory. For examples of some of the earliest critiques by legal scholars, see, e.g., Henry C. Simons, *Personal Income Taxation: The Definition of Income as a Problem of Fiscal Policy* (Chicago: University of Chicago Press, 1938); Louis Eisenstein, *The Ideologies of Taxation* (New York: Ronald Press, 1961); Walter J. Blum and Harry Kalven, *The Uneasy Case for Progressive Taxation* (Chicago: University of Chicago Press, 1963). For more recent critiques from philosophers, see Liam Murphy and Thomas Nagel, *The Myth of Ownership: Taxes and Justice* (New York: Oxford University Press, 2002).

[20] Thomas L. Haskell, *The Emergence of Professional Social Science: The American Social Science Association and the Nineteenth-Century Crisis of Authority* (Urbana: University of Illinois Press, 1977); Robert H. Wiebe, *The Search for Order, 1877–1920* (New York: Macmillan, 1966); Samuel P. Hays, *The Response to Industrialism, 1885–1914* (Chicago: University of Chicago Press, 1957).

[21] Richard T. Ely, "Report of the Organization of the American Economic Association," *Publications of the American Economic Association* 1 (1886), 6–7. American intellectual

A particular group of "new school" or "ethical" political economists proved to be the crucial hinge or connective tissue between the growing social hostility toward the old order and the rise of the new fiscal polity.[22] These young, German-trained, progressive public finance economists led the conceptual campaign for the graduated taxation of incomes, profits, and inheritances. As part of what legal historians have referred to as the "first great law & economics movement," academics such as Henry Carter Adams, Richard Ely, and especially Edwin R. A. Seligman not only trafficked in a new wave of transatlantic ideas about changing conceptions of the self, society, economy, and the state. They also made European ideas palatable for an American audience that was generally suspicious of foreign influences and entanglements. These progressive public finance experts soon became the visionaries or architects of the modern fiscal state.[23]

The emergence of this new fiscal polity had enormous implications for modern American economic, social, and political life. First, the new fiscal regime reallocated across both income classes and national regions the economic responsibility of financing the growing needs of a modern industrialized democracy. Second, this fiscal reordering redefined the social meaning of modern citizenship. Third, it facilitated the beginnings of a fundamental change in political arrangements and institutions. And, fourth, the new fiscal order helped underwrite the subsequent expansion of the American liberal state.

historians have identified the significance of progressive taxation to the general reform impulse of the time period. "The graduated income tax, based on the idea that everyone owes a debt to society proportional to his ability to pay," James T. Kloppenberg has written, "was perhaps the quintessential progressive reform." Kloppenberg, *Uncertain Victory: Social Democracy and Progressivism in European and American Thought, 1870–1920* (New York: Oxford University Press, 1986), 355.

22 Scholars have regularly referred to this new generation of thinkers as "new school" or "ethical" economists. Mary O. Furner, *Advocacy and Objectivity: A Crisis in the Professionalization of American Social Science, 1865–1905* (Lexington: University Press of Kentucky, 1975); Nancy Cohen, *The Reconstruction of American Liberalism, 1865–1914* (Chapel Hill: University of North Carolina Press, 2002); Bradley W. Bateman, "Make a Righteous Number: Social Surveys, the Men and Religion Forward Movement, and Quantification in American Economics," *History of Political Economy* 33 (2001), 57–85.

23 Herbert Hovenkamp, "The First Great Law and Economics Movement," *Stanford Law Review* 42:4 (1989), 993–1058; Barbara H. Fried, *The Progressive Assault on Laissez Faire: Robert Hale and the First Law and Economics Movement* (Cambridge, Mass.: Harvard University Press, 1998). As Hovenkamp has noted, the progressive political economists influenced American law because their "books on taxation read as much like legal treatises as economic texts – they seemed to the courts to be as much 'law' as 'economics.'" Hovenkamp, "The First Great Law and Economics Movement," 1008–9.

From the beginning, the late-nineteenth-century social movement for fundamental tax reform was driven by populist and progressive calls for a more egalitarian fiscal system. By replacing the national structure of regressive, hidden, disaggregated, and politicized consumption taxes with graduated, transparent, centralized, and professionally administered taxes, revenue reformers were seeking to force those segments of society that had the greatest taxpaying ability – namely, wealthy individuals and corporations in the Northeast – to share the burden of funding the demands of a modern, industrial state.[24] The goal was not to radically redistribute wealth, but rather to ensure that those who had the greatest taxpaying capacity were contributing their fair share.

Determining what constituted a "fair" share was, to be sure, problematic. Progressive reformers understood that "fairness" was a mutable idea, yet they hewed to their fundamental principle that the existing system of indirect and regressive taxation was inherently unfair. The intellectuals and political leaders who ultimately helped lead this tectonic turn in American public finance were thus animated by desires to address the fiscal injustices identified by Conrad Carl and other social activists. As Congressman Cordell Hull (D-Tenn.), one of the chief architects of the 1913 progressive income tax, explained: "I have no disposition to tax wealth unnecessarily or unjustly, but I do believe that the wealth of the country should bear its just share of the burden of taxation and that it should not be permitted to shirk that duty."[25]

Hull and other proponents of the progressive tax movement believed that with a fundamental restructuring of American public finance, citizens would begin to reimagine their civic duties and democratic obligations. In an age when the social dimensions of American democracy became paramount – when "the identification with the common lot," as the social reformer Jane Addams explained, was "the essential idea of democracy" – new forms of taxation based on rejuvenated egalitarian principles could recalibrate thinking about fiscal citizenship.[26] Belonging to a broader

[24] Charles Postel, *The Populist Vision* (New York: Oxford University Press, 2007); Elizabeth Sanders, *Roots of Reform: Farmers, Workers, and the American State, 1877–1917* (Chicago: University of Chicago Press, 1999); Michael Kazin, *The Populist Persuasion: An American History* (New York: Basic Books, 1995).

[25] *Congressional Record* 61st Cong., 1st sess. (1909), 44:536, 533.

[26] Jane Addams, *Democracy and Social Ethics* (New York: Macmillan Co., 1902), 11. For more on Addams and her theories of American social democracy, see Louise W. Knight, *Citizen: Jane Addams and the Struggle for Democracy* (Chicago: University of Chicago Press, 2005), Ch. 15. On the importance of associational sentiments to the age, see generally, Michael McGerr, *A Fierce Discontent: The Rise and Fall of the Progressive*

political and social community meant that taxes were no longer simply the price paid for government services and benefits. Instead, the new democratic meaning of civic identity was based on the idea that each citizen owed a debt to society in proportion to his or her "ability to pay." Tax reform, simply put, was used to reconfigure the relationship between citizens and the state. It was used to renegotiate a new social contract, to reinvigorate the "imagined community" of the modern American polity.[27]

As part of this reconstituted social contract, wealthy citizens would take on the social responsibility of doing their part to underwrite badly needed public goods and services. In the process, citizens as taxpayers would come to accept, and in many cases embrace, the growing powers of the modern state as it solved new problems, created the basis of economic development, and provided aid and assistance to the community in times of stress and crisis. They would also become more engaged with civic life and the operations of the polity. Solidarity, ethical duty, and political consciousness, in sum, would be embodied in the concept of direct and progressive taxation.

Within the formal realm of partisan politics, the changed conception of taxation also became part of the institutional means for the gradual demise of the late-nineteenth-century party system. While the tariff was among the central policy issues that defined the main cleavage between the two national parties in the late nineteenth century, the rise of direct and graduated taxation in the early twentieth century signaled the start of a more complex and sophisticated system of fiscal governance.[28] During the

Movement in America, 1870–1920 (New York: Free Press, 2003); Maureen A. Flanagan, *America Reformed: Progressives and Progressivisms, 1890s–1920s* (New York: Oxford University Press, 2007); Eldon J. Eisenach, *The Lost Promise of Progressivism* (Lawrence: University Press of Kansas, 1994). For a recent summary of the scholarship on this time period and the importance of democratic aspirations, see Robert D. Johnston, "The Possibilities of Politics: Democracy in America, 1877–1917," in *American History Now*, ed. Eric Foner and Lisa McGirr (Philadelphia: Temple University Press, 2011), 96–124.

27 Benedict Anderson, *Imagined Communities: Reflections on the Origins and Spread of Nationalism* (London: Verso Books, 1983). For a defense of the current U.S. income tax based on similar principles of fiscal citizenship, see Lawrence Zelenak, *Learning to Love Form 1040: Two Cheers for the Return-Based Mass Income Tax* (Chicago: University of Chicago Press, 2013).

28 On the importance of the tariff to the party period, see Richard L. McCormick, *Party Period and Public Policy: American Politics from the Age of Jackson to the Progressive Era* (New York: Oxford University Press, 1988); Richard Franklin Bensel, *The Political Economy of American Industrialization, 1877–1900* (New York: Cambridge University Press, 2000); John J. Coleman, *Party Decline in America: Policy, Politics, and the Fiscal State* (Princeton: Princeton University Press, 1996).

earlier party period, the tariff and excise taxes were determined mainly by legislative log-rolling, and the collection of import duties was conducted by custom houses, peopled by political appointees. In the modern era, the new taxes on individual incomes, business profits, and wealth transfers required more sophisticated and technical knowledge about the sources of income and the definition of the tax base, not to mention new regulations and rules governing the complex process of collection and remittance.

As such, new tax laws, policies, and regulations became the vanguard for the rise of the proto-administrative state. In the process of placing new ideas about taxation into action, powerful political leaders and entrepreneurial government bureaucrats helped create the administrative framework that would ensure the future vitality and durability of these new laws. If, as Max Weber noted, "a stable system of *taxation* is the precondition for the permanent existence of bureaucratic administration," American progressives understood that the converse was also true.[29] Effective administration was essential to the future of the new tax regime. As American politics became more fractured and pluralistic, as partisanship declined and the power of interest groups rose, the relative complexity of modern tax laws led the way in the development of a new regime of statecraft – one that was less beholden to political parties and more receptive to the bureaucratic operations of professional experts.[30]

Finally, and perhaps most importantly, the revenues generated by this new tax regime became the lifeblood of the burgeoning regulatory and administrative social-welfare state. In contrast to the traditional tariff regime, which was concerned mainly with protecting domestic industries rather than raising revenue, the new system of direct and progressive taxation generated significant public revenues. Over time, as this new tax system became the leading source of government receipts, it financed an

[29] Max Weber, "Bureaucracy" in *From Max Weber: Essays in Sociology*, ed. H. H. Gerth and C. Wright Mills (New York: Oxford University Press, 1958), 208 (emphasis in the original).

[30] Michael E. McGerr, *The Decline of Popular Politics: The American North, 1865–1928* (New York: Oxford University Press, 1988); Elisabeth S. Clemens, *The People's Lobby: Organizational Innovation and the Rise of Interest Group Politics in the United States, 1890–1925* (Chicago: University of Chicago Press, 1997). By focusing on the origins of administrative power, this study joins other recent socio-historical legal scholarship that seeks to trace the early roots of the modern American administrative state. See, e.g., Jerry L. Mashaw, *Creating the Administrative Constitution: The Lost One Hundred Years of American Administrative Law* (New Haven: Yale University Press, 2012); Nicholas Parrillo, *Against the Profit Motive: The Salary Revolution in American Government, 1780–1940* (New Haven: Yale University Press, 2013).

array of public goods and services associated with a new vision of American liberalism – a vision that stressed what contemporaries like philosopher John Dewey referred to as the creation of a "Great Community."[31] Indeed, by the end of the 1920s, the intellectual, legal, and administrative framework of the modern fiscal polity was firmly set in place.[32]

Gradually, the new national tax regime prospered and fueled the rise of the American positive state, especially during the Second World War when the income tax became institutionalized as a socially and culturally legitimate mass tax.[33] In fact, by the end of the twentieth century, the progressive income tax had become the central foundation of modern American public finance, generating in fiscal year 2000 nearly 60 percent of federal receipts and roughly 40 percent of average state government revenue.[34] A historical analysis of the broad social forces, innovative ideas, political conditions, and contingent historical events that precipitated this critical and consequential turn in U.S. tax policy is, therefore, crucial in understanding the subsequent development of twentieth-century American liberalism.

The new fiscal regime, to be sure, did not completely vanquish or displace all aspects of the earlier tax system. Nor was it simply a linear or uncontested advance in American institutional development free of latent tensions and paradoxes. The historical process of political change and regime building frequently comes with deep ironies and unintended consequences. During critical periods of American political development,

[31] John Dewey, *The Public and Its Problems* (New York: Henry Holt & Co., 1927), 144; Josiah Royce, *The Hope of the Great Community* (New York: Macmillan Co., 1916).

[32] Throughout the 1920s, individual and corporate income tax revenues accounted for roughly 60 percent of total federal receipts. Carter, *Historical Statistics*, Table Ea588–593.

[33] Bartholomew H. Sparrow, *From the Outside In: World War II and the American State* (Princeton: Princeton University Press, 1996); Carolyn C. Jones, "Class Tax to Mass Tax: The Rise of Propaganda in the Expansion of the Income Tax during World War II," *Buffalo Law Review* 37:3 (1989), 685–737; James T. Sparrow, *Warfare State: World War II Americans and the Age of Big Government* (New York: Oxford University Press, 2011), 122–33.

[34] *Statistical Abstract of the United States: 2002* (Washington, D.C.: Government Printing Office, 2001), Table No. 464, 315. The recent economic downturn has diminished income tax revenues, which in 2010 accounted for roughly 50 percent of total federal receipts. *Statistical Abstract of the United States: 2012* (Washington, D.C.: Government Printing Office, 2012) Even so, these figures support George Mowry's early claims that "the modern democratic social service state probably rests more upon the income tax than upon any other single legislative act." Mowry, *The Era of Theodore Roosevelt and the Birth of Modern America, 1900–1912* (New York: Harper, 1958), 263.

new intellectual and institutional structures are regularly layered on top of previous ones, in an entangled, incongruous, and at times even antagonistic relationship.[35] In the process, the long-term implications of immediate ideas and actions are often beyond the view of historical actors. If ideas, as Max Weber suggested, can act like "switchmen" altering the course of history, it is often unclear what the final station along the material tracks of history will ultimately be.[36]

The reform-minded political economists who led the conceptual revolution in American public finance could not foresee the far-reaching and unintended consequences of their ideas and actions. In the process of attacking the benefits theory and exalting the ability-to-pay rationale, these influential thinkers severed the theoretical link between state spending and revenue generation. Whereas the benefits theory held that taxes were the price paid for public goods and services, the ability to pay rationale focused exclusively on the social and ethical obligations of paying taxes, with little regard for the spending side of the budget.[37]

Progressive social scientists, to be sure, were concerned about efficient government spending, about rationalizing the budgetary process.[38] But when it came to imagining how the new fiscal polity could address the social dislocations of modern industrial capitalism, they seemed to focus narrowly on revenue extraction – on who paid what in taxes. They seemed to overlook how progressive public spending could counter the regressive incidence of certain taxes. Responding to the historical conditions they inherited, particularly the growing concentrations of wealth and the increasing social antagonism toward the prevailing fiscal system, reformers appeared unable to see how their short-term reactions to the

[35] Morton Keller, *Regulating a New Economy: Public Policy and Economic Change in America, 1900–1933* (Cambridge, Mass.: Harvard University Press, 1990), 2; Karen Orren and Stephen Skowronek, *The Search for American Political Development* (New York: Cambridge University Press, 2004); Robert C. Lieberman, "Ideas, Institutions, and Political Order: Explaining Political Change," *American Political Science Review* 96:4 (2002), 697–712.

[36] Weber, "Social Psychology of the World's Religions," in *From Max Weber*, 280.

[37] Mid-twentieth-century public finance economists were among the first thinkers to lament how the ability-to-pay rationale severed the theoretical link between spending and taxation. Richard A. Musgrave and Alan T. Peacock, "Introduction," in *Classics in the Theory of Public Finance*, ed. Richard A. Musgrave and Alan T. Peacock (London: Macmillan, 1958), xiii–xxiii.

[38] Charles H. Stewart, *Budget Reform Politics: The Design of the Appropriation Process in the House of Representatives, 1865–1921* (New York: Cambridge University Press, 1989); Jonathan Kahn, *Budgeting Democracy: State Building and Citizenship in America, 1890–1928* (Ithaca: Cornell University Press, 1997).

existing regime would have perverse, long-term implications. By eliding the fiscal state's enormous spending powers, these theorists and activists narrowed the range of permissible tax-and-*transfer* policy options. By stigmatizing all consumption taxes as outdated expressions of the benefits principle, they limited the imagination of future American tax theorists and lawmakers. By privileging the ability-to-pay rationale, they created a kind of fiscal myopia that continued to afflict American policy analysts, legislators, and interest groups well into the twentieth and twenty-first centuries.

The symptoms of this fiscal myopia became more evident when viewed from a comparative perspective later in the twentieth century. When other Western industrialized democracies began experimenting with broad-based, regressive consumption taxes as a way to finance modern social-welfare spending, the United States resisted this seemingly global trend. Other modern democracies were willing to try crude forms of consumption taxes as supplements to income taxation; together these taxes generated tremendous revenue that was spent to counter the regressive incidence of consumption taxes.[39] By contrast, the United States refrained from moving beyond income as the primary base for national taxation. As a result, rather than develop a comprehensive view of the fiscal state's tax-and-transfer powers, policymakers in the United States became mired in a preoccupation with the progressivity of the American income tax system, with the process of extracting revenue, with "soaking the rich." They failed to see how the regressive incidence of broad-based consumption taxes could be countered by progressive state spending on social-welfare provisions.[40]

This fiscal myopia, to be sure, was not due solely to intellectual currents. Raw political power and conflicting American visions of civic identity contributed to the disconnected nature of fiscal policymaking. Given the checkered American historical experience in denying full citizenship

[39] Peter Lindert, *Growing Public: Social Spending and Economic Growth since the Eighteenth Century* (New York: Cambridge University Press, 2004); Junko Kato, *Regressive Taxation and the Welfare State: Path Dependence and Policy Diffusion* (New York: Cambridge University Press, 2003); Harold L. Wilensky, *Rich Democracies: Political Economy, Public Policy, and Performance* (Berkeley: University of California Press, 2002), Ch. 12; Monica Prasad and Yingying Deng, "Taxation and the Worlds of Welfare," *Socio-Economic Review* 7:3 (2009), 431–57.

[40] As Monica Prasad has recently argued, the American focus on consumption and progressive taxation during this critical period may have closed off paths toward a European-style welfare state. Monica Prasad, *The Land of Too Much: American Abundance and the Paradox of Poverty* (Cambridge, Mass.: Harvard University Press, 2012).

to individuals based on class, race, ethnicity, gender, and religion, it is not surprising that the modern fiscal state developed a compromised and schizophrenic profile – one that neglected the importance of social-welfare spending on dependents and subordinated groups. Not only did the peculiar institution of slavery have an enduring impact on American political development, nearly every aspect of the historical formation of civic identity has been shaped at one time or another by what Rogers Smith has dubbed the "inegalitarian ascriptive traditions of Americanism."[41]

Comparative historical differences in political institutions, likewise, partially explain the origins of this fiscal myopia. As political scientist Sven Steinmo has demonstrated, the United States, with its fragmented political decision-making structures, has traditionally kept tax and spending decisions divided, while other countries with more corporatist decision-making institutions have melded the consideration of tax and spending policies.[42] Still, the fiscal ideas that began to circulate in the late nineteenth century and that gained increasing currency among influential political leaders and lawmakers in the early twentieth century reinforced rather than mitigated these political and institutional tendencies. Consequently, one of the deep-seated paradoxes at the heart of the modern American fiscal state was that a tax reform movement geared toward addressing the many social ills of modern urban-industrial society may have done as much to frustrate as it did to advance the possibilities of a progressive fiscal state.[43]

41 Robin L. Einhorn, *American Taxation/American Slavery* (Chicago: University of Chicago Press, 2006); Rogers M. Smith, *Civic Ideals: Conflicting Visions of Citizenship in U.S History* (New Haven: Yale University Press, 1997); Gary Gerstle, *American Crucible: Race and Nation in the Twentieth Century* (Princeton: Princeton University Press, 2001). Molly Michelmore has recently chronicled how "liberal state-builders" throughout the twentieth century perpetuated this fiscal myopia by maintaining the conceptual separation between indirect social-welfare benefits and the more salient direct taxes that paid for such benefits. Molly C. Michelmore, *Tax and Spend: The Welfare State, Tax Politics, and the Limits of American Liberalism* (Philadelphia: University of Pennsylvania Press, 2012).

42 Sven Steinmo, *Taxation and Democracy: Swedish, British and American Approaches to Financing the Modern State* (New Haven: Yale University Press, 1993). For more on the stealth nature of U.S. social-welfare spending, see Christopher Howard, *The Hidden Welfare State: Tax Expenditures and Social Policy in the United States* (Princeton: Princeton University Press, 1999); Suzanne Mettler, *The Submerged State: How Invisible Government Policies Undermine American Democracy* (Chicago: University of Chicago Press, 2011).

43 If the U.S. experience with state-level sales taxes is any indication, it is certainly possible that the United States could have adopted a regressive consumption tax base without any accompanying progressive spending. Katherine S. Newman and Rourke L. O'Brien,

Long before these unintended consequences materialized, the fiscal order that took shape at the turn of the century marked the ascendancy of a new and particular mode of governance, one that had broad egalitarian potential. Certain elements of the old fiscal order continued to linger into the mid-twentieth century and later. The tariff remained a perennial part of international trade policy. The property tax continued to finance most local government activities. And party politics and the pressures of federalism continued to shape overall fiscal policy.[44] Nonetheless, a system of direct and graduated taxation based on the progressive notion of "ability to pay," premised on a rejuvenated sense of democratic citizenship, and administered by bureaucratic experts, gradually became the hallmarks of the modern American fiscal state.

The turn-of-the-century transformation in American public finance and the attendant rise of the modern American fiscal state raise several fundamental questions: How and why was this significant shift in the U.S. system of public finance possible? What were the historical factors that affected, and were affected by, this dramatic change in fiscal policy? How was this new fiscal power distributed and shared within the structure of American federalism? Who were the key historical agents who helped create the modern fiscal polity? Why were social groups, reform-minded political economists, progressive lawmakers and jurists, and key government bureaucrats able to alter tax policy during the turn of the twentieth century but not earlier? And, most importantly, how did the rise of this new fiscal order reconfigure the meaning of modern American citizenship and alter existing institutional arrangements? These important questions frame the analysis of this study.

The origins and consequences of the modern American fiscal state are thus the subject of this book. It begins mainly as a story about ideas, about the conceptual shift in the way that theorists and policy analysts examined and argued about taxation. But it proceeds as a tale about how new fiscal ideas were put into action and enacted into law, about how this conceptual shift was received by lawmakers, judges, administrators, and ordinary Americans. It is not meant to be a "whiggish" history, reifying uncontested and linear progress or valorizing the modern fiscal state. For

Taxing the Poor: Doing Damage to the Truly Disadvantaged (Berkeley: University of California Press, 2011).

44 Keller, *Regulating a New Economy*; Coleman, *Party Decline in America*; Kimberley S. Johnson, *Governing the American State: Congress and the New Federalism, 1877–1929* (Princeton: Princeton University Press, 2007).

as we shall see, the emergence of the modern fiscal polity was marked by institutional struggles, historical contingencies, and surprising paradoxes.

Nor is this a narrative of declension, harping on the lost opportunities and insidious machinations of robber barons and special interests. The aim, instead, is to uncover the rich complexities of the historical process of American state formation, to show how the rise of a new fiscal order dramatically altered the distribution of tax burdens, the meaning of modern citizenship, the existing regime of American statecraft, and the range of possibilities for robust government action.

Ultimately, this transformation was a qualified success. It did not go as far as some reformers and activists had envisioned. It did not radically redistribute wealth, as some radical populists had hoped. It did not maintain the use of World War I profits taxes as an antitrust tool, nor did it experiment with national sales taxes after the conflict, as some fiscal experts and lawmakers had hoped. By averting the last path – the possibility of a national sales tax – the new fiscal order, ironically, seemed to limit the potential development of a more holistic public response to the dislocations of modern industrial capitalism. It appeared to arrest the development of a robust fiscal state that could use progressive social-welfare spending to counter regressive forms of taxation. Still, this new fiscal polity – as imperfect as it may have been – laid the foundation for, and held out the promise of, a new more progressive American state.

Conflicts over taxation have, of course, persisted throughout American history. From the Revolutionary Era's demands for "no taxation without representation" to the more recent calls for a "flat tax" or for steeply progressive taxes on millionaires, taxation has remained a perennial political issue in American society and culture.[45] One reason for this is because taxation is one of the most widely and persistently experienced relationships that citizens have with their state. Taxation reminds us that the private and public realms are inextricably intertwined, rather than separate and distinct. "Private liberties have public costs," legal theorists Stephen Holmes and Cass Sunstein have written. "Individual freedom is both constituted and bolstered by collective contributions." Since the extraction of contributions often entails potentially conflicting

[45] Charles Adams, *Those Dirty Rotten Taxes: The Tax Revolts That Built America* (New York: Free Press, 1998); Robert E. Hall and Alvin Rabushka, *The Flat Tax*, 2nd ed. (Stanford: Hoover Institution Press, 1995); Steve Forbes, *Flat Tax Revolution: Using a Postcard to Abolish the IRS* (Washington, D.C.: Regnery Publishers, 2005).

interests, debates about taxation in liberal democracies are also continually reproduced rather than resolved. In American history, the latent tension at the center of taxation has meant that the relationship between individual citizens and the state has been constantly renegotiated and revised.[46]

Yet if debates about taxation are an inherent part of liberal democracies, they took a consequential turn in the United States in the late nineteenth and early twentieth centuries. For it was during these decades that potent social movements, confronting the massive economic disparities of the Gilded Age, were able to press for effective tax reform. Responding to the growing social antipathy toward the *ancien* tax regime, a group of reform-minded intellectuals began the conceptual campaign to transform the existing fiscal order. Through their writings, arguments, and actions, they convinced powerful lawmakers to seize the opportunities posed by economic crises to move the demands for direct and graduated taxes from the political margins – where independent third parties had for decades been clamoring unsuccessfully for fundamental tax reform – to the center of American political and legal discourse. Once the legal foundations were in place, government officials subsequently used the national emergency of the Great War to build the administrative capacity necessary to consolidate the powers of the nascent fiscal polity. The results of their efforts were evident during the postwar decade when the formal calls for retrenchment belied the progressive resolve and institutional resiliency of the new fiscal order.

There were, of course, other pivotal moments in the historical development of the American fiscal state. But it was the turn of the century that provided the critical context, the contingent opportunities, as well as the human agency and political will necessary to create a dramatic shift in the way that Americans envisioned modern fiscal relations. The Founding Era and the Early Republic were, to be sure, formative periods in the early institutional design and development of a modern fiscal-military state. But for all that the Founders did to redeem the republic after the fiscal failures of the Articles of Confederation, they also established the

[46] Stephen Holmes and Cass R. Sunstein, *The Cost of Rights: Why Liberty Depends on Taxes* (New York: W. W. Norton, 1999); Charles Tilly, *Democracy* (New York: Cambridge University Press, 2007), 143–5; Isaac William Martin, Ajay K. Mehrotra, and Monica Prasad, "The Thunder of History: The Origins and Development of the New Fiscal Sociology" in *The New Fiscal Sociology: Taxation in Comparative and Historical Perspective*, ed. Isaac William Martin et al. (New York: Cambridge University Press, 2009), 1–29.

traditional tax regime that subsequent generations of Americans assailed as regressive, unfair, and ineffective.[47]

The Civil War, likewise, began the U.S. experiment with national direct and graduated taxes. But these wartime levies were expressly created as temporary measures, as fleeting attempts to highlight the shared sacrifices and social obligations of a liberal democracy at war.[48] It was not until the 1880s and '90s, when the broad structural forces of modern industrial capitalism ignited social antagonisms amid swelling inequalities and economic crises, that the foundations for a truly modern concept of the fiscal polity began to take shape. Even though the New Deal and World War II were seminal events, the fiscal achievements of those eras were ultimately built on the intellectual, legal, and administrative foundations that took root at the turn of the century.[49] For it was at that time that social groups, political activists, reform-minded intellectuals, key lawmakers, jurists, and government administrators undertook the imaginative and emotional spade work necessary to lay the basis for the first major transformation in American tax law and policy.

In explaining the turn-of-the-twentieth-century fiscal transformation, scholars have generally offered three conventional accounts. The first focuses primarily on the functional demand for greater public revenue, particularly during moments of national conflict. "State building in America was stimulated during periods of sustained warfare," writes

[47] Max Edling, *A Revolution in Favor of Government: Origins of the U.S. Constitution and the Making of the American State* (New York: Oxford University Press, 2003); Roger H. Brown, *Redeeming the Republic: Federalism, Taxation, and the Origins of the Constitution* (Baltimore: Johns Hopkins University Press, 1993); Dall W. Forsythe, *Taxation and Political Change in the Young Nation, 1781–1833* (New York: Columbia University Press, 1977); Calvin Johnson, *Righteous Anger at the Wicket States: The Meaning of the Founders' Constitution* (New York: Cambridge University Press, 2005). On the significance of slavery to the antebellum fiscal system and American democracy, see Einhorn, *American Taxation/American Slavery*.

[48] Richard Franklin Bensel, *Yankee Leviathan: The Origins of Central State Authority in America, 1859–1877* (New York: Cambridge University Press, 1990), 332–5; Heather Cox Richardson, *The Greatest Nation of the Earth: Republican Economic Policies During the Civil War* (Cambridge, Mass.: Harvard University Press, 1997), 112–37; Steven A. Bank, Kirk J. Stark, and Joseph J. Thorndike, *War and Taxes* (Washington, D.C.: Urban Institute Press, 2008), Ch. 2; Christopher Shepard, *The Civil War Income Tax and the Republican Party, 1861–1872* (New York: Algora Publishing, 2010).

[49] Mark Leff, *The Limits of Symbolic Reform: The New Deal and Taxation, 1933–1939* (New York: Cambridge University Press, 1984); Sparrow, *From the Outside In*; Jones, "Class Tax to Mass Tax;" Sparrow, *Warfare State*, 122–33.

political scientist and legal scholar Sheldon D. Pollack, "and both state building and war making required that political leaders adopt more aggressive revenue strategies to finance their expanded activities."[50] This narrative builds on a vast literature of European state building to suggest that American political development was remarkably similar, that despite initial variations the U.S. experience fit within a broader structural pattern and social scientific model of historical change.

These theory-driven explanations of Western state formation have been insightful. With their macro-level, comparative analyses, historical social scientists have demonstrated persuasively how wars and the extraction of tax revenues have been instrumental to the creation of nation-states; how rulers and lawmakers throughout time have sought to maximize revenue given certain rational constraints; how differing political cultures, values, and historical institutions have determined the variation of tax regimes across place and time; and how social resistance to modern industrialization and state centralization has determined comparative differences in the origins of tax regimes. Indeed, in many of these structural-functionalist accounts, the social and political responses to the exogenous shocks of international conflicts come to define nation-states. As Charles Tilly has succinctly put it: "war makes states."[51]

[50] Sheldon D. Pollack, *War, Revenue, and State Building: Financing the Development of the American State* (Ithaca: Cornell University Press, 2009), 293. See also Sparrow, *From the Outside In*; Bensel, *Yankee Leviathan*, and the essays contained in *Shaped by War and Trade: International Influences on American Political Development*, ed. Ira Katznelson and Martin Shefter (Princeton: Princeton University Press, 2002).

[51] Charles Tilly, ed., *The Formation of National States in Western Europe* (Princeton: Princeton University Press, 1975); *Coercion, Capital, and European States, AD 990–1990* (New York: Basil Blackwell, 1990); Michael Mann, "State and Society, 1130–1815: An Analysis of English State Finances," in *States, Wars, and Capitalism: Studies in Political Sociology*, ed. Michael Mann (New York: Basil Blackwell, 1988), 73–123; Margaret Levi, *Of Rule and Revenue* (Berkeley: University of California Press, 1988); Carolyn Webber and Aaron Wildavsky, *A History of Taxation and Expenditure in the Western World* (New York: Simon and Schuster, 1986); Steinmo, *Taxation and Democracy*; Kimberly J. Morgan and Monica Prasad, "The Origins of Tax Systems: A French-American Comparison," *American Journal of Sociology* 114:5 (2009), 1350–94. See also Richard Bonney, ed., *The Rise of the Fiscal State in Europe, c. 1200–1815* (New York: Oxford University Press, 1999); John Brewer, *The Sinews of Power: War, Money, and the English State, 1688–1783* (London: Century Hutchinson, 1988). Charles Tilly, "War Making and State Making as Organized Crime," in *Bringing the State Back In*, ed. Peter Evans, Dietrich Rueschemeyer, and Theda Skocpol (Cambridge: Cambridge University Press, 1985), 169–87, 170. For a recent reappraisal of the importance of war to the global development of progressive taxation, see Kenneth Scheve and David

These broad, comparative studies have contributed immensely to our understanding of the relationship between taxation and state building. They have also begun to influence the growing interdisciplinary subfield of American Political Development (APD). Students of APD, in their efforts to emphasize the importance of historically created political institutions, have largely been preoccupied with social policy and the ways in which public spending has supported the development of the American social-welfare state. Yet, in "bringing the state back in,"[52] these scholars have continued to leave out one of the state's most potent sources of power and control: its ability to tax. In this sense, applying the models of Western state formation to the U.S. experience can help reveal how taxation was, and continues to be, an essential component of modern American political and economic development.

Yet while the work of comparative historical social scientists has been instructive, these accounts frequently discount the importance of historical contingency and human agency. Absent from many of these wide-ranging narratives is a strong sense of the plasticity of the past. Instead, overly deterministic theories and models of change are frequently deployed to neatly categorize the messiness of history. Though these scholars recognize the importance of "critical junctures" to the "path-dependent" process of political development, they generally pay much greater attention to the sequence of broad structural forces and to the "positive feedback" mechanisms that keep initial policy choices on a particular institutional path. In so doing, they often overlook the contested nature of pivotal decisions, the possibilities of numerous critical junctures, and the potential paths not taken.[53]

Strasavage, "The Conscription of Wealth: Mass Warfare and the Demand for Progressive Taxation," *International Organization*, 64:4 (2012), 529–61.

[52] See the essays contained in the now classic volume, *Bringing the State Back In*. For a sampling of the vast literature on social spending, see, e.g., Theda Skocpol, *Protecting Soldiers and Mothers: The Political Origins of Social Policy in the United States* (Cambridge, Mass.: Harvard University Press, 1992); *The Politics of Social Policy in the United States*, ed. Margaret Weir et al. (Princeton: Princeton University Press, 1988).

[53] Paul Pierson, *Politics in Time: History, Institutions, and Social Analysis* (Princeton: Princeton University Press, 2004); James Mahoney, "Path Dependency in Historical Sociology," *Theory & Society* 29:507–48 (2000). This is not to suggest that historical social scientists and ADP scholars ignore contingency. Their focus on the historical sequence of institutional development underscores moments of possibility. But the potential for change is often limited to the temporal sequence of *institutional* processes, suggesting that tensions in broad structural forces are the main drivers of contingent development. Yet even these institutional processes are shaped by groups and

Broad structural forces were, of course, critical to the formation of the American fiscal state. The turn-of-the-century strains of modern industrial capitalism and the pressures of war, as the following chapters will show, dramatically affected the contours of the new fiscal order. Yet, little was natural or inevitable about how these forces would specifically shape the new order. Social movements, political activists, public intellectuals, powerful lawmakers, and key government administrators all engaged in a highly contested, contingent, and uncertain battle over the ideas, laws, and institutions that would come to define the new fiscal polity. Cyclical economic crises and the Great War were significant triggers of change, but they acted more as catalysts than underlying causes. The broad comparative histories of state building, moreover, generally neglect how different individuals and groups struggled and fought to shape the emergence of the modern state according to their various ideals and visions. In these all-encompassing narratives, individuals and groups are generally swept along by ineluctable structural forces, and in their place independent variables such as war and the functional need for revenue are inserted as the dominant historical actors.

The complex process of American state formation cannot be explained solely with reference to changes in broad structural factors or functional needs. Powerful individuals and organizations made choices and took actions that altered the course of history. They seized the opportunities provided by the changing forces of modernity to stress the social democratic thrust behind turn of the century tax reform. For these historical actors, taxation was about much more than just raising revenue. It was also about social justice, democratic civic identity, and rational and effective administration. "Whereas in former years the income tax was adopted chiefly from considerations of revenue," noted progressive political economist Edwin Seligman in 1894, "there is of late a growing tendency, especially in the more democratic communities, to utilize the income tax as an engine of reparation – a means of attaining greater justice."[54]

A second and more historically attuned explanation of the fiscal transformation contends that if this era was a moment of change, it was merely

individuals using scarce resources during particular historical periods. See James T. Kloppenberg, "Institutionalism, Rational Choice, and Historical Analysis," *Polity* 28:1 (1995), 125–8.

54 Edwin R. A. Seligman, "The Income Tax," *Political Science Quarterly* 9:610 (1894), 616.

a palace revolution – a form of sophisticated conservatism designed to blunt more radical calls for wealth redistribution. Mirroring the work of an earlier generation of revisionist American historians, who argued that the turn of the century was not an age of progressive reform but rather an expression of U.S. "corporate liberalism,"[55] New Left legal historians have maintained that the tax jurisprudence of late-nineteenth-century "classical legal thought" was animated by a desire to solidify an "anti-redistribution principle" into the foundations of American tax laws and policies. The income tax movement, according to this line of reasoning, was infused with a "centrist" logic that permitted relatively autonomous lawmakers to become "the trustees" of the capitalist system. Thus, the tax reform movement was not "an expression of real economic democracy through a reduced burden on the poor and middle classes," Robert Stanley has argued, "but a rejection of the far more fundamental institutional change advocated by intellectuals and street dissidents of both left and right." The limited redistributive effects of changes in early tax laws and policies were portrayed as evidence of the state's hollow rhetoric of social justice. From this perspective, the origins of the income tax system were thus seen implicitly as missed opportunities to implement true democratic and egalitarian reform.[56]

[55] Leading examples of the corporate liberal interpretation of this time period remain William A. Williams, *Contours of American History* (Cleveland: World Publishing Co., 1961); James Weinstein, *The Corporate Ideal in the Liberal State, 1900–1918* (Boston: Beacon Press, 1968); Gabriel Kolko, *The Triumph of Conservatism: A Reinterpretation of American History, 1900–1916* (New York: Free Press, 1963); Martin J, Sklar, *The Corporate Reconstruction of American Capitalism, 1890–1916* (New York: Cambridge University Press, 1988); James Livingston, *Origins of the Federal Reserve System: Money, Class, and Corporate Capitalism, 1890–1913* (Ithaca: Cornell University Press, 1986); Jeffrey R. Lustig, *Corporate Liberalism: The Origins of Modern American Political Theory, 1880–1920* (Berkeley: University of California Press, 1982).

[56] Morton J. Horwitz, *The Transformation of American Law, 1870–1960: The Crisis of Legal Orthodoxy* (New York: Oxford University Press, 1992), 19–27; Robert Stanley, *The Dimensions of Law in the Service of Order: Origins of the Federal Income Tax, 1861–1913* (New York: Oxford University Press, 1993), 12, 230–1. For examples of the corporate-liberal interpretation as applied to later periods of American fiscal history, see Ronald F. *King, Money, Time, and Politics: Investment Tax Subsidies and American Democracy* (New Haven: Yale University Press, 1993); James O'Connor, *The Fiscal Crisis of the State* (New York: St. Martin's Press, 1973). Economic historians have similarly claimed that Congress's ability to allocate federal spending to key states "played a critical role in forging the political coalition that passed the income-tax amendment." Bennett D. Baack and Edward John Ray, "Special Interests and the Adoption of the Income Tax in the United States," *Journal of Economic History* 45:3 (1985), 607–25.

There is some credence to the corporate liberal interpretation. Some "centrist" lawmakers like Missouri Congressman Uriel Hall supported the income tax as "a measure to kill anarchy and keep down socialists."[57] These critiques, however, tend to overestimate the ability of corporate-liberal lawmakers and reformers to absorb challenges from the political left and right. Abundant evidence, especially during the World War I period, shows how progressive reformers were able to take advantage of economic crises and national emergencies to overcome conservative resistance and substantiate social democratic claims on the state. They were able to do so because they had a pragmatic, rather than radical or reactionary, notion of redistribution. Their ultimate goal was not to redistribute wealth in any extreme sense, nor was it to maintain the fiscal status quo. Rather, they sought to reallocate the costs of underwriting a modern state across geographical regions and socioeconomic classes. As Cordell Hull put it, they sought to ensure that the rich "not be permitted to shirk" their fiscal and civic duties.[58]

In focusing on the limits of the fiscal state, the standard centrist accounts have not only underestimated the potency of the tax reform movement. More importantly, they have obscured what was actually accomplished during this formative period of American history. The dramatic shift from a regressive, hidden, disaggregated, and politicized tax system to a graduated, transparent, and centrally and professionally administered one was a tremendous achievement. This transformation may not have gone as far as some dissent activists, theorists, and legislators had hoped, but it ultimately laid the foundation for a revolution in American fiscal relations. The idea that this was purely a palace revolution, like the structural-functional explanations of state formation, provides only a partial accounting of a considerably more complex and consequential historical moment.

A third group of explanations emphasizes neither structural forces nor corporate liberal motives, but rather the teleological march of democratic egalitarianism. For an older generation of scholars, reared during and by the New Deal order, the turn-of-the-century fiscal revolution was part and parcel of the Progressive Era's victories of "the people" over "the

[57] Hall quoted in Stanley, *Dimensions of Law*, 117. Because Stanley ends his account with the creation of the 1913 income tax, he overlooks how the subsequent development of the fiscal state, especially during World War I, challenges his thesis about the dominance of centrist thinking and institutions.

[58] *Congressional Record* 61st Cong., 1st sess. (1909), 44:536, 533.

interests." Like many other reforms of the age, the movement for direct and graduated taxes was depicted as required prehistory, a precursor to the triumphal arrival of New Deal liberalism. With one eye on Franklin D. Roosevelt as savior, this older progressive historiography described the unfolding of events leading up to the creation of the 1940s mass income tax as necessary preconditions for a fated rendezvous with America's fiscal destiny. Writing during and immediately after the New Deal, scholars such as Sidney Ratner, Roy and Gladys Blakey, and Randolph Paul extolled the virtues of the income tax movement as an unqualified victory of democratic egalitarianism and as prologue to the advent of the New Deal order.[59]

Like the structural accounts of taxation, the older progressive histories generally discount the contingencies in the development of a new democratic fiscal regime. In the process, they underestimate how the New Deal and World War II accomplishments were built on an intellectual, legal, and administrative foundation that was firmly established well before the 1930s and '40s. In presupposing the explosive and triumphal arrival of the New Deal, these narratives overlook the many contested junctures that existed in the long progression toward the institutional establishment of the modern income tax. Similarly, while the 1940s adoption of the mass income tax did, in fact, lead to a second transformation in American fiscal history, one in which direct and graduated taxes became firmly institutionalized, this second revolution would not have been possible without the early-twentieth-century conceptual sea change. The intellectual shift in American public finance that laid the basis for the legal and administrative framework for direct and graduated taxes was absolutely indispensable. Recovering the historical significance of this earlier transformation, without reproducing the linear and teleological

[59] The historical development of direct and graduated taxes was, for Ratner, a story about "the endeavor of the American people . . . to forge taxes which would be not only sources of revenue, but also instruments of economic justice and social welfare." Sidney Ratner, *American Taxation, Its History as a Social Force in Democracy* (New York: W. W. Norton, 1942), 9. In their classic study of the legislative history of the income tax, the Blakeys similarly contended that "no other important tax is more in harmony with the ideals of democracy." Roy G. Blakey and Gladys C. Blakey, *The Federal Income Tax* (New York: Longmans, Green and Co., 1940), 559, 577. And for Randolph Paul, a former tax lawyer in the New Deal Treasury Department, the establishment of a mass income tax suggested "that the majority of the people have won a battle in the campaign for democratic control of taxation." Randolph E. Paul, *Taxation in the United States* (Boston: Little Brown and Co., 1954), 764.

narrative of progressive historiography, is one of the central aims of this study.

Even though the older progressive historiography may be outdated and overshadowed by the more recent corporate liberal accounts, its emphasis on the achievements of reformers is a welcome reminder of what is possible. In some respects, then, this book seeks to revitalize the older progressive histories to underscore both the achievements and limits of the modern American fiscal state. It thus joins other recent analyses that employ what historian W. Elliot Brownlee refers to as a "democratic-institutionalist" approach – an approach that "recognizes the power of democratic forces" outside of the state, as well as "the influence of governmental institutions," including the importance of ideas, in shaping policy.[60]

Unlike other neo-progressive accounts, however, this study stresses the role of law, juridical institutions, and legal professionals and processes in the creation of a new fiscal order. It seeks to uncover the social and political assumptions that undergirded a period of significant legal and institutional change. Law, in this sense, was a crucial lingua franca. It was, as Alexis de Tocqueville observed, "a vulgar tongue," available to all Americans, including the grassroots social activists seeking to challenge the existing tax system.[61] Meanwhile, law was also the traditional language of state power. It was the discourse that progressive political economists used to influence jurists and legislators. And it was the idiom

[60] W. Elliot Brownlee, *Federal Taxation in America: A Short History* (New York: Cambridge University Press, 1996), 266; "Historical Perspective on U.S. Tax Policy Toward the Rich," in Joel B. Slemrod, ed., *Does Atlas Shrug? The Economic Consequences of Taxing the Rich* (New York: Russell Sage Foundation, 2002), 29–74; "The Public Sector," in Stanley L. Engerman and Robert E. Gallman, eds., *The Cambridge Economic History of the United States, Volume III: The Twentieth Century* (Cambridge: Cambridge University Press, 2000), 1013–60; W. Elliot Brownlee, ed., *Funding the Modern American State, 1941–1995: The Rise and Fall of the Era of Easy Finance* (New York: Cambridge University Press, 1996). Other recent studies following in the "democratic-institutionalist" mold include, Elizabeth Sanders, *Roots of Reform*, Ch. 7; Steven R. Weisman, *The Great Tax Wars: Lincoln – Teddy Roosevelt – Wilson, How the Income Tax Transformed America* (New York: Simon & Schuster, 2002); Richard Joseph, *The Origins of the American Income Tax: The Revenue Act of 1894 and Its Aftermath* (Syracuse, N.Y.: Syracuse University Press, 2004); Joseph J. Thorndike, *Their Fair Share: Taxing the Rich in the Age of FDR* (Washington, D.C.: Urban Institute Press, 2012); Prasad, *The Land of Too Much*.

[61] Alexis de Tocqueville, *Democracy in America*, Vol. I, ed. Philips Bradley (New York: Vintage Books, 1990), 280.

that government administrators relied upon to create and maintain the bureaucratic autonomy of the new fiscal polity.

A particular focus on legal underpinnings, furthermore, reveals the complex and contradictory consequences of the new fiscal order. This book thus illustrates what socio-legal scholars have referred to as "law's double role" – that is, law's ability both to facilitate and contain social, economic, and political transformations.[62] The leading historical actors in the making of the modern American fiscal state turned to law, juridical institutions, and legal processes not only to achieve the immediate economic goal of reforming a regressive and antiquated tax system, but to advance a new sense of civic obligation, to improve existing modes of governance, and perhaps most importantly to lay the institutional foundations for the activist state. In the process, they also domesticated more radical calls for wealth redistribution and limited the possibilities of using the full tax-and-transfer powers of the fiscal state to address the many social dislocations of modern industrial capitalism. Tax law both fostered and frustrated broader reforms.

To comprehend the significance of the dramatic changes wrought by the creation of a new fiscal polity, one must first appreciate the pervasiveness of the *ancien régime* and the growing social antagonism toward the intransigency of the old order. Chapter 1 begins with a portrait of the late-nineteenth-century fiscal landscape. It shows how leading jurists like Judge Thomas M. Cooley and ordinary American workers like members of the Knights of Labor identified all that was wrong with the existing tax

[62] Robert A. Kagan, Bryant Garth, and Austin Sarat, "Facilitating and Domesticating Change: Democracy, Capitalism, and Law's Double Role in the Twentieth Century," in *Looking Back at Law's Century*, ed. Austin Sarat, Bryant Garth, and Robert A. Kagan (Ithaca: Cornell University Press, 2002), 2. By stressing the importance of legal concepts, formal statutes and regulations, the lawmaking process, the administrative institutions that gave force to new tax laws, and the role of legal professionals in the fiscal state-building process, this study joins a growing literature at the intersections of legal history, the new political history, and the role of law in American state-building. For a sampling of this literature, see generally Daniel R. Ernst, "Law and American Political Development, 1877–1938," *Reviews in American History* 26:1 (1998); John D. Skrentny, "Law and the American State," *Annual Review of Sociology* 32 (2006), 213–44; William E. Forbath, "Politics, State-Building, and the Courts, 1870–1920," in *The Cambridge History of Law in America*, Vol. II, ed. Michael Grossberg and Christopher Tomlins (New York: Cambridge University Press, 2008), 643–96; William J. Novak, "The Myth of the 'Weak' American State," *American Historical Review* 113 (2008), 752–72; Julian E. Zelizer, *Governing America: The Revival of Political History* (Princeton: Princeton University Press, 2012).

system. Despite the obvious defects, the economic inequities of existing taxes persisted mainly because they were rooted in a highly politicized system of "courts and parties,"[63] as well as a traditional social contract ideology that characterized taxes as the price for government benefits. Other reform movements like Henry George's single tax and the rising tide of American socialism inspired and at times distracted and debilitated the halting movement for fundamental tax reform. Nevertheless, by the end of the 1880s, there was a growing and relentless social animus toward the existing tax system. "Taxes," as Conrad Carl observed as early as 1883, were a topic that "deeply interested the workingmen."[64]

Agrarian associations and certain segments of organized labor may have provided the social pressure for dramatic changes at the turn of the century. But as we shall see in Chapter 2, broader structural forces led to unforeseen events that ultimately provided reformers with opportunities to hasten the decline of the old fiscal order. Industrialization, urbanization, and mass migration compelled governments at all levels to confront the increased need for public goods and services, and thus for greater public revenue. At the same time, the economic cycle of industrial capitalism, punctuated by financial downturns, strained the traditional sources of public funding. Together these broad trends exacerbated the massive inequalities of the era and precipitated a protracted crisis in American public finance – a crisis whereby the growing demand for state action outpaced the supply of government revenues. A group of reform-minded academics and political activists sought to resolve this crisis. In so doing, they proved to be the crucial hinge between the growing social antagonism toward the old order and the rise of a new fiscal polity.

Over time, tax reformers and powerful lawmakers absorbed the teachings of the progressive public finance economists. They did so in order to overcome institutional obstacles such as the U.S. Supreme Court's 1895 invalidation of the first national peacetime income tax. Chapter 3 shows how these thinkers responded to the Court's ruling by navigating an intellectual middle ground between conservative forces opposed to direct and graduated taxes and seemingly more radical calls for fiscal change. From urban union halls to rural chautauquas to the corridors of official political

[63] Skowronek, *Building a New American State*. For recent reassessments of Skowronek's classic work and the period of "courts and parties," see Richard R. John, "Ruling Passions: Political Economy in Nineteenth-Century America," *Journal of Policy History* 18:1 (2006), 1–20; see also the essays in the "Roundtable: Twenty Years after Building a New American State," in *Social Science History* 23:3 (2003).

[64] "Testimony of Conrad Carl," 419.

power, these theorists educated everyday Americans and their political representatives about the importance of fundamental tax reform.

The process of building the basis for a new tax regime was not limited, however, to the federal level. Indeed, the struggle to establish the intellectual, legal, and administrative foundations of a new fiscal polity also existed at the state and local level, where reformers concentrated their efforts on challenging the outmoded general property tax. Chapter 4 examines subnational tax reforms. Initially, activists at the state level were loath to give up on a general property tax that was traditionally designed as a fair and effective levy on wealth. Still, the early attempts to salvage the property tax through administrative improvements created the intellectual space and institutional opportunity for states and commonwealths to experiment with new revenue sources including an income tax. When Wisconsin became the first state to administer an effective income tax in 1911, others followed suit, demonstrating how subnational governments were fast becoming factories of fiscal innovation.

One salient similarity between state and federal efforts to institute progressive taxation was the attempt to use the state's taxing powers to control the bourgeoning power of corporate capital. Indeed, using tax policy to contain corporate power was an intermediary step in the process of amending the Constitution in response to the U.S. Supreme Court's resistance to the income tax. Chapter 5 chronicles the process whereby reformers exploited the social anxieties surrounding corporate capitalism to create the constitutional foundations, the first permanent income tax laws, and the administrative framework that would soon become the heart of the modern fiscal state. Influential political leaders evoked the lessons of the progressive political economists in efforts to convince fellow legislators to accept what William Jennings Bryan referred to as the global sweep of the progressive income tax movement. They also turned to the rise of American managerial capitalism to harness the information producing powers of the new corporate behemoths, and to tax the profits, salaries, and dividends generated by these industrial giants. If the academic theorists were the architects of the new fiscal polity, the lawmakers soon became the contractors seeking to follow the blueprints of reform.

Not long after the legal foundations were in place, U.S. entry into the Great War provided the seminal triggering event that crystalized the taxing, spending, and borrowing powers of the new fiscal polity. Indeed, it was during the national war emergency that government administrators – many of whom were legal professionals – played a central role in building the institutional and administrative apparatus of the new fiscal order. Chapter 6 shows how a particular group of Wall Street lawyers turned entrepreneurial bureaucrats worked in a corporatist policy environment to create, manage, and defend a robust tax regime necessary to wage a global war. Through the crucible of conflict these Treasury lawyers became the bricklayers of the modern fiscal polity. Many of the corporate professionals who converged on Washington as "dollar-a-year" men to assist in the war mobilization effort were unlikely supporters of a powerful fiscal state. But the war experience transformed them. Former corporate lawyers such as Russell C. Leffingwell, Daniel C. Roper, and Arthur A. Ballantine returned home after the war with a great interest in sustaining and promoting the fiscal state's relative autonomy – an autonomy they helped forge during the war emergency.

After the war, the development of the fiscal polity went through a highly contingent period of consolidation. Chapter 7 takes up the postwar period. Under the stewardship of Andrew Mellon, Treasury Secretary during the Republican-dominated 1920s, a paradoxical process of retrenchment took place. On the one hand, Mellon and like-minded Republicans swiftly dismantled the steeply progressive rate structure of the wartime tax regime and repealed such anti-monopoly measures as the excess-profits tax. But at the same time these policymakers realized that the transformation in American political and legal culture wrought by decades of social unrest and intellectual agitation and triggered by the Great War had ushered in a new understanding of the relationship between citizens and their state. Even when the U.S. Supreme Court stepped into the fray to limit the reach of the Sixteenth Amendment, its rulings ironically provided the administrative framework necessary to secure the future of an income-based tax system.

Though the 1920s are regularly characterized as a "return to normalcy," the tax laws and policies of the postwar decade did not, in the end, signal an end to progressive reform. Rather, they were a vindication of the progressives' social democratic aims. The bold new ideas about the fiscal state articulated by social groups, reform-minded intellectuals, and lawmakers well before the war had by the end of the 1920s become an accepted part of the vocabulary of mainstream American political, economic, and social discourse.

Nearly five decades after Conrad Carl boldly articulated the injustices of national indirect and regressive taxes, the foundations of a new fiscal order were securely in place. Carl, himself, would not have recognized the modern system of public finance that existed in his grandchildren's lifetime. But he would have been relieved to know that the working-man was no longer the sole "pack-horse that carries all the burden." He would have been reassured that the rich were not permitted to shirk their just share of the tax burden. And he would have been pleased to have witnessed the early steps in the making of the modern American fiscal state.[65]

[65] Ibid.

PART I

THE OLD FISCAL ORDER

1

The Growing Social Antagonism

Partisan Taxation and the Early Resistance to Fiscal Reform

> For more than a generation the slavery agitation, the war to which it led and the problems growing out of that war have absorbed political attention in the United States. That era has passed, and a new one is beginning, in which economic questions must force themselves to the front. First among these questions, upon which party lines must soon be drawn and political discussion must rage, is the tariff question.
>
> – Henry George

On May 22, 1878, Thomas M. Cooley, the eminent jurist and legal scholar, delivered a paper at the annual meeting of the American Social Science Association (ASSA). Founded in 1865 as an organization devoted to studying the social questions of the day, the ASSA by the late 1870s had become a well-known, if unstable, national association of reformers, educators, and civic leaders. ASSA officials had long been admirers of Judge Cooley's writings, which by this time included a widely read treatise on constitutional law, an edited version of *Blackstone's Commentaries*, and a recently published tract on the law of taxation. Though the ASSA had extended several invitations to Cooley to participate in prior meetings, it was not until 1878, when he was returning from a visiting lectureship at the recently established Johns Hopkins University, that the Michigan Supreme Court justice agreed to take part in the organization's May meeting.[1]

Late spring was giving way to early summer when the members of the ASSA gathered in Cincinnati, Ohio, to learn about and debate topics

[1] Frank B. Sanborn to Thomas M. Cooley, March 3, 1875; June 24, 1876; June 13, 1877, Box 6, Thomas M. Cooley Papers, Bentley Historical Library, University of Michigan, Ann Arbor, Michigan [hereinafter TMCP]. On the origins of the American Social Science Association and its role in the professionalization of the social sciences see Thomas L. Haskell, *The Emergence of Professional Social Science: The American Social Science Association and the Nineteenth-Century Crisis of Authority* (Urbana: University of Illinois Press, 1977).

as wide-ranging as education reform, the "silver question," charitable administration, temperance, and the like. During the second evening of the conference, Judge Cooley took the stage to outline the "Principles that Should Govern the Framing of Tax Laws." Speaking before the association's general session, Cooley directed his remarks not at legal professionals but to the larger audience of engaged citizens interested in understanding and improving a rapidly changing American society.[2]

In comments that would come to resemble the complaints lodged by Conrad Carl, the Arnos, and others, Cooley described all that was wrong with the prevailing fiscal order. He began by criticizing the national system of import duties and excise taxes. "As indirect taxes," Cooley explained, these levies "are collected eventually of consumers," and thus "when laid upon the necessities or conveniences of life . . . fall most heavily upon the poorer classes," where they are "often exceedingly oppressive." The protective tariff, Cooley continued, was particularly troublesome because it had become detached from its origins as a central source of public revenue. It had, instead, become a tool of international trade policy, designed to protect privileged domestic industries.[3]

To be sure, the tariff had been seen by many as much more than just a source of external public revenue. As Cooley's University of Michigan colleague Henry Carter Adams noted, the tariff was initially used mainly as a geo-political tool to combat British naval imperialism after the Revolutionary War. But over time this historically specific purpose became lost in the continued use of import duties to protect domestic industries. By the late 1870s, economic experts like H. C. Adams were consistently claiming that the early manipulation of tax policy led directly to the late-nineteenth-century abuse of the tariff to protect privileged interests.[4] For

[2] Thomas M. Cooley, *Principles That Should Govern in the Framing of Tax Laws* (St. Louis: G. I. Jones, 1878); "Social Science; Second Day's Session of the American Association," *Washington Post*, May 22, 1878, 1; Frank B. Sanborn, "Social Science at Cincinnati," *The Independent... Devoted to the Consideration of Politics, Social and Economic Tendencies, History, Literature and the Arts*, June 27, 1878, 4.

[3] Cooley, *Framing of Tax Laws*, 8–9.

[4] Henry Carter Adams, *Taxation in the United States, 1789–1816* (Baltimore: Johns Hopkins University Press, 1884). This book began as Adams's doctoral thesis at Johns Hopkins, where he received one of the university's first doctoral degrees. "First Bestowal of Degrees," Johns Hopkins University Flyer, June 13, 1878, Box 1, Henry Carter Adams Papers, Bentley Historical Library, University of Michigan, Ann Arbor, MI [hereinafter HCAP]. See also William J. Barber, "Political Economy in the Flagship of Postgraduate Studies: The Johns Hopkins University," in *Economists and Higher Learning in the Nineteenth Century*, ed. William J. Barber (New Brunswick, N.J.: Transaction Publishers, 1993). On the importance of the tariff for Anglo-American relations during the early

a Jacksonian Democrat like Cooley, who adamantly opposed the use of public power to benefit special private interests, the tariff was clearly a form of "usurpation" and "a plain abuse of governmental power."[5]

The state and local general property tax fared no better. It too was "a system full of incongruities and inequalities," Cooley contended, "under which assessors openly, notoriously, and shamelessly disregard their duty." This dereliction of administrative responsibility led to "the most prominent evil in state taxation," namely "the habitual undervaluation" of real property, "and the neglect to assess at all a large proportion of all" personal property. To counter these defects, Cooley recommended the creation of new and more effective forms of taxation. Though he was no income tax advocate, Cooley argued that direct taxes theoretically offered "the least opportunity for concealment, evasion, and fraud," and thus taxed "the members of the community generally, and so near as may be in proportion to their respective incomes." One place to begin, Cooley suggested, was to tax "stocks in corporations which have a practical monopoly in their line."[6]

Cooley's remarks typified the prevailing view of American taxation. Extracted from his recently published tax law treatise, his ASSA presentation summarized the technical defects as well as the broad inequities of the existing tax system. Like most well-respected treatise writers, Cooley seemed to encapsulate the accepted views of American jurisprudence. As one of the country's most prominent jurists, he frequently became the first and last word on a variety of legal topics, including taxation. His remarks at the ASSA thus reflected the growing disillusionment and frustration with the existing late-nineteenth-century system of public finance.[7]

In many ways, Thomas Cooley was a seminal figure in the conceptual revolution of American public finance. His investigations of nineteenth-century federal and state taxation stressed the maldistribution of fiscal burdens. His studies identified the highly disagreeable and political nature of national tax policy and the pervasive malfeasance of state and local tax assessments. His thoughts on the philosophical justifications

republic, see Paul A. Gilje, *Free Trade and Sailors' Rights in the War of 1812* (New York: Cambridge University Press, 2013).

5 Cooley, *Framing of Tax Laws*, 8–9; Alan R. Jones, *The Constitutional Conservatism of Thomas McIntyre Cooley: A Study in the History of Ideas* (New York: Garland, 1987).

6 Cooley, *Framing of Tax Laws*, 14, 17, 19, 20.

7 Jones, *Constitutional Conservatism of Thomas McIntyre Cooley*; Paul D. Carrington, "'The Common Thoughts of Men': The Law-Teaching and Judging of Thomas McIntyre Cooley," *Stanford Law Review* 49 (1997), 495–546.

for taxes, as merely the quid pro quo for the benefits of government protection, and his skepticism of the income tax expressed the passive sense of fiscal citizenship that dominated the times. His ambivalence toward the scale and scope of governmental taxing powers, moreover, illustrated the general American unease with concentrated power, as well as the particular tensions inherent in the transition from the *ancien* tax regime to the modern fiscal state. Even Cooley's long and distinguished legal career, which encompassed nearly every aspect of the growing profession – from small town practitioner, to court reporter, to esteemed jurist, academic, and treatise writer, to federal railroad administrator – seemed to mirror the turbulent changes in late-nineteenth-century American politics and governance. Indeed, not only did his career trajectory track the shift from the party period of statecraft to the rise of the proto-administrative state; it also reflected the increasing role that professional expertise played in the articulation of the modern American fiscal polity. Cooley, in sum, was a key transition figure. Although many of his ideas were part of an increasingly antiquated fiscal order, his critiques of the existing tax system provided an entry point for subsequent revenue reformers.[8]

In detailing the deficiencies of the prevailing tax system, however, Cooley was hardly alone. Rather, he represented a relatively common, late-nineteenth-century American perspective on law, economy, and society. Other thinkers frequently agreed with his assessments, as did many political leaders and social reformers. His writings also appealed to a general audience of educated readers, and an emerging generation of academic tax experts who relied on his work – sometimes as a useful foil – for their teaching, research, and policy advocacy.[9] Although generations of modern scholars have disagreed about Cooley's motivations and legacy, nearly all concur that he was an acute observer of late-nineteenth-century American law and political economy.[10] Among his many insights,

[8] Jones, *Constitutional Conservatism of Thomas McIntyre Cooley.*

[9] Richard T. Ely to Thomas M. Cooley, February 13, 1888; Edwin R. A. Seligman to Thomas M. Cooley, November 9, 1886; November 15, 1892, TMCP. Evidence of Cooley's popularity and influence, as well as the lucrative potential of his writings, can be seen from the numerous solicitations he received from publishers and readers interested in his work on taxation. See, e.g., W. H. Burroughs to Thomas M. Cooley, Dec. 18, 1874; Banks & Brothers to Thomas M. Cooley, Oct. 8, 1875, Box 6; Edwin R. A. Seligman to Thomas M. Cooley, Nov. 15, 1892; Dec. 3, 1892, Box 5; Richard T. Ely to Thomas M. Cooley, Feb. 13, 1888, Box 3, TMCP.

[10] While an earlier generation of scholars depicted Cooley as an apologist for laissez-faire constitutionalism and corporate capitalism, recent revisionist accounts have described

one of the most accurate was his identification of the "often exceedingly oppressive" application of indirect national taxes on "the poorer classes."[11]

The Inequities of Existing Taxes

While few seemed to doubt Cooley's general assertion that indirect national taxes were unfair, many economic experts were more circumspect about the ultimate impact or incidence of particular levies, especially the tariff. Most, in fact, considered the final effect of customs duties rather uncertain. The British philosopher and political economist, Henry Sidgwick, claimed in 1883 that "there is no theoretical means of determining" the consequences of a tariff on domestic consumers or producers. American economists concurred, adding that a multitude of empirical factors made any theoretical conclusions highly suspect. In one of his early tax treatises, Edwin R. A. Seligman, the Columbia University professor who would become one of the leading supporters of direct and progressive taxes, verified the seemingly insurmountable challenges in determining the ultimate impact of the tariff. The elements that affect the incidence of import duties "are so numerous and so complex that an investigation of the actual effects of a tax upon any one class of commodities

the complex ambivalence of the jurist's writings and actions. For an example of the former interpretation, see Benjamin R. Twiss, *Lawyers and the Constitution: How Laissez Faire Came to the Supreme Court* (Princeton: Princeton University Press,1942); Clyde S. Jacobs, *Law Writers and the Courts: The Influence of Thomas M. Cooley, Christopher G. Tiedman, and John F. Dillion upon American Constitutional Law* (Berkley: University of California Press, 1954); Arnold M. Paul, *Conservative Crisis and the Rule of Law: Attitudes of Bar and Bench, 1887–1895* (Itacha: Cornell University Press, 1960). On the revisionist view of Cooley and his generation of jurists, see, e.g., Jones, *The Constitutional Conservatism of Thomas McIntyre Cooley*; Herbert Hovenkamp, *Enterprise and American law, 1836–1937* (Cambridge, Mass.: Harvard University Press, 1991); Charles W. McCurdy, "Justice Field and the Jurisprudence of Government-Business Relations: Some Parameters of Laissez-Faire Constitutionalism, 1863–1897," *Journal of American History* 61:4 (March 1975), 970–1005; Robert Stanley, *Dimensions of Law in the Service of Order: Origins of the Federal Income Tax, 1861–1913* (New York: Oxford University Press, 1993); Howard Gillman, *The Constitution Besieged: The Rise and Demise of Lochner Era Police Powers Jurisprudence* (Durham, N.C.: Duke University Press, 1993); William J. Novak, *The People's Welfare: Law and Regulation in Nineteenth-Century America* (Chapel Hill: University of North Carolina Press, 1996); Jeffrey Sklansky, *The Soul's Economy: Market Society and Selfhood in American Thought, 1820–1920* (Chapel Hill: University of North Carolina Press, 2002); David M. Rabban, *Law's History: American Legal Thought and the Transatlantic Turn to History* (New York: Cambridge University Press, 2013), 21–7.

11 Cooley, *Framing of Tax Laws*, 8.

would require for its proper solution, not only an acquaintance with the details of theory itself," wrote Seligman, "but also an intimate knowledge of all the forces influencing the supply of, and the demand for, the commodities affected." For most late-nineteenth-century economic commentators, then, the answer to the question of "Who paid the tariff?" remained highly uncertain.[12]

The same was not true of the regional effects of protectionism. As contemporaries at the time duly noted and as modern economic historians have corroborated, the nineteenth-century tariff had a clear and significant impact in redistributing wealth from agricultural sections of the country, namely the South and West, to the industrial centers located in the Northeast. More specifically, the protective tariff shielded Northeastern manufacturers by increasing the domestic prices of competing imports; it provided an implicit subsidy to domestic import-competing producers.

Meanwhile, customs duties harmed Southern exporters of raw materials such as cotton and tobacco and Midwestern exporters of wheat and corn by effectively taxing their exports. Southern and Western leaders were well aware of the distributive impact of import duties during the antebellum era, and they continued to complain decades after the Civil War about how Northeastern manufacturers benefited from protectionism at the expense of Southern and Western exporters. It is "to the evident advantage of the whole cotton-growing section," opined one Southern newspaper in 1878, "that any legislation on the subject of important duties should provide for the admission" of cotton as "free of duty." Although cotton as an export was not explicitly on the duty list, the editors seemed to understand that exporters effectively suffered from the tariff. The editorial called upon Southern lawmakers at the Capitol to "see the importance of this matter and use all their influence to free the Cotton States from this tax."[13]

[12] Henry Sidgwick, *The Principles of Political Economy* (London: MacMillan, 1883), 492; Edwin R. A. Seligman, *The Shifting and Incidence of Taxation*, 2nd ed. (New York: MacMillian, 1899 [1892]), 374. On the uncertainty of tariff incidence among economic experts at the time, see Douglas Irwin, *Against the Tide: An Intellectual History of Free Trade* (Princeton: Princeton University Press, 1996), 111–13.

[13] "Cheaper Bagging for Baling Cotton; The South's Interest in Tariff Reform," *Georgia Weekly Telegraph*, January 1, 1878, at 3; Jeremy Atack and Peter Passell, *A New Economic View of American History from Colonial Times to 1940* (New York, 1994), 139–40; Richard Franklin Bensel, *The Political Economy of American Industrialization, 1877–1900* (New York: Cambridge University Press, 2000), 458–68. Douglas Irwin has recently shown how late-nineteenth-century protectionism provided domestic

Exporters of raw materials like cotton were not the only ones harmed by the tariff. Social critics underscored how the consuming public perceived import duties as inequitable, even though economic experts agreed that the incidence of indirect taxes like the tariff was highly ambiguous. Writing in 1885, the British legal scholar Sir Henry Maine proclaimed the American tariff to be "as oppressive as ever a nation has submitted to." Many ordinary Americans and social commentators agreed. The "essential character of our protective policy," noted the *New York Times*, "artificially and cruelly increases the cost of clothing, of bedding, of shelter, of tools, and of a thousand necessaries of daily life." By taxing everyday consumption goods, the prevailing system was inherently regressive, extracting more from those with less. In comments that echoed Conrad Carl's testimony before the Senate committee, the popular journal *Christian Union* criticized how "more than three-quarters of the average savings of mechanics, laborers, and small farmers are constantly absorbed by indirect taxation and its necessary effects," while "not more than one-quarter... of the savings of the capitalist class is taken in the same way." Even worse, some critics contended, was that these indirect taxes remained insidiously hidden because they were folded into the final price of consumer goods. Citizens were frequently oblivious to their presence. Because "the masses are entirely unconscious of the extent to which they are bled," contended the *Washington Post*, "it would be easier to find a hundred men who can quote Homer and Virgil, than one man who can tell the taxes he has paid on the clothes he has or the dinner he has just eaten."[14]

Some dissonance clearly existed between the formal, ambiguous economic incidence of the tariff and the public perception of import duties. The same, however, was not true of the state and local general property tax. By the late nineteenth century, nearly everyone agreed that the

manufacturers with a smaller subsidy than nominal tariff rates would indicate, how agricultural exporters bore the brunt of high tariffs, and how protectionism was slightly harmful to consumers who spent much of their income on exported products, namely food. Most significantly, Irwin has estimated that the tariff redistributed roughly 8 percent of GDP among various producer groups and consumers. Douglas Irwin, "Tariff Incidence in America's Gilded Age," *Journal of Economic History* 67:3 (2007), 582–607.

14 Sir Henry Maine, *Popular Government: Four Essays* (London, 1895), 247; "Taxing Food," *New York Times*, June 1, 1891, 4; "Industrial Problems," *Christian Union*, August 20, 1885, 8; "Methods of Taxation," *Washington Post*, August 6, 1883, 2. For more on the popular perception that the tariff led to a high cost of living, see Mark Aldrich, "Tariffs and Trusts, Profiteers and Middlemen: Popular Explanations for the High Cost of Living, 1897–1920," *History of Political Economy* (forthcoming).

general property tax, which dominated state and local government revenues, was an abject failure – both because it failed to generate adequate revenue and because it disproportionately affected those taxpayers who held real and visible property. Since it was a direct levy, many believed that the general property tax was progressive. It generally could not be shifted onto others, and because real property was a principal form of wealth, the tax theoretically could extract more from those who had greater economic power. Yet, in the midst of an industrial age when finance capitalism was radically transforming the markers and vessels of wealth and income, the general property tax no longer operated as it had in an earlier, more agricultural era.[15]

As Cooley's comments suggested, many believed that the rampant under-assessment and outright evasion of state and local property taxes disproportionately affected small property owners. Not only were corporations and wealthy individuals eager to hide their taxable property, the process of valuing property was woefully inadequate. As the historian Clifton K. Yearley has illustrated, "the states' general tax systems were uniformly primitive, while the myriad forms of evasion were quite sophisticated." In most states, locally elected or appointed, part-time assessors calculated and collected the general property tax. Charged with the responsibility of determining the value of their neighbors' property, local assessors had neither the expertise nor the gumption to measure accurately the value of real estate or personal intangible property such as stocks, bonds, mortgages, and other financial assets. Consequently, tax experts throughout the country proclaimed that the property tax discriminated against less affluent property owners, particularly farmers, whose limited holdings of land, livestock, and machinery were corporeal and in plain sight. The urban rich, by contrast, held much of their wealth in the form of salaries or intangible personal property such as financial assets, which often escaped assessment. Expressing the consensus among political economists and tax officials, Seligman noted in 1890 that the state and local general property tax "pressed hardest on those least able

[15] Clifton K. Yearley, *The Money Machines: The Breakdown and Reform of Governmental and Party Finance in the North, 1860–1920* (Albany: State University of New York Press, 1970), xii–xv; Morton Keller, *Affairs of State: Public Life in Late Nineteenth Century America* (Cambridge, Mass.: Harvard University Press, 1977), 323–5; R. Rudy Higgens-Evenson, *The Price of Progress: Public Services, Taxation, and the American Corporate State, 1877–1929* (Baltimore: Johns Hopkins University Press, 2003), 13–14; Jon C. Teaford, *The Rise of the States: Evolution of American State Government* (Baltimore: Johns Hopkins University Press, 2002), 42–53.

to pay" and that no other institution had "evoked more angry protest," or "more earnest dissatisfaction."[16]

Such pervasive beliefs about the disproportionate tax burden had significant political ramifications. As long as Americans perceived the prevailing tax system as unjust, there appeared to be a wellspring of social support for fiscal reforms, including direct and progressive taxes on individual incomes, business profits, and wealth transfers. When it came to the protective tariff, some analysts argued that voters would have no trouble locating the origins of their problems. "The prompt rise in prices of the common necessaries of life," an editorial written during the height of the 1890 tariff debates observed, "is bringing the Republican tariff home to the masses of voters in a way highly unsatisfactory to those who made that tariff." The editorial's partisan remark expressed how by the late nineteenth century the setting of import duties had become a new kind of political problem. In the antebellum era, the tariff had been a divisive issue over national sovereignty, slavery, and states' rights, but by the 1880s the consistent log-rolling over the setting of import duties had made the tariff a different kind of partisan, sectional issue. As Cooley noted in his remarks before the ASSA, tariff policy had long been decoupled from its historical origins to become an endemic political issue.[17]

The Political and Social Dynamics of Taxation

The tariff had its origins in the antebellum economic policy of raising revenue, protecting American "infant industries" from foreign competition, and avoiding political debates over slavery. By the late nineteenth century, however, the tariff raised less revenue and had become predominantly a political instrument – both internationally and domestically. Import duties had dominated federal revenues before the Civil War, accounting for, on average, roughly 85 percent of total national receipts. But as early as 1880 that figure had dipped below 60 percent.[18]

[16] Yearley, *Money Machines*, 66; Edwin R. A. Seligman, "The General Property Tax," *Political Science Quarterly* 5:1 (1890), 62; Glenn W. Fisher, *The Worst Tax? A History of the Property Tax in America* (Lawrence: University Press of Kansas, 1996).

[17] "Object Lessons in Tariff," *New York Times*, October 9, 1890, at 8; Cooley, *Framing of Tax Laws*. On the importance of the tariff for antebellum political economy, see Robin L. Einhorn, *American Taxation/American Slavery* (Chicago: University of Chicago Press, 2006); Mark Thornton and Robert B. Ekelund, Jr., *Tariffs, Blockades, and Inflation: The Economics of the Civil War* (New York: Rowman & Littlefield, 2004).

[18] *Historical Statistics of the United States: Earliest Times to the Present, Millennial Edition*, ed. Susan B. Carter et al. (New York: Cambridge University Press, 2006), 5-83–5-90,

As tariff revenue declined, protectionism became embroiled in broader geopolitical battles over international trade. As historian Morton Keller has explained, the "tariff was the most prominent and persistent category of nineteenth-century American economic policymaking" mainly because it was premised on the U.S. economy's need to export raw materials and protect infant industries. Other industrialized nations had different priorities. For the British, with their global empire and mature industries, free trade was sacrosanct, at least until the early 1900s. The continental powers of Germany and France, by contrast, mirrored American rationales. German economic theorists, led by Friedrich List, contended that protectionism was necessary to enable a newly unified German nation-state to ascend from the agricultural to the industrial stage of modern economic development. Many German lawmakers agreed, instituting a form of protectionism that shielded domestic industries and was used as a cudgel for international trade negotiations. In this early era of globalization, when innovations in technology and transportation led to the increasing integration of the world economy, countries like France that relied heavily on agricultural exports also embarked upon protectionism. As a result, the United States found itself using the tariff both as a shield for domestic manufacturers, and as a negotiating tool to open markets for its agricultural exports.[19]

In addition to affecting international trade policy, the tariff also became one of the defining domestic political issues of the last third of the nineteenth century. Tariff administration afforded both major political parties the opportunity to appoint party loyalists to lucrative posts as custom house officials. This rampant political patronage was seen by many tariff critics as a growing sign of government corruption.[20] Yet

Table Ea588–593. During the antebellum era, proceeds from the tariff fell below 75 percent of federal revenue only during the van Buren administration when brisk federal land sales contributed significantly to the federal treasury. John Mark Hansen, "Taxation and the Political Economy of the Tariff," *International Organization*, 44 (1990), 527–51.

19 Morton Keller, *Regulating a New Economy: Public Policy and Economic Change in America, 1900–1933* (Cambridge, Mass.: Harvard University Press, 1990), 192–3; Frank Trentmann, *Free Trade Nation: Commerce, Consumption, and Civil Society in Modern Britain* (Oxford, Oxford University Press, 2008); Paul Wolman, *Most Favored Nation: The Republican Revisionists and U.S. Tariff Policy, 1897–1912* (Chapel Hill: University of North Carolina Press, 1992); Percy Ashley, *Modern Tariff History: Germany, United States, France* (London: Murray, 1904).

20 Robert D. Marcus, *Grand Old Party: Political Structure in the Gilded Age, 1880–1896* (New York: Oxford University Press, 1971); Ari Hoogeboom, *Outlawing the Spoils: A History of the Civil Service Reform Movement, 1865–1883* (Urbana: University of

the politics of tariff administration was minor compared to the partisan combat that determined the setting of import duties. Democrats and their general disdain for government-sanctioned special privileges favored low rates and free trade, while Republicans with their nationalistic ideology were the standard-bearers for high duties. Cooley, as a longtime Jacksonian Democrat, did not hide his contempt for a Republican policy that he believed had become unhinged from its historical and egalitarian roots, and thus was a "misuse" and "usurpation" of public power.[21]

Unsurprisingly, Republican legislators disagreed with Cooley. From the end of Reconstruction through the 1890s, Republican lawmakers, representing traditional Northeastern industrial interests and newly mobilized Western producers, consistently supported the protective tariff as a central pillar in their program for economic development. They believed that a policy of regulating the inflow of foreign goods into American markets and society was one principal way to enforce national identity. In the U.S. House of Representatives, Republicans during this period voted more than nine times out of ten for tariff protection. Although some Democrats, especially those from more economically developed sections of the country, occasionally supported protectionism, most favored downward revisions to the duty list. And a few even advocated unregulated free trade. Indeed, when Grover Cleveland, the first post–Civil War Democrat elected president, explicitly attacked the tariff "as a vicious, unequitable, and illogical source of unnecessary taxation," Democrats hardened their opposition to protectionism. Cleveland's unambiguous 1887 assault on the tariff disciplined members of his party and provided voters with a stark policy distinction between Democrats and Republicans.[22]

At the same time that President Cleveland was leading the Democratic charge against protectionism, Republicans were consciously and

Illinois Press, 1961). On the importance of political appointments in the context of the postal service, see Richard R. John, *Spreading the News: The American Postal System from Franklin to Morse* (Cambridge, Mass.: Harvard University Press, 1998).

21 Cooley, *Framing of Tax Laws*, 9. On the Jacksonian-Democratic roots of Cooley's politics, see Jones, *The Constitutional Conservatism of Thomas McIntyre Cooley*, 41–3; Hovenkamp, *Enterprise and American Law*, 28–30.

22 Bensel, *Political Economy of American Industrialization*, Tables 7.1 and 7.2, 470–1; Cleveland quoted in Sidney Ratner, *American Taxation: Its History as a Social Force in Democracy* (New York: W. W. Norton, 1942), 157; Joanne Reitano, *The Tariff Question in the Gilded Age: The Great Debate of 1888* (University Park: Pennsylvania State University Press, 1994); Andrew Wender Cohen, "Smuggling, Globalization, and America's Outward State, 1870–1909," *Journal of American History* 97:2 (2010), 371–98.

FIGURE 1.1. "Difference Between Trimming a Hedge and Cutting it Down." In this 1888 W.A. Allen political cartoon from *Harpers Weekly*, President Cleveland is depicted trimming the tariff "protection hedge," while wayward children representing Northeast manufacturing interests complain to Uncle Sam, who replies: "Now don't come around tellin' me that story about cuttin' down the hedge and bein' eat up by the free-trade b'ars." Courtesy of The Library of Congress, Prints and Photographs Division, Washington, D.C.

carefully crafting a tariff policy attuned to regional disparities. The tariff had historically stoked sectional tensions, pitting Northeast industrialists against the agrarian regions of the South and West. But in the post-bellum period Republicans strengthened their hold over protectionism by appealing to new constituents in the West. By adding items such as wool, hides, and grains to the duties list after the Civil War, North-eastern Republicans were able to bring some Western and Midwestern farming interests into the protectionist fold. Furthermore, Republicans linked revenues generated by the tariff to particular spending programs. The Republican agenda of integrating and developing the national economy included expenditures for internal improvements in infrastructure, as well as the repayment of Civil War debts held by European and Union bondholders.[23]

But the greatest example of how Republicans were able to inextricably link tariff revenue to federal spending was through the provision of Civil War pensions – the nation's first proto-welfare measures. Since the pensions went to Union Army veterans, Republicans were able to solidify their support for the tariff in the North and West, while further marginalizing the resistance of Southern Democrats. By tying tariff revenues to the financing of internal improvements, repayment of Union bondholders, and veterans' pensions, the Republicans skillfully highlighted the spending benefits that accompanied protectionism. In the process, they bolstered the theory that taxation ought to be based on the reciprocal benefits provided by government in exchange for tariff revenue. For both parties, the tariff became a contentious issue that could be mobilized to maintain party discipline and loyalty, among not only party members but also voters.[24]

Standing behind the partisan politics of protectionism were the economic interests that profited from high import duties. Whenever Congress considered revisions to the duty list, organizations such as the American Iron and Steel Association, the Boston Home Market Club, the Wool Manufacturers' Association, and the American Protective Tariff League disseminated pro-tariff pamphlets, raised campaign funds, and lobbied lawmakers on behalf of protectionism. As the names of these lobbying

[23] Elizabeth Sanders, *Roots of Reform: Farmers, Workers, and the American State, 1877–1917* (Chicago: University of Chicago Press), 217–20.

[24] Richard F. Bensel, *Sectionalism and American Political Development, 1880–1980* (Madison, Wis.: University of Wisconsin Press, 1984), 60–103. On the social welfare roots of Civil War pensions, see Theda Skocpol, *Protecting Soldiers and Mothers: The Political Origins of Social Policy in the United States* (Cambridge, Mass.: Harvard University Press, 1992), 112–14.

groups indicate, Northern manufacturing interests, particularly within the iron and steel industry as well as makers of raw wool, were the ones who arguably benefited the most from the Republican Party's defense of protectionism. Although it is unclear whether protectionism was indispensable to the existence of protected industries, as tariff advocates claimed, the owners of these industries believed it was a subsidy worth fighting for.[25]

Tariff opponents countered that a government shield from competition facilitated economic collusion and the concentration of corporate power in the form of trusts and other monopolies. Decades before the sugar magnate Henry O. Havemeyer famously confessed in 1899 that the protective tariff was "the mother of all trusts," critics of protectionism had linked the tariff with the growth in corporate consolidation.[26] Evoking a long anti-monopoly tradition, Southern and Western Democrats railed against "the iniquitous tariff system" that made "combinations, pools, and trusts possible." Congressman Benton McMillin (D-Tenn.), an early advocate of progressive income taxes and antitrust laws, was a leading foe of a tariff regime that he believed fostered the concentration of economic power. "While the Government has thrown up its tariff walls without," McMillin reminded lawmakers, "monopolists have joined hands within for the purpose of putting up prices and plundering the people through the devices known as trusts, pools, and combines."[27]

Populist lawmakers like McMillin were not the only ones who protested the monopoly-inducing powers of the tariff. Proprietary capitalists, fearful of the growing powers of large-scale national corporations, were equally critical of protectionism. Reformers like Henry Demarest Lloyd favored free trade as a means of preserving a nation of small entrepreneurs. As editor of the American Free Trade League's broadsheet,

[25] Bensel, *Political Economy of American Industrialization*, 462; Reitano, *The Tariff Question*, 115–16; F. W. Taussig, *The Tariff History of the United States* (New York: G. P. Putnam's Sons, 1888). On the importance of protectionism to the iron and steel industry during this period, see Bennett Baack and Edward Ray, "Tariff Policy and Comparative Advantage in the Iron and Steel Industry, 1870–1929," *Explorations in Economic History* II (Fall 1973): 6–8.

[26] *Preliminary Report on Trusts and Industrial Combinations, Vol. 1, Testimony* (Washington, D.C.: GPO, 1900), 100; Byron W. Holt, *The Tariff, the Mother of Trusts* (n.p.: New England Free Trade League, 1899).

[27] *Congressional Record*, 50th Cong., 1st sess. (1888), 19, pt. 4:3373, 3305; Roy G. Blakey and Gladys C. Blakey, *The Federal Income Tax* (New York: Longmans, Green and Co., 1940), 13–15. For a recent reevaluation of the antimonopoly tradition during this time period, see Richard R. John, "Robber Barons Redux: Antimonopoly Reconsidered," *Enterprise & Society* 13:1 (March 2012), 1–38.

the *People's Pictorial Taxpayer*, Lloyd consistently voiced his concern about how high tariffs were fostering economic concentration. With political cartoons titled "How the Tariff Robs the Farmer and Every Workingman to Benefit the Monopolist," Lloyd sought to advance the League's mission of revealing the "baleful effects of levying a tax on such foreign products as compete with our own."[28]

With commercial interests exerting pressure on the tariff question, even prominent academic thinkers who favored trade liberalization were frequently hesitant to come out against protectionism. Throughout the mid-nineteenth century, American economic theorists, subscribing to the "exceptionalist" nature of the New World, rejected the classical free-trade ideas of Adam Smith and John Stuart Mill. Relying on a religiously inflected view of political economy, protectionists such as Henry C. Carey taught generations of antebellum Americans about the importance of shielding domestic infant industries.[29] By the last decades of the nineteenth century, however, as accelerating industrialization undermined the uniqueness of U.S. circumstances, and as the empirical justification for the infant industry rationale began to dissolve, other economic writers challenged protectionism, though with great caution. Williams College professor Arthur Latham Perry vigorously defended free trade and harshly criticized protectionism in his classroom, only to have his views censured by the college's prominent alumni. Even the Harvard professor Frank W. Taussig, who in the 1880s was fast becoming the leading American expert on the tariff, held a rather agnostic view on the infant industry argument. In fact, his conclusions that the merits of protectionism hinged on a case-by-case basis only seemed to further politicize the already partisan tariff issue.[30]

National politics surrounding the tariff also implicated a different kind of struggle over the meaning of protection, one that went beyond regional and class interests to implicate traditional gender roles. As historian Rebecca Edwards has shown, both national parties molded their

[28] *Pamphlets of the Hour on Tariff and Free Trade* (1875), 85; Giles B. Stebbins, *The American Protectionist Manual* (Detroit: Thorndike Nourse, 1883), 78–9; Reitano, *Tariff Question*, 72.

[29] Joseph Dorfman, *The Economic Mind in American Civilization, 1865–1918* (New York, 1969), 6–7; James L. Huston, *Securing the Fruits of Labor: The American Concept of Wealth Distribution, 1765–1900* (Baton Rouge: Louisiana State University Press, 1998); Abraham D. H. Kaplan, *Henry Charles Carey: A Study in American Economic Thought* (Baltimore: Johns Hopkins University Press, 1931).

[30] Judith Goldstein, *Ideas, Interests, and American Trade Policy* (Ithaca: Cornell University Press), 83–91; Irwin, *Against the Tide*, 97–8; Dorfman, *Economic Mind*, 61.

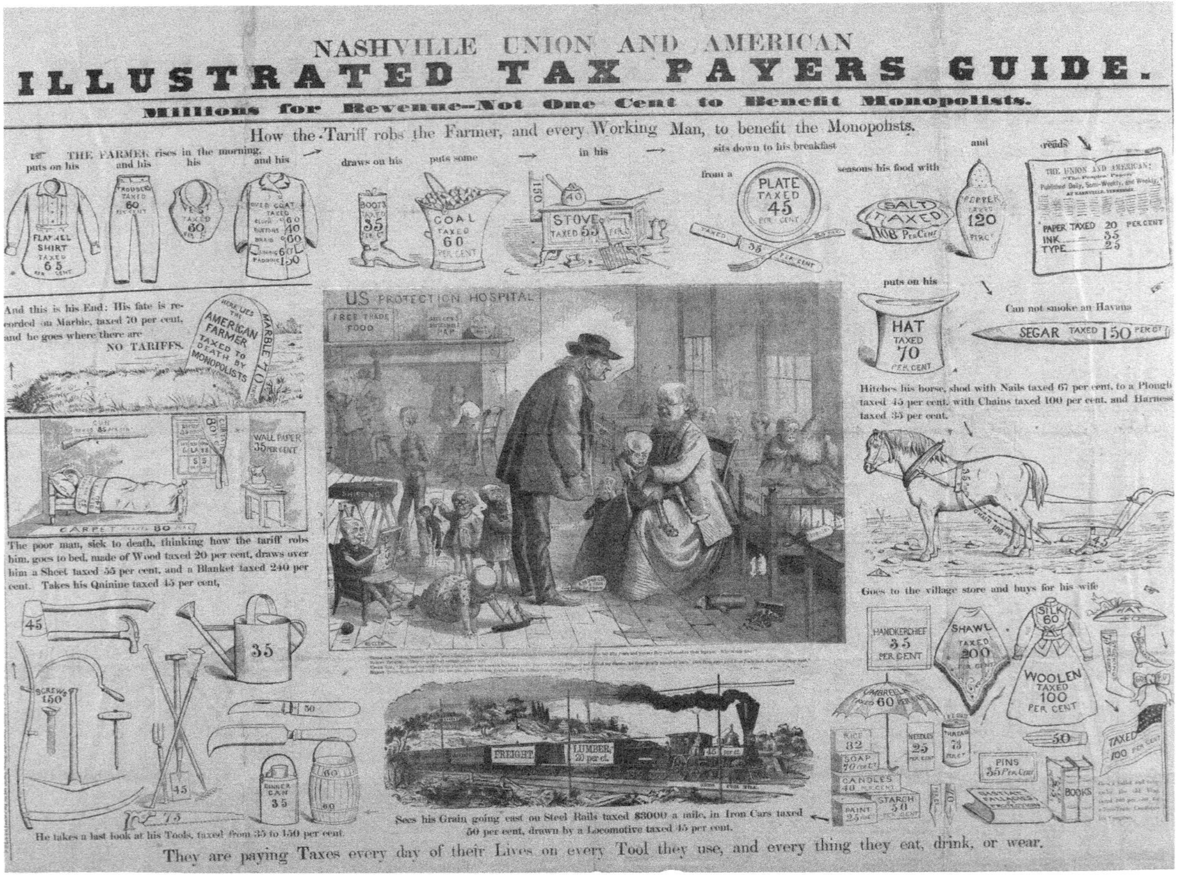

FIGURE 1.2. "How the Tariff Robs the Farmer and Every Workingman." The border of this political cartoon lists the many everyday items that were on the tariff's duty list, from clothes, to food, to the tools used by farmers and workingmen. The cartoon in the center shows Uncle Sam confronting "Mammy Tribune" about why her "infant manufacturers" continue to need tariff protection. Courtesy of The New York Historical Society.

contrasting positions on "tariff reform" to fit reigning gender ideologies. For Republicans, the tariff did more than just protect domestic manufactures; it also "protected" the world of "female domesticity." By using high tariffs to preserve the jobs and purported higher wages of male breadwinners, Republicans claimed that they were "protecting the home," shielding women and children from the ravages of the formal labor market, so that they could attend to their separate domestic sphere. As members of the "party of the home," Republicans mobilized a late-nineteenth-century rhetoric of family values to contend that under protectionism workingmen could keep "their wives at home and their children in school."

Low-tariff Democrats offered a contrasting rationale for opposing high tariffs, but without challenging the prevailing ideology of separate spheres. In the 1880s, Democrats argued that the shifting of high duties onto everyday consumption items unnecessarily increased the cost of living. This, in turn, hindered the male wage earner's ability to support his family, and thus threatened the privileges and obligations of masculinity. As numerous government investigations of tenement houses and working-class life had illustrated, indirect taxes like the tariff seemed to threaten a male breadwinner's entitlement to be the master of his dependent family.[31]

Both parties also used gender dynamics to mobilize support for their differing positions on protectionism. While Democrats appealed to women as consumers by arguing that tariffs were harming the purchasing power of working and middle-class families, Republicans countered that women ought to be more concerned about maintaining high wages and the challenge that free trade posed to the employment of their wage-earning husbands. Even though most women at this time did not have the franchise, political leaders realized that women had great influence on everyday decisions at home – including those that shaped the votes of their husbands. Female political activists in the 1880s, moreover, identified with tariff reform or "free trade" as a central pillar of civic improvement. Republicans and Democrats were bitterly divided over the tariff, but they seemed to agree that tax policy could be used instrumentally to

[31] Rebecca Edwards, *Angels in the Machinery: Gender in American Party Politics from the Civil War to the Progressive Era* (New York: Oxford University Press, 1997), 68–82. On the importance of measuring "cost of living" to political debates during this time period, see Thomas A. Stapleford, *The Cost of Living in America: A Political History of Economic Statistics, 1880–2000* (New York: Cambridge University Press, 2009), Chapter 1.

maintain gender hierarchy. By the end of the century, a new group of professional social scientists would not only challenge the national politics of the tariff, they would also seek to invert this traditional, gendered division between home and market.[32]

Political tensions and their implications for social relations were not limited to the national level. Politics intruded on state and local taxation as well. In addition to massive evasion and administrative limitations, the subnational general property tax was crippled by political corruption. The office of tax assessor was frequently a less than desirable patronage position. "In nominating conventions," one Utah political leader explained as late as 1912, the position of property tax assessor "is usually the last place filled, and the nominee is more likely to be chosen because of the particular section from which he came, or on account of his past services to the party, . . . rather than because of his special fitness for the office." As officials beholden to the authority of political parties, property tax assessors were also exposed to the disciplining efforts of party bosses. Such "general demoralization," David A. Wells, a former Civil War tax official and popular economic commentator observed, was inevitable "where assessors are dependent for their tenure of office on political favoritism."[33]

The dependency of state and local tax assessors was even more pronounced in the context of valuing business property, especially taxable property owned by large-scale corporations. Tax reformers claimed that just as the protective tariff privileged large national business corporations and fostered the creation of monopolies, the ineptly administered property tax afforded these corporations a similar benefit at the state and local level. Although the tangible assets of railroads, streetcars, and other businesses were subject to the same taxes as those levied on individuals,

[32] Edwards, *Angels in the Machinery*, 68–82; Amy Dru Stanley, *From Bondage to Contract: Wage Labor, Marriage, and the Market in the Age of Slave Emancipation* (New York: Cambridge University Press, 1998), 148–57, 166–74. On the changing role of women in a more capacious notion of politics and public action, see Paula Baker, "The Domestication of Politics: Women and American Political Society, 1780–1920," *American Historical Review* 89:3 (1984), 620–47; Elisabeth S. Clemens, *The People's Lobby: Organizational Innovation and the Rise of Interest Group Politics in the United States, 1890–1925* (Chicago: University of Chicago Press, 1997); Alice Kessler-Harris, *In Pursuit of Equity: Women, Men, and the Quest for Economic Citizenship in 20th-Century America* (New York: Oxford University Press, 2001).

[33] *Final Report of the Board of Commissioners on Revenue and Taxation for the State of Utah* (Salt Lake City: Arrow Press, 1913), 13 (quoted in Teaford, *Rise of the States*, 44); David A. Wells, "Principles of Taxation," *Popular Science Monthly* 48:1 (1895), 1–14.

subservient assessors notoriously undervalued corporate property by colluding with business officials, accepting bribes, and participating in a host of corporate tax evasion techniques. Such malfeasance was not limited to urban districts. Elite farmers and other rural property owners complained vociferously about having to bear a disproportionate tax burden. The decentralized administration of property taxes and the broad discretion granted to rural assessors, however, permitted farmers and rural residents to partake in their own form of self-help property tax relief by concealing their property or engaging in other forms of malfeasance.[34]

Like the partisan tariff, the late-nineteenth-century politics of state and local property taxation also shaped broader social relations and civic visions. Early women's suffragists, for instance, linked their payment of state and local property taxes to demands for the franchise. Invoking the Revolutionary slogan "no taxation without representation," women like Abby and Julia Smith of Glastonbury, Connecticut, protested that it was inconsistent and illegal to impose the fiscal obligations of citizenship upon female property owners while denying them the reciprocal voting rights of citizenship. Because the Smith sisters were ultimately successful in securing the franchise, their protests and those of many other suffragists demonstrated the empowering aspects of tax law, how taxes could be used as a vehicle for political mobilization.[35]

Like other aspects of the legal system, tax laws could bolster egalitarian claims, but they could also be used to contain progressive reform and maintain historical hierarchies. In the post-Reconstruction decades, for example, Southern states eagerly and quickly introduced poll taxes along with literacy and property qualifications for voting, as part of the elite white supremacist agenda of disenfranchising racial minorities and poor whites, and denying them the rights of full citizenship. Poll taxes, of course, were not new; they had existed throughout American history as a head or capitation tax, with occasional connections to suffrage. In the 1890s, however, Southern Democrats, seeking to consolidate their political and social authority and secure white supremacy, transformed the meaning of a poll tax into a levy that became directly linked to the

[34] Higgens-Evenson, *Price of Progress*, 39–51; Yearley, *Money Machines*, 53, 63; Ransom E. Noble Jr., *New Jersey Progressivism before Wilson* (Princeton: Princeton University Press, 1946), 11.

[35] Linda K. Kerber, *No Constitutional Right to Be Ladies: Women and the Obligations of Citizenship* (New York: Hill & Wang, 1998), 81–123; Carolyn C. Jones, "Dollars and Selves: Women's Tax Criticism and Resistance in the 1870s," *University of Illinois Law Review* (1994), 265–310.

franchise – one that had to be paid in order to vote. Mississippi led the way in 1890 with a two-dollar poll tax and other voting restrictions that technically adhered to the U.S. Constitution's Fifteenth Amendment, but effectively eliminated African Americans and poor whites from state and local politics. Other Southern states soon followed suit, as tax laws continued to be used as political tools to maintain social and political power.[36]

Judicial Deference to Partisan Taxation

The late-nineteenth-century partisan nature of taxation was fortified by a deferential judiciary. As contemporary treatise writers observed, the Anglo-American legal tradition had long vested legislatures with a nearly unrestricted taxing power. Judges had rather limited discretion in constraining the legitimate application of a variety of taxes. As a result, nineteenth-century American courts were generally willing to permit legislatures, with their ostensibly democratic decision-making powers, to determine the broad parameters of tax policy, as long as lawmakers did not run afoul of constitutional limitations. "With regard to the precise mode of exercising the taxing power," wrote Francis Hilliard in one of the first modern American tax law treatises, "the legislature, unless restricted by some constitutional provision, seems to be invested with entire discretion." Courts, of course, had the responsibility to determine how constitutional provisions constrained a legislature's discretion, but for Hilliard and other treatise writers the existing state and national case law seemed to suggest that legislatures had a "very broad extent" of taxing power.[37]

Cooley concurred that the "power of taxation" was one of the primary prerogatives of the state; it was "an incident of sovereignty" that

[36] Kessler-Harris, *In Pursuit of Equity*, 22–64. Mississippi Constitution of 1890, Article 12, Sections 241, 243; *Voting in Mississippi: A Report of the United States Commission on Civil Rights* (Washington, D.C.: The Commission, 1965), 3–5. C. Vann Woodward, *The Strange Career of Jim Crow* (New York: Oxford University Press, 1974), 83–5; Alexander Keyssar, *The Right to Vote: The Contested History of Democracy in the United States* (New York: Basic Books, 2000), 111–12; Frank B. Williams, Jr. "The Poll Tax as a Suffrage Requirement in the South, 1870–1901," *Journal of Southern History* 18:4 (November 1952), 469–96.

[37] Francis Hilliard, *The Law of Taxation* (Boston: Little, Brown 1875), 3, 5; William Henry Burroughs, *A Treatise on the Law of Taxation as Imposed by the States and Their Municipalities* (New York: Baker, Voorhis & Co., 1877), 5–7; James McIlvanie Gray, *Limitations of the Taxing Power: Including Limitations upon Public Indebtedness* (San Francisco: Bancroft-Whitney Co., 1906), 123–30, 228–9.

"acknowledges no limits." Yet, unlike Hilliard, Cooley was more explicit in addressing the potential limitations. His *Treatise on the Law of Taxation* was meant to emphasize "those fundamental principles which restrict the power to tax." As a common-law jurist, he had great faith in courts.[38] But Cooley demonstrated throughout his legal analysis that federal courts overruled only the most egregious violations of congressional taxing authority. "Of public policy in matters of federal taxation, the congress must judge," wrote Cooley. "Every tax must discriminate, and only the authority that imposes it can determine how and in what direction." There were undoubtedly instances "when a burden is imposed which it is impossible to bear; one which is laid not for the purpose of producing revenue, but in order to accomplish some ulterior object which general government lacks the power otherwise to accomplish." Yet "even in such cases," Cooley concluded, "it is held that the presumption that correct motives have controlled the legislative action must preclude the judiciary from inquiring into the purpose of the legislation."[39]

The treatise writers reflected the existing case law and the U.S. Supreme Court's general deference toward Congress's taxing powers. The U.S. Constitution required "direct" taxes to be apportioned among the states by population. Throughout most of the nineteenth century, however, the Supreme Court interpreted this restriction narrowly, implicitly granting Congress great leeway in exercising its taxing powers. In a series of decisions stretching from 1796 to 1880, the Court ruled that a variety of levies – including taxes on carriages, the gross receipts of certain corporations, the circulation of state bank notes, and even individual earnings – were not direct taxes requiring apportionment.[40] In each of these cases, the justices conceded that the direct tax clause was a formal restriction on Congress's taxing power. But since the prevailing view was that only poll and land taxes were the types of direct levies requiring apportionment,

[38] Jones, *Constitutional Conservatism of Thomas McIntyre Cooley;* Kunal M. Parker, *Common Law, History, and Democracy in America, 1790–1900: Legal Thought before Modernism* (New York: Cambridge University Press, 2011), 204–9.

[39] Cooley, *A Treatise on the Law of Taxation: Including the Law of Local Assessments* (Chicago: Callaghan and Co., 1876), iv, 74–5; Stanley, *Dimensions of Law*, 82–5. In his tax law lectures, Cooley similarly observed the importance of judicial deference in fiscal matters – a lesson that was passed on to the next generation of tax scholars, including Henry Carter Adams. Henry Carter Adams, "Tax Lectures," in Box 26, Folder 1; "Lectures on Taxation – By Judge Cooley, 1882," Bounded Materials, Box 15, HCAP.

[40] U.S. Constitution, Article I, Section 9; *Hylton v. United States*, 3 Dall. (3 U.S.) 171 (1796); *Pacific Ins. Co. v. Soule*, 7 Wall. (74 U.S.) 433 (1868); *Veazie Bank v. Fenno*, 8 Wall. (75 U.S.) 533 (1869); *Springer v. United States*, 102 U.S. 586 (1881).

the Court upheld these other levies as indirect taxes. In the process, the justices confirmed that the direct tax clause tacitly provided Congress with great latitude. As Justice Nathan Clifford explained in upholding a succession tax, the direct tax clause was less a restriction than a provision that "vests the power in Congress to lay and collect taxes, duties, imposts, and excises to pay the debts and provide for the common defence and public welfare."[41]

For many lawmakers, the Court's decisions confirmed a presumption of plenary congressional authority over taxation. As Senator John Sherman (R-Ohio), an early and staunch defender of the income tax, proclaimed, the "Constitution gives to Congress more unlimited power over the subject of taxation than almost any other. We have the power to levy taxes almost without limit."[42] Accordingly, congressional politics became nearly the sole determinant of tax policy, including the setting of import duties. The Court did cast doubt on such plenary taxing powers in 1895 when, as we shall see, it strikingly departed from long-held precedents to strike down the 1894 income tax, but for much of the nineteenth century judicial deference guaranteed that federal taxation would remain a highly partisan issue.[43]

Indeed, given that customs duties were clearly deemed indirect taxes by the courts as well as Congress, they became a dominant yet inconspicuous source of federal revenue. Customs duties, however, were not simply imposts, levied at a flat rate on all imported goods, but rather were tariffs with varying enumerated rates on different products. This subtle yet significant distinction between an impost and a tariff was one reason why legislative log-rolling over the setting of import duties became the defining characteristic of late-nineteenth-century tax policy. As a result, congressional leaders from the two national parties regularly negotiated legislative agreements about the details of the duty list and the benefits of protectionism.[44]

The judicial deference to party politics in the realm of tax legislation did not mean, however, that taxpayers could not challenge tariff appraisals or classifications – something they did with great frequency in appeals to the U.S. Treasury Department and after 1890 the newly created Board of United States General Appraisers, the predecessor of the U.S. Customs

41 *Scholey v. Rew*, 90 U.S. 331, 346 (1874).
42 *Congressional Globe*, 41st Cong., 3rd sess., (1871), 43, pt. 1, Appendix, 61.
43 *Pollock v. Farmers' Loan & Trust Company*, 158 U.S. 601 (1895).
44 Einhorn, *American Taxation/American Slavery*, 154–6.

Court. Rather, the extent of federal judicial deference to Congress on revenue legislation illustrated how national tax policy remained one area where democratically elected lawmakers seemed to be supreme. Over time, the growing complexity of the national tax laws, especially after World War I, would imbue the Treasury Department with increased bureaucratic autonomy and help accelerate the transition from a state of "courts and parties" to a modern administrative polity. But for the time being, the Gilded Age judiciary seemed content to allow the dueling political parties to determine the contours and details of a tax policy that was hidden in plain sight.[45]

Just as the federal Constitution and courts bolstered the politics of protectionism, state constitutions and courts provided similar support for the existing subnational general property tax. In both cases, the judiciary generally deferred to legislatures and administrators. Though many Northern industrial states had constitutional clauses requiring "uniform" property taxes, these provisions, as interpreted by state courts, did not prevent state legislatures from classifying different types of property into distinct categories. Nor did the courts generally interfere in the arbitrary and capricious nature of property tax assessments.[46] For instance, Wisconsin, which would become a leader in state and local tax reform in the early twentieth century, had a constitutional uniformity clause that read: "The rule of taxation shall be uniform and taxes shall be levied upon such property as the legislature shall prescribe."[47] The Wisconsin courts, however, rarely used their powers of judicial review to overturn what appeared to be politically motivated and unequal property tax assessments. While federal courts were deferring to Congress's sweeping tax powers, state courts seemed equally reluctant to challenge the findings of local property tax assessments. In principle, these courts could intervene, as the Wisconsin Supreme Court acknowledged, to prevent "errors of

[45] Customs Administrative Act of 1890, §9, 26 Stat. 131–142; William H. Futrell, *The History of American Customs Jurisprudence* (New York, 1941), 131–40; John Dean Goss, *The History of Tariff Administration in the United States from Colonial Times to the McKinley Administrative Bill* (New York: Columbia University Press, 1891), 76–87; Stephen Skowronek, *Building a New American State: The Expansion of National Administrative Capacities, 1877–1920* (New York: Cambridge University Press, 1982); Brian Balogh, *A Government Out of Sight: The Mystery of National Authority in Nineteenth-Century America* (New York: Cambridge University Press, 2009).

[46] Fisher, *The Worst Tax?* Chapter 4; Einhorn, *American Taxation/American Slavery*, 204; Simeon Leland, *The Classified Property Tax in the United States* (Boston: Houghton Mifflin Co., 1928).

[47] *Wisconsin Constitution*, Section 1, Article VIII.

judgment and mistakes of fact" made by local assessors. But as long as such errors were "exceptional and happen[ed] in good faith, not affecting the principle or the general equality of the assessment," they were deemed constitutional. Indeed, only the most overt and egregious types of malfeasance compelled the Wisconsin court to strike down an assessment, such as when all the lands in a particularly diverse township were assessed at precisely the same value.[48]

State courts, like their federal counterparts, may have granted legislatures great latitude in levying equal taxes for public purposes, but legal experts were ambivalent about the unfettered powers of state legislatures. Though Cooley viewed Congress's taxing powers as plenary, he was deeply concerned about the taxing powers of state lawmakers. On the one hand, Cooley recognized that the democratic decision-making powers of legislatures, particularly in the realm of tax policy, ought to be respected by courts. On the other hand, he feared that unrestricted taxing powers could be used to privilege special interests and monopoly power ahead of the public purpose. Thus, Cooley combined the principles of judicial self-restraint with his concern for government neutrality and formal equality. "The constitutional requirement of equality and uniformity only extends to such objects of taxation as the legislature shall determine to be properly subject to the burden," Cooley declared in his path-breaking and widely read constitutional treatise. "The power to determine the persons and the objects to be taxed is trusted exclusively to the legislative department; but over all those the burden must be spread or it will be unequal and unlawful as to those who are selected to make the payment." State courts could intervene only when it was "plain and palpable" that such sweeping legislative fiscal powers were in "no degree" for the public benefit.[49] Judge Cooley, himself, on occasion declared certain state tax laws as violations of the emerging doctrine of "public purpose." But these cases seemed to be the exceptions that proved the rule.[50]

48 *Marsh v. Supervisors*, 42 Wis. 502 (1877); *Hersey v. Board of Supervisors*, 37 Wis. 75 (1875); *Bradley v. Lincoln County*, 60 Wis. 71 (1884).

49 Thomas M. Cooley, *A Treatise on the Constitutional Limitations Which Rest Upon the Legislative Power of the States* (New York: Da Capo reprint, 1872), 515, 494–5.

50 *East Saginaw Manufacturing Co. v. City of East Saginaw*, 19 Mich. 259 (1969); *People v. Salem*, 20 Mich. 452 (1870); Horwitz, *Transformation of American Law*, 22–4; Stanley, *Dimensions of Law*, 82–4. For more on how these decisions emanated from Cooley's general Jacksonian political philosophy, see Hovenkamp, *Enterprise and American Law*, 28–30; Sklansky, *Soul's Economy*, 210; see also Alan Jones, "Thomas M. Cooley and

Benefits Theory and the Social Contract Foundations of Fiscal Citizenship

The judicial deference toward legislative taxing powers was just one institutional reason why the nineteenth-century's politically entrenched tax system seemed immutable. The broad social and political theories that undergirded the existing regressive tax regime provided an even stronger ideological justification for the status quo – a justification that would pose a formidable challenge for progressive tax reformers.

For most nineteenth-century thinkers, taxes were quite simply the price that individual citizens paid in exchange for the benefits of government protection. Dubbed the "benefits" or "compensatory" theory of taxation, this logic reflected a laissez-faire view of state authority that stressed a stark distinction between public power and private rights.[51] Citizens paid taxes, under this principle, to ensure that the neutral and limited state could provide individuals with equal physical and financial security, not only from each other but from the public powers of the sovereign. The benefits principle was thus based, first and foremost, on the logic of reciprocal exchange: citizens paid taxes in return for state protection.[52]

Cooley was, once again, emblematic of this line of thought. Although he was a moderate supporter of tax reform, ideologically the jurist was a transition figure who subscribed to the prevailing benefits theory of taxation. "The citizen and the property owner owes to the government the duty to pay taxes," Cooley proclaimed, so "that the government may be enabled to perform its functions." The taxpayer "is supposed to receive his proper and full compensation in the protection which the government affords to his life, liberty and property, and in the increase to the value of his possessions by the use to which the money contributed is applied." In his remarks before the ASSA, Cooley succinctly summarized the benefits theory of taxation when he reiterated "persons should be taxed for the

'Laissez-Faire Constitutionalism': A Reconsideration," *Journal of American History* 53:4 (March 1967), 751–71.

[51] Francis A. Walker, "The Principles of Taxation," *Princeton Review*, 2 (July 1880), 93.

[52] Present-day tax theorists continue to define the benefits principle by reference to a reciprocal exchange, though they often apply the rationale to user fees like gasoline taxes, as opposed to the general benefits provided by public goods. Robert W. McGee, *The Philosophy of Taxation and Public Finance* (Norwell, Mass.: Kluwer Academic Publishers, 2004), 58–9; David N. Hyman, *Public Finance: A Contemporary Application of Theory to Policy* (Mason, Ohio: Thomson Learning, 2008), 411–12.

support of government in proportion to the revenue they enjoy under its protection."[53]

In elaborating on the reciprocal relationship between tax payments and government protection, Cooley admitted the difficulty of applying the benefits theory in practice. "If it were practicable to do so, the taxes levied by any government ought to be apportioned among the people according to the benefit which each receives from the protection the government affords: but this is manifestly impossible," wrote Cooley. "The value of life and liberty and of the social and family rights and privileges cannot be measured by any pecuniary standard." Nonetheless, for Cooley and others, the criterion of reciprocal exchange remained an ideal worth pursuing, a form of rough justice. "Experience has given us no better standard," conceded Cooley. Benefits theory "is applied in a great variety of forms, and with more or less approximation to justice and equality." In the end, Cooley concluded, "what is aimed at is, not taxes strictly just, but such taxes as will best subserve the general welfare of the political society."[54]

Other jurists and policymakers concurred, though with varying degrees of enthusiasm. Some followed what was referred to as "the insurance model" of taxation, which suggested that a sliding scale existed between tax payments and government benefits: "pay me so much money, and I guarantee you so much protection," one Massachusetts tax commission reported. Meanwhile, others had a more diffuse notion of benefits. "Taxes are revenue collected from the people for objects in which they are interested – the contributions of the people for things useful and conducive to their welfare," wrote one legal treatise writer.[55]

Still others contrasted the abstract and practical underpinnings of taxation. The jurist W. H. Burroughs, who corresponded with Cooley as he drafted his own tax treatise, held a more social and pragmatic view of taxation. "In theory, the taxpayer receives compensation for the taxes paid in protection the government affords," acknowledged Burroughs, "but the foundation of the taxing power is political necessity. Taxes are sacrifices made for the public good." Burroughs seemed to subordinate the

[53] Cooley, *Law of Taxation*, 2; Cooley, *Framing of Tax Laws*, 7.

[54] Cooley, *Law of Taxation*, 16–17.

[55] *Report of the Commissioners Appointed to Inquire into the Expediency of Revising and Amending the Law Relating to Taxation and Exemption Thereof* (Boston: Wright & Potters State Printers, 1875), 9; Robert Desty, *The American Law of Taxation* (St. Paul: West Publishing Co., 1884), 2.

government protection rationale to public necessity.[56] Subsequent generations of theorists, as we shall see in the following chapter, would extend this logic, focusing specifically on the significance of equal sacrifice. Melding the ideas of John Stuart Mill with the teachings of the German Historical School of Economics, a new generation of professionally trained American political economists led by Richard T. Ely, Henry Carter Adams, and Edwin R. A. Seligman would use the notion of "ability to pay" to show how direct and progressive taxes could forge a reinvigorated sense of social sacrifice, civic identity, and fiscal citizenship.

Yet for Cooley and his cohort a robust notion of fiscal citizenship remained relatively foreign. Instead, they embraced the promise and perils of a more circumscribed and highly individualistic view of taxation. Rooted in classical liberal visions of social contract and possessive individualism, the benefits theory of taxation reflected atomistic notions of selfhood, consent, and reciprocal exchange. In the age of slave emancipation, and during the height of free labor ideology, political and social theorists reinforced the belief that taxes ought to be part of the political pact between autonomous, self-possessive citizens and their representative republic. In this sense, the relationship between the state and its citizens represented a natural limit on the taxing powers – a limit that appealed to those who valued the liberating aspects of traditional social contract theory. Only those who fell within the polity's sphere of power were identified as taxpaying citizens. As Cooley explained, quoting an early U.S. Supreme Court decision, "the power of taxation, however vast in its character, and searching in it extent, is necessarily limited to subjects within the jurisdiction of the state." This constraint itself, Hilliard agreed, could act as "a sufficient security against erroneous and oppressive taxation." Conversely, the benefits theory's inherent limit on taxing authority meant that individual citizens could use taxation to acknowledge their willingness to be a part of a political and social community. By paying taxes, independent individuals exercised their volition and free will when they consented to be governed by a sovereign that provided protection in exchange for loyalty and tax payments.[57]

If the benefits theory of taxation embodied the liberating aspects of contractual relations, it also contained, critics asserted, a narrow,

[56] W.H. Burroughs to Thomas M. Cooley, December 18, 1874, Box 6, TMCP; W.H. Burroughs, *Treatise on the Law of Taxation*, 1.

[57] Cooley, *Law of Taxation*, 15; Hilliard, Law *of Taxation*, 4–5. On the dominance of contract thinking during the postbellum era, see Stanley, *From Bondage to Contract*.

market-oriented view of fiscal citizenship. Under the benefits theory, taxes were akin to a commercial transaction. Members of a polity had no social obligations or civic duties beyond the quid pro quo of paying taxes and receiving governmental protection. If taxation was one of the most commonly and consistently experienced relationships between Americans and their government, benefits theory appeared to limit that important relationship – and the civic identity that emerged from it – to the cash nexus. Citizenship itself was reduced to a commodity. The benefits principle seemed to subordinate the social aspects of the *social* contract. For a subsequent group of theorists and political activists, such an impoverished vision of taxes and community would be unacceptable. But during the last decades of the nineteenth century few doubted this logic and characterization of taxes.

To be sure, the benefit rationale was not a systematic and internally consistent theory, as critics and even supporters like Cooley pointed out. It frequently had contradictory implications that made it less of an intellectually coherent principle than a politically convenient ideology. Even Adam Smith's first maxim of taxation was a highly ambiguous endorsement of the notion that taxes ought to be based solely on the benefits conferred by government protection. "The subjects of every state," wrote Smith, "ought to contribute towards the support of the government, as nearly as possible, in proportion to their respective abilities; that is, in proportion to the revenue which they respectively enjoy under the protection of the state." By conflating the notion of taxing according to "respective abilities" with reference to state protection, Smith provided intellectual credibility to a rather flexible view of taxation.[58]

The theoretical malleability of the benefits rationale proved to be a huge boon for legislators. When lawmakers evoked the benefits principle, they frequently did so in the context of state and local property taxes, contending that the revenues from property taxes were used to provide fire and police protection as well as the legal protection of property and contract rights more generally. Even on the national stage, as we have seen, congressional leaders claimed that the tariff protected domestic industries, and by implication high wages, from foreign competition. In reality, the tariff regime was a complex and messy amalgamation of international trade policy, party patronage, and log-rolling. But that

[58] Cooley, *Law of Taxation*, 16–17. Adam Smith, *An Inquiry into the Nature and Causes of the Wealth of Nations*, ed. Edwin Cannan (New York: Modern Library, 1937 [1776]), Vol. II, Book V, Chapter II, Part II.

did not prevent Republican lawmakers from defending high tariffs as a beneficial form of government protection. Although this was a different form of protection than envisioned by conventional benefits theory, the amorphous nature of the benefits principle permitted national political leaders to argue that the customs duties and internal excise taxes were the prices paid for all sorts of government benefits, from tariff protection to internal improvements to Civil War pensions. Given this malleability, the benefits principle could even be used by the most unlikely of theorists to attack protectionism.[59]

Indeed, American thinkers not usually associated with progressive reform evoked the benefits rationale to condemn the protective tariff and support a flat income tax. Along with Cooley, William Graham Sumner, the Yale professor and leading American proponent of laissez faire, and David Wells derided the protective tariff as a form of state capitalism. They depicted protectionism as an unwarranted benefit, as an illegitimate exercise of public power. "Any favor or encouragement," wrote Sumner, "which the protective system exerts on one group of its population must be won by an equivalent oppression exerted on some other group." By imposing customs duties, "government gives a license to certain interests to go out and encroach on others" Sumner concluded. It permits a "subtle, cruel, and unjust invasion of one man's rights by another." The solution, as Sumner explained to a congressional committee in 1878, was to shift the federal government's sources of revenue from the tariff to a flat income tax with an exemption level set at the minimal cost of living. "I am in favor of an income tax as a matter of public finance," Sumner informed lawmakers. "If we had an income tax and could do away with tariff taxes, the result, I think, would be very beneficial to the whole community."[60]

Other economic analysts agreed, suggesting that the durability of the tariff regime was the inevitable consequence of corrupt administration and lawmaking. Not only was the appointment of key Collectors of Customs deeply embedded in the spoils system of party patronage, the setting of duty lists and rates was the result of intense lobbying and special interest politics. "The anomalous and disgraceful tariff now existing,"

[59] David A. Wells, *The Theory and Practice of Taxation* (New York: D. Appleton and Co., 1911), 408–12; Jonathan B. Wise, *An Argument for a Protective Tariff* (Cambridge: University Press, John Wilson and Son, 1880), 25–7.

[60] William G. Sumner, "The Argument against Protective Taxes," *Princeton Review*, 1 (March 1881), 241; Sumner, *Protectionism* (New York: Holt, 1888), vii, 165; House Misc. Doc. 29 (45th Congress, 3rd Session), S.S. 1863, 206.

Wells announced, "is the result of the labors of men, who have gone to Washington as representatives of particular interests, and have fought and lobbied and log-rolled until they have got what they wanted, without caring in the least how their success may have affected other equally meritorious interests."[61]

Though many influential thinkers supported income taxes as a replacement for the tariff, they did not endorse progressive or redistributive tax policies. Cooley, in fact, believed that income taxes were an ideal that could not be achieved, at least not in the United States where "the objections to it are so serious that it seems improbable it will ever be resorted to as a permanent means of revenue." Even if income taxes were administratively feasible, Cooley feared that graduated rates or the principle of progressivity "once admitted" could permit legislatures to impose "the whole burden of government on the few who exhibit most energy, enterprise and thrift."[62]

Wells, as the former Civil War Commissioner of Internal Revenue, had some limited faith in the income tax. After all, he had helped usher in and administer the country's first income tax laws. But he too resolutely opposed any form of graduated rates or even a basic exemption level. "Any government," wrote Wells, "whatever name it may assume, is a despotism, and commits acts of flagrant spoliation, if it grants exemptions or exacts a greater or lesser rate of tax from one man than from another." Such discriminations, Wells concluded, were "purely arbitrary" and hence "an act of charity which every American ought to reject upon principle and with scorn." Wells went even further. Deploying the Republican Party's rhetoric of separate gendered spheres, Wells maintained that progressive taxes of any sort were a form of emasculating charity. "Equality and manhood," he concluded, "demand and require uniformity of burden in whatever is the subject of taxation."[63]

Still, theorists like Wells, Sumner, and Cooley held out hope that a uniformly applied income tax could one day replace the state capitalism of the protective tariff. In so doing, these conservative thinkers unwittingly planted the seeds of a seismic shift in American thinking about taxation. Meanwhile, a younger generation of professionally trained political

[61] James Parton, "The Power of Public Plunder," *North American Review* 133 (July 1881), 43–64; David A. Wells, "Reform in Federal Taxation," *North American Review* 133 (December 1881), 611–28.

[62] Cooley, *Framing Tax Laws*, 10; *Law of Taxation*, 20.

[63] David A. Wells, "The Communism of a Discriminating Income Tax," *North American Review* 130 (1880), 236–46.

economists soon began turning their attention to the tariff and the social scientific study of public finance. These German-trained academics would join their intellectual predecessors in condemning protectionism, though with a radically different view of public power – one that favored the state as an ethical agency of progressive reform.

Social Movements and the Obstacles to Tax Reform

Before the progressive political economists would come to challenge their elders, a variety of social groups were already growing increasingly antagonistic to the existing fiscal order. While Cooley, Hilliard, and other legal experts were deriding the current state of fiscal affairs, populist leaders and reformers were expressing their own hostility not only toward the prevailing tax laws but toward the entire system of industrial capitalism. Indeed, the Great Upheaval of the 1880s, with its rising tide of labor strikes, its boycotts and protests, and its explosive growth in populist organizing, provided an important backdrop for the social and political pressures driving progressive tax reform. The decade's turmoil also shaped an emerging group of public intellectuals who would soon become the social democratic advocates for working-class demands.[64]

For some tax activists, the working masses appeared to be an ideal constituency. Many ordinary Americans believed that, as consumers, they bore the brunt of the existing tariff and the excise taxes. Similarly, farmers contended that their visible property made them vulnerable to the inequities of the woefully antiquated state and local property tax. Organized laborers and farmers thus seemed to be a potential group that reformers could mobilize in support of fundamental fiscal reform. And given the growing tensions between labor and the American judiciary in the 1880s, political and social reformers believed they could harness the electoral power of the working masses to improve the existing tax system.[65]

64 Bruce Laurie, *Artisans into Workers: Labor in Nineteenth-Century America* (New York: Hill and Wang 1989); Nell Irving Painter, *Standing at Armageddon: The United States, 1877–1919* (New York: W. W. Norton and Co., 1989); Sanders, *Roots of Reform*; Leon Fink, *Progressive Intellectuals and the Dilemmas of Democratic Commitment* (Cambridge, Mass.: Harvard University Press, 1999), 52.

65 Sanders, *Roots of Reform*; Clemens, *The People's Lobby*; William E. Forbath, *Law and the Shaping of the American Labor Movement* (Cambridge, Mass.: Harvard University Press, 1991).

The reformers were only partly correct. Elected representatives of agrarian regions would eventually lead the legislative charge for progressive taxes in the early twentieth century, but in the last decades of the nineteenth century fundamental tax reform seemed unlikely for several reasons. First, as we have seen, the expanding protective tariff and the revenues it generated for Civil War pensions commanded the allegiance of many a tiller and toiler and thereby frustrated any coherent and cohesive opposition to protectionism. Second, the national excise levies on alcohol and tobacco faced little resistance because of their hidden and insidious application. The excise tax on alcohol may not have been salient to ordinary Americans, but its complex relationship to the dynamics of the temperance movement made this levy remarkably intractable.

Third, and perhaps most important, other reform movements attracted working-class attention that fragmented the popular support for direct and graduated taxes. Henry George's single-tax movement, arguably the most potent fiscal reform campaign of its time, eschewed any levies beside an exclusive tax on land rents. Although many American socialists supported graduated taxes, their primary focus on protective labor legislation and other industrial reforms similarly meant that their attention was frequently focused elsewhere. More radical elements of the American left, including those who held out hope for a proletariat revolution, believed that graduated income and wealth-transfer taxes were insufficient solutions to the growing ills of modern capitalism. These divided loyalties, in sum, forestalled any widespread and sustained support for genuine tax reform.

As a whole, the social unease with basic tax reform reflected the general nineteenth-century American ambivalence toward centralized authority. While many hailed the virtues of private initiative, there was no denying the persistent, if inconspicuous, exercise of public power – particularly with the protective tariff.[66] Dismantling an entrenched fiscal system thus meant challenging not just the tariff, but an entire structure of statecraft. By the late 1880s, some social groups appeared ready for the task. An emerging labor-farmer political alliance and the ongoing demands from independent political parties for direct and graduated taxes illustrated not only the growing hostility to the existing regressive tax regime, but also the range of alternative proposals floated by social groups. For the most part, however, these organizations and their ideas remained on the margins of national politics.

[66] Keller, *Regulating a New Economy*; Balogh, *Government Out of Sight*.

Legislative Optimism and Divided Allegiances over the Tariff

Organized workers and farmers may have been divided and distracted, but that did not mean that they had no interest in tax reform. Despite the judicial opposition to labor laws, many working-class leaders in the 1880s still had faith in the transformative powers of law and legal institutions. They embraced the language of law as a vulgar tongue. With the courts consistently using injunctions to outlaw strikes and boycotts, some labor reformers believed that the legislative arena, as imperfect as it was, might be the best place to air their grievances.[67] Leaders of the Noble Order of the Knights of Labor, the leading late-nineteenth-century organization of farmers and laborers, conceded in 1886 that the privileged classes dominated the legislative process, that "any attempt on the part of the people to influence or create law is met by discontent and opposition." Yet this was a distortion of American democracy, the labor leaders claimed. "Law making should be the expression of the will of the people – not as exists, that of the conclave," intoned an editorial in the Knights' official newsletter, the *Journal of United Labor (JUL)*. "Therefore, as a body, the people should become the law-makers and this right embraces each and every individual." Echoing the sentiments of the new generation of political economists who at the same time were challenging the so-called natural laws of laissez faire, labor leaders emphasized the malleability of laws like the tariff. "The fact that man creates law presupposes change of law," the *JUL* editorial observed. "Law is obligatory only so long as it occupies a place on our statute books. The changes of commercial and domestic affairs attending progressive development call for changing enactments."[68]

Rank-and-file members of the Knights of Labor – ordinary farmers and workers – similarly believed that the power of the ballot box and political petitions could be harnessed to reform the fiscal system and curb monopoly power. As one farmer's wife explained in one of her many letters to the *JUL* in 1888, "the great issues ov this hour" are "the rites ov the farmers and laborers (for their interests are identical and the same), as ginst the hydra-headed monster that is suckin our life's blood – hi taxation and monopoly." To slay this monster, she recommended

[67] Leon Fink, *Workingmen's Democracy: The Knights of Labor and American Politics* (Urbana: University of Illinois Press, 1983); Clemens, *The People's Lobby*; Forbath, *Law and the Shaping of the American Labor Movement*.

[68] "The Functions of Law," *Journal of United Labor*, April 16, 1887. For more on the Knights of Labor, see Fink, *Workingmen's Democracy*.

that readers "use that God-given defence – baptised in the blood ov the Revolutionary War – the ballot and vote for no man who is tu make or execute the laws in this country who is not one ov our number and true to our interests."[69] In her own homespun terms, this ordinary American also provided readers with the text for a petition requesting that congressional leaders nominate members of the producing class for national office: "We the undersigned – farmers, shopkeepers and wage-workers – ask the leadin political parties ov the kongressional district of ___ tu nominate a kandidate for Kongress from *our Ranks*, that we may have konfidence in his *Fidelity* tu our interests. If neither ov the leadin parties nominate such a man we will do so ourselves; and we further pledge our *word and sacred honor* tu each other *not to vote for eny other congressional kandidate.*"[70] Petitions like these, frequently with more specific demands, were regularly sent to congressional leaders during debates over tax reform.[71]

Although members of the Knights and other labor associations may have been eager to participate in the legislative process, they received little guidance from their national leaders when it came to the issue of tax reform. Even in the late 1880s, as the tariff became the dominant political question of the day, national leaders of the Knights attempted to remain above the partisan fray. When a local assembly member from Iowa wrote to the *Journal of United Labor* in 1887 requesting "a synopsis of the arguments showing the advantages of a high tariff and the disadvantages of free trade," the editors responded with characteristic caution. Admitting that they had "decided opinions on the subject of 'protection,' as

[69] Merlinda Sisins, "Farmers and Mechanics, Likewise Laborers, All Interested in the Question of Taxation, Letter No. I," *Journal of United Labor*, June 23, 1888.

[70] Merlinda Sisins, "Two Heavy Burdens; High Taxation and Organized Monopoly Destroying the Farmer and Wage-Worker," *Journal of United Labor*, August 30, 1888 (emphasis in the original). These and other letters in the labor press demonstrate not only how the Knights reached out to working women, but also how issues important to women often stretched well beyond hearth and home. In this sense, women were active participants in the social response to the regressive tax system. For more on working-class women and political reform, see generally Susan Levine, *Labor's True Woman: Carpet Weavers, Industrialization, and Labor Reform in the Gilded Age* (Philadelphia: Temple University Press, 1984); Alice Kessler-Harris, *Gendering Labor History* (Urbana: University of Illinois Press, 2006); Edwards, *Angels in the Machinery*.

[71] See, e.g., Kansas Farmers' Alliance of Riley County to Hon. John Davis, January 18, 1894, Fifty-Third Congress – Petitions; Ways and Means (HR 53A-33.10), Box 180, Folder "Tax on Incomes, September 9, 1893–April 30, 1894," National Archives and Record Administration, Washington, D.C. For more on the popular calls for an income tax, see Elmer Ellis, "Public Opinion and the Income Tax, 1860–1900," *Mississippi Valley Historical Review* 27:2 (1940), 225–42.

it is called – opinions which many other equally well-read members of the Order do not share," the editors replied that "it would not be the correct thing to promulgate our individual ideas, which would possibly not even find endorsement among the majority, as the official sentiment of the Order." The editors did not, however, minimize the gravity of the tariff issue. "There are few topics of more interest to wage earners than the question of custom house protection to our industries," the editors concluded. "Let the different Local Assemblies make this a subject for debate, preceded by study." Among the important authors and works to consult, the editors recommended Henry George.[72]

Labor leaders demurred on the topic of protectionism for good reason. It was a highly divisive issue for wage earners and farmers. Protariff Republicans attempted to appeal to workers as consumers by linking high duty goods such as wool products with promises to reduce internal excise taxes on alcohol and tobacco. Yet while customs duties may have hurt workers as consumers, the tariff also appeared to benefit laborers in protected industries. Not only did the tariff shelter domestic manufacturers and thus create and preserve jobs that might not have otherwise existed in the face of foreign competition, it also supposedly led to higher wages – a point that high-tariff Republicans frequently raised during congressional debates. Representative William McKinley (R-Ohio), a leading tariff advocate, pointed to a petition sent by the Iron and Steel and Glassblowers assemblies of the Knights and other unions in 1888 to proclaim that he had the support of at least "a half million working men of the United States in opposing" tariff reduction. Lawmakers like McKinley did not hesitate in drawing direct links between the tariff and the benefits it provided. Workers from the Ohio trade unions specifically acknowledged in their petition: "we receive our share of the benefits of protection on the industries we represent. We therefore emphatically protest against any reduction of the duties that will bring us on a level with the low price paid for labor in Europe. We insist upon the maintenance of a strong protective tariff in order to maintain an American standard of wages for American workingmen."[73]

Workers in unprotected industries, by contrast, had "no need for the protective tariff," as one shoemaker put it, because "the duty" was a "very iniquitous proposition." As early as 1882, the nascent American Federation of Labor (AFL) even went so far as to renounce officially the

72 "Protection v. Free Trade," *Journal of United Labor*, April 9, 1887.

73 *Congressional Record*, 50th Cong., 1st sess. (1888), 19, pt. 5:4406.

TABLE 1.1. *Alcohol Excise and Federal Government Revenue, Internal and Total, 1880–1913 (in thousands of nominal dollars)*

Year	Alcohol Excise Tax Revenue	Total Federal Internal Revenue	Alcohol as % of Total Internal Revenue	All Federal Revenue	Alcohol as % of All Federal Revenue
1880	$74,015	$123,982	60%	$333,527	22%
1890	107,696	142,595	76%	403,081	27%
1894	116,674	147,168	79%	306,355	38%
1900	183,420	295,316	62%	567,241	32%
1910	208,602	289,957	72%	675,512	31%
1913	230,146	344,424	67%	714,403	32%

Source: Historical Statistics of the United States: Millennial Edition, ed. Susan B. Carter et al. (New York: Cambridge University Press, 2006), Table Ea588–593.

protective tariff in its convention platform. Unsurprisingly, the Amalgamated Association of Iron and Steel Workers initially refused to join the AFL because of its anti-tariff stance. Over time, however, constituent AFL unions acting independently endorsed protectionism for their respective industries. As a result, the tariff remained a divisive issue among organized labor throughout the turn of the century.[74]

Hidden Excise Taxes and the Dynamics of Prohibition

If the protective tariff divided working-class loyalties, excise taxes seemed to prevent fiscal changes in more subtle and complex ways. Throughout the late nineteenth century, excise taxes on alcohol, tobacco, and other sundry items remained a significant source of federal revenues and a constant thorn for quotidian consumers. From 1880 to 1913, the excise levy on alcohol alone accounted for between 60 and 79 percent of total internal revenue (which did not include tariff revenue), and 22 to 38 percent of all federal receipts (see Table 1.1).

74 "Testimony of Mr. Horace M. Eaton," Washington, D.C., September 21, 1899, 360–1, in *Report of the Industrial Commission*; Molly Ray Carroll, *Labor and Politics: The Attitude of the American Federation of Labor Toward Legislation and Politics* (New York: Houghton, Mifflin, 1923), 133–4; Lewis L. Lorwin, with the assistance of Jean Atherton Flexner, *American Federation of Labor: History, Policies and Prospects*. (Washington: Brookings Institution, 1933), 436–7.

As indirect taxes, though, the excise levies on alcohol often escaped the notice of everyday consumers. Because these taxes were "so adroitly mingled in the price" of an item, wrote the Virginia lawyer and legislator John Randolph Tucker, the consumer "sees only the greed of the merchant, and does not dream of the exactions of his government." The hidden nature of such "unconscious exaction," Tucker observed, explained why citizens had become negligent in their "watchfulness of the fiscal operations of government." As a Southern lawmaker opposed to centralized authority, Tucker did not hide his disdain for how indirect national taxes were harming ordinary citizens. "The government, in effect, becomes irresponsible to him for the real injury it inflicts," Tucker concluded, "because he feels none. Though robbed, 'let him not know it, and he's not robbed at all.'"[75]

Although he was not seeking to enhance the powers of the federal government, Tucker, like others, believed that taxpayers and citizens had a right to see and understand how their national government was extracting public revenues. In fact, many progressive tax reformers concurred that the hidden aspects of indirect taxation undermined effective political and civic engagement. The University of Wisconsin political economist and labor reformer Richard T. Ely observed how increasing concentrations of wealth combined with indirect taxation were making elite citizens disconnected from the democratic process. Ely identified a new leisure class of individuals – "a considerable and increasing class living in great comfort on incomes of large proportions" – as one of the most politically and socially apathetic. In concealing their wealth and shirking their fiscal responsibilities, the members of this new leisure class, Ely wrote, were often "careless and indifferent about their public duties, knowing that their income is not affected by high or low taxation. They appear to pay nothing to government, and as it seems to cost them nothing, they too often care little for it."[76]

An emerging leisure class was only part of the problem. Even more disconcerting for Ely and other social reformers was the class of "professional people," the "lawyers, physicians, and teachers," who had "opportunities for personal cultivation and for gathering knowledge," and whose "influence ought to be large and beneficial." As long as this group of educated citizens was only tangentially affected by the prevailing indirect tax

[75] John Randolph Tucker, "Evils of Indirect Taxation," *Forum* (February 1887), 633.

[76] Ely, *Taxation in American States and Cities* (New York: Thomas Y. Crowell and Co., 1888), 289.

system, they too would remain detached from practical politics. To combat this political and civic apathy, economic thinkers and reformers touted the increased transparency and government accountability that came with more salient and direct taxes on incomes, profits, and wealth transfers. A direct tax on income, Ely contended, was "precisely the kind of tax needed" to reengage citizens with the political process and to promote good government. "It is beyond question," Ely optimistically concluded, that a fairly administered income tax "would change the attitude of a large portion of the community towards government."[77]

Though they supported the move to direct and graduated taxes, social groups and activists appeared uncertain about how new taxes on income and wealth might fit a broader reform agenda. Early advocates for Prohibition – the twentieth-century "noble experiment" that had its roots in the temperance movements of the nineteenth century – were ambivalent about supporting direct and progressive taxes. On the one hand, temperance advocates feared that if these new taxes came to replace the existing levies on alcohol, the final price of distilled spirits would decline and consumption would increase. Seen in this light, the excise levies were welcomed "sin" taxes that demonstrated the public disapproval of alcohol and tobacco. Early pragmatic Prohibitionists viewed the liquor tax as a necessary penalty or stigma on the production and sale of alcohol, and hence as an implicit temperance tool. In some cases, they were even able to use the national liquor tax as an effective state-level enforcement mechanism. Members of the Anti-Saloon League, therefore, approved of the federal liquor tax as a badge of shame that could further "Prohibition by indirection."[78]

On the other hand, some Prohibitionists supported new taxes on income and wealth as substitutes for the excise levies on alcohol. They believed that the federal government's reliance on alcohol taxes as a source of revenue prevented national lawmakers from seriously considering the moral merits of nationwide Prohibition. The Prohibition Party opposed measures like the excise taxes that might permanently legitimize the liquor traffic.[79] Lawmakers understood that they could even use alcohol excise taxes to wipe out the liquor traffic. As Representative

[77] Ibid., 290.

[78] Richard F. Hamm, *Shaping the Eighteenth Amendment: Temperance Reform, Legal Culture, and the Polity, 1800–1920* (Chapel Hill: University of North Carolina Press, 1995), Chapter 5.

[79] John J. Rumbarger, *Profits, Power, and Prohibition: Alcohol Reform and the Industrializing of America, 1800–1930* (Albany: SUNY Press, 1989), 72, 87–8, 120–1.

Richmond P. Hobson (R-Ala.) noted when he introduced the resolution that would become the Eighteenth Amendment: if lawmakers were serious about using taxation as a temperance tool, "Congress could make every State in the country dry" by simple majority. Enacting enormous liquor taxes could easily increase prices to the point of shutting down the entire industry. But because national legislators were reliant on the revenue from alcohol excise taxes, there was little chance they would kill the golden goose. The goal for "drys" like Hobson was to find an alternative revenue source that could help wean the national state off of its addiction to liquor tax revenue. New taxes on incomes, profits, and wealth transfers were thus a welcomed first step toward national Prohibition.[80]

Temperance advocates supported replacing the liquor levy with new taxes for a second reason: to undermine the brewers' moral claims that they were patriotically supporting the national government by paying the tax. Some of the country's largest brewers had originally formed the United States Brewers' Association to protest the Civil War excise tax, but by the turn of the century many of these same distillers were arguing that the tax legitimated the production and sale of alcohol. The excise, they maintained, came with Uncle Sam's seal of approval. Unsurprisingly, temperance activists sought to defile that seal. By severing the government's reliance on liquor for revenue, and in the process removing the government's imprimatur, members of the Woman's Christian Temperance Union contended that the income tax could be used indirectly to advance the full nationwide prohibition of alcohol.[81] Although dry advocates and tax reformers potentially had similar interests, looming concerns about the possible adverse impact of removing the "sin" tax kept temperance activists divided in their support for new national taxes. Caught between these opposing views, most early Prohibitionists were unable to integrate the two reforms, and consequently the movement for progressive tax reform remained fractured and sterile in the 1880s.

[80] *Congressional Record*, 63rd Cong., 3rd sess. (1915), 52, pt. 1:602; Richmond Pearson Hobson, *The Truth about Alcohol* (Washington, D.C.: Government Printing Office, 1914); K. Austin Kerr, *The Politics of Moral Behavior: Prohibition and Drug Abuse* (Reading, Mass.: Addison-Wesley, 1973), 97–102.

[81] Daniel Okrent, *Last Call: The Rise and Fall of Prohibition* (New York: Scribner, 2010), 53–8; Hamm, *Shaping the Eighteenth Amendment*, 92–122. See also Jan-Willem Gerritsen, *The Control of Fuddle and Flash: A Social History of the Regulation of Alcohol and Opiates* (Leiden: Brill, 2000); Wilbur R. Miller, *Revenuers and Moonshiners: Enforcing Federal Liquor Law in the Mountain South, 1865–1900* (Chapel Hill: University of North Carolina Press, 1991).

The Distraction of Other Reform Movements: The Single Taxers and the Socialists

The ambivalence of organized labor and Prohibitionists only partially explains the ineffectiveness of late-nineteenth-century tax reform. An equally crucial obstacle throughout the post-Reconstruction decades was the distraction that other social issues and seemingly more radical tax proposals posed for progressive change. For many populist groups, comprehensive fiscal reform was subordinate to other issues like the "silver question," railroad regulation, and anti-monopoly concerns. Likewise, alternative ideas and movements such as Henry George's immensely popular single tax and the newly emergent American socialist organizations sapped valuable reformist energy away from the campaign for graduated wealth and income taxes.

In its purest form, the single tax called for the exclusive use of a single levy on land values, specifically rent, to curb land speculation and raise revenue for a limited state. Henry George believed that land speculation was the root cause of nearly all the problems of modern industrial life. With one simple solution – a tax on the increase in land values – George claimed that modern capitalist society could do away with the excessive returns, or what George referred to as the "unearned increment," of an exploitive rentier class without having to build a robust regulatory and administrative state.[82] Spawned by George's writings, the single-tax movement, which in its many variants frequently veered from its creator's initial pronouncements, was an irresistible magnet for reform organizations – a kind of flypaper for social movements. Although the single tax did not gain traction in the United States until the early twentieth century, when it was adopted in isolated areas, it had great popular appeal in the late nineteenth century.[83] Lured by George's anti-capitalist rhetoric and

[82] George, *Progress and Poverty*; Arthur N. Young, *The Single Tax Movement in the United States* (Princeton: Princeton University Press, 1916); Peter Speek, *The Single-tax and the Labor Movement* (Ph.D. dissertation, University of Wisconsin, 1915). To understand George's ideas within the context of late-nineteenth-century American thought, see John Thomas, *Alternative America: Henry George, Edward Bellamy, Henry Demarest Lloyd and the Adversary Tradition* (Cambridge, Mass.: Harvard University Press, 1983); Sklansky, *Soul's Economy*.

[83] On the early-twentieth-century popularity of the single tax in the Pacific Northwest, see Robert D. Johnston, *The Radical Middle-Class: Populist Democracy and the Question of Capitalism in Progressive Era Portland, Oregon* (Princeton: Princeton University Press, 2003), 159–76; Lawrence M. Lipin, "'Cast Aside the Automobile Enthusiast': Class Conflict, Tax Policy, and the Preservation of Nature in Progressive-Era Oregon, *Oregon Historical Society* 107:2 (2006), 165–95.

his biblical references, activists of all stripes were attracted to the single tax, to varying degrees, as the inexorable solution to the social, political, and economic dislocations of modern industrial capitalism. Farmers understandably were weary of a levy on land, even if it was directed at speculators and not small producers, but laborers and small merchants readily embraced George and his ideas.[84]

Published the year after Cooley's tax treatise, George's *Progress and Poverty* was particularly popular among urban workers who had little in the way of property holdings.[85] The *Journal of United Labor* regularly circulated excerpts of the book. The preamble of the Knights' constitution echoed George's demand that "all lands now held for speculative purposes be taxed to their full value." And even when labor leaders demurred on the issue of taxation, they did not hesitate in encouraging rank-and-file members to consult George's book. Soon after it was published, Richard Ely observed that "tens of thousands of laborers have read *Progress and Poverty*, who have never before looked between the two corners of an economic book."[86]

The single tax also had adherents among urban religious leaders. "I owe my first awakening to the world of social problems to the agitation of Henry George," recalled social gospel leader, Walter Rauschenbusch, who referred to George as the "single-minded apostle of a great truth." Single-tax leagues, often created by church groups drawn to George's reference to his evangelical Christian faith, emerged throughout the country. When George ran for mayor of New York City in 1886, he had the backing of several labor leaders, including Samuel Gompers, and reform-minded ministers like Washington Gladden and Rauschenbusch. George did not win the election, finishing behind Abraham Hewitt but ahead of Theodore Roosevelt, yet the strength of his candidacy indicated the broad urban support for his ideas and proposals.[87]

84 George, *Progress and Poverty*, 359–60; Henry George, *The Science of Political Economy* (New York: Robert Schalkenbach Foundation 1897), 150–1; Jeffrey A. Johnson, *"They Are All Red Out Here": Socialist Politics in the Pacific Northwest, 1895–1925* (Norman: University of Oklahoma Press, 2008), 104–11.

85 George, *Progress and Poverty*; Charles A. Barker, *Henry George* (New York: Oxford University Press, 1955).

86 Knights of Labor, "Constitution of the General Assembly," Demand IV, Preamble. Ely, quoted in Philip S. Foner, *History of the Labor Movement in the United States. Vol. 2. From the Founding of the American Federation of Labor to the Emergence of American Imperialism* (New York: International Publishers, 1955), 120.

87 Walter Rauschenbusch, *Christianizing the Social Order* (New York: Macmillan Co., 1914), 394; David Scobey, "Boycotting the Politics Factory: Labor Radicalism and the

Despite his political setbacks, George's ideas filtered into everyday discussions of the working class, as the writings of rank-and-file members of the Knights revealed. "Landlordism can be rendered perfectly harmless," wrote Samuel B. Shaw of Eastport, Maine, in the pages of the *JUL*, "if it is compelled to return to the community in the shape of a tax the money it demands from men as the price for the privilege of living." An ardent single taxer, Shaw went so far as to proclaim that the "single tax on land values" was "the only final solution to the labor problem." Another single-tax supporter put the matter in more legal terms: "Laws that enable the land speculator to rob labor of its earnings must be supplanted by the laws that place land under collective ownership, through the appropriation of ground rents to be applied to the public welfare." And still others saw the single tax as a way to address "the labor problem" without assenting to the "slavery of socialism."[88] The growing affinity toward Henry George and the single tax invariably drew attention away from other more moderate and practical tax reform proposals.

While many ordinary workers enthusiastically absorbed George's ideas, national labor leaders were more skeptical. The editors of the Knights' newsletter, for instance, acknowledged that the single tax, with its communitarian assumptions, "would be an immense advance and materially better the condition of the toilers." But they doubted that the single tax by itself could provide all the cascading benefits and thus be the panacea that George and his disciples claimed. As the *JUL* editors explained, the single tax would not "be sufficient of itself to give labor its full earnings or anything approaching them." The social problems of modern urban industrial life were simply too numerous and complex for one policy prescription. The single tax "will not cause an exodus from the cities to the country," the editors intoned. "It will not enable those engaged in trades and city occupations to become independent farmers. It will not prevent the masses of city toilers from being crushed and ground between the upper and nether millstone of money monopoly and unrestricted competition." And most important of all, the single tax would

New York City Mayoral Election of 1884," *Radical History Review* 28–30 (1984), 280–325; Thomas, *Alternative America*, 220–7. On the popularity of single-tax leagues, see Barker, *Henry George*; Young, *The Single Tax Movement in the United States*; Speek, *The Single Tax and the Labor Movement*.

88 Samuel B. Shaw, "A Single Tax," *Journal of United Labor*, June 6, 1889; M. Ritchie, "Whose Fault Is It?" *American Federationist* (August 1895), 102; Sara Mifflin Gay, "Is the Single Tax Enough to Solve the Labor Problem?" *The Arena* (May 1896), 956–9.

not alter the ownership of the means of production. "The capitalist, the machine owner, the speculator will still exact from the toiler the greater portion of his earnings," concluded the editors, questioning the efficacy of the single tax. "Much will remain to be done in addition to taxing the soil to its full value so long as the control of capital and machinery remain in the hands of the few."[89]

The reference to the ownership and control of capital and machinery was, of course, an allusion to more radical methods of confronting the excesses of industrial capitalism. The growing, though still nascent, American socialist organizations of the 1870s and 1880s were rather heterogeneous in their make-up and aims. Whereas more radical elements of American socialism endorsed the public ownership of railroads and utilities, other factions sought to provide immediate and practical assistance to industrial workers. What these groups had in common was that they, like the single taxers, drew valuable energy away from mainstream tax reform.[90]

Although the 1880 fusion between the Socialist Labor party and the Greenback Party led to the endorsement of a graduated income tax as a secondary aim, American socialists for the most part were more concerned with other issues. Moderate socialists wanted to ameliorate day-to-day working conditions, while radicals promulgated an ideology of public ownership and proletariat revolution. Supporting a progressive income tax did not fit easily with either of these two objectives. For those socialists focused on tangible and immediate changes, political activism was aimed toward securing better wages, working conditions, and the rights to organize and assemble, not the more abstract and long-term objective of fundamentally restructuring the American fiscal order. Meanwhile, for unreconstructed Marxists, progressive taxes were explicitly a capitalist tool – a palliative premised on the perpetuation, not the abolition, of private property and rigid social classes. Even the short-term goal of tariff reform was frequently dismissed as insufficient. When the Milwaukee socialist, Victor Berger, attempted to insert a plank into the Socialist Party platform calling for tariff reduction, more radical

[89] "Is the Single Tax Sufficient?" *Journal of United Labor*, September 19, 1889.

[90] Daniel Bell, *Marxian Socialism in the United States* (Ithaca: Cornell University Press, 1996); Ira Kipnis, *The American Socialist Movement 1897–1912* (New York: Columbia University Press, 1952); Stanley, *Dimensions of Law*, 77–8. As we shall see in Chapter 3, the progressive political economists who stressed the moderate aspects of direct and graduated taxes also believed that radical socialists would not support steeply graduated taxes.

elements within the party rebuked Berger's proposals and rejected the proposal.[91]

Ironically, radical socialists and single taxers resisted progressive taxation for opposite, though equally fundamental, reasons. Whereas direct and graduated taxes did not go far enough for those socialists who advocated proletariat revolution and the public ownership of the means of production, they went too far for Henry George and his acolytes. Henry George's single tax was based on a totalizing social theory that attempted to solve all the problems of modern capitalism with a single cure-all, as the *JUL* editors noted. In short, George was a laissez-faire ideologue who wanted to preserve the sanctity of private property while limiting state action to the collection of an exclusive tax on economic rent. The narrowness of relying on only one solution to the myriad of problems confronting modern society revealed the conservative anti-statist nature of George's theory. Put simply, Henry George's single tax retained a sense of radical individualism as it sought to address what George saw as the root of all evil: the private appropriation of land rent.

As some labor leaders attempted to point out, George's single-tax idea was, in the end, a narrow and conservative proposal – one that used the rhetoric of anti-capitalism to disguise an adherence to private enterprise and a limited vision of social change. "Henry George's theory that the taxation of land values will relieve the work-people employed in factories, mines and mills of their present misery and poverty is a snare and a delusion," declared one labor newspaper. "No sensible trade unionist will take any stock in George's patent medicine."[92] The socialist leader, Daniel DeLeon, similarly, disavowed the single tax, after having initially supported George's candidacy for New York City mayor. DeLeon dismissed the single tax as a "charlatan boom," supported by "half-antiquated, half-idiotic reasoning."[93]

Still, organized workers differed in their commitment to the single tax. Just as they were divided over the tariff, many wage workers were frequently ensnared by the single tax's attraction and populist appeal. As a result, single-tax supporters and socialists alike loathed the existing fiscal

[91] Bell, *Marxian Socialism in the United States*, 73–5. See also, Victor L. Berger, *The Wool Schedule: Protection, Free Trade, and the Working Class, A Socialist View of the Tariff* (New Castle, Penn.: Free Press, 1911).

[92] *Cigar Maker's Official Journal*, April, May, 1887, quoted in Foner, *History of the Labor Movement*, 148. See also, Speek, *The Single Tax and the Labor Movement*, 116.

[93] L. Glen Seretan, *Daniel DeLeon: The Odyssey of an American Marxist* (Cambridge, Mass.: Harvard University Press, 1979), 25–7.

TABLE 1.2. *Nineteenth-Century Independent Parties Favoring an Income Tax*

Year	National Party	Priority of Platform Plank
1880	Greenback Party	9th Demand for Graduated Income Tax, as part of Property Tax Reform
1884	Antimonopoly Party	8th Demand for Graduated Income Tax tied to Tariff Revision
1884	Greenback National Party	5th Demand for Graduated Income Tax, as part of Property Tax Reform
1888	Union Labor Party	6th Paragraph Calling for Graduated Income Tax
1892	People's Party	3rd Demand within "Finance" section of Platform
1892	Socialist Labor Party	9th Demand within "Social Demands," tied to Inheritance Tax

Source: Donald B. Johnson, ed., *National Party Platforms, Vol. 1: 1840–1956* (Urbana: University of Illinois Press, 1978).

system, but were nonetheless slow to turn their collective and focused attention to the progressive tax cause.

Early and Ineffective Political Support for Progressive Taxes

The single-tax movement and the growth of American socialism may have hindered the progressive tax campaign, but that did not mean that the numerous political reform associations that emerged in the late nineteenth century were uninterested in transforming the fiscal system – far from it. In the same year that Cooley was outlining his *Principles for Framing Tax Laws*, several independent political parties throughout the country were calling for graduated taxes on income and wealth transfers as part of their official party platforms. From the Granger Movement, to the mainstream American Socialist Party, to the Greenback and Anti-monopoly Party, to the People's Party, agrarian-based organizations and local unions convinced several independent political parties that progressive taxation was a salient issue among farmers, laborers, and small merchants. But, as the names of some of the parties themselves suggest, taxation was frequently subordinated to other issues, especially monetary reform[94] (see Table 1.2).

[94] Donald B. Johnson, ed., *National Party Platforms, Vol. I: 1840–1956* (Urbana: University of Illinois Press, 1978).

These and other populist political parties urged Congress to adopt graduated taxes. After the Civil War, income and inheritance taxes expired in the early 1870s, lawmakers had on several occasions attempted unsuccessfully to resuscitate these levies. By the late 1880s and early 1890s, the social pressure was mounting. Agrarian associations and other activist groups were petitioning Congress to consider reviving direct and graduated taxes on incomes, profits, and inheritances.[95] But for the most part the strongest calls for reform remained along the peripheries of national political power.

Similar forces were stirring at the state level, where political parties outside of the mainstream had long advocated for reforming the general property tax. Numerous independent political parties mainly from the West and Midwest exerted tremendous, though often varied, pressure on state-level Democratic Parties to adopt graduated taxes on incomes and inheritances. The Greenback and Populist Parties, for instance, were the most consistent supporters of the income tax at the state and national level. Prohibitionists, as we have seen, had a rather ambivalent reaction to income taxes, ignoring it in some years and endorsing it in others.[96]

Despite the growing social demands for progressive taxation, the movement failed to gain significant political traction during the 1880s. None of the bills to revive the national income tax introduced in Congress carried a majority, and none of the independent political parties clamoring for tax reform was able to sustain serious electoral victories. Many national lawmakers, harking back to the Civil War experience, believed that progressive taxes were best reserved for emergencies or serious crises. And intense log-rolling between Democrats and Republicans over the details of import duties kept most legislators sufficiently preoccupied. The emergent agrarian and labor political parties, like most social movements before and since, foundered on the shoals of the entrenched American two-party political system. With the economy growing steadily, if unevenly, throughout the 1880s, and with most Americans voting as part of a "core electorate," with intense partisanship and consistent participation,

95 Kansas Farmers' Alliance of Riley County Kansas to Hon. John Davis, Jan. 18, 1894; H. J. Whitmansk (Secretary of the Granby, MA Grange) to Hon. Samuel W. McCall, Jan. 25, 1894; Citizens of Rica, Colorado to Rep. John G. Bell, [n.d.], 53rd Congress – Petitions; Ways & Means (HR53A-33.10), Box 180, Folder "Tax on Incomes, Sept. 9, 1893–Apr. 30, 1894," Records of the U.S. House of Representatives, National Archives and Records Administration, Washington, D.C.; Ratner, *American Taxation*, 148.

96 Bensel, *Political Economy of Industrialization*, 159–61.

agrarian and labor social movements had little hope of supplanting either of the national parties that they resisted joining.[97]

With single taxers, socialists, and other political activists preoccupied with other reforms, the campaign for direct and graduated taxes seemed to be going nowhere in the 1880s. The social antagonism toward the prevailing fiscal system no doubt remained alive, as the numerous third-party political platforms and the unsuccessful congressional calls for reviving the income tax suggested. Even though economic experts were unsure about the incidence of indirect consumption taxes, the public perception was clear: import duties and national excise taxes were regressive; they extracted more from those who had less. At the same time, the tariff stoked still unsettled sectional tensions, as it protected core Northeast manufacturers at the expense of peripheral Southern and Western consumers and agricultural interests. State and local property taxes posed a similar set of problems. Taxpayers and reformers consistently complained about how evasion, corruption, and incompetent administration combined to make general property taxes disproportionate, applying more to those who had corporeal and visible forms of property and wealth.

Yet, despite the frustrations with the status quo, the opposition to the late-nineteenth-century fiscal order remained fractured and distracted. Protectionism divided loyalties among ordinary American workers. The economic impact of excise taxes remained relatively hidden. And other issues, including monetary reform, anti-monopoly crusades, the single tax, and labor organizing absorbed the attention of political and social activists. Consequently, tax reformers were unable to harness the mounting social dissatisfaction to dislodge the existing regime of high import duties, excise levies, and the subnational general property tax.

Indeed, these taxes were a deeply entrenched part of the late-nineteenth-century party system. The tariff was one of the central issues of partisan national debates between high-rate Republicans and low-duty Democrats. In many ways, the tariff was the glue that held the party period together; it was among the central economic issues the provided

[97] Mark Lawrence Kornbluh, *Why America Stopped Voting: The Decline of Participatory Democracy and the Emergence of Modern American Politics* (New York: New York University Press, 2000), Chapter 1; Michael McGerr, *The Decline of Popular Politics: The American North, 1865–1928* (New York: Oxford University Press, 1988); Lawrence Goodwyn, *Democratic Promise: The Populist Movement in America* (New York: Oxford University Press, 1976).

cohesion and stability for each of the dominant parties.[98] The administration of property taxes similarly was embedded in the system of state and local party patronage. Constitutional restrictions and judicial deference to legislative taxing powers, as Cooley and other treatise writers noted, only seemed to fortify the enveloping reach of party machines over tax policy. Underpinning the judicial and political support for the existing system was an ideology of taxation that viewed taxes as simply the price for government protection. Drawn from classical liberalism's reliance on social contract theory, this perspective on taxation rested on notions of limited government and on an even more limited sense of fiscal citizenship.

Still, beneath the seemingly static state of the fiscal system, broader structural forces were taking shape in the late 1880s and early 1890s that would soon provide public finance theorists and reformers with an opportunity to disrupt the prevailing tax regime. Chief among these forces were the changing social, political, and economic conditions, as well as the power of new ideas about taxation. Increasing economic inequality seemed to galvanize the social opposition to the existing tax system. The increasing rise of intangible wealth in the form of financial assets further undermined the already dysfunctional property tax. At the same time, the federal budget's move from deficits to large surpluses combined with the maturation of domestic industries and Civil War pensioners appeared to undermine the political support for the existing tariff regime. Progressive intellectuals, seeking to bridge the worlds of quotidian concerns and public policymaking, contributed to these changing economic and social conditions by propagating their ideas and beliefs about the importance of state action, and the growing need for direct and graduated taxes.

Thomas Cooley could not have anticipated these profound changes when he took the stage in 1878 to deliver his paper to the American Social Science Association. In fact, he publicly doubted that the income tax in the United States "will ever be resorted to as a permanent means of revenue."[99] But unlike many of his more conservative colleagues, Cooley did not always resist social change. In many ways, he helped instigate the fundamental transformation in American public finance that was

[98] Richard L. McCormick, *The Party Period and Public Policy: American Politics from the Age of Jackson to the Progressive Era* (New York: Oxford University Press, 1986), 208–9; Joel H. Silbey, *The American Political Nation, 1838–1893* (Stanford: Stanford University Press, 1991), 81–8.

[99] Cooley, *Framing Tax Laws*, 10; *Law of Taxation*, 20.

about to take place. Through his legal writings and his correspondence, he assisted a new group of tax experts, including his junior University of Michigan colleague Henry Carter Adams, with their efforts to reconfigure the meanings and implications of American fiscal governance.[100]

For some progressives, Cooley was a foil to be attacked. For others, he was a model to be emulated, though with some important modifications. Either way, the eminent jurist was instrumental in the development of a succeeding generation of thinkers and reformers who would come to challenge the institutional inertia of the existing fiscal system. In time, Cooley would come to represent the seminal transition in American law and political economy that was taking place at the turn of the century – a transition between the gradual decline of an old tax regime and the rise of the modern American fiscal state.

[100] Henry Carter Adams to Thomas M. Cooley, December 16, 1879, Box 1; Ely to Cooley, February 13, 1888, Box 3; Seligman to Cooley, December 3, 1892, Box 5, TMCP.

2

The Gradual Demise

Modern Forces, New Concepts, and Economic Crisis

> If, then, there is to be real, effective national government, there must be a power of taxation coextensive with its powers, wants, and duties.
>
> – Joseph Story

As the social antagonism toward an antiquated, politicized, and highly disagreeable tax regime increased, broader material forces in the Gilded Age were already fueling the potential for a dramatic transformation in the American system of public finance. At the national level, structural and demographic pressures were gradually undermining the logic of the tariff and, in the process, eroding the Republican Party's political coalition for protectionism. By the early 1890s, a consistent federal government surplus, growing anxiety about the corrupt liberalization of Civil War pensions, a mature industrial economy, and the increasing traction of free-trade ideas were all casting doubt on the necessity and durability of the tariff regime. More importantly, the tremendous inequality and growing disparity in wealth that accompanied American economic expansion also heightened the awareness of the regressive impact of the prevailing fiscal regime.

While the broad historical forces of modernity were providing the underlying, structural pressures for a fiscal revolution, it was an emerging generation of American economic experts and tax reformers who were leading the conceptual shift in economic and legal ideas that would ultimately help usher in a new fiscal order. German-trained, American political economists like Richard T. Ely, Henry Carter Adams, and Edwin R. A. Seligman were at the forefront of the intellectual and political movement for the graduated taxation of incomes, profits, and wealth transfers. Responding to the social and political dislocations of their times, these theorists and activists played a pivotal role in supplanting the "benefits theory" of taxation, and its attendant vision of the state as a passive protector of private property, with a more equitable principle of taxation based on one's "faculty" or "ability to pay." Through their efforts and achievements, these economic experts became the visionaries or architects of the modern American fiscal state.

The intellectual campaign for direct and progressive taxation was a crucial catalyst in the rise of the new fiscal order. But there were also several seminal historical events that triggered the transition and signaled the demise of the *ancien régime*. The Panic of 1893 precipitated a deep and unprecedented economic depression – arguably the nineteenth century's worst economic downturn – that, in turn, unleashed a torrent of social and political pressure for reform. Political economists, social activists, and lawmakers seized on the economic crisis to enact a federal income tax in 1894 – the country's first peacetime income tax. While the law initially appeared to be a victory for tax reformers, the celebration was short-lived. In the following year, the U.S. Supreme Court took the unprecedented step of striking down the income tax as a violation of the Constitution's direct tax clause. By the summer of 1895, the future of the new fiscal polity appeared highly tenuous and uncertain. The High Court's decision forced tax activists, including the progressive political economists who were leading the paradigm shift in tax theories, to redouble their efforts to transform the existing fiscal order.

The Modern Forces Undermining the Old Tax Regime

The late-nineteenth-century Republican Party's high-tariff regime was a byproduct of the Civil War and its aftermath. The soaring postwar federal public debt and the promise to provide increasingly generous pensions for veterans and their dependents strengthened the reliance on tariff revenues. But by the last decades of the nineteenth century, these principal rationales for supporting high import duties seemed to be crumbling. From the end of Reconstruction to the beginning of the 1890s depression, consistent annual budget surpluses, fueled by tariff revenue and internal excises, were leading to a steady decline in the national public debt and to the annual interest payments on that debt. While the national debt reached, in nominal terms, a post-Reconstruction high of roughly $2.3 billion in 1879, by 1893 that figure had dipped well below $1 billion. The direct beneficiaries of this trend – American and European bondholders – no doubt were delighted to have their debts repaid. But, as tariff reformers pointed out, if the main purpose of customs duties was to raise revenue, and if the immediate impetus for high duties was the repayment of war loans, then the rapidly diminishing public debt suggested that perhaps import duties ought to be declining as well. A "tariff for revenue only," the longtime slogan of economic reformers, once again became a common refrain among tariff reformers, free-traders, and low-tariff Democratic lawmakers.[1]

Consistent annual surpluses may have strained the tariff regime, but increased spending on Civil War pensions – the other central justification for high customs duties – only appeared to solidify support for the tariff. Despite an aging population of veterans, the increasing expansion of Union Army pensions, which by the 1890s accounted for roughly 40 percent of the total federal budget, tightened the link between tariff revenue and social insurance provisions. Indeed, spending on veterans' pensions was one area that traditional tax theorists could identify as an example of the benefits theory underlying the existing tariff regime.[2]

Ironically, though, while the Republican Party was able to maintain the political loyalty of veterans and their dependents with expanded pension benefits, the increasing government largess called into question the fairness of the program's administration. Detractors claimed that the overly generous pension program was riddled with fraud and political corruption, and that it unnecessarily bolstered the high-tariff regime. "The assertion that our pension system is a worthy monument of the generous gratitude of the American people sounds like a fiendish mockery," exclaimed Civil War veteran and journalist Carl Schurz. "No people have ever been more shamelessly victimized than the American people have been in this shameless pension business." Such criticism continued well into the early twentieth century, placing continuous pressure on the Republicans' existing tariff regime.[3]

By the late 1880s, however, few tariff supporters argued that the main objective of high import duties was to generate significant revenue. They

[1] Susan B. Carter et al., eds. *Historical Statistics of the United States Millennial Edition*, Table Ea584–587; *Tariff for Revenue Only: Speech of Hon. S.B. Maxey, of Texas, in the Senate of the United States, January 23, 1883* (Washington, D.C., 1883); American Tariff League, *The Tariff Review*, Vol. 2 (1888).

[2] Theda Skocpol, *Protecting Soldiers and Mothers: The Political Origins of Social Policy in the United States* (Cambridge, Mass.: Harvard University Press, 1995), 272–85. Federal spending on veteran's compensation and pensions reached a nineteenth-century high in 1893 with nearly $160 million or 42 percent of the annual national budget. *Historical Statistics of the United States*, Table Ea636–643.

[3] Carl Schurz, "The Pension Scandal," *Harper's Weekly*, May 5, 1894, 410; *Historical Statistics of the United States*, Table Ea636–643; Maris A. Vinovskis, "Have Social Historians Lost the Civil War? Some Preliminary Demographic Speculations" in *Toward a Social History of the American Civil War: Exploratory Essays*, ed. Maris A. Vinovskis (New York: Cambridge University Press, 1990), 1–30, 27.

believed, instead, that protection from international competition was vital to the continued maturation of American industries. But even here there was growing skepticism that the "infant industries" of an earlier era still needed to be shielded from global commerce. For many political activists, American economic and political expansion suggested that protectionism had outlasted its usefulness. In fact, by the last decades of the century, a robust and mature economy placed the United States near the top of all industrialized nations. Meanwhile, economic ideas about the overwhelming long-term benefits of free trade began to percolate through the American academy into popular discourse. These forces combined to create a vulnerable opening in the Republican Party's high-tariff regime and the fiscal order of which it was a part.

Throughout the late nineteenth century, the United States experienced tremendous, if uneven, economic growth. Driven mainly by an abundance of natural resources, technological innovations, and increasing factor inputs and productivity, economic expansion transformed the nation into one of the world's leading industrial, capitalist economies by the end of the century. From a comparative perspective, the United States by the 1880s had per capita real income levels that were among the highest in the world. Although American prosperity was astonishingly disparate, the general standard of living in the United States outpaced many countries, including leading European imperial powers. France and Germany, for instance, had per capita real gross domestic product figures in the 1880s that were roughly three-fourths of U.S. levels. By the start of the twentieth century, the United States was on pace to surpass the United Kingdom and all other advanced industrializing nations in terms of economic growth (see Chart 2.1). Even if specific sectors of American commerce benefited, in the short term from tariff protection, the overall resource-based, industrial prosperity called into question the need for a high-duties tariff policy.[4]

[4] Angus Maddison, *Monitoring the World Economy, 1820–1992* (Paris: OECD Publishing, 1995), 194–206; Monica Prasad, *The Land of Too Much: American Abundance and the Paradox of Poverty* (Cambridge, Mass.: Harvard University Press, 2012), Chapter 3. For succinct summaries of American economic development during this period, see generally Robert E. Gallman, "Economic Growth and Structural Change in the Long Nineteenth Century," in *The Cambridge Economic History of the United States, Volume II: The Long Nineteenth Century*, ed. Stanley L. Gallman and Robert E. Engerman (New York: Cambridge University Press, 2000); Kenneth L. Sokoloff and Stanley L. Engermann, "History Lessons: Institutions, Factor Endowments, and Paths of Development in the New World," *Journal of Economic Perspectives* 14 (2000), 217–32; Gavin Wright, "The Origins of American Industrial Success, 1879–1940," *American Economic Review* 80:4 (1990), 651–68.

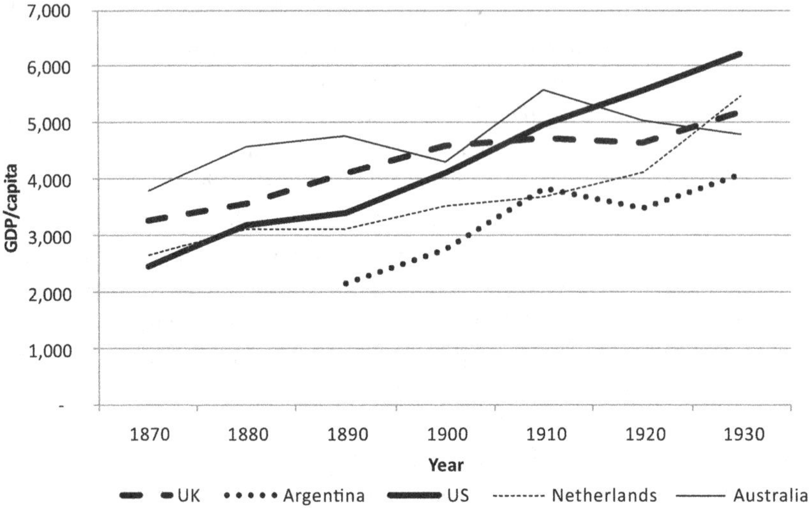

CHART 2.1. Industrializing Nations: Real GDP per Capita, 1870–1930.
Source: Angus Maddison, *Monitoring the World Economy, 1820–1992* (Paris: OECD Publishing, 1995), 194–206.

Unparalleled economic growth brought with it a sea change in the structure of the American economy, which further imperiled the "infant industry" argument. Nineteenth-century technological improvements related to the second industrial revolution linked a continental nation and helped create a mass market for production and distribution. As the railroads and telegraph systems spread, enormous integrated industrial corporations emerged to exploit the economies of scale provided by the new, high-volume technologies.[5] Accordingly, manufacturing began to displace agriculture as the sector of the economy with the largest share of output and employment. And as colossal new industrial corporations began to usher in a new era of American capitalism, the calls for protection from "ruinous competition abroad" seemed to fall on deaf ears. By the early 1890s, American industrial firms were coming to dominate the international market for manufactured goods. These same businesses,

[5] Alfred D. Chandler Jr., *The Visible Hand: The Managerial Revolution in American Business* (Cambridge, Mass.: Harvard University Press, 1977); David Bunting, *The Rise of Large American Corporations, 1889–1919* (New York: Garland Press, 1987); Martin J. Sklar, *The Corporate Reconstruction of American Capitalism, 1890–1916* (New York: Cambridge University Press, 1988).

desperately seeking overseas markets for their output, would have the most to gain from lower duties and increased free trade.[6]

If accelerating American industrialization was eroding certain economic arguments for protectionism, the massive inequality of the Gilded Age was putting added social pressure on the need to transform a regressive fiscal order. Although precise statistical data from this time period are limited, present-day economic historians have estimated that the distribution of wealth and income in the United States became increasingly concentrated during the late nineteenth century. By the 1890s, according to one set of modern projections, the wealthiest 1 percent of American families held more than two-thirds of the nation's total assets. The maldistribution of wealth was mirrored by income disparities. In the postbellum era, as economic historians Jeffery G. Williamson and Peter H. Lindert have shown, the United States "drifted along at high inequality levels up to the 1890s," reaching an "uneven plateau" of persistent income disparity that likely peaked during World War I.[7]

Contemporary social critics were highly cognizant of these trends in inequality. Not only did Henry George and other populist leaders use the visible signs of poverty amidst plenty as a rationale for seemingly radical proposals, like the single tax, empirical studies at the time also underscored the degree of economic inequality. In 1889, Thomas G. Sherman, a single-tax advocate and founding member of the New York law firm of Sherman & Sterling, conducted a crude investigation of existing wealth disparities. With some rather grand comparative extrapolations,

[6] Joanne Reitano, *The Tariff Question in the Gilded Age: The Great Debate of 1888* (University Park: Pennsylvania State University Press, 1994), 47; Robert E. Gallman and Edward S. Howle, "Trends in the Structure of the American Economy since 1840," in *The Reinterpretation of American Economic History*, ed. Robert W. Fogel and Stanley L. Engerman (New York: Harper & Row, 1971). As late as 1879, agriculture accounted for about half of the total value added in the economy's commodity output; at that same time, manufacturing was responsible for roughly a one-third share. Within two decades, the two sectors had completely reversed positions. Manufacturing became the dominant segment of the economy by 1899, with a 53 percent share of output, while the agricultural proportion dropped to roughly one-third. Robert E. Gallman, "Commodity Output, 1839–1899," in *The Conference on Research in Income and Wealth, Trends in the American Economy in the Nineteenth Century*, Studies in Income and Wealth, vol. 24 (1960), 26 (all figures are in constant 1879 dollar).

[7] Robert E. Gallman, "Trends in the Size Distributions of Wealth in the Nineteenth Century: Some Speculations," in *Six Papers on the Size Distribution of Wealth and Income*, ed. Lee Soltow (New York: National Bureau of Economic Research, 1969), 1–30, 10; Jeffrey G. Williamson and Peter H. Lindert, *American Inequality: A Macroeconomic History* (New York: Academic Press, 1980), 75–82.

Sherman concluded that the richest 6 percent of American families owned roughly two-thirds of the country's wealth.[8] Sherman's estimates were severely criticized by experts like Edwin Seligman who challenged the methodology of Sherman's study, but agreed with the central message that economic inequality was on the rise.[9]

The federal statistician and lawyer George K. Holmes verified Sherman's intuition with a more sophisticated assessment of economic figures. Using data from the 1890 census, Holmes estimated that the top 9 percent of American families owned over 70 percent of the nation's wealth. Holmes was no proponent of radical wealth redistribution, but he warned that "there is always the danger that [the rich] will get too large a hold upon the wealth, the resources and the labor of the country," in which case "the most effective and practicable remedies are progressive taxes on incomes, gifts and inheritances." Only through such measures could society ensure "a distribution . . . most conducive to social welfare."[10]

These empirical findings reached a wide audience, and thus intensified the political and social resentment toward the existing tax system. Congressional leaders arguing for an income tax regularly evoked Sherman's study, despite its defects, during the legislative debates over the 1894 income tax. Social leaders, likewise, highlighted the connection between inequality and the existing tax system. Referring to Holmes's study, labor leader Eltweed Pomeroy declared that American society had reached an unprecedented and unbearable level of inequality: "Today the sun looks down on the most unequal and inequitable distribution of wealth that has probably ever been seen." Among the primary causes of

[8] John L. Thomas, *Alternative America: Henry George, Edward Bellamy, Henry Demarest Lloyd and the Adversary Tradition* (Cambridge, Mass.: Harvard University Press, 1983); Thomas G. Sherman, "The Owners of the United States," *Forum* (November 1889), 262–73. Although Sherman explicitly linked the American disparity in wealth to "the machinery of public taxation," which he claimed "fell exclusively on the working class" and had "been used so unscrupulously for private profit," he refrained from supporting "a graduated income tax" or "a heavy succession tax," contending that his study was "a simple investigation of facts." Ibid., 273.

[9] Thomas G. Sherman to Edwin R. A. Seligman, April 23, 1895; May 16, 1895, Cataloged Correspondence, Edwin R. A. Seligman Papers, Butler Library, Columbia University, New York, N.Y. [hereinafter ERASP].

[10] George K. Holmes, "The Concentration of Wealth," *Political Science Quarterly* 8:4 (Dec. 1893), 589–600. See also Charles B. Spahr, *An Essay on the Present Distribution of Wealth in the United States* (New York: Thomas Y. Crowell & Co, 1896). Holmes's estimates, in particular, were later ratified by modern economic historians who found his work to be a "rather remarkable confirmation" of their own studies. Gallman, "Trends in the Size Distributions of Wealth," 11.

this new concentration of wealth, Pomeroy identified as the most significant "indirect and inequitable taxation" and the "special and monopoly privilege" created by the tariff.[11]

In addition to the material forces undermining the tariff, economic ideas about the long-term benefits of free trade also gradually began to challenge the dominance of protectionism. To be sure, Adam Smith's scathing criticism of eighteenth-century British mercantilism was well known among American economic writers. But in the United States, protectionism had a particular appeal. Henry C. Carey, the Pennsylvania publisher and economic commentator, trained generations of antebellum students through his writings to believe in the virtues of high customs duties. Likewise, John Stuart Mill's temporary and tempered support for protectionism "in some particular cases" emboldened many American tariff promoters. In fact, Carey, who himself was a convert from free trade, approvingly paraphrased Mill in arguing that "the road to absolute freedom of trade lies through perfect protection."[12]

Still, by the 1880s, just as the revenue needs for the tariff were diminishing, so too were the theoretical rationales for protectionism. The leading American economic treatises of the time, written by Francis A. Walker and Arthur Latham Perry, supported free trade, as did a number of popular tracts and pamphlets written by tariff reformers. Walker, a prominent professor of political economy and the first president of the American Economic Association (AEA), lent great intellectual credence to free-trade ideas when he identified the institutional inertia that often led to the "undue continuance of protective duties." Although Walker conceded that protectionism might be justified as a temporary economic policy, "the time seldom comes," he warned, "when those who represent a protected industry are willing to admit that government assistance is no

[11] *Congressional Record*, 53rd Cong., 2nd sess. (1894), 26, pt. 7:6714; Eltweed Pomeroy, "The Concentration of Wealth and the Inheritance Charge," *American Federationist*, July 1895, 1. On the emergence of social scientific studies of economic inequality and poverty during this time period, see Alice O'Connor, *Poverty Knowledge: Social Science, Social Policy, and the Poor in Twentieth-Century U.S. History* (Princeton: Princeton University Press, 2009), Chapter 1.

[12] Henry C. Carey, *The Harmony of Interests: Agricultural, Manufacturing, and Commercial* (Philadelphia: J. B. Skinner, 1851), 67; Rodney T. Morrison, *Henry C. Carey and American Economic Development* (Philadelphia: American Philosophical Society, 1986); John Stuart Mill, *Principles of Political Economy* (London: Longmans, Green, [1848], 1909), 920; Joseph Dorfman, *The Economic Mind in American Civilization, 1865–1918* (1969), 6–7; Douglas A. Irwin, *Against the Tide: An Intellectual History of Free Trade* (Princeton: Princeton University Press, 1996), Chapter 8.

longer needed." As we shall see, one of Walker's most successful students, Henry Carter Adams, would soon continue his mentor's critique of protectionism by promoting direct taxes on incomes and inheritances as replacements for customs duties. In time, Adams would become a pioneer in the American study of public finance, and a representative of the growing academic consensus behind tariff reform and the movement for national taxes on incomes, inheritances, and business profits. A handful of young, progressive economists among Adams's cohort would continue to favor protectionism, but by the end of the nineteenth century, free-trade ideas were beginning to dominate American academic discourse.[13]

While structural and intellectual forces were undermining the national, high-tariff regime, a similar, though less pronounced, deterioration of the old fiscal order was occurring at the state and local level. As late as 1890, the general property tax continued to dominate subnational government revenues, accounting for over 70 percent of annual state receipts and roughly 90 percent of total local government funding. Yet despite raising badly needed revenue, the property tax was riddled with defects, as Justice Thomas Cooley and others noted. As we have seen in the previous chapter, taxpayer evasion, political corruption, limited administrative capacity, the decreasing visibility of personal property, and judicial neglect all hampered the property tax's ability to raise sufficient public revenue in a fair and effective manner. Consequently, the property tax failed to keep up with the growing demands on state and local government spending – demands that increased exponentially in the late nineteenth century as the forces of modernity impinged upon American public life.[14]

In fact, the new pressures of mass migration, rapid urbanization, and accelerated industrialization had their greatest impact on the state and local level. Between 1870 and 1900, roughly four million immigrants entered the United States per decade, a figure that was double

[13] Francis Amasa Walker, *First Lessons in Political Economy* (New York: Henry Holt & Co., 1889), 175; A. W. Coats, "Henry Carter Adams: A Case Study in the Emergence of the Social Sciences in the United States, 1850–1900," *Journal of American Studies*, 2:2 (October 1968), 177–97.

[14] George C. S. Benson et al. *The American Property Tax: Its History, Administration, and Economic Impact* (1865), 65; Clifton K. Yearly, *The Money Machines: The Breakdown and Reform of Governmental and Party Finance in the North, 1860–1920* (Albany: State University of New York Press, 1970), Glenn W. Fisher, *The Worst Tax? A History of the Property Tax in America* (Lawrence: University Press of Kansas, 1996).

the decennial average of previous periods. Many of these immigrants settled in expanding urban areas and found work in burgeoning industrial factories.[15] The mutual attraction of cities and immigrants led to a voracious demand for state and municipal public goods and services. As ships teeming with immigrants landed on American shores, and workers migrated internally from rural farms and "island communities" to industrial factories and urban centers, state and local infrastructure and social services became increasingly strained.[16] In the last third of the nineteenth century, calls for increased local government spending were especially strident during what one historian has called the "halcyon days of urban promoters," when "boosters of each city believed that the best way to guarantee prosperity in the future was to create the state's smoothest streets, fastest transportation system, most efficient garbage removal, biggest schools, and best fire and police protection."[17]

The combination of increased demand for government spending, especially among cities, and a decreasing supply of property tax revenue placed great pressure on subnational public finance. As we shall see in Chapter 4, improving state and local tax systems was a pressing concern for reformers. Indeed, subnational changes not only presaged what might be possible at the federal level, they also reflected how political activists and economic thinkers believed that a new fiscal order could do much more than simply reallocate tax burdens. The reformers at the center of the conceptual revolution in public finance were all active in state and local tax reform. From their experiences with subnational governments, they understood full well that changing the mindset about the fiscal basis of modern statecraft also meant reconfiguring the social obligations of citizenship and building the bureaucratic capacity of the nascent administrative state.

[15] *Historical Statistics of the United States*, Table ad21–24. The proportion of Americans living in urban areas (defined as locations with more than 2,500 persons) more than doubled between 1870 and1900, and the share of those living in large cities (defined as locations with more than 100,000 persons) nearly quadrupled. *Historical Statistics of the United States*, Table Aa 684–698; Table Aa 699–715.

[16] Richard H. Wiebe, *The Search for Order, 1877–1920* (New York: Hill and Wang, 1966); Samuel P. Hays, *The Response to Industrialism, 1885–1914* (Chicago: University of Chicago Press, 1957).

[17] R. Rudy Higgens-Evenson, *The Price of Progress: Public Services Taxation and the American Corporate State, 1877–1929* (Baltimore: Johns Hopkins University Press, 2003), 25–38; David P. Thelen, *The New Citizenship: Origins of Progressivism in Wisconsin, 1885–1900* (Columbia: University of Missouri Press, 1972), 133–4.

"New School" Economists, "Ability to Pay," and a Contested Vision of Fiscal Citizenship

The American political economists who envisioned a new fiscal order were part of a larger cohort of German-trained professional social scientists who sought to dismantle the orthodox theories of classical economic liberalism. Reacting to the social dislocations of modern industrial capitalism, this younger generation of aspiring academics and new liberals disavowed traditional notions of self-reliant individualism. They, instead, sought to demonstrate – through their writing, teaching, and public advocacy – the mutual interdependence of modern social relations. In their efforts to establish what they referred to as a "new school" of American political economy, these heterodox economists became part of the first group of social scientists to sever their ties to the traditional field of moral philosophy and place their fledgling discipline on a firmer professional standing. Together with many other economic reformers, including several social gospel ministers, these maverick intellectuals formed the American Economic Association (AEA) in 1885 as part of a professionalization project designed to secure the status, prestige, and legitimacy of their "scientific" expertise.[18]

These young academics, as historian Mary Furner has shown, struggled throughout the professionalization process to reconcile their desire for social democratic reforms with their intellectual commitment to scientific objectivity. Initially, the reform-minded economists who founded the AEA sought to use their training to disrupt the conventional means of studying and understanding economic and social problems. Eschewing timeless universals and deductive methods, these thinkers used empirical facts and inductive reasoning to show how economic relations were embedded in a larger social and institutional matrix – a matrix that was often constituted empirically by law and legal institutions and processes. For these thinkers, the state was an "ethical agency." And because law was the official language of the state, as well as a malleable human creation, these reform-minded academics believed that legal reform was the means toward fundamental fiscal change. These "new school" or

[18] Thomas L. Haskell, *The Emergence of Professional Social Science: The American Social Science Association and the Nineteenth Century Crisis of Authority* (Urbana: University of Illinois Press, 1977); A. W. Coats, "The American Economic Association and the Economics Profession," *Journal of Economic Literature* 23:4 (December 1985), 1697–1727; Dorothy Ross, *The Origins of American Social Science* (New York: Cambridge University Press, 1991).

"ethical economists," as they came to be known, were thus part of what legal historians have referred to as the "First Great Law & Economics Movement."[19]

A New School of American Public Finance

Among the new school of professionally trained economists, there were several who were interested in public finance. Occupying influential teaching posts throughout the country, academics such as Henry Carter Adams, Richard T. Ely, and Edwin R. A. Seligman dedicated much of their careers to the empirical and theoretical study of taxation. Bound by common experiences, yet somewhat disparate family backgrounds, these reform-minded theorists helped launch the systematic study of American public finance, or what they referred to – borrowing from their German mentors – as the "science of finance."[20] H. C. Adams, who spent the majority of his academic career at the University of Michigan, focused his early scholarship on government revenues, taxation, and expenditures, and wrote some of the earliest, most influential American treatises on budgets and public debts. When he was appointed chief statistician of the Interstate Commerce Commission in 1887 by his former Michigan colleague Judge Thomas M. Cooley, Adams's attention turned away from fiscal issues to the regulation of railroads, the topic for which he is best remembered today.[21]

Ely, likewise, began his academic career with an interest in public finance, before turning to other topics. When he was a junior faculty

[19] Mary O. Furner, *Advocacy & Objectivity: A Crisis in the Professionalization of American Social Science, 1865–1905* (Lexington: University Press of Kentucky, 1975); Richard T. Ely, *Social Aspects of Christianity and Other Essays* (New York: Crowell, 1889), 118; Herbert Hovenkamp, "The First Great Law & Economics Movement," *Stanford Law Review* 42:4 (April, 1990), 993–1058; Barbara H. Fried, *The Progressive Assault on Laissez-faire: Robert Hale and the First Law and Economics Movement* (Cambridge, Mass.: Harvard University Press, 1998).

[20] On the origins of academic public finance as a distinct subfield of American economics, see Marianne Johnson, "American Academic Public Finance: The First Fifty Years," *History of Political Economy* (forthcoming).

[21] Nancy Cohen, *The Reconstruction of American Liberalism, 1865–1914* (Chapel Hill: University of North Carolina Press), 155–9; Joseph Dorfman, "Introduction," in *Two Essays by Henry Carter Adams: Relation of the State to Industrial Action and Economics and Jurisprudence*, ed. Joseph Dorfman (New York: A. M. Kelley, 1969); A. W. Coats, "Henry Carter Adams: A Case Study in the Emergence of Social Sciences in the United States, 1850–1900," *Journal of American Studies* 2:2 (October 1968), 177–97; Lawrence Bigelow et al., "Henry Carter Adams, 1851–1921," *Journal of Political Economy* 30:2 (April 1922), 201–11.

member at the Johns Hopkins University in the 1880s, Ely investigated state and local tax issues as a member of the Baltimore and Maryland tax commissions. His interest in labor issues also led him to analyze the protective tariff and author a tepid critique of protectionism. But, like Adams, Ely turned his attention to other matters later in his career. By the time he joined the University of Wisconsin faculty in 1892 as the first full-time professor of economics, Ely began shifting his focus from public finance to agricultural economics and industrial relations.[22]

By contrast, Seligman, who spent nearly his entire life associated with Columbia University, first as a student and then as a faculty member, was committed throughout his career to the study of public finance. After graduating with both a law degree and a doctorate in political economy, he began his lifelong commitment to the "science of finance" with a series of articles in the late 1880s and several significant and highly influential tax treatises in the following decades. Active both within and outside of the academy, Seligman was involved in nearly every important issue of progressive reform. Yet, he is best remembered today for his scholarly and civic achievements in public finance. Early in his career, Seligman was tapped to be one of the editors of the newly created, Columbia-sponsored journal, the *Political Science Quarterly*. He was also the faculty member assigned to supervise and edit public finance texts for a Columbia University Press book series. As a result of these institutional commitments and because of his proficiency in several foreign languages, Seligman became the de facto translator of continental texts on fiscal policy. He would later modestly recount to his Columbia colleague Wesley C. Mitchell that this "mere accident of departmental organization" would lead to his lifelong commitment to the study of taxation. To be sure, there were other writers who contributed to the emerging American literature on public finance. But it was Adams, Ely, and especially Seligman who were not only representative of their

[22] Richard T. Ely, *Ground under Our Feet: An Autobiography* (New York: Arno Press, 1938); Benjamin G. Rader, *The Academic Mind and Reform: The Influence of Richard T. Ely in American Life* (Lexington: University of Kentucky Press, 1966). On the important role that Ely played in developing Wisconsin's economic institutionalism and its pioneering work in law and economics and public finance, see Malcolm Rutherford, *The Institutionalist Movement in American Economics, 1918–1947: Science and Social Control* (New York: Cambridge University Press, 2011), 187–90; Marianne Johnson, "Public Finance and Wisconsin Institutionalism, 1892–1929," *Journal of Economic Issues* 45:4 (2011), 965–83.

generation of maverick economic thinkers, but who were also the pivotal historical figures guiding the conceptual shift in U.S. tax theory.[23]

Many of the reform-minded economists were united by their personal backgrounds, particularly their religious and ethical upbringings. Though Ely, Adams, and Seligman were each reared in rather different environments, they all shared, from an early age, a desire to channel their particular religious and ethical sensibilities toward addressing the ills of modern industrialism. Ely was raised in the agricultural region of upstate New York by a family of ardent Presbyterians dedicated to egalitarianism and social change. Although his parents had hoped that young Richard would one day join the ministry, Ely did not develop clerical ambitions. Still, among his contemporaries, Ely was the most deeply and directly engaged with the Social Gospel Movement. He developed a close relationship with Washington Gladden and other reform-minded ministers. He was a frequent lecturer on the Chautauqua circuit of adult education, helping to establish their Political Economy Clubs. And he wrote eloquently and passionately about how social Christianity informed economic science. Indeed, as Ely explained, his generation of political economists comprised the "ethical school" precisely because they "consciously adopt an ethical ideal," and because they "endeavor to point out the manner in which it is to be attained, and even encourage people to strive for it."[24]

[23] Pier Francesco Asso and Luc Fiorito, eds., "Edwin Robert Anderson Seligman, Autobiography," in *Documents from and on Economic Thought*, Vol. 24C, ed. Warren J. Samuels (Amsterdam: JAI Press, 2006), 47–187; Joseph Dorfman, "Edwin Robert Anderson Seligman," *Dictionary of American Biography*, Suppl. 2 (1958), 606–9; Carl S. Shoup, "Seligman," in *International Encyclopedia of the Social Sciences*, ed. David L. Sills (New York: Macmillan, 1968); Wesley C. Mitchell, "Tribute," in *Edwin Robert Anderson Seligman, 1861–1939* (Stamford, Conn.: Overlook Press, 1942), 60; "In Memoriam: Edwin Robert Anderson Seligman," *Political Science Quarterly* 54:3 (September 1939), 3. For more on Columbia University as an early incubator of institutionalist economics, see Rutherford, *Institutionalist Movement in American Economics*, 223–57.

[24] Ely, *Ground under Our Feet*, 79–87; Rader, *Academic Mind and Reform*, 32–3, 64–5; Kate F. Kimball (Executive Secretary, The Chautauqua Literary and Scientific Circle) to Richard T. Ely, Nov. 15, 1892, Box 5, Correspondence March–Nov. 1892, Richard T. Ely Papers, Wisconsin Historical Society, Madison, Wis.; Ely, *Social Aspects of Christianity*, 118. On the intellectual links between the Social Gospel Movement and the progressive political economists, see Thomas C. Leonard, "Religion and Evolution in Progressive Era Political Economy: Adversaries or Allies?" *History of Political Economy* 43:3 (2011), 429–69; R.A. Gonce, "The Social Gospel, Ely, and Commons's Initial Stage of Thought," *Journal of Economic Issues* 30:3 (1996), 641–65; Bradley W. Bateman, "Clearing the Ground: The Demise of the Social Gospel Movement and the Rise of Neoclassicism in American Economics," in *From Interwar Pluralism to Postwar*

Henry Carter Adams followed a similar path. He was born and raised in rural Iowa, the son of a Congregational minister and abolitionist leader, who also aspired to mold his son into a minister. But like Ely, Adams did not share his family's zeal for the ministry. Even at an early age, he acknowledged his recurring religious doubts. After graduating from Grinnell College in 1874, Adams reluctantly entered Andover Theological Seminary, but soon left to pave his own path toward ethical reform. He received a fellowship to study at the Johns Hopkins University, as one of its first doctoral students, and thus embarked upon his academic career. When Adams informed his father about his decision to become a scholar and reformer rather than a minister, he emphasized the religious aspects of his new career choice. Quoting scripture, Adams informed this father that providing the "voters of this country" with "a political education" was now his calling. "It is work of a lower order than dealing directly – profoundly – with the souls of men," Adams admitted, "but it is work which a follower of Christ may do."[25]

Unlike Ely and Adams, Seligman was raised in a more cosmopolitan and urbane environment. As the child of an affluent German-Jewish banking family, Seligman was reared in the open New York City environment of Reform Judaism. Relatively early in his adult life he became a prominent member of Felix Adler's Society for Ethical Culture. Like his many brothers and sisters, Edwin was educated at home from a very early age, tutored by Horatio Alger Jr., who corresponded with Seligman throughout his life. With a steady dose of instruction in foreign languages, politics, and history, Seligman excelled at his studies. Through his family's regular travels abroad, he became particularly proficient in several European languages. And at the age of eleven he began his formal education by attending the Columbia Grammar School on the Upper West Side of Manhattan.[26] Though each of these scholars in various ways absorbed moral and ethical values that would in time shape their scholarship and

Neoclassicism, ed. Mary S. Morgan and Malcolm Rutherford (Durham: Duke University Press, 1998), 29–52.

[25] Coats, "Henry Carter Adams," 179–83; Henry C. Adams to Mother, Oct. 23, 1870; Henry C. Adams to Father, June 12, 1876, Correspondence 1876 Jan.–June, Box 1, Henry Carter Adams Papers, Bentley Library, University of Michigan, Ann Arbor, MI [hereinafter HCAP].

[26] Asso and Fiorito, "Edwin Robert Anderson Seligman, Autobiography,"; Horatio Alger Jr. to Seligman, Feb. 21, 1876; May 7, 1876; Apr. 1, 1876, Cataloged Correspondence; "Seligman Report Cards," Box 58 – Father, School, and College, ERASP; Carl S. Shoup, "Seligman." Scholars have generally attributed Seligman's ethical inclinations to his family's commitment to Reformed Judaism, overlooking his connections to Adler's Ethical

reform activities, they also learned, as part of their professional acculturation, to privilege an "intellectual gospel" over the Social Gospel or any of its moral variants.[27]

Similar backgrounds inclined the new generation of public finance economists toward social change. Their experiences with the harsh material realities of late-nineteenth-century American life further fortified their reformist tendencies. Not only did the structural forces of rapid industrialization and urbanization heighten economic disparities, the uneven development of modern American capitalism also fueled class conflict and labor unrest during this period. The public salience of the "labor question" thus was not lost on the aspiring political economists. After searching desperately for work in New York, Ely resolved as early as 1880 to become an advocate for the working class. When Adams began his graduate training at Johns Hopkins in the late 1870s, he was struck, as he walked the streets of Baltimore, by the extent of urban poverty. Although Seligman was the scion of a prestigious banking family, he was empathetic to the needs and wants of trade unionism, as his early scholarship on the cooperative movement and Christian socialism suggested. Indeed, nearly this entire generation of American academic activists struggled with the longstanding dilemma of attempting to bridge the world of educated opinion with that of the working masses. For those progressive intellectuals who became interested in public finance, overcoming the chasm between highbrow theories and the material world of the masses meant educating lawmakers, policy analysts, and the broader public about the need for dramatic fiscal reform.[28]

Personal backgrounds and contemporary conditions may have shaped the ideas and beliefs of the new school of American economists. But an even more resounding influence came from their shared graduate training

Culture Society. See, e.g., Ross, *Origins of American Social Science*, 103. But, according to his son, Eustace, Edwin Seligman had "broken with Judaism psychologically, intellectually, and every other way" relatively early in life. Interview with Eustace Seligman, Columbia University Oral History Collections, September 3, 1974, Butler Library, Columbia University, New York, N.Y.

27 For more on how these public finance economists privileged science over religion in their development as tax scholars and reformers, see generally Ajay K. Mehrotra, "'Render unto Caesar...' Religion/Ethics, Expertise, and the Historical Underpinnings of the Modern Tax System," *Loyola University of Chicago Law Journal* 40:2 (Winter 2009), 321–67. See, also Furner, *Advocacy & Objectivity*.

28 Ely, *Ground under Our Feet*, 164–5; Ross, *Origins of American Social Science*, 105; Edwin R. A. Seligman, "Owen and Christian Socialists," *Political Science Quarterly* 1:2 (1886), 206–49; Leon Fink, *Progressive Intellectuals and the Dilemmas of Democratic Commitment* (Cambridge, Mass.: Harvard University Press, 1977).

Henry Carter Adams (1851–1921)

Richard T. Ely (1854–1943)

Edwin R. A. Seligman (1861–1939)

FIGURE 2.1. The Progressive Public Finance Economists. These three reform-minded academics helped pioneer the American study of public finance, and led the intellectual movement for direct and graduated taxation.

and experience abroad. Following the path of their American mentors, a cohort of aspiring academics sojourned to Germany in the late nineteenth century to complete or complement their graduate training. As historian Daniel T. Rodgers has shown, "Germany was an intellectual mecca and a key station on an increasingly well-traveled career path" for reform-minded American social scientists. As one of the oldest of the group, Ely helped initiate the transatlantic transfer of ideas and pedagogy. "Studying in Germany," he wrote to his mother, was "a pleasure to every student. You learn here, and only here, how to do independent, real scientific work." Ely attended the University of Heidelberg, where he completed his doctorate in 1879 under the guidance of Karl Knies. He also brought the German seminar model of teaching back to Johns Hopkins, where he began his teaching career. Adams, who received one of the first doctorates granted by an American university (Johns Hopkins), also completed his graduate studies at Heidelberg and the University of Berlin, where he studied with Adolph H. G. Wagner, one of Germany's leading authorities on public finance. Seligman, who had family ties in Germany and often visited Europe during his childhood, also studied in Heidelberg and Berlin, under the tutelage of Knies, Wagner, Gustav Schmoller, and other well-known German economists.[29]

Their German training had a significant impact on the reform-minded American economists. Unlike some of their more conservative colleagues who also studied in Germany, members of the new school were deeply indebted to, and became great admirers of, the scholars who made up the German Historical School of Economics. Although historians of economic thought have disagreed about the coherency of a so-called "school" of German economic historicism, most concur that German academics such as Wilhelm G. F. Roscher, Gustav Schmoller, Karl Knies, and Adolph Wagner – to name only a few – coalesced during the second half of the nineteenth century as a group of thinkers who sought to challenge the metaphysical laws of British classical political economy. Ely, Adams, and Seligman each studied under some of these leading German scholars. And Seligman, who had the greatest affinity for German culture, maintained

[29] Daniel T. Rodgers, *Atlantic Crossings: Social Politics in a Progressive Age* (Cambridge, Mass.: Harvard University Press, 1998), 86, 96–7; James T. Kloppenburg, *Uncertain Victory: Social Democracy and Progressivism in European and American Thought, 1870–1920* (New York: Oxford University Press, 1986), 207–8; Jurgen Herbst, *The German Historical School in American Scholarship: A Study in the Transfer of Culture* (Ithaca: Cornell University Press, 1965); Joseph Dorfman, "The Role of the German Historical School in American Economic Thought," *American Economic Review* 45:2 (1955), 17–28; Ely, *Ground under Our Feet*, 41–7; Asso and Fiorito, "Edwin Robert Anderson Seligman, Autobiography," 163–5.

a substantive correspondence with his teachers long after his days as a student.[30]

Led by Roscher, who in the 1840s began the assault on deductive, a priori systems of economic thought, the subsequent generation of German historicists contended that universal economic laws were incoherent outside of their social, political, and economic context. Like the German school of jurisprudence, which Roscher explicitly sought to emulate, the German historical economists believed that human societies were not governed by natural laws. Instead, Roscher and his colleagues contended that social and economic relations were contingent upon historical and institutional contexts. These scholars used the term "historical" in its broadest sense to stress not only the significance of the past, but to renounce generalizing theories in favor of a fidelity to the particularity of actual events. Similarly, they used the term "institution" to refer to a broad category of norms and other socially created constraints on human behavior. From this vantage point, scholars such as Schmoller critiqued the tenets of classical and neoclassical economic theory, and took a normative position on the role of the state in guiding the economy and society. In contrast to the laissez-faire commitment of classical theory, the German historical economists argued that the increasing complexity and interdependence of modern society required a changing and more active role for the positive state.[31]

It was this emphasis on social context and historical contingency and the normative appeal to state action that had the greatest influence on the young American political economists trained at the foot of the German Historical School. Many of these American scholars came back to the United States with a more radical and fervent desire for reform. In their roles as teachers and publicly engaged academics, these progressive

[30] Furner, *Advocacy & Objectivity*, 54–5; Herbst, *The German Historical School*, 134–5; Heath Person, "Was There Really a German Historical School of Economics?" *History of Political Economy* 31:3 (1999), 547–62; "Notebooks from Classes in Berlin," Box 86, Lecture Notes Taken by Edwin R. A. Seligman; Gustav Cohn to Seligman, April 21, 1886, Feb. 10, 1909; Johannes Conrad to Seligman, Oct. 15, 1896; Karl Knies, Feb. 8, 189; Gustav Schmoller, Oct. 31, 1896; Adolph Wagner to Seligman, March 13, 1909, Cataloged, ERASP. Gustav Cohn and Seligman carried on an extensive transatlantic correspondence, and Cohn was delighted that "a community of scientific inquiry is establishing itself between the U.S. and Germany." Cohn to Seligman, April 21, 1886, ERASP.

[31] *The German Historical School: The Historical and Ethical Approach to Economics*, ed. Yuichi Shionoya (London: Routledge, 2001); Pearson, "Was There Really a German Historical School of Economics?" 548–9; Joseph Dorfman, *The Economic Mind in American Civilization*, 131–4; Furner, *Advocacy and Objectivity*, 48–9.

intellectuals adopted the pedagogical seminar style of the German universities and absorbed the substantive lessons of their German mentors. In the process, they helped forge not only a new view of economics, but also a distinct form of American new liberalism – a new liberalism that advocated using the powers of the state to address the social strife of modern industrial capitalism.[32]

Nowhere was the influence of German historicism on American new liberalism more apparent than among those American scholars who were interested in fiscal reform. Ely, Adams, and Seligman, in particular, returned from their postgraduate experiences in Germany with a serious interest in understanding public finance, or what their German teachers referred to as *Finanzwissenschaft*, the "Science of Finance."[33] Having read Schmoller's historical tracts and listened to Wagner's calls for a redistributive tax policy, Ely, Adams, and Seligman began to pioneer the rigorous and systematic study of American public finance. But first they had to translate the general philosophy of the German Historical School for an American audience. In keeping with the historicism they learned from their German mentors, the reform-minded American economists needed to graft continental ideas onto the stock of Anglo-American thought; they needed, in other words, to make German economic theories palatable for modern American institutions and culture. This was no easy task.

When Ely began teaching at Johns Hopkins, he became one of the first Americans to import German economic historicism to the United States. He specifically identified the German Historical School as the model for the American new school of heterodox economists. Although he was careful not to dismiss completely the contributions of Adam Smith and the "English or Manchester school of political economy," Ely described those ideas as outdated. He proclaimed that a more scientific method, a Teutonic viewpoint that emphasized an historical and institutional approach, was now carrying the day. For these German scholars, Ely maintained, political economy "is not regarded as something fixed or unalterable, but as a growth and development changing with society." Acknowledging the plasticity of the supposedly "natural laws" of political economy meant doing something, taking action to correct the excesses of modern

[32] Rodgers, *Atlantic Crossings*, 76–111; Ross, *Origins of American Social Science*, 98–140; Kloppenberg, *Uncertain Victory*, 241–3.

[33] Wilhelm Von Roscher, *System der Finanzwissenschaft* (Stuttgart, 1886); Adolf Wagner, *Finanzwissenschaft*, Erster Theil, 3te Aufl. (Leipzig, 1883).

industrialism. The young economists who subscribed to the historical school do not, Ely explained, "acknowledge laissez-faire as an excuse for doing nothing while people starve, nor allow the all-sufficiency of competition as a plea for grinding the poor." Instead, this "younger political economy," Ely concluded with his characteristic evangelical tone, "denoted a return to the grand principles of common sense and Christian precept."[34]

Other new school economists soon followed Ely's lead. In one of his first published essays, Seligman claimed that German scholars like Roscher, Knies, and Schmoller were the first thinkers to place economic ideas on a "truly scientific basis" because they understood "the necessity of treating economics from the historical stand-point." Seligman contended that it was these German thinkers – and now their American disciples – who discarded "the exclusive use of deductive method" and called for the "necessity of historical and statistical treatment." It was they who denied "the existence of immutable natural laws in economics, calling attention to the interdependence of theories and institutions, and showing that different epochs or countries require different systems." It was the German Historical School, Seligman continued, that abandoned any "belief in the beneficence of the absolute laissez-faire system" and maintained "the closer interrelation of law, ethics, and economics," while refusing to accept "the assumption of self-interest as the sole regulator of economic action." Finally, and most important for Seligman, the new school shared with its German teachers the desire to address contemporary problems. Once it was free from the reigning orthodoxy of laissez-faire, "the new school, devoid of all prepossessions, devoted itself to the task of grappling with the problems which the age had brought with it." These were the main principles, Seligman argued, that their German mentors had bequeathed to the new school of American political economy.[35]

The American new school was not, however, a simple imitation of German historical economics; suggesting that it was would belie the true lessons of historicism. Both schools of thought were rather a function of historically specific social, political, and economic conditions. Thus, the message of the German Historical School was a manifestation of an

[34] Richard T. Ely, "The Past and Present of Political Economy," *Overland Monthly and Out West Magazine* 2:9 (September 1883), 225–35, 233–5.

[35] Edwin R. A. Seligman, "Change in the Tenets of Political Economy with Time," *Science* (Supplement; April 23, 1886), 375–82, 381.

industrial era. "The new school is the product of the age, of the *zeitgeist*, not of any particular country," explained Seligman, "for the underlying evolutionary thoughts of a generation sweep resistlessly throughout all countries whose social conditions are ripe for change." Even English economists – those most ardent supporters of timeless economic and legal doctrines – Seligman argued, could not resist the force of the *zeitgeist*. John Stuart Mill "himself had gone through an evolution and was sincere enough to express his disbelief in the old economy, and to a certain extent in his own book." This commitment to the relativity of economic and legal doctrines – a commitment that the reform-minded economists acquired mainly during their German education – became an essential part of their overall fiscal vision.[36]

While Ely and Seligman embraced the process of transplanting German ideas onto American soil, Adams had a more cautious approach. He had always been more skeptical of the radical proposals of German socialists, like mandatory public education, which Adams decried as an idea where "all the children shall be brought up by the state." Writing to his mother during his studies in Germany, Adams ridiculed European socialism as "a dream of a new creation in which the nature of man as well as social organization must be entirely remodeled." Such a communal view of society "cannot exist and spread in America," wrote Adams, "because we love our homes to [sic] much. Men are too exclusive in their habits to want commonality in everything." Adams, more so than some of his new school colleagues, understood the institutional constraints posed by American political culture. In this way, he was perhaps more consistent in self-reflexively applying historicism to his own particular context.[37]

Adams may have harbored reservations about the American reception of European socialism, but he was by no means an apologist for capital. On the contrary, during the labor turmoil of the Gilded Age, Adams, along with many of his new school colleagues, was an adamant

[36] Ibid., 381–2. At the same time that the new school economists were molding transatlantic ideas for an American audience, U.S. jurists were performing a similar function for American law. Kunal M. Parker, *Common Law, History, and Democracy in America, 1790–1900: Legal Thought before Modernism* (New York: Cambridge University Press, 2011), 230–47; David M. Rabban, *Law's History: American Legal Thought and the Transatlantic Turn to History* (New York: Cambridge University Press, 2013), Chapter 11.

[37] Henry C. Adams to Mother, August 4, 1878, Correspondence Jan.–June 1876, Box 1, HCAP.

supporter of the American labor movement and its calls for greater equality in industrial relations. For a younger, rebellious generation of thinkers such support often came at a steep price, however. Adams's academic career, for instance, was dealt a serious setback in 1886 when his employment contract with Cornell University was not renewed because of his public comments suggesting that labor deserved "proprietary rights" in industrial capital.[38] Coming on the heels of one of the most violent years of labor strife, at a time when many Americans feared the rising tide of socialism, Adams's comments were interpreted by prominent Cornell alumni and administrators as unequivocal support for labor's "crusade against capital." Ultimately, Adams was able to secure a position at the University of Michigan after assuring administrators there that he was no socialist. Still, Adams's encounter with the political constraints on academic freedom colored much of his subsequent scholarship and informed his generation of social scientists about the limits of American academic freedom. These limits would, in turn, circumscribe their advocacy for a new and robust fiscal polity.[39]

Adams was not alone in his encounters with the limits of academic freedom. Ely and several other reform-minded economists faced similar political pressures. Indeed, defining the parameters of academic freedom became an essential part of the professionalization process. Forced to realize that American professors did not enjoy the same intellectual liberty or political support as their German counterparts, the new school economists learned to moderate their views on controversial issues and their support for a new fiscal polity. After his ordeal at Cornell, Adams, for instance, began to couch his otherwise more daring pronouncements on law and political economy with an appeal to "English liberty" and the long-established cultural values of American institutions.[40] Surely, these collisions with political power during the early stages of the professionalization of the social sciences tempered nearly every aspect of the

[38] Henry C. Adams, "The Labor Problem," *Scientific America Supplement* (August 21, 1886), 8861–3.

[39] Dorfman, "Introduction," 36; Furner, *Advocacy & Objectivity*, 133–8. When Adams was attempting to secure a teaching position at Johns Hopkins, his colleague and mentor Thomas M. Cooley recalled to his wife how he was skeptical that Adams's "style" would fit in at Hopkins. Thomas M. Cooley to Wife, Feb. 25, 1878, Folder: Typescript 1878, Box 6, Thomas M. Cooley Papers, Bentley Historical Library, University of Michigan, Ann Arbor, MI.

[40] Rader, *Academic Mind and Reform*, 136–50; Henry C. Adams, "Discussion of the Interstate Commerce Act," *Michigan Political Science Association Publications* 1:1 (1893), 137–43, 143.

economists' theories, including their views on public finance.[41] Although it is doubtful that Ely, Seligman, or Adams wholly embraced the radically redistributive tax theories of some of their German mentors, any sympathy they may have had was certainly diminished after they witnessed firsthand how American society responded to academic support for anything remotely resembling European socialism.

Importing German Historicism to the American "Science of Finance"

When the German-trained public finance economists set out to draft the theoretical blueprints for a new fiscal state, they were operating in relatively unchartered territory. For most of the nineteenth century, there was little scholarly discussion in the United States about the general economic principles of taxation beyond the politically controversial tariff.[42] The taxing powers of state and local governments in the United States were, of course, necessary to promote a "well-regulated" society, and, as we have seen, state and local property taxes were topics of discussion among some economic writers and social commentators. Yet, few contemporary scholars investigated the political and economic power that lay behind the federal government's ability to levy taxes. As late as 1880, the senior American political economist Francis A. Walker could confidently claim that "The body of English literature in finance is shabby in the extreme." The main explanation for the "feebleness and emptiness of the English literature in this department," Walker explained, was the lack of serious scholarly attention given to taxation. "Most of our political economists have not dealt with the subject at all, or have done so very perfunctorily." The young, reform-minded economists set out to change all that.[43]

Proceeding from somewhat similar intellectual origins, Adams, Ely, and Seligman began the American engagement with the "science of finance." They did so by applying the historicism of the new political

[41] Furner, *Advocacy & Objectivity*, 147–62. For more on academic freedom in the United States during this period, see Walter P. Metzger, *Academic Freedom in the Age of the University* (New York: Columbia University Press, 1955); Matthew W. Finkin and Robert C. Post, *For the Common Good: Principles of American Academic Freedom* (New Haven: Yale University Press, 2009), 1–52.

[42] As Henry Carter Adams noted, one of the tasks of his generation of academics was to teach students "that there is more in Polt. Economy than the mere discussion of Free Trade and Protection." Furner, *Advocacy & Objectivity*, 130.

[43] William J. Novak, *The People's Welfare: Law and Regulation in Nineteenth-Century America* (Chapel Hill: University of North Carolina Press, 1996); Francis A. Walker, "The Principles of Taxation," *Princeton Review* 2 (1880), 92–114, 93–4. Walker was Henry Carter Adams's mentor at Johns Hopkins. Coats, "Henry Carter Adams."

economy to public finance issues such as the tariff, public debts, and, of course, the income tax. Adams began the scholarly engagement. His doctoral thesis was a historical analysis of the protective tariff, and his early treatises focused on public debts and the budget-making process. In his dissertation, Adams illustrated how political pressures during the early years of the republic – namely the need to respond to Britain's attempts to curtail the naval powers of the United States – transformed the tariff from a simple revenue-generating device into a protectionist tool to combat British naval imperialism. This early manipulation of tax policy, Adams argued, gained institutional momentum and gradually became the de facto rationale for the nineteenth-century use of the tariff to protect domestic industry. Building on his mentor Francis Walker's observations, Adams believed protectionism was an historical accident sustained mainly by politics and institutional inertia, not economic logic. It was a policy that could and ought to be corrected. Adams's normative message seemed clear: he wanted to ensure that "tariff reform means tariff for revenue only."[44]

In one of his earliest publications, Ely took a similar, though more diffident, position. Evoking Adams's historical study, Ely concurred that the tariff had been distorted from its original objectives. But unlike Adams, who took a strong stand against protectionism, Ely eschewed the two extremes of trade policy and tried to navigate a middle path between free trade and protectionism. "I am unable to believe that any one policy respecting international commercial relations is an absolutely correct policy for all times and places," Ely declared. Given his sympathies with the working class, Ely was careful not to condemn all import duties, for he understood that there was some credence to the claims that the tariff protected jobs as well as industries. Nonetheless, through an inductive and comparative analysis, Ely ultimately concluded that many of the contentions of tariff supporters with regard to labor were unfounded. It was America's abundance of natural resources, its technological innovations, and its labor productivity, Ely believed, that were far more important to higher wages than protectionism.[45]

Contesting the tariff was a key part of creating a new fiscal order. But an even more crucial task was to scrutinize the broad underlying

44 Henry C. Adams, *Taxation in the United States, 1789–1816* (Baltimore: Johns Hopkins University Press, 1884), 79.

45 Richard T. Ely, *Problems of To-day: A Discussion of Protective Tariffs, Taxation, and Monopolies* (New York: Thomas V. Crowell Col., 1888), 39.

philosophical principles of taxation and their connection to fiscal citizenship. This required delineating between the divergent social and political theories that undergirded the two contending justifications for taxation: the "benefits principle" and the "ability-to-pay" or "faculty" rationale. Neither of these doctrines was unique to the American context; their coterminous development could be traced back throughout the Western world for centuries. Even Adam Smith, in his first maxim of taxation, had fused the two notions. Subsequent political economists, particularly John Stuart Mill, would refine the ability-to-pay rationale, but in popular discourse the two theories were frequently conflated.[46]

American tax theorists, building on the work of Mill, sought to decouple these two central justifications for taxation. They attempted to expose the anachronistic social theory that underpinned the benefits principle. Their goal was to debunk the dominant benefits rationale, and replace its language and logic with a new way of thinking about taxation. In the process, they intended to use the ability-to-pay or faculty rationale as a political tool to galvanize support for a modern fiscal state.[47]

In criticizing the benefits theory, Ely, Adams, and Seligman singled out its antiquated political and civic implications. For many contemporary theorists, as the previous chapter illustrated, the benefits doctrine was based mainly on the notion of reciprocal obligations. It relied on a traditional – and critics would argue impoverished – notion of the social contract to justify nearly every exercise of the sovereign's taxing powers. Taxes, under this theory, were simply the price that citizens paid for the benefit of government protection and spending.[48]

46 Harold M. Groves, *Tax Philosophers: Two Hundred Years of Thought in Great Britain and the United States*, ed. Donald J. Curran (Madison: University of Wisconsin Press, 1974); Carolyn Webber and Aaron Wildavsky, *A History of Taxation and Expenditure in the Western World* (New York: Simon & Schuster, 1986). As Smith explained, "The subjects of every state . . . ought to contribute towards the support of the government, as nearly as possible in proportion to their abilities that is in proportion to the revenue which they respectively enjoy under the protection of the state." Adam Smith, *Wealth of Nations*, ed. Edwin Cannan (New York: Modern Library, 1937 [1776]), 777.

47 The continuous coexistence of the benefits and ability-to-pay theories illustrates how the history of ideas is rarely about the complete victory of one concept over another. As the historian Neil Duxbury has noted, "Ideas – along with values, attitudes, and beliefs – tend to emerge and decline, and sometimes they are revived and refined. But rarely do we see them born or die." Neil Duxbury, *Patterns of American Jurisprudence* (New York: Oxford University Press, 1995), 2–3.

48 Thomas M. Cooley, *A Treatise on the Law of Taxation: Including the Law of Local Assessments* (Chicago: Callaghan and Co., 1876), 2; Cooley, *Principles That Should Govern in the Framing of Tax Laws* (St. Louis: G. I. Jones, 1878), 7.

The reform-minded tax experts adamantly disagreed with this principle. Using no less an authority than Judge Cooley as his foil, Ely claimed that taxes could no longer be justified based on "the old fiction of reciprocity." In attempting to define "taxes," Ely was careful in explaining that they were "not exchanges" or "payments" for public goods and services. "The sovereign power," wrote Ely, "demands contributions from citizens regardless of the value of any services which it may perform for the citizen." Thus, taxes were simply "one-sided transfers of economic goods or services demanded of the citizens . . . by the constituted authorities of the land, for meeting the expenses of government, or for some other purpose, with the intention that a common burden shall be maintained by common contributions or sacrifices." Given the extensive interdependence of modern industrial life, Ely continued, no serious person could maintain "the old legal fiction that taxes are paid for protection." This traditional justification for taxation was "so palpable an absurdity that it is strange that it could ever have gained the currency which it now enjoys," Ely concluded.[49]

Adams echoed Ely's sentiments. Classical benefits theory, wrote Adams, ignored how "[t]he modern State . . . assumes duties far beyond the primitive functions of protection to life and property." While such a "*quid pro quo* theory of taxation may have served fairly well under conceptions of governmental activity held in the early part of the century," Adams intoned, "it must be regarded at present as somewhat antiquated."[50] Adams, who believed in distinguishing between the theoretical justification for taxation and the "lawyer's point of view," subscribed, instead, to what he referred to as a "contributory theory of a tax" – a principle that expressly acknowledged the social aspects of taxation. Direct and graduated levies on incomes, profits, and inheritances, were justified under such a theory because they embodied the ethical duty of social unity that citizens of a community owed to each other and to the larger commonwealth. Unlike the contending "purchase theory" or "benefit theory" of tax – which stressed an atomistic and consumerist relationship between the citizen-taxpayer and the state – Adams explained that a contributory theory was based on "solidarity of social interest."[51]

49 Richard T. Ely, *Taxation in American States and Cities* (New York: Crowell, 1888), 14, 13, 6–7.

50 Henry C. Adams, *Science of Finance* (New York: Henry Holt & Co., 1898), 300.

51 Ibid., 301–2.

In this context, Adams was careful in using "contribution" to connote that taxes ought to be seen as part of the organic or collective nature of the state. Indeed, Adams was drawn to the study of public finance precisely because it inextricably intertwined the public and private realms. Contribution "implies that all the functions undertaken by the State are such as minister to common wants, and in large measure to wants which cannot be segregated or specialized to individuals or to classes," wrote Adams. "A sense of organic unity and of interdependence and a consciousness of common rights and common duties go along with the idea of contribution." Privileging the social over the individual was, therefore, an essential element in the campaign to displace the benefits theory and legitimate the principle of taxpaying ability.[52]

Seligman went even further in condemning the political theory that buttressed the benefits principle. He argued that the benefits doctrine was based, at its core, on an outmoded conception of citizenship:

> It is now generally agreed that we pay taxes not because the state protects us, or because we get any benefits from the state, but simply because the state is a part of us. The duty of supporting and protecting it is born with us. In a civilized society the state is as necessary to the individual as the air he breathes; unless he reverts to stateless savagery and anarchy he cannot live beyond its confines. His every action is conditioned by the fact of its existence. He does not choose the state, but is born into it; it is interwoven with the very fibers of his being; nay, in the last resort, he gives to it his very life. To say that he supports the state only because it benefits him is a narrow and selfish doctrine. We pay taxes not because we get benefits from the state, but because it is as much our duty to support the state as to support ourselves or our family; because, in short, the state is an integral part of us.[53]

With these striking words, Seligman articulated visions of a new and revitalized sense of civic identity, one that went well beyond traditional social contract rationales to capture a citizen's "ability to pay," or what Seligman referred to as their taxpaying "faculty." In this sense, Seligman and his colleagues disparaged the traditional notion of an individualized contract between a taxpayer and the state – a contract buttressed by the benefits principle. In its place, they sought to forge a more abstract yet

[52] Ibid., *Science of Finance*, 301–2. Writing to Seligman in 1904, Adams affirmed that "the science of finance is *par excellence* the branch of economic science which lays stress upon the organic or collective conception of social relations." Henry Carter Adams to Seligman, June 20, 1904 in "The Seligman Correspondence II," ed. Joseph Dorfman *Political Science Quarterly*, 56:270–86 (June 1941), 275 (emphasis in the original).

[53] Edwin R. A. Seligman, *Essays in Taxation* (New York: Macmillan, 1895), 72.

robust covenant, one that stressed taxation as a social obligation that yielded collective gains.

Indeed, the terms "faculty" and "ability to pay" soon became staunch, social democratic justifications for a new fiscal order. But, as we shall see in the following chapter, some of the progressive public finance economists were careful to distance their support for graduated taxes from the type of radically redistributive proposals forwarded by Adolph Wagner and other German public finance scholars and reformers. Like his new school colleagues, Seligman understood that American political culture placed limits on the degree and extent of fundamental fiscal reform.

If the reform-minded economists concurred that the benefits rationale was obsolete for a modern, highly interdependent society, they also disapproved of benefits doctrine because it was framed in an idiom of market relations. With their emphasis on the importance of ethical duty and social bonds, these theorists loathed how the benefits doctrine commodified the relationship between citizens and the state. Taxes "are one-sided transfers of goods or services, and are not mutual," Ely emphasized. "The citizen pays because he is a citizen, and it is his duty as a citizen to do so. It is one of the consequences which flow from the fact that he is a member of organized society," Ely concluded. "Only an anarchist can take any other view."[54]

Since individual citizens were part of a greater community, taxation based on a transactional notion of mutual exchange or barter seemed wholly out of place. It seemed to contradict the ethical responsibility and social solidarity that tax activists and economic theorists believed was at the center of a new sense of political belonging. The older understanding of social life had begun to lose force as an explanatory metaphor in a rapidly changing and increasingly interdependent world. If the state had a reciprocal duty as part of the social contract, it was not to simply protect life and property, but rather to ensure that fiscal sacrifices were equitably distributed among all community members. In sum, the progressive economists saw the benefits doctrine as a misrepresentation of the social obligations of modern citizenship.

These reformers were critical of benefits theory for pragmatic reasons as well. When it came to applying the benefits rationale to the structure of an actually existing tax system – to practical questions like whether the wealthy should pay more than the poor – critics contended that

[54] Ely, *Taxation in American States and Cities*, 13.

the benefits principle was intrinsically incoherent. The "give-and-take theory," as Seligman disparagingly referred to it, left the issue of degrees of taxation "inconclusive." Seligman argued that the benefits principle could be used to defend both a progressive tax as well as a regressive one. Because "most of the public expenses are incurred to protect the rich against the poor," Seligman coyly noted, the benefits theory would dictate that "the rich ought to contribute not only actually, but relatively more." Thus, if the justification for taxation under the benefits doctrine was the protection of private property, those with more property had more to protect and hence ought to have a larger tax burden.[55]

Yet at the same time, proponents of the benefits theory, Seligman maintained, could also demonstrate that "the very reverse is true." Because "the millionaire who is able to hire his own watchmen, his own detectives, his own military guard, and who often relies more on his individual efforts than on the government for the protection of his property causes the state less expense than the man of smaller means who must depend entirely on the government," wrote Seligman, taxes based on benefits could mean that "the poor man should then pay relatively more than the rich man." Even variants of the benefits doctrine that viewed taxes in terms of "the cost of services to government," and not "the value of protection" granted to individuals, were for Seligman "untenable." Benefits doctrine, however it was defined, was "indefensible" because, as Seligman succinctly stated: "It is absolutely impossible to apportion to any individual his exact particular share in the benefits of governmental activity. The advantages are quantitatively immeasurable."[56]

To be sure, the faculty theory, as the progressive political economists acknowledged, had its own problems, especially when it came to designing a practical tax system. For this and other reasons, the theorists placed different levels of faith in an income tax as the culmination of ability-to-pay logic. Ely remained resolutely confident that a graduated income tax could equitably reallocate fiscal burdens and reinvigorate civic and political participation. Adams, by contrast, supported income taxes as just one part of a broader vision of more radical fiscal changes at nearly all levels of government. "It can not be questioned that ability to pay

[55] Edwin R. A. Seligman, "Progressive Taxation in Theory and Practice," *Political Science Quarterly* 9:1/2 (1894), 7–222, 82. See also, Seligman, "The Theory of Progressive Taxation," *Political Science Quarterly* 8:2 (1893), 220–51.

[56] Seligman, "Progressive Taxation in Theory and Practice," 83–4.

is the only just and practicable basis for the apportionment of taxes, or that ability increases with increasing income at a rate more rapid than the increase of income itself," wrote Adams. Yet, he saw the taxing system not "as the sole means of social reform, but as a check upon the industrial tendencies during the period in which a general scheme of social reform" could come into existence."[57]

Similarly, Seligman believed that the income tax was an incremental, practical step toward the ideal of taxing one's ability to pay. But, ultimately, taxation according to faculty was, for Seligman, an aspirational aim – an ideal type that might not be achieved in practice but that could be a useful touchstone for policymakers. By striving to capture a citizen's ability to pay, an income tax could help, as Seligman put it, round "out the existing tax system in the direction of greater justice." In this way, the theory of faculty or ability to pay was, for these progressive economic thinkers, less about concrete tax laws or a consistent fiscal philosophy than it was a rhetorical device, a set of key words, used to inspire political and social support for a new fiscal order.[58]

Though the public finance economists may have disagreed about the development of concrete revenue laws, they seemed to agree that benefits theory provided an inconsistent and hence incoherent intellectual basis for creating a modern tax system. Did this mean that the benefits justification had no place in tax theory and fiscal policy discussions? What about those transactions where one could, indeed, identify a quid pro quo between the state and the taxpayer? For the political economists such payments were not only rare, they did not deserve to be called taxes. Seligman conceded that "some payments made by individuals for particular" government services "should represent as nearly as possible the cost of service to the government." But these payments, Seligman concluded, "are not taxes." They were, instead, merely "fees or tolls."[59]

57 Henry C. Adams, "Arguments for Progressive Taxation," MSS, "Tax Bound Folder," Box 14, HCAP; "Suggestions for a System of Taxation," *Michigan Political Science Association Publications* 1:2 (1894), 49–79.

58 Seligman, "The Income Tax," *Political Science Quarterly* 9:4 (1894), 610–48; Daniel T. Rodgers, *Contested Truths: Keywords in American Politics since Independence* (Cambridge, Mass.: Harvard University Press, 1998).

59 Seligman, "Progressive Taxation in Theory and Practice," 85–6. Seligman similarly made an analytical distinction between the state's "taxing powers" and "taxes." The former was a general plenary power exercised by government, and the latter was simply one form of that broader power. Nineteenth-century "special assessments" at the municipal level were an example of the sovereign's taxing powers, but they were not "taxes" per se. Seligman, "The Classification of Public Revenues," *Quarterly Journal of Economics*

The distinction was critical. It suggested that Seligman and his like-minded colleagues still believed that the benefits theory had an important, though subordinate, role to play in public finance discourse. After all, there was no other way to define a toll, a fee, or a special assessment accurately without some reference to the benefits conferred by the state. Yet when it came to financing pure public goods and services – those goods and services like national defense, law enforcement, and public roads that could be enjoyed by all individuals without increasing the cost of the goods and services for each individual – the best justification for taxes was the criterion of ability to pay. Thus, according to Seligman, not only was the benefits principle inconsistent in structuring tax rates; in the end, it also failed to reflect the true meaning of a tax.

The progressive political economists' relentless attacks on the benefits principle appeared to be laying the foundations for a pernicious, unintended consequence. By privileging the ability-to-pay principle over the benefits rational, these thinkers were severing the link between government spending and revenue collection. The faculty theory's obsession with economic power and egalitarian taxes neglected to address how taxation and government transfers could go hand in hand to ameliorate the massive economic inequalities and social dislocations of modern industrial life. Although these intellectuals could not have foreseen how they were creating this blind spot in progressive thinking, the early stages of American fiscal myopia were becoming manifest.

For their part, the reform-minded public finance economists conceded that they were simply expressing an idea that had been a neglected part of American tax policy. They maintained that American fiscal experts had long recognized the social dimension of taxation. W. H. Burroughs in his 1877 legal treatise had maintained that "the foundation of the taxing power is political necessity. Taxes are sacrifices made for the public good." Academics and treatise writers were not the only ones who understood the social relations underpinning taxation. Even tax administrators acknowledged the collective component of taxation. As Ely pointed out, the Massachusetts Tax Commission had identified as early as 1875 "the correct doctrine of taxation." The commission's final report, to which Ely approvingly cited at length, stated that "a man is taxed not to pay the state for its expense in protecting him, and not in any respect as a

7:3 (1893), 286–321. For more on the importance of special assessments to nineteenth-century municipal governance, see Robin Einhorn, *Property Rules: Political Economy in Chicago, 1833–1872* (Chicago: University of Chicago Press, 1991).

recompense to the state for any service in his behalf, but because his original relations to society require it." Ely believed that social cohesion, not any notion of radical individualism, justified taxation. "All the enjoyments which a man can receive from his property come from his connection with society," the Massachusetts report continued. "Cut off from all social relations a man's wealth would be useless to him. In fact, there could be no such thing as wealth without society."[60] Identifying the social underpinnings of American taxation helped the reform-minded economists with their campaign to reform the existing fiscal regime. The next step was to place these ideas into action to reform the existing tax system.

Applying Theory to Practice: An Early Salvo at the Property Tax

When it came to applying the abstract ideas of faculty or ability to pay to concrete conditions, the new school political economists turned, first, to an easy target: the general property tax. As we have seen, by the late nineteenth century the state and local property tax was the favorite target of nearly every economic commentator. Yet, unlike other critics, the young public finance economists used inductive, empirical, and historical methods to discredit the property tax. Their examinations focused on how the property tax no longer corresponded to modern industrial conditions – how the levy, because of changing social and economic conditions, no longer conformed with what they saw as the touchstone of modern taxation: the principle of ability to pay.

While the ownership of real property was at one time a fair representation of a citizen's tax-paying ability, the reformers believed that with the rise of industrial capitalism, real property was no longer an accurate measure of taxpaying faculty. The institutional convergence of large-scale manufacturing and finance capital had profoundly altered the social conceptions of property. The increasing prevalence of intangible personal property, in the form of stocks, bonds, and other financial assets, allowed citizens to conceal their wealth in what contemporary tax administrators referred to as "hidden assets." With real property no longer the primary marker of wealth and tax-paying ability, fiscal experts and reformers

[60] W. H. Burroughs, *A Treatise on the Law of Taxation* (New York: Baker, Voorhis & Co., 1877), 1; Ely, *Taxation in American States and Cities*, 14 (quoting Thomas Hills et al., *Report of the Massachusetts Commission on Taxation* [Boston: Wright & Porter, 1875]).

believed that a property tax was insufficient in accurately gauging a citizen's ability to meet his or her social obligations.[61]

Ely began his systematic assessment of the property tax when he was appointed to the Baltimore and Maryland tax commissions in the mid-1880s. Capitalizing on his official government position, he gathered an enormous amount of data on how the property tax actually functioned in numerous North American cities and several American states. Ely was left appalled by the "worthless" system of state and local taxation that existed at the time. Struck by how unfair the process of assessing property was in application, Ely dissented from the Commission's rudimentary recommendations for more stringent enforcement of existing laws, and issued his own supplemental report calling for a radical overhaul of state and local tax systems.[62]

Ely also used his experience on the tax commissions to publish a groundbreaking treatise on subnational taxation. In it he made the case for the superiority of the income tax mainly in terms of equity and social justice. The income tax "is the fairest tax ever devised," Ely wrote, "it places a heavy burden when and where there is strength to bear it, and lightens the load in case of temporary or permanent weakness. Large property does not always imply ability to pay taxes, as taxes should come from income; even when assessed on property it is only an indirect device for estimating income." Why not remove the indirect device of taxing property, Ely reasoned, and take a more direct approach at seizing one's ability to pay by imposing an income tax? The income tax, he concluded, was "beneficial because it places a heavy load only on strong shoulders"[63]

Seligman provided an even more detailed critique of how the property tax deviated from the principle of ability to pay. He made three principal points. First, he demonstrated with comparative evidence that the property tax was not exceptional to American conditions, as many commentators had claimed. Second, because it was not unique or timeless, the American property tax was susceptible to the forces of historical change. Third, and perhaps most important, Seligman illustrated how the

[61] Yearley, *Money Machines*; William G. Roy, *Socializing Capital: The Rise of the Large Industrial Organization* (Princeton: Princeton University Press, 1999), 122–41; Higgens-Evenson, *Price of Progress*.

[62] Richard T. Ely, "Supplementary Report on Taxation in Maryland," in *Report of the Maryland Tax Commission to the General Assembly* (Baltimore: King Bros., 1888), 93–200.

[63] Ely, *Taxation in American States and Cities*, 288–9.

property tax was currently out of place "because property is no longer a criterion of faculty or tax-paying ability." With changes in economic and social conditions, Seligman asserted "[t]he standard of ability has been shifted from property to product."[64]

Like Ely, Seligman believed that the emergence of modern, industrial capitalism meant that the general property tax in its current form had outlived its usefulness, at least at the state level. At its origins, the property tax was a wealth tax, but by the late nineteenth century, wealth could no longer simply be equated with real property. "Not the extent but the productivity of wealth constitutes the test," wrote Seligman. Revenue or the flow of wealth – not its mere physical embodiment – was the true measure of one's faculty or ability to pay. The property tax, moreover, had become increasingly unproductive in generating public revenue. It could no longer be collected effectively in an age of finance capital because it could not get at the increasing forms of intangible wealth. The new type of "hidden" wealth remained concealed from tax rolls.[65]

Since wealthy investors and taxpayers had little incentive to reveal their true wealth, the existing property tax also "puts a premium on dishonesty and debauches the public conscience." But most significantly, for Seligman, the property tax was no longer practical because "[i]t presses hardest on those least able to pay" – those who held more limited assets largely in real property that could not be concealed from the property tax rolls. In light of these problems, Seligman believed that the income tax was "infinitely superior in practice." With his characteristic zeal, the Columbia professor concluded that "the general property tax is so flagrantly inequitable that its retention can be explained only through ignorance or inertia. It is the cause of such crying injustice that its abolition must become the battle cry of every statesman and reformer."[66] Seligman's clarion call to action was not lost on policymakers. As we shall see in Chapter 4, state-level lawmakers agreed with the political economists' assessments of the property tax, and through a gradual process of institutional change, they set out to reform a subnational fiscal system that had become increasingly obsolete.

64 Edwin R. A. Seligman, "The General Property Tax," *Political Science Quarterly* 5:1 (1890), 24–64, 62.

65 Ibid.

66 Ibid.

Economic Crisis and the 1894 Income Tax

The intellectual campaign for direct and graduated taxes was a critical element in the development of the modern American fiscal state. Yet, if the broad structural changes sweeping the nation and new ideas about taxation and civic identity were the long-term underlying causes of the seismic shift in American public finance, the short-term triggers for this transformation were the seminal events that closed out the century. The Panic of 1893, which precipitated a deep and severe economic contraction, fueled populist rage against the existing social, political, and economic order. As labor strife intensified and economic disparities widened, populist calls for reviving progressive taxes on incomes, inheritances, and business profits quickly moved from the margins of third-party political platforms to the center of American political debate. National lawmakers took notice.

The 1893 Panic and New Political Opportunities for Reform

The economic depression of the mid-1890s that provided the impetus for the 1894 tax law had deep and complex roots. To be sure, the same broad structural changes in the economy – the shift, that is, from a rural agricultural economy to an urban industrial one – that were straining the existing public finance regime also provided the context for the economic crisis. More specifically, though, uncertainty surrounding the "silver question" and monetary policy, a global recession that began in France in 1889 and spread quickly to other leading European nations, falling prices for agricultural staples, and a general decline in U.S. railroad expansion and building construction all contributed to what economic historians have identified as "among the severest depressions in the United States."[67]

The panic itself began in the spring of 1893 when a stock market crash prompted a nationwide run on bank deposits and an ensuing tightening of credit. Months earlier, the collapse of the Philadelphia and Reading Railway Company and a decline in U.S. Treasury reserves signaled the

[67] Charles Hoffmann, *The Depression of the Nineties: An Economic History* (Westport, Conn.: Greenwood Publishing, 1970); Douglas Steeples and David O. Whitten, *Democracy in Desperation: The Depression of 1893* (Westport, Conn.: Greenwood Press, 1998). On the similarities of panic-induced economic crises, see generally Charles P. Kindleberger, *Manias, Panics, and Crashes: A History of Financial Crisis* (New York: Basic Books, 1989).

start of a recession. The downturn was accelerated by the swelling tide of business and bank failures. And an overall loss of confidence in the economy following the stock market crash only seemed to exacerbate the situation. Despite a slight upturn in 1895, the depression lasted well into 1897. The magnitude of the contraction over that five-year period was astonishing. Banks and businesses were suspended or failed at an alarming rate, and unemployment reached a peak of nearly 20 percent, according to one modern estimate. In fact, unemployment did not fall below 10 percent until 1899, when annual national output began to match pre-depression levels. As labor leader Samuel Gompers observed, "the great number of idle, unemployed workers, the almost countless ... men and women" were "suffering the pangs of hunger, the poignancy of distress and dependence."[68]

The 1890s depression, of course, put even greater pressure on public revenues and a national tariff system that many believed was incapable of functioning during a national calamity. The federal budget had been running significant annual surpluses for several years, but that trend reversed in the mid-1890s due to the economic slump. While tax experts had long been critical of the tariff regime, the gravity of the business downturn and its effects on American life led other economic experts to join the growing chorus of tariff critics. Writing at the start of the 1890s depression, University of Chicago labor economist Robert Hoxie observed that "the customs revenue system, through inherent inflexibility and instability, is incapable of serving as an adequate source of public revenue in times of emergency." Because moments of national crisis were crucial testing grounds, "no nation could be found willing to base its finances on a system that must fail it in time of stress," Hoxie continued. "This conclusion then is really equivalent to a general condemnation of the customs revenue system as the main source of a national income."[69]

The depression also reignited populist demands for fiscal reform. An unparalleled wave of labor strikes – highlighted by the Pullman Strike of 1894 – followed by a conservative backlash heightened class and sectional anxieties. Southern and Western populists reached out to lawmakers to

[68] Steeples and Whitten, *Democracy in Desperation*, 42–65; Samuel Gompers in *Report of Proceedings of the American Federation of Labor, 1893* (Bloomington, Ind.: American Federation of Labor, 1893), 12–23.

[69] *Historical Statistics of the United States*, Table Ea584–587; Robert F. Hoxie, "Adequacy of the Customs Revenue System," *Journal of Political Economy* 3:1 (1894), 39–72, 71.

express their desire to use direct and progressive taxes both as a tool to attack growing concentrations of wealth and as a pragmatic source of government revenue. "The most effective weapon for use against the Plutocratic policy is the graded income tax," wrote one St. Louis newspaper editor to William Jennings Bryan. "There is nothing which those Eastern Plutocrats dread so much as that and it is a weapon which the Democrats should have used long ago to stop the piling up of pensions." Acknowledging that the depression had strained public revenues, the editor contended that "an income tax on abnormal incomes is far preferable to replacing the duty on sugar or even to an increase of the internal revenue tax on whiskey."[70]

Southern and Western elites were not alone in seizing on the economic crisis to push for tax reform. Ordinary farmers and their agricultural associations throughout the country articulated similar concerns. Petitions like the one from the Kansas Farmers' Alliance of Rile County flooded House and Senate offices demanding a new income tax law. Specifically, the Kansas farmers requested a national tax on all incomes above $5,000 (roughly $138,000 in 2012 dollars). This was an exemption level that clearly put nearly all everyday farmers and wage earners out of reach.[71] Similarly, agrarian associations in the Northeast also recognized that an income tax could help alleviate the uneven distribution of fiscal burdens. A petition sent by a Massachusetts Grange to its congressional representative on the House Ways and Means Committee seemed to summarize how many farmers felt: "The American Farmer has heretofore and is now paying more than his just proportion of taxation, and believing that an internal revenue tax upon incomes will tend to equalize the burden of taxation, Resolved: That the members of Granby Grange No. 157 Request

[70] Charles Postel, *The Populist Vision* (New York: Oxford University Press, 2007), 131–2; Elizabeth Sanders, *Roots of Reform: Farmers, Workers, and the American State, 1877–1917* (Chicago: University of Chicago Press, 1999), 217–32; Lawrence Goodwyn, *The Populist Movement: A Short History of Agrarian Revolt in America* (New York: Oxford University Press, 1978), 208–10; John D. Hicks, *The Populist Revolt: A History of the Farmers' Alliance and the People's Party* (Omaha: University of Nebraska Press, 1961), 321–3; Ratner, *Taxation and Democracy in America*, 172–3.

[71] Kansas Farmers' Alliance of Riley County to Hon. John Davis, January 18, 1894; Fifty-Third Congress – Petitions; Ways and Means (HR 53A-33.10), Box 180, Folder "Tax on Incomes, September 9, 1893 – April 30, 1894," National Archives and Record Administration, Washington, D.C. [hereinafter NARA I]; relative value of U.S. dollar amounts calculated using consumer price index. Available at: http://www.measuringworth.com/uscompare/relativevalue.php.

our Representatives in Congress and also our Senators to use their best efforts to place such a law upon the Statute Books of our Country."[72]

Opponents of tax reform were equally alarmed by the Panic of 1893. But rather than view the crisis as an indictment of the prevailing tax system, many saw it as a harbinger of even more dramatic and dangerous changes. Fearful of "the communism of the Populists and Socialists," wealthy individuals and commercial interests charged that the proposed 1894 income tax was an attack on private property and republican liberty. The New York State Chamber of Commerce contended that it would be "unwise to impose a tax on incomes" because the law would adversely impact the most vulnerable persons in society. In a congressional petition that became a template for income tax opponents across the country, the Chamber wrote: "The experience of the year 1893 shows that the incomes of persons engaged in agriculture, industry and trade vary with the prosperity of the country, so that people generally do not know from one year to another how much they may have earned. Persons who draw regular salaries, widows and orphans whose estates are managed by Courts, and other persons living on fixed incomes, would sustain the brunt of this burden, while they are least able to pay it." The Chamber conveniently neglected to mention that the proposed high exemption level would likely mean that only the wealthiest of "widows and orphans" would be liable for income taxes. Nor did they acknowledge that, unlike other forms of taxation, an income tax would actually vary with economic conditions, decreasing during difficult times when taxpayers earned less.[73]

The First Peacetime Income Tax

Regardless of their position on the income tax, national lawmakers understood that the 1893 panic initiated a reconsideration of the existing fiscal regime. The economic contraction together with the prevailing high import duties reduced government revenues and forced both national parties to reevaluate their positions on tax policy. Republicans continued

[72] H. J. Witmark, Secretary of Granby Massachusetts Grange, to Samuel W. McCall, January 25,1894, Fifty-Third Congress – Petitions; Ways and Means (HR 53A-33.10), Box 180, Folder "Tax on Incomes, September 9, 1893 – April 30, 1894," NARA I.

[73] "Memorial from the Chamber of Commerce of the State of New York, March 1, 1894," Fifty-Third Congress – Petitions; Ways and Means (HR 53A-33.10), Box 180, Folder "Tax on Incomes, September 9, 1893–April 30, 1894," NARA I. This New York petition became the template for dozens of other local chambers of commerce and boards of trade, who submitted nearly identical petitions to the Ways and Means Committee. Ibid.

to maintain their support for protectionism, though the downturn forced them to reassess rate schedules. Meanwhile, Democrats who controlled both Houses of Congress and the White House during the panic began to reconsider new forms of internal revenue. Led by Western and Southern populists like William Jennings Bryan and Benton McMillin (D-Tenn.) in the House and William V. Allen (Populist-Neb.) and William A Peffer (Populist-Kan.) in the Senate, an alliance of Populists and insurgent Democrats exploited the economic turmoil and the projected shortfall in federal revenues to help enact the first peacetime income tax. Many mainstream Democrats, including the powerful chairman of the House Ways and Means Committee William L. Wilson (D-W. Va.), feared that an income tax would jeopardize pragmatic tariff reform. But the populist leaders saw the economic crisis as an opportunity to create radically redistributive tax laws and policies.[74]

Like the progressive public finance economists, lawmakers were influenced by transatlantic forces, the extent of the economic crisis, and the growing evidence of economic inequality in American society. During the early consideration of the 1894 income tax law, Bryan asked the U.S. State Department to investigate the details of existing revenue laws in several European nations. The findings, which Bryan prominently added to the *Congressional Record*, suggested that there was an emerging global convergence toward income taxation. England, Austria, Switzerland, Italy, and several German states all had income taxes with varying exemption levels and progressive rates. The conspicuous absence of an income tax in the United States weighed heavily on Bryan and other lawmakers. Income tax proponents proclaimed that the glaring omission was proof of American backwardness and the need for the United States to catch up to other "civilized nations." Meanwhile, detractors celebrated the comparative anomaly, arguing that it evidenced how "un-American" the income tax truly was, and how its continued absence could prevent the arrival of creeping European socialism on American shores.[75]

Congressional leaders, unsurprisingly, were also cognizant of how the economic crisis drew attention to the increasing concentration of wealth.

[74] Ratner, *Taxation and Democracy*, 168–92; Richard J. Joseph, *The Origins of the American Income Tax: The Revenue Act of 1894 and Its Aftermath* (Syracuse, N.Y.: Syracuse University Press, 2004), 47–61. For a recent assessment of the influence of Bryan and the populists on American constitutional development, see Gerard N. Magliocca, *The Tragedy of William Jennings Bryan: Constitutional Law and the Politics of Backlash* (New Haven: Yale University Press, 2011).

[75] *Congressional Record*, 53rd Cong., 2nd sess. (1894), 26, pt. 1:584–91.

Referring to the growing mass of unemployed workers and to the studies of inequality conducted by Thomas Sherman and George Holmes, legislators like Senator William Allen, "the intellectual giant of populism," rhetorically asked whether such trends in inequality were sustainable: "How many years will it be until the total wealth of this nation shall have passed into the hands of a very few thousand men, and the great masses of the people, male and female, become a vast agricultural and mining peasantry, practically slaves?" To prevent that day from arriving, Allen and other income tax advocates contended that affluent Americans had a civic responsibility to reform the existing tax system.[76]

In language that echoed the claims made by Ely, Adams, and Seligman, populist lawmakers reframed the elite hostility to income taxes as an abdication of the social responsibility that accompanied great wealth and power. Responding to Republican charges that an income tax was inherently "unjust and inquisitorial," Allen retorted that these arguments were simply a "subterfuge" for the true motivations of income tax opponents: their selfish desire to shift the burden of taxation onto others. The true objection to the income tax, Allen intoned, is "the argument of avarice; it is the argument of cupidity; it is the argument of the man who loves his lucre better than he loves his country, who wants to escape with his whole fortune, who wants to shirk his responsibility as a citizen, who wants to cast the burden of conducting the Government upon the poor and distressed and those least able to bear it."[77]

To remind wealthy Americans of their civic duty, Allen and other legislators paid particular attention to the scope of the new income tax. The pending bill expressly provided that "every citizen of the United States and every person residing therein" was subject to the income tax. This citizenship-based system of taxation meant that individuals and corporations would be responsible for paying taxes on their worldwide income. Fleeing to a foreign jurisdiction would not absolve American citizens of their national civic and fiscal responsibilities. In the post–World War I period, as we shall see, taxing income across international borders would become a highly charged issue. But in 1894, this seemingly technical aspect of the law illustrated just how aware lawmakers were of the links between taxation, nationalism, and citizenship.[78]

[76] Ibid.; *Congressional Record*, 53rd Cong., 2nd sess. (1894), 26, pt. 7:6714; Hicks, *Populist Revolt*, 282–3.

[77] *Congressional Record*, 53rd Cong., 2nd sess. (1894), 26, pt. 7:6716.

[78] Ibid.; Wilson-Gorman Tariff Act of 1894, Sec. 54; Joseph, *Origins of the American Income Tax*, 67–9. Although the modern U.S. system of international taxation did not

Though they rarely acknowledged the new school economists as their explicit inspiration, legislators used the idiom of fiscal citizenship and ethical obligations, as well as the specific language of "ability to pay," in support of the pending 1894 income tax bill. In fact, there was a remarkable similarity between the rhetoric used by congressional income tax supporters and the writings of the progressive public finance economists – right down to the metaphors that were employed. The "income tax is the most equitable and just way of taxation, putting the burden of taxation upon the shoulders of those who are most able to bear it, and takes it from the shoulders of those who are least able to bear it," proclaimed Georgia representative Henry Talbert in words that expressly echoed Ely's treatise. Similarly, Illinois Congressman George W. Fithian, citing to Sherman's study of inequality, defended an "income tax levied upon owners of these immense fortunes" because quite simply "they have the means and ability to pay."[79]

Other lawmakers evoked biblical references that stressed the importance of taxpaying capacity. Missouri Congressmen Uriel S. Hall, an early advocate of the income tax, charged that ignorant foes of the income tax "certainly never read Moses in Deuteronomy, where he advocates collecting taxes according to means and ability to pay." In their enthusiasm to cite "distinguished writers on political economy," some leaders were even willing to twist canonical texts. Bryan, for example, claimed that Adam Smith unequivocally backed taxation based on one's ability to pay, eliding how Smith's maxim also justified taxation based on benefits.[80]

To be sure, lawmakers also used the benefits principle to justify the 1894 income tax. As pragmatic legislators, they deployed any claim that might persuade their colleagues and constituents. But the most astute congressional arguments seemed to recognize that direct levies based on a taxpayer's means or ability held the potential to do much more than simply reallocate fiscal burden. Basing taxation upon ability or faculty also opened up new avenues for enhanced civic engagement. The salience

take shape until World War I and the 1920s, the 1894 law's focus on the worldwide income of U.S. citizens has remained a fundamental part of U.S. international tax law. Michael J. Graetz and Michael M. O'Hear, "The 'Original Intent' of U.S. International Taxation," *Duke Law Journal*, 46:5 (March 1997), 1020–1109; Reuven S. Avi-Yonah, "The Structure of International Taxation: A Proposal for Simplification," *Texas Law Review* 74: (1996), 1301–61.

79 "Speech of Hon. George W. Fithian," *Congressional Record*, 53rd Cong., 2nd sess. (1894), 26, Appendix: 67–72, 71; 26, pt. 2:1608, 160.

80 *Congressional Record*, 53rd Cong., 2nd sess. (1894), 26, pt. 2:1676; Joseph, *Origins of the American Income Tax*, 89–90.

of direct taxes could have positive effects on political participation. In his support for the income tax, Mississippi Congressman John Williams expressly recognized Ely's groundbreaking treatise and quoted from it at length to show how the new levy was "a tax which will interest the taxpayer in watching the politicians in order to see that they do not lay too heavy burdens upon the backs of the people; in order to see that government is neither extravagantly nor dishonestly administered." For Williams and others, the income tax's promise of re-engaging citizens with their polity was one of the new law's greatest attributes.[81]

For their part, income tax opponents did not hesitate in exploiting civic identity claims, but they did so in an attempt to turn the tables on the populists. New York Congressmen Bourke Cockran, for example, contended that with a relatively high exemption level of $4,000 ($110,000 in 2012 dollars) the middle-class and working poor would not be eligible to pay the pending income tax, and they would accordingly be deprived of their opportunity to participate actively in political and civic negotiations. From this perspective, "taxation instead of being a sign of servitude was a badge of freedom," and high exemption levels were thus a denial of liberty and citizenship. Income tax advocates, however, reminded their opponents that the proposed income tax was merely a supplement to a larger tariff regime, and that national taxation was just one part of a broader fiscal order that included many forms of regressive taxes. "If taxation is a badge of freedom," William Jennings Bryan caustically responded to Cockran, "let me assure my friend that the poor people of this country are covered all over with the insignia of freemen."[82]

Ultimately, the income tax measure, which began as a separate bill, was absorbed into the Wilson-Gorman Tariff Act and enacted in the summer of 1894 without President Cleveland's signature. Republicans and a few Northeastern Democrats in the Senate eviscerated the tariff reductions in the House bill, yet they were unable to defeat the income tax provision. The final bill thus appeared to be a compromise, one that yielded some higher custom duties, especially on sugar, in exchange for the new income tax. This was an arrangement that income tax opponents seemed willing to live with, at least for the time being. But the political compromise, particularly the Senate's inability to maintain the House's dramatic reduction of import duties, infuriated President Cleveland and other Democratic political leaders. The defection of leading Senate Democrats

[81] *Congressional Record*, 53rd Cong., 2nd sess. (1894), 26, pt. 2:1604–5.
[82] Ibid., 1656.

like David Hill signaled the decline of the Cleveland administration's ability to retain national party discipline and loyalty. Sectional and material interests seemed to win out over party allegiance.[83]

The details of the 1894 income tax were also the result of compromise. While numerous social groups and populist lawmakers demanded a permanent progressive rate structure, the law was scheduled to expire after five years and contained only a flat 2 percent tax rate. The relatively high exemption level of $4,000 guaranteed a certain amount of de facto graduation, but in the end the levy was clearly a "class tax" on the wealthy just as its opponents claimed. For the economic experts and lawmakers who were consciously trying to build a new fiscal state, this aspect of the tax squarely fit their primary desire to reallocate economic burdens. Although the law did not go as far in redistributing wealth as some populists and socialists had hoped, the measure did counter the perceived regressive aspects of the existing tax regime. Likewise, the broad legislative definition of the tax base, which included all "gains, profits, or income," including gifts and inheritances, demonstrated that the new law was focused on tapping taxpaying capacity. Moreover, the global application of the tax base to the worldwide income of American individuals and business associations (but not partnerships) further solidified the notion that the levy was premised not on the benefits that a particular government might provide in creating wealth and income, but on the notion that, no matter where they resided in the world, well-heeled U.S. citizens – individuals and corporations alike – had a social obligation and an ethical duty to share the burden of financing the modern American state.[84]

Yet for all of its achievements, the 1894 law lacked several critical elements that troubled state-builders and tax experts. In its efforts to define a broad base, the law did not differentiate between wage income earned by a growing class of professionals and the "unearned" incomes of wealthy Americans who were living off invested capital. Similarly, the inclusion of wealth transfers, such as gifts and inheritances, in the

[83] F.W. Taussig, "The Tariff Act of 1894," *Political Science Quarterly* 9:4 (Dec. 1894), 585–609; Ratner, *Taxation and Democracy*, 179–192. Although the Democrats endured several key defections, the Wilson-Gorman Tariff was passed mainly along partisan lines in both houses of Congress. For a more detailed analysis of voting on the 1894 law, see Robert Stanley, *The Dimensions of Law in the Service of Order: Origins of the Federal Income Tax, 1861–1913* (New York: Oxford University Press, 1993), 128–32.

[84] Wilson-Gorman Tariff Act of 1894, Sections 27–37; Joseph, *Origins of the U.S. Income Tax*, 51–3.

tax base muddied the conceptual and legal definition of income by taxing equally both periodic windfalls as well as regular flows of income. Finally, and perhaps most importantly, the 1894 law contained an anemic administrative mechanism for collecting the tax. Unlike the English income tax, the 1894 law relied mainly on self-assessment and collected only a few types of income directly at their source through a crude form of withholding. Whereas the British used a scheduler system that required nearly all income taxes to be remitted by the payor, the 1894 American levy used the principle of "stoppage at the source" only for government salaries and corporate dividends.[85] These and other drawbacks, as we shall see, would become important issues in subsequent iterations of the tax laws, especially during the post–World War I period when rationalizing the legal definition of income, maintaining the bureaucratic machinery for tax collection, and securing the social legitimacy of graduated taxes would become pivotal for the consolidation of the new fiscal order.

A Judicial Obstacle: The Road to *Pollock*

Initially, the enactment of the first peacetime income tax was hailed by supporters as "a wonderful success," and denounced by detractors as "a penalty set on thrift" and "a condemnation of industry and providence."[86] Opponents of the income tax had expended a great deal of energy in unsuccessfully resisting the enactment of the 1894 bill. It did not take long, however, for these tax reform foes to shift their focus from Congress to the courts. During legislative debates, several lawmakers including New York Senator David Hill had contended that an income tax would not survive constitutional scrutiny. Despite a long line of Supreme Court precedents to the contrary, opponents were confident that the 1894 income tax would be struck down either as a violation of the "direct tax" clause or the constitutional requirement that all taxes be "uniform."[87]

[85] Charles F. Dunbar, "The New Income Tax," *Quarterly Journal of Economics* 9:1 (October 1894), 26–46; Seligman, "The Income Tax," 610–48. Unlike the Civil War income tax, which adopted a crude form of withholding for corporate interest and dividends, the 1894 law did not require corporations to remit interest income. For more on the history of the corporate tax during this period, see Steven A. Bank, *From Sword to Shield: The Transformation of the Corporate Income Tax, 1861 to Present* (New York: Oxford University Press, 2010).

[86] "The Income Tax Feature of the New Tariff Law," *The Chautauquan* 20:1 (October 1894), 93.

[87] U.S. Constitution, Article I, Section 2. The pertinent section of this clause requires that "direct taxes shall be apportioned among the several states ... according to their

Tax reformers gave the constitutional objections short shrift, both before and after the enactment of the new income tax. During the legislative debates, Nebraska Senator William Allen, a former lawyer and judge, reminded his colleagues of the sustained precedents supporting the constitutionality of an income tax. From the 1796 decision upholding a tax on carriages to the more recent 1881 case validating the Civil War income tax, the U.S. Supreme Court had consistently interpreted the "direct tax" clause narrowly to conclude that only poll and land taxes were direct taxes requiring apportionment. Likewise, the Court had ruled that the "uniformity clause" governed the geographical application of federal tax laws – that they were uniform throughout the nation. The clause was generally not interpreted to apply to the rate structure of a particular tax or to distinctions between specific taxpayers. Thus, for Allen and other informed jurists, the constitutionality of an income tax in 1894 was a "settled" legal question.[88]

In his published assessments of the new income tax, Seligman similarly disparaged the constitutional opposition, particularly the claims based on the direct tax clause. After reiterating his longstanding belief that "among economists there is no absolute agreement as to the exact distinction between direct and indirect taxes," the Columbia professor conceded that from a legal perspective it was critical to determine what the framers of the Constitution meant when they used the term "direct tax." As a trained lawyer, who interacted frequently with prominent jurists and whose work was regularly cited by the courts, Seligman understood that legal fictions often trumped economic reality. In this context, he believed the High Court had been consistent in its prior rulings. Given the lack of explicit historical evidence about the original meaning of "direct" taxes, the Court had concluded for nearly a century that the term "direct" tax ought to be construed narrowly. "The Supreme Court of the United States is thus undoubtedly correct in assuming that the only direct taxes contemplated by the Constitution were the poll tax

respective numbers." U.S Constitution, Article I, Section 8. The latter portion of this section states that "all duties, imposts, and excises shall be uniform throughout the United States."

[88] *Hylton v. United States*, 3 U.S. 171 (1796); *Springer v. United States*, 102 U.S. 586 (1881). In between these two cases, the Court regularly upheld other national taxes by interpreting the direct tax clause narrowly. See, e.g., *Scholey v. Rew*, 90 U.S. (23 Wall.) 331 (1874); *Veazie Bank v. Fenno*, 75 U.S. (8 Wall.) 533 (1869); *Pac. Ins. Co. v. Soule* 74 U.S. (7 Wall.) 433 (1868); *Congressional Record*, 53rd Cong., 2nd Sess. (1894), 26, part 7: 6707.

and the general property tax, chiefly the land tax," wrote Seligman. By implication, then, the Supreme Court held "in a number of cases that the income tax was not a direct tax within the meaning of the constitution." Given the longstanding precedents, Seligman maintained that the 1894 law would easily pass constitutional muster. "There is no reason to suppose" Seligman confidently claimed, that this long line of judicial authority "will be reversed." Rather, "all attempts to declare the income tax unconstitutional," Seligman firmly concluded are "foredoomed to failure."[89] Indeed, few contemporary observers believed that the Court would even consider scrutinizing the 1894 income tax.

Yet to the surprise of many experts, including Seligman, the Supreme Court did agree to examine the constitutionality of the 1894 income tax in the case of *Pollock v. Farmers' Loan & Trust Company*. In the winter and spring of 1895, the Court consolidated three individual cases, conducted two separate hearings, and issued two separate rulings, as well as numerous dissenting opinions. The plaintiffs in *Pollock*, or what came to be known as the Income Tax case, were individual shareholders of business corporations that were charged with remitting income taxes on rental properties. The wealthy stockholders attempted to enjoin the corporations from paying the tax. When the lower courts dismissed the suits, the plaintiffs appealed to the U.S. Supreme Court.[90]

Throughout the proceedings, both sides invoked the authority of legal and economic experts to bolster their positions. Although the cases analyzed several distinct issues, the Court's decision and reasoning turned mainly on an interpretation of the direct tax clause, and more specifically whether a levy on rents from real estate constituted a direct tax. In their briefs on behalf of the taxpayers challenging the law, the eminent corporate lawyers Joseph H. Choate, William D. Guthrie, George F. Edmunds, and Clarence A. Seward crafted an innovative, if at times ahistorical, argument against the tax. Each of these lawyers had developed impeccable credentials as elite jurists, having represented some of the country's largest business corporations and wealthiest individuals. With the weight of precedent against them, they needed to use all of their legal acumen

89 Seligman, "The Income Tax," 634–5; Seligman, "Is the Income Tax Constitutional?" 49.

90 *Pollock v. Farmers' Loan & Trust Co.* 158 U.S. 601 (1895); Edward B. Whitney, "The Income Tax and the Constitution," *Harvard Law Review*, 20: 280–96 (February 1907); Ratner, *Taxation and Democracy in America*, 195–6.

and creativity to make the claim that the Court had been operating under an erroneous view of direct taxes for nearly a century.[91]

Even before they filed their first brief, the taxpayer's counsel contacted Seligman for his advice. The professor had long been a champion of the graduated income tax, and by the mid-1890s he had become one of the leading academic authorities on taxation. Yet because of his reputation as an objective and unbiased expert, Seligman was willing to assist both sides of the legal controversy. Joseph Choate and Seligman were personal acquaintances, and Choate directed his colleague Clarence Seward to solicit Seligman's guidance on the original constitutional meaning of the term "direct tax." Having read Seligman's work on the general property tax and his recent evaluation of the 1894 income tax, Seward floated an idea that must have struck the professor as highly implausible if not ludicrous. Seward requested Seligman's assistance in trying to determine whether state governments had historically levied an income tax that was deemed to be a direct tax.[92] Seligman expressly stated in his recently published article that "at the time the constitution was discussed there were no direct income taxes in existence." He acknowledged that Massachusetts made an early and feeble attempt at an income tax. But Seligman did not think that levy amounted to a separate tax worth considering seriously because it was effectively administered as an "adjunct of the property tax," rather than as a "distinct form of taxation."[93]

Still, Seward seized on the Massachusetts exception. In a series of personal correspondences, he asked Seligman to catalog examples of other states that may have blended their income taxes with an assessment of property. Seward's purpose was clear: "I wish to show, if I can, that those income taxes" in the states "were added to the other tax against the taxpayer, from which resulted a lump sum, which lump sum was collected by a general assessment upon all his property."[94] By supposedly uncovering a lost tradition of state-level direct income taxes, Seward hoped to

[91] Francis R. Jones, "Pollock v. Farmers' Loan and Trust Company," *Harvard Law Review* 9:3 (1895), 198–211. Ratner, *Taxation and Democracy*, 196–9; W. Elliot Brownlee, *Federal Taxation in America: A Short History* (New York: Cambridge University Press, 1996), 47–9.

[92] Joseph H. Choate to Seligman, Jan. 31, 1894; Feb. 19, 1894; April 11, 1894, Catalogued Correspondence, ERASP.

[93] Seligman, "The Income Tax," 634.

[94] C. A. Seward to Seligman, January 23, 1895, 2, Uncataloged Correspondence, Box 2, ERASP.

convince the Court that the framers did, indeed, believe that the apportionment requirement of the direct tax clause applied to income taxes. Seward clarified his intent in subsequent private letters. Referring to the taxes of the early Republic, Seward confidently informed Seligman that "the phrase 'direct taxes' included the very income tax so collected which [state residents] were then paying for Federal purposes. It was, therefore, to the income tax of the period, as well as to the then poll and land taxes, that the [constitutional] safeguard applied."[95]

Seward was rather persistent. After consulting some of the historical sources that Seligman recommended, including Treasury Secretary Oliver Wolcott Jr.'s 1796 public finance study, Seward boldly submitted to Seligman that he was able to demonstrate that several states levied direct taxes on income during the early Republic. Ignoring the central message and thrust of Seligman's published historical research, Seward wrote in an "entirely confidential" letter that "various of the States before the Constitutional Convention... were in the habit of imposing and collecting an income tax." Harping on the Massachusetts example, Seward concluded "therefore, the income tax, *eo nomine*, was known to and was being paid by the people of the country at the time when the Constitution was adopted."[96]

Seligman must have been startled by Seward's blatant misinterpretation of the historical record. In an attempt to dissuade Seward, Seligman shared with the attorney portions of a book manuscript that he had been researching about the comparative history of the income tax. In it Seligman demonstrated that while there were numerous instances of state and local "faculty taxes" in the colonial period and early Republic, these levies "were not direct taxes in the contemplation of the Constitution." Seligman obviously believed that the framers did not have income or faculty taxes in mind when they drafted the direct tax clause.[97]

Unsure whether Seward would heed his counsel, Seligman took matters into his own hands. He contacted the government lawyers defending the income tax, and he hastily began preparing for publication the portion of the manuscript that he had shared with Seward. Though this article would not be published until shortly after the final income tax decision

[95] C. A Seward to Seligman, Jan. 24, 1895, Uncataloged Correspondence, Box 2, ERASP.

[96] C. A Seward to Seligman, Jan. 28, 1895, Uncataloged Correspondence, Box 2, ERASP.

[97] C. A. Seward to Seligman, April 25, 1895; May 1, 1895, Uncataloged Correspondence, Box 2, ERASP. The broader book manuscript would eventually become Seligman's treatise on the income tax. *The Income Tax: A Study of the History, Theory, and Practice of Income Taxation at Home and Abroad* (New York: Macmillan Co., 1911).

was delivered, it illustrated what Seligman likely conveyed to Seward in their private correspondence, namely that the original meaning of the Constitution's direct tax clause did not apply to the early forms of income taxation. "To claim, then, that our colonial taxes on faculty were income taxes," Seligman sternly concluded in the article, "betrays a confusion of thought and an ignorance of economic distinctions."[98]

Seward may have been disheartened by Seligman's ultimate position on the constitutional meaning of direct taxes. A rebuke of his own selective and strategic use of history was not what the lawyer had hoped to learn from the good professor. Nevertheless, Seward relegated his differences with Seligman as merely a "personal disagreement." After compensating the Columbia professor handsomely for his consultation, Seward and his colleagues conveniently and completely ignored Seligman's historical and legal findings.[99] Instead, taxpayers' counsel claimed in their briefs and oral arguments before the Court that "at the date of the Constitution (1787), the words 'direct taxes' and 'indirect taxes' were household words." Contrary to Seligman's more nuanced and complex comparative-historical analysis, Seward argued that direct taxes "had been used in Europe as meaning taxes which fell directly upon property and its owners, like a land tax or a tax on incomes." Because their goal was to broaden the constitutional definition of "direct taxes," Seward and his colleagues contended that the mere existence of state income taxes in the early Republic suggested that the Constitution's use of the term "direct taxes" included "all such taxes as the states were then levying and collecting, under the name of 'direct taxes.'"[100] This last point must have surely infuriated Seligman, who had made exactly the opposite argument.

The taxpayers' counsel similarly used the work of Thomas M. Cooley selectively and instrumentally to make their case that the 1894 income tax also violated the Constitution's uniformity clause. As we've seen in the previous chapter, Cooley's tax treatise provided for a great deal of congressional discretion in the formation of national tax laws and policies.

98 Seligman, "The Income Tax in the American Colonies and States," *Political Science Quarterly* 10:2 (June 1895), 221–47, 247.

99 Seward to Seligman, April 24, 1895; May 16, 1895, Uncataloged Correspondence, Box 2, ERASP. Seligman was paid $250 for his time, a tidy sum, but an insignificant one given Seligman's family wealth. Seward to Seligman, May 16, 1895.

100 "Argument of Mr. Seward for the Appellants," *Pollock v. Farmers' Loan & Trust Co.*, 157 U.S. 429 (1895), in *Landmark Briefs and Arguments of the Supreme Court of the United States: Constitutional Law*, Vol. 12, ed. Philip B. Kurland and Gerhard Casper (1975), 359.

The corporate lawyers attacking the income tax elided this central aspect of Cooley's scholarship – just as they ignored Seligman's historical analysis – and focused instead on Cooley's criticism of tax exemptions. Citing liberally to the work of the Michigan jurist and other treatise writers, the taxpayers argued that the $4,000 exemption level and the other exceptions in the 1894 law violated the Constitution's "uniformity" clause, as well as the implied limitations on Congress's taxing powers.[101]

Although the taxpayers' lawsuits contained other challenges, the claims based on the "direct tax" clause were the fulcrum upon which the Court's decision ultimately pivoted. This was also the central issue that captured the attention of the lawyers defending the income tax, Attorney General Richard Olney and private lawyer James C. Carter, a highly respected New York corporate attorney and former president of the American Bar Association.[102] These lawyers had tremendous confidence that the Court would respect its existing precedents and continue to define the direct tax clause narrowly to exclude income taxes. In his own private correspondence with Seligman, Carter dismissed Seward's historical argument about the original meaning of "direct taxes" as "faint and feeble lights." When Seligman suggested that Carter and Olney amend their initial brief to address Seward's historical claim more forcefully, Carter confidently maintained that the "direct tax" clause was not a serious challenge. The historical evidence, Carter believed, "must have been part of the familiar knowledge of the men who decided the case of Hilton v. the United States [sic]" – the 1796 decision which upheld a tax on carriages as an "excise" and not a direct tax. "It would be impossible to put this Court into any condition of knowledge or information which would give it anything like the advantages possessed by the Court at that time," wrote Carter. "So far as the question depends upon the intention of the framers of the Constitution, the authority of that case [*Hylton v. United States*], it seems to me, must be accepted as final."[103]

[101] Thomas M. Cooley, *A Treatise on the Law of Taxation, Including the Law of Local Assessments*, 2nd ed. (Chicago: Callaghan, 1886); "Argument of Mr. Seward for the Appellants," 359. Attorney General Richard Olney believed that the lack of uniformity was the plaintiff's strongest claim. Morton J. Horwitz, *The Transformation of American Law, 1870–1960: The Crisis of Legal Orthodoxy* (New York: Oxford University Press, 1992), 25–6.

[102] Carter had been retained as counsel for the corporate managers who were being sued by shareholders for paying the income tax according to the withholding provisions of the 1894 law. Ratner, *Taxation and Democracy*, 196–9.

[103] James C. Carter to Professor Edwin R. A. Seligman, March 20, 1895, Uncataloged Correspondence, Box 2, ERASP.

Attorney General Olney seemed to agree, though he was reluctant to take anything for granted. In April 1895, a majority of the Court had already struck down portions of the income tax as unconstitutional, but because the Court was equally divided over the critical issue of whether a general tax on individual and corporate income was a direct tax, the justices immediately agreed to rehear the case to determine the fate of the full income tax statute. Thus, before the rehearing, Olney and his office filed a detailed, supplemental brief clarifying the historical meaning of the terms "duty" and "direct tax." In that brief and in his oral arguments, Olney addressed the Court's initial decision that a tax on rents derived from real estate was identical to a tax on real estate itself. Quoting directly from Seligman's forthcoming article, the attorney general attempted to debunk the notion that the early state-level faculty taxes were direct taxes. Olney, in sum, recapitulated what economic and legal experts had been saying all along, namely that the direct tax clause was originally meant to apply only to poll and land taxes, and that a levy on the income derived from land was not equivalent to a direct tax on land itself.[104]

Yet what was most noteworthy about Olney's arguments was how he used the language of taxpaying faculty to justify the modern state's taxing powers. Using terms that echoed the writings of the new school public finance economists and the drafters of the 1894 income tax, Olney contended that Congress had the legislative discretion to impose taxes based on taxpaying capacity. "What then is this tax in its true nature and essence?" Olney asked during his final dramatic oral argument. "It is an assessment upon the taxpayer on account of his money-spending power as shown by his revenue for the year." To rule against the tax, Olney reasoned, would be to destroy the state's most vital source of power and paralyze the process of political development. To give new life to "the doctrine of apportionment of public burdens" would be to tend toward "the direction of disintegration." And, perhaps most importantly, to rely on the outmoded application of benefits theory to justify taxation would be to perpetuate the inequalities of the existing tax system. "To impose taxes solely upon the principle of the ensuing advantages realized would, in effect, largely exempt the more fortunate and wealthy classes and place the greater part of the burden upon those least able to bear it," Olney concluded.[105]

104 "Historical Argument on the Meaning of Words 'Direct Tax' and 'Duty' in Constitution," in *Landmark Briefs and Arguments*, 765–856, 801–2.

105 "Argument of Mr. Olney for the United States," in *Landmark Briefs and Arguments*, 970, 976.

On May 20, 1895, the Court handed down its final decision on the income tax. It reaffirmed its earlier ruling striking down the tax on rents from real estate as an unapportioned direct tax. Just as he had in the prior ruling, Chief Justice Melville Fuller concluded that "a tax upon . . . realty and a tax upon the receipts therefrom were alike direct." Writing for a 5–4 majority, Fuller was unwilling to concede that there was a fundamental distinction between the flow of wealth and its ultimate source. Any tax upon the productive yields of property was, for the majority, a tax on the property itself. Notwithstanding "the speculative views of political economists or revenue reformers," the Court held that the original meaning of direct tax included not just land, but also the yield from real and personal property. Ridiculing the government's argument, the Court caricatured Olney's position as a form of legal sophistry. It was implausible, Fuller wrote, that "rents received, crops harvested, interest collected, have lost all connection with their origin, and, although once not taxable, have become transmuted, in their new form, into taxable subject-matter – in other words, that income is taxable, irrespective of the source from whence it is derived."[106] Simply put, Fuller believed that if a tax on real property required apportionment under the direct tax clause, so too did a tax on the income derived from real property. For him, the source of income was dispositive.

Fuller also addressed the long line of Supreme Court precedents interpreting the direct tax clause. He did so by distinguishing the facts in *Pollock* from the earlier cases. Whereas *Hylton* was based upon a carriage tax and *Springer v. United States* analyzed a tax on professional salaries, *Pollock's* focus on rents from real estate, Fuller reasoned, set it apart as a new and separate judicial question. With this clever legal maneuver, Fuller was able to ensure the constitutional death of the 1894 income tax. While the first *Pollock* decision, delivered roughly a month earlier, was silent on several poignant issues, Fuller's second opinion unequivocally rejected the entire income tax law. It concluded that because the taxation of rents from real property was an integral part of the income tax law, invalidating that provision meant that the entire income tax section was unconstitutional.[107]

If the Fuller opinions dealt with the dry and technical details of the income tax law, Justice Stephen J. Field's early concurrence expressed the more dramatic and deep-seated ideological fears and anxieties that attended the rising campaign for progressive taxation. As an elder

[106] *Pollock v. Farmers' Loan & Trust Co.*, 158 U.S. 601 (1895), 618, 627, 629.
[107] Ibid., 623–7.

statesmen and senior member of the Court, Field embodied the neo-Jacksonian aversion to "class" legislation and centralized political power. In remarks that reiterated the writings of conservative economic experts like David Wells and William Graham Sumner, Fields described the movement for fundamental tax reform as the first step down a slippery slope toward class warfare. "The present assault on capital is but the beginning," wrote Fields. "It will be but the stepping-stone to others, larger and more sweeping, till our political contests will become a war of the poor against the rich; a war constantly growing in intensity and bitterness."[108] Whereas progressive political economists like Ely, Adams, and Seligman saw class tensions, exacerbated by the growing disparity of wealth, as the impetus for a more equitable distribution of fiscal burdens, Fields and other supporters of the status quo viewed this same tension in more millennial and catastrophic terms.

The majority's judicial logic and Field's alarmist rhetoric did not go unchecked by the dissenting justices. They not only railed against Fuller's "cavalier reversal of precedence," they deployed a global perspective and the progressive vocabulary of tax reformers to argue that the Court had unfairly arrested national political development. Referring to Field's concurrence, Justice Henry Billings Brown – no advocate of wealth redistribution – noted how the Court seemed determined to hamstring the national government. "Even the specter of socialism is conjured up to frighten congress from laying taxes upon the people in proportion to their ability to pay them," wrote Brown, using the keywords of the new school economists. "It is certainly a strange commentary upon the constitution of the United States and upon a democratic government that congress has no power to lay a tax which is one of the main sources of revenue of nearly every civilized state. It is a confession of feebleness in which I find myself wholly unable to join."[109]

Justice Howell E. Jackson, who had been absent during the first hearing, went even further in linking the distributional aspects of the income tax with the growing needs of a modern state. "The practical operation of the decision, wrote Jackson, "is not only to disregard the great principles of equality in taxation," but the further principle that in the

[108] *Pollock v. Farmers' Loan & Trust Co*, 157 U.S. 429, 607 (1895) (Fields, J., concurring); Stanley, *Dimensions of Law*, 159. The classic article on Field's judicial philosophy remains: Charles W. McCurdy, "Justice Field and the Jurisprudence of Government-Business Relations: Some Parameters of Laissez-Faire Constitutionalism, 1863–1897," *Journal of American History* 61:4 (March 1975), 970–1005.

[109] *Pollock v. Farmers' Loan & Trust Co.*, 158 U.S. 601, 686–95 (1895) (Brown, J., dissenting), 695.

imposition of taxes for the benefit of the government the burdens thereof should be imposed upon those having most ability to bear them." Jackson agreed with Olney and tax reformers about the importance of taxpaying capacity, and therefore he saw the majority position as inverting the distributional aspects of the tax system and impeding American political development. "This decision, in effect, works out a directly opposite result, in relieving the citizens having the greater ability, while the burdens of taxation are made to fall most heavily and oppressively upon those having the least ability," wrote Jackson. "Considered in all its bearings, this decision is, in my judgment, the most disastrous blow ever struck at the constitutional power of congress. It strikes down an important portion of the most vital and essential power of the government in practically excluding any recourse to incomes from real and personal estate for the purpose of raising needed revenue to meet the government's wants and necessities under any circumstances."[110] Jackson's dissent summarized how nearly all revenue reformers viewed the majority opinion.

Ultimately, the *Pollock* decision was a critical juncture in the development of the modern American fiscal state. For tax reform opponents, the Court's invalidation of the 1894 income tax law was a signal victory and a bulwark against what many like Justice Field saw as imminent class warfare. Despite the mounting strains of urban industrialism and the growing economic disparities, many conservative thinkers, jurists, and lawmakers continued to believe that the existing national system of tariffs and excise taxes was more than sufficient. For others, including the new school public finance economists who were the vanguard of the intellectual and political campaign for a new fiscal order, the Court's actions came as a shock. Progressive activists wondered how a mere five justices could overturn a century worth of legal precedents, especially during an economic crisis that revealed all that was wrong with the existing tax regime.

Pollock, in the end, posed a fateful choice for tax reformers: they could accept the decision as the new law of the land and devise other less dramatic ways to ameliorate the inequities of the existing fiscal order while searching for new ways to reconfigure notions of national citizenship and find badly needed public revenue. Or they could intensify their efforts by elaborating on the underlying philosophical principles and material conditions that called for a new set of progressive taxes on incomes, inheritances, and profits. They chose the latter.

[110] Ibid., 696–707 (Jackson, J., dissenting), 706.

PART II

THE RISE OF THE MODERN FISCAL STATE

3

The Response to *Pollock*

Navigating an Intellectual Middle Ground

> The ideas of economists and political philosophers, both when they are right and when they are wrong, are more powerful than is commonly understood. Indeed, the world is ruled by little else. Practical men, who believe themselves to be quite exempt from any intellectual influences, are usually the slaves of some defunct economist.
>
> – John Maynard Keynes

In July 1896, little more than a year after the Supreme Court handed down its final decision in *Pollock*, Democratic leaders gathered in Chicago for their national convention. Amid the scorching summer heat, convention delegates scrambled to select a presidential candidate and finalize a party platform. The growing concern over monetary policy not only propelled the "money question" to the top of the convention agenda; it also catapulted a young and still relatively unknown Nebraska populist and income tax advocate onto the national political stage. With his eloquent and electrifying "cross of gold" speech, William Jennings Bryan captured the nomination and became the standard bearer for the temporary fusion of the People's Party and the Democratic Party.[1]

Although bimetallism became the dominant political issue, 1896 also marked the first year that demands for a graduated income tax were part of a national party platform. The Democrats' absorption of a portion of the People's Party meant that the calls for the progressive taxation of incomes, profits, and inheritances were no longer relegated to the margins of American political and academic discourse. Since the early 1880s, reform-minded economic thinkers and populist activists had been planting the intellectual seeds for a tax reform movement; they had been

[1] "Big Political Guns Reach Town," *Chicago Daily Tribune*, July 2, 1896, 3; "The Fighting Has Begun," *New York Times*, July 3, 1894, 1. Charles Postel, *The Populist Vision* (New York: Oxford University Press, 2007); Michael Kazin, *Godly Hero: The Life of William Jennings Bryan* (New York: Random House, 2007), 53–65.

advancing for years the need for graduated taxes based on the notion of one's faculty or financial means. By the mid-1890s, those seeds were gradually germinating. The theoretical claims of taxation based on ability to pay and the independent political parties' demands for graduated taxes had converged and seeped into the 1894 congressional debates, the judicial dissents in *Pollock*, and now, finally, onto the official platform of one of the country's two leading political parties. Indeed, the official Democratic platform echoed decades of independent political party demands and directly responded to *Pollock* by calling on "Congress to use all the constitutional power which remains after that decision, or which may come from its reversal by the court as it may hereafter be constituted, so that the burdens of taxation may be equally and impartially laid, to that end that wealth may bear its due proportion of the expenses of the Government."[2]

The Democratic-Populist demands for overturning *Pollock* were the culmination of a year's worth of discontent. The immediate reaction to the Supreme Court's decision was hardly surprising. Conservatives defended the Court as the "ultimate bulwark" against "the wave of socialist revolution." At the height of the hearings, the economic commentator David Wells had reiterated the general laissez-faire opposition to any law that sought to alter "the distribution of wealth by direct or indirect compulsion" or any measure that "diminished the incentives for personal accumulation." Meanwhile, many tax activists, including some of the country's leading jurists, denounced *Pollock* as "utterly inconsistent" with prior rulings, and as a judicial usurpation of political power. Labor leaders, likewise, characterized the decision as "cowardly" and as added evidence that the "court undoubtedly leans, consciously or unconsciously, to the interests of wealth and capital." Yet many elite critics and working-class commentators alike presciently noted that *Pollock* might not be the last word on fundamental tax reform. "They make a great mistake who think to find in the decision of the Supreme Court the final

[2] Donald B. Johnson, ed. *National Party Platforms, Vol. 1: 1840–1956* (Urbana: University of Illinois Press, 1978), 98. The People's Party in its 1896 platform also demanded "a graduated income tax to the end that aggregated wealth shall bear its just proportion of taxation" In addition, the platform identified "the recent decision of the Supreme Court relative to the Income Tax law as a misinterpretation of the Constitution and an invasion of the rightful powers of Congress over the subject of taxation." Ibid., 105. By the end of the century, state-level Democratic parties were also increasingly adopting an income tax plank after years of pressure from independent parties. Richard F. Bensel, *The Political Economy of American Industrialization, 1877–1900* (New York: Cambridge University Press, 2000), 159–61.

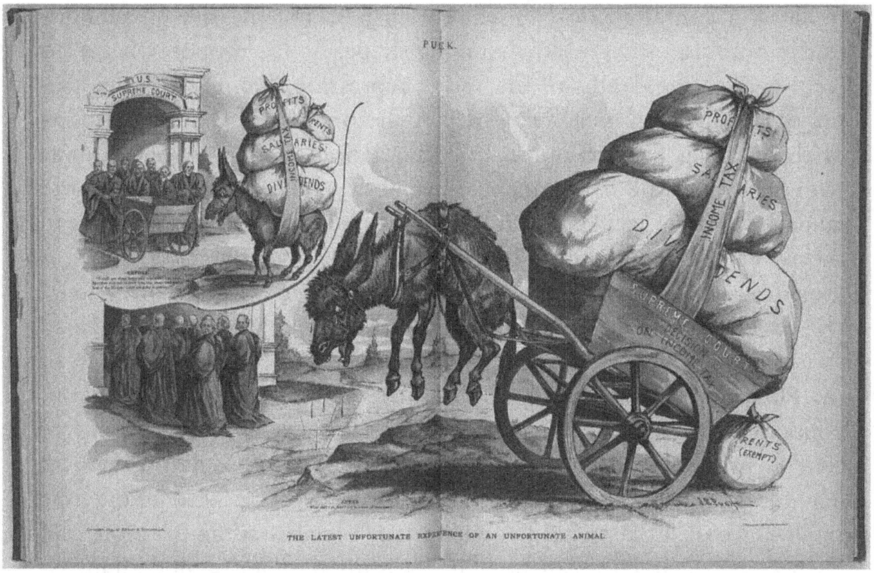

FIGURE 3.1. "The Latest Unfortunate Experience of an Unfortunate Animal." This before and after political cartoon demonstrates how critics of the U.S. Supreme Court believed that the Court's judicial intervention unnecessarily burdened a tax that was perfectly capable of taxing accumulated wealth. The *Pollock* decision, as represented by the wagon, impeded the Democratic donkey from taxing such concentrated wealth. Courtesy of the Library of Congress, Prints & Photographs Division.

word against the so-called socialistic tendencies of the moment," wrote one newspaper editor. "The people, whether for good or ill, will speak that word." Others were more forthright and prescriptive. One labor leader called upon the people to amend the Constitution "as speedily as possible."[3]

It would take nearly two decades, however, before tax activists could muster the political will and power necessary to overturn *Pollock* with a constitutional amendment. During that time, material forces and several seminal historical events ensured that tax reform remained a pressing national political, economic, and social issue. As a result, the three key features of the modern fiscal polity – a more equitable allocation of tax

[3] Sidney Ratner, *Taxation and Democracy in America* (New York: John Wiley & Sons, Inc. 1967), 213–14; David Wells, "Is the Existing Income Tax Unconstitutional?" *Forum* 19 (1895), 537; Francis J. Jones, "Pollock v. Farmers' Loan and Trust Co." *Harvard Law Review* 9 (October 1895), 198–211; S.B. Hoefgen, "Income Tax Decision," *American Federationist* (June 1895), 58–71.

burdens, a revitalization of fiscal citizenship, and the rise of administrative authority – were slowly taking shape. As the economy began to recover from the depths of the 1890s depression, the massive inequalities of the time continued to exert pressure on the distributional aspects of the existing fiscal regime. Similarly, a brief but consequential war with Spain in 1898 over American naval hegemony in the New World launched an overseas U.S. military empire and drew greater attention to the need for increased public funds to maintain an empire – one that was growing both at home and abroad. Fought under the guise of national self-determination for Cuba, the Spanish-American War also heightened concerns about fiscal citizenship. The resulting American annexation of the Philippines, Guam, and Puerto Rico raised anew questions about political belonging and the salience of taxation to renewed visions of civic identity.[4] Finally, the turn of the century also brought a wave of new ideas and vigor about the interdependency of social relations, the significance of professional knowledge and efficient administration, and the need for an activist state to address the dislocations of modern industrialism. Thus, as one century came to a close and another began, the central intellectual pillars of a new American fiscal state were visibly taking shape.

While modern forces as well as contingent historical events continued to provide the critical context for the conceptual revolution in public finance, economic ideas and the work of progressive thinkers drove the intellectual transformation in tax law and policy, paving the groundwork for the subsequent legal and popular acceptance of a new fiscal order. Although *Pollock* posed a serious institutional obstacle to the tax reform movement, activists used the decision as an opportunity to redouble their efforts. Some social leaders, in fact, reacted to the invalidation of the 1894 income tax with half-hearted pleasure. They welcomed *Pollock* as an opportunity to enact an even more robust levy – one that differentiated between various sources of income and radically redistributed economic resources and power.

[4] David Traxel, *1898: The Birth of the American Century* (New York: Random House, 1999); Emily S. Rosenberg, *Spreading the American Dream: American Economic and Cultural Expansion, 1890–1945* (New York: Hill & Wang, 1982). For more on the importance of American colonialism and the development of civic identity in Puerto Rico, see Jose A. Cabranes, "Citizenship and the American Empire: Notes on the Legislative History of the United States Citizenship of Puerto Ricans." *University of Pennsylvania Law Review* 127:2 (1978), 391–492.

This critique from the political left was, of course, not new. European socialists had for years been touting the redistributional potential of progressive taxation. But for the American political economists who were the intellectual vanguard of the tax reform movement, and who were seeking to dispel the notion that progressive taxation was somehow antithetical to American institutions and culture, the opposition from socialists and similar-minded critics proved to be quite formidable. The reform-minded academics needed to distance themselves from these radical views, while maintaining strong support for progressive taxation.

In the wake of *Pollock*, therefore, the young public finance economists needed to defend their vision to recreate a tax system based on the notion of faculty or ability to pay. They needed to navigate between two extremes: the opposition from the political right and left. For political conservatives like Justice Field and David Wells, who were wedded to a classical, night-watchman view of the state, the move to a graduated income tax was equated with European state socialism. The new school economists had witnessed firsthand – often to their personal and professional detriment – the overwhelming power that such conservative critics held, particularly in delineating the bounds of academic freedom. Addressing these opponents, the progressive public finance economists sought to demonstrate that support for moderately graduated taxes on incomes, profits, and inheritances could be compatible with the evolving American liberal tradition.

The reform-minded economists faced a more amorphous, though equally formidable, type of opposition from the political left, where both Henry George's single tax and the ideas of socialist economic theorists challenged the promise of a moderate fiscal state. As we have seen in Chapter 1, the populist attraction to the single tax distracted important social constituencies from the tax reform movement. But many socialists saw the single tax for what it was: a rearguard response to the changes wrought by industrial capitalism. Karl Marx himself had castigated Henry George's *Progress and Poverty* as "simply an attempt, decked out with socialism, to save capitalist domination and indeed to establish it afresh on an even wider basis than its present one."[5] The American economists picked up on this critique. In their efforts to diffuse the potential populist appeal of the single tax, Richard Ely, Francis Walker, Edwin Seligman,

[5] Marx quoted in Charles A. Barker, *Henry George* (New York: Oxford University Press, 1955), 356.

and others sought to debunk the amateur economic analysis of the single-tax movement by unmasking the "ultra-conservative" social theory that underpinned the single tax on land rent.[6]

The new school of American professional economists may not have taken George's amateur and "unscientific" theories seriously. But for them, a far more potent intellectual challenge from the political left came in the guise of their German mentors who had been advocating for a more radically redistributive form of taxation. Leading this charge was Adolph Wagner, the Berlin economist with whom many of the political economists had studied during their German sojourn. Wagner's calls for using taxes to address directly the vast inequalities in wealth had a far more receptive audience in Germany than in the United States, where his American disciples were careful to decouple progressive taxation from state socialism. By steering between these two camps of political opposition – between conservative critics who equated a progressive taxation with socialism and populist reformers who advanced more radical forms of taxation – the progressive economists combined their theories with other prevailing economic ideas of the time to show that the movement for direct and progressive taxation was, in fact, an assault on privilege that did not amount to an inexorable move toward state socialism.

Questioning Income

Even before the 1894 income tax was enacted, social critics and academic theorists had questioned one of its most central elements: the use of a flat, uniform rate on all income as the best method for capturing a citizen's taxpaying ability. The Supreme Court's decision to strike down the law provided these critics with an opportunity to reassert claims about the distributional impact of adopting a new fiscal system. The editors of the *American Federationist*, the official journal of the American Federation of Labor (AFL), for instance, took a rather unconventional view of *Pollock*. Rather than criticizing the Court for striking down a statute that many believed had the potential to shift the burden of taxation onto those with a greater ability to pay, the editors thanked the justices for doing away

[6] Richard T. Ely, *Taxation in American States and Cities* (New York: Crowell, 1888), 16; "The Single Tax Debate," *Journal of Social Science*, 27 (1890); Francis A. Walker, "Henry George's Social Fallacies," *North American Review*, 137:321 (August 1883), 147–57. See also Thomas Bender, *Intellect and Public Life: Essays on the Social History of Academic Intellectuals in the United States* (Baltimore: Johns Hopkins University Press, 1997), 57–8, 134–5.

with a law that did not go far enough in redistributing income and wealth. Because the 1894 law did not distinguish between different sources of income, the editors contended that it was "at variance with the people's desire." Since the law taxed income from labor and property equally, with a flat rate as opposed to graduated rates, the measure did not seriously address the growing maldistribution of wealth and power. Moreover, since the tax did not differentiate between the income "earned" by the ordinary worker through "the sweat of his brow" from the "unearned" income extracted by the capitalist and landlord, the law ignored the most fundamental aspects of taxation and belied the principle of ability to pay.[7]

The exemption levels of the 1894 levy, of course, excused the vast majority of ordinary American workers from paying the income tax.[8] But that seemed irrelevant to the editors who were intent on agitating for an even more robust income tax law. They resolutely held to the principle – shared by many in the laboring class as well as the academy – that those with "unearned" income innately had a greater ability, and hence a great social responsibility, to pay more taxes. Just as other tax reformers and lawmakers had sought to design a law that taxed the "unearned" income from capital and other property at a greater rate than the earnings from labor, the editors held out hope for a more potent income tax law.[9] They thus concluded that *Pollock* "simply wipes out a law that was made odious to the great mass of our people." Because of "the manifest injustice imposed upon many of our people by the mutilated measure, we feel like tendering to the majority of the United States Supreme Court our sincere thanks for their last kindly act in connection with the so-called income tax law." The editors' remarks reflected an intuition about tax fairness that was shared by many Americans at the time.[10]

That common intuition was expressed in more sophisticated terms by the reform-minded public finance economists. Nearly all tax experts agreed with Richard Ely that industrial capitalism had created a new leisure class, as well as a sector of society with enormous personal wealth rooted in intangible assets like stocks and bonds. And most economic observers concurred that this new type of financial wealth was only

7 "Income Tax Decision," *American Federationist* (June 1895), 58–71.

8 With a flat rate of 2 percent applied to all household incomes above $4,000 ($110,000 in 2012 dollars), the 1894 would have touched only a small fraction of Americans. The Revenue Act of 1894, 28 Stat. 570 (1894).

9 *Congressional Record*, 53rd Cong., 2nd sess. (1894), 26, pt., 1:584–91.

10 "Income Tax Decision," 71.

marginally affected by the national system of indirect taxation and the subnational property tax.[11] But rather than wholeheartedly embrace an income tax as a way to reallocate fiscal burdens or promote good government, some political economists like Henry Carter Adams cautiously questioned whether the monetary value of income was a sufficient "measure of the relative ability of citizens to pay for the support of the State."[12]

Writing in one of the first American public finance treatises, Adams was restrained in his ultimate support for the income tax. He concurred with his progressive colleagues that ability to pay was the sound theoretical foundation for a modern tax system. "Assuming the ability to pay to be the just measure of payment," Adams wrote, "income is accepted as the surest test of ability." He was skeptical, however, that in practice income could accurately measure a citizen's taxpaying faculty. "The difficulty of obtaining the correct statement of income," Adams noted, was aggravated by "the great variety of forms in which incomes exist." During a simpler age, lawmakers could be more confident that "incomes would be homogenous" and that a given tax would lead to "the same treatment applicable to all." But in a more modern, industrial world, "in society as it exists," wrote Adams in 1898, "incomes are not homogenous. They do not reflect the same industrial conditions or measure with accuracy the energy expended to secure them."[13]

Adams had in mind at least three different categories of income. The first was "income from services" by which he meant "wages, salaries, professional fees," and the like. The second was "income from property," which itself could be subdivided into income from land in the form of rent and income from capital in the form of interest or profits. Finally, there was "income of property" by which he meant intergenerational wealth transfers, such as inheritances. For Adams, each of these sources of income was accompanied by differing economic and social conditions, and hence entailed different tax treatment. For example, since the first category of "income from services" (e.g., wages and salaries) was considered

[11] Ely, *Taxation in American States and Cities*, 289.

[12] Henry Carter Adams, *The Science of Finance: An Investigation of Public Expenditures and Public Revenues* (New York: Henry Holt and Co., 1898), 357. In writing this treatise, Adams drew heavily on his lecture notes from the classes he taught and those he attended under the tutelage of Judge Thomas Cooley. See Henry Carter Adams, "Tax Lectures," in Box 26, Folder 1; "Lectures on Taxation – By Judge Cooley, 1882," Bounded Materials, Box 15, Henry Carter Adams Papers, Bentley Historical Library, University of Michigan, Ann Arbor, MI [hereinafter HCAP].

[13] Adams, *Science of Finance*, 357.

"both terminable and uncertain, while rent and interest are by comparison considered as perpetual and certain," the difference warranted "a distinction in the law of taxation by which income from property is rated higher than income from effort."[14]

Similarly, Adams argued that "property of income" received by one-time bequests ought to be taxed at an even higher rate than either wage or capital income. Because an inheritance was a type of "accidental or fortuitous income to the individual, and from the social point of view represents a transfer of property and not an increase in wealth," it ought to be treated "differently in the framing of tax laws from the manner in which the ordinary consistently recurring personal or property income are treated." Given that the various sources of income "reflect diverse economic conditions and are subject to varying economic tendencies," Adams concluded, "the amount of money received during the twelve months is no satisfactory measure of the relative ability of citizens to pay for the support of the state."[15] As he learned from his mentor, Thomas Cooley, "a man may grow rich with having no income," which Adams interpreted to mean that wages alone were an insufficient measure of taxpaying ability.[16] Adams was not willing to settle for using an undifferentiated income tax as an exclusive metric or proxy for one's taxpaying capacity. The income tax may have placed a "heavy load only on strong shoulders," to use Ely's vivid phrase, but that did not mean that this load weighed the same for all shoulders.

The social leaders and theorists who questioned the details of the 1894 law in the wake of *Pollock* were not turning their backs on the tax reform movement. Rather, they were seeking to push that movement to its logical ends. The growing social and political demands for new and graduated taxes to replace the existing national system of tariffs and excise taxes were, first and foremost, rooted in a desire to create a fairer and more just system of public finance. As Seligman had explained, even a moderate

[14] Ibid., 358. Adams also presciently believed that the "the family unit is, in fact, the social unit, and as such should receive consideration in the framing of tax laws." More specifically, Adams recommended that "an abatement should be made on account of the" possible "death or incapacity of the head of household." Ibid., 358. Modern tax law scholars eventually took up Adams's claims about the family as the appropriate taxable unit. See, e.g., Boris Bittker, "Federal Income Tax and the Family," *Stanford Law Review* 27:6 (July 1975), 1389–463.

[15] Ibid., 357–60. Ely, *Taxation in American States and Cities*, 288.

[16] Henry Carter Adams, "Lectures on Taxation – By Judge Cooley, 1882," Bounded Materials, Box 15, HCAP.

income tax like the 1894 law helped to round "out the existing tax system in the direction of greater justice."[17]

For some, though, justice meant going beyond the enactment of a merely symbolic, flat income tax; it meant interrogating the substantive rationale of the faculty principle that was at the heart of a new and fledgling fiscal order. When the editors of the *American Federationist* thanked the Supreme Court for striking down the 1894 law, they were only partially insincere. The "mutilated measure" that emerged from congressional compromises was surely better than no income tax at all.[18] Yet, it left unanswered crucial questions about the specific meaning of "income" or "ability to pay." Reform-minded political economists like Henry Carter Adams took up those salient questions. Adams's differentiation of income by source and his recommendations that income derived from personal labor be taxed at a lower rate than capital income or inheritances suggested that the practical implementation of an income tax was a complex legal and political exercise – one that required thinking broadly about not only the disparate sources of income and wealth, but also about how different kinds of taxes fit within a systematic analysis of public finance.[19]

In Defense of Progressive Taxation

Between the *Pollock* decision and the introduction in 1908 of the constitutional amendment that would eventually overturn that ruling, tax reformers and theorists continued to emphasize the egalitarian aspects of progressive taxation. Questioning the generic and undifferentiated use of income as the proper tax base was only one way of reallocating the tax burden and promoting greater economic justice. An equally important method was examining the rate structure, the choice between a flat rate, which led to proportional taxation, and graduated rates which ensured

17 Edwin R. A. Seligman, "The Income Tax," *Political Science Quarterly* 9:4 (1894), 610–48, 610.

18 "Income Tax Decision," 59.

19 Although Adams's ideas about differentiating between different sources of income would gain some traction in the early 1920s, the tax code would eventually invert Adams's logic to provide a preferential tax rate for capital gains income. For more on the history of the capital gains tax preference, see Marjorie E. Kornhauser, "The Origins of Capital Gains Taxation: What's Law Got to Do with It?" *Southwestern Law Journal* 39:4 (1985), 869–928; Leonard Burman, *The Labyrinth of Capital Gains Tax Policy: A Guide for the Perplexed* (Washington, D.C.: Brookings Institution Press, 1999), Chapter 2.

progressivity. The lawmakers who drafted the 1894 law had bracketed the critical question of rate structure in their efforts to enact a compromise measure. But for the reformers and theorists trying to transform American public finance, the distinction between proportion and progressive taxes was vital. This distinction implicated the foundational social and political theory undergirding taxation. "The real contest between the principles of proportion and progression," Seligman explained, "turns about the fundamental question as to the basis of taxation – the theory of benefits or the theory of ability."[20] Seligman and his colleagues acknowledged that the benefits theory could theoretically support either proportional or graduated taxes, depending on how one viewed the role of the state. Yet these theorists strategically linked a uniform rate with the benefits theory as part of their political project to displace the doctrine of benefits with their favored approach of faculty or ability.[21]

The distinction between proportional and progressive taxation also implicated a second fundamental concern among political activists: how taxes could be used to reconfigure a new understanding of fiscal citizenship. Requiring those who earned more to pay more – progressively more not merely more in absolute dollars – meant highlighting the social debts one owed to society. If wealth was created not solely by individual effort but through the support of state and society, then wealth was obviously a social product with attendant social and ethical responsibilities. For the public finance economists, the growing interdependency of modern industrial life required more affluent Americans to recognize their civic obligations and responsibilities in underwriting the emergence of a burgeoning regulatory, social-welfare state.

Demands for graduated taxes were constrained, however, by the institutional limits of a fledgling administrative state. Though a flat income tax posed its own set of practical concerns, moving to a graduated rate structure added a layer of complexity that suggested the need for increased bureaucratic capacity. Whereas a flat rate tax could rely on third-parties to report or withhold a fixed percentage of a taxpayer's income, a progressive rate structure required taxing authorities to verify and assess the total amount of a citizen's earnings and income. This meant obtaining

20 Edwin R. A. Seligman, "Theory of Progressive Taxation," *Political Science Quarterly* 8:2 (1893), 220–51, 224.

21 D. P. O'Brien, "Introduction to Volume VIII," in *The History of Taxation, Vol. VIII*, ed. D. P. O'Brien (London: Pickering & Chatto, 1999); Walter J. Blum and Harry Kalven Jr. *The Uneasy Case for Progressive Taxation* (Chicago: University of Chicago Press, 1953), 64–8.

and processing more information from third parties and taxpayers alike, and enforcing the collection of new taxes – no small feat for any turn-of-the-century government agency.[22] Despite these institutional obstacles, tax reformers remained optimistic. In fact, many believed that adopting progressive taxes could help propel the administrative development necessary for a new system of governance – one that was less beholden to the partisanship of party politics and more receptive to the bureaucratic operations of professional experts.

To be sure, stressing the importance of progressive rates was also one way to respond to *Pollock* and maintain the momentum of the tax reform movement. But continued calls for new, graduated levies also galvanized the conservative opposition. As a result, foes of progressive taxation aroused the traditional American resistance toward centralized power. Given these popular anxieties, the reform-minded political economists sought to embed their calls for a moderate fiscal polity within the comfortable and well-respected confines of American political culture.

They did so in three ways. First, they uncovered and underscored the long history of progressive faculty taxes in the United States. In the process, they sought to illustrate that these levies were not insidious, antidemocratic foreign imports. Second, they showed how the faculty theory had a long and noble, if at times muddled, intellectual lineage that could be traced back to the liberal Anglo-American political economic tradition. Finally, they sought to demonstrate the theoretical incompatibility of graduated rates and state socialism. In sum, tax experts were determined to dispel the myth that progressive taxation was antithetical to American values and liberal democracy. Although they did not always agree on the administrative feasibility of progressive taxes, they concurred that direct and progressive levies were the ideal method of taxation for modern American society.

Retracing the History of American Progressive Faculty Taxes

To counter the conservative charge that progressive taxes were somehow un-American or undemocratic, tax activists turned to the historical

[22] For more on the limits of turn-of-the-century American administrative capacity, see Stephen Skowronek, *Building a New American State: The Expansion of National Administrative Capacity, 1877–1920* (New York: Cambridge University Press, 1982); Theda Skocpol, "Bringing the State Back In: Strategies of Analysis in Current Research," in *Bringing the State Back In*, ed. Peter B. Evans, Dietrich Rueschemeyer, and Theda Skocpol (Cambridge: Cambridge University Press, 1985), 3–43.

and comparative record. In his academic writings, as well as his private correspondence with Clarence Seward during the *Pollock* hearings, Seligman had demonstrated that "faculty" taxes on the earnings of artisans and skilled professionals had been in existence in the United States since colonial times. Initially, Seligman's main point was to show that these early graduated faculty taxes were not considered "direct" taxes by contemporaries, and therefore the framers of the Constitution did not have these levies in mind when they drafted the Constitution's direct tax clause. But the mere existence of graduated faculty taxes in the colonies and later several states also demonstrated that progressive taxes on incomes or profits were not alien to American experiences or democratic ideals.[23]

In his more public pronouncements, Seligman was even more straightforward. Writing in the popular journal *Forum*, the Columbia professor explained that the claim that progressive income taxes were contrary to American ideals or the precepts of liberal democracy was "absurd." In fact, the experience of other advanced, democratic nation-states suggested that there was a tight link between greater democracy and direct taxation. "It is a matter of common knowledge that the income tax has been most fully developed precisely in the most democratic countries, like Switzerland, England, and Australia," wrote Seligman, "and that the whole tendency toward democracy, even in non-republican states, has gone hand in hand with the extension of property and income taxation."[24]

Historical and comparative examples did little, however, to assuage conservative critics. Tax reform opponents like Senator David Hill and economic commentator David Wells objected to any kind of discrimination in setting tax rates, including the rather generous exemption level

[23] C. A. Seward to Seligman, April 25, 1895; May 1, 1895, Uncataloged Correspondence, Box 2, Edwin R.A. Seligman Papers, Butler Library, Columbia University, New York, N.Y. [hereinafter ERASP]; Seligman, "The Income Tax in the American Colonies and States," *Political Science Quarterly* 10:2 (June 1895), 221–47, 247.

[24] Edwin R. A. Seligman, "Is the Income Tax Constitutional and Just?" *Forum* 19 (1895), 48–56, 54. Present-day scholars have similarly suggested a correlation between expanding democracy and progressive taxation. Daron Acemoglu and James A. Robinson, "Why Did the West Extend the Franchise? Democracy, Inequality, and Growth in Historical Perspective," *Quarterly Journal of Economics* 115:4 (2000), 1167–99; Charles Boix, *Democracy and Redistribution* (Cambridge: Cambridge University Press, 2003); Peter H. Lindert, *Growing Public: Vol. 1, Social Spending and Economic Growth since the Eighteenth Century* (New York: Cambridge University Press, 2004). For a recent empirical study that stresses the importance of war over democracy, see Kenneth Scheve and David Stasavage, "The Conscription of Wealth: Mass Warfare and the Demand for Progressive Taxation," *International Organization* 64:4 (2010), 529–61.

in the 1894 law. "The great republican principle of equality before the law, and constitutional law itself," wrote Wells, "preclude any exemption of income derived from like property." Wells was referring to the Constitution's uniformity clause, which stated that "all duties, imposts and excises shall be uniform throughout the United States." Many critics seized upon this constitutional provision to resist progressive taxation. Although the Court in *Pollock* did not rely on the uniformity clause to strike down the 1894 law, reform opponents frequently cited the provision as a reason why progressive taxes were anathema to American law and society.[25]

For their part, tax reformers did not perceive the uniformity clause as a formidable barrier. The uniformity clause, viewed from the "lawyer's point of view" as H. C. Adams often put it, did not bar exemption levels or even graduated rates. The clause simply meant, as Seligman explained, that "taxation should be uniform as between the several States." Taxes had to be geographically nondiscriminatory from state to state, or "uniform throughout the United States," as the Constitution specifically stated. But territorial uniformity did not require absolute uniformity.[26] Nearly all jurists had come to a similar conclusion. Decades earlier, Justice Joseph Story had determined that the main purpose of the uniformity clause was "to cut off all undue preferences of one state over another in the regulation of subjects affecting their common interests." Justice Cooley concurred, noting that the Supreme Court had "repeatedly" held that attempts at absolute uniformity would, in fact, be "destructive of the principle of uniformity and equality in taxation." And even the majority of the justices in *Pollock* had refrained from addressing whether the 1894 law had violated the uniformity clause.[27]

Still, in the process of analyzing the uniformity clause, the progressive political economists underscored the social, as well as the legal, legitimacy of progressive taxation. "When we speak of uniform and equal taxation,

[25] David A. Wells, "An Income Tax: Is It Desirable?" *Forum* 18 (1894); U.S. Constitution, Article 1, Section 8, Clause 1.

[26] Henry Carter Adams, *Science of Finance*, 298, 310; Seligman, "Is the Income Tax Constitutional and Just?" 51; U.S. Constitution, Article 1, Section 8.

[27] Joseph Story, *Commentaries on the Constitution of the United States: With a Preliminary Review of the Constitutional History of the Colonies and States, Before the Adoption of the Constitution* (Boston: Hillard, Gray, 1833), 342; Thomas M. Cooley, *The Law of Taxation* (Chicago: Callaghan, 1924), 706 (quoting *Pacific Exp. Co. v. Seibert*, 142 U.S. 339).

we mean substantial uniformity, substantial equality," wrote Seligman. Absolute equality, Seligman conceded, was neither a viable goal nor a desirable objective. "All that government can hope to achieve is to treat all the individuals in the same class equally and uniformly. But this does not mean that no distinction can be made between classes."[28]

In fact, American state governments had for years used property tax exemptions, graduated rates on corporate income, and varying rates of inheritance taxes without violating the principle of uniformity in taxation. In each of these cases, Seligman explained, "the individuals in the class are treated uniformly, but a distinction is made between the classes." When such distinctions were made with the consent of the governed and for the benefit of the commonweal, the main purpose of uniformity could be achieved. "The object of uniformity is to secure equality or justice," Seligman reminded *Forum* readers. "Yet the final test of equal justice must be sought in the well-considered public policy. It is the social consensus or the public sentiment which in the last resort is our only test of justice in taxation, as of justice in other human relations. If, therefore, certain distinctions or exemptions are made in the interest of the whole community and for the sake of the public welfare, the substantial equality demanded by the Constitution is attained."[29]

Seligman's references to respecting public opinion and social values illustrated how the public finance economists approached the issue of progressivity – and overall tax reform – with a great deal of caution. Though they understood that their new school of political economy was at the forefront of American economic science and social reform, when it came to presenting their ideas to popular audiences, they were careful to temper their support for dramatic institutional change by acknowledging the importance of public sentiments and social consensus.

The Origins of the Faculty Principle

Addressing the perceived constitutional barriers to progressive taxation may have defused some of the conservative opposition. But tax reformers understood that if they wanted to convince others of the merits of graduated rates, they needed to trace the Anglo-American pedigree and logical consistency of ideas like the faculty principle. By doing so, they

28 Seligman, "Is the Income Tax Constitutional and Just?" 52, 53.
29 Ibid.

believed they could give progressive taxation greater intellectual credence and authority.

Seligman was once again at the forefront. By 1900, he had become one of the leading international scholars of public finance. His writings frequently appeared in the top academic journals – in the United States and abroad – as well as the leading popular periodicals of the day. He regularly advised state and local governments about fiscal policy. And his tax treatises, particularly his *Essays in Taxation*, had been republished in several subsequent editions. His peers recognized that Seligman had become the leading American authority on public finance. In a glowing review of his work, Henry Carter Adams declared that "no student of finance, in this country, at least, will feel he has a right to an opinion until he has read whatever Professor Seligman may have written."[30]

There was, to be sure, no shortage of material to read. During the turn of the century, Seligman was at the peak of his prolific writing career. In addition to his regular essays and reviews, he was still hard at work on a comprehensive book about the comparative history of the income tax – a project that he had mentioned in his correspondence with Clarence Seward during the *Pollock* case. Perhaps more important, Seligman was also revising his book on progressive taxation for a new edition and a French translation, just as American reformers were intensifying their response to *Pollock*, and as leading French statesmen and intellectuals were making their own case for progressive taxation.[31]

In the second edition of his progressive taxation treatise, Seligman carefully melded the ideas of other economic thinkers to show that the faculty theory was firmly rooted in the works of well-respected (and noncontroversial) American and British political economists. As in much

[30] Edwin R. A. Seligman, *Essays in Taxation* (New York: Macmillan, 1895); Henry Carter Adams, "Review of *Essays in Taxation* by Edwin R. A. Seligman," *Annals of the American Academy of Political and Social Science* 7 (March 1896), 146–9, 147. Although Adams criticized Seligman for neglecting to analyze U.S. subnational taxation in detail, overall he believed the volume constituted "the most important contribution to the science of finance which has thus far appeared from the pen of an American author" Ibid., 149.

[31] Edwin R. A. Seligman, *Progressive Taxation in Theory and Practice*, 2nd ed. (Princeton: American Economic Association, 1908). While France did not adopt an income tax until 1917, Seligman's translation of his treatise into French was part of the decades-long agitation for a graduated income tax in France. James T. Kloppenberg, *Uncertain Victory: Social Democracy and Progressivism in European and American Thought, 1870–1920* (New York: Oxford University Press, 1986), 355–6; Robert E. Kaplan, *The Forgotten Crisis: The Fin-de-Siècle Crisis of Democracy in France* (Oxford: Berg Publishers, 1995).

of his scholarship, Seligman was most effective not as an original thinker, but as a synthesizer and popularizer of the ideas and works of others.[32] Though he would soon become the American economist most directly connected to tax reform and the faculty theory, Seligman acknowledged his intellectual debts to predecessors. In the process, he attempted to convince others that graduated taxes based on the principle of taxpaying capacity had the imprimatur of some of the world's most respected economic theorists.

Seligman began by identifying Francis A. Walker as the originator of the faculty principle of taxation. Walker had passed away in 1897, but he was still revered by many academics and political leaders as the moderate voice of American political economy. Walker's service in the Union Army and the U.S. Census Bureau, his teaching career at Yale, and his stewardship of the Massachusetts Institute of Technology all marked him as a highly acclaimed academic and civic leader. His popular textbook on political economy and his role in helping establish the American Economic Association and the American Statistical Association, likewise, earned him an international reputation as a liberal yet moderate spokesman for the emerging American economics profession.[33]

In an influential 1888 article, Walker had proposed that taxation ought to be based not on the property held by an individual, nor by the amount of consumption one enjoyed, nor even by the regular earnings one received. Rather, he argued that a "faculty tax" based on an individual's "native or acquired power of production" was the "most equitable form of public contribution." Unlike an income tax, which "accepts indolence, shiftlessness, and worthlessness as a sufficient ground for excuse from public contribution," a faculty tax measured by one's "natural powers," Walker contended, "constitutes the only theoretically just form of taxation, men being required to serve the state in the degree in

[32] Adams, "Review of *Essays in Taxation* by Edwin R. A. Seligman." For more on Seligman as synthesizer and popularizer of the economic literature on taxation, see Pier Francesco Asso and Luca Fiorito, "Editors' Introduction," in "Edwin Robert Anderson Seligman, Autobiography (1929)" in Warren J. Samuels, ed., *Documents from and on Economic Thought* (Amsterdam: JAI Press, 2006), 149–78.

[33] James P. Munroe, *A Life of Francis Amasa Walker* (New York: Henry Holt & Co., 1923); B. Newton, *The Economics of Francis Amasa Walker: American Economics in Transition* (New York: A. M. Kelley, 1968); Mary O. Furner, *Advocacy & Objectivity: A Crisis in the Professionalization of American Social Science, 1865–1905* (Lexington: University Press of Kentucky, 1975), 40–8; Dorothy Ross, *The Origins of American Social Science* (New York: Cambridge University Press, 1990), 77–85.

which they have ability to serve themselves."[34] An individual's naturally endowed ability was thus, for Walker, the theoretically sound basis for taxation.

Seligman embraced Walker's ideas, but he reworked them to argue that faculty ought to mean more than just naturally endowed abilities. Ever the pragmatist, Seligman focused on the results or consequences of one's natural abilities. Thus, he advocated a revised faculty theory that examined how one's innate powers were deployed. The faculty theory, he wrote, includes also "the opportunity of putting these powers to use, as well as the manner in which the powers are actually employed and the results of their use as measured by the periodic or permanent accretion to the producer's possession." Whereas Walker wanted to isolate an individual's endowed productive capabilities as a basis of taxation, Seligman sought to merge productive ability with consumptive power. Faculty to Seligman meant "not only powers of production or results of powers of production, but also the capacity to make use of these powers or of these results – the capacity in other words of enjoying the consequence of the exertions."[35] Seligman's focus on "accretion" of possessions and the "enjoying" of the "consequences of exertions" would subsequently become touchstones for future tax theorists. In the 1920s, as we shall see, Seligman's prized student Robert Murray Haig would further develop the conceptual, economic definition of income.[36]

By introducing consumptive powers into Walker's definition of faculty, Seligman not only made his version of faculty more practical, he also helped soften the redistributive potential of progressive taxation. Graduated taxes based on one's endowed, natural productive capabilities had far-reaching and coercive implications in radically redistributing wealth – perhaps even more so than Walker had anticipated. Seligman seemed to understand the possible unfairness of endowment taxation. He certainly knew that it would not hew well with the traditional American ambivalence toward centralized power. Although Walker had acknowledged the practical limitations of his faculty theory, it was Seligman who sought to correct those limitations by turning to an analysis of how endowed

[34] Francis A. Walker, "The Bases of Taxation," *Political Science Quarterly* 3:1 (March 1888), 1–16, 14, 15.

[35] Seligman, *Progressive Taxation in Theory and Practice*, 291.

[36] Robert Murray Haig, "The Concept of Income – Economic and Legal Aspects," in *The Federal Income Tax*, ed. Robert Murray Haig (New York: Columbia University Press, 1921), 1–28.

abilities were actually put to use, how they were exercised to gain economic power.[37]

Seligman thus integrated consumptive powers into the theory of faculty not only to moderate the practical implications of the faculty principle, but also to bring Walker's ideas into line with British theories about taxation. Illustrating how the "ability-to-pay" rationale emanated from a longstanding and revered Anglo-American tradition was one way, Seligman reasoned, to lend these theories greater intellectual credence. Yet constructing this genealogy proved to be challenging. Adam Smith, for instance, had been inconsistent in distinguishing between benefits theory and the ability to pay, frequently conflating the two in his support for proportional taxation. As a result, Smith was emblematic of what Seligman referred to as "the individualistic, the give-and-take theory" of taxation that the reform-minded political economists were seeking to displace.[38]

John Stuart Mill seemed to be a more hospitable intellectual ally, though Mill posed his own problems for American supporters of progressive taxation. Unlike Smith, Mill was an unequivocal proponent of the ability-to-pay doctrine. He believed that taxation according to an individual's means led to an "equality of sacrifice" that was the central lodestar for public finance. "All are thought to have done their part," wrote Mill, "when each has contributed according to his means, that is, has made an equal sacrifice for the common object." Equality of sacrifice, for Mill, meant "apportioning the contribution of each person toward the expense of government so that he shall feel neither more nor less inconvenience from his share of the payment than every other person experiences from his."[39]

[37] In recent years, tax scholars and philosophers have revived an interest in exploring the philosophical aspects of taxation based on natural endowments. See, e.g., Daniel Shaviro, "Endowment and Inequality," in *Tax Justice: The Ongoing Debate*, ed. Joseph J. Thorndike and Dennis Ventry Jr. (Washington, D.C.: Urban Institute Press, 2002), 123–48; Liam Murphy and Thomas Nagel, *The Myth of Ownership: Taxes and Justice* (New York: Oxford University Press, 2004); Kirk J. Stark, "Enslaving the Beachcomber: Some Thoughts on the Liberty Objections to Endowment Taxation," *Canadian Journal of Law & Jurisprudence* 18 (2005), 47–68; Lawrence Zelenak, "Taxing Endowment," *Duke Law Journal* 55 (2006), 114.

[38] Adam Smith, *An Inquiry into the Nature and Causes of the Wealth of Nations*, ed. Edwin Cannan (New York: Modern Library, 1937 [1776]), 777; Seligman, *Progressive Taxation in Theory and Practice*, 165.

[39] John Stuart Mill, *Principles of Political Economy with Some of Their Applications to Social Philosophy*, ed. William J. Ashley (London: Longmans, Green & Co., 1909, [1848]), 804–5; see also Henry Sidgwick, *The Principles of Political Economy* (London: MacMillan, 1901 [1883]), 566–71.

Mill may have provided American reformers with the theoretical provenance that they were seeking, but Mill did not use his maxim of equality of sacrifice to endorse progressive taxation. In fact, Mill opposed graduated rates, except in the case of inheritance taxes. He anticipated what subsequent economists would later refer to as the thorny problem of interpersonal welfare comparisons to argue that it was practically impossible to determine a set of optimal progressive tax rates that could achieve equality of sacrifice.[40] The notion of fine-tuning tax laws to ensure equality of sacrifice between individuals in different income classes "seems to me too disputable altogether," wrote Mill, "and even if true at all, not true to a sufficient extent to be made the foundation of any rule of taxation." Unsatisfied with the practical limits of his theory, Mill instead endorsed a second-best position: proportional taxation with exemption levels for the costs of subsistence.[41]

Although the classical writings of British political economists did not appear to endorse directly the claims for progressive taxation made by American reformers, the melding of faculty theory with the notion of equal sacrifice became an important cornerstone for the ideas of the public finance economists. Equality of sacrifice, for them, was a corollary to the faculty theory. It implied that taxes ought to be structured so as to exact the same amount of disutility from each individual. The principle of equal sacrifice ought to reduce the consumptive aspects of one's faculty, or diminish the "accretion" of possessions and the "enjoying" of the "consequences" of one's "exertions," to use Seligman's language. Ultimately, equal sacrifice based on individual faculty was, for Seligman and like-minded reformers, an aspirational aim, an ideal type that pointed directly toward progressive taxation. "If we never can reach an ideal,

[40] British economist Lionel Robbins is generally acknowledged to be one of the first scholars to reject completely the possibility of interpersonal comparisons of ordinal utilities. Robbins, *An Essay on the Nature and Significance of Economic Science* (London: Macmillan, 1932); Robbins, "Interpersonal Comparisons of Utility: A Comment," *Economic Journal* 48:192 (1938), 635–41. D. P. O'Brien, ed., *The History of Taxation*, Vol. VIII (London: Pickering & Chatto, 1999), xii. For more on the history of the theoretical problem of interpersonal comparisons of utility, see Mark Blaug, *Economic Theory in Retrospect*, 5th ed. (Cambridge: Cambridge University Press, 1997), 320–2.

[41] Mill, *Principles of Political Economy*, 807. Seligman seized upon Mill's acceptance of subsistence exemption levels as an exception that swallowed the rule. The Columbia professor contended that "according to Mill's own theory no really equitable fixed minimum of subsistence can be determined. If equality of sacrifice is the only defense of the exemption of the minimum of subsistence, we could not stop with this; for human wants shade into each other by imperceptible gradations." Seligman, *Progressive Taxation in Theory and Practice*, 234–5.

there is no good reason why we should not strive to get as close to it as possible," wrote Seligman. "Equality of sacrifice, indeed, we can never attain absolutely or exactly, because of the diversity of individual wants and desires, but it is nevertheless most probable that in the majority of normal and typical cases, we shall be getting closer to the desired equality by some departure from proportional taxation."[42]

By blending a revised version of Walker's faculty theory with Mill's notion of equality of sacrifice, Seligman was able to construct a theoretical basis for progressive taxation that took into account both productive potential as well as consumptive power. Seligman's revised version of faculty recognized that wealth had the capacity to produce even more wealth, and therefore the affluent had a greater obligation to support the state. "[I]t is evident that the possession of large fortunes or large incomes in itself affords the possessor a decided advantage in augmenting his possessions," wrote Seligman. "The facility of increasing production often grows in more than arithmetical proportion."[43] This growth was not simply natural; it was fostered by the broader context created by state and society. Consequently, wealthy citizens had a financial responsibility to the commonwealth that also grew in more than arithmetical proportion.

At the same time, taxation entailed a sacrifice on the consumptive powers of individuals, and this burden ideally ought to be dispersed so as to extract an equal sacrifice from all taxpayers. Measuring accurately the extent of such sacrifice was, however, nearly impossible. Consequently, Seligman ambivalently concluded, in the second edition of his classic text on progressivity, that progressive taxation was a concept that was ahead of its time. "While it is highly probable that the ends of justice would be more nearly subserved by some approximation to a progressive scale," he wrote, "considerations of expediency as well as the uncertainty of the interrelations between various parts of the entire tax system should tend to render us cautious in advocating any general application of the principle." The future success of progressive taxation in America, Seligman concluded, rested not on economic theories, but rather on "the state of social consciousness and the development of the feeling of civic obligation."[44]

[42] Seligman, *Progressive Taxation in Theory and Practice*, 292.

[43] Ibid.

[44] Ibid., 302. In his first edition, Seligman was much more supportive of graduated rates: "on the whole less injustice will be done by adopting some form of progression than by accepting the universal rule of proportion." Seligman, *Progressive Taxation in Theory and Practice* (Baltimore: American Economic Association, 1894), 193.

Once again, reformers moderated their support for institutional development by deferring to changing public sentiments about the degree of social cohesion.

With these concluding remarks, Seligman summarized the true promise of the faculty principle. His emphasis on "social consciousness" and "civic obligation" demonstrated tax activists' understanding that social conditions determined the fate of fundamental tax reform. Promoting progressive taxation based on the notion of ability to pay, for these reformers, was less about developing a coherent and unassailable economic theory of taxation, than it was about advancing a political and social reform movement based on ethical duties and social solidarity. Faculty and ability to pay were key words that could arouse and empower tax activists in their efforts to overturn *Pollock* and build the foundation for a new fiscal order. Seligman's tentative defense of progressivity was far from electrifying, to be sure.[45] But that did not mean that he and other tax experts had lost faith in the ability of their ideas to help transform the existing tax system. On the contrary, the faculty principle remained the cornerstone of the intellectual campaign for moderate and feasible tax reform.[46]

Progressive Taxation for Progressive Capitalists

Tracing the American historical experience with faculty taxes and uncovering the intellectual genealogy of the faculty principle may have reassured some critics of the political and social legitimacy of progressive taxation. Mill and Walker were highly regarded by some of the most conservative of American economic commentators, and hence the links between their work and calls for progressive taxation may have assuaged some concerns. Nonetheless, the perceived link between graduated taxes and state socialism remained a formidable challenge for reformers and theorists.

[45] As one reviewer had explained, Seligman's "attitude is that of an apologist for progressive taxation; and it must be added, that the apology is not a very convincing one." A. C. Miller, "Review of *Progressive Taxation in Theory and Practice* by Edwin R. A. Seligman," *Journal of Political Economy* 2:4 (1894), 596–9, 597.

[46] Legal scholars and philosophers have leveled a withering critique against the "ability-to-pay" rationale as an intellectually incoherent concept. These ahistorical critiques, however, elide the political and social context in which these key words were deployed. For a sample of these critiques, see generally Harry Kalven and Walter J. Blum, *The Uneasy Case for Progressive Taxation* (Chicago: University of Chicago Press), 67–71; Liam Murphy and Thomas Nagel, *The Myth of Ownership: Taxes and Justice* (New York: Oxford University Press, 2002), 20–37.

Taxation based on the principle of ability to pay may have been rooted in the American democratic tradition, but tax reform opponents maintained that the new progressive levies were a form of "creeping socialism" that was incompatible with American liberalism. Many old-guard economic commentators erroneously assumed that "progressive taxation necessarily implies socialism and confiscation," wrote Seligman, explicitly citing the writings of David Wells. But that was not the case. "It is quite possible to repudiate absolutely the socialistic theory of taxation and yet at the same time advocate progression," explained Seligman. Thus, in addition to providing historical and comparative evidence of the correlation between liberal democracy and progressive taxation, the public finance economists also sought to demonstrate that the adoption of moderately graduated taxes on incomes, profits, and wealth transfers would not lead inexorably toward state socialism.[47]

This was no easy task at the time. The searing reminders of the tensions between labor and capital seemed to be everywhere, and the echoes of Justice Field's alarmist concurrence in *Pollock* still resonated throughout American society, particularly within the halls of the academy. In the decade that straddled *Pollock*, the nascent American social science professions endured several challenges to academic freedom that ossified the distinction between impermissible social advocacy and the "rigors" of scientific objectivity. The progressive political economists were not immune to this disciplining trend. Ely recanted much of his radicalism and sympathy with labor after he had been accused in 1894 of teaching socialism and anarchism at Wisconsin. Consequently, his scholarship moved away from public finance, labor relations, and government regulation and toward the seemingly more innocuous topic of agricultural economics. H. C. Adams and Seligman, by contrast, continued to articulate the case for fundamental tax reform, though with a moderate and temperate inflection.[48]

For Seligman, conservative complaints that the adoption of progressive taxes would inevitably lead to socialism were empirically unfounded and politically motivated attacks intended to alarm ordinary citizens. Throughout American history the "socialistic" tag had been strategically deployed by opponents of nearly all types of reform. "The cry of Socialism has always been the last refuge of those who wish to clog the wheels

[47] Seligman, "The Theory of Progressive Taxation," 222.

[48] Rader, *Academic Mind and Reform*, 131–3; Furner, *Advocacy & Objectivity*, 157–62; Ross, *Origins of American Social Science*, 231–2.

of social progress or to prevent the abolition of long-continued abuses," wrote Seligman. "The Factory Laws were in their time dubbed socialistic. Compulsory education and the public post office system were called socialistic. There is scarcely a single tax which has ever been introduced, which has not somewhere or other met with the same objection." And it was not only at the federal level or solely in the United States that foes of change objected to new levies with misplaced charges of socialism: "the new inheritance tax in some of our commonwealths and in England," Seligman recounted, as well as "the new property tax in Holland and Prussia" faced the same criticism. "But the argument nowhere carried any weight."[49]

The political economists quickly dismissed the charges of "creeping socialism." The "objection scarcely deserves a refutation," Seligman noted dismissively. Not only because it had long been a tired and spurious political scare tactic used to impede reform, but because it was an expression of the increasingly obsolete social and political theory of laissez-faire individualism. For Adams, there was a clear distinction between European-style socialism and the "new individualism" that had taken hold in the United States at the turn of the century. Opponents of tax reform seemed unwilling to acknowledge the new social realities. They maintained that the individual naturally preceded the state and society. New school economists and other tax reformers sought to undermine this belief of the pre-social state of nature. "The State grows up naturally, spontaneously, and men are born into the State," wrote Ely even after his Wisconsin ordeal over academic freedom. "The basis of the State is human nature, and the State is the natural condition of men."[50] In their desperate efforts to hold on to a romantic view of the past, conservative opponents of tax reform were oblivious to the political and economic consequences of modern industrialism. The conservative complaint of creeping socialism, Seligman concluded, "entirely misconceives the relations of the individual to the state."[51]

Though the public finance economists were highly critical of the conservative opposition, their advocacy for moderately graduated taxation did not translate into a wholehearted acceptance of European-style

[49] Seligman, "Is the Income Tax Constitutional and Just?" 53–4.

[50] Adams, *Science of Finance*, 76–7; Richard T. Ely, *The Social Law of Service* (New York: Eaton & Mains, 1896), 167.

[51] Seligman, "Is the Income Tax Constitutional and Just?" 54.

socialism. In the process of navigating between the poles of political and intellectual opposition, Seligman and his colleagues were quick to point out that the type of state socialism they had witnessed during their travels to Germany was unlikely to take hold in the United States. The traditional American aversion to centralized power would not permit it. Thus, in addition to debunking conservative myths about creeping socialism, the professionally trained economists also challenged the ideas of some of their most revered German mentors.

Adolph Wagner, for example, had long been a staunch proponent of socialism and an advocate of using steeply progressive taxes to mitigate the growing economic inequalities generated by industrial capitalism. As early as 1881, in his monumental study of public finance, *Finanzwissenschaft*, Wagner emphasized the modern tendency of the scope of government to increase with higher levels of economic activity. This so-called "law" of the "increasing expansion of public, and particularly state, activities," was for Wagner, the historical political economist, neither an ironclad rule nor a prediction of future political activity. It was, instead, what subsequent commentators referred to as a "regularity," or "observable uniformity" in the "absolute and relative expansion of the public sector within the national economy, particularly of government services for communal purposes and at the cost of the growth in the private sector."[52]

Among the governmental activities that Wagner endorsed, none perhaps was more important than redistributing national income through progressive taxes. Using tax law as a "regulating factor in the distribution of national income and wealth" was an elementary aspect of what Wagner referred to as the *sozialpolitisch* or "social-welfare" concept of taxation. Unlike the "purely financial" purpose of taxation, which was directed at raising the necessary revenue to provide basic public goods and services, the "social-welfare" function meant using taxation to mitigate the maldistribution of wealth created by industrial capitalism. "It is

[52] Adolph Wagner, "Three Extracts on Public Finance," in *Classics in the Theory of Public Finance*, ed. Richard A. Musgrave and Alan T. Peacock (New York: St. Martin's Press, 1994), 1–15, 8. A veritable cottage industry of studies attempting to test empirically the viability of Wagner's law emerged during the post–World War II decades. For a summary and critique of this literature based on a careful, historical assessment of Wagner's work, see Richard M. Bird, "Wagner's 'Law' of Expanding State Activity," *Public Finance* 26 (March 1971), 1–26; Alan Peacock and Alex Scott, "The Curious Attraction of Wagner's Law," *Public Choice* 102:1/2 (2000), 1–17.

legitimate, nay essential," wrote Wagner, "to establish a second criterion of taxation beside the purely financial one: a criterion of social welfare, by virtue of which taxation is not merely a means of raising revenue, but at the same time intervenes to improve the distribution of income and wealth resulting from free competition." In this sense, taxation played a critical compensatory role in Wagner's science of finance. "The redistribution of national income in favor of the lower classes is a conscious aim of modern social policy," explained Wagner. To achieve that goal, Wagner supported "progressive taxation of higher incomes" and the rejection of "purely proportional taxation." Anticipating H. C. Adams's analysis, Wagner also called for higher taxes on income from land and investments as compared to wages, as well as extra levies on chance gains and windfall profits.[53]

Wagner did not expressly address how progressive taxes by themselves could "improve the distribution of income and wealth." It was presumed that steeply graduate taxes coupled with social-welfare spending would ameliorate inequalities. The tax-and-transfer process as a whole would work together to achieve social justice. This was a logical premise for a German scholar immersed in Bismarck's social-welfare state.[54] But for the American public finance economists, such social spending could not be assumed. When Adams, Ely, and Seligman transplanted the ideas of their German mentors onto American soil, they stressed the importance of taxation based on ability to pay, but in the process they overlooked Wagner's critical assumption about social-welfare spending. The Americans, thus, advanced a one-sided view of the fiscal state – a view that lacked a significant commitment to the social-welfare spending component of the tax-and-transfer process.

While Wagner stood "firmly by this conception" that the social-welfare aspects of taxation could be "extended to interfere with the uses of individual incomes and profits," he cautioned his readers not to reify even the most basic principles of taxation. Such principles were, after all, "relative in time and place," Wagner explained; "they depend upon cultural, economic and technical conditions, upon current public opinion, ideals of justice and constitutional law. If these change, the principles of taxation

[53] Wagner, "Three Extracts," 8, 9, 14. For more on Wagner and his influence on German economic policy, see Kenneth Barkin, "Adolf Wagner and German Industrial Development," *Journal of Modern History* 41:2 (1969), 144–59.

[54] Richard A. Musgrave, "The Role of the State in Fiscal Theory," *International Tax and Public Finance* 3 (1996), 247–58.

change too; they are in part not purely logical categories, but historical ones." This message about the importance of historical context was not lost on Wagner's American students.[55]

Indeed, many new school economists concurred with their German mentor about both the social welfare aspects of fiscal policy – that taxes ought to be used for much more than just generating public revenues – and about the significance of historical context. Applying their German historicist training to their own conditions, the American economists concluded, however, that Wagner and other socialists promoted a conspicuous level of government intervention that was wholly distasteful to most late-nineteenth-century Americans. Even though the reform-minded economists disparaged laissez-faire positions, particularly the benefits theory of taxation, for ignoring the social aspects of modern conditions, some recoiled at the broad and dramatic implications of Wagner's redistributive tax policies. "From the principle that the state may modify its strict fiscal policy by considerations of general national utility, to the principle that it is the duty of the state to redress all inequalities of fortune among its private citizens, is a long and dangerous step," warned Seligman. "It would land us not only in socialism, but practically in communism."[56] Wagner's particular brand of socialism proved too much for Seligman and the more moderate American reformers.

To be sure, the progressive political economists did not always agree on the meaning of socialism and its feasibility for turn-of-the-century American circumstances. For Ely and other members of the Social Gospel movement the "true aim of the best socialism," was not to foment proletariat revolution, but to provide the means for "general social amelioration which proposes to sacrifice no class, but to improve and elevate all classes."[57] To that end, Ely frequently chastised his academic colleagues for not pursuing more radical reforms, for moving too slowly with their efforts to address growing inequalities. The academic reformers also failed to maintain a consistent viewpoint over time, as the pressures on academic freedom and a changing political climate continued to constrain their writings and teachings. Seligman's views on socialism, for instance,

55 Wagner, "Three Extracts," 10. Seligman's contact with Wagner went well past his student days, as he corresponded with his former mentor throughout much of his early career. See, e.g., Adolph Wagner to Edwin Seligman, March 13, 1909, Series I: Catalogued Correspondence, ERASP.

56 Seligman, *Progressive Taxation in Theory and Practice* (1908), 131.

57 Richard T. Ely, *The Strength and Weakness of Socialism* (New York: Chautauqua Press, 1899), 7, 179.

gradually changed throughout his life. During his early career, he was fascinated by Robert Owen and the Christian Socialists, describing them as "the eloquent and enthusiastic apostles of socialism." Toward the end of this career, after he witnessed firsthand the unanticipated and explosive growth of the World War I fiscal-military state, the Columbia professor became increasingly cautious and politically conservative, frequently defending what he called "progressive capitalism" in public debates.[58]

At the turn of the century, however, Seligman remained rather moderate in his evaluation of socialism and its links to graduated taxes. This may have been because he was becoming more interested at the time in the historical materialism of socialist theory. In addition to revising his progressive tax treatise and continuing his work on the history of the income tax, he was also making a foray into the philosophy of history. His modestly entitled monograph *The Economic Interpretation of History* (1902) had as much to say about the imminent rise of socialism as it did about the nature of historical knowledge. One of the primary aims of the popular book was to sever the traditional Marxist theory of historical change, which Seligman agreed with, from the prescriptive tenets of conventional Marxist socialism, which he profoundly rejected. "Socialism is a theory of what ought to be; historical materialism is a theory of what has been," wrote Seligman. "The one is teleological, the other is descriptive. The one is speculative idea, the other is a canon of interpretation. It is impossible to see any necessary connection between such divergent conceptions."[59] By decoupling historical materialism from scientific socialism, Seligman believed he could also extenuate the distance between progressive taxation and state socialism. If he could convince readers that economic determinism did not necessarily lead to socialist revolution, he hoped that he could also bolster the case that progressive

[58] Edwin R. A. Seligman,"Owen and the Christian Socialists," *Political Science Quarterly* 1:2 (1886), 206–49, 206; W. Elliot Brownlee, "Tax Regimes, National Crisis, and State-Building in America," in *Funding the Modern American State, 1941–1995: The Rise and Fall of the Era of Easy Finance*, ed. W. Elliot Brownlee (New York: Cambridge University Press, 2003), 37–107, 57; O.G. Villard, *Debate between Prof. E.R.A Seligman (Affirmative) and Prof. Scot Nearing (Negative)* (New York: Fine Arts Guild, 1921).

[59] Edwin R. A. Seligman, *The Economic Interpretation of History* (New York: Columbia University Press, 1902), 108. With this text, Seligman solidified his reputation among subsequent scholars as being a strong influence on a wide swath of early-twentieth-century social scientists, including Charles Beard. See, Richard Hofstadter, *The Progressive Historians: Turner, Beard, Parrington* (New York: Knopf, 1968), 196–200; Karen Orren and Stephen Skowronek, *The Search for American Political Development* (New York: Cambridge University Press, 2004), 210.

taxation was not the first step toward the collective ownership of the means of production and exchange.[60]

Ely concurred with Seligman, though for different reasons. While Seligman questioned the teleology of the socialist vision of change in order to scrub economic determinism of its socialist stain, Ely challenged the inevitability of socialist change in order to emphasize the importance of individual volition. Like his Social Gospel colleagues, Ely had great faith in the power of religion and collective action. Unreconstructed socialists who believed in an economic determinism "as inflexible as cast iron" were as oblivious to true historical change, Ely contended, as the conservatives who refused to admit the transformations wrought by industrial capitalism. Though he agreed with Seligman that material economic forces played an important role in shaping history, Ely refused to give up on the notion that human agency and collective social action could shape all kinds of reform – including tax reform.[61]

[60] American historians who have examined Seligman's endeavor into the philosophy of history have generally concluded that by abandoning Marx's socialism, Seligman became an apologist for industrial capitalism, or at the very least that he provided liberal historians with a more domesticated version of economic determinism. Ross, *Origins of American Social Science*, 186–91; Brian Lloyd, *Left Out: American Pragmatism, Exceptionalism and the Poverty of American Marxism, 1890–1922* (Baltimore: Johns Hopkins University Press, 1997). More specifically, Brian Lloyd has maintained that Marx's historical materialism was inseparable from his scientific socialism, and that Seligman severed the two for purely political purposes. For Seligman, Lloyd writes, "the whole point of divorcing a materialist philosophy of history from Marx's socialist economics was to make available a realist justification for his advocacy of market capitalism and Darwinian gradualism." Lloyd, *Left Out*, 86. In fact, Lloyd building on Dorothy Ross's work sees the limited vision of Seligman's liberal historicism as symptomatic of all of American social science. "The liberal professor's need to pillage so wantonly the analytic holdings of the Marxist tradition points up the limited resources American social science offered the historically minded at the turn of the century," writes Lloyd. "Seligman, in a word, consorted with Marx for the same reason Dewey kept company with Hegel: neither could squeeze a conception of 'the social' from the politically palatable but analytically desiccated body of Anglo-American empiricism" Ibid., 87. Lloyd's claims are difficult to square given Seligman's fidelity to German historicism rather than Anglo-American empiricism, especially when one considers the influence Seligman had on other ostensibly less moderate commentators, such as Charles Beard. See Clyde W. Barrow, "From Marx to Madison: The Seligman Connection in Charles Beard's Constitutional Theory," *Polity* 24:3 (spring 1992), 379–97; Peter Novick, *That Noble Dream: The "Objectivity Question" and the American Historical Profession* (New York: Cambridge University Press, 1988), 94.

[61] Ely, *Socialism: An Examination of its Nature, its Strength and its Weakness, with Suggestions for Social Reform* (New York: Thomas Y. Crowell & Company, 1894), 176–7. For more on Ely's ties to the social gospel and his views on socialism, see Rader, *Academic Mind and Reform*, 62–5; Kloppenberg, *Uncertain Victory*, 233–4.

New school economists also criticized the logical fallacy underpinning the opposition to graduated taxes. In his 1898 public finance treatise, H. C. Adams explained how progressive taxation complemented American capitalism and was logically irreconcilable with the theory of state socialism. Of course, Adams had always been skeptical of the socially regenerative potential of European-style socialism. Perhaps his Congregationalist rearing had inoculated him from accepting the collectivist assumptions of socialism. Nevertheless, Adams supported progressive taxation. He argued that it was logically consistent with private property and the profit motive. In fact, he believed that "extreme socialists" would reject graduated taxation. The socialist ideal, he wrote, "is of a society in which government is the one great industrial corporation. Their purpose is the establishment of a society that does not recognize private property, or, indeed, a private income except in the form of public salary or public wages." The traditional socialist, Adams reasoned, "approves the centralization of industrial power, since this brings the industrial organization more nearly to his ideal." A moderately progressive tax system respected the notion of private property by preserving it, rather than using confiscatory taxes to eliminate all private property. For a true socialist, "therefore, to advocate such a use of the taxing power as to obstruct this tendency toward centralization is illogical in the extreme."[62]

By the same token, Adams contended that proponents of industrial capitalism ought to embrace progressive taxation because of its ability to maintain a level playing field for market participants:

> Progressive taxation efficiently carried out would, other things remaining the same, tend toward the equalization of private incomes and result in a more equitable distribution of industrial power. It would be logical for one who defends the institution of private property, and who believes in the theory of voluntary initiative in industry, to advocate progressive taxation as an essential condition to the maintenance of those industrial relations in which his ideal of society may be realized; but for the socialist, whose theory of social organization is opposed to that of voluntary association, such an advocacy is illogical and absurd.[63]

Progressive taxes that merely reallocated fiscal burdens without radically redistributing wealth, Adams reasoned, were wholly consistent with American liberal institutions and values.

[62] Henry Carter Adams, *Science of Finance*, 344. On Adams's Congregationalist background, see A. W. Coats, "Henry Carter Adams: A Case Study in the Emergence of the Social Sciences in the United States, 1850–1900," *Journal of American Studies* 2:2 (1968), 177–97.

[63] Adams, *Science of Finance*, 344.

Ely agreed with Adams about the necessity of equalizing economic power. For him, American-style social democracy or what he referred to as "modern socialism" did not "propose to abolish private property." "Quite the contrary," Ely reasoned, social democracy "proposes to extend the institution of private property in such manner as to secure to each individual in society property in an annual income." One way to secure such equality was to use graduated taxes on incomes, profits, and inheritances to control wealth and reconfigure the financial obligations of modern citizenship.[64]

Like other progressive reformers, the public finance economists defended graduated taxes as part of the broader effort to reorient American thinking about the role of the polity in economy and society. The rising interdependence of modern industrial life, the lived social experiences of their times, compelled reform-minded economists to question classical liberal notions of the relation between the self-possessive individual and the laissez-faire state, and the so-called natural divide between public and private. By stressing the need for progressive taxation, and dispelling the myth of creeping socialism, these progressive thinkers were attempting to provide a new vocabulary of ethical duty and social solidarity – a new twentieth-century idiom that could be used to displace the autonomous individualism that had been at the center of nineteenth-century American jurisprudence and liberal ideology.

Marginalism, Minimum Sacrifice, and the Moderate Fiscal State

In their efforts to draw new mental metaphors about the fiscal basis for government action, the reform-minded theorists had to engage with new economic ideas that could, in principle, challenge the notion of a moderate fiscal state. In their efforts, moreover, to navigate between the conservative opposition to tax reform and the socialistic calls for radical wealth redistribution, the progressive economists needed to explain how graduated rates could mitigate increasing economic inequality without undermining the principal tenets of market capitalism. They wanted, in sum, to show that a new fiscal order could both achieve social justice and maintain economic growth. The rise of marginal utility analysis at the turn of the twentieth century was one set of economic ideas that appeared to contest such a vision of a moderate fiscal state.

[64] Richard T. Ely, *Strength and Weakness of Socialism*, 16–17.

A variant of neoclassical political economy, marginal utility analysis, or marginalism as it was often referred to, triggered a paradigm shift in economic theory. The foundations of marginalsim could be traced to the 1870s, if not earlier, when several European economic thinkers were independently yet simultaneously reorienting the classical theory of value. Marginalism gained ascendancy in the United States in the late nineteenth century with the work of Seligman's Columbia colleague John Bates Clark, who at least initially was greatly influenced by his own German training with Karl Knies and by the writings of Henry George.[65]

Building on the work of the British political economist Alfred Marshall, American marginalists like Clark believed that value was a function of individual utility and that utility was determined by the law of diminishing returns. Unlike classical theory, which held that the value of a commodity was determined by the labor costs incurred to create it, marginalism dictated that a commodity's value turned on the subjective worth, or utility, a consumer placed on such a commodity. This value, in turn, depended upon how much of the commodity the consumer already had. As one's income grew and as they acquired an increasing amount of a given good, one tended to value the last unit of the acquired good less than previous units. "In careful statements of the law of value," Clark explained, "allowance is made for the fact that, as an income grows larger, there is not a continuous quantitative increase in the consumption of all the articles that are early secured. Some articles for consumption are never duplicated at all; and others which are duplicated have, after one unit has been supplied, a comparatively slight utility."[66]

Clark used marginalism mainly to analyze industrial productivity. He sought to explain and justify how the workers' wages and the returns from capital were determined by the last "incremental" unit of labor or capital that was added to the production process. Under perfectly competitive markets, Clark reasoned, capital and labor would flow to their highest marginal returns, and as a result each would have a right to that share of wealth that corresponded to its respective marginal contribution

[65] John F. Henry, *John Bates Clark: The Making of a Neoclassical Economist* (London: Macmillan Press, 1995); R. D. Black, A. W. Coats, and C. D. W. Goodwin, *The Marginal Revolution in Economics* (Durham: Duke University Press, 1973). Harvard economist Joseph Schumpeter identified Clark as "the master of American marginalism." Joseph A. Schumpeter, *History of Economic Analysis* (London: Allen & Unwin, 1954), 868–70.

[66] Clark, *Distribution of Wealth*, 213.

to the production process. From this, Clark concluded, marginalism could be used as a normative principle of distributive justice. The market allocation of wages was not only efficient, it was fair. Marginalism, thus, provided new support for competitive capitalism at a time when tensions in American industrial relations and fears of socialism were perhaps at their height. Marginal utility analysis soon became not only a central pillar of neoclassical economics, but also the dominant paradigm in American economics.[67]

Yet, if Clark's marginal theory of productivity was embraced as a "scientific" justification for the prevailing distribution of wealth between labor and capital, other economic thinkers at the time applied marginalism to tax policy in potentially more radical ways. Theorists like British political economist F. Y. Edgeworth and American academic Thomas N. Carver carried marginalism and the notion of "minimum sacrifice" to their logical extremes to provide a theoretical justification for steeply progressive taxes. As a firm utilitarian, Edgeworth sought to justify progressive taxation on the grounds that it could maximize total social welfare. He pursued this aim indirectly by arguing that one way to maximize social utility was to minimize the disutility from taxation. "The condition that the total net utility procured by taxation should be a maximum," wrote Edgeworth, "reduces to the condition that the total disutility should be minimum." And from this, "it follows in general that the marginal disutility incurred by each taxpayer should be the same." Applying the law of diminishing marginal utility to income, Edgeworth thus concluded that "higher incomes should be cut down to a certain level." Limiting taxation only to the wealthy, however, limited the state's revenue capacity, as Edgeworth acknowledged: "there will not be enough taxation to go around." The theoretical resolution lay in designing a system that consistently taxed those who were better off. "The solution," Edgeworth declared, "in the abstract is that the richer should be taxed for the benefit of the poorer up to the point at which complete equality of fortunes is attained."[68]

[67] Ibid. Ross, *Origins of American Social Science*, 118–22; Blaug, *Economic Theory in Retrospect*, 406–9. For more on the comparative aspects of marginalism and American institutionalism during this period, see, Marion Fourcade, *Economists and Societies: Discipline and Professions in the United States, Britain, and France, 1890s to 1990s* (Princeton: Princeton University Press, 2008), 81–4.

[68] F. Y. Edgeworth, "The Pure Theory of Taxation," *Economic Journal* 7:28 (1897), 550–71, 552–3.

Although many contemporary commentators latched on to Edgeworth's theoretical conclusion about equalizing fortunes, the British thinker was cautious and skeptical about radically redistributive taxes. Thus, while he recognized that his position "in the abstract" led to the "*acme* of socialism," he maintained that his theoretical position "is immediately clouded over by doubts and reservations." The most significant of these related to the incentive effects of steeply progressive taxes. Edgeworth acknowledged that high rates of income taxation could discourage individuals from generating income, thus inhibiting economic growth. Citing to the scholarship of his Cambridge colleague, Henry Sidgwick, Edgeworth explained that "a greater equality in the distribution of produce would lead ultimately to a reduction in the total amount to be distributed in consequence of a general preference of leisure to the results of labor on the part of the classes whose shares of produce had increased." Other practical reservations such as dealing with incommensurate, individual utility functions, the population effects of redistributive taxes, and the problem of tax avoidance and evasion further clouded Edgeworth's theoretical case for radically redistributive taxation. Ultimately, Edgeworth contended that minimum sacrifice, or what he referred to as "equimarginal sacrifice," was "the sovereign principle of taxation." But he acknowledged that "practical wisdom" would deter the lawmaker "from moving directly towards" this theoretical ideal.[69]

Edgeworth was not the first scholar to meld marginalism with a theory of "minimum" tax sacrifice. Oberlin College economist Thomas Carver made a similar argument earlier, though with less mathematical sophistication.[70] Like Edgeworth, Carver based his support for progressive taxes on purely utilitarian grounds. Although Edgeworth's writings were more prominent, frequently appearing in the flagship journals of the British economics profession, Carver anticipated much of Edgeworth's reasoning.[71] From the utilitarian premise of promoting "the greatest happiness to the greatest number," Carver reasoned that the state should

69 Ibid., 556, 553 (emphasis in the original). Denis Patrick O'Brien and John Presley, *Pioneers of Modern Economics in Britain, Vol. 2* (London: Macmillan Press, 1981), 89–91.

70 T. N. Carver, "The Ethical Basis of Distribution and Its Application to Taxation," *Annals of the American Academy of Political and Social Science* 6 (July 1895), 79–99. Laurence S. Moss, "The Seligman-Edgeworth Debate about the Analysis of Tax Incidence," *History of Political Economy* 35:2 (2003), 205–40.

71 In fact, Edgeworth approvingly quoted Carver at length in his article. Edgeworth, "The Pure Theory of Taxation," 556.

develop a tax system aimed at creating the least amount of total disutility; "ought not the test of justice in taxation," he asked rhetorically, "be *the least evil to the least number*?" If so, and if taxation entailed two types of "evil," namely "the sacrifice to the one who pays the tax" and "the repressive effect which a tax may have on industry and enterprise," then finding the proper mix of these two evils was critical.[72]

Addressing the two evils of taxation, for Carver, meant promoting two different types of taxes. "The minimum amount of repression is secured by imposing an equal sacrifice on all members of the community, but the minimum amount of sacrifice is secured by collecting the whole tax from those few incomes which have the lowest final utility." In other words, limiting the disincentives for economic productivity meant creating a flat tax that required each individual to carry a proportional fiscal burden. But limiting the personal disutility of the incidence of taxation meant adopting a highly progressive income tax aimed at soaking the rich. Squaring this circle was a tremendous challenge. To do so, Carver turned to the sources of large incomes. He argued that because "large incomes are more often due to the possession of special talents, or ground rents, or patents and other forms of monopoly, or inherited property, . . . it would seem that a moderate application of the principle of requiring a larger sacrifice from those with large incomes would not only reduce the total sacrifice but would have very little repressive effect." With this intuition, Carver concluded "that a moderately progressive tax would conform more nearly with the principle of the least evil to the least number than any other method of distributing the burdens of taxation."[73]

Carver and Edgeworth were careful to constrain the implications of their ideas. Indeed, Edgeworth explicitly acknowledged that in theory his analysis could lead to the "acme of socialism." Neither writer, however, was a socialist. And thus both tempered the consequences of their writings by reiterating the need for practical restraint in designing tax policy and progressive rates.[74] Yet that did not prevent critics like Seligman

72 Carver, "The Ethical Basis of Distribution and Its Application to Taxation," 95 (emphasis in the original). For more on Carver, see David Charles Lewis, "Carver, Thomas Nixon," in *The Biographical Dictionary of American Economists, Vol. I*, ed. Ross B. Emmett (London: Thoemmes Continuum, 2006), 126–7. See also Carver's autobiography, *Recollections of an Unplanned Life* (Los Angeles: W. Ritchie Press, 1949).

73 Carver, "The Ethical Basis of Distribution and Its Application to Taxation," 97, 98.

74 Although his early writings reflected a general sympathy for the moral and ethical obligations inherent in progressive taxation, Carver's writings became increasingly

from using Carver and Edgeworth as foils for their own vision of a moderate fiscal state. For the Columbia professor, the reservations that Edgeworth and Carver held about the practical implications of their "minimum sacrifice" theory undermined their relevance and significance. Seligman unmercifully disparaged Edgeworth's analysis, perhaps because the two academics had been engaged in an ongoing scholarly battle about the incidence of taxation. "A theory which according to the confessions of its author is so completely inapplicable is perhaps of no real validity," wrote Seligman, referring to Edgeworth's writings on progressive taxation. "Its impracticability renders it subject to grave suspicion."[75]

Seligman was more charitable toward Carver. But here too he believed that the minimum sacrifice theory did little to advance fiscal science, and even less for the institutional design of tax law and policy. Seligman commended Carver for identifying and disentangling the two types of marginal sacrifice associated with taxation: (1) the direct sacrifice placed on the taxpayer and (2) the indirect sacrifice felt by those who were deprived of the economic activity discouraged by taxation. Nevertheless, he contended that Carver's indirect sacrifice "has no necessary relation to the progressive scale." Different types of taxes, Seligman surmised, would have different incentive effects completely independent of the rate structure. Decoupling the tax base from tax rates was one way to isolate the incentive effects of progressivity. Thus, if the issue of progressivity as it applied to the direct sacrifice placed upon a taxpayer could be detached from the disincentive effects of what Carver referred to as "indirect sacrifice," then "there was no reason why taxes on general property or income or land or inheritances should not be arranged according to a well-nigh confiscatory scale." And if Carver's theory did not provide a limit on progressivity, then Seligman concluded it "becomes equivalent to the confiscatory or socialist theory" of progressive taxation.[76]

There was, of course, an unacknowledged tension in Seligman's critiques of Edgeworth and Carver. Although he criticized Edgeworth for

conservative, and perhaps even reactionary, over time as he became a staunch critic of the New Deal and redistributive social-welfare policies. See Thomas N. Carver, *Recollections of an Unplanned Life* (Los Angeles: W. Ritchie Press, 1949); Lewis, "Carver, Thomas Nixon," 127.

75 Seligman, *Progressive Taxation in Theory and Practice*, 286. For more on the differences between Seligman-Edgeworth, see, Moss, "The Seligman-Edgeworth Debate about the Analysis of Tax Incidence."

76 Seligman, *Progressive Taxation in Theory and Practice* (1908), 288, 289.

being impractical, Seligman's own conclusions on the optimal rate of graduated taxes were hardly unequivocal. In fact, both scholars were similarly dubious that their theories could be reliable guides for lawmakers. Like Mill before him, Seligman anticipated that using marginalism to justify progressive taxes implied an interpersonal comparison of subjectivity that was frequently untenable. "Mathematics cannot help us here," he wrote in reference to previous studies, "because the very first condition fails us – the power to gauge with accuracy the mathematical relations of the marginal utilities."[77] Likewise, while Seligman unfairly conflated Carver's view with confiscatory taxes, the same charge could, and often was, leveled against Seligman himself. Why then did Seligman choose to depict the ideas of political moderates like Edgeworth and Carver as dangerously radical?

Part of the answer rested with the desire to stress the moderate aspects of the progressive tax reform project. Pragmatic reformers such as Seligman understood that the ideas of academics, no matter how sincere or cautious, could be manipulated and distorted by critics. Given the consistent contemporary fears of "creeping socialism," Seligman was quick to quash even theoretical models that might taint progressive taxes with a radical hue. By dismissing Edgeworth and Carver as irrelevant and perhaps even dangerous, Seligman was seeking to sanitize even further his tempered support for graduated taxes. Even though *Pollock* had been decided a decade before Seligman began revising his treatise on progressive taxation, which included his criticism of Edgeworth and Carver, the Supreme Court's decision continued to resonate within American political and legal discourse. Any activist serious about fundamental tax reform, thus, needed to keep in mind the political, as well as the theoretical, implications of new economic ideas.

In fact, within a few years, as the movement for a constitutional amendment overturning *Pollock* began to gain momentum, Seligman would once again revise his position on progressive taxation for a changing political climate. In composing the second edition of his treatise on progressive taxation – a treatise aimed more at economic experts (at home and abroad) than lawmakers or ordinary citizens – Seligman was careful and cautious in his analysis of graduated taxes, supporting them with a great deal of reservation. By 1911, when a constitutional amendment was slowly gaining traction in state legislatures, Seligman published

77 Ibid., 283.

his magnum opus on the history and theory of the income tax. In that wide-ranging and thorough text, as we shall see in Chapter 5, Seligman expressly came out in support for the pending constitutional amendment and progressive income taxes. Aimed at a more general readership, the income tax treatise went even further in illustrating that graduated taxes on income and other forms of wealth were a fundamental part of liberal democracy and the American creed.[78]

While Seligman was making progressive taxation safe for American consumption, Henry Carter Adams was underscoring the importance of private industry for the future of the moderate state. Though he abhorred the extreme individualism at the center of classical political economy, Adams continued to believe that economic progress was driven mainly by private industry rather than state action. In this sense, Adams shared Seligman's faith in "progressive capitalism." The two theorists retained an allegiance to the profit motive and the productive powers of capital. And that allegiance in turn restrained their advocacy for redistributive tax policy. They held these views not because of any affinity for the distributional consequences of modern American capitalism; both scholars, after all, disdained the massive inequality caused by industrialization.

Rather, Adams and Seligman placed great faith in legal change to address some of the ills of industrial capitalism. In his 1896 presidential address before the American Economic Association, Adams described how state action through law and legal institutions shaped nearly all economic and social relations. "Every change in the social structure, every modification of the principle of political or industrial association, as well as the acceptance of a new social ideal," Adams announced, "must be accompanied by a corresponding change in those rights and duties acknowledged and enforced by law." With such confidence in the power of formal rules, Adams stressed how law and government intervention could mitigate the evils of "unguarded competition."[79]

[78] Edwin R. A. Seligman, *The Income Tax: A Study of the History, Theory, and Practice of Income Taxation at Home and Abroad* (New York: Macmillan, 1911). This treatise, which went through numerous editions and was translated into several languages, was arguably Seligman's most influential text.

[79] Henry C. Adams, "Economics and Jurisprudence: Delivered at the Meeting of the Association in Baltimore, Maryland, December 28, 1896," *Economic Studies* 2:1 (February 1897), 7. Adams first presented his ideas on the connections between "Economics and Jurisprudence" a decade earlier when he contributed an article to the famous *Science* debate about the emerging American economics discipline. Henry C. Adams, "Economics and Jurisprudence," *Science* 8 (July 2, 1886), 15–19.

More specifically, Adams believed the positive state had two principal legal responsibilities in monitoring industrial society. The first was to raise the "ethical plane of competitive action" so as to ensure that the long term interests of the public good were not compromised by the short-term objectives of narrow-minded economic actors. The second was to regulate those unique industries known as "natural monopolies," which were immune to competitive, market forces. In both cases, Adams advocated that tax law and policy had a central role to play, by punitively taxing businesses that deviated from an agreed upon ethical plane and by extracting the financial rents secured by natural monopolies.[80]

Though Adams was willing to exercise the coercive powers of the state to regulate industry, he recoiled at the thought of steeply progressive taxes that might inhibit economic growth. Like Edgeworth and Carver, Adams was concerned about the potential impact that progressive taxation might have on incentives to generate income and wealth. Adams was especially concerned about not disturbing what he referred to as the "patrimony of the State." As a thorough-going historicist, Adams admitted that the "patrimony of the State is not a thing that is fixed, but that it changes with the ideas of political and industrial rights entertained by the people." Still, Adams made preserving economic incentives, and the state's right to tap such economic growth, a fundamental part of his fiscal vision. The "first fiscal axiom of the Science of Finance," declared Adams in the opening pages of his pioneering 1898 treatise, is that a "sound financial policy will not impair the patrimony of the State."[81] Unlike Wagner, Adams and his cohort of American thinkers seemed reluctant to use the full fiscal powers of the positive state to address the excesses of modern industrialism. In their preoccupation to maintain the "patrimony of the State," they appeared unable to imagine how the tax-and-transfer process could function as a holistic part of the new fiscal state.

To be sure, Adams was genuinely concerned about the growing disparity of wealth, or what he called the "disparity of possessions."[82] But he

80 Henry C. Adams, "Relation of the State to Industrial Action," *Publications of the American Economic Association* 1:16 (January 1887): 471–549, 507–8; Adams, *Science of Finance*, 305–6. For more on the links between Adams's early scholarship and his later career, see Joseph Dorfman, "Henry Carter Adams: The Harmonizer of Liberty and Reform," in *Two Essays by Henry Carter Adams: Relation of the State to Industrial Action & Economics and Jurisprudence*, ed. Joseph Dorfman (New York: Columbia University Press, 1954), 3–56.

81 Adams, *Science of Finance*, 3.

82 Adams, *Public Debts*, 50; *Science of Finance*, 3.

harbored an even greater fear that steeply progressive taxes would jeopardize the state's main source of sustenance. As he informed his students, an "inequitable apportionment" of the tax burden "checks industrial enterprise." Though he did not clarify what he meant by "inequitable," he confirmed that "it is not taxation, but unjust taxation that dampens industrial order."[83] Similarly, in his lectures on taxation, Adams stated that a "mark of a good system of taxation" was that "it should tend to close rather than widen the breech between classes." But this assertion did not translate into a policy prescription of fundamental wealth redistribution. In fact, closing "the breech between the classes" was, he informed his students, one of the last aims of a "good system of taxation," well behind meeting "the adequate wants of the state," and having "elasticity for expansion and contraction." Like his social-democratic colleagues, Adams did not lose sight of the ultimate life blood of the emerging liberal state. "The patrimony of the State consists in a flourishing condition of private industries," wrote Adams. For him, the modern state was the one institution that could mitigate inequality without destroying future prosperity.[84]

In the years between *Pollock* and the ratification of the Sixteenth Amendment, tax reformers began to articulate more clearly what they had envisioned for the emerging fiscal polity. Rather than putting an end to fundamental tax reform, *Pollock* had given political activists an opportunity to redefine the parameters and promise of a new fiscal order. For some social commentators and academics, this meant questioning whether an undifferentiated reliance on an income tax – a reliance that ignored the varied sources of income and wealth – was a sufficient means to address the growing inequality of the Gilded Age or the growing need

83 Henry Carter Adams, "Lecture IV: The Apportionment of Taxes" 3; "Lecture I on Taxation: General Principles of Taxation," Box 26, Folder 2 "Lecture on Taxation – 1896," HCAP.

84 Adams, *Science of Finance*, 3, 6, 5. Richard Ely appeared to share Adams's notion of the importance of industrial development, though he clearly favored a more even distribution of the ownership of capital. As he explained in his popular *Introduction to Political Economy* textbook: "What socialists object to is not capital but the private capitalist. They desire to nationalize capital and to abolish capitalists as a distinct class by making everybody, as a member of the community, a capitalist; that is, a partial owner of all the capital in the country." Ely, *Introduction to Political Economy* (New York: Chautauqua Press, 1889), 241. Like his new school colleagues, Ely was eager "to defang socialism for American audiences." Kloppenberg, *Uncertain Victory*, 280–2.

for greater public revenue. Other reformers confronted more directly the fears inherent in Justice Field's concurrence about an income tax signaling the inexorable rise of socialism in America. Progressive political economists led by Seligman, Ely, and Adams sought to dispel this myth of "creeping socialism" by showing that graduated taxes on incomes, profits, and inheritances were not only part of a long history of American taxation, but also that progressive levies based on one's ability to pay were supported by a venerable group of distinguished Anglo-American thinkers.

In the process of accentuating the moderate aspects of their fiscal vision, the public finance economists also distanced themselves and their ideas from more radical views of taxation. Although they had all studied with German historical economists, who called for using progressive taxes to redistribute income and wealth, the U.S. reformers remained skeptical that American political culture was willing to accept such European-style statism. Indeed, in their relentless efforts to allay American anxieties about progressive taxation, the tax theorists even challenged the work of other Anglo-American academics who employed new ideas about diminishing marginal utility. They did all of this, in the end, to demonstrate that the shift from an indirect, regressive system of national taxation to a more direct and progressive one was more about reallocating the burdens of financing a modern state, and less about radically redistributing income or wealth. A new, moderate American fiscal state could take the place of the obsolete nineteenth-century statecraft of excise taxes and tariffs without undermining traditional American values and institutions.

These ideas about transforming the existing fiscal structure had broad implications. Not only did the dense and turgid economic treatises influence elite lawmakers, like federal judges and national legislators;[85] the popular writings of these academics also caught the attention of social reformers, as well as ordinary citizens struggling to cope with the everyday incidence of the existing tax regime. For many quotidian taxpayers, the increasing burdens of taxation were perhaps most strongly felt at the subnational level, where state and local property taxes continued to dominant turn-of-the-century tax policy. Thus, tax activists understood that if they were to transform the existing mindset about taxation, they needed to usher in a completely new fiscal order, one that attended to

[85] Herbert Hovenkamp, "The First Great Law & Economics Movement," *Stanford Law Review* 42:4 (1990), 993–1058, 1008–9.

state and local as well as federal concerns. Challenging the dysfunctional, nineteenth-century property tax by trying to enhance the administrative capacity of subnational taxing authorities and by searching for alternative sources of revenue would become the hallmarks of the state-level aspects of the new fiscal order.

4

The Factories of Fiscal Innovation

Institutional Reform at the State and Local Level

> It is one of the happy incidents of the federal system that a single courageous State may, if its citizens choose, serve as a laboratory; and try novel social and economic experiments without risk to the rest of the country.
>
> – Justice Louis D. Brandeis

The economic experts and fiscal reformers who responded to the *Pollock* decision by paving a progressive, middle path between the status quo and radically redistributive taxes focused much of their efforts on dismantling the national system of indirect and regressive import duties and excise taxes. But they did not lose sight of the importance of subnational tax reform. In some ways, *Pollock* channeled reform efforts toward improving state and local fiscal regimes. By foreclosing, at least for the time being, the possibility of a national income tax, the U.S. Supreme Court indirectly pushed fiscal reformers to concentrate their efforts at the subnational level. But economic experts and political activists were already protesting the defects of the property tax well before the Court struck down the 1894 federal income tax. Recall that the new school of American political economists began their assault on benefits theory with an early salvo against the state and local general property tax. They were not alone. Journalists, lawmakers, political reformers, and concerned citizens alike detested the capricious assessment and unequal distributional consequences of the existing subnational property tax regime.

Between the end of Reconstruction and the conclusion of the First World War, the growing dissatisfaction with the prevailing property tax was a driving force for state and local tax reform. Exacerbated by the modern forces of urban industrialization, particularly the accelerating emergence of corporate capitalism, the defects of the existing property tax regime became increasingly pronounced at the turn of the century. As one concerned Wisconsin citizen succinctly explained, "The two great administrative problems before our people at this time are, first, the control of corporate wealth, and, second, the establishment of a rational system of taxation."[1]

Indeed, nearly every economic commentator and political activist in the late 1800s singled out state and local general property taxes as abject failures of American law and public policy. In 1878, Justice Cooley reflected the view held by most lawyers and jurists at the time when he informed members of the American Social Science Association that the existing subnational tax system was "full of incongruities and inequalities." More specifically, Cooley identified the dysfunctional assessment of personal property as "the most prominent evil in state taxation." Similarly, the British jurist James Bryce observed the "serious evil" that accompanied not only the underassessment of property by local officials, but also "the fact that so large a part of taxable property escapes taxation." Referring to how the wealthy could conceal their "intangible wealth," Bryce note that these "difficulties help to explain the occasional bitterness of feeling among American farmers as well as the masses against capitalists, much of whose accumulated wealth escapes taxation, while the farmer who owns his land, as well as the workingman who puts his savings into the house he lives in, is assessed and taxed upon his visible property."[2]

As we have seen, reform-minded political economists like Richard T. Ely, Henry Carter Adams, and Edwin R. A. Seligman went even further, identifying how and why the property tax had become an anachronistic relic of a bygone era. "The general property tax as actually administered," Seligman explained with his characteristic aplomb, "is beyond all doubt one of the worst taxes known in the civilized world." It was a levy that "pressed hardest on those least able to pay," and no other fiscal institution had "evoked more angry protest," or "more earnest dissatisfaction." In 1909, new liberal journalist and public intellectual Herbert Croly expressed the view of most educated Americans when he concisely lamented that the property tax "has become both unjust and unproductive."[3]

[1] H. S. Wilson to Nils P. Haugen, September 1, 1910, Box 56, Nils P. Haugen Papers, State Historical Society of Wisconsin, Madison [hereinafter SHSW].

[2] Thomas M. Cooley, *Principles that Should Govern in the Framing of Tax Laws* (St. Louis: G. I. Jones, 1878), 14, 17; James Bryce, *The American Commonwealth*, Vol. I (London: Macmillan & Co., 1889), 209–10.

[3] Edwin R. A. Seligman, "The General Property Tax," *Political Science Quarterly* 5:1 (1890), 62; Edwin R. A. Seligman, *Essays in Taxation* (New York: Macmillan &

In many ways, the increasing social animus toward the general property tax paralleled the antagonism toward national import duties and excise taxes. The entire nineteenth-century fiscal system, in fact, seemed ill-equipped to deal with the growing demands of a nascent modern, regulatory, administrative, social-welfare state. The existing levies and assessment processes appeared insufficient to generate badly needed public revenue. The same broad, structural and demographic factors and key historical events that compelled national reformers and lawmakers to reconsider the existing federal tax system also forced many of these same activists to question the prevailing subnational fiscal regime. In fact, the modern forces of mass migration, rapid industrialization, and accelerating urbanization pressed hardest on state and local governments, especially during moments of economic crisis, such as the reoccurring financial panics that frequently triggered downturns in the business cycle.[4]

Similarly, the hastening rise of corporate capitalism aggravated the failings of both the tariff regime and the property tax. National activists persuasively pointed to protectionism as "the mother of all trusts" and thus as a driver of corporate consolidation.[5] Meanwhile, state and local reformers understood that the property tax's greatest flaw was its inability to reach new forms of wealth, like the growing salaries of corporate managers and intangible personal property such as stocks and bonds. Unlike real and visible property, which had been the backbone of the property tax for generations, the increasing prevalence of money incomes, corporate securities, and other financial assets meant that these new forms of personal property frequently went undetected and therefore untaxed. "The omission of this kind of property from assessment," the Wisconsin

Co., 1895), 61; Herbert Croly, *The Promise of American Life* (New York: Macmillan, 1909), 318.

[4] Jon Teaford, *The Rise of the States: Evolution of American State Government* (Baltimore: Johns Hopkins University Press, 2002); R. Rudy Higgens-Evenson, *The Price of Progress: Public Services, Taxation, and the American Corporate State, 1877–1929* (Johns Hopkins University Press, 2003); Morton Keller, *Affairs of State: Public Life in Late Nineteenth Century America* (Cambridge, Mass.: Harvard University Press, 1977), 319–42, 538–41; Clifton K. Yearley, *The Money Machines: The Breakdown and Reform of Governmental and Party Finance in the North, 1860–1920* (Albany: SUNY Press); Glenn W. Fisher, *The Worst Tax? A History of the Property Tax in America* (Lawrence: University Press of Kansas, 1996).

[5] "Mr. Havemeyer, The Tariff, and the Trust," *Literary Digest* (June 24, 1899), 720; Kevin Phillips, *Wealth and Democracy: A Political History of the American Rich* (New York: Random House, 2003), 242.

Tax Commission complained in 1898, "is perhaps the most noticeable of all defects in the administration of our tax laws."[6]

The continued underassessment of personal property had broad and profound implications. It not only decreased the supply of government revenues at a time when the demand for public goods and services was exploding; it also made compliance with the property tax highly arbitrary, capricious, and unfair. Consequently, the deteriorating property tax undermined the rule of law and popular faith in public power. Citizens had little confidence in a system riddled by corruption and malfeasance. Unsure whether their neighbors were paying their fair share of the property tax, many otherwise responsible Americans did little to reveal their own property holdings, however nominal, to the local tax assessor. As a result, the ineffectual property tax was fostering a culture of deceit that itself eroded civic engagement, democratic participation, and fiscal citizenship. If the stealth nature of the tariff and federal excise taxes disconnected citizens nationally from the general government, the failing property tax seemed to have a similar effect on the links between citizens and their state and local authorities.

Faced with these problems, tax activists understood that if they were to usher in a new fiscal order, they needed to address the myriad of issues related to the subnational tax system. State and local tax reform was, thus, a pivotal part of all three elements of the emerging modern American fiscal polity. First, by making the property tax fairer and more effective, reformers could reallocate the economic burdens of taxation in a more equitable manner. Second, by searching for new forms of direct and graduated subnational taxes, advocates for fiscal change could make taxation more salient for citizens and thereby reconfigure notions of fiscal citizenship. In the process, they could also restore trust in government, as they assuaged the traditional American aversion to centralized power. Finally, by improving the tax assessment process, they could create the administrative capacity that was at the heart of American political and economic development. Just as they did at the national level, economic experts led the way in educating lawmakers and concerned citizens about the need for a changed mindset about the basis for modern public finance – at all levels of government.

[6] Wisconsin Tax Commission, *Report of the Wisconsin State Tax Commission* (Madison, Wis.: Democrat Printing Co., 1898), 109–10. The Wisconsin commission, like nearly all other state commissions, also noted "frequent instances of an almost open and avowed practice of favoring particular interests and industries or classes of property." Ibid., 78.

Indeed, a new set of reform-minded political economists took up the intellectual campaign to transform the fiscal order by focusing mainly on state and local tax reform. Led by the likes of Thomas S. Adams, Charles J. Bullock, and Carl C. Phlen, progressive economic thinkers worked with the first generation of new school political economists, as well as with state builders and business leaders, both to advance the tax reform movement and to make it more suitable for American political culture. Following in the footsteps of the reform-minded economists who pioneered the study of public finance in the United States, this second cohort of theorists focused much of their initial energies on subnational tax reform. Together with their senior colleagues, they created professional organizations like the National Tax Association, which soon became the country's leading professional association of public finance scholars, state and local tax administrators, and concerned citizens interested in reforming American tax laws and policies.[7]

Although there was a great deal of conceptual similarity between national and subnational tax reform, there was one major practical difference. Whereas national activists and lawmakers sought to use new forms of direct and graduated levies as replacements for the existing indirect and regressive tax regime, reformers at the state and local level were loath, at least initially, to give up on a property tax that was traditionally designed as a fair and effective levy on wealth. Rather than abandon the general property tax, reformers and tax officials sought to salvage it through a number of institutional and administrative innovations. By improving the property tax instead of scrapping it, tax experts believed they could make the levy live up to its historical, egalitarian roots.

As historians have shown, revenue reformers adopted three main types of administrative improvements to try to save and improve the property tax. First, they attempted to rationalize the assessment process by centralizing it at the state – rather than the local – level. The creation of state tax commissions charged with supervising and disciplining local

[7] Yearley, *Money Machines*, 167–9, 187–91; Higgens-Evenson, *Price of Progress*, 68–9. For more on the history of the National Tax Association, see generally Albert Luther Ellis III, "The Regressive Era: Progressive Era Tax Reform and the National Tax Association – Roots of the Modern American Tax Structure" (Ph.D. dissertation, Rice University, 1991); Ferdinand P. Schoettle, "The National Tax Association Tries and Abandons Tax Reform, 1907–30" *National Tax Journal* 32 (1979), 429–44; Ajay K. Mehrotra and Joseph J. Thorndike, "From Programmatic Reform to Social Science Research: The National Tax Association and the Promise and Perils of Disciplinary Encounters," *Law & Society Review* 45:3 (2011), 593–630.

assessors and providing expert guidance on property valuations was one method that removed the assessment process from the ambit of locally elected or politically appointed officials and placed it in the realm of centralized, professional experts. Second, during the late nineteenth century, many states attempted to persuade owners of "hidden" personal property to reveal their new forms of wealth by "classifying" different types of personal property into distinct categories taxed at lower rates. This required not only revising revenue laws but also amending the "uniformity" clauses of many state constitutions. Finally, many states attempted to rescue the property tax by relegating it to the local level and seeking out new sources of revenue. Whereas the property tax was traditionally assessed and collected by both local and state governments with overlapping and often conflicting jurisdictions, the movement for "separating the sources" of the property tax was intended to rationalize and routinize the tax on real property exclusively as a local levy. Allowing the property tax to devolve to the local level, of course, forced many state governments to experiment with new sources of tax revenue, including levies on corporations and inheritances, as well as taxes on individual and business earnings.[8]

In the last quarter of the nineteenth century, many states also began thinking about tax policy as a regulatory tool, as a way to curb and monitor the emergence of Big Business. Over time, as the institutional pressures of fiscal federalism took hold, corporate taxes would become a challenging and controversial topic for state tax officials who were seeking to centralize taxing authority away from localities, while at the same time resisting and in some cases accommodating the growing dominance of federal fiscal powers.[9] Thus, many tax reformers, especially those who sat on state tax commissions, were eager to ensure that subnational administrative improvements inured only to the benefit of state governments – at least until the crisis of the Great War shattered the

[8] Jon Teaford has referred to these three particular developments – classification, centralization, and separation of sources – as the "triad of tax reforms." Teaford, *Rise of the States*, 47. While this chapter builds on the work of Teaford and others, the main focus is on how these administrative improvements not only paved the way for new sources of revenue, namely progressive taxes on incomes, profits, and inheritances; but also, more importantly, how subnational tax reform as a whole bolstered the central elements of a new fiscal order.

[9] On the importance of intergovernmental grants-in-aid to the development of the first New Federalism during this period, see Kimberly S. Johnson, *Governing the American State: Congress and the New Federalism, 1877–1929* (Princeton: Princeton University Press, 2007).

notion that state and local tax officials could arrest the expansion of the national fiscal state.[10]

The subnational administrative improvements to the property tax proved insufficient by themselves to meet the skyrocketing demand for public revenues. Indeed, the stubborn persistence of the property tax, at the local if not the state level, illustrated how even the dramatic transition to a new fiscal regime entailed accommodating, rather than simply replacing, previously existing political and economic arrangements. Still, the early administrative reforms meant to salvage the property tax created the institutional space for state governments to experiment with new revenue streams, particularly newly revived levies on individual and business income. In fact, Wisconsin's adoption of the first effective state-level income tax in 1911 not only became a model for many other states, it also helped shape national efforts to implement a graduated tax on individual incomes and business profits. In the end, pioneering progressive states like Wisconsin illustrated how subnational governments were not only essential "laboratories" of democratic reform, as Justice Louis Brandeis would later suggest, but also creative and productive factories of fiscal innovation.[11]

The Growing Dissatisfaction with the General Property Tax

Late-nineteenth-century reformers were reluctant to abandon the general property tax because it was historically a direct and highly symbolic levy on wealth. From the colonial era through the early Republic, as Treasury Secretary Oliver Wolcott Jr.'s 1796 survey demonstrated, a vast assortment of state and local taxes were levied on land, buildings, farm stock, and personal assets – all property owned mainly by the affluent and prosperous. The only thing that was more diverse than the types of

10 Given the rich diversity of subnational tax systems and regional differences in social and economic conditions, this chapter does not attempt to catalogue all tax reforms in every state or locality. Rather, the aim is to focus on those key changes in leading – mainly northern industrial – states and cities that are representative of turn-of-the-century subnational fiscal reform. For an interesting taxonomy of state-level public finance reforms throughout the United States in this time period, see generally, Higgens-Evenson, *Price of Progress.*

11 W. Elliot Brownlee, *Progressivism and Economic Growth: The Wisconsin Income Tax, 1911–1929* (Port Washington, N.Y.: Kennikat Press, 1974); *New State Ice Co. v. Liebmann*, 285 U.S. 262 (1932) (Brandeis, J., dissenting), 311. For more on the many ways in which states were "factories of reform," see Teaford, *Rise of the States*, and Morton Keller, *Regulating a New Economy: Public Policy and Economic Change in America, 1900–1933* (Cambridge, Mass: Harvard University Press, 1990).

property taxes enacted in this period was the radically different assessment and collection procedures used by various state and local governments. This administrative heterogeneity reflected differing regional political cultures and changing economic and social conditions.[12]

From the early Republic to the end of the nineteenth century, the property tax gradually became the main source of state and local public revenue. Once the federal Constitution prevented states and localities from taxing imports or exports, subnational government units were compelled to search for other sources of revenue. At first, states and commonwealths relied on several different types of funding beyond taxes, including revenue from land sales, tolls, and licensing fees. Although a variety of property taxes had been part of the statutes of most states, these taxes generated little revenue, accounting for only 30 percent of all state government revenues as late as the 1840s. But by the 1890s, an all-encompassing general property tax came to dominate subnational government revenues, generating over 50 percent of all state government revenues, and nearly 80 percent of all subnational revenue.[13] In subsequent decades, as state governments relegated the property tax to localities and began experimenting with other revenue streams, the percentage of property tax revenue began to decline steadily, just as state-level receipts from income and sales taxes started to climb (see Table 4.1).[14]

[12] Oliver Wolcott Jr., "Direct Taxes," December 14, 1796, in *American State Papers: Documents, Legislative and Executive of the United States*, 10 vols., comp. Walter Lowrie and Matthew St. Clair Clark (Washington, D.C.: Gales and Seaton, 1832–61); Alvin Rabushka, *Taxation in Colonial America* (Princeton: Princeton University Press, 2008); Robert A. Becker, *Revolution, Reform, and the Politics of American Taxation, 1763–1783* (Baton Rouge: Louisiana State University Press, 1980); Roger H. Brown, *Redeeming the Republic: Federalists, Taxation, and the Origins of the Constitution* (Baltimore: Johns Hopkins University Press, 1993). Frequently, a state's commitment to slavery determined the degree of democratic participation in fiscal policymaking, as well as the effectiveness of tax assessment and collection. Robin L. Einhorn, *American Taxation, American Slavery* (Chicago: University of Chicago Press, 2006).

[13] John Joseph Wallis, "American Government Finance in the Long Run: 1790–1990," *Journal of Economic Perspectives* 14:1 (winter 2000), 61–82. Wallis has shown how early-nineteenth-century state budgets were funded mainly by "asset income," or revenues from "tolls on canals, dividends from bank stock, and revenues from land sales as well as indirect taxes on business." Ibid., 67.

[14] *Historical Statistics of the United States, Colonial Times to 1970, Part 2* (Washington, D.C.: Bureau of the Census, 1975), pp. 1106–8; U.S. Bureau of the Census, *Census of Governments, 1967 Vol. VI, No. 5* (Washington, D.C.: Government Printing Office, 1967); Jens Peter Jensen, *Property Taxation in the United States* (Chicago: University of Chicago Press, 1931), 2–3.

TABLE 4.1. *State and Local Government Receipts by Source, 1890–1932, as Percentage of Total*

	1890	1902	1913	1922	1927	1932
Property Tax	76%	67%	66%	64%	60%	57%
Licensing Fees	5%	6%	6%	5%	5%	6%
Income Taxes (Corporate and Individual)	–	–	–	2%	2%	2%
Sales Tax	–	3%	3%	3%	6%	10%
Other Taxes	–	12%	11%	9%	9%	10%
Miscellaneous General Revenue	19%	12%	15%	16%	18%	15%
Total	100%	100%	100%	100%	100%	100%

Source: Historical Statistics of the United States, Colonial Times to 1970, Part 2 (Washington, D.C.: Bureau of the Census, 1975), 1106–8; U.S. Bureau of the Census, *Census of Governments, 1967 Vol. VI, No. 5* (Washington, D.C.: Government Printing Office, 1967); *Report on Wealth, Debt and Taxation at the Eleventh Census: 1890 Part II, Valuation and Taxation* (Washington, D.C.: Government Printing Office, 1895), 412–13.

The Rise and Fall of the General Property Tax

The late-nineteenth-century dominance of the property tax was due in part to the gradual consolidation of revenue laws. Over time, the myriad of different types of special levies on property became subsumed under the rubric of a "general property tax." Rather than tax different types of property at various rates, the general property tax was intended, at least in theory, to tax all property universally at a uniform rate, with limited exceptions. The commitment to a universal property tax base and a uniform rate resonated with common understandings of fairness; it was seen by many as a fiscal expression of democratic equality.

The general property tax, moreover, was viewed by tax experts as an embodiment of the ability-to-pay principle. For economic theorists like Carl C. Plehn, a University of California at Berkeley professor who was the leading authority on California public finance, property traditionally represented an accurate measure of an individual's ability to support the state and society. Like Seligman and the progressive public finance economists, Plehn was a student of the German historical school. Thus, while he ascribed to the ability-to-pay theory, he recognized that changing historical conditions altered the practical means for capturing a citizen's taxpaying ability. By the late nineteenth century, Plehn explained, "property forms but one of the many indices of ability."[15]

Because of the vast diversity of property taxes, the process of consolidating existing rules into a general property tax was methodically incremental. Reaching back to their colonial heritage, Northeastern states began revising their tax laws in the mid-1800s to expand the property tax base and simplify rate structures. In the early 1850s, Connecticut combined its multiple levies on real and personal property into one general property tax that established a single rate of 3 percent for all property. Neighboring states such as New York, Massachusetts, and Pennsylvania made similar efforts to rationalize the property tax into one broad and simple levy. So too did Western states like California, which in its 1879 constitution and subsequent revenue laws broadened the general property tax base to include the net value of mortgages, or what many contemporaries referred to as "credits." Earlier, antebellum Southern states had also begun the process of adopting "uniformity" clauses to their constitutions not to broaden the tax base but to preserve the power of slaveholding elites.[16]

The movement for a general property tax as a replacement for special and assorted levies on property seemed to peak in the Midwest. States like Illinois and Ohio not only enacted statutes in the mid-nineteenth century calling for the consistent taxation of all real and personal property, they also added clauses to their state constitutions requiring uniform and universal property taxation. These provisions were frequently a reaction to the inequities stemming from the granting of special tax privileges to antebellum business corporations such as financial institutions. In 1848, Illinois's second state constitution empowered the General Assembly to levy "a tax by valuation, so that every person and corporation shall pay

[15] Carl C. Plehn, "The General Property Tax in California," *American Economic Association Economic Studies* 2:3 (1897), 111–97, 121. Plehn approvingly cited to Seligman's scholarship and proudly self-identified himself as "an adherent of the faculty theory of taxation." Ibid. Carl C. Plehn, *Introduction to Public Finance* (New York: Macmillan Co., 1896), 83–5. Carl C. Plehn to E. R. A. Seligman, January 26th, 1895; April 27th, 1895; November 19, 1895, Catalogued Correspondence, Edwin R. A. Seligman Papers, Rare Book and Manuscript Collection, Butler Library, Columbia University, New York, N.Y.

[16] Benson, "A History of the General Property Tax," 43–4; John Christopher Schwab, "History of the New York Property Tax," *Publications of the American Economic Association* 5:5 (1890), 17–108; Charles J. Bullock, "The Taxation of Property and Income in Massachusetts," *Quarterly Journal of Economics* 31:1 (November 1916), 1–61; Plehn, "General Property Tax in California," 126–7; Einhorn, *American Taxation, American Slavery*, 207–50.

a tax in proportion to the value of his or her property." Although the Illinois law that followed the constitutional revision exempted property held by governmental units and religious and charitable organizations, it technically levied a tax on "all real and personal property in the state," which included "the value of agricultural tools, implements, and machinery." The law, moreover, provided that all personal property, including "all moneys, credits, bonds or stocks and other investments" be assessed at "fair cash value."[17]

Ohio's 1851 constitution was even more specific: "Laws shall be passed taxing by a uniform rule all moneys, credits, investments in bonds, stocks, joint-stock companies or otherwise; and also all real and personal property, according to its true value in money."[18] The law, following the constitutional amendment, was even more detailed, requiring individuals and corporations to list and verify by oath the value of sixteen types of taxable property:

> the number of horses, ... cattle, ... mules and asses, ... sheep, ... hogs, ... pleasure carriages (of whatever kind), ... the total value of all articles of personal property, ... the number of watches, ... piano-fortes, ... the average value of the goods and merchandise which a person is required to list as a merchant, ... the value of property which such a person is required to list as a banker, broker, or stock-jobber, ... the average value of the materials and manufactured articles which such person is required to list as a manufacturer, ... moneys on hand, or on deposit subject to order, ... the amount of all moneys invested in bonds, stocks, joint stock companies, annuities, or otherwise.[19]

With this nearly exhaustive catalog, Ohio's property tax revenues skyrocketed in the short term. Between 1851 and 1853, property tax receipts nearly doubled from $4.9 million to $8.8 million, as the value of assessed personal property climbed from $116 million to $230 million. Given this immediate success, other states soon followed Illinois and Ohio, in some cases even copying property tax provisions verbatim.[20]

[17] Illinois Constitution (1848), Article IX, Section 2; Robert Murray Haig, *A History of the General Property Tax in Illinois* (Urbana; University of Illinois Press, 1914), 94–7; *Revised Statutes of the State of Illinois*, Chapter 120, Revenue, Sections 1, 3, 25 (Chicago: Chicago Legal News Co., 1883).

[18] Ohio Constitution (1851), Article XII, Section 2; Jensen, *Property Taxation in the United States*, 44–5.

[19] Benson, "History of the General Property Tax," 48–52.

[20] Oliver C. Lockhart, "Assessment of Intangible Property in Ohio under the Uniform Rule," *Proceedings of the Seventh Annual Conference of the National Tax Association* (Madison, Wis.: National Tax Association, 1913), 74–5; Haig, *History of the General Property Tax in Illinois*, 38.

Initially, some states may have been able to generate sufficient revenues from the general property tax. But by the last decades of the nineteenth century the levy appeared incapable of keeping up with the growing demands precipitated by the modern forces of industrial capitalism. As the demographic and structural pressures of urban industrialism mounted, state and local officials faced pressures to improve the existing infrastructure and provide more and better public goods and services. At the same time, the general property tax had become deeply embedded in patronage politics, and hence the levy was grossly inefficient in raising adequate revenue in a fair or effective manner.

Caught between an increasing demand for government services and a decreasing supply of public revenue, states and localities were forced to take on enormous levels of debt to balance their budgets. In some cases, rising debt levels were a sign of increased creditworthiness, but the increased debt created even greater demand-side pressure in the form of annual interest payments. The financial squeeze came to a head in the 1890s when the economic depression not only exacerbated both ends of the fiscal dilemma, but also compelled policymakers to reconsider the existing system of public finance. Some sought to constrain the increasing size of government, while others attempted to reform the property tax and search for alternative forms of financing.

Demand-Side Pressures

Between 1880 and 1900, the two greatest spending demands on subnational governments were for education and the care of dependents. Although the movement for free public schools originated earlier in the century, by the 1870s many states – led by California and New York – had begun the process of establishing a comprehensive system of common school funding supported mainly by state property taxes. Once in place, state expenditures on free public education grew rapidly. In California, for example, real per capita spending on common schools increased from \$2.69 in 1880 to \$4.60 by 1900. New Jersey witnessed a similar rise, with real per capita spending climbing from \$1.35 to \$3.48 over the same period. States were not alone in footing big educational bills. In Massachusetts, Illinois, Wisconsin, and several other states, local taxes increasingly became the main source of educational spending, especially once the property tax became consigned to towns and counties.[21]

[21] Higgens-Evenson, *Price of Progress*, 27–9; Fletcher Harper Swift, *A History of Public Permanent Common School Funds in the United States, 1795–1905* (New York: Henry Holt & Co., 1911).

After education, the second largest discretionary expenditure in this period was for the general welfare of what contemporaries referred to as the "indigent insane." Frequently classified as spending on "insane asylums," or "charitable and penal institutions," these state-level expenditures were more sporadic throughout the country and significantly lower than educational spending. Nevertheless, in states like New York, which was a leader in mental health reform, spending on indigent care accounted for a significant portion of the annual budget. During the 1890s, when the Empire State led the nation in consolidating local dependent-care institutions, state spending on asylums skyrocketed. By 1897, New York spent more than any other state or commonwealth in the country on care for the indigent, with roughly $0.80 per capita devoted to such expenditures.[22]

While states were tending mainly to schools and social-welfare institutions, local governments throughout the country were using their discretionary property tax revenues to manage the multitude of other issues that accompanied the rise of urban industrialism. Like the states that created them, municipal corporations were burdened throughout the last decades of the nineteenth century with annual debt payments, which frequently accounted for roughly a quarter of most large cities' annual budgets.[23] Besides debt payments, cities and other minor civil units were responsible for providing the public goods and services that most ordinary Americans had come to rely on: water and sewer mains, streets and bridges, mass transport and sanitation, police and fire protection, libraries, and in many cases local schools.[24] New York City, for instance, spent an increasing amount of its annual budget in the 1880s and '90s on parks, street cleaning, and public works. Likewise, Chicago and Philadelphia could boast that their public sector spending rivaled the grand old municipalities of Europe. Even in less urban areas, American towns and municipalities competed to demonstrate their commitment to public works and economic growth. During these halcyon days of local promotion, as historian David Thelen has shown, "boosters of each city believed that the best way to guarantee prosperity in the future was to create the state's

[22] Higgens-Evenson, *Price of Progress*, 34–7.

[23] Eric H. Monkkonen, *The Local State: Public Money and American Cities* (Stanford: Stanford University Press, 1995).

[24] By the end of the nineteenth century, municipal special assessment taxes – based on the benefits theory – were becoming increasingly rare, and thus localities relied more on general property tax revenues. For more on nineteenth-century special assessment property taxes, see Robin L. Einhorn, *Property Rules: Political Economy in Chicago, 1833–1872* (Chicago: University of Chicago Press, 1991); Stephen Diamond, "The Death and Transfiguration of Benefit Taxation: Special Assessments in Nineteenth-Century America," *Journal of Legal Studies* 12:2 (1983), 201–41.

smoothest streets, fastest transportation system, most efficient garbage removal, biggest schools, and best fire and police protection."[25]

Shrinking Supply and the Fiscal Mismatch

As the demands on state and local budgets were mounting, the potential supply of public revenue was gradually diminishing. As we have seen, the general property tax was riddled with flaws. Many saw the distributional impact of the tax as unfair because it was more likely to tax those with real and visible property, such as farmers and rural residents, than those who held their wealth in cash or intangible personal property. In the process of taxing real property – mainly land – state and local governments were in a sense harnessing the public sector's role in identifying and enforcing capitalist property rights. Real property was more "legible" to the state, though problems of accurate valuation persisted. By contrast, taxing personal property required a great deal of intrusion to make it "legible." Cash salaries, household goods, and particularly intangible assets were much more difficult to locate, assess, and tax.[26]

Many commentators also believed that the defective and unreliable assessment of property taxes fostered a culture of duplicity that undermined democratic values and confidence in public power. Because the general property tax relied on taxpayers to reveal and verify all their property holdings, including their true salaries and the fair market value of their financial assets, and because locally elected or politically appointed assessors had little incentive or skill in taxing property accurately, tax evasion was rampant in the late nineteenth century. "Before the enactment of Prohibition," one historian has noted, "probably nothing in American life entailed more calculated or premeditated lying than the general property tax."[27]

[25] Edward D. Durand, *The Finances of New York City* (New York: Macmillan Co., 1898), 292, 384 (Diagram E). From 1876 to 1896, annual spending in New York City on street cleaning increased over fourfold, spending on public parks rose over threefold, and spending on public works more than doubled. Ibid., 292. Jon C. Teaford, *The Unheralded Triumph: City Government in America, 1870–1900* (Baltimore: Johns Hopkins University Press, 1984), 217–50; David Thelen, *The New Citizenship: Origins of Progressivism in Wisconsin, 1885–1900* (Columbia: University of Missouri Press, 1972), 247.

[26] Yearley, *Money Machines*, 74–5. James C. Scott, *Seeing Like a State: How Certain Schemes to Improve the Human Condition Have Failed* (New Haven: Yale University Press, 1998), 23–4.

[27] Keller, *Affairs of State*, 322–24; Yearley, *Money Machines*, 41.

TABLE 4.2. *State and Local Government Debt Levels, 1880–1927 (in millions of nominal dollars and as percent of all public debt)*

Year	State Debt	State Debt as % of All Public Debt	Local Debt	Local Debt as % of All Public Debt	All Public Debt
1880	$297	9.2%	$826	25.7%	$3,213
1890	228	10.1%	905	40.1%	2,255
1902	230	7.0%	1,877	57.1%	3,285
1913	379	6.8%	4,035	72.0%	5,607
1922	1,131	3.4%	8,978	27.1%	33,072
1927	1,971	5.9%	12,910	38.7%	33,393

Source: Historical Statistics of the United States: Millennial Edition, ed. Susan B. Carter et al. (New York: Cambridge University Press, 2006), 5-83–5-90, Table Ea588–593; John Joseph Wallis, "American Government Finance in the Long Run: 1790 to 1990," *Journal of Economic Perspectives* 14:1 (winter 2000), 61–82, Table 2, 66.

The property tax's greatest drawback, at least from the perspective of progressive reformers, was its crucial link to patronage politics. As the "money machine" for a state of "courts and parties," the property tax was a central institutional impediment to the development of effective and efficient, administrative statecraft. While these drawbacks may have been tolerable in earlier times, the turn-of-the-century pressure for greater public revenue exacerbated the levy's many foibles. The general property tax, in sum, seemed to have outlived its usefulness. It was, as Seligman aptly explained, "a relic of mediaevalism... foredoomed to failure."[28]

One sign of the dramatic mismatch between the increasing demand for subnational spending and the decreasing supply of revenue was the tremendous increase in state and local borrowing that occurred at the turn of the century. With municipal governments leading the way, subnational debt levels escalated. Whereas state and local government debt accounted for only about 35 percent of all government borrowing in 1880, that figure jumped to roughly 50 percent by 1890 and nearly 65 percent by 1902. Within this category, local debt accounted for approximately one-quarter of all public borrowing in 1880, and more than 57 percent by 1902 (see Table 4.2).

Rising municipal debt at the turn of the century was a reflection not only of increased demand for public goods and services, but also of the growing creditworthiness of local governments. This trend continued until World War I placed tremendous pressure on federal government

[28] Seligman, *General Property Tax*, 56.

debt. Because cities bore the brunt of public borrowing and spending, they were also the government entities that had to cope with the chaos of the budgeting process, trying to match limited revenues with growing spending demands. With debt levels rising and budgets in turmoil, state and local officials were eager to improve their existing revenue systems and experiment with new forms of taxation.[29]

Given the prominence of the property tax for subnational revenues and its salience to taxpayers, it is hardly surprising that economic experts and concerned citizens tried to improve this levy as part of their broader efforts to transform the prevailing fiscal regime. The resurgent popularity of Henry George's single tax at the turn of the century, furthermore, placed added pressure on those reformers who wanted to abandon the property tax completely. Although the single tax gained traction only in particular locales such as in the Pacific Northwest, George's stinging indictment of land speculators made it difficult for activists and lawmakers to abandon property-based taxation, despite its increasingly obvious weaknesses. Thus, before government officials experimented with alternative sources of new revenue, they attempted to salvage the general property tax.[30]

Salvaging the Property Tax

At first, policymakers tried to make the property tax live up to its egalitarian roots by seeking to increase taxpayer compliance. Early attempts ranged from mere jawboning by tax officials to the more creative and highly coercive practice of outsourcing tax investigations to private parties. Throughout the late nineteenth century, tax officials attempted to use the authority of their government offices to persuade taxpayers of their

[29] Wallis, "American Government Finance in the Long Run: 1790 to 1990," Table 2, 66; John B. Legler, Richard E. Sylla, and John Joseph Wallis, "U.S. City Finances and the Growth of Government, 1850–1902," *Journal of Economic History* 48:2 (1988), 347–56; Jonathan Kahn, *Budgeting Democracy: State Building and Citizenship in America, 1890–1928* (Ithaca: Cornell University Press, 1997), 8–15.

[30] Arthur N. Young, *The Single Tax Movement in the United States* (Princeton: Princeton University Press, 1916); John L. Thomas, *Alternative America: Henry George, Edward Bellamy, Henry Demarest Lloyd and the Adversary Tradition* (Cambridge, Mass.: Belknap Press, 1983). For more on the popularity of the single-tax in the Pacific Northwest, see, Robert D. Johnston, *The Radical Middle-Class: Populist Democracy and the Question of Capitalism in Progressive Era Portland, Oregon* (Princeton: Princeton University Press, 2003), 159–76.

civic duties. Recall that Richard Ely frequently praised the 1875 Massachusetts State Tax Commission because it explicitly maintained the primacy of the state over the individual, as it attempted to cajole citizens to meet their tax obligations.[31] Other state and local officials tried similar tactics. In Ely's own 1888 supplement to the Report of the Maryland Tax Commission, he appealed to the "conscientious convictions" of a citizen's "duty to the commonwealth" to "pay taxes on their personalty."[32]

The Ohio Experiment with Tax Inquisitors

When such public pleading fell on deaf ears – as it frequently did – some tax authorities took more creative measures. In the 1880s, Ohio empowered several of its largest and leading counties to hire external, private investigators or "tax inquisitors" to counter evasion. An 1888 statute extended the scope of the law permitting all counties "to employ any person to make inquiry and furnish the county auditor the facts as to any omissions of property for taxation and the evidence necessary to authorize him to subject to taxation any property improperly omitted" from the tax rolls. The Ohio legislature singled out personal property as the main source of evasion. In fact, the compensation of inquisitors was tied directly to "the returns of omitted moneys, credits, investments in bonds, stocks, joint stocks, annuities, or other valuable interests." Using information provided by county assessors, private individuals like C. E. and Henry Morgentaler – two brothers who became leading tax investigators – set out to earn up to 20% (the legal limit) of all the delinquent state and local tax revenues they could help find and collect. Several other states and a few cities followed Ohio's lead in hiring "tax inquisitors" or "tax ferrets."[33]

[31] Richard T. Ely, *Taxation in American States and Cities* (assisted by John H. Finley) (New York: T. Y. Crowell & Co., 1888), 14, fn. 2 (quoting *Report of the Massachusetts Commissioners Appointed to Inquire into the Expediency of Revising and Amending the Law relating to Taxation and Exemption therefrom* [Boston: Wright & Porter, 1875]).

[32] "Supplementary Report by Dr. Ely," in *Report of the Maryland Tax Commission to the General Assembly January, 1888* (Baltimore: King Brothers, 1888), 103; Yearley, *Money Machines*, 47–8.

[33] Act of April 23, 1885, 66th General Assembly, Adjourned Session, 82 Ohio Laws 152; Act of April 10, 1888, 68th General Assembly, Regular Session, 85 Ohio Law 170–1; Thomas N. Carver, *Ohio Tax Inquisitor Law* (New York: American Economic Association, 1898); E. A. Angell, "Tax Inquisitor System of Ohio," *Yale Review* 5 (Feb. 1897), 355–8; Nicholas Parillo, *Against the Profit Motive: The Salary Revolution in American Government, 1780–1940* (New Haven: Yale University Press, 2013), Chapter 5.

Outsourcing parts of the tax information and collection process was, of course, nothing new. The ancient Athenians and Romans used "tax farming" as an effective, if at times abusive, way to raise revenue.[34] But in modern times, and in the New World, even the phrase "tax inquisitor" conjured up images of an omnipotent and ruthless Leviathan. This language in turn lent credence to those critics who feared that the income tax movement was the thin edge of an inquisitorial wedge. Ohio's unique blending of public and private authority also presaged the type of national corporatism or business-government cooperation that would take shape during and after the Great War. At the same time, it demonstrated to reformers the importance of insulating tax assessors from local politics. Because tax inquisitors were usually from outside of the counties that hired them, they were less likely to be prone to the pressures of local politics or social norms. And because they frequently were responsible for several counties, they developed professional expertise in the process of gathering important tax information. These two aspects of tax ferreting – insulation from local politics and the development of professional knowledge – would not be lost on tax reformers.[35]

Even so, for many progressive reformers, Ohio's so-called innovative method of tax investigation was hardly an improvement. "Such an invasion of the privacy of life is shocking to any one who appreciates the traditions of English liberty," recounted one former Ohio tax commissioner. Relying on the profit motives of private investigators also seemed to be in tension with appeals to civic virtue and the goal of developing reciprocal trust between the state and its citizens. Compelling individuals to pay property taxes through more punitive enforcement measures or greater extrinsic motivation led some tax officials to charge that Ohio's inquisitor system undermined the intrinsic motivation that loyal citizens might feel in paying taxes because they understood that it was part of their civic duty. The use of inquisitors was thus an affront "to men's honor"

[34] Carolyn Webber and Aaron Wildavsky, *A History of Taxation and Expenditure in the Western World* (New York: Simon and Schuster, 1986), 113–19; A. H. M. Jones, "Taxation in Antiquity," in A. H. M. Jones, *The Roman Economy: Studies of Ancient Economic and Administrative History* (Oxford: Oxford University Press, 1974), 151–86, 154–5; Margaret Levi, *Of Rule and Revenue* (Berkeley: University of California Press, 1988), Chapter 4. Unlike the earlier forms of "tax farming," the Ohio experiment was limited to using private investigators to uncover hidden property, rather than actually collect the tax. Carver, *Ohio Tax Inquisitor Law*.

[35] Parillo, *Against the Profit Motive*, Chapter 5.

and an assault on the significance of social bonds, ethical obligations, and trust in public power.[36]

Little wonder, then, that Ohio's tax inquisitor system bore little fruit. In the dozen or so years that it was in effect, it increased tax revenues only marginally, especially when one considers the steep bounties paid to the inquisitors. According to one set of estimates, the total assessed value of personal property in Ohio increased steadily from 1880 until 1893 when the ensuing economic recession dramatically affected all property values. In that period, the total assessed value of personal property rose from $456 million to $563 million. But the value of net mortgages or credits, arguably the largest and most difficult category of personal property to assess, only grew from $101 to $114 million during that same period.[37] A more careful look at the operations of tax inquisitors in Cuyahoga County (which includes Cleveland) reveals that during a twelve-year period roughly $840,000 of tax revenue was generated by private investigators, who earned over $240,000 for their services. The state thus netted only $600,000 over these dozen years. Such data led Ohio tax experts to conclude that even with the outsourcing of tax investigations, "the amount obtained is a mere bagatelle compared with that which escapes taxation."[38]

One reason for the mixed results of the Ohio inquisitor system was the ubiquity of political corruption. Although private tax investigators were intended to counter the dishonesty of taxpayers and the malfeasance of local assessors, the inquisitors themselves were frequently entangled in their own perfidy. The Morganthaler brothers, who held a virtual monopoly on government contracts for tax investigation in Cuyahoga County, were alleged to have received their information about the holders of stocks and bonds through bribes to leading corporations. Once this graft became public, fewer citizens were willing to put their

36 Angell, "Tax Inquisitor System in Ohio," 369–70. Present day public finance scholars have made similar arguments about how increasing external motivations with more punitive enforcement measures might "crowd out" internal motivations related to civic virtue. Bruno S. Frey, "A Constitution for Knaves Crowds Out Civic Virtues," *Economic Journal* 107:443 (July 1997), 1043–53.

37 Carver, *Ohio Tax Inquisitor Law*, 190–1.

38 Angell, "Tax Inquisitor System in Ohio," 370, 372; Yearley, *Money Machines*, 47. Despite the legal limit of 20 percent, creative and entrepreneurial tax inquisitors were frequently able to negotiate higher yields for their work. Angell, "Tax Inquisitor System in Ohio," 369.

faith in a system of tax rules and state power that was riddled with malfeasance.[39]

Even when private auditors operated honestly, the tax inquisitor system suffered from a fatal flaw: local assessors ultimately controlled the flow of information to and from private contractors. City and county tax officials decided which delinquent taxpayers were worthy of intense private investigation, and they determined what do to with the information provided by the inquisitors. Thus, as long as local assessors remained beholden to party bosses and the influence of special political interests, there was little hope that private firms could do much to disturb the status quo of underassessment. Party politics could not be so easily dislodged by private pecuniary incentives.[40]

Once reformers and government officials realized that tinkering with the existing collection system would not be enough to salvage the property tax, they turned to more fundamental changes to the substance and administration of their tax codes. Between 1880 and 1920, several states attempted to improve their respective property tax regimes by centralizing the assessment process at the state, rather than local, level; by classifying various types of property into different rate structures; and by dividing jurisdictional authority over different types of property between states and localities. These three central reforms did not necessarily evolve in any particular sequential order. Nor were any of them panaceas for the prevailing problems. But as a whole they not only reflected the general ethos of subnational tax reform at the turn of the century. They also helped facilitate a fundamental transformation in American experience with the developing system of public revenues.

Centralization

Tax reformers understood quite clearly that the *local* assessment of property was the primary reason for the administrative failures of the general property tax. Locally elected or politically appointed assessors did not have the autonomy or the temerity to value their neighbors' property accurately. Nor did many of them have the expert financial knowledge to appraise certain types of property, like corporate assets, which often

39 Carver, *Ohio Tax Inquisitor Law*, 182–7. For more on the allegations of tax ferret abuse and the root causes and consequences of their rise and fall, see Parillo, *Against the Profit Motive*, Chapter 5.

40 Carver, *Ohio Tax Inquisitor Law*, 182–7; Ernest L. Bogart, *Financial History of Ohio* (Urbana, Ill.: University Press, 1912), 241.

stretched across several different local jurisdictions. Consequently, the highly diverse practices of municipal and county assessors undermined state lawmakers' attempts to standardize and rationalize property assessments. And, of course, the growing amount of intangible wealth only seemed to exacerbate these problems. For some experts, the assessment process and not the tax base was the crucial – and nearly hopeless – linchpin to any type of fundamental fiscal reform. As the Harvard economist and Massachusetts tax reformer Charles Bullock succinctly put it: "Under a purely local system of administration, there never was and never will be a generally satisfactory assessment of either income or property."[41]

Others concurred, pointing to the broad implications of ineffective, decentralized assessments. Thomas S. Adams, a political economist at the University of Wisconsin who was one of Ely's former students and his first external hire at Madison, became one of the leading supporters of greater state supervision of property tax assessments. As a member of the Wisconsin State Tax Commission, Adams focused on how the political nature of local assessments fostered a culture of deceit among taxpayers, and in the process undermined faith in good government and the rule of law. Whereas many tax officials believed that the dishonesty of taxpayers was the main cause of undervaluation, Adams contended that a lax and corrupt system of local assessment was the true culprit. "The American taxpayer is the most maligned creature in all the annals of fiction," proclaimed Adams. "He has been compared, confused and used synonymously with the liar. As a matter of fact, when confronted with an equitable tax and a fearless assessor, he is amazingly honest. It is the locally elected property assessor, bent on conciliating voters and on keeping his own underpaid job, who has demoralized the American property tax and made it in the past a by word for chicanery, inefficiency and inequality."[42]

For reformers like T. S. Adams, the ineffectiveness of locally assessed property taxes had profound distributional and political implications. "The statute under which taxation is now carried on is really class legislation, molded in favor of the possessors of intangible property," Adams informed Wisconsin legislators. "The smaller property-owners bear the

[41] Charles J. Bullock, "The State Income Tax and the Classified Property Tax," in *Proceedings of the Tenth Annual Conference under the Auspices of the National Tax Association* (New Haven: National Tax Association, 1917), 369; Teaford, *Rise of the States*, 47–9.

[42] T. S. Adams, "The Significance of the Wisconsin Income Tax," *Political Science Quarterly* 28 (December 1913): 569–85, 575.

whole burden." The inequitable application of the property tax fostered a pervasive environment of deceit and distrust. "We all engaged in the scramble," Adams charged. "Democracy is failing in one of the most important phases of government – that of collecting the necessary revenues in an equitable manner. It might be termed a great conspiracy, in which democracy corrupts its citizens and, in turn, is corrupted." Citizens were losing faith in their so-called self-governing, local institutions. And that loss of faith was only further undermining a positive culture of taxpayer compliance.[43]

To counter the defects of local property assessments, reformers turned to permanent state tax commissions to centralize administrative procedures. State commissions had a rich, historical heritage. They had existed throughout the nineteenth century in Northern states as temporary, investigative bodies charged with gathering data about the actual workings of the general property tax. By collecting abundant proof of the failings of the property tax, and by outlining new collection methods introduced by neighboring states, these temporary commissions provided "advisory suggestions" to their state legislatures, including ways to rationalize and simplify existing tax laws and calls for more frequent and precise methods of valuation. Yet, the early temporary commissions lacked any direct supervision over the process of local assessments; they were merely ephemeral reporting agencies.[44]

The first sign of change came in the 1890s, when Indiana created the first permanent state tax commission with executive influence over local assessments. The Hoosier State's pioneering efforts, which were soon copied by other states, grew out of the general, modern tendency toward administrative consolidation.[45] To be sure, citizens wedded to local autonomy looked upon centralization with some suspicion. They noted that it was frequently state tax administrators, eager to enhance their own power and prestige, who were the most forceful advocates for centralization. Still, tax experts throughout the country contended that

[43] "Praise Income Tax," *Milwaukee Journal*, May 24, 1911; "Income Tax Hearing," (Milwaukee) *Evening Wisconsin*, May 24, 1911.

[44] James W. Chapman, *State Tax Commissions in the United States* (Baltimore: Johns Hopkins Press, 1897), 89; Seligman, *Essays in Taxation*, 609–21.

[45] Sections, 115–30, "An Act Concerning Taxation," in *Laws of the State of Indiana, 57th Regular Session of the General Assembly*, January 1891; Donald W. Kiefer, *Indiana Public Finance, Past and Present: Report of the Commission on State Tax and Financing Policy* (Indianapolis: Indiana Commission on State Tax and Financing Policy, 1974), 14–15.

political and administrative concentration was a seemingly inevitable part of modern life. "The most striking feature of the present is the universal and rapid progress toward centralization of fiscal control," declared T. S. Adams. "And the banner of reform is being carried by the State Tax Commission."[46]

In Indiana, the reform banner contained two significant improvements. The 1891 statute, first, revised the status and authority of the county tax assessor. Whereas historically county assessors had nearly complete autonomy, after 1891 they became midlevel officials who operated below the guidance of state commissioners and above local members of the administrative machinery. The second, and perhaps more innovative reform, was the creation of a permanent state commission itself, which not only consolidated the operations of assessing corporate property and equalizing local assessments, but also supervised the entire tax system.[47] As part of its duties, the Indiana commission adjudicated appeals between taxpayers and local assessors. It also prescribed standardized forms and assessment procedures, organized an annual conference for local assessors, and occasionally visited counties to inspect local conditions and the work of assessors. In sum, the commission embodied Progressive-Era faith in the ability of professionals and expert knowledge to tame and discipline local partisan politics.[48]

Despite its ambitions, the Indiana State Tax Commission failed to live up to the expectations of most revenue reformers. While the changes enacted by the 1891 law led to significant, short-term improvements in property assessments, especially corporate property, which increased by nearly threefold between 1890 and 1891, the state commission ultimately lacked powerful authority over local assessments; it was given only the power of advisory supervision.[49] Consequently, the perennial

[46] T. S. Adams, "The Separation of the Sources of State and Local Revenues," *Journal of Political Economy* 16:1–12 (January 1908), 5; Harley L. Lutz, *The State Tax Commission: A Study of the Development and Results of State Control over the Assessment of Property for Taxation* (Cambridge, Mass.: Harvard University Press, 1918), 3–4.

[47] "An Act Concerning Taxation." See also Timothy E. Howard, "The Tax Law of 1891," in *Report of the Proceedings of the Annual Conference Convention of the State Board of Tax Commissioners and the County Assessors of the State of Indiana for the year Nineteen Hundred and Ten* (Indianapolis: State Printing and Binding, 1910), 32–40.

[48] "An Act Concerning Taxation"; William A. Rawles, *Centralizing Tendencies in the Administration of Indiana* (New York: Columbia University Press, 1903), 272–7.

[49] *Conference Convention of the County Assessors and the State Board of Tax Commissioners of the State of Indiana* (Indianapolis: State Printing and Binding, 1899).

problem of accurately assessing personal property, particularly intangible wealth, persisted – not only in Indiana but in nearly every state that adopted permanent tax commissions. Though the total assessment of personal property in Indiana increased by nearly 25 percent in 1891 alone, most commentators agreed that "the evasion of intangibles was but little affected by the administrative reforms." Other states that followed Indiana's lead witnessed similar fleeting and uneven success. As Harley Lutz, one of Bullock's former Harvard students, noted in his nearly exhaustive study of state tax commissions, "the figures for intangible personal property reveal most clearly the failure of the uniform rule, even under centralized administration. The total assessment of intangibles has usually stood still, or has increased but slowly, while many of the individual items have declined."[50]

The centralization of administrative authority did not single-handedly save the property tax, but it was a development that foreshadowed other innovations. In time, fiscal experts and lawmakers would realize that state commissions needed more than mere advisory supervision. Those states that began experimenting with new sources of revenue like the income tax quickly realized that they needed to bolster the powers of their central administrators. Vanguard states like Wisconsin soon learned that by transferring the authority for assessments from the ambit of local political amateurs to qualified state financial experts, they could strengthen nearly all aspects of tax administration.[51] But before reformers turned to new revenue streams backed by enhanced centralized authority, they attempted to rescue the property tax by ironically reverting back to the policies that existed before the movement for a uniform and universal general property tax – policies that taxed different classes of property at different rates.

Classification

Because the general property tax's greatest defect was its inability to reach intangible wealth, reformers and tax officials focused their efforts on rectifying this particular aspect of the prevailing subnational tax system. Some argued that intangible property, and perhaps even all personal property,

[50] Lutz, *State Tax Commission*, 181, 175, 632–3; Teaford, *Rise of the States*, 49.

[51] Raymond V. Phelan, "Centralized Tax Administration in Minnesota and Wisconsin," in *State and Local Taxation, First National Conference under the Auspices of the National Tax Association* (New York: Macmillan Co., 1908), 97–106.

ought to be excluded from state and local tax rolls.[52] More pragmatic reformers understood, however, that formally exempting personal property, or even just intangible assets, from taxation would raise the ire of important political constituencies, particularly farmers and owners of urban realty. Even though in practice these two groups probably bore the brunt of the existing property tax burden because personal property frequently escaped assessment, statutorily exempting personal property or intangible wealth could be seen as capitulating to moneyed interests. "The influence of the farmers and the owners of city reality," Bullock confidently predicted in 1909, "will long make the total exemption of intangible property a political impossibility."[53]

If exempting personal or intangible property was out of the question, the next best alternative was to provide taxpayers with a greater incentive to reveal such "hidden" wealth. After all, the quasi-voluntary nature of property assessments hinged, initially at least, on taxpayers accurately listing their personal and intangible wealth. Thus, reformers argued that by placing intangible assets into a separate category or class of property, and taxing that class at a lower rate, taxpayers would respond by revealing more of their intangible wealth. This, in turn, would lead to significantly higher amounts of assessed personal property, which would – or so the argument went – yield greater tax revenue, despite the lower classified rate. Ancillary benefits would soon follow: other classes of property would bear a less oppressive burden, capital would remain within the newly classified tax jurisdiction and new investments might flow in, and, perhaps most importantly, the new found honesty of holders of financial assets would restore faith in the rule of law and effective government. These advantages were all premised on the notion that it was better to tax some intangible wealth than to allow all of it to escape assessment. This expediency-based argument soon became the dominant rationale for the classification movement.[54]

[52] Simeon Leland, *The Classified Property Tax in the United States* (Boston: Houghton Mifflin Co., 1928), 131–2.

[53] Charles J. Bullock, "The Taxation of Intangible Property," in *State and Local Taxation, Second International Conference* (Columbus, Ohio: International Tax Association, 1909), 127–37.

[54] Charles J. Bullock, "A Classified Property Tax," in *State and Local Taxation, Third International Conference* (Columbus, Ohio: International Tax Association, 1910), 95–105; E. H. Wolcott, "Classification of Property for Purposes of Taxation," in *Proceedings of the National Tax Association* (Ithaca: National Tax Association, 1915), 346–57; Leland, *Classified Property Tax*, 131–2.

It was not the only justification, however. Public finance economists, like Charles Bullock, who was arguably the most active proponent of classification, provided even more sophisticated equity-based rationales – rationales that illustrated how notions of ability to pay and the faculty theory of taxation reached deep into subnational tax reform. In meeting after meeting with lawmakers, concerned citizens, and other tax experts, Bullock stressed that "it is under modern conditions imperative that we should classify property in a scientific manner and pass from a general to a classified property tax."[55] Building on the work of Seligman and Henry Carter Adams, Bullock explained that a "scientific manner" of classification entailed recognizing that different types of property held different economic capacities to contribute to the public good.

In their earlier scholarship, Seligman and H. C. Adams had raised doubts about income and property serving as practical proxies for the ability-to-pay principle. As we saw in the previous chapter, Adams was highly skeptical that an undifferentiated income tax could truly capture the diversity of individual economic powers and hence taxpaying capacities. And Seligman and Adams both had earlier questioned the accuracy of the theory underpinning the general property tax, namely that all property was identical and hence that "each possessor" of property had the same "relative duty to pay for the support of the State."[56]

Bullock went a step further. Not only did he reject the notion that all property was always and everywhere homogenous, he also advocated for classification in practical terms. Rather than appeal to the social conscience or moral probity of citizen-taxpayers, as some new school political economists were wont to do, Bullock framed the case for classification in a more commercial idiom. "Diversification of rates of taxation," he informed a gathering of the National Tax Association (NTA), "agrees with the ordinary business principle of adjusting charges and prices to 'what the traffic will bear.' No railroad charges as much for carrying logs as for carrying furniture, but the discrimination in favor of logs, by enabling that traffic to move, contributes to the revenue of the road and decreases the charges upon furniture and other traffic of higher grade." Similarly, Bullock reasoned, taxing intangibles at a lower rate would

[55] Bullock, "A Classified Property Tax," 98. Bullock to Seligman, April, 10, 1892; Feb. 27, 1919, Catalogued Correspondence, ERASP.

[56] Seligman, *Essays in Taxation*; Henry Carter Adams, *The Science of Finance: An Investigation of Public Expenditures and Public Revenues* (New York: Henry Holt and Co., 1905).

bring them onto tax rolls, possibly increasing revenues, and reducing the fiscal burden on real property.[57]

The reference to market pricing, and the use of the phrase "what the traffic will bear," was, to be sure, a strange inversion of the faculty principle. It did not reference the organic relationship between the individual and the state, nor did it emphasize the growing civic duty of the wealthy to pay their fair share of underwriting a modern, urban-industrial polity. Instead, the idea of "adjusting taxation to what property will bear" appealed to the pecuniary intuition of businessmen who dominated middle-class reform organizations like the NTA – in ideology, if not in numbers.[58] As a pragmatic reformer, with strong ties to the Boston Chamber of Commerce, Bullock understood that the ability-to-pay principle had to be reframed for different audiences. Though the link between taxpaying capacity and market price may have been theoretically tenuous, in practice it resonated with the constituency that many activists and fiscal experts were trying desperately to reach, namely middle-class and elite business leaders.[59]

By the early twentieth century, the classification movement was much more than an academic exercise. As Bullock noted in his NTA presentations, by 1907, the commonwealths of Pennsylvania and Maryland already had over a decade worth of experience in classifying and taxing intangibles at a lower rate. Pennsylvania, in fact, led the modern classification movement. In 1885, it adopted a fixed low rate for personal property including intangible assets such as mortgages, debts, notes, and stocks and bonds of foreign corporations. Other nearby states soon followed.[60] Connecticut enacted a similar low-rate tax in 1889, though it did so indirectly by charging a low registration fee for financial assets, a fee that exempted such assets from the higher property tax rolls. Maryland, expressly using Pennsylvania as a model, adopted its own low-rate

[57] Bullock, "A Classified Property Tax," 103–4. Bullock's relentless advocacy for classification seemed to influence even those tax commissioners and business representatives who were more ambivalent about moving away from uniform taxation. Arthur S. Dudley, "The Doctrine of Classification," in *Proceedings of the National Tax Association* (Madison, Wis.: National Tax Association, 1914), 351–63.

[58] Bullock, "A Classified Property Tax," 104; Ellis, "Regressive Era;" Yearley, *Money Machines*, 187–8.

[59] Charles J. Bullock to James McKibben, August 11, 1909, Folder 350–17, "Taxation – Federal Taxation on Corporate Earnings," Case 67, Boston Chamber of Commerce Collection, Baker Library Historical Collections, Harvard Business School, Boston, Mass.; E. H. Wolcott, "Classification of Property for Purposes of Taxation."

[60] Leland, *Classified Property Tax*.

classification system in 1896, though it applied only to the local, not the state, portion of the levy.[61]

Several other states and localities throughout the country mimicked these states. The details of the various classified taxes varied, of course, with some states adopting a partial system of classification that placed nearly all personal property in a lower rate, while others like Minnesota gradually implemented a more comprehensive classification system, whereby several different types of property were classified separately and taxed either at lower rates or with a lower percentage of assessment. By the mid-1920s, roughly sixteen states had one form of classification or another.[62]

For many states and commonwealths, moving to a classified system was a significant challenge. Recall that many had adopted constitutional provisions guaranteeing a uniform rate on all property as part of the rise of the general property tax movement. Such provisions prevented these states from experimenting with classification. Indeed, it was no coincidence that the leaders of the classification movement were two states (Pennsylvania and Connecticut) that did not have such constitutional restrictions.[63] In some cases, those states that resisted the earlier move toward constitutionalized uniform rates were also the ones able to convince their citizens to ratify constitutional amendments permitting classification. Other states were not nearly as successful: constitutional amendments failed in California, Illinois, Louisiana, Oregon, Ohio, and Utah in 1912 alone.[64]

Like centralization, the early success of classification proved to be limited. After Pennsylvania began the classification process, the assessment of personal property skyrocketed. Between 1885 and 1905, the total amount

[61] K. M. Williamson, "The Present Status of Low-Rate Taxation of Intangible Property," in *Proceedings of the Eighteenth Annual Conference on Taxation under the Auspices of the National Tax Association*, (New York: National Tax Association, 1926), 90–128; Fred R. Fairchild, "Registration Taxes on Intangibles, with Special Reference to the Connecticut Chose-in-Action Tax," in *Proceedings of the National Tax Association* (New York: National Tax Association 1920), 152–62.

[62] J. G. Armson, "Two Years' Experience in Minnesota with the Three-Mill Tax on Money and Credits," in *Conference on State and Local Taxation, Sixth Annual Conference, Under the Auspices of the National Tax Association* (Madison, Wis.: National Tax Association, 1913), 239–48; Leland, *Classified Property Tax*; Teaford, *Rise of the States*, 48.

[63] Leland, *Classified Property Tax*, 297, 315.

[64] Ibid., 85.

of assessed personal property in Pennsylvania climbed from roughly $145 million to over $885 million, a sixfold increase. Much of this early success was due to the increasing assessment of intangible wealth, which was aided by a crude and early form of withholding.[65] By 1909, the Keystone State could boast that its assessment of intangibles was about one-half the value of real property assessments, a figure that dwarfed other states. With its highly sophisticated and comprehensive classification system, Minnesota may have been the most successful model of the classification movement. Within two years of its implementation, Minnesota's comprehensive classification system yielded nearly a tenfold increase, as the value of assessed "money and credits" rose from about $14 million in 1910 to just under $136 million by 1912.[66]

Not all states, however, enjoyed such success. Although classifying property may have increased the tax base, such increases did not always counteract or offset the lower rate of classified property. In other words, states and localities were not adequately compensated for their efforts to nudge more personal property onto assessment rolls. Even when they were, many taxpayers still continued to shroud their personal property. States like Pennsylvania and Minnesota could claim that their citizens understood that with lower rates, there was less of an incentive to conceal intangible wealth. But not all citizens in those states or elsewhere reacted similarly to such incentives. In Iowa, the total yield of low-rate taxes on moneys and credits actually declined from 1910 to 1921. Classification might have reduced tax evasion, but it certainly did not eliminate it. As a result, property tax revenues decreased in several states that followed the classification movement.[67]

Still, many experts agreed that classification, like centralization, was a necessary early step in the overall trend toward progressive tax reform. "Classification is not a panacea for all the ills of state and location taxation," wrote the University of Chicago political economist Simeon E.

65 John A. Smull et al., *Smull's Legislative Handbook and Manual for the State of Pennsylvania* (Harrisburg, Penn.: Harrisburg Publishing Co., 1907), 705; Williamson, "Present Status of Low-Rate Taxation of Intangible Property," 91–4; Leland, *Classified Property Tax*, 301, Table 55.

66 Williamson, "Present Status of Low-Rate Taxation of Intangible Property," 90–128, 99, 102, 112; Armson, "Two Years' Experience in Minnesota with the Three-Mill Tax on Money and Credits," 242–3.

67 Fairchild, "Registration Taxes on Intangibles," 160–2; Williamson, "Low-Rate Taxation of Intangible Property," 113; Teaford, *Rise of the States*, 49.

Leland, a leading advocate of the classification movement, "but it is an essential element in a tax system which shall conform to the highest attainable standards of equity and expediency developed by American taxation experience."[68]

Separation of Sources

In addition to classification and centralization, fiscal experts also advocated that states and localities divide control over the property tax as a way to salvage the levy. In most parts of the country, states and localities frequently shared the property tax as a main source of revenue. This overlapping and often conflicting jurisdictional authority led to two primary problems. First, the local diversity of levies and assessment procedures meant that property owners potentially faced a variety of taxes on the same set of property. This was particularly troublesome for large business corporations whose operations spanned across local and even state lines, and who became the most vociferous critics of "multiple taxation." Unsurprisingly, local political machines frequently exploited these business concerns by extracting payments in exchange for underassessment and other forms of intentional neglect.[69]

The second, perhaps more significant, drawback was the structural and economic incentive that local officials had to under assess property in their jurisdiction. State property tax liabilities were apportioned by the property values established by local assessors. When local tax officials under/assessed property for state tax purposes, they ensured that their constituents bore a lighter state burden. "Local assessors," explained Lawson Purdy, a New York lawyer and one of the founding members of the NTA, "were induced to make low assessments in order to save their own localities from paying a proper share of revenue to the State." As a result, they essentially shifted a portion of the state levy onto other counties and townships. This, of course, meant that every locality had an incentive to keep assessments as low as possible. A "race to the bottom" ensued, and nearly every county and township competed with its neighbors to set a low, but plausible, assessment of local property. Initially, state boards of equalization and then later state tax commissions

[68] Leland, *Classified Property Tax*, 419.

[69] Theodore Sutro, "Double and Multiple Taxation," in *State and Local Taxation, Second International Conference* (Columbus, Ohio: International Tax Association, 1909), 547–57; Yearley, *Money Machines*.

were established to try to correct this problem, but these administrative improvements, by themselves, were less than satisfactory.[70]

A more robust remedy to the shortcomings of a shared property tax base was to separate or segregate revenue sources between states and localities. Hailed by leading experts like Seligman as "the first and most important step" in subnational fiscal reform, separation of revenue sources soon became the most popular and the most scrutinized method of salvaging the property tax.[71] By divorcing the revenue base and relegating the property tax to localities, reformers contended, state governments could be liberated to tap more appropriate revenue sources such as business corporations, which not only owed their existence to state legislatures, but also frequently operated across local jurisdictions. Although some of the early state tax commission reports gestured toward the separation of sources, it was not until the turn of the century that the movement gained momentum.[72]

In an essay published in 1894, Henry Carter Adams set out a blueprint for the fiscal division of revenue sources among national, state, and local governments. Using data from the 1890 census as a measure of the relative spending of the different levels of government, Adams suggested that the property tax ought to be the main source of revenue exclusively reserved for localities, and that states should resort to levies on corporations. Though Adams conceded that "segregation of the sources of revenue is by no means a novel idea," he presciently observed that it would have great appeal among Americans because it resonated with constitutional notions of fiscal federalism.[73]

Indeed, separation of sources did appeal to many Americans. It did so not only because of its inherent similarity to other aspects of federalism, but because it provided solace both for proponents of local autonomy, or what contemporaries referred to as "home rule" or the "local option," as well as those who favored administrative centralization. By making the property tax the exclusive purview of localities, separation would

70 Lawson Purdy, "Outline of a Model System of State and Local Taxation," in *State and Local Taxation, First National Conference*, 54–74, 56; Bryce, *American Commonwealth, Vol. I*, 107–9; Teaford, *Rise of the States*, 51–2.

71 Seligman, "Tax Reform in the United States," in *Proceedings of the Ninth Annual Conference under the Auspices of the National Tax Association* (Ithaca: National Tax Association, 1915), 186–98.

72 Yearley, *Money Machines*, 194.

73 Henry Carter Adams, "Suggestions for a System of Taxation," *Michigan Political Science Association Publications* 1:2 (May 1894), 49–74. Adams later elaborated on this essay in a chapter in his public finance treatise. Adams, *Science of Finance*, 489–506.

eliminate the local incentive for underassessment. At the same time, separation of sources would grant townships and counties the freedom to assess property without competing pressures to keep assessments low. In the absence of a state property tax, low local assessments would simply lead to higher local rates to raise the required funds; no one county or municipality would benefit from assessing property below its fair market value. Without having to look over their shoulders at state authorities, moreover, local officials would have complete control over local property taxes. "The simplest plan indeed," wrote Seligman, "is to have a separation of state and local taxation, with local option on the part of the localities to tax or to exempt from taxation whatever classes of property they see fit." As H. C. Adams – a lingering skeptic of centralized authority – concluded, separation "would tend to decentralize political power and, consequently may be regarded as in harmony with the development of local self-governance."[74]

Proponents of centralization welcomed the notion of states and commonwealths abandoning the property tax to localities, and focusing on more effective means of revenue. Iowa State University political economist John Brindley bristled at how counties in the Hawkeye State ruthlessly competed for shares of railway taxes. By consolidating corporate taxes at the state level, Brindley believed Iowa could rid itself of such local predatory competition. He and other fiscal experts thus saw in separation the potential for "more centralization in the revenue systems of the American commonwealths."[75] There were, of course, still some reformers wedded to administrative centralization who, like Bullock and T. S. Adams, believed that the "home rule" benefits of separation were dubious. But by the second decade of the twentieth century several states had already begun the process of separating the sources of state and local taxation. Frequently, they did so in conjunction with other reforms including the creation of permanent state tax commissions.[76]

74 Edwin R. A. Seligman, "Recent Reports on State and Local Taxation," *Political Science Quarterly* 22:2 (June 1907), 297–314, 313; Adams, "Suggestions for a System of Taxation," 59; Adams, *Science of Finance*, 501.

75 John Brindley, *History of Taxation in Iowa*, 166–7, 1, 45–69, 162–6, 208–12.

76 Charles J. Bullock, "Local Option in Taxation," in *State and Location Taxation, Fifth Annual Conference* (Columbus, Ohio: National Tax Association, 1912). T. S. Adams warned NTA members in 1907 that local fiscal "liberty may denigrate into license." He maintained that "real progress lies in the direction of centralization, not decentralization, of fiscal control." Adams, "Separation of the Sources of State and Local Revenues as a Program of Tax Reform," 517.

One reason for the spread of separation was the early success it had in states like California. Lawmakers in Pennsylvania and New York may have initiated the ad hoc and incremental process of testing new forms of revenue like liquor licenses and corporate franchise fees, while they allowed the property tax to gravitate toward localities through benign neglect. But the full-fledged, deliberate embrace of separation did not occur until California eagerly and enthusiastically adopted the idea in 1910. Four years earlier the Commission on Revenue and Taxation, led by the Berkeley political economist Carl Plehn, issued a report calling for the separation of revenues sources along the lines suggested by H. C. Adams and other experts.[77] Identifying the separation of revenue sources as "the one feasible pathway for reform," the commission counseled lawmakers to allow localities to "tax only the private or individual real estate and tangible property within their boundaries," because the "activities of the local governments... redound distinctly, directly, and peculiarly to the benefit of local real estate owners." Likewise, the Plehn Commission reasoned that state authorities had the right to tax "all those industries, and classes of property sometimes called 'corporate,'" by which the commission meant levies on the gross earnings of the state's leading businesses, especially public service corporations. An intrastate enterprise, unlike municipal real estate, the report explained, "does not have, in the same sense, a local situs." Rather, it "extends over many communities, serves all, and all contribute to its income."[78]

In implementing the separation of sources, California reformers were not interested merely in securing adequate revenue for the different levels of government, though that was one concern. They also sought to provide an intellectual link between their separation plan and the broader philosophical revolution in public finance triggered by reform-minded political economists. They sought, in short, to balance equity with expediency. The report's language and logic, in fact, illustrated how subnational tax reform struggled to reconcile the apparent theoretical tension between the benefits principle and the ability-to-pay rationale.

The separation of revenue sources seemed to deploy both principles. Unlike in the national context, where progressive public finance

[77] *Report of the Commission on Revenue and Taxation of the State of California, 1906* (Sacramento: Superintendent of State Printing, 1906).

[78] Ibid., 77, 79. California used a creative means to tax the gross receipts of public utilities as a proxy for the property values of these corporate entities. Steven M. Sheffrin, "Tax Reform Commissions in the Sweep of California's Fiscal History," *Hastings Constitutional Law Quarterly* 37:4 (2010), 661–88, 665–6.

economists like Ely, Adams, and Seligman unequivocally privileged ability to pay over the benefits principle, state and local reformers relied on both ideas. With Plehn as its primary author, the California report showed how economic theorists and reformers were able to relegate benefits theory to a subordinate position without completely abandoning it. Reserving the property tax for localities, where the quid pro quo of the benefits principle was most clearly visible, and permitting the state to tax corporate earnings, which reflected a company's taxpaying capacity, appeared to be one way to ensure that both rationales had their proper place in the complex matrix of intergovernmental tax policy.

Yet, at the same time, the California commissioners were also supporters of the ability-to-pay principle. One of the primary goals of their recommendation to separate state and local tax revenues was to challenge the premise that the uniform and equal taxation of all property everywhere accurately captured the varying taxpaying abilities of different individuals and property interests. Just as supporters of the classification movement questioned a homogenous understanding of property, proponents of separation were similarly skeptical that all economic interests could, or even ought to, be taxed equally. From their perspective, one of the great benefits of separation was that it eviscerated the need to equalize local property assessments; without a state property tax, there would be no need to apportion the state levy based on local property values. "The crude assumption that each and every interest should be taxed in the same way in proportion to the property which it uses," wrote the Plehn Commission, "is one of the fundamental inequities of our present system." Blind adherence to this assumption, the commissioners warned, "prevents us from taxing each interest in accordance with its ability to pay." Only by recognizing that "property forms but one of the many indices of ability," as Plehn had put it earlier, would lawmakers be free to tax other, perhaps more accurate, measures of taxpaying faculty.[79]

Tax experts reflecting on the separation movement tended to agree that an efficient, administrative division of revenue sources was an important, though intermediary, step in creating a fair and effective tax regime. "Separation," wrote Vassar College political economist Mabel Newcomer, "is not in itself a reform, but opens the way to reform." Newcomer

[79] *Report of the Commission on Revenue and Taxation of the State of California, 1906*, 79; Plehn, "The General Property Tax in California," 121. On the importance of California's 1910 reforms to the broader context of the state's many reform movements, see Sheffrin, "Tax Reform Commissions in the Sweep of California's Fiscal History."

was a Seligman student who conducted one of the first comprehensive studies of the separation movement.[80] As part of her analysis, Newcomer acutely noted that separation did not explicitly implicate distributional questions; it did not directly address whether individual tax burdens ought to be determined by the benefits received or the taxpaying faculty of citizens. That issue, Newcomer concluded, had already been settled. "Ability, as measured by progressive rather than proportional taxes, is now the generally accepted principle for dividing the burden among individuals," she proclaimed in 1917. "Although progressive taxes are at best a crude measure... they at least approach our present conception of justice." Separation did address the intergovernmental "administration and division of revenues." In doing so, it indirectly implicated distributional issues by paving the way for state governments to experiment with new taxes that might better capture a citizen's taxpaying ability. The search for administrative improvements, in other words, provided the opportunity for institutional innovations – innovations that could help build a new, more just and powerful fiscal polity.[81]

California's experience in implementing the Plehn Commission's proposals appeared originally to bode well for the future of the separation movement. Two years after an initial defeat in 1908, Californians ratified the constitutional amendment necessary to establish the separation of revenue sources.[82] The resulting tax system replaced the state-level property tax with a gross-earnings levy on railroads, street cars, light, heat and power corporations, and telephone and telegraph companies, as well as other public service corporations.[83] Several constituencies welcomed the

[80] Mabel Newcomer, *Separation of State and Local Revenues in the United States* (New York: Columbia University Press, 1917), 23. Seligman was one of the few Columbia professors who had female doctoral students. He held Newcomer in rather high regard as one of his best students, and he helped her secure her position at Vassar as well as with the U.S. Treasury Department, working with T. S. Adams. Seligman to Newcomer, [n.d.]; Seligman to T.S. Adams, May 3, 1921, Catalogued Correspondence, ERASP.

[81] Newcomer, *Separation of State and Local Revenues*, 15–17. Like her mentor, Newcomer went on to apply a comparative and historical perspective on municipal finance and its relation to increased centralization. Mabel Newcomer, *Central and Local Finance in Germany and England* (New York: Columbia University Press, 1937). Like Seligman, she also participated in numerous state and national public finance advisory committees. "Newcomer, Mabel," in *Current Biography* (New York: H. W. Wilson, 1944), 491–3.

[82] Mansel G. Blackford, *The Politics of Business in California, 1890–1920* (Columbus: Ohio State University Press, 1977), 156–7; Marvel M. Stockwell, *Studies in California Taxation, 1910–1935*, Vol. 7 (Los Angeles: University of California Press, 1939).

[83] The state also retained the poll tax and inheritance levy, both of which contributed mainly to local school districts. Carl C. Plehn, "Results of Separation in California," in

new revenue regime. Farmers believed that it more fairly distributed the tax burden. Businessmen, eager to relieve themselves of the chaotic diversity of county taxes and the exploitation by local party bosses, preferred a more stable and predictable state tax bill. And even local political leaders, some of whom had been the main opponents of separation because they feared it would erode their tax bases, adapted to their exclusive use of property taxes.[84]

In the short run, the Golden State's deliberate separation of tax bases yielded significant returns. Revenues from corporate taxes alone increased nearly fourfold between 1905 and 1915, from $4 million to over $15 million, with the levy on railroads and street railways leading the way. Part of the success was due to progressive Governor Hiram Johnson's leadership in enacting corporate tax hikes in 1913 and 1915 to fund his increased spending on schools and indigent care. But this early success could also be traced to the 1906 commission's recommendations to separate tax sources. In a temporary moment of self-congratulation, Carl Plehn informed his NTA colleagues that by 1915 "every one of the fondest hopes of the commission have been more than abundantly fulfilled."[85]

Ultimately, though, California's separation of revenue sources, like the other attempts to salvage the property tax, proved to be an ephemeral achievement. While the new corporate levies generated a sizeable increase in state revenues, they failed to keep up with escalating spending. Even Plehn soberly acknowledged that his home state faced "a crisis in our fiscal affairs."[86] Because state revenues had become heavily reliant on the prosperity of corporations, a downturn in the business cycle spelled a relative decline in the growth of state tax revenues. Although overall corporate tax revenues jumped precipitously since the adoption of separation, the year-to-year increase was dampened by economic downturns. "It was soon evident," reported California State Senator Newton W. Thompson with some disappointment, "that the revenues of the state were dependent almost entirely upon general business conditions and the prosperity of those utilities taxed directly for its support." The percentage decline in revenue, moreover, came at a time when the Golden State's

Proceedings of the Ninth Annual Conference under the Auspices of the National Tax Association (Ithaca: National Tax Association, 1915), 52.

[84] Blackford, *Politics of Business in California*.

[85] Plehn, "Results of Separation in California," 50–8, 55. David R. Doerr, *California's Tax Machine: A History of Taxing and Spending in the Golden State*, ed. Ronald Roach (Sacramento: California Taxpayers' Association, 2000).

[86] Plehn, "Results of Separation in California," 55.

progressive leaders were calling for greater state spending to help those groups badly hit by the economic recession.[87]

There were other drawbacks to separation in California. Because public service corporations accounted for the vast majority of corporate tax revenues, the state's regulation of these businesses, particularly its setting of rates to benefit consumers, cut against the state's own interest in maximizing tax revenue. "Regulation of public utilities resulting, usually, in substantial decreases in rates materially affected state revenues," Thompson explained candidly. Likewise, competition from municipal public utilities and private firms also reduced the profits of state public service corporations and hence diminished the state treasury. In short, California's experience with the separation of sources was a limited success.[88]

More thoughtful proponents of tax reform, however, recognized that California's experiment may not have been an accurate measure or execution of the principles of separation. "To my mind the ultimate solution is to be found in what I am accustomed to consider as true separation as distinct from segregation," noted Plehn. "This is the establishment of new and independent taxes for state purposes." The distinction between "separation" and "segregation" was, for Plehn and others, more than merely semantic. Whereas "segregation" simply referred to a tentative division of labor between governmental units, "true separation" implied that states and commonwealths would have the freedom to pave new revenue paths. "The separation of state and local revenues is not a cure, but it will help to make a cure possible," observed Seligman.[89]

Part of the cure was the search for new sources of tax revenue. Though many states experimented with new levies on corporations as well as individual wealth transfers, most reformers understood that a tax on individual incomes and business profits held the greatest promise for fundamental and comprehensive fiscal reform – at both the national and subnational levels. "There are a good many such taxes which might be considered," Plehn informed his NTA colleagues, "but they are all makeshifts except one, namely, the income tax."[90]

87 Newton W. Thompson, "Separation of State and Local Revenues," in *Proceedings of the Ninth Annual Conference Under the Auspices of the National Tax Association* (Ithaca: National Tax Association, 1915), 42–9, 44.

88 Thompson, "Separation of State and Local Revenues." As Jon Teaford has put it, "by protecting its private consumer, the state was robbing itself of funds needed to finance the public utility commission and other state agencies." Teaford, *Rise of the States*, 54.

89 Plehn, "Results of Separation in California," 58; Seligman, *Essays in Taxation*, 351.

90 Plehn, "Results of Separation in California," 58.

The Search for New Sources of State Revenue

The early attempts to salvage the property tax may have failed to restore the levy to its egalitarian roots as a fair and effective tax on wealth. But centralization, classification, and separation of sources each did their part incrementally to help shape the administrative backbone of subnational fiscal reform. Without these institutional innovations, it is unlikely that renewed attempts to experiment with new revenue sources – many of which had been tried before only to languish on the statute books of several states and commonwealths – would have been fruitful. Indeed, the enhanced state-level bureaucratic capacity created by the triad of centralization, classification, and separation of sources facilitated the emergence of levies on business corporations, estates and inheritances, motor vehicles and gasoline, and especially individual and business incomes.

Corporate Levies and Inheritance Taxes

The separation of sources, in particular, was instrumental in furthering the state-level taxation of business corporations. Once states deliberately abandoned the property tax to localities, corporations became an increasingly attractive source of public revenue, as California's experience suggested, and just as some experts had hoped. Corporations, after all, had long been the special creatures of state charters, and even with the advent of general incorporation laws, it was states and not localities or the national government that breathed life into business corporations and gave them the special legal privilege of limited liability. Consequently, as taxing authority became more centralized, states regularly charged corporations a variety of fees and taxes. But they did so in a rather haphazard way. From the early levies on corporate property to capital-stock taxes to incorporation and licensing fees, states and commonwealths enacted a wide variety of laws throughout the late nineteenth century to raise revenue from corporations and attract and retain capital investments. With over a dozen different corporate tax bases employed by various states and commonwealths, fiscal experts were left bewildered by the unbridled patchwork of subnational corporate levies. "We have in the United States a chaos of practice – a complete absence of principle," bemoaned Seligman.[91]

[91] Edwin R. A. Seligman, "Taxation of Corporations I," *Political Science Quarterly* 5:2 (June 1890), 269–308, 269. Other tax experts later echoed Seligman's sentiment. "Chaos

By the early 1900s, however, state corporate taxes appeared to be converging toward the dual aim of raising revenue and regulating the growth of large-scale business corporations. Although tax experts remained unsure about the ultimate incidence of corporate taxes, state lawmakers and tax officials welcomed the public funds that corporate taxes generated. Indeed, as the pressures of meeting the needs of a growing urban-industrial society mounted, state governments solidified their taxation of corporations, particularly on the earning capacity of these growing economic organizations. For a number of Northeastern industrial states and commonwealths, corporate levies – of one kind or another – remained a consistent source of revenue. At the turn of the century, Pennsylvania regularly accumulated about a third of its annual receipts from corporate taxes, mainly from its tax on capital stock.[92] And in their well-known competition for corporate charters, New Jersey and Delaware engaged in a fierce "race to the bottom," as they tried to outdo one another by luring companies with increasingly permissive and manager-friendly incorporation laws that generated significant revenues for each of these states. During the height of this competition, New Jersey consistently generated more than half of its annual revenue from corporate taxes.[93]

The "charter mongering" between New Jersey and Delaware also contributed to a wave of corporate consolidations frequently identified as the great American merger movement. This unprecedented combination of manufacturing firms created some of the country's largest business corporations and intensified social anxieties about the rise of corporate capitalism in the United States.[94] Political activists were especially

is the only descriptive term applicable to existing conditions in Commonwealth taxation," U.S. Department of Commerce and Labor, Bureau of the Corporations, *Taxation of the Corporations II – Middle Atlantic States* (Washington, D.C.: Government Printing Office, 1910), 8.

92 M. L. Faust, "Sources of Revenue of the States with a Special Study of the Revenue Sources of Pennsylvania," *Annuals of the American Academy of Political and Social Science* 95 (May 1921), 113–22, 120–1.

93 Christopher Grandy, New *Jersey and the Fiscal Origins of Modern American Corporation Law* (New York: Garland Press, 1993); Higgens-Evenson, *Price of Progress*, 41, 122-3 (Figure 4). For more on New Jersey and Delaware's competition for corporate charters, see generally William L. Cary, "Federalism and Corporate Law: Reflections upon Delaware," *Yale Law Journal* 83:4 (March 1974); Roberta Romano, *The Genius of American Corporate Law* (Washington, D.C.: American Enterprise Institute Press, 1993).

94 Naomi R. Lamoreaux, *The Great Merger Movement in American Business, 1895–1904* (New York: Cambridge University Press, 1985); Ralph L. Nelson, *Merger Movements in American Industry, 1895–1956* (Princeton: Princeton University Press, 1959), 36–9;

concerned that large-scale, national conglomerates would harm the economic prospects of local merchants and manufacturers. As a result, state lawmakers began directing tax policy toward these large-scale industrial organizations not only to raise badly needed revenue, but still more to try to curb the growth of big business. Tapping the deep-seated American anti-monopoly tradition, reformers contended that regulatory taxes ought to be used to diminish the growing power of these new colossal industrial firms. This meant replacing the chaotic patchwork of corporate levies, with a coherent and principled approach toward taxing a corporation's fiscal abilities.[95]

Even though economic experts were unsure whether corporate levies were ultimately borne by shareholders, workers, or consumers, taxes on corporate earnings quickly became a favored method of raising revenue and attacking corporate power. "There is a marked tendency in all these States toward making earning power the basis of taxation for quasi-public corporations," wrote George Clapperton of the U.S. Industrial Commission in 1901. "Properly directed, this must be regarded as the correct principle and capable of practical application to such corporations under existing industrial conditions." Clapperton's remarks referred specifically to public utilities, but the principle soon spread to cover all corporations.[96] The progressive public finance economists' concept of taxing all citizens – individuals and corporations alike – according to their ability to pay was gaining ever more traction beyond the halls of the academy and the confines of scholarly conferences.

The intergenerational transfer of wealth through inheritances and estates also became a relatively lucrative source of state revenue and a target for those who wanted to mitigate the growing concentrations of wealth. Such wealth-transfer taxes, to be sure, were not new. The earliest uses of a tax on inherited property could be traced back to the ancient Egyptians, as well as the Greeks and Romans, who used it to fund the pensions of military veterans.[97] In the United States, the federal

Martin Sklar, *The Corporate Reconstruction of American Capitalism, 1890–1916* (New York: Cambridge University Press, 1988).

95 Bryce, *American Commonwealth*, 519–20; Higgens-Evenson, *Price of Progress*, 39–51.

96 George Clapperton, *Taxation of Corporations: Report of Systems Employed in Various States Prepared under the Direction of the Industrial Commission* (Washington, D.C.: Government Printing Office, 1901), 8–9; "Favors an Income Tax," *New York Times*, March 28, 1901, 5.

97 Carolyn Webber and Aaron B. Wildavsky, *A History of Taxation and Expenditure in the Western World* (New York: Simon and Schuster, 1986),

government taxed the transactions associated with intergenerational wealth transfers only temporarily, during the early Republic and the Civil War. Inheritances and gifts were also included as part of income in the 1894 federal law struck down by *Pollock*. And, as we have seen in the previous chapter, the fiscal exigencies of the Spanish-American War compelled national lawmakers to return to the inheritance tax provisionally to fund the war effort.[98]

Yet, well before the federal government began using inheritance taxes as a transitory measure to fund military excursions, states and commonwealths had already laid claim to this revenue stream. During the antebellum period, several states followed Pennsylvania's lead and levied inheritance taxes to fund internal improvements and pay down debt. But with high exemption levels and relatively low rates, these taxes raised a limited amount of revenue and mainly seemed to serve the symbolic purpose of attempting to check dynastic wealth.[99] In the Gilded Age, as industrial fortunes accumulated and the demands for public goods and services increased, states and commonwealths once again returned to the inheritance tax – not only to secure revenue lost with the abandonment of the property tax, but to make a political statement about reallocating the tax burden. The latter message was not lost on the rich, some of whom endorsed the inheritance tax. "Of all forms of taxation, this seems the wisest," wrote the Pittsburgh steel magnate Andrew Carnegie in 1889. "By taxing estates heavily at death the state marks its condemnation of the selfish millionaire's unworthy life."[100]

In several leading industrial states, inheritance levies with moderate rates and low exemption levels became significant sources of revenue. By 1900, New York reaped roughly one-fifth of its annual receipts from the levy, while in Illinois and Pennsylvania the tax accounted for between 9 and 13 percent of total revenues. The Empire State became particularly adept at taxing the swollen fortunes of its well-heeled citizens, many of whom resided in New York City. With politicians like Governor Theodore Roosevelt supporting steeply progressive inheritance and income taxes, lawmakers in Albany integrated revised versions of the wealth-transfer tax into New York's complex matrix of revenue sources.

98 Randolph Paul, *Taxation in the United States* (Boston: Little, Brown, 1954); Steven A. Bank, Kirk J. Stark, and Joseph J. Thorndike, *War and Taxes* (Washington, D.C.: Urban Institute Press, 2008).

99 Max West, *The Inheritance Tax* (New York: Columbia University Press, 1908), 97–101.

100 Andrew Carnegie, "Wealth," *North American Review*, June 1889, 653–64.

In 1912 alone, the inheritance tax generated $12 million for New York, making it the leading source of state receipts.[101]

Elsewhere, the inheritance tax foundered on the shoals of judicial objections and ineffective statutory design. In states like Ohio, Michigan, and Minnesota, inheritance taxes were struck down for a variety of reasons as violations of state constitutions.[102] When inheritance levies in other places passed judicial scrutiny, they frequently suffered from complex and unproductive technical details. High exemption levels, low rates, and distinctions between heirs all contributed to increased complexity and decreased inheritance tax revenues. Connecticut's 1890 inheritance tax, for instance, imposed a flat 0.5 percent tax on personal property to direct heirs that exceeded $10,000, and levied a progressive tax on collateral heirs that maxed out at only 3 percent. Likewise, Wisconsin's inheritance tax applied a complex rate structure, contingent upon the heir's relationship with the donor, to any amount of property transferred in excess of $25,000.[103] With these policy limitations, the United States trailed other Western industrialized nations in its productive use of inheritance taxes. Still, New York's early success with the inheritance tax meant that some states and commonwealths believed they had an early and vested interest in such wealth-transfer taxes – an interest that they were loath to relinquish when the federal government pursued such taxes during the Great War and afterwards.[104]

Despite the varying experiences with inheritance and corporate taxes, many analysts remained optimistic that new state-level taxes could lead to the devolution of property taxes to the local level. "The experience of New York with the inheritance tax, and the experience of a number of

[101] Solom Heubner, "The Inheritance Tax in the American Commonwealths," *Quarterly Journal of Economics* 18:4 (August 1904), 529–50, 546; Frank A. Fetter, "Changes in Tax Laws of New York in 1905," *Quarterly Journal of Economics* 20:1 (1905), 151–6; Lucius Beers, "Increase of Inheritance Taxes in New York," *Columbia Law Review* 14:3 (1914), 229–40.

[102] Max West, "Recent Inheritance-Tax Statutes and Decisions," *Journal of Political Economy* 6:4 (September 1898), 437–56.

[103] West, "Recent Inheritance-Tax Statutes"; John Harrington, "The Inheritance Tax," *Annals of the American Academy of Political and Social Science* 58 (March 1915), 87–94.

[104] Frank A. Fetter, "The German Imperial Inheritance Tax," *Quarterly Journal of Economics* 21:2 (February 1907), 332–4; Max West, "The Inheritance Tax," in *Studies in History, Economics and Public Law* 4:2 (1908), 231–2; Keller, *Regulating a New Economy*, 212. For more on the rise of New York City's economic elite, see Sven Beckert, *The Monied Metropolis: New York City and the Consolidation of the American Bourgeoisie, 1850–1896* (New York: Cambridge University Press, 2001).

states with corporation taxes," proclaimed the tax expert Max West in 1908, "show that by these two methods of taxation alone most if not all of the state governments could pay all of their expenses, leaving the taxes on property to the local divisions." West was another Seligman student, one who dedicated his brief career to studying the comparative history of inheritance taxes.[105] And, as a Seligman acolyte, West touted how the inheritance tax "accords as well as any other one tax with the principle of ability." West contended that actually existing inheritance taxes were justified by what he dubbed the "accidental-income argument," which rested on "the fortuitous nature of acquisitions by inheritance and bequest." These wealth transfers, West explained, "are sudden and perhaps unexpected accretions of property without labor on the part of the heir, and manifestly increase his ability to pay taxes." The lack of labor meant that these accidental incomes were a form of "unearned increment" that increased the economic power of heirs. And as such, they were precisely the types of economic accretion that ought to be taxed by graduated inheritance levies.[106]

Taxing corporations and individual wealth transfers was one way to implement the faculty principle advanced by the progressive political economists. But that did not mean that benefits theory had no place in state and local tax reform. Relegating the property tax to the local level was, as we have seen, premised on the belief that counties and municipalities could best provide property-owning taxpayers with the type of public goods and services they expected in return for their tax payments. Technological innovations, meanwhile, ensured that state governments also retained certain elements of taxation based on reciprocal benefits. The growth of motor vehicles, for example, led states and localities to register and license the cars, trucks, buses, and taxis that began operating

[105] West, "The Inheritance Tax," 232. West was one of Seligman's first graduate students. And as he did for many of his other students, Seligman assisted West in securing a job with the Department of Agriculture. When West died suddenly in a tragic accident, Seligman solicited funds from friends and colleagues to start a charitable fund for West's dependents. West to Seligman, December 6, 1895; Jane Addams to Seligman, [n.d.], Charles Bullock to Seligman, Feb. 27, 1919, Catalogued Correspondence, ERASP.

[106] Max West, "The Theory of Inheritance Tax," *Political Science Quarterly* 8:3 (September 1893), 426–44, 434–5; West, *The Inheritance Tax*, 118–9. The "accidental-income argument" also explained the distinction between direct and collateral heirs. The latter were taxed more heavily, wrote West, because "there is a distinct increase of taxpaying ability; and the more distant the relationship, the more truly may the acquisition be said to be accidental." Ibid., 435.

along state and municipal roads. Revenues from motor vehicle registrations and licensing fees gradually became an important revenue stream for state treasuries. So, too, did gasoline and other excise taxes.

In a classic example of benefits theory, the revenues from state gasoline taxes frequently were earmarked directly for building and maintaining roads. Although these various excises only generated a marginal amount of state revenue in the pre–World War I era, by the 1920s they became increasingly important. The gasoline tax, in particular, presaged the growth of state sales taxes, which in the 1930s would come to challenge income taxes as the main source of state level revenues. The explosion of these sales taxes during the Great Depression would not only undermine the dominance of the ability-to-pay logic. They would, in time, prevent the federal government from encroaching on a revenue source initially claimed by the states.[107]

The Wisconsin Income Tax

While the early seeds of the state sales tax were being planted, that other mainstay of late-twentieth-century state tax revenue – the income tax – was already beginning to blossom. Just as political momentum at the national level was mounting for a federal constitutional amendment overturning *Pollock*, vanguard progressive states were taking the lead in adopting graduated income taxes based squarely on the principle of ability to pay. No state did more for the historical development of the subnational income tax than Wisconsin, which in 1911 adopted the first effective levy on individual and business incomes – a levy that was soon copied by many other states and that also shaped national tax policy.[108]

To be sure, state and local income taxes had existed since the colonial era and the early Republic. Seligman, after all, labeled his specific version of the ability-to-pay principle the "faculty" theory mainly because

[107] Joseph H. Beale, "The Progress of the Law, 1923–4, Taxation," *Harvard Law Review* 38:3 (1925), 281–96; Keller, *Regulating a New Economy*, 66–9; Robert Murray Haig et al., *The Sales Tax in the American States* (New York: Columbia University Press, 1934). On the importance of road building for the development of subnational administrative capacity, see Michael R. Fein, *Paving the Way: New York Road Building and the American State, 1880–1956* (Lawrence: University Press of Kansas, 2008).

[108] Brownlee, *Progressivism and Economic Growth*; John D. Buenker, *The History of Wisconsin, Vol. IV, the Progressive Era, 1893–1914* (Madison: State Historical Society of Wisconsin, 1998); Thelen, *New Citizenship*.

the country's first income taxes were referred to as "faculty taxes."[109] Yet, despite this long tradition, early state income taxes rarely generated significant revenue. Like personal property, income was assessed mainly by untrained assessors who were locally elected or politically appointed. Thus, like intangible assets, earnings frequently failed to show up on tax rolls. As Bullock had stated both publicly and in his private correspondence with other academics, rigorous state supervision was critical for the assessment of just about any tax base. Bullock was not the only political economist who doubted the future viability of an American income tax. In fact, when Wisconsin first began the process of considering an income tax, T. S. Adams acknowledged that the prevailing consensus among economic experts was stacked against the Badger State's efforts: "Today the economists of this country have lined up in opposition to the state income tax in an array so nearly unanimous that the outside world would be justified in asserting that current American political economy is against the income tax."[110]

Even Seligman was initially skeptical. Although he had long supported moderately graduated income taxes as a means toward capturing a citizen's economic faculty, the Columbia professor questioned whether the United States had the administrative capacity or the social and political will at the turn of the century to levy an effective tax on individual incomes and business profits. As late as 1911, he remained particularly skeptical that state governments had the bureaucratic competency to administer an income tax. "The income tax as it exists to-day in the American commonwealths does not merit serious consideration," he boldly proclaimed in the first edition of his income tax treatise. "More and more it is being realized by state officials and state tax commissions that any hope for a satisfactory state income tax is illusory."[111]

[109] Edwin R. A. Seligman, "The Income Tax in the American Colonies and States," *Political Science Quarterly* 10:2 (June 1985), 221–47; Seligman, *The Income Tax: A Study in the History, Theory, and Practice of Income Taxation at Home and Abroad* (New York: Macmillan Co., 1914), 4; Buenker, *The Income Tax and the Progressive Era* (New York: Garland Publishing, 1985), 1–2.

[110] Bullock, "The State Income Tax and the Classified Property Tax," 369; Charles Bullock to Edwin R. A. Seligman, June 3, 1911, Box 25, Folder 1, TSAP; T. S. Adams, "The Place of an Income Tax in the Reform of State Taxation, *Bulletin of the American Economic Association* 4:2 (1911), 302.

[111] Seligman, *The Income Tax*, 419. For more on the early skepticism and challenges of state income tax administration, see Clara Penniman and Walter W. Heller, *State Income Tax Administration* (Chicago: Public Administration Service, 1959), 1–8.

Given the range of forces arrayed against the income tax, Wisconsin's fiscal reformers understood that they had a long and arduous road ahead of them. In addition to the doubts about administrative capacity, activists and tax officials in the Badger State also had to deal with other institutional obstacles, namely judicial impediments and, perhaps most importantly, a political culture that favored local autonomy over centralized authority. Like most Midwestern states, Wisconsin had a uniformity clause as part of its constitution. A pithy single sentence, this clause did not provide much relief from the arbitrary and capricious application of politically motivated local assessments, which were generally upheld by the courts.[112] The Wisconsin Supreme Court did intervene to prevent "errors of judgment and mistakes of fact" made by local assessors, but as long as such errors were "exceptional and happen in good faith, not affecting the principle or the general equality of the assessment," they were deemed constitutional. Only the most overt and egregious types of malfeasance compelled the court to strike down an assessment. Amending the uniformity clause to permit graduated income taxes was, thus, a pivotal early priority for Wisconsin's tax reformers.[113]

Reformers and tax officials were able to take on such daunting obstacles like amending the state constitution mainly because the state benefited from a particular confluence of economic, political, and institutional factors. Like other states, Wisconsin was battered in the late nineteenth century by the fiscal mismatch of increasing public demands and a shrinking source of state revenues. The economic recession of the 1890s placed particular pressure on the state treasury. But the downturn also led to the formation of a unique political coalition that challenged the conservative core of Wisconsin's Republican Party. The fiscal dilemma and the economic slump, as historian David Thelen has shown, united "workers and businessmen, foreign born and native born, Populist and Republicans, drinkers and abstainers, Catholics and Protestants" behind a whole host of progressive reforms, including tax reform, which "was the most popular and powerful of the state's reform movements."[114]

[112] Wisconsin Constitution (1848), Article VIII, Section 1. The Clause read: "The rule of taxation shall be uniform and taxes shall be levied upon such property as the legislature shall prescribe." Ibid.

[113] *Marsh v. Supervisors*, 42 Wis. 502 (1877); see also *Hersey v. Board of Supervisors*, 37 Wis. 75 (1875); *Bradley v. Lincoln County*, 60 Wis. 71 (1884).

[114] David Thelen, *New Citizenship*, 204–7, 288.

As a result of this unique political coalition, a long line of progressive governors including Robert M. La Follette Sr. provided the executive leadership necessary to improve the state's fiscal regime. Tax reform, in fact, was one of the two major planks of La Follette's first gubernatorial campaign in 1896. After falling short in that election but winning the governor's office in 1900, La Follette helped initiate Wisconsin's march toward a graduated income tax by creating the state's first permanent tax commission, which brought together leading government officials and academic tax experts, including T. S. Adams.[115]

Working with Adams on the tax commission was Nils P. Haugen, a lawyer and former U.S. congressman, who was the leading income tax activist within La Follette's progressive Republican wing. Known as La Follette's "first lieutenant," Haugen represented the Norwegian immigrant agricultural region that was at the base of La Follette's political coalition.[116] Along with Adams and Haugen, the other pivotal revenue reformers were Kossuth K. Kennan, a Milwaukee railroad lawyer, who had long advocated for a state tax commission to rationalize the various state and local tax laws, and Charles McCarthy, the head of the state's legislative reference library and the fountainhead of many of Wisconsin's innovative progressive laws.[117] The collaboration between these men, in particular the extensive cooperation between Adams and Haugen, illustrated the special institutional links that existed in Madison between the state government and the flagship university campus, a link that explained why Wisconsin was one of the nation's leading incubators of progressive reforms. Contemporaries described this distinctive reciprocal relationship as the "Wisconsin Idea" – a term coined by McCarthy that captured his belief that social scientific knowledge ought to be used

[115] David P. Thelen, *Robert M. La Follette and the Insurgent Spirit* (Boston: Little, Brown, 1976), 29; Brownlee, *Progressivism and Economic Growth*; Buenker, *The History of Wisconsin.*

[116] Nils P. Haugen, *Pioneer and Political Reminiscences* (Evansville, Wis.: Antes Press, 1930); Robert La Follette to Nils Haugen, September 24, 1911; Haugen to La Follette November 2, 1911, Box 56, Haugen Papers, SHSW; Buenker, *History of Wisconsin*, 442–3. For more on Haugen, see Stuart D. Brandes, "Nils P. Haugen and the Wisconsin Progressive Movement" (Master's thesis, University of Wisconsin, 1965).

[117] Emanuel L. Philipp, *Political Reform in Wisconsin: A Historical Review of the Subjects of Primary Election, Taxation, and Railway Regulation* (Milwaukee, 1910), 109–11; Kossuth Kent Kennan, "The Wisconsin Income Tax," *Quarterly Journal of Economics* 26:1 (November 1911), 169–78; Joseph A. Ranney, "Law and the Progressive Era, Part 2: The Transformation of Wisconsin's Tax System, 1887–1925," *Wisconsin Lawyer* 67 (August 1994): 22–25, 62–3.

to solve the problems and improve the everyday lives of the community's citizens.[118]

Together with Adams and others, Haugen spearheaded the political campaign for a state income tax as a complete replacement for the antiquated property tax. Just as California's reformers had hoped they could replace the property tax with corporate levies, Adams and Haugen naively believed that an income tax could almost immediately become a fiscal workhorse completely replacing the state property tax. As a lawyer trained under the tutelage of Thomas Cooley, Haugen understood that if the income tax was to become a part of the state's fiscal system, the proper constitutional foundations needed to be established. Thus, amending the state constitution's uniformity clause became a top priority.[119]

By mobilizing those most disgruntled with the existing property tax, especially among his own agrarian constituency, Haugen was able to convince the state legislature in 1903 to consider a constitutional amendment permitting a graduated state income tax.[120] Approved as part of a larger tax overhaul, which included the adoption of a graduated inheritance tax and modifications to existing corporate taxes, the amendment called for a simple addition to the uniformity clause: "Taxes may also be imposed on incomes, privileges and occupations, which taxes may be graduated and progressive, and reasonable exemptions may be provided." Milwaukee's socialist leaders were instrumental in paving the way for the constitutional amendment, hoping that it would lead to the adoption of more radically redistributive tax policies. After some early technical setbacks, the income tax amendment was overwhelmingly approved in a 1908 statewide referendum by a margin of 2 to 1.[121]

Establishing the constitutional foundations for a progressive income tax, however, was only part of the battle. Income would be no easier to assess than intangible personal property. As long as the assessment

118 Charles McCarthy, *The Wisconsin Idea* (New York: Macmillan Co., 1912); Buenker, *History of Wisconsin*, 573–7.

119 Haugen, *Pioneer and Political Reminiscences*; Brandes, "Nils P. Haugen and the Wisconsin Progressive Movement."

120 Haugen, *Pioneer and Political Reminiscences*, 158–9. John O. Stark, "The Establishment of Wisconsin's Income Tax," *Wisconsin Magazine of History* (autumn 1987): 27–45.

121 Fredrick C. Howe, *Wisconsin, An Experiment in Democracy* (New York: Scribner's Sons, 1912), 133–9; *Wisconsin Constitution*, Article VIII, Section 1; T. S. Adams, "The Wisconsin Income Tax," *American Economic Review* 1 (December 1911), 906–9; *Wisconsin: A Guide to the Badger State* (Madison, Wis.: Wisconsin Library Association, 1941), 60–2.

and supervision process was left in the hands of local officials there was little hope of effectively raising revenue in an equitable manner. Economic experts and activists in Wisconsin, therefore, advocated the centralization of tax assessments at the state rather than the county level. In what was perhaps the boldest of reforms, they sought to remove tax administration from the ambit of local political machines and place that responsibility with the state's growing cadre of bureaucratic experts.

The calls for greater administrative centralization, as we have seen, were not unique to Wisconsin; nor were they divorced from the self-interest of reformers. Proponents of centralization, like Adams and Haugen, may have sincerely, perhaps even naively, believed that solving the administrative problems of the tax assessment process would be some kind of panacea. Once thoroughgoing civil service reforms had been adopted and politics had been separated from the assessment process, supporters contended, the bureaucratic autonomy would exist to allow the state income tax to replace the property tax. Neither Adams nor Haugen, however, mentioned that the administrative reforms they proposed necessarily meant that a great deal of political and economic power would also be bestowed upon the state tax commission, on which they both served. For Adams, the social scientist, the fortification of fiscal powers was an inexorable function of centralization; for Haugen, it was a political opportunity to further his policy goals – a fact that did not escape the lawmakers who opposed the income tax.

Assuaging concerns about the consolidation of robust administrative authority also meant confronting a political culture that seemed wedded to the notion of local autonomy or "home rule." In a series of private correspondence with H. S. Wilson, the president of the State Normal School in River Falls, Haugen expressed his views on the pernicious aspects of local tax assessments. Although Haugen had gradually persuaded Wilson that income was the proper measure of taxation based on ability, the local school administrator continued to resist any form of bureaucratic centralization. "I am not yet ready to turn over local taxation with all of its glaring evils to some centralized authority," wrote Wilson in the summer of 1910. "This is not in harmony with the American Spirit." Haugen acknowledged in response that "the sentiment in favor of what Americans believe is local self-government is the greatest objection that we have to meet in order to improve our taxation system." But what Americans' believed to be self-government was, in Haugen's estimation, completely illusory. "There is absolutely no choice in an American town, city or village as to the kind of government under which the local community desires to live," wrote Haugen. "The jacket is cut and fitted by central authority and the local community must wear it no matter how great the misfit may be."[122]

Those who held on to the antiquated notion of local self-government amid the dramatic changes of turn-of-the-century industrial capitalism, Haugen argued, were not only out of touch with the interdependency of modern life, they were also paradoxically eroding popular faith in good government. Those who held on to the American myth of local self-government, Haugen contended, undermined rather than enforced the efficacy of law. "The difficulty now is that the rule adopted for taxation, as well as other purposes, is entirely out of harmony with local sentiment and the law cannot be enforced for that reason probably as much as for any other," Haugen informed Wilson.[123] When Wilson persisted, conceding that he could not so easily abandon "the fetish of local self-government," Haugen reiterated his claim that effective local sovereignty over fiscal matters was a chimera. "Our method of electing local assessors," Haugen wrote, "has nothing whatever to do with the fundamental idea of local self-government. It serves as a pre-text for disregard of the law and results in local mis-government instead of self-government." Adopting a centrally administered income tax was one way to make the law conform to the local sentiment in favor of a fair and effective fiscal system – it was one way to close the gap between the law on the books and law in action.[124]

Yet, what Haugen feared even more than the deterioration of law and the loss of faith in public power was the notion of American exceptionalism reflected in Wilson's letters. Wilson's invocation of the "American Spirit" was representative of a much broader concern among provincial officials about the unique nature of American statecraft. Haugen felt compelled to correct this misconception. Using Germany as a comparative example, and citing Adolph Wagner as his authority, Haugen provided Wilson with a detailed quantitative analysis of how German public finance was, in fact, saturated with local self-government. From

[122] H. S. Wilson to Nils Haugen, July 24, 1910; Haugen to Wilson, July 26, 1910, Box 56, Haugen Papers, SHSW.

[123] Ibid. Haugen conveyed a similar sense of how the law had been divorced from "the public conscience" in his May 1910 address to the Wisconsin's Banker's Association, when he declared: "Local self-government as far as taxation goes is a howling farce. No respect is paid to the law. It may be that the public conscience condemns it and the local assessor responds to that sentiment rather than to the provisions of the law." "Income Tax in Place of Personal Property Tax," *Milwaukee Free Press*, May 26, 1910.

[124] Wilson to Haugen, September 1, 1910; Haugen to Wilson, September 19, 1910, Box 56, Haugen Papers, SHSW.

this Haugen concluded that "the local self-government which we enjoy is the privilege of ignoring the law – setting it aside – and leaving the offender to go unpunished or unrebuked." If this is what Wilson meant by self-government, Haugen sardonically remarked, "there is probably less self-government in Germany than in the United States." Simply put, Haugen believed that what passed for "American self-government," was often no form of government at all, especially when considered from a comparative perspective.[125]

In challenging the traditional reliance on local authority, reformers like Haugen were also using tax policy to forge a new and broader sense of citizenship. Like the progressive political economists, Haugen believed that, in an increasingly interdependent social world, individual citizens needed to recognize that they had civic obligations and responsibilities that stretched beyond their local communities to the larger realm of state and even national government. Wilson himself seemed to understand this when he informed Haugen that he shared the goal of restoring the republican ideals of civic virtue through a new form of American liberalism. "What we need in this respect," wrote Wilson, "are higher ideals of citizenship and political practices that are in accordance with these ideals. Can it be that we are a nation of degenerates, a people so absorbed in individual gain that we are willing to sacrifice the public welfare for personal profit?"[126]

Haugen believed not, but he fundamentally disagreed with Wilson about how to shape democratic faith and public consciousness to meet changing historical conditions. Frontier Wisconsin residents during the antebellum era could perhaps express their loyalty to local institutions through the "civic grammar" and "fiscal syntax" of navigating complex intergovernmental fiscal regimes, but in a modern urban-industrial age citizens needed to view their responsibilities and obligations more broadly.[127] They needed to rethink their imagined community as stretching beyond the confines of local parameters. Fostering the legitimacy of

[125] Haugen to Wilson, July 26, 1910, Haugen Papers, SHSW; Haugen, *Pioneer and Political Reminiscences*, 158–9.

[126] Wilson to Haugen, September 1, 1910, Box 56, Haugen Papers, SHSW.

[127] Merle Curti, *The Making of an American Community: A Case Study of Democracy in a Frontier County* (Stanford: Stanford University Press, 1959), 270. In his analysis of Trempealeau County, Wisconsin, Curti noted that despite the "fantastic labyrinth of intergovernmental finance," loyal citizens expressed their political allegiances by mastering the "civic grammar" and "fiscal syntax" of the intergovernmental finance. Ibid.

a state-level income tax, along with the centralization of fiscal administration, was an important step in forging this new civic identity. In future years, the federal constitutional amendment permitting progressive income taxes and subsequent national tax laws would replicate this process of realigning fiscal citizenship with the tenets of American new liberalism.

As Haugen was trying to convince Wisconsinites like Wilson of the virtues of a centrally administered income tax, lawmakers in Madison were drafting the details of the new income tax law. Although Haugen and Adams were perhaps the most vocal experts supporting the income tax concept, the legislative drafting process was guided mainly by McCarthy and the economist D. O. Kinsman, an early income tax skeptic.[128] Under McCarthy and Kinsman's leadership, the bill appeared to be moving in a slightly different direction. Whereas Haugen and Adams confidently believed an effectively administered income tax could be a wholesale replacement for the general property tax, McCarthy and Kinsman were more cautious. Concerned about the growing revenue demands on the state, McCarthy and Kinsman proposed that the new income tax simply replace the levy on personal property. In the McCarthy-Kinsman version of the bill, the tax on real property would be maintained.[129]

Haugen and Adams were not pleased by this change of direction, but they gradually came to support the final version of the bill.[130] With the backing of Milwaukee's Socialists, the legislature enacted a progressive income tax that began with a 1 percent tax on all personal incomes

[128] Like Seligman, Kinsman's objections to the income tax were based mainly on administrative grounds. In 1903 he concluded that "failure will continue to accompany the tax until our industrial system takes on such form as to make possible the use of some method other than self-assessment." Delos O. Kinsman, *The Income Tax in the Commonwealths of the United States* (Ithaca: American Economic Association, 1903), 121.

[129] Brownlee, *Progressivism and Economic Growth*, Chapter 3; Stark, "Establishment of Wisconsin's Income Tax"; Adams to Haugen, December 24, 1910; Adams to Haugen, April 1, 1910, Box 56, Haugen Papers, SHSW. "Genesis of Wisconsin's Income Tax: An Interview with D. O. Kinsman," *Wisconsin Magazine of History*, September 1937, 4. McCarthy apparently feared that Adams's feedback on the pending legislation had the potential of "killing the whole matter." McCarthy to Adams cited in Buenker, *History of Wisconsin*, 552.

[130] "Unexpected Fight on Income Tax Measure," *Milwaukee Free Press*, May 3, 1911; G. D. Van Dencook, "Income Tax Bill Hits Rocky Road," (Milwaukee) *Evening Wisconsin*, May 3, 1911. "Let the income tax be as faulty as it may," Adams informed legislators with some resignation, "and if in any way it tends to remove taxation of personal property, it would have moved in the right direction." "Income Tax Hearing," (Milwaukee) *Evening Wisconsin*, May 24, 1911.

over $1,000 (roughly $25,000 in 2012 dollars) and reached a maximum rate of 6 percent for incomes greater than $12,000 (about $300,000 in 2012 dollars). As lawmakers promised, and as some of Wisconsin's most affluent citizens feared, the tax affected only the wealthiest of taxpayers. More important, the income tax effectively replaced only the taxation of personal property, leaving the levy on real property intact. It did so by eliminating several types of intangible personal property such as stocks and bonds from the tax rolls, and by permitting taxpayers an "offset," or credit, against their income tax liability for any taxes paid on the remaining forms of taxable personal property. In an effort to placate local interests, the new law provided that revenues from the new income tax would be shared between state and local governments.[131]

Although lawmakers did not agree to have the income tax replace the entire property tax, they did adopt the administrative changes that Adams and Haugen had recommended. Indeed, nearly two-thirds of the statute was dedicated to administrative reforms. The new law centralized the assessment process, taking it away from local officials and placing it in the hands of professional experts supervised by the state tax commission. These professionals were chosen not because of any political affiliations but rather by their performance on rigorous civil service exams, which tested financial and tax expertise. Even skeptical political economists, like Seligman, who initially doubted the feasibility of state income taxes, by 1915 viewed the new Wisconsin law as "a revolution in administrative methods."[132]

Having lost their battle in the legislature, opponents of the income tax turned to the courts for relief. Just months after it was enacted, lawyers for a Wisconsin realtor challenged numerous provisions of the new law, including the consolidation of administrative powers. The Wisconsin Supreme Court made quick work of the case. In a unanimous decision upholding the statute, the court explicated the democratic roots and comparative context of the income tax movement, noting how the levy signaled "a very important change in the general taxation policy of the state." The new law, wrote Chief Justice John B. Winslow on behalf of

[131] *Wisconsin Session Laws* (1911), Section 1087m-8(1) and (2), Chapter 658; Kennan, "The Wisconsin Income Tax"; Seligman, *The Income Tax*, 421; J. C. Stamp, "The Tax Experiment in Wisconsin," *Economic Journal* 23:89 (March 1913), 142–6. Relative dollar values calculated using MeasuringWorth, available at: http://www.measuringworth.com/uscompare/.

[132] Seligman, *The Income Tax*, 421; Stamp, "The Tax Experiment in Wisconsin"; Higgens-Evenson, *Price of Progress*, 85.

the court, "is but the concrete embodiment of a popular sentiment which has been abroad for some time." More specifically, the court noted that the 1908 constitutional amendment had explicitly paved the way for the graduated income tax. This "change was ratified by the people at the general election," wrote Winslow, "and thus was clearly expressed by both the legislature and the people the idea that some form of general taxation in addition to or in place of property taxation might well be adopted."[133]

As part of his general defense of the law, Winslow also noted the successful comparative history of the income tax. Echoing the language of the reform-minded economists as well as the comments made by Governor Francis McGovern when he signed the bill, the court assertively claimed that "the income tax is no new and untried experiment in the field of taxation." Identifying the venerable tradition of income taxes in "many of the civilized governments of the world" and among "twenty of our own states," as well as "for a brief period by the government of the United States," the court concluded that "taxation should logically be imposed according to ability to pay, rather than upon the mere possession of property." Thus, in enacting the new law, Winslow contended that "the legislature is only adopting a scheme of taxation which has been approved for many years by many of the most enlightened governments of the world, and has the sanction of many thoughtful economists."[134]

The court's specific references to the "ability-to-pay" principle demonstrated that the conceptual revolution undertaken by the reform-minded academics was having a profound impact on legal actors and the development of American jurisprudence. The notion of basing taxation on an individual's economic power, and not just merely the benefits received by state action, was seeping into broader parts of American life. Acceptance of an income tax centered on faculty was no longer limited to the ideas and writings of theorists, or the pronouncements of populist lawmakers; progressive jurists were beginning to embrace the fiscal revolution that was spreading throughout the country. By linking ability to pay to the

[133] *State ex rel. Bolens v. Frear*; *Winding v. Frear*. The Court consolidated these two cases as the *Income Tax Cases*, 148 Wis. 456 (1911), 504. "Believes Income Tax Law Invalid," *Milwaukee Sentinel*, November 16, 1911; "Income Tax Law Is Argued," *Milwaukee Free Press*, November 21, 1911.

[134] *Income Tax Cases*, 505. In signing the bill, Governor McGovern attached a lengthy memo that stated in part that "the plan of adjusting pubic burdens according to ability has been in successful operation for many years in Switzerland, Austria, France, England, Norway, Sweden, Denmark, Holland, and the German states." "Governor Calls Income Tax Just," *Milwaukee Sentinel*, July 14, 1911.

use of income taxes in "civilized" communities and "enlightened governments," the Wisconsin justices, moreover, illustrated their recognition of the broader global context in which American law was operating. By endorsing a workable state income tax, that was fair and effective, they believed that they were helping lead their state, and their nation, out of its backward and uncivilized era and into a new period of economic and political development.[135]

If tax reformers found some comfort in the court's ruling on the substance of the income tax, they were especially reassured by the judicial approval of the administrative modifications. Pointing to particular constitutional provisions that governed the election and appointment of local officials, the plaintiffs claimed that the newly created state powers of assessment violated "the constitutional guaranties of local self-government." In response, the court ruled that "the office of assessors of income," created by the new law, was neither a "county, city, town, or village" office, nor was it an office "existing in substance at the time of the adoption of the constitution, or essential to the existence or efficiency of either of said municipal divisions of the state." The court concluded, instead, that the centralized administration of assessments was "an entirely new office... whose election or appointment may be provided for in any way that the legislature may in its discretion direct."[136]

Within a decade of its initial enactment, the Wisconsin income tax had achieved some significant, albeit limited, success. By 1920, the income tax generated over $15 million, accounting for roughly 14 percent of total annual receipts for state and local governments. By contrast, the general property tax continued to be the main source of subnational government revenues, yielding about $77 million or 73 percent of total revenues in 1920.[137] Although it did not completely eclipse the property tax as the state's main source of revenue – as Adams and Haugen had hoped – the

[135] *Income Tax Cases*, 505.

[136] Ibid., 511. Many observers, including the staunchly anti–income tax *Milwaukee Sentinel*, viewed the court's deference to the legislature as the death knell for the inchoate movement to repeal the income tax. "Income Tax Law Valid, Says Court," *Milwaukee Sentinel*, January 10, 1912.

[137] Harold M. Groves, "The Wisconsin State Income Tax," in *The Wisconsin Blue Book* (Madison, Wis.: Democratic Print Co., 1933), 51–61, 58 (Table I). Groves's estimates may be conservative given that they include amounts for state and local revenues, not just state government receipts. Still, the point remains that the income tax was a growing source of revenue for Wisconsin. See *The Wisconsin Blue Book, 1921* (Madison, Wis.: State Printing Board, 1921), 355, 539, 541. I am indebted to Jon Teaford for pointing out this distinction.

income tax began the incremental process of diminishing the reliance on an obsolete system of taxing personal property.

Reflecting back on the early success of the new income tax, Wisconsin reformers also noted the importance of the administrative changes, particularly the appointment of expert state assessors and the method of collecting tax information at the source. "The greatest discovery of the Wisconsin income tax is the non-political assessor of incomes," T. S. Adams declared. This ensured that the tax system contained a "set of officers not dependent for the retention of their offices upon the favor of the people whom they assess." For Adams, such administrative reform marked a seminal moment in the historical development of American taxation. "The appointment of a body of protected tax officials marks a new epoch in the fiscal history of the state of Wisconsin, possibly in that of the United States," gushed Adams. "It is very largely their work that has made the income tax a success."[138]

The efficiency of income tax collections was facilitated further by the tax commission's subsequent adoption of regulations that required parties paying salaries, dividends, and interest to provide the tax commission with information about the taxpayers receiving such income. This crude form of information reporting, or what contemporaries referred to as a form of "stoppage at the source," underscored the importance of third-party reporting for a quasi-voluntary system of tax compliance. With these administrative changes, the Wisconsin income tax law became an effective source of revenue, and soon became the model for several other states, and even the federal government.[139]

Perhaps more important, the administrative reforms enacted as part of the 1911 income tax law dramatically changed the way Wisconsin managed the assessment and collection of taxes. A process traditionally controlled by local politics gradually came under the domain and supervision of a relatively autonomous group of bureaucratic experts who could rely on technical improvements, like the adoption of information withholding, to secure badly needed tax revenues. Despite the overwhelming

[138] T. S. Adams, "The Significance of the Wisconsin Income Tax," 572.

[139] Kossuth Kent Kennan, "The Wisconsin Income Tax," *Annals of the American Academy of Political and Social Science* 58 (March 1915): 65–76; Thomas E. Lyons, "The Wisconsin Income Tax," *Annals of the American Academy of Political and Social Science* 58 (March 1915), 77–86. Present-day tax scholars have stressed the importance of third-party reporting for an effective income tax. For a summary of this recent literature, see Joel Slemrod, "Cheating Ourselves: The Economics of Tax Evasion," *Journal of Economic Perspectives* 21:1 (Winter 2007), 25–48.

skepticism of many tax experts, Wisconsin activists were able to respond to the turn-of-the-century fiscal challenges by overcoming the legal, institutional, and social resistance to tax reform. Amending constitutions, enhancing bureaucratic authority, and confronting popular aversion to consolidated power were all necessary steps in building a modern fiscal polity. By taking on these challenges, reformers not only addressed growing inequality while securing a stable source of revenue; they also helped forge a new vision of civic identity, as they laid the foundation for the subsequent growth of the public sector.

In many ways, Wisconsin's experiment with the income tax was a microcosm of the broader revolution in American public finance. Like many other states and the federal government, Wisconsin was coping with the pressures of modernity. The Badger State was trying to meet the growing demand for public goods and services with an outdated and ineffective revenue system, amid tremendous economic inequality. But not all governments responded to these broad socioeconomic forces in the same way. There was no single, universal solution. Whereas some states and commonwealths failed to reform their property taxes or to seek out new sources of revenue, activists and officials in Wisconsin and elsewhere were able to serve as incubators of progressive fiscal innovations, exploiting new ideas and creating new institutions to mediate the challenges of a modern, urban-industrial society. Although the development of an effective state-level income tax may have precluded other, more radical fiscal changes, the early success of the tax reform movement emboldened other activists and politicians at the state and national level to pursue a similar set of fundamental reforms.

5

Corporate Capitalism and Constitutional Change

The Legal Foundations of the Modern Fiscal State

> A change in definition is such a simple and natural way of changing the constitution from what it is to what it ought to be, and the method is so universal and usually so gradual in all walks of life, that the will of God, or the will of the People, or the Corporate will, scarcely realizes what has happened.
>
> – John R. Commons

While industrial states and commonwealths were actively trying to salvage the property tax and seek out new sources of revenue, the federal government appeared to be drifting passively along the existing fiscal path of relying on import duties and excise taxes. William McKinley's defeat of William Jennings Bryan in the 1896 presidential contest solidified this institutional inertia. McKinley's victory not only signaled a critical electoral realignment toward the Republican Party and the end of the Populist Party; it also seemed to dash the future hopes of tariff reformers. In fact, in the following year, President McKinley and a Republican-controlled Congress raised tariff rates to their highest levels since the Civil War, thus, reinforcing the Republican Party's – and the nation's – commitment to a high-tariff regime.[1]

The Spanish-American War, to be sure, forced lawmakers to find new revenue sources. But that "splendid little war" proved to be too short to puncture the status quo fiscal system; nearly all of the new levies enacted to finance the war were repealed shortly after the end of the conflict. The economic recovery that followed also did little to alter the existing

[1] Charles Postel, *The Populist Vision* (New York: Oxford University Press, 2007), 269–70; Walter Dean Burnham, *Critical Elections and the Mainsprings of American Politics* (New York: W. W. Norton & Co., 1970), 71–90; Charles V. Stewart, "The Federal Income Tax and the Realignment of the 1890s," in *Realignment in American Politics: Toward a Theory*, ed. Bruce A. Campbell and Richard J. Trilling (Austin: University of Texas Press, 1980), 263–87; F. W. Taussig, *The Tariff History of the United States*, 6th ed. (New York: G. P. Putnam's Sons, 1914), 321–60.

federal tax regime. Between 1900 and 1907, with the economy growing at a steady pace, revenues from import duties and internal excise taxes flooded the U.S. Treasury with annual surpluses that temporarily diminished the total national debt. Given the political and economic context, there appeared to be little impetus at the national level for fundamental fiscal reform.[2]

Yet, despite the apparent calm and continuity in federal tax policy that marked the decade following the Spanish-American War, broader structural forces were once again gradually exerting pressure on the existing regime of national indirect and regressive taxes. In due time, these historical forces would collide with seminal events to provide reformers with an opportunity to adopt a corporate excise tax and a constitutional amendment overturning *Pollock*. Among the many structural strains shaping the tax reform movement, demand-side pressures on the federal budget were paramount. Military-related spending, in particular, continued to dominate federal expenditures. Outlays for veterans' pensions and compensation averaged roughly $140 million annually, accounting for more than a quarter of annual federal spending. The brief conflict with Spain enhanced the power and prestige of the United States in the world community; it also initiated the international policing of American economic and geopolitical interests. With new territories spread throughout the globe, a newly revamped national military became the guardian of America's nascent overseas empire. Accordingly, spending on the War Department increased steadily, especially under the leadership of Secretary of War Elihu Root.[3]

An equally significant concern among many ordinary Americans was the increasing cost of living, which became directly associated with the resurgent tariff regime. Although the annual rate of inflation was, by historical standards, rather moderate during the early 1900s (averaging about 2 percent annually), the perception among many workers and

[2] Steven A. Bank, Kirk J. Stark, and Joseph J. Thorndike, *War and Taxes* (Washington, D.C.: Urban Institute Press, 2008), 51–2; Paul Studenski and Herman Edward Krooss, *Financial History of the United States* (New York: McGraw Hill, 1952), 235–7; *Historical Statistics of the United States Millennial Edition*, ed. Susan B. Carter, et al. (New York: Cambridge University Press, 2006), Series Y, 254–7.

[3] Robert P. Saldin, *War, the American State, and Politics since 1898* (New York: Cambridge University Press, 2010), Ch. 2. See also Paul A.C. Koistinen, *Mobilizing for Modern War: The Political Economy of American Warfare, 1865–1919* (Lawrence: University Press of Kansas, 1997); Lewis L. Gould, *The Spanish-American War and President McKinley* (Lawrence: University Press of Kansas, 1980); Hugh Rockoff, *America's Economic Way of War: War and the U.S. Economy from the Spanish-American War to the Persian Gulf War* (New York: Cambridge University Press, 2012), Chapter 3.

consumers was that the widening scale and scope of import duties was inexorably raising the price of the "necessaries of life," while unduly "protecting" domestic monopolies. Attention to how the tariff was fueling inflation and the power of the trusts became even more pronounced after 1907 when a new financial panic triggered a downturn in the business cycle and revived concerns about federal deficits. The panic and ensuing recession soon reduced annual federal revenues, put added pressure on the party discipline backing the tariff regime, and once again brought to the fore the growing disparities in economic wealth and power. These structural factors became important catalysts for the renewed demands for a change in the existing fiscal order.[4]

As scholars have long noted, these broad forces provided the crucial context for the development of the modern income tax regime. Standard historical accounts of the origins of the 1909 corporate tax, the Sixteenth Amendment, and the enactment of the 1913 national income tax tend to focus mainly on how high-level political actors responded to these wide-ranging, structural factors to establish a new tax system.[5]

[4] "The Increased Cost of Living," *American Economist* (August 22, 1902), 95; Mark Aldrich, "Tariffs and Trusts, Profiteers and Middlemen: Popular Explanations for the High Cost of Living, 1897–1920," *History of Political Economy* (forthcoming); Hugh Rockoff, "Banking and Finance, 1789–1914," in *The Cambridge Economic History of the United States, Vol. II, The Long Nineteenth Century*, ed. Stanley L. Engerman and Robert G. Gallman (New York: Cambridge University Press, 2000), 665; Milton Friedman and Anna Jacobson Schwartz, *A Monetary History of the United States, 1867–1960* (Princeton: Princeton University Press, 1971), 152–74.

[5] These conventional historical narratives, to be sure, differ dramatically in their interpretations. For some, the corporate tax and constitutional amendment were rooted in the efforts of "centrist" lawmakers and thinkers who, acting as trustees of capital, were seeking to restore conservative calm in the face of social unrest and party fracture. See, e.g., Robert Stanley, *Dimensions of Law in the Service of Order: Origins of the Federal Income Tax, 1861–1913* (New York: Oxford University Press, 1993), Chapter 5. In a similar vein, other scholars have contended that Congress used its discretionary spending power over veterans' pensions and military installments to forge a vital political coalition in favor of the constitutional amendment and the income tax law. See Bennett D. Baack and Edward John Ray, "Special Interests and the Adoption of the Income Tax in the United States," *Journal of Economic History* 45:3 (September 1985), 607–25. Still others have depicted the Sixteenth Amendment and the first permanent, peacetime income tax as unvarnished victories for a diverse set of liberal activists, from peripheral agrarian associations to progressive urban reformers, who were demanding greater tax justice. The classic and perhaps best political account in this traditional progressive vein remains John Buenker, *The Income Tax and the Progressive Era* (New York: Garland Press, 1985). See also Sidney Ratner, *American Taxation: Its History as a Social Force in Democracy* (New York: W. W. Norton, 1942); *Taxation and Democracy in America* (New York: W. W. Norton, 1967); Randolph E. Paul, *Taxation in the United States* (Boston: Little, Brown, 1954); Roy and Gladys Blakey, *The Federal Income Tax* (London: Longmans, Green,

Though these conventional explanations provide a rich narrative of the formal political battles behind the income tax movement, they frequently neglect the pivotal role that the rise of corporate capitalism played in fortifying the central legal pillars of the emerging fiscal state. The "corporate reconstruction of American capitalism," to use historian Martin J. Sklar's well-known phrase, not only helped initiate the first constitutional amendment since Reconstruction; it also bolstered the future promise of the new fiscal order in several other ways.[6]

First, the growing concentration of capital in the Northeast commercial sector provided income tax advocates, particularly those from the agrarian South and West, with an easy target. They could point to the wealthy shareholders and managers of the new, large-scale industrial firms as the type of individual taxpayers that had the faculty and ability to bear a growing share of the burdens of underwriting increased governmental expenditures. In this sense, the consequences of the great merger movement gave reformers an opportunity to place the ability-to-pay logic into action, to move the calls for direct and progressive taxes beyond the halls of the academy into the corridors of national power. At the same time, given the deep-seated, American anti-monopoly tradition, the rise of corporate capitalism also intensified the U.S. aversion to concentrations of economic power – an aversion that was most clearly visible when American national tax policy was placed in a comparative perspective.

Second, the colossal corporations themselves were seen as sources of tax revenue and as citizens in their own right – citizens that had a social responsibility to contribute to the commonwealth. Many of the economic and legal thinkers leading the intellectual revolution behind the tax reform movement had written about corporate taxation as a key component in building a new fiscal polity and a modern sense of civic identity. As early as 1878, Justice Thomas Cooley had recommended a tax on "stocks in corporations which have a practical monopoly in their line."[7] Early-twentieth-century thinkers and policymakers, similarly, stressed the social and ethical obligations that accompanied the power and influence of the new industrial giants. From this perspective, the enormous profits generated by these new businesses were viewed not merely as individual,

1940); Elizabeth Sanders, *The Roots of Reform: Farmers, Workers and the American State, 1877–1917* (Chicago: University of Chicago Press, 1999), 220–30.

[6] Martin J. Sklar, *The Corporate Reconstruction of American Capitalism, 1890–1916: The Market, the Law, and Politics* (New York, Cambridge University Press, 1988).

[7] Thomas M. Cooley, *Principles that Should Govern in the Framing of Tax Laws* (St. Louis: G. I. Jones and Co., 1878), 14, 17, 19, 20.

private gains, but as social wealth, produced and augmented by the broader state and collectivity. As Henry Carter Adams had explained, strategically deploying the language of Henry George, surplus profits were "an unearned increment to the corporation that should be directed through the machinery of taxation to the benefit of the citizens from which it accrues."[8] Simply put, the broader commonwealth, acting through the powers of the state, had a right to extract a portion of these corporate profits in the name of associational duties and social solidarity.

Finally, and perhaps most importantly, the transition to a "corporate-administered" stage of American capitalism also led to dramatic changes in economic organizations and administrative procedures that gave state builders new "tax handles" with which to assess and collect personal and business incomes.[9] As income and economic power became concentrated in large, integrated business corporations, it became easier for government authorities to identify and access sources of tax revenue. Corporate and individual income, in short, became more visible and "legible" for taxing authorities.[10]

With the 1909 corporate excise tax preceding the broader 1913 income tax, government officials were able to leverage the information provided by corporations to strengthen the tax collection process. In fact, lawmakers drafting the early income tax law would deploy the ideas of the progressive political economists, whom they depicted as politically neutral experts, to create a crude form of income tax withholding. In due time, the early American adoption of third-party reporting of revenue information would become particularly vital in strengthening the bureaucratic capacity of tax compliance. In these and other ways, the accelerating rise of Big Business in America at the turn of the century facilitated the development of the modern fiscal state.

8 Henry Carter Adams, "Suggestions for a System of Taxation," *Michigan Political Science Association Publications* 1:2 (May 1894), 60. H.C. Adams *Description of Industry: An Introduction to Economics* (New York: Henry Holt & Co., 1918), 261–2; H.C. Adams "Corporate Taxation," Mss Box 26, Henry Carter Adams Papers, Bentley Library, University of Michigan, Ann Arbor, Mich.

9 The term "tax handles" is generally associated with the work of early developmental economists. See, e.g., Richard Musgrave, *Fiscal Systems* (New Haven: Yale University Press, 1969), 125; Harley H. Hinrichs, "Determinants of Government Revenue Shares among Less-Developed Countries," *Economic Journal* 75 (September 1965), 546–56. Political and economic historians have, of course, also recognized the importance of changing economic organization to the development of tax regimes. W. Elliot Brownlee, *Federal Taxation in America: A Short History* (New York: Cambridge University Press, 2003); Martin Daunton, *Trusting Leviathan: The Politics of Taxation in Britain, 1799–1914* (Cambridge: Cambridge University Press, 2001), 14–15.

10 James C. Scott, *Seeing Like a State: How Certain Schemes to Improve the Human Condition Have Failed* (New Haven: Yale University Press, 1998).

A Crucial Context for Fiscal Reform

A number of historical factors prompted national lawmakers in 1909 to adopt a corporate excise tax and a proposed constitutional amendment overturning *Pollock*. These forces bore a remarkable resemblance to the structural strains that occasioned the adoption of the 1894 income tax. The modern currents of mass migration and urban industrialization that had begun in the late nineteenth century continued, albeit unevenly, well into the early decades of the twentieth. A new wave of European immigration, in fact, seemed to peak in the years that straddled the new century. So too did the growing number of Americans moving from rural farms to urban factories.[11] And just as the adoption of the 1894 income tax was preceded by a financial panic that triggered a massive economic depression, the 1909 corporate tax and constitutional amendment also came in the aftermath of a financial panic and an economic recession. The latter economic crisis began with the San Francisco earthquake and fire of 1906. That disaster not only devastated the city and its inhabitants, it also set in motion a series of events that undermined confidence in Northeastern financial institutions.[12]

With a fragile national economy still reeling from the San Francisco disaster, a failed speculative endeavor in the fall of 1907 revealed systemic flaws in New York's money markets. These defects alarmed investors and set off a run on several of New York's leading banks and brokerage houses. As depositors began demanding their money and banks became insolvent, Wall Street financier J. P. Morgan intervened, as he had done in the past, to support the failing financial institutions. Without a central bank to supply greater credit, and with the U.S. tethered to the rigid gold standard, private capital in the form of Morgan's individual wealth and his influence over the banking community appeared to be the only solution to the economic crisis.[13]

[11] Roger Daniels, *Guarding the Golden Door: American Immigration Policy and Immigrants since 1882* (New York: Hill & Wang, 2004); Timothy J. Hatton and Jeffrey G. Williamson, *The Age of Mass Migration: An Economic Analysis* (New York: Oxford University Press, 1998).

[12] Robert F. Bruner and Sean D. Carr, *The Panic of 1907: Lessons Learned from the Perfect Storm* (New York: John Wiley and Sons, 2009); O. M. W. Sprague, *History of the Crises under the National Banking Act* (Washington, D.C.: Government Printing Office, 1910).

[13] O. M. W. Sprague, "The American Crisis of 1907," *Economic Journal* 18:71 (1908), 353–72; Ron Chernow, *The House of Morgan: An American Banking Dynasty and the Rise of Modern Finance* (New York: Atlantic Monthly Press, 1990), 121–30; Bruner and Carr, *Panic of 1907*.

Morgan's rescue may have averted a devastating stock market crash, but the consequences of the panic were still felt throughout the country for the next several years. Hundreds of small banks across the nation failed, commodity prices fell dramatically, and unemployment skyrocketed. Although the recession that followed was not nearly as severe as past downturns, the dismal economic climate compelled reformers and lawmakers to reconsider the role of the state in the economy. Not only did tax activists exploit the economic conditions to press for fiscal reforms, but monetary experts used the crisis to advance their campaign for that other great Progressive-Era institutional achievement – the creation of the Federal Reserve Bank.[14]

Like the earlier downturn of the 1890s, the recession that followed the 1907 panic also drew greater public attention to the prevailing disparities in wealth and income. Just as empirical studies of economic inequality had appeared in the earlier slump, economic experts and social commentators once again underscored how industrialization widened the growing gulf between rich and poor. Although there was a dearth of accurate data on income and wealth, academics, journalists, and social activists used the emerging discipline of statistical science to infer trends in the rising concentration of wealth. Many of these tracts were written by students of the leading new school economists. Frank H. Streightoff, who studied with Edwin Seligman and Henry R. Seager at Columbia, and taught at DePauw University and later Indiana University, researched and wrote his 1912 study "The Distribution of Incomes in the U.S." in the wake of the recession. Though Streightoff was cautious in painting a precise picture of the overall distribution of income and wealth, he used available data to conclude that because of stagnant real wages over the past twenty years, little progress had been made in closing the disparities of income and wealth.[15]

Other commentators were more forthright. Willford I. King, the Wisconsin statistician and political economist who studied under Richard Ely, expressly updated the earlier studies conducted by George Holmes and Charles Spahr to show that by 1910 there was "considerable evidence to indicate that a larger fraction of the income is now concentrated

[14] Allan H. Meltzer, *A History of the Federal Reserve, Vol. 1: 1913–1951* (Chicago: University of Chicago Press, 2001), 128–9; William Greider, *Secrets of the Temple* (New York: Simon and Schuster, 1987), 273–5. For more on the beginnings of the Federal Reserve as the centerpiece of corporate liberal reform, see James Livingston, *Origins of the Federal Reserve System: Money, Class, and Corporate Capitalism, 1890–1913* (Ithaca: Cornell University Press, 1986).

[15] Frank H. Streightoff, *The Distributions of Incomes in the United States* (New York: Columbia University Press, 1912).

in the hands of a few of the very rich, than was the case twenty years ago." King's statistical analysis illustrated that, at the other end of the economic spectrum, the "poorest two-thirds of the people own but a petty five or six per cent of the wealth and the lower middle class possesses a still smaller share." The driver of these disparities was, for King, quite clear. "The greatest force in the last three decades making for income concentration has been the successful organization of monster corporations," King contended. "The promoters and manipulators of these concerns have received, as their share of the spoils, permanent income claims, in the shape of securities, large enough to make Croeus appear like a pauper."[16]

The new statistical studies of wealth and income concentration, like their predecessors, helped shape public opinion. Just as the earlier investigations had found their way into the labor press and congressional debates, the studies by King, Streightoff, and others were similarly influential, making their way into labor party debates over socialism and economic discussions among academics, religious leaders, and even business groups.[17] Social Gospel ministers like Walter Rauschenbusch became increasingly alarmed by the ravages of economic inequality. Referencing the recent studies of inequality, Rauschenbusch believed that it was necessary to level the existing concentrations of wealth. "Wealth – to use a homely illustration – is to a nation what manure is to a farm," Rauschenbusch wrote using his gift for vivid metaphors; "if the farmer spreads it evenly over soil, it will enrich the whole. If he should leave it in heaps, the land would be impoverished and under the rich heaps the vegetation would be killed."[18]

[16] Willford I. King, *The Wealth and Income of the People of the United States* (New York: Macmillan Co., 1915), 231–2, 80, 218–19. Despite King's criticism of "monster corporations," his normative proposals were rather conservative and dismissive of progressive calls for a "living wage." Ibid. King's conservatism may also be a reflection on how his mentor, Richard Ely, by 1915 had himself grown increasingly wary of state intervention. Benjamin G. Rader, *The Academic Mind and Reform: The Influence of Richard T. Ely in American Life* (Lexington: University of Kentucky Press, 1966).

[17] Morris Hillquit and John A. Ryan, *Socialism, Promise or Menace?* (New York: Macmillan Co., 1914), 123–5; Scott Nearing, *Financing the Wage-earner's Family: A Survey of the Facts Bearing on Income and Expenditures in the Families of American Wage-earners* (New York: B. W. Huebsch, 1913), 105; National City Bank of New York, *U.S. Securities, Government Finance, Economic and Financial Conditions* (New York: National City Bank of New York, 1916), 7–8.

[18] Walter Rauschenbusch, *Christianity and the Social Crisis* (New York: Macmillan, 1907), 281. On the significance of Rauschenbusch to modern social Christianity, see Christopher H. Evans, *The Kingdom is Always but Coming: A Life of Walter Rauschenbusch* (Grand Rapids, Mich.: Wm. B. Eerdmans Publishing Co., 2004).

The renewed attention to inequality also reinvigorated the single-tax movement, which had always been a meddlesome distraction for income tax advocates. Although professional economists like Seligman and Ely remained dubious and highly critical of the single tax, prominent citizens such as Philadelphia industrialist Joseph Fels reignited popular interest in using the tax system – particularly the single tax on the "unearned increment" of land values – to regulate monopoly power. In 1909, a decade after Henry George's death, Fels created a foundation to help spread and popularize George's teachings on land reform and the single tax.[19]

The single tax, however, failed to gain much traction in the United States, outside of a few pockets of acceptance. Part of the reason was because more practical supporters of the single tax believed that a graduated income tax was a more politically plausible alternative. "While I believe in a single tax," the labor leader Jacob G. Schonfarber informed lawmakers, "I do not think we could radically put single tax into effect all over this country at once, because it would cause a revolution, and I believe the way we want to grow on this is by evolution. I do not want to see a revolution."[20] In this way, the revived interest in the single tax fueled the calls for fundamental fiscal reform without succumbing to the dogmatic demands of Henry George.

Despite the striking parallels between the 1890s and the 1900s, there was one critical distinction between the two periods: the changing landscape of corporate consolidations, or what King described as the rise of "monster corporations" in the early twentieth century. Between 1895 and 1904, during the great merger movement, manufacturing firms consolidated at a remarkable, breakneck pace due to a confluence of historical factors. During that brief period, nearly two thousand companies combined with former rivals to create some of the nation's largest industrial corporations – many of which continue to exist today.[21]

[19] Arthur N. Young, *The Single Tax Movement in the United States* (Princeton: Princeton University Press, 1916), 163–84; Arthur P. Dudden, *Joseph Fels and the Single-Tax Movement* (Philadelphia: Temple University Press, 1971), 199–245; Brownlee, *Federal Taxation in America*, 53–4.

[20] "Testimony of Jacob G. Schonfarber," Washington, D.C., December 5, 1899, in *Report of the Industrial Commission, Vol. VII* (Washington: Government Printing Office, 1901), 444–46; Robert D. Johnston, *The Radical Middle Class: Populist Democracy and the Question of Capitalism in Progressive Era Portland, Oregon* (Princeton: Princeton University Press, 2003), 159–76.

[21] Naomi R. Lamoreaux, *The Great Merger Movement in American Business, 1895–1904* (New York: Cambridge University Press, 1895); Robert L. Nelson, *Merger Movements in American Industry, 1895–1956* (Princeton: Princeton University Press, 1959); Alfred

The great merger movement was an unprecedented and highly consequential event. The nineteenth-century canal companies and railroads, to be sure, had pioneered American managerial capitalism. But whereas the earlier transportation businesses relied mainly on the issuance of public and private debt, the great merger movement hastened the institutional convergence of industrial manufacturing and finance capital. With the rise of corporate consolidations came the accelerating expansion of capital markets. Banks and financial firms prospered, as a result, and the ownership of large business corporations gradually became more dispersed as the American spirit of financial speculation and the ideology of "shareholder democracy" began to take shape. The broadened base of corporate ownership was ironically accompanied by a growing concentration of wealth in the hands of those who dominated the giant corporate organizations.[22]

Contemporaries reacted to the growth of Big Business with great ambivalence. Some celebrated the enormous industrial corporations as the ideals of economic efficiency and as essential vehicles for the mobilization of capital and the implementation of scientific management. Many others, by contrast, were more suspicious of the new corporate behemoths and the "robber barons" who owned and led them. Tapping into the deep-seated American anti-monopoly tradition, critics characterized large corporations as rapacious financial predators that disregarded the rule of law and common morality in their relentless efforts to expand and entrench their economic empires. Indeed, corporations, many of which were consolidated as holding companies or "trusts," were depicted in popular culture as economic octopuses stretching their many tentacles

D. Chandler, Jr. *The Visible Hand: The Managerial Revolution in American Business* (Cambridge, Mass.: Harvard University Press, 1977); David Bunting, *The Rise of Large American Corporations, 1889–1919* (New York: Garland Publishing, 1987).

22 William G. Roy, *Socializing Capital: The Rise of the Large Industrial Corporation in America* (Princeton: Princeton University Press, 1997); Vincent P. Carosso, *Investment Banking in America: A History* (Cambridge, Mass.: Harvard University Press, 1970); Lawrence E. Mitchell, *The Speculation Economy: How Finance Triumphed over Industry* (San Francisco: Berrett-Koehler, 2007); Julia C. Ott, *When Wall Street Met Main Street: The Quest for an Investors' Democracy* (Cambridge, Mass.: Harvard University Press, 2011); David Hochfelder, "'Where the People Could Speculate': The Ticker, Bucket Shops, and the Origins of Popular Participation in Financial Market, 1880–1920," *Journal of American History* 93:2 (2006), 335–58. The increasing separation of ownership and control of corporate businesses would, of course, become a great concern for a subsequent generation of corporate law scholars and policymakers. Adolf A. Berle Jr. and Gardiner C. Means, *The Modern Corporation and Private Property* (New York: Macmillan, 1932).

into nearly every aspect of American life. Accordingly, social commentators feared that the concentration of economic and political power amassed in these large businesses would threaten republican values and the core ideals of a liberal democracy. These tensions were reflected in tax policy, as the owners and operators of these big businesses – and in many cases the corporations themselves – became the targets of reformers seeking to reallocate the tax burden.[23]

Most supporters of progressive taxation, however, did not want to radically redistribute the tremendous wealth generated by the new corporate economy. They wanted, instead, to recalibrate the existing imbalance of tax burdens. Following the political economists who had been advancing the theoretical superiority of taxing individuals and businesses according to their "ability to pay," legal experts and other tax reformers seized on the growing power of Big Business and the increasing disparities in wealth to reinvigorate the tax reform movement. They began by focusing on corporations and their owners and managers as targets of a new income tax. Reformers were aided in their efforts, ironically, by the U.S. Supreme Court itself. With a new composition of justices, the Court validated important tax measures from the Spanish-American War that opened the way for lawmakers and reformers to reconsider the durability of *Pollock*. These decisions, together with pivotal presidential leadership, revived the campaign for fundamental fiscal reform.

A Rejuvenated Reform Movement

As early as the 1890s, even before the tremendous trend toward business consolidations, the growing power of interstate corporations pushed economic theorists to reconsider the optimal taxation of these large-scale national businesses. As we have seen in the previous chapter, the late-nineteenth-century system of state and local corporate taxes, based mainly on tangible property, was far from coherent or consistent. To counter the reigning "chaos" and to rationalize the taxation of corporations operating across state lines, economic experts like Edwin R. A. Seligman, Henry

[23] Frank Norris, *The Octopus: A Story of California* (New York: Doubleday, 1901); Matthew Josephson, *The Robber Barons: The Great American Capitalists, 1861–1901* (New York: Harcourt Brace, 1934). For examples of scholarship that has celebrated the contributions of the corporations and the capitalists who led them, see Allan Nevins, *Study in Power: John D. Rockefeller, Industrialist and Philanthropist* (New York: Scribner, 1953); Maury Klein, *The Change Makers: From Carnegie to Gates: How the Great Entrepreneurs Transformed Ideas into Industries* (New York: Henry Holt, 2004).

Carter Adams, Francis Walker, and others had contended that the federal government ought to intervene by taxing the earning power of large multistate corporations.[24] The *Pollock* decision had put an end to such initial proposals for a federal tax on interstate corporations. But the Court's subsequent decisions, first, upholding the 1898 national inheritance tax in *Knowlton v. Moore*, then, validating the corporate excise taxes on sugar and oil refineries in *Spreckels Sugar Refining Co. v. McClain*, once again opened up possibilities for fiscal state-builders.[25]

The two Supreme Court decisions did not challenge *Pollock*, but they did provide some solace to progressive reformers. By limiting the application of the direct tax clause, the decisions maintained the use of national taxing powers to attack certain concentrations of wealth. In *Knowlton*, the Court upheld the 1898 succession tax as an indirect "death duty." Because inheritance taxes were historically considered "as being imposed, not on property real or personal... but as being levied on the transmission or receipt of property occasioned by death," they were deemed to be indirect duties not direct taxes. Taxes on the mere transfer of property, the Court concluded, were not direct levies requiring apportionment. Similarly, in *Spreckels*, the Court ruled that a gross receipts tax imposed on sugar and oil refiners to help fund the Spanish-American War was not a direct tax requiring apportionment, but rather that it was an indirect excise. "Clearly the tax is not imposed upon gross annual receipts as property," wrote Justice John M. Harlan for the majority, "but only in respect of carrying on or doing the business of refining sugar." Although neither decision expressly undermined the holding of *Pollock*, each evidenced the Court's reluctance in extending the reach of the direct tax clause. Even this slight hesitation, as we shall see, gave some legal experts a chance to question the durability of *Pollock*.[26]

The decision upholding the corporate excise tax also provided an opening for those activists focused on taxing the rising "monster corporations." Reformers seized the new opportunity. Influential thinkers and civic leaders like Francis Walker reaffirmed that corporations had an obligation, a social duty under the tenets of fiscal citizenship, to pay a reasonable share of the growing tax burden. Writing near the height of the

[24] Edwin R. A. Seligman, "The Taxation of Corporations II," *Political Science Quarterly* 5:3 (September 1890), 464; Francis Walker, *Double Taxation in the United States* (New York: Columbia University Press, 1895), 131; Adams, "Corporate Taxation."

[25] *Knowlton v. Moore*, 178 U.S. 41 (1900); *Spreckels Sugar Refining Co. v. McClain*, 192 U.S. 397 (1904).

[26] *Knowlton*, 178 U.S. 41, 81; *Spreckels Sugar Refining Co.*, 192 U.S. 397, 411.

merger boom and soon after the *Knowlton* decision, Walker – the American theorist who had initiated the conceptual campaign for taxation based on natural ability – stressed the distributional concerns that underpinned a national corporate income tax: "Theoretical justice requires, first, that the tax shall reach the actual income earning power of the business, and, secondly, that the burden shall be equitably apportioned among the parties that receive the income." The latter phrase suggested that Walker, like most political economists, was well aware that the incidence of a corporate tax was contingent on a number of factors, that shareholders, workers, or creditors (and possibly other parties) might be the ultimate payers of the levy.[27]

Indeed, economic experts and lawmakers had been grappling for decades with the challenges of trying to tax corporations and their shareholders. "Governments are everywhere confronted by the question of how to reach the taxable capacity of the holders of these securities, or of the associations themselves," wrote Seligman. "Whom shall we tax and how shall we tax them in order to attain substantial justice? Perhaps no question in the whole domain of financial science has been answered in a more unsatisfactory way." Ultimately, there was no conclusive solution to this dilemma.[28]

As present-day scholars have shown, the original motives behind U.S. corporate taxation consisted of a mix of regulation and remittance. Many contemporaries believed that corporations were organic and real business associations that had their own collective identity, and thus tax law could be used as a cudgel to curb and regulate the growing power of these big businesses. By contrast, others contended that corporations were simply aggregations of individuals; they were artificial entities that had no metaphysical presence beyond serving the will of their individual owners. From this perspective, the corporate tax was geared simply toward raising revenue effectively by remitting taxes aimed squarely at stockholders.[29]

[27] Francis Walker, "The Taxation of Corporations in the United States," *Annals of the American Academy of Political and Social Science* 19 (1902), 1–20. See also "Testimony of Edwin R.A. Seligman," Washington, D.C., December 6, 1899, in *Report of the Industrial Commission on Transportation, Vol. IV* (Washington: Government Printing Office, 1900), 602.

[28] Edwin R. A. Seligman, "The Taxation of Corporations I," *Political Science Quarterly* 5:2 (June 1890).

[29] This debate over regulation or remittance has come to dominate the recent legal-historical literature on the origins of the U.S. corporate tax. See, e.g., Marjorie E. Kornhauser, "Corporate Regulation and the Origins of the Corporate Income Tax," *Indiana Law Journal* 66 (1990), 53; Reuven S. Avi-Yonah, "Corporations, Society, and the State: A

There is, to be sure, sufficient historical evidence to support both of these dominant interpretations. The corporate tax was both a means toward regulating corporate capital and a vehicle for collecting taxes aimed at shareholders. Still, a comparative examination of corporate taxation suggests that the United States, unlike other Western industrialized nation-states, had a particular preoccupation at the turn of the century with using tax policy to discipline capitalists. In this sense, the twin goals of regulation and remittance were not antithetical to each other, but rather reinforcing. Just as bootleggers and Baptists came together to support Prohibition, anti-corporate regulators and administrative revenue reformers could agree, at least in principle, on the need for a corporate tax, even if their motivations differed. The growing contemporary consensus for some kind of corporate tax, and the American obsession with taxing capitalists, can be seen most clearly by placing U.S. corporate tax policy in a broader comparative perspective – one that goes below the national level and beyond the American nation-state.

Between Regulation and Remittance: Comparative Perspectives

At the U.S. subnational level, as we have seen, corporations were regularly embedded in the taxing web of industrial states and commonwealths. Throughout the antebellum era, American state governments attempted to apply their varying property taxes to corporations. And as they reformed their fiscal structures at the turn of the century, corporations consistently remained at the center of their taxing efforts, as California's experience shows. When they separated their sources of revenue, state lawmakers in the Golden State used corporate income taxes to further the dual aims of remitting badly needed revenue and regulating the growing power of Big Business.[30]

In this way, the development of state-level corporate tax law and policy was part and parcel of the broader intellectual currents sweeping through American public finance. The key words "ability to pay" and

Defense of the Corporate Tax," *Virginia Law Review* 90 (2004), 119; Steven A. Bank, "Entity Theory as Myth in the Origins of the Corporate Income Tax," *William & Mary Law Review* 43 (2001), 173; Steven A. Bank, "A Capital Lock-In Theory of the Corporate Tax," *Georgetown Law Journal* 94 (2006), 889.

30 Carl C. Plehn, "Results of Separation in California," in *Proceedings of the Ninth Annual Conference under the Auspices of the National Tax Association* (Ithaca: National Tax Association, 1915), 50–8. David R. Doerr, *California's Tax Machine: A History of Taxing and Spending in the Golden State*, ed. Ronald Roach (Sacramento: California Taxpayers' Association, 2000).

"faculty" applied as much to individuals as to corporations, which by 1886 were deemed by the U.S. Supreme Court to be legal persons entitled to equal protection under the Fourteenth Amendment.[31] Taxing corporations based not only on their property holdings, but also on their earning capacity, was thus one pivotal way to put into practice the dramatic shift in the philosophical foundations of American tax policy.

In comparing the development of state tax laws, national officials echoed the significance of taxing corporations according to their earning capacity or ability to pay. "There is a marked tendency in all these States toward making earning power the basis of taxation for quasi-public corporations," wrote George Clapperton of the U.S. Industrial Commission in 1901. "Properly directed, this must be regarded as the correct principle and capable of practical application to such corporations under existing industrial conditions."[32] By 1909, federal tax officials conceded that even the precise definition of "taxation" itself had shifted. In language remarkably similar to Richard Ely's 1888 definition of a tax, the U.S. Bureau of Corporations opined that a tax "is a payment exacted by government as a source of general revenue and not as an equivalent of a specific benefit."[33]

The Bureau admitted that there were still two prevailing theories of taxation – benefits and ability to pay. But it stressed that "the preference is commonly given to the theory that each person, natural or artificial, should contribute to governmental support according to his ability to pay." In fact, the Bureau went on to emphasize that corporations provided "a place where the theoretically perfect test – ability to earn – can be applied in practice as a means of ascertaining the proper amount of taxes to be paid." Unlike individuals, for whom faculty or ability to pay was difficult to measure and perhaps even more daunting to administer, corporations were uniquely situated to measure future earning power. "The market value of the stock depends not wholly upon past earnings, but also, and chiefly, upon the supposed ability to earn in the future," wrote the Bureau. Consequently, corporations faced a tax "burden which

[31] *County of Santa Clara v. Southern Pacific Railroad*, 118 U.S. 394 (1886).

[32] George Clapperton, *Taxation of Corporations: Report on Systems Employed in Various States Prepared Under the Direction of the Industrial Commission* (Washington, DC: Government Printing Office, 1901); "Favors an Income Tax," *New York Times*, March 28, 1901, 5.

[33] U.S. Department of Commerce & Labor, Bureau of the Corporations, *Taxation of Corporations: New England I* (1909), 3; Richard T. Ely, *Taxation in American States and Cities* (New York: Crowell, 1888), 14 (for his definition, Ely was quoting an even earlier 1875 Massachusetts Tax Commission report).

is theoretically correct," and which "may well be taken into account when one discusses whether it is to the public interest to encourage the formation of corporations." By the end of the merger boom, government officials became well aware of how corporate consolidations and the concomitant expansion of capital markets were making corporate profits and the earnings of shareholders and managers not only more visible but also more "legible."[34]

Another reason American thinkers, jurists, and government officials embraced the direct taxation of corporations was the acceptance of new continental theories about corporate personality. Transatlantic ideas were once again shaping tax debates. In earlier years, the new school political economists learned a great deal from their overseas mentors working in the tradition of the German historical school. Now, a new group of American legal and economic theorists was adopting Germanic ideas about the collectivist nature of corporations as real or natural, not merely artificial, entities. Legal perceptions about the corporation as a real entity – with its own sense of legal personhood and the attendant responsibilities of fiscal citizenship – supported the demands for a separate corporate tax. The work of the German jurist Otto von Gierke, the leading continental proponent of depicting corporations as real entities, had a tremendous impact on American scholars. The University of Chicago Professor Ernst Freund incorporated many of Gierke's ideas into his own classic 1897 monograph *The Legal Nature of Corporations*.[35]

American jurists accepted Freund's juridical notion of corporations as real and separate legal entities mainly because it resonated with the deep-seated, American anti-monopoly tradition and with the changing material conditions of a modern industrializing nation. Recall that nearly every progressive reformer – from the political economists to the founders of settlement houses to the Social Gospel ministers – believed that the increasing interdependency of modern life had challenged the classical notion of individualism. In an urban-industrial society, these reformers contended, a greater concern for solidarity and community interests had supplanted the dominance of atomistic individualism. The importance of

34 Ely, *Taxation in American States and Cities*, 16; Scott, *Seeing Like a State*.

35 Ernst Freund, *The Legal Nature of the Corporation* (Chicago: University of Chicago Press, 1897). On the influence of continental legal theories for American law, see generally Horwitz, *Transformation II*, 179–80; Ron Harris, "The Transplantation of the Legal Discourse on Corporate Personality Theories: From German Codification to British Political Pluralism and American Big Business," *Washington & Lee Law Review* 63 (2006), 1421–78.

the collectivity over the individual was perhaps best expressed in commercial life. "We have almost come to the point," Henry Carter Adams proclaimed at the height of the corporate merger boom, "where the individuality of business conduct is swallowed up in its collective character so that the individual point of view is now the exception rather than the rule."[36]

Given the growing attention to collective privileges and duties, it is no surprise that the theory of the corporation as a real, separate entity was ascendant. Even the U.S. Supreme Court had recognized that the corporation was a metaphysical person entitled to equal protection under the Fourteenth Amendment. In the 1886 landmark case of *Santa Clara v. Southern Pacific Railroad*, the Court succinctly concluded that "the Fourteenth Amendment to the Constitution, which forbids a State to deny to any person within its jurisdiction the equal protection of the laws, applies to these corporations." More specifically, the Court held that California was prohibited, under the Equal Protection Clause, from taxing corporate and individual property differently. Although the decision did not expressly promote the view of a corporation as a natural or metaphysical entity, it embedded corporate property rights into American constitutional jurisprudence.[37]

In the process of imbuing corporations with the legal property rights of personhood, the Court unwittingly helped reformers make the case for a separate layer of corporate taxation. For if corporations were legal persons with constitutional rights, they were also members of the body politic, and thus their legal rights came with reciprocal social duties and responsibilities, including contributing to the commonwealth. From this perspective, *Santa Clara* not only provided legal legitimacy to newly emergent concentrations of economic power; it also made these new business organizations parties to the newly reconfigured social contract. The notion of corporations having separate legal personalities corresponded, moreover, with the hostile intentions ascribed to these giant economic entities. If the industrial corporation could be seen in American social thought and popular culture as a ravenous octopus seeking to extend its tentacles throughout American society, then surely such economic

[36] Henry Carter Adams to Edwin R. A. Seligman, June 20, 1904, in "The Seligman Correspondence II," ed. Joseph Dorfman, *Political Science Quarterly* 56 (June 1941), 270–86, 275.

[37] *County of Santa Clara v. Southern Pacific Railroad*, 118 U.S. 394 (1886); Horwitz, *Transformation II*, 66–76.

associations could be seen as occupying a distinct space in the body politic and the legal order.[38]

While newly emergent legal theories about the corporation may have supported reformers' calls for a U.S. corporate tax, there was still something peculiarly American – and adversarial – about the historical development of the taxation of corporate capital. Whereas U.S. thinkers and lawmakers viewed corporations as both dangerous concentrations of capital and as conduits that could be used to tax business owners, British experts were much less equivocal. For them, the corporation was truly an artificial entity that had no earning capacity of its own. For tax purposes, English corporations were the functional equivalent of partnerships. Accordingly, the British mainly used their "company" income tax as an indirect collection device aimed at shareholders.[39]

Comparative tax experts reflected on the differences in Anglo-American corporate tax policy. In England, "corporations, except for convenience of collection of the tax, are not treated as taxable entities," wrote the scholar Harrison B. Spaulding. "The underlying theory is that the income tax is to be imposed only on individuals and in accordance with their taxable capacity." For the British, this meant that

> a corporation is regarded merely as a device by means of which a number of individuals can conveniently do business, and it is not looked upon as a separate object of taxation. It is not in itself a potentially taxable person, but is an aggregation of persons who may or may not be taxable. It is necessary for some purposes that corporations be regarded as separate legal entities, but the British do not extend this conception to the field of income tax.[40]

The contrasting Anglo-American visions of the corporation also illustrated a long and peculiar material history of American antagonism between business and government. The U.S. treatment of corporations as separate legal entities was a doctrine, Spaulding noted, that "is so well settled, and has been established so long, that it has no doubt had its effect on the popular mind."[41]

[38] Gregory A. Mark, "The Personification of the Business Corporation in American Law," *University of Chicago Law Review* 54 (1987), 1441–83, 1465–6. On the cultural significance of corporations in this time period, see Alan Trachtenberg, *The Incorporation of America: Culture and Society in the Gilded Age* (New York: Hill & Wang, 1982).

[39] Rob McQueen, *A Social History of Company Law: Great Britain and the Australian Colonies, 1854–1920* (Surrey: Ashgate, 2009), Ch. 5.

[40] Harrison B. Spaulding, *The Income Tax in Great Britain and the United States* (London: P. S. King & Sons, 1927), 86–7.

[41] Ibid., 92. The U.S.–U.K. differences in corporate law and taxation also reflected the different ownership structure and power relations between owners and managers in

That effect could be seen perhaps most clearly in the general American aversion toward concentrated economic power – an aversion that was best expressed in the public distrust of large-scale business corporations. "In any discussion of the development of ideas regarding corporations in the United States, it must be remembered that they have frequently been regarded as possible or actual sources of evil, and accordingly are objects of suspicion," wrote Spaulding. "Practically all 'big business' is carried on by means of corporations," and thus "there is a feeling that if corporations are heavily taxed the tax will fall most heavily on the wealthier part of the community." Unlike their British counterparts, Spaulding noted, Americans seemed conflicted; their laws seemed to contradict their politics. The U.S. political theory of laissez-faire capitalism seemed to be in tension with an actually existing tax system that punished capitalists. "While in the United States Socialism as a political creed has little following," Spaulding concluded, "yet in few countries have there been tax laws so pleasing to Socialists as those of the United States."[42]

Spaulding's acute observation captured the ambivalence at the heart of American corporate tax policy. Although many experts and lawmakers welcomed the economic growth and prosperity that attended the rise of corporate capitalism, they also feared its social and political repercussions. To counter the excesses of industrialism, theorists argued that corporations ought to be seen not merely as the agents of individual economic actors, but rather as separate legal entities with significant social responsibilities. "Everywhere," wrote Edwin Seligman at the tail end of the merger boom, corporations "form a problem of increasing importance

the two countries. Steven A. Bank, *Anglo-American Corporate Taxation: Tracing the Common Roots of Divergent Approaches* (New York: Cambridge University Press, 2001), 142–6. Business historians have long recognized that before World War I family structured companies general dominated the British corporate landscape. See Alfred D. Chandler Jr., *Scale and Scope: The Dynamics of Industrial Capitalism* (Cambridge, Mass.: Harvard University Press, 1994), Chapter 7; Brian R. Cheffins, "Law, Economics, and the UK's System of Corporate Governance: Lessons from History," *Journal of Corporate Law Studies* 1:1 (June 2001), 71–91.

42 Spaulding, *Income Tax in Great Britain and the U.S.*, 93–4. British historians have corroborated Spalding's interpretation. "Corporate taxation did not have a purchase in British fiscal policy, for it contradicted the assumption that firms were agents rather than taxable entities," Martin Daunton has explained. English "corporation taxation did not, as in the United States, connect with hostility to big business or with opposition to the federal income tax." Martin Daunton, *Just Taxes: The Politics of Taxation in Britain, 1914–1979* (New York: Cambridge University Press, 2002), 93.

and present an admirable example of what is meant by taxation from a *social* rather than individual point of view."[43]

This social point of view meant that the growing interdependency of modern life required a major readjustment of the tax system – a readjustment in which the centralized state could become a much needed political and social counterbalance to the corporate concentration of economic power. Just as state-level reformers like T. S. Adams, Charles Bullock, and Nils Haugen resisted the demands for maintaining "home rule" and local autonomy, activists at the national level similarly fought for the growth and consolidation of federal power. "It is evident," wrote Francis Walker "that the enlargement of federal control is a matter of necessity in many ways, and the need of it will become more and more urgent as the economic relations of different parts of the country become more intimate and the organization of business more centralized. This solidarity of economic life must find a more appropriate expression in the law."[44]

From the Theorists to the Lawmakers

It did not take long for influential national politicians to consider ways of translating the growing interdependency of modern economic life into new tax legislation. In December 1906, President Theodore Roosevelt elaborated on his earlier calls for a "tax on wealth," by recommending that Congress consider a progressive inheritance tax and "if possible a graduated income tax." These seemingly offhanded remarks alarmed economic elites and their representatives in Congress, who feared that the "cowboy" president might follow through on these proposals. Yet, throughout the rest of his presidency and his political life, Roosevelt vacillated in his support for direct and progressive taxation. At times he echoed previous reformers by urging the United States to join other "civilized countries" in adopting such levies. And on other occasions he proposed that the federal government rely only on inheritance taxes, leaving income taxes to the states. Ultimately, Roosevelt did little during his presidential administration to further the movement for direct and progressive taxation.[45]

43 Seligman, "Pending Problems in Public Finance," *Proceedings of the Congress of Arts and Sciences, Universal Exposition, St. Louis* ed. Howard J. Rodgers (Boston: Houghton, Mifflin and Co., 1906) (emphasis added). This essay was subsequently republished in Seligman's hugely popular *Essays in Taxation* (1913).

44 Walker, "Taxation of Corporations."

45 Buenker, *Income Tax and the Progressive Era*, 51–4; Ratner, *American Taxation*.

Roosevelt's tepid endorsements emboldened centrist lawyers and tax experts. In 1906, former Attorney General Wayne MacVeagh commended Roosevelt for drawing attention to the tax reform movement. But unlike the new liberal reformers who saw the movement for direct and progressive taxes as a way to "round out the existing tax system in the direction of greater justice," as Seligman had put it, MacVeagh believed that conceding to a moderate income tax could help maintain social stability and preserve well-heeled fortunes.[46] Like Roosevelt himself, MacVeagh was astonished that the president's calls for a moderate tax on swollen wealth had terrified the ultra-rich. The wealthy seemed oblivious to the way ordinary Americans perceived the growing power of corporations and widening economic disparities. "Capitalists exhibit a singular stupidity in resisting every attempt to impose upon them their proper share of the public burdens," proclaimed MacVeagh. Economic elites failed to understand how moderate taxation could defuse more radical calls for wealth redistribution. If Roosevelt's comments and the *Knowlton* decision, upholding the inheritance tax, signaled the impending taxation of accumulated wealth, MacVeagh's central goal was "to impress upon the public mind the necessity of proper limits upon such taxation."[47]

Although MacVeagh's remarks may have reflected a conservative reaction to changing historical circumstances, many other experts sincerely believed that the heightened anxieties surrounding corporate consolidations and increasing inequality could reinvigorate genuine and profound fiscal reform. The *Knowlton* decision, for example, prompted several economic and legal experts to reopen the discussion about the continued validity of *Pollock*. Seligman's soon-to-be Columbia colleague, Wesley C. Mitchell, summarized the holding and reasoning in the inheritance tax case to demonstrate that the Court had been absorbing the lessons about the economic distinctions between direct and indirect taxes – distinctions that the justices in *Pollock* seemed to ignore. Likewise, Seligman's student Max West posited the case for amending the Constitution to overturn *Pollock*, rather than relying on challenging the Court's presumed

[46] Edwin R. A. Seligman, "The Income Tax," *Political Science Quarterly* 9:14 (December 1984), 610–48, 610.

[47] Wayne MacVeagh, "The Graduated Taxation of Incomes and Inheritances," *North American Review* 182:595 (June 1906), 824–8, 827; Buenker, *Income Tax and the Progressive Era*, 51–4; Stanley, *Dimensions of Law in the Service of Order*, 188–9.

inconsistencies with a new income tax law.[48] The Harvard economist Charles J. Bullock published a lengthy two-part historical analysis of the direct tax clause – in the *Political Science Quarterly*, no doubt with Seligman's editorial approval – to show that the clause was a "relic of the great compromise upon the subject of slavery," and as such that it "had no basis in any rational scheme for regulating taxation."[49]

Recent academic work and state-level tax reforms further boosted the growing interest in direct and progressive taxation. Legal experts like Frank J. Goodnow began turning their attention to taxation with the publication of an influential tax treatise modeled after Thomas Cooley's earlier work. Even those experts who were dubious about the administrative efficacy of an income tax – such as the Wisconsin economist D. O. Kinsman who had initially resisted the adoption of state-level income taxes – acknowledged that a new "spirit of reform" seemed to have swept through many states since *Pollock*. The "present period of income tax activity" by states and commonwealths acting as "political laboratories," Kinsman conceded in 1909, prepared the way for more far reaching changes at the national level.[50]

Yet, the strongest case for challenging the existing constitutional obstacle to the income tax came from Edwin B. Whitney, the former attorney general who had lost the *Pollock* case. Writing in the *Harvard Law Review*, Whitney presented a legal brief – disguised as an academic article – that attempted to retry *Pollock* before the legal academy, if not the Court. From Whitney's perspective, the Court's most recent support for the federal succession tax suggested that the meaning of the direct tax clause "still remains in doubt." Though Whitney stated that the aim of his article was not "to comment upon the advisability of a court's reversing its own previous decisions upon a point of political controversy," he did not hide his disappointment in how his defense of the 1894 income tax was defeated by the historical "accident" of "the odd judge in a five

[48] Wesley C. Mitchell, "The Inheritance Tax Decision," *Journal of Political Economy* 8:3 (1900), 387–97; Max West, "The Income Tax and the National Revenues," *Journal of Political Economy* 8:4 (1900), 433–51.

[49] Charles J. Bullock, "The Origin, Purpose and Effect of the Direct-Tax Clause of the Federal Constitution, II," *Political Science Quarterly* 15:3 (1900), 452–81, 452–3. See also Bullock, "The Origins, Purpose and Effect of the Direct-Tax Clause of the Federal Constitution, I," *Political Science Quarterly* 15:2 (1900), 217–39.

[50] Frank J. Goodnow, *Selected Cases on the Law of Taxation* (Chicago: Callaghan and Co., 1905); Delos O. Kinsman, "The Present Period of Income Tax Activity in the American States," *Quarterly Journal of Economics* 23:2 (Feb. 1909), 296–306, 304, 296.

to four decision."[51] Indeed, Whitney went on to predict that a "future income tax law, varying perhaps slightly in its substantial provisions" would create a constitutional dilemma for the Court. It would force the justices to determine whether the pre-*Pollock*

> series of decisions should be given greater weight because they were unanimous upon the point involved, and because one of them was substantially contemporaneous with the Constitution, and was enunciated by men who were witnesses as well as judges as to the meaning of the words used in that instrument, or whether another decision [*Pollock*] should be given greater weight because it was later in point of time, and was regarded by five out of the nine judges then comprising the court as distinguishable from the earlier ones, or as overruling them.[52]

With this less-than-subtle comparison, the former attorney general encouraged fiscal state-builders to maintain the pressure for a genuine legal transformation of the prevailing tax regime.

Whitney's plea did not go unheeded. In fact, his argument persuaded many influential lawyers and lawmakers including a newly elected President William Howard Taft. Swept into the White House as a tariff reformer, Taft had intimated that a carefully crafted income tax, designed to make up for lost revenues from lower import duties, might pass constitutional muster.[53] Encouraged by these comments, a group of agrarian Southern Democrats, led by Cordell Hull (D-Tenn.) in the House and Joseph W. Bailey (D-Tex.) and William E. Borah (D-Idaho) in the Senate, joined forces with a cadre of Midwestern progressive Republicans, led by Senators Robert La Follette (R-Wis.) and Albert C. Cummins (R-Iowa), in drafting a new income tax law. Aligned against these income tax advocates were the core congressional members of the Old Guard Republican Party, led by Nelson W. Aldrich (R-R.I.), the powerful chair of the Senate Finance Committee, and Rep. Joseph G. Cannon (R-Ill.), the Speaker of the House.[54]

Although national legislators had attempted unsuccessfully to introduce an income tax several times in the wake of *Pollock*, the 1909 congressional debates occurred amidst a unique confluence of historical forces favoring tax reform. The heightened social anxieties surrounding the power of Big Business and increasing economic inequality, the

[51] Edward B. Whitney, "The Income Tax and the Constitution," *Harvard Law Review* 20:4 (1907), 280–96, 280, 286, 289.

[52] Ibid., 288–9.

[53] Ratner, *American Taxation*, 268–9; Paul, *Taxation in the United States* 90–1.

[54] Ratner, *American Taxation*, 280–9.

William E. Borah (1865–1940)

Cordell Hull (1871–1955)

Nelson W. Aldrich (1841–1915)

FIGURE 5.1. The Lawmakers. Among the key legislators, Representative Cordell Hull (D-Tenn.) and Senator William E. Borah (D-Ida.) were firm supporters of the income tax. Senator Nelson W. Aldrich (R-R.I.) was a staunch opponent. Courtesy of the Library of Congress, Prints & Photographs Division, photographed by Harris & Ewing, LC-DIG-hec-15593, LC-DIG-hec-20332, LC-DIG-hec-16628.

recession-induced federal deficit, the Court's support for inheritance and corporate excise taxes, the expert calls for fiscal reform, and perhaps most importantly the potential splintering of the Republican Party – all seemed to suggest that the time for significant tax reform had arrived. Southern Democrats certainly believed that they had a rare opportunity to replace the existing indirect tax regime, which Hull described as an "infamous system of class legislation," with a more equitable and effective tax system. The protective tariff and national excise taxes not only fell on those least able to bear such fiscal burdens, Hull contended during the congressional debates; they virtually exempted "the Carnegies, the Vanderbilts, the Astors, the Morgans, and the Rockefellers, with their aggregated billions of hoarded wealth." The principal goal for Hull and the other national lawmakers who rallied behind the income tax in 1909 was to reallocate the nation's tax burden, not to redistribute the wealth generated by corporate-industrial development.[55]

In his calls to "tax wealth not poverty," Hull cited the well-known economic thinkers and jurists who had come out in favor of a graduated income tax as the best means to tax a citizen's ability to pay.[56] In fact, Hull used language nearly identical to what Ely and the other progressive political economists had written decades earlier in support of the income tax as "the fairest, the most equitable system of taxation that has yet been devised." In doing so, Hull illustrated how the conceptual revolution in American public finance that had been taking place for decades in academic journals and conferences was once again reaching the corridors of national power, just as it had during the turmoil over the 1894 income tax.

Hull and his colleagues firmly believed that by replacing the national structure of regressive indirect consumption taxes with direct and graduated levies on incomes, profits, and inheritances, they could help usher in a new fiscal order. They could, in short, force those segments of American society that had the greatest taxpaying ability – namely wealthy citizens and corporations in the Northeast – to share the burden of underwriting the growing demands of a modern, industrial state. "I have no disposition to tax wealth unnecessarily or unjustly," Hull informed his fellow legislators, "but I do believe that the wealth of the country should bear its

[55] *Congressional Record*, 61st Cong., 1st sess. (1909), 44:536.

[56] *Congressional Record*, 61st Cong., 1st sess. (1909), 44:532–6. Hull corresponded with Seligman and other political economists often about how the U.S. government could compile more accurate tax statistics and help simplify the income tax. Cordell Hull to Edwin R. A. Seligman, April 16, 1915; July 11, 1918, ERASP; F. W. Taussig to Cordell Hull, October 2, 1917, Box 2, Folder 5, Cordell Hull Papers, Tennessee State Library and Archives, Nashville, TN.

just share of the burden of taxation and that it should not be permitted to shirk that duty."[57] Hull's remarks, to be sure, reflected the self-interest of a Southern Democrat who was eager to shift the burden of taxation from the periphery to the industrial core of the Northeast. But, at the same time, Hull seemed to understand that by stressing the civic responsibilities that accompanied great individual wealth, he was also helping create an institutional beachhead for the subsequent development of a modern fiscal polity.

With the growing support for an income tax, lawmakers drafted a proposal for such a levy as part of the pending 1909 tariff bill. Senators Joseph Bailey and Albert Cummins collaborated on a proposal that provided for a 2 percent flat tax on the net income of individuals and corporations in excess of $5,000.[58] Modeled after the 1894 income tax law, the Bailey-Cummins proposal was a direct challenge to *Pollock*. Echoing Hull's sentiments, Bailey and Cummins explained that the central aim of the bill was to ensure that wealthy citizens and owners of large corporations paid their fair share of the national tax burden. There was no better way to do that, Bailey argued, than to shift the tax base from consumption to income. Relying on the key words that new school public finance economists had been advancing for decades, the Texas senator stressed the distributional equity that came from a tax that "rose and fell with a man's ability to pay," rather than the amount of goods he consumed.[59] Cummins concurred, declaring that the income tax proposal should be seen "not as an assault upon wealth, but as an assault upon the vicious principle of exemption of wealth."[60] Some supporters of the income tax questioned the strategy of directly challenging the Court with a new income tax law that was nearly identical to the one that had been struck down. They preferred a constitutional amendment overruling *Pollock* as a wiser tactic.

[57] *Congressional Record*, 61st Cong., 1st sess. (1909), 44:536, 533; Ratner, *American Taxation*, 272.

[58] Roy G. Blakey and Gladys C. Blakey, *The Federal Income Tax* (New York: Longmans, Green, and Co., 1940), 30–6. Interestingly, the Bailey-Cummins income tax provided for a tax credit for those stockholders with income less than $5,000 who might be susceptible to the double taxation of corporate income. This provision indicated that even at this early stage in the development of U.S. corporate taxation, lawmakers were thinking about ways to integrate the individual and corporate tax. Steven A. Bank, *From Sword to Shield: The Transformation of the Corporate Income Tax, 1861 to Present* (New York: Oxford University Press, 2010), 62–6.

[59] *Congressional Record*, 61st Cong., 1st sess. (1909), 44:1351, 1538, 2447; Blakey and Blakey, *Federal Income Tax*, 37.

[60] *Congressional Record*, 61st Cong., 1st sess. (1909), 44:2447.

Unsurprisingly, the most ardent opposition to the proposed income tax came from the conservative representatives of Northeastern capital. Rhode Island Senator Nelson Aldrich, the key Republican spokesman for protectionism, attempted to kill the income tax bill through a variety of procedural maneuvers designed to postpone discussion and voting on a measure that Aldrich and other Republicans realized would divide the party and undermine protectionism. To unite his fellow Republicans, President Taft brokered a compromise. In a June message to Congress, the president proposed as an alternative to the Bailey-Cummins income tax bill: a corporate excise tax, and a resolution to amend the Constitution to permit an income tax without apportionment. Taft had shifted his earlier position on the constitutionality of an income tax, recognizing that a direct challenge to the Court could undermine the integrity of an institution that he revered and would later in his career join.[61]

Yet, what was most astonishing about Taft's congressional message was the reasoning he used to support a new corporate tax. Alluding to the Supreme Court's recent validation of the 1898 corporate tax on sugar and oil refineries (*Spreckels*), Taft described the corporate levy as "a perfectly legitimate and effective system of taxation," one that provided the added advantage of monitoring and perhaps curbing the growth of corporate capitalism. With the new tax, Taft contended, "we are incidentally able to possess the government and the stockholders and the public of the knowledge of the real business transactions and the gains and profits of every corporation in the country." By enacting such corporate transparency, Taft contended, the United States could take "a long step toward that supervisory control of corporations which may prevent a further abuse of power."[62] With Taft's vital leadership, the combination of a corporate excise tax and a constitutional amendment permitting a direct income tax appeared to assuage both sides.

The compromise proposal gave both parties an opportunity to frustrate the aims of their opponents while gaining a toehold for their own position. For liberal tax reformers, the proposed constitutional amendment provided an opportunity to settle the income tax issue once and for all. In addition, the corporate tax, and particularly the collateral provision providing for the publicity of corporate records, pushed the existing tax system toward a more equitable equilibrium while making corporations more transparent. For conservative tax opponents, the corporate excise tax was one way to forestall the passage of the Bailey-Cummins

[61] Buenker *Income Tax and the Progressive Era.*

[62] *Congressional Record*, 61st Cong., 1st sess. (1909), 44:3344.

income tax bill. "I shall vote for a corporation tax as a means to defeat the income tax," Aldrich famously declared. For him and other conservative Republicans wedded to the power and prestige that came from protectionism, maintaining the party's disciplined support for the tariff was crucial. "I am willing," Aldrich declared, "to accept the proposition of this kind for the purpose of avoiding what, to my mind, is a great evil and the imposition of a tax in time of peace when there is no emergency, a tax which is sure in the end to destroy the protective system."[63] Ultimately, income tax opponents like Aldrich were confident that the proposed constitutional amendment would fail and that the corporate tax would eventually be repealed.

The Road to Ratification

To the chagrin of conservatives like Aldrich, the movement to ratify the constitutional amendment gradually gained significant momentum, and the corporate tax slowly became an established part of a newly emergent fiscal order. The ratification process began in earnest in 1910, as roughly twenty of the necessary thirty-six states approved the amendment in that year. A decisive turning point came in July 1911 when New York became the thirty-first, and arguably the most important, state to ratify the Sixteenth Amendment. With New York's vital support, the ratification process gained steady steam, and by February 1913 the requisite number of states had ratified the proposed amendment. Less than a year later, the Sixty-second U.S. Congress seized the political moment to pass the Underwood-Simmons Tariff Act of 1913, which provided for a modest graduated federal income tax.[64] As one of the centers of Northeast economic concentration, New York State played a critical role in helping establish one of the essential legal foundations of modern American fiscal governance.[65]

The road to ratification was not, however, a smooth one, nationally or within the Empire State. New York's path in particular was paved with numerous political potholes – most prominent of which was the opposition to the amendment articulated by the governor of New York, and one of Seligman's law school classmates and oldest friends, Charles Evan Hughes. Although Governor Hughes did not directly object to the idea

[63] *Congressional Record*, 61st Cong., 1st sess. (1909), 44:3929.

[64] Underwood-Simmons Act, 38 Stat. 114 (1913).

[65] For more on the origins of the Sixteenth Amendment, see generally Buenker, *The Income Tax and the Progressive Era.*

of an income tax, his opposition to the proposed language of the Sixteenth Amendment led to a tumultuous battle in New York's ratification process – a battle that lasted two years and included an initial defeat of the proposed amendment in 1910.

Seligman v. Hughes

On January 5, 1910, at the opening session of the New York State Legislature, Governor Hughes delivered a special message regarding the proposed income tax amendment. Acknowledging receipt of the proposed constitutional amendment, Hughes began by reading its specific language: "Article XVI: The Congress shall have power to lay and collect taxes on income from whatever source derived without apportionment among the several states, and without regard to any census or enumeration."[66] As a prominent lawyer and esteemed member of the New York Bar, Hughes had no objections to the latter half of the proposed amendment, which excluded apportionment among the several states. After all, this was the language that directly addressed *Pollock*. Hughes admitted "this power should be held by the Federal Government so as properly to equip it with the means of meeting National exigencies." What did offend the governor, however, were the four words that read: "from whatever source derived." He believed that this language gave Congress the ability to destroy the fiscal powers and the political sovereignty of the individual states by taxing the interest on their debt obligations. "To place the borrowing capacity of the State and of its governmental agencies at the mercy of the Federal taxing power," Hughes proclaimed, "would be an impairment of the essential rights of the State which, as its officers, we are bound to defend."[67]

More specifically, Hughes feared that Congress would have the power to tax "the income derived from bonds issued by the State itself, or those issued by municipal governments organized under the State's authority." Such a grant of federal power, Hughes believed, would abrogate an implied constitutional restriction. "The immunity from Federal taxation that the State and its instrumentalities of government now enjoy," Hughes argued, "is derived not from any express provision of the Federal Constitution, but from what has been deemed to be necessary implication. Who

66 U.S. Constitution, Article XVI.

67 State of New York, Senate, *Special Message from the Governor Submitting to the Legislature Certified Copy of a Resolution of Congress Entitled "Joint Resolution Proposing an Amendment to the Constitution of the United States,"* January 5, 1910, 3.

can say that any such implication with respect to the proposed tax will survive the adoption of this explicit and comprehensive amendment?" Citing *Pollock* and other Supreme Court decisions, Hughes contended that the implied constitutional restriction against federal taxation of state and local securities was enshrined in American jurisprudence, and that the proposed amendment as written was a potential threat to this long-held tradition. In some ways, Hughes's objections echoed what state-level tax experts, like National Tax Association founder Allen Ripley Foote, had feared, namely that the centralization of federal fiscal powers would undermine the states' "sovereign power of taxation."[68]

But Hughes did not base his opposition to the amendment solely on constitutional or legal grounds. He also argued that a federal tax on state and local bonds would inhibit individual states and municipalities from effectively tapping the capital markets. "In order that a market may be provided for State bonds, and for municipal bonds, and that thus means may be afforded for State and local administration, such securities from time to time are exempted from taxation. In this way lower rates of interest are paid than otherwise would be possible," Hughes explained. "To permit such securities to be the subject of Federal taxation is to place such limitations upon the borrowing power of the State as to make the performance of the functions of local government a matter of federal grace."[69]

As historian John D. Buenker has documented, the fallout from the Hughes message was predictable. Fellow Republicans and anti-income tax newspapers supported the governor's comments, while Democrats and pro-income tax reformers assailed the speech as an example of the power of moneyed interests. Prominent Republicans who had played an instrumental role in drafting the constitutional amendment such as New York's U.S. Senator Elihu Root attempted to defuse the potency of Hughes's remarks by assuring state legislators that the amendment was not designed to allow the federal government to supersede the fiscal power of states and localities. Indeed, as Root pointed out, the congressional debates over the specific language of the amendment showed that the central aim of the amendment was to repudiate *Pollock's* newly expansive view of the "direct tax" clause. In a letter to the New York State

68 Ibid. Allen Ripley Foote, "Annual Address of the President," *Conference on State and Local Taxation, Sixth Annual Conference under the Auspices of the National Tax Association* (Madison, Wis.: National Tax Association, 1913), 19–27.

69 State of New York, Senate, *Special Message from the Governor*.

Legislature, Root expressly stated that the sole objective of the amendment was to address the constitutional obstacle posed by *Pollock*, and that apportionment, and not control over state and local fiscal policy, was the true target of the proposed amendment.[70]

Similarly, Professor Seligman, a self-proclaimed "good Republican," also rebuked his old friend the governor as well as the legislature for taking Hughes's message too seriously and for ignoring the democratic will of the people. Seligman, as we have seen, had always favored a national income tax ahead of any state-level attempts to administer such a levy. Among the many administrative challenges he identified in the 1894 federal income tax, the most important was that an effective income tax had to be collected at the source of its creation and distribution, and that only the federal government – in an age of national flows of capital and people – could administer such a system of "stoppage-at-the-source." An income tax designed to capture one's ability to pay could be best administered at a centralized level where income across state lines could be assessed, reported, and collected. The ratification process and Hughes's resistance afforded Seligman an opportunity to make the case, once again, for a national income tax.

Indeed, Seligman was completing his magnum opus on the income tax when Hughes articulated his opposition to the constitutional amendment. In the preface to his new treatise, Seligman explicitly stated his overriding goal: "As it seems probable that we shall before long have an income tax in the United States my chief object in writing this book has been to set the subject in a somewhat clearer light and to aid the legislator in constructing a workable scheme."[71] In addition to providing a workable scheme, Seligman aimed to convince every lawmaker and reader of the book that a progressive income tax was the historically appropriate method of taxation for a modern, industrial society. Yet, even before the treatise was published, Seligman brashly challenged Hughes's objections with an article derived from the broader book manuscript.

70 Root was instrumental in drafting the specific language of the Sixteenth Amendment, especially the emphasis on identifying the income tax as a "direct tax" that could be levied "without apportionment by population"; April 27, 1909, copy of "Joint Resolution Proposing an Amendment to the Constitution of the United States;" "S.J. Res. No. 25" in Container No. 191: Corporation Tax Amendment, 1909, Elihu Root Papers, Manuscript Division, Library of Congress, Washington, D.C. [ERP]. Buenker, *Income Tax and the Progressive Era*, 278–9. For more on the congressional debates over the specific language of the amendment, see Bruce Ackerman, "Taxation and the Constitution," *Columbia Law Review* 99:1 (January 1999), 1–57, 36–9.

71 Edwin R. A. Seligman, *The Income Tax: A Study of the History, Theory, and Practice of Income Taxation at Home and Abroad* (New York: Macmillan Co., 1911), v.

Writing in the pages of the *Political Science Quarterly*, which Seligman still edited, the Columbia professor contended that Hughes's opinion was "erroneous in three respects." First, the governor had confused the legal precedents, overlooking how *Pollock* was an aberration to a well-established tradition of judicial support for a national income tax. Second, Hughes did not understand how market forces would balance out any tax effects on state and local bonds, neutralizing to a degree the economic benefits of tax exemption. And finally and most importantly Seligman argued that his old friend and classmate did not understand how the historical evolution of centralized political power was a result of changing economic and social life. "The conditions which existed when the constitution was framed are no longer existent," Seligman wrote. "During the last century ... the development of the underlying economic and social forces has created a nation, and this development calls for uniform national regulation of many matters which were not dreamed of by the founders." Using a comparative analysis, Seligman concluded that economic and legal progress should not be hindered by antiquated attachments to the ideas of state and local self-governance. "Let us not make a fetish of 'self-government,'" proclaimed Seligman, "and let us not oppose central authority in those cases where self-government means retrogression rather than progress." State-level tax administrators, as we have seen, were making similar arguments in their attempts to centralize assessments of local taxes.[72]

Despite the views of Seligman, Root, and the many others who challenged Hughes, the income tax amendment did not survive the resistance of the Republican majority in the New York Assembly. The amendment was put to a vote three times during the 1910 session, and all three times the Republican majority resoundingly defeated it. But the fate of the Sixteenth Amendment in New York did not end with the 1910 legislative session, for when the political tides changed dramatically later that year, delivering both the legislature and the governor's mansion to the Democrats, the congressional proposal for an income tax amendment received new and considerably greater consideration.[73]

With a Tammany Hall majority in the legislature and Democratic Governor John A. Dix in office, the 1911 legislative session provided a more receptive audience for the proposed income tax amendment. Yet, the

[72] Edwin R. A. Seligman, "The Income Tax Amendment," *Political Science Quarterly* 25:2 (June 1910), 193–219, 214.

[73] Buenker, *The Income Tax and the Progressive Era*, 278–80.

dire warnings of Governor Hughes, who was then an Associate Justice of the U.S. Supreme Court, continued to resonate with many state legislators. This time, Professor Seligman took no risks in voicing his support for the constitutional amendment and the income tax. Realizing perhaps that his influence could be expanded beyond the pages of his academic writings, Seligman testified again before a state legislative committee in 1911 – this time with a renewed sense of purpose.

Appearing last after a long Saturday afternoon of witnesses, Seligman clearly displayed his disapproval not only with Governor Hughes's objections, but with those Republican assemblymen who had retained their political positions, despite the previous fall's Democratic landslide. Essentially, Seligman reiterated his comments that Hughes and his ilk did not realize: (1) that the proposed amendment would simply restore the constitutional status quo pre-*Pollock*; (2) that an efficient capital market would take into consideration the different tax effects of state and local bonds and all other securities; (3) that even if the federal government did limit the fiscal powers of states and localities, the increased revenue of an income tax could potentially benefit all, and not just the federal government; and (4) that the political will of the people, representing the spirit of the age, was behind the amendment. Seligman peppered his second argument, the economic analysis, with a personal attack on Hughes. After he explained the economic logic of how an efficient capital market would take into consideration the tax status of securities, Seligman concluded: "If any of my students at Columbia had made the same mistake as Governor Hughes, I should have flunked him dead."[74]

In a similar tone, Seligman reminded the remaining Republican assemblymen of the political warning he had issued in his earlier testimony, given in the previous legislative session. Back then, Seligman had forewarned the senators that by rejecting the amendment the lawmakers would be ignoring the political power of the people at their own peril. "It was my good fortune," Seligman stated in his 1911 testimony, "to say to the Senate committee that though I was as good a Republican as any of those present, I believed the party would be snowed under at the polls, if it refused to accept the amendment. The Republican Party

[74] "Corrects Hughes on Income Tax," *New York Times*, May 21, 1911, 12; "Says Hughes Made Mistake," *Washington Post*, May 21, 1911. Seligman appeared to be gesturing toward the economic concept that tax-exempt securities like state and local bonds came with an "implicit tax" due to the lower market interest rates they commanded compared to taxed securities. Harry Watson, "Implicit Taxes," in *The Encyclopedia of Taxation and Tax Policy*, ed. Joseph J. Cordes, Robert D. Ebel, and Jane G. Gravelle (Washington, D.C.: Urban Institute, 1999), 167–8.

was snowed under and one of the reasons was its failure to observe my warning."[75] Seligman's brash rebuke of Republican lawmakers was intensified when his expertise became self-evident even among his critics. During that same testimony, a Republican member of the judiciary committee attempted to impeach Seligman's expertise in taxation. Holding up a public finance text, he asked the professor whether he had read the whole book through. The question caused a great deal of amusement among onlookers, and some embarrassment for the lawmaker, when he realized that he was holding up one of Seligman's own treatises.[76]

Seligman's comments, especially his rebuke of Hughes's economic logic, caused quite a stir. The anti-income tax *New York Times*, for instance, not only gave Seligman's comments prime news coverage, it also published a scornful editorial and several letters to the editor questioning Seligman's assumptions about the efficiency of the capital markets. Even John Burgess, Seligman's mentor, came out against the income tax. State Democrats, for their part, used Seligman's comments as a club to beat away continued Republican resistance to the amendment. Just as the Republicans in the previous year had used Hughes's message as political cover for their rejection of the constitutional proposal, many Democrats in 1911 used Seligman's comments, and his credentials as an objective expert, to curry more support for the amendment. Even though Seligman attempted to clarify that he was attacking "the reasoning not of Gov. Hughes, but of those who shelter themselves under his great reputation," the impact of his testimony had already been felt, just as the political momentum for the amendment was gradually building.[77]

With the Democrats controlling both the New York Senate and Assembly, and with the support of newly elected Governor John Dix, the income tax amendment sailed through the 1911 session on firm partisan lines. The change in the legislature's political composition was, to be sure, the major factor leading to New York's approval of the amendment. But Seligman's writings and testimony may also have had a significant effect

75 Buenker, *Income Tax in the Progressive Era*, 288. Though Seligman claimed to be a "good Republican" before the New York State lawmakers, his political leanings would soon shift to Theodore Roosevelt's progressive Bull Moose Party. Frank J. Goodnow to Seligman, September 9, 1912, Cataloged Correspondence, ERASP. According to Seligman's son, Eustace, his father would also become a firm supporter of Franklin Roosevelt and the New Deal. Interview with Eustace Seligman, September 3, 1974, Columbia Oral History Collections, Butler Library, Columbia University, New York, N.Y.

76 Buenker, *Income Tax in the Progressive Era*, 288.

77 "The Income Tax Hearing," *New York Times*, May 23, 1911, 10; "Mr. Fish at Issue with Prof. Seligman," *New York Times*, May 30, 1911; "Prof. Seligman Says His Remarks on the Income Tax Were Misunderstood," *New York Times*, May 25, 1911.

in tipping the balance. His challenge of Hughes's message galvanized the pro-income tax forces by lending them the prestige and prominence of a well-known, and ostensibly neutral, expert in the field. This influence extended well beyond New York since Seligman's challenge to Hughes's logic was instrumental in other states where governors protested the amendment on similar grounds. New York's approval of the amendment also tipped the balance in favor of ratification. And once the Republican National Party became divided after the 1912 Taft-Roosevelt split, the proposed constitutional amendment gained further traction and was ultimately ratified in 1913. It was not long before Seligman's position against Hughes was vindicated. In the 1916 Supreme Court decision of *Brushaber v. Union Pacific*, Justice Hughes assented to a unanimous decision that essentially refuted his earlier position on the general powers of the Sixteenth Amendment.[78]

The Lasting Legislative Influence of the Progressive Political Economists

When Congress began drafting the 1913 income tax law, soon after the ratification of the Sixteenth Amendment, the lasting influence of the progressive political economists was readily apparent. Not only did lawmakers regularly invoke the logic and language of "faculty," "earning capacity," and "ability to pay" to support a broad-based graduated income tax, they also directly cited Seligman's recently published income tax treatise as an example of how the pending legislation had the backing of an unbiased, neutral expert. Such appeals to objective expertise helped defuse claims that Southern and Western populist lawmakers were supporting progressive income taxes for purely self-interested reasons.

At the same time, key legislators such as Hull and Borah pointed to the theoretical work and the comparative historical evidence of the public finance economists to argue for a differentiated income tax, one that attended to the distinction between different sources of income. They also evoked Seligman's comparative research in calling for a crude and early form of withholding. To be sure, the general concept of an income tax still faced stern resistance during the legislative drafting process, and even after its initial implementation. But the ratification of the Sixteenth Amendment gave the tax reform movement a new found democratic legitimacy – one that pro-income tax lawmakers exploited as they evoked the many lessons of the new school of American economic thinkers.

[78] *Brushaber v. Union Pacific Railroad Co.*, 240 U.S. 1 (1924).

Among the many conservative critiques of the pending income tax law, a pervasive and frequent charge was that it was an "inquisitorial" levy. Since the Civil War, income tax opponents had been decrying the tax as an intrusive invasion of privacy. Although reformers regularly pointed out that assessing income was no more invasive than administering subnational property taxes, this did little to allay privacy concerns.[79] Yet, by the time lawmakers began considering a new income tax, the cries of intrusiveness were falling on deaf ears. In their private correspondence, key lawmakers dismissed these claims as "the natural re-action against any interference at all by Government," as Elihu Root informed U.S. Attorney General George W. Wickersham. "The protest is not rational at all. It is purely instinctive just as a man winks his eye when a bug gets in it."[80]

If political leaders had become desensitized to the claim that an income tax was intrusive, they seemed more attentive to the criticism that tax reform advocates were abandoning principles and capitulating to the populist uproar. Critics like Senator Henry Cabot Lodge (R-Mass.) contended that by designing the income tax as a "class tax" aimed solely at the rich, supporters of the bill were succumbing to "popular prejudice."[81] Senator Borah assailed this criticism by pointing to the academic origins of the American income tax movement. "The income tax had its impetus not with men seeking popular favor," proclaimed Borah, "but in a thorough, conscientious, persistent investigation upon the part of those who have gone to the sources of information and have studied the statistics which are available from almost all the countries of the world." With this appeal to the neutral and objective knowledge of experts, Borah attempted to defuse the claim that he and the other drafters of the income tax bill were acquiescing to the demands of radical populism.[82]

Borah further supported his assertions of apolitical expertise by referring to Seligman's newly published income tax treatise. Though Borah conceded that he could "quote many" learned thinkers, he chose "a short paragraph from one who occupied a most eminent position in one of the great universities of this country, and who, I presume, cares as little

79 Steven R. Weisman, *The Great Tax Wars: Lincoln – Teddy Roosevelt – Wilson, How the Income Tax Transformed America* (New York: Simon and Schuster, 2002), 97, 104.

80 Elihu Root to George W. Wickersham, July 28, 1909, Container No. 67, General Correspondence, S-Z 1909, ERP.

81 *Congressional Record*, 63rd Cong., 1st sess. (1913), 50:3838–41.

82 Ibid.

about popular favor as any many who could possibly be called into this discussion." Without mentioning Seligman directly, Borah quoted a section from the Columbia professor's new book that placed the income tax in its proper social and economic context: "Under existing conditions in the United States the burdens of taxation, taking them all in all, are becoming unequally distributed and the wealthier classes are bearing a gradually smaller share of the public burden. Something is needed to restore the equilibrium; and that something can scarcely take any form except that of an income tax."[83] For Seligman, Borah, and other income tax advocates, restoring the fiscal equilibrium – not punishing wealth and success – was the principal objective.

The details of the 1913 law, in fact, embodied the desire to correct the fiscal equilibrium. In addition to lowering import duties significantly and expanding the free list, the Underwood Tariff enacted a "normal" tax of 1 percent on individual annual incomes that exceeded $3,000 ($4,000 for married couples), and a graduated "surtax" rate ranging from 1 to 6 percent on annual incomes beginning at $20,000 and reaching the top bracket of $500,000. Given these relatively high exemption levels, legislators ensured that the new levy was a "rich man's tax" aimed at recalibrating existing fiscal burdens.[84] Their goal was to ensure that the "idle rich" as depicted in John Scott Clubb's famous 1913 political cartoon were doing their share to keep the treadmill of government expenses going (see Figure 5.2).

The adoption of a progressive rate structure, which was a departure from the flat tax of the 1894 law, also showed how the arguments of the progressive political economists had come to shape congressional thinking. In his newly published treatise, Seligman reiterated his support for graduated taxes based on objective criteria. In his 1894 treatise on progressivity, Seligman had acknowledged that the challenges of

[83] Ibid., 3841. Borah's quote was taken directly from Seligman's treatise. Seligman, *The Income Tax*, 640. Seligman regularly sent his scholarship to Borah. The lawmaker once responded: "I can assure you Prof. Seligman, I never fail to read what I find you have written, and I thank you for kindly sending me" your scholarship. William E. Borah to Seligman, February 25, 1911, ERASP.

[84] Section II(A), subdividion (2), Underwood Tariff Act of October 3, 1913, 38 Stat. 166. In 2012 dollars, the exemption level for single taxpayers would be roughly $72,000 (for couples it would be about $96,000), and the first graduated "surtax" rate would begin at approximately $478,000. Relative value of U.S. dollar amounts calculated using consumer price index. Available at: http://www.measuringworth.com/uscompare/relativevalue.php.

FIGURE 5.2. "The New Man on the Job." In this 1913 John Scott Clubb political cartoon, the "working class" is delighted to see that the "income tax" collar is ensuring that "the idle rich" is doing his part to keep the treadmill of "governmental expenses" going. Courtesy of the Library of Congress, Prints & Photographs Division, LC-USZ62-84130.

comparing interpersonal marginal utility had undermined most conventional defenses of progressivity. Still, he defended progressivity on more objective grounds.[85]

[85] Seligman, *Progressive Taxation in Theory and Practice*, 144–5.

This defense became even stronger in Seligman's new income tax treatise. There he reminded his readers that "if we take a general view and treat of the average man – and the government can deal only with classes, that is, with average men – it seems probable that on the whole less injustice will be done by adopting some form of progression than by following the universal rule of proportion." By taking this "general view" based on class distinctions, Seligman attempted to avoid the difficulties of trying to compare the subjective, marginal utilities of different individuals, while, at the same time, addressing the massive inequality that was at the center of the tax reform movement. "A strictly proportional rate," Seligman concluded, "will be a heavier burden on the typical average poor man than on the typical average rich man."[86] This was hardly an electrifying defense of graduated rates. Even so, Seligman's measured tone served its purpose, especially for the lawmakers who were reading his work and exalting it as a model of academic integrity and neutrality. Indeed, the writings of the political economists provided legislators, some of whom were undoubtedly pursuing the self-interest of their constituents, with a guise of expert neutrality.

Other parts of the new income tax also exhibited the lasting influence of the reform-minded economists. Like the 1894 law, the new income tax applied to "every citizen of the United States, whether residing at home or abroad."[87] This commitment to worldwide taxation based on citizenship reinforced the notion that the new levy was linked not to the benefits conferred by any particular sovereign state, but rather to the principle that all American citizens – no matter where they lived – had a social obligation and ethical duty to pay their fair share of U.S. tax burdens based on their ability to pay. Simply put, wealthy Americans could not abdicate their civic and fiscal responsibilities by moving overseas. This was a central message of the conceptual revolution in favor of direct and graduated taxes.

The new law also extended this concept of fiscal citizenship to corporate entities. By replacing the 1909 corporate excise tax, which was premised on taxing businesses for the privilege of operating in corporate form, with a 1 percent tax on net corporate *income*, lawmakers stressed

[86] Seligman, *Income Tax*, 32–3. For more on Seligman's commitment to progressivity, see Herbert Hovenkamp, "The First Great Law & Economics Movement," *Stanford Law Review* 42:4 (1990), 1003–5.

[87] Section II(A), subdivision (1), Underwood Tariff Act, 38 Stat. 114, 166 (1913).

that corporations, like individuals, were subject to the same responsibilities and duties embodied by direct taxation. For those legislators who believed that affluent shareholders ultimately bore the burden of the corporate income tax, this semantic modification furthered the goal of readjusting the fiscal equilibrium. With these provisions, congressional leaders like Borah could sincerely claim that expert guidance had led them to craft a law that forced the wealthier classes to bear their fair share of the public tax burden.[88]

There was, of course, a rich historical irony to congressional claims about expert neutrality. Though it served Borah's purpose to depict Seligman and the other progressive theorists as somehow insulated from "popular favor," the progressive economists themselves were deliberately and deeply engaged in a political project. They began their conceptual assault on the benefits principle, and the anemic and commodified notion of fiscal citizenship that it represented, with the hopes and aspirations of advancing an intellectual revolution in the basis of American public finance. By 1913, the seeds of their earlier ideas were coming to fruition at a time when lawmakers needed to pose these experts and their conceptual proposals as neutral and objective. These thinkers did not object initially to politicians deploying their key words and ideas in the process of constructing the legal foundations of the fiscal state. In fact, they welcomed this attention.[89] But as the powers of this new polity grew, especially during the First World War, some theorists became more reluctant to support a highly robust wartime tax regime.

Still, in 1913, the progressive political economists were gratified that a fundamental shift in thinking about fiscal governance was affecting the development of pending legislation. Indeed, some lawmakers even picked up on the particular details and implications of new economic ideas, such as the theoretical distinction between different sources of individual income. Recall that Henry Carter Adams and others had argued in the 1880s and '90s that any new tax on income ought to differentiate between the sources of income, taxing "earned" income from labor at a lower rate

[88] Section II(G) (a), Underwood Tariff Act, 38 Stat. 114, 172 (1913); *Congressional Record*, 63rd Cong., 1st sess. (1913), 50:3841.

[89] Cordell Hull to Edwin R. A. Seligman, April 16, 1915; William E. Borah to Edwin R. A. Seligman, Feb. 25, 1911, Cataloged Correspondence, Edwin R. A. Seligman Papers, Rare Book and Manuscript Collection, Butler Library, Columbia University, New York, N.Y.

than the "unearned" income from capital investments.[90] This idea gained currency in the Senate, when several legislators evoked Adams's ideas and Seligman's comparative evidence of the British income tax to advocate for some type of "discrimination in favor of vocational income as against property income." Ultimately, a preference based on "the character of income" was not adopted in 1913, but the idea of taxing "earned" income at a lower, preferential rate would loom large in the early decades of the income tax regime, and eventually find its way into the 1920s tax code.[91]

Far more successful was the idea of instituting a crude form of income tax withholding, or what contemporaries referred to as "stoppage at the source." Building on the Civil War withholding system, and borrowing from the British experience, the new collection method required institutions that were making disbursements to individuals to withhold and remit a portion of high salaries, dividends, interest, and rents as partial tax payments.

Once again, Seligman's scholarship, with its focus on the pivotal role played by large American corporations, was instrumental. Alabama Congressman Oscar Underwood, the primary sponsor of the pending 1913 law and an early advocate of withholding, quoted Seligman's income tax treatise at length to show how an academic expert had determined from careful comparative evidence that "stoppage at the source" could be especially effective in the United States. Reading directly from Seligman's income tax book, Underwood explained that the accelerating rise of American corporate capitalism had made "stoppage at the source" particularly appealing:

> In the United States the arguments in favor of this method are far stronger than in Europe, because of the peculiar conditions of American life. In the first place, nowhere is corporate activity so developed and in no country of the world does the ordinary business of the community assume to so overwhelming an extent the corporate form. Not only is a large part of the intangible wealth of individuals composed of corporate securities, but a very appreciable part of business profits consists of corporate profits.[92]

Accordingly, Underwood concluded – quoting Seligman again – that withholding could be particularly effective in the United States. "The arguments that speak in favor of a stoppage-at-source income tax abroad

90 Henry Carter Adams, *The Science of Finance: An Investigation of Public Expenditures and Public Revenues* (New York: Henry Holt and Co., 1898), 357.

91 *Congressional Record*, 63rd Cong., 1st sess. (1913), 50:3815, 3838.

92 *Congressional Record*, 62nd Cong., 2nd sess. (1912), 48:3587 (Underwood quoting Seligman, *The Income Tax*, 661–2).

hence apply with redoubled force here," Underwood declared. "The stoppage-at-source scheme lessens to an enormous extent the strain on the administration; it works, so far as it is applicable, almost automatically; and where enforced it secures to the last penny the income that is rightfully due."[93]

In the end, Underwood's use of Seligman's research proved effective. As part of the new tax law, Congress enacted a "stoppage at the source" system of withholding. It required any person or organization making payments of more than $3,000 in salary, interest, or other fixed income to withhold and remit tax payments on behalf of the individual taxpayer. Yet, because the statute itself was ambiguous about how this early form of withholding would be implemented, Congress granted the Treasury Department great latitude in developing the necessary bureaucratic details and machinery. In this way, the 1913 income tax law became the vanguard for the growth of the proto-administrative state. As we shall see in the following chapter, this legally delegated power to the executive branch would be critical in consolidating the growing powers of the wartime fiscal state.[94]

Even before the war began, though, the U.S. Treasury Department was compelled to elaborate on the tax collection process. Less than a month after the enactment of the 1913 income tax law, the Treasury Department issued two detailed regulations outlining the specific requirements of the new withholding system. These regulations provided precise guidance on which financial institutions in the chain of fiduciary agents had the legal duty to collect and remit taxes. They also stressed the significance of ascertaining accurate tax information and using institutions like large-scale, industrial corporations as deputized tax-collecting agents.[95] The importance of these administrative developments did not escape the notice of legal experts like Garrard Glenn, a New York commercial lawyer and occasional Columbia Law School lecturer, who identified "collection

93 Ibid.

94 Section II, subsection D, Underwood Tariff Act, 38 Stat. 114 (1913). The provision, moreover, applied only to individual, not corporate, taxpayers, and it required withholding only for the tax liability related to the normal tax, not the graduated surtax rates.

95 U.S. Treasury Department Regulations, October 25, 1913; October 31, 1913; Roger Foster, *A Treatise on the Federal Income Tax under the Act of 1913* (Rochester, N.Y.: Lawyers Cooperative Publishing Co., 1913). For more on these and similar administrative developments in this period, see generally, Joseph J. Thorndike, "Reforming the Internal Revenue Service: A Comparative History," *Administrative Law Review* 53 (2001), 717–80.

at the source" as "the new law's most salient, if not its most popular feature."[96]

In Glenn's estimation, the congressional delegation of authority to the executive branch to elaborate on the collection process was wholly legal and rather banal. What caught Glenn's attention, however, was how the regulations empowered a form of private, third-party reporting and remittance that appeared revolutionary. In the case of interest payments, for example, the regulations required debtor corporations and financial institutions to remit withheld taxes along with certificates of ownership identifying the taxpayer/creditor. Similar rules were established for dividends, rents, and other annual fixed charges. "Thus in every case of deduction at the source," wrote Glenn, "the Government ends by not only getting the tax, but by knowing whom it is taxing."[97]

This state-sponsored information gathering would have far reaching consequences, illustrating the double role that this legal innovation played. On the one hand, the process of collecting taxpayer information facilitated greater social control and surveillance by state actors. Just as the poll tax was used in the post-Reconstruction South as a local tool to reestablish racial domination and subordination, the greater "legibility" of national taxpayers through withholding and information reporting could give federal officials unprecedented social knowledge and power. Conservative critics, after all, had long opposed the income tax on similar grounds as an "inquisitorial" levy.[98]

On the other hand, because the 1913 income tax was a class tax created by political elites aimed at economic elites, there was perhaps less fear that the new-found tax information would be exploited for dangerous purposes. On the contrary, the withholding and information gathering aspect of the new law may have bolstered faith and confidence in the new fiscal state. By securing the tax at the source and verifying the accurate taxpayer, the new law demonstrated that the income tax was much more than a "centrist" sop to the masses. Indeed, in many ways, greater tax information gathering and knowledge production was essential to fulfill the theoretical aspirations of the new fiscal polity. A progressive income tax based on an individual's ability to pay could

[96] Garrard Glenn, "The Income Tax Law and Deduction at the Source," *Columbia Law Review* 13 (1913), 714–26.

[97] Ibid., 721.

[98] Scott, *Seeing Like a State*. In this sense, tax compliance was a means of creating model taxpaying citizens. Assaf Likhovski, "'Training in Citizenship': Tax Compliance and Modernity," *Law & Social Inquiry* 32:3 (2007), 665–700.

not exist without some method of accurately measuring an individual's income or taxpaying faculty. "We might as well face the fact," Glenn conceded, "that the Government cannot go very far with taxation of incomes without being forced to adopt an inquisitorial system for discovering objects of taxation."[99] For many ordinary Americans, who were expressly exempt from the income tax and who supported it as a means toward restoring the fiscal equilibrium, a robust system of third-party remittance and information reporting could also give the new fiscal state greater social and political legitimacy. If quotidian workers and farmers, who paid their share of taxes to the national government through excise taxes and import duties, could be assured that national tax authorities were monitoring and collecting income taxes from the wealthier classes, these ordinary working-class Americans were more likely to support the new fiscal regime.

The process of collecting income taxes at the source also implicated the blurring line between public power and private rights. Because large-scale corporations were frequently the source of annual payments subject to withholding – namely, managerial salaries and interest and dividend payments to individual bond and stockholders – these private corporate entities, in effect, became quasi-public tax collectors. As Glenn explained, the Supreme Court had long upheld the use of a business corporation as "an agent of the Government for the collection of the tax."[100] But the new regulations went a step further. They "laid upon this citizen turned tax gatherer the additional duty of collecting from the creditor a statement identifying himself as such." The new industrial corporations were certainly up to this important information gathering task. With their rational and routinized systems of accounting, business corporations contained a surfeit of financial information. In many ways, the rise of managerial capitalism facilitated the development of the fiscal state. By becoming deputized tax collectors and third-party reporters, private business entities thus became central arenas for the mutual and reciprocal constitution of state and society.[101]

99 Glenn, "Income Tax Law," 723.

100 Ibid., 725. Although he mistakenly attributed this language to Justice Field, Glenn correctly cited to the Civil War income tax case that upheld the B & O Railroad's withholding of interest and dividends. *United States v. B. & O.R.R.* 84 U.S. 322 (17 Wall. 322) (1872).

101 Glenn, "Income Tax Law," 725; Ajay K. Mehrotra, "American Economic Development, Managerial Capitalism, and the Institutional Foundations of the Modern Income Tax," *Law & Contemporary Problems* 73:1 (2010), 25–62. Present-day tax experts

The harnessing of private authority for the purposes of public tax collection proved relatively effective. Although the individual income tax by itself only generated a modest figure of roughly $40 million or less than 6 percent of total revenue in fiscal year 1915, Treasury officials and lawmakers remained optimistic about the subsequent development of the levy. Indeed, over time, salaries and dividends withheld by business corporations became leading sources of personal income tax revenue. Historians have estimated that during the early years of the tax "businessmen... accounted for about eighty-five percent of the income reported, and almost ninety percent of the tax paid." Contemporary estimates corroborate that salaries and dividends accounted for 44 percent of personal income tax revenue in 1916, with those figures jumping to nearly 80 percent by 1920.[102]

To harness business corporations as modern day customs houses, government officials knew that they needed to enhance national administrative capacities and inform citizens about the mechanics of the new tax system. They understood that "the people of the country, unaccustomed to an income tax, must be educated to the law," and that "administrative methods must develop with experience." The latter entailed increasing the bureaucratic capacity of the Bureau of Internal Revenue, the executive agency responsible for administering the new law.[103] Educating the people was a more challenging task, one that was taken up by legislators as they addressed not only their constituents, but also that key critical

have recognized the importance of the modern corporation to tax collection. "The key to effective taxation is information, and the key to information in the modern economy is the corporation," the public finance economist Richard Bird has written. "The corporation is thus the modern fiscal state's equivalent of the customs barrier at the border." Richard M. Bird, "Why Tax Corporations?" *Bulletin for International Fiscal Documentation* 56 (2002), 199.

102 U.S. Treasury Department, *Annual Report of the Secretary of the Treasury on the State of the Finances for the Fiscal Year Ended June 30 1915* (Washington, D.C.: Government Printing Office, 1916), 53; Buenker, *Income Tax and Progressive Era*, 14; U.S. Treasury Department, U.S. Internal Revenue, *Statistics of Income Compiled from the Returns for 1916* (Washington, D.C.: Government Printing Office, 1918); U.S. Treasury Department, U.S. Internal Revenue, *Statistics of Income Compiled from the Returns for 1920* (Washington, D.C.: Government Printing Office, 1922).

103 *Annual Report of the Treasury of the State of the Finances for the Fiscal Year Ended June 30, 1915* (Washington, D.C.: Government Printing Office, 1916), 135; *Annual Report of the Treasury of the State of the Finances for the Fiscal Year Ended June 30, 1914* (Washington, D.C.: Government Printing Office, 1915), 31. Between 1913 and 1915, the headquarters of the Bureau of Internal Revenue grew from 277 to 530, while the number of field officers increased from 3,700 to 4,200. Thorndike, "Reforming the Internal Revenue Service," 741–2.

intermediary group of professionals responsible for helping enforce the law: private lawyers.

On February 4, 1914, Cordell Hull took the case for the effective administration of the income tax directly to the New York State Bar Association. In a lengthy speech to a crowded assembly hall, Hull outlined the causes and consequences of the new fiscal regime. Borrowing liberally once again from Seligman's treatise, Hull reminded his fellow brethren of the bar and bench that the income tax was rooted in a hard-fought battle for social and economic justice. "The incorporation of this tax as a part of the newly adopted fiscal policy of this country marks the culmination of a contest that has been waged in its behalf throughout the Nation for 20 years," announced Hull. This contest hinged on creating a tax system based on the principle of ability to pay, and "ability to pay, as demonstrated by worldwide experience, is best measured by net income." To those who questioned whether an income tax limited to the wealthy was an ideal way to enact the faculty principle, Hull responded by reminding such critics that the national income tax was just one part of a larger tax system. Since the vast majority of Americans were already paying excise taxes and import duties on everyday goods, an income tax with a high exemption level was meant to "equalize the tax burdens."[104]

Yet, Hull did not rule out the possibility that, in due time, the income tax might be expanded to include more citizens. At the moment, the income tax, "like all new laws," he proclaimed, "must first be understood by the people and become adjusted to the intricate business conditions of the country before its administration could be expected to prove entirely convenient and satisfactory." To turn the class tax into a mass tax at this early stage "might result in the breaking down of its administration." But, in what would turn out to be his most prescient remark, Hull acknowledged that "in the future, when the revenue demands from this source shall become greater and the present law becomes thoroughly understood and adjusted to business conditions, it will be easy to lower the exemption, further extend the provisions of the law, and otherwise

[104] Cordell Hull, "Address of Hon. Cordell Hull of Tennessee," *Congressional Record*, 63rd Cong., 2nd sess. (1914), 51, pt. 17 (Appendix): 102–6. "Income Tax Law to Stand," *New York Times*, January 29, 1914. Hull frequently reflected back on his pivotal role in drafting the earliest and most significant tax laws. As he informed Seligman, perhaps with some exaggeration, "I feel some pride in having written both the Income Tax Acts of 1913 and 1916, and the federal estate tax of 1916." Cordell Hull to Seligman, [n.d.] 1921, ERASP.

round it into more comprehensive and permanent form."[105] That time would come much sooner than perhaps even Hull anticipated.

A broader web of taxpaying individuals, Hull noted, also held out the potential of increasing tax consciousness across a great swath of citizens. By shifting revenue sources from indirect and "hidden" taxes on consumption to direct and visible levies on income, the new fiscal regime could re-engage wealthy citizens, just as Richard Ely and the new school political economists had suggested. "Unlike the intangible, indirect tariff act," Hull explained, the direct tax on income "enables every citizen to see and know the exact amount of taxes he contributes to the Government, and to know that every dollar he pays goes into the Federal Treasury."[106] Making taxation more salient for affluent citizens was one way to reignite their sense of civic responsibility and duty.

Another way to bolster fiscal citizenship, Hull claimed, was for his audience of lawyers to educate the country's economic elite about the administrative aspects of the new law. As a former commercial lawyer and judge, Hull was well aware that members of the New York Bar were trusted advisors to the nation's leading businesses and many affluent citizens. By reaching out to this group of lawyers, he sought to underscore all the virtues of a "stoppage at the source" collection method "by which the Government might intercept the tax on certain large classes of income before it reached the owner and taxpayer."[107]

Hull, likewise, sought to assuage those critics who were concerned that the new withholding system was a radical departure from conventional collection methods and the first step toward the "inquisitorial" state. Quoting directly from Seligman's income tax study, Hull reminded his listeners that there was nothing new about withholding: "England, Italy and other countries have long employed this method with splendid results." He implored the country's leading lawyers to inform their clients that they "should make a reasonable effort... to conform to the law." The initial success of withholding and third-party information reporting in the first year of the income tax suggested that wealthy individuals and leading business had already begun to absorb the administrative requirements of the new law. By complying with "collection at the source," these citizens "have shown a spirit of patriotism characteristic of true

[105] Hull, "Address of Hon. Cordell Hull of Tennessee," 105.
[106] Richard T. Ely, *Taxation in American States and Cities* (New York: Crowell, 1888); Hull, "Address of Hon. Cordell Hull of Tennessee," 105.
[107] Hull, "Address of Hon. Cordell Hull," 105.

American citizens."[108] As we shall see, some of the country's leading lawyers would heed Hull's words, especially after the experience of World War I transformed many reluctant legal professionals into enthusiastic fiscal state-builders.

By attending to how the new fiscal polity actually operated, how it would take on the massive administrative task of collecting a new source of revenue, reformers demonstrated that they were concerned not only about the ideas that undergirded the new fiscal order, but also with "the state-in-action," with the legal and institutional means that would give force to such economic and social ideas. For the progressive political economists, and the lawmakers who were absorbing their ideas and proposals, building the legal foundations of a new fiscal state was thus not only about implementing a new ideational perspective on public finance. The process of integrating the law with state-building required much more. It required greater attention to the means and methods of tax collection, to the processes and conduct of fiscal governance. "The state," John Commons would later write, "is what its officials do."[109] And in the realm of fiscal policy, what legislators wanted fiscal officials to do is harness the information-gathering and remittance powers of the new "monster corporations" to make the tax regime fairer and more effective.

[108] Ibid.

[109] John R. Commons, *The Legal Foundations of Capitalism* (New York: Macmillan, 1924), 122. Building on Commons's observation, the legal realist Karl Llewellyn echoed this notion when he proclaimed that "What officials do about disputes is, to my mind, the law itself." Karl Llewellyn, *The Bramble Bush* (New York: Oceana, 1930), 12.

PART III

CONSOLIDATING THE NEW FISCAL ORDER

6

Lawyers, Guns, and Public Monies

The U.S. Treasury, World War I, and the Administration of the Modern Fiscal State

> Wartime brings the ideal of the State out into very clear relief, and reveals attitudes and tendencies that were hidden. In times of peace the sense of the State flags in a republic that is not militarized. For war is essentially the health of the State.
>
> – Randolph Bourne

On the evening of April 2, 1917, with Europe engulfed in the bloodshed and turmoil of the Great War, President Woodrow Wilson convened a special, joint session of Congress. The European conflict had been escalating in recent months, and Germany's unrestricted submarine warfare meant that the United States could no longer remain neutral. Speaking before national lawmakers, Supreme Court justices, and members of the diplomatic corps, Wilson urged U.S. entry into the war, proclaiming that the "world must be made safe for democracy." With trepidation in his voice, the president acknowledged the magnitude of his request. "It is a fearful thing," he intoned, "to lead this great peaceful people into war, into the most terrible and disastrous of all wars, civilization itself seeming to be in the balance."

Waging a total war entailed a great many sacrifices, not the least of which was the need to distribute the burdens of financing the conflict in a fair and effective manner. "The granting of adequate credits to the Government," Wilson noted, referring to the importance of public borrowing, was essential. But equally significant was the need to ensure that such debts were backed "as far as they can equitably be sustained by the present generation, by well conceived taxation." With these words, the president articulated how a combination of borrowing and taxes borne by present and future generations would ultimately fund the American war effort.[1]

[1] "Must Exert All Our Power" *New York Times*, April 3, 1917, 1; "Full Text of Address by the President to Congress," *Los Angeles Times*, April 3, 1917, 11.

The ensuing wartime crisis and the need to craft "well conceived taxation" soon became a crucial catalyst for the consolidation of the modern fiscal state. With the legal foundations in place by 1913, the Wilson administration was able to underwrite the war effort by dramatically expanding the scale and scope of the new tax regime. Ratification of the Sixteenth Amendment and the subsequent enactment of the first peacetime, graduated income tax provided wartime lawmakers with the opportunity to reinforce the tectonic shift in American tax law and policy. As historian David M. Kennedy has observed, the wartime tax regime "occasioned a fiscal revolution in the United States." The Great War, in short, was a watershed event in the consolidation of the modern American fiscal state.[2]

Like other aspects of war mobilization, this fiscal revolution required an enormous infusion of national administrative resources. Nowhere was this more evident than within the corridors of the U.S. Treasury Department – the executive agency responsible for creating, managing, and defending wartime fiscal policies. Prosecuting a global war, and administering a tax system that included such novel and difficult to decipher provisions as an "excess-profits" levy, demanded an unprecedented amount of bureaucratic capacity. The tremendous responsibility of orchestrating this expansion in fiscal capacity fell mainly upon Wilson's Treasury Secretary (and son-in-law) William Gibbs McAdoo.[3]

The dramatic changes in tax laws and policies and the particular contours of the wartime proto-administrative state were not inevitable or

[2] David M. Kennedy, *Over Here: The First World War and American Society* (New York: Oxford University Press, 1980), 112. For more on the significance of World War I to American state formation, see Thomas J. Knock, *To End All Wars: Woodrow Wilson and the Quest for a New World Order* (New York: Oxford University Press, 1992); Ronald Schaffer, *America in the Great War: The Rise of the War Welfare State* (New York: Oxford University Press, 1991); Marc A. Eisner, *From Warfare to Welfare State: World War I, Compensatory State-Building, and the Limits of the Modern Order* (University Park: Pennsylvania State University Press, 2000); Ellis W. Hawley, *The Great War and the Search for Modern Order: A History of the American People and Their Institutions, 1917–1933* (New York: St. Martin's Press, 1979); Barry Karl, *The Uneasy State: The United States from 1915 to 1945* (Chicago: University of Chicago Press, 1983); Christopher Capozzola, *Uncle Sam Wants You: World War I and the Making of the Modern American Citizen* (New York: Oxford University Press, 2008).

[3] As Robert D. Cuff aptly noted, "an administrative army marched into Washington before a military force sailed overseas." Cuff, *The War Industries Board: Business-Government Relations during World War I* (Baltimore: Johns Hopkins University Press, 1973), 1; W. Elliot Brownlee, *Federal Taxation in America: A Short History* (Cambridge: Cambridge University Press, 1994), 24, 51, fn.4.

preordained. The political malleability created by the crisis provided fiscal state-builders with a unique opportunity to determine the future framework of American tax law and policy, but the ultimate shape of that contested framework remained highly contingent. In this sense, the wartime fiscal revolution was not merely a functional response to the need for revenue; nor was it an abrupt end to wholesale progressive tax reform, as some scholars have suggested.[4] The wartime tax regime embodied, instead, a complex continuation of the conceptual shift in public finance advanced by prewar progressive intellectuals and political leaders, as well as a constraint on the social-democratic ambitions of some populist tax reformers.

Although the wartime tax system may not have gone as far as some activists had hoped, the unprecedented turn toward a system of steeply graduated taxes fundamentally altered the distribution of economic obligations, the meaning of fiscal citizenship, and perhaps most significantly the burgeoning powers of the administrative state. These three key elements of the expanding fiscal polity, in turn, furthered the development of a new strand of modern, American liberalism – one committed to using the powers of the state to advance progressive and egalitarian ideals.[5]

Among the Treasury officials who took part in creating the wartime tax regime, a group of elite lawyers was central to the project of building wartime administrative capacity. These government lawyers were midlevel entrepreneurial bureaucrats, operating just below the main line of hierarchical authority and well above the quotidian tasks of clerical staff. Some, like Daniel C. Roper, the Commissioner of Internal Revenue, and Thomas B. Love, an Assistant Treasury Secretary, were longtime Southern Democrats and Wilson supporters who fit easily into the wartime administration.[6] Others seemed more out of place. Wall Street

4 John F. Witte, *The Politics and Development of the American Income Tax* (Madison: University of Wisconsin Press, 1985); Robert Higgs, *Crisis and Leviathan: Critical Episodes in the Growth of American Government* (New York: Oxford University Press, 1987), Chapter 7; James Weinstein, *The Corporate Ideal in the Liberal State, 1900–1918* (Boston: Beacon Press, 1968), 214–54.

5 On the importance of the Wilson administration to the development of modern American liberalism, see generally John Milton Cooper, Jr., *Woodrow Wilson: A Biography* (New York: Vintage, 2011), Ronald J. Pestritto, *Woodrow Wilson and the Roots of Modern Liberalism* (Oxford: Rowman & Littlefield, 2005).

6 It should come as no surprise that attorneys working for President Woodrow Wilson – the lawyer/scholar turned statesman who arguably did the most to advance the intellectual campaign for the administrative state – were at the forefront of using tax laws and policies to develop the administrative infrastructure of the modern state. Woodrow Wilson, *The*

Republicans Russell C. Leffingwell and Arthur B. Ballantine were early Treasury Department consultants who quickly rose to more prominent positions. They were more emblematic of the elite corporate attorneys who viewed the rise of the wartime fiscal state and their role in its emergence with a combination of pride and consternation.

Enlisting the expertise and social connections of these legal professionals was critical to the development of fiscal capacity. Just as Cordell Hull appealed to the New York Bar in his 1914 pleas to inculcate a taxpaying culture among America's wealthiest classes, so too did the Wilson administration seek out lawyers like Roper, Love, Leffingwell, and Ballantine as key intermediaries between the state and its citizens. Through their efforts, these Treasury lawyers were able to put the ideas of the progressive public finance economists into action by developing the vital institutional capacity necessary to implement a tax system based on the notion of ability to pay. In sum, these government attorneys helped lock in a pattern of financing that would have far-reaching implications beyond the immediate crisis of the war – and, in some cases, even beyond what the lawyers, themselves, had envisioned.

The Treasury lawyers contributed to the consolidation of the new fiscal order in several ways. First, as leading members of the bar, they used their particular social and professional networks – developed through attendance at elite law schools, employment at leading corporate law firms, and service to the nation's largest businesses and wealthiest individuals – to staff and train their offices with like-minded legal professionals committed to the Department's core institutional mission of building public trust. Instilling greater faith in the discretionary powers of an executive agency was vital, mainly because it facilitated the transition from a patronage-laden tariff regime to an income-based tax system administered by professional policymakers and bureaucrats.

Second, the lawyers used their practical legal skills to help consolidate Treasury's administrative authority. Their legal expertise was necessary to guard the Department's jurisdictional control, to limit the reach of other government entities, and to manage the daily details of financing a global war. Melding their claims to professionalism with their expertise and desire to wield state power, the Treasury lawyers were active participants in the creation of a distinctively legal administrative state.[7]

State: Elements of Historical and Practical Politics: A Sketch of Institutional History and Administration (Boston: D. C. Heath and Co., 1889).

7 The role of expertise and social networks in American state-building has been explored in several recent studies, see, e.g., Mary O. Furner and Barry Supple, eds., *The State*

Third, as intellectual stewards, the lawyers helped formulate broad policies regarding the mix of war financing options.[8] They used their contacts, skills, and experience to search for legally viable alternative sources of revenue, to channel Treasury efforts in constitutionally permissible directions, and to remind key policymakers that the choice between taxation and public debt implicated the dynamics of patriotism, wartime sacrifice, and fiscal citizenship.

Fourth, and perhaps most important, the wartime Treasury lawyers were moderators of social forces and ideological tensions. Operating as classic, Tocquevillian arbitrators of conflicting societal interests, they sought to mediate between populist leaders who wanted to use the war crisis to radically reconstruct American political economy and more conservative forces that wanted to retain or extend the regressive prewar system of tariffs and consumption taxes. In an earlier era, the reform-minded public finance economists advanced their ideas and visions about a new, conceptual basis of taxation by navigating between the extremes of radical populism and laissez-faire conservatism. Now, during the war emergency, the Treasury lawyers engaged in a similar negotiation between the two ends of the political spectrum.[9]

In carrying out these tasks, the lawyers were not always altruistic guardians of the public purse. In their patriotic zeal to build public trust, they did not lose sight of their own professional and personal self-interest, particularly when they considered their postwar opportunities. In their attempts to create an Americanized version of an ideal-typical Weberian

and Economic Knowledge: The American and British Experiences (New York: Cambridge University Press, 1990); Daniel P. Carpenter, *The Forging of Bureaucratic Autonomy: Reputations, Networks and Policy Innovations in Executive Agencies, 1862–1928* (Princeton: Princeton University Press, 2001); Michael Bernstein, *A Perilous Progress: Economists and Public Purpose in Twentieth-Century America* (Princeton: Princeton University Press, 2001).

8 Stephen Skowronek has identified lawyers as the American state's "most important intellectual resource." Skowronek, *Building a New American State: The Expansion of National Administrative Capacities, 1877–1920* (New York: Cambridge University Press, 1982), 32. Although Skowronek was referring to the role of nineteenth-century government lawyers, his emphasis on the "intellectual skills and human talents" that lawyers brought to the resolution of crisis situations applies equally well to the World War I Treasury Department lawyers. Ibid., 31–4; see also Willard Hurst, *The Growth of American Law: The Law Makers* (Boston: Little Brown, 1950), 334–5.

9 Alexis De Tocqueville, *Democracy in America*, 2 vols. (New York: Vintage Books, 1945 [1835]), vol. 1, 282–8. The broader role of professionalism in moderating conflicting forces and maintaining order is also identified with the social theory of Emile Durkheim, *The Division of Labor in Society*, trans. Joseph Ward Swain (New York: Free Press, 1933).

bureaucracy, they maintained their allegiance to a highly marketable profession and not a rigid civil service system.[10] In trying to mediate between social interests, they nonetheless retained an unyielding and self-serving faith in corporate capitalism as the engine of economic growth and prosperity.

Despite being the "counterpoise to the democratic element," the Treasury lawyers helped build the administrative foundations of the new fiscal polity.[11] By weaving direct and progressive taxation further into the fabric of a new legal and bureaucratic regime, they bolstered patterns of public financing that would usher in a new fiscal order and fundamentally transform American life – well beyond what these government lawyers could have anticipated. By building the administrative capacity necessary to effectuate the ideas of the public finance economists, the Treasury lawyers also ironically exacerbated the fiscal myopia that would accompany the institutionalization of the ability-to-pay logic. As we have seen, tax experts were generally oblivious to how their advocacy for a new tax regime based on the principle of faculty or taxpaying capacity severed the links between tax and spending policies. In their drive to promote the ability-to-pay rationale, they lost sight of how the spending side of fiscal policy could be used to address issues of distributional justice. The Treasury lawyers, in the process of building the administrative apparatus to support the faculty principle, became complicit in narrowing the reach of the rising fiscal polity. Like the progressive political economists, the government lawyers unwittingly limited the promise and possibilities of a holistic tax and transfer regime.

Wartime Statism, Fiscal Revolution, and the Infusion of Administrative Resources

As part of the war mobilization effort, the federal government significantly expanded its powers and reach over American society. Overall federal spending, for instance, skyrocketed from a paltry 0.2 percent of Gross Domestic Product (GDP) in 1914 to about 3.2 percent by 1919.[12] Within months of U.S. entry into the war, several new federal agencies were

[10] Max Weber, "Bureaucracy" in *From Max Weber: Essays in Sociology*, ed. Hans H. Gerth and C. Wright Mills (Oxford: Oxford University Press, 1946), 196–245.

[11] Tocqueville, *Democracy in America*, 282.

[12] *Historical Statistics of the United States: Millennial Edition*, ed. Susan B. Carter et al. (New York: Cambridge University Press, 2006), Table Ea584–587, Table Ca9–19.

created, including the Food Administration to regulate the price, production, and distribution of foodstuffs; the National War Labor Board to manage industrial relations; and most notably the War Industries Board, which under the leadership of financier Bernard M. Baruch attempted to coordinate and streamline the military-industrial procurement process. In what was perhaps the most intense form of government intervention in the economy, the Wilson administration also took control of the railroads, pooling the various lines to create an integrated, national system of transportation. By the eve of the war, a form of American corporatism was firmly in place, as "the federal government, the industrial community, and the military services had developed complex, modern, and professionalized structures, each dependent upon the others."[13]

To underwrite the unprecedented institutional interdependence between state and society, the national tax system underwent its own transformation. Ratification of the Sixteenth Amendment and the subsequent enactment of a progressive income tax in 1913 provided a basis from which lawmakers could launch a more robust tax regime. The war emergency soon provided the federal government with an opportunity to exercise assiduously its new taxing powers.[14] With high exemption levels and moderately graduated rates, the early prewar versions of the federal income tax, as we have seen, affected only a small fraction of American citizens and added little to the national fisc. In fiscal year 1914, as the tariff and excise taxes continued to dominate federal revenues, only about 2 percent of the labor force paid income taxes, and income tax receipts, accordingly, made up fewer than 10 percent of total federal revenues.[15]

By the end of the war, however, levies on income and profits had eclipsed all other forms of taxation. Marginal individual income tax rates soared to a top figure of 77 percent, the percentage of the labor force filing

[13] Paul A. C. Koistinen, *Mobilizing for Modern War: The Political Economy of American Warfare, 1865–1919* (Lawrence: University Press of Kansas, 1997), 4. See also Hugh Rockoff, *America's Economic Way of War: War and the U.S. Economy from the Spanish-American War to the Persian Gulf War* (New York: Cambridge University Press, 2012), Chapter 5; Hew Strachan, *Financing the First World War* (Oxford: Oxford University Press, 2004); Steven A. Bank, et al., *War and Taxes* (Washington, D.C.: Urban Institute Press, 2008), Chapter 3.

[14] Witte, *Politics and Development of the Federal Income Tax*, 79–87; Brownlee, *Federal Taxation in America*, 47–58.

[15] United States Treasury Department, *Annual Report of the Secretary of the Treasury on the State of the Finances for the Fiscal Year Ended June 30, 1914* (Washington, D.C.: Government Printing Office, 1915), 149.

TABLE 6.1. *Maximum Marginal Tax Rates and Tax Revenues by Source, Fiscal Years 1913–1921 (nominal dollar amounts in millions)*

Year	Top Marginal Tax Rate	Individual Income Tax Revenue	Corporate Income Tax Revenue	War Profits and Excess Profits Tax	Total Income and Profits Tax Revenue	Total Tax Revenue as % of Total Federal Revenues
1913	7%	$28	$43	–	$71	10%
1914	7%	41	39	–	80	12%
1915	7%	68	57	–	125	16%
1916	15%	173	172	–	345	31%
1917	67%	795	504	$1,639	2,938	80%
1918	77%	1,128	653	2,506	4,287	83%
1919	73%	1,270	744	1,432	3,445	51%
1920	73%	1,075	637	989	2,700	48%
1921	73%	719	366	335	1,421	35%

Sources: Historical Statistics of the United States; *Annual Reports of the Treasury Department, 1914–1921;* Roy G. Blakey and Gladys C. Blakey, *The Federal Income Tax* (New York: Longmans, Green, and Co., 1940), Table 20, 512.

income taxes climbed to nearly 20 percent, and monies generated by income and profits taxes accounted for roughly half of all federal revenues in fiscal year 1919 (see Table 6.1). Although exemption levels decreased substantially, the wartime tax system had a distinctive "soak-the-rich" characteristic. In fact, the effective tax rate of the nation's wealthiest households (those making more than $50,000) soared from roughly 3 percent in 1916 to 22 percent within two years.[16]

Taxes were not the only source of funding for the robust wartime state; government borrowing and the use of newly created monetary powers were also critical.[17] Government bonds, artfully dubbed "Liberty

[16] *Historical Statistics of the United States*, Series Ea758–772; Thomas Piketty and Emmanuel Saez, "Income Inequality in the United States, 1913–2002" (2004), available online at: http://emlab.berkeley.edu/users/saez/piketty-saezOUP04US.pdf. For those few taxpayers who had annual incomes that exceeded $1 million, the effective tax rate skyrocketed from 10 percent to over 70 percent between 1916 and 1918. W. Elliot Brownlee, "Historical Perspectives on U.S. Tax Policy toward the Rich," in *Does Atlas Shrug? The Economic Consequences of Taxing the Rich*, ed. Joel B. Slemrod (New York: Russell Sage Foundation, 2000), 45.

[17] In addition to the conventional sources of war financing – taxes, public borrowing, and money creation – the United States also resorted to more implicit "taxes" related to price controls and the draft. Rockoff, *America's Economic Way of War*, 24–7. 126, 129.

Loans," provided significant revenue. As a result, total public debt as a percentage of GDP increased from 0.2 percent in 1914 to roughly 4.3 percent by 1919.[18] Lenient monetary policy also provided a convenient, if often unacknowledged, source of financing. From June 1916 to June 1919, the money supply increased by over $11 billion, and consumer prices shot up nearly 66 percent. Although budget surpluses and a more stable money supply resurfaced after the war, debt financing and rampant inflation proved to be key components in the wartime mix of funding sources. In fact, economic historians have estimated that the American war effort was financed with roughly 30 percent from taxes, 30 percent from money creation, and the remaining 40 percent from public borrowing. As we shall see, wartime government officials, especially the Treasury lawyers, agonized over the distributional implications of these different funding sources.[19]

From a historical and comparative perspective, the economic results of U.S. war financing were mixed. On the one hand, the wartime fiscal policies provided European Allies and the American Expeditionary Forces with sufficient resources to win the war, and the First World War mix of financing was an improvement over the Civil War when the North resorted mainly to debt financing and the printing of new money. Calls to share the sacrifice of blood and treasure during the Great War did not fall on deaf ears; the prewar demands for using taxation to forge a reinvigorated sense of civic identity continued to resonate. Yet, if one measures the economic success of wartime financing by focusing on the state's ability to extract tax revenue from a broad base of citizen-taxpayers while limiting the costs of inflation, the American financing of World War I was not nearly as successful as World War II. During the latter conflict, taxes constituted a significantly larger percentage of revenue, and

[18] In nominal terms, the federal budget deficit climbed from roughly $400 million in 1914 to over $13 billion by 1919. Total public debt consequently soared from about $1 billion to over $25 billion during the same period. *Historical Statistics of the United States*, Series Ea584–587.

[19] Charles Gilbert, *American Financing of World War I* (Westport, Conn.: Greenwood Publishing, 1970), 177–99, 212–13; Bartholomew H. Sparrow, *From the Outside In: World War II and the American State*(Princeton: Princeton University Press, 1996), 298–302; Milton Friedman and Anna J. Schwartz, *A Monetary History of the United States, 1867–1960* (Princeton: Princeton University Press, 1963), 189–239; Hugh Rockoff, "Until It's Over, Over There: The U.S. Economy in World War I," in *The Economics of World War I*, ed. Stephen Broadberry and Mark Harrison (Cambridge: Cambridge University Press, 2005), 310–43; Rockoff, *America's Economic Way of War*, 125, Table 5.2.

inflation was much lower mainly because of greater productivity and stable rates of savings.[20]

Comparatively, U.S. financing of the Great War was economically superior to that of nearly all other major participants in the conflict. To be sure, mobilization for mass warfare compelled nearly all belligerents to dramatically increase progressive taxes as a response to social calls for greater equality of sacrifice. Still, the specifics of war financing differed in each of the countries. Only Great Britain, which followed a path similar to the United States, was able to fund roughly one-fifth of its war expenditures with taxes, though it suffered from an increasing price level that exceeded American inflation. France, Russia, and Italy, by contrast, raised little from taxes and were forced to rely on tremendous amounts of public borrowing and inflation-inducing money creation, which greatly undermined their postwar credit and economies. Similarly, Germany's early optimism for a quick victory led it to rely heavily on loans. The comparative success of the United States, in part, explains why World War I was vital to the early development of American geopolitical power.[21]

During the early stages of mobilization, lawmakers seemed intent on financing the war evenly with current taxes and debt financing. Even before the United States officially entered the conflict, the 1916 Revenue Act demonstrated the federal government's resolve. It provided sharply higher income tax rates, a tax on the business profits of munitions manufacturers, and a graduated federal inheritance tax. Supported by progressive groups like the American Committee on War Finance and the Association for an Equitable Federal Income Tax, the new law had broad appeal, especially since it came on the heels of the U.S. Supreme Court's

[20] Hugh Rockoff, "The United States: From Ploughshares to Swords," in *The Economics of World War II: Six Great Powers in International Comparison*, ed. Mark Harrison (Cambridge: Cambridge University Press, 1998); Rockoff, *America's Economic Way of War*, Chapter 6; Sparrow, *From the Outside In*; James T. Sparrow, *Warfare State: World War II Americans and the Age of Big Government* (New York: Oxford University Press, 2011), Chapter 4.

[21] Kenneth Scheve and David Stasavage, "The Conscription of Wealth: Mass Warfare and the Demand for Progressive Taxation," *International Organization* 64 (fall 2010), 529–61; Paul Studenski and Herman E. Krooss, *Financial History of the United States: Fiscal, Monetary, Banking, and Tariff, including Financial Administration and State and Local Finance* (New York: McGraw-Hill, 1963), 280–1. Gilbert, *American Financing of World War I*, 221–4; Michael H. Hunt, *The American Ascendancy: How the United States Gained and Wielded Dominance* (Chapel Hill: University of North Carolina Press, 2007), Chapter 2.

validation of the 1913 income tax – a decision that emboldened lawmakers to forcefully use their new found fiscal powers.[22]

As the war progressed, lawmakers sought to continue to minimize borrowing to restrain inflation and spread the war costs fairly across generations and between socioeconomic classes. In his 1917 message to Congress, President Wilson stated, "so far as practicable the burden of the war should be borne by taxation of the present generation rather than by loans." Treasury Secretary McAdoo reiterated that "fifty percent of the war costs should be financed by" taxation, contending that "one of the most fatal mistakes that governments have made in all countries has been the failure to impose fearlessly and promptly upon the existing generation a fair burden of the cost of war."[23] The desire to balance the war costs with an eye toward intergenerational equity illustrates how the Wilson administration was mindful of its social and ethical obligations to monitor the distributional effects of war financing. The Treasury lawyers echoed this initial message of seeking distributional equity, especially when other Department officials began to veer from the original commitment.

Yet, while the 1916 law solidified the taxing powers of the national government, the most radical departures – and certainly the most controversial – came after the United States officially entered the war in April 1917. Initially, McAdoo anticipated that of the $3.5 billion needed for the war new taxation could provide $1.8 billion. These optimistic projections were soon dashed, however. By the summer of 1917, war costs were expected to be closer to $15 billion, with taxation making up less than $2 billion. "With each fresh calculation," McAdoo later recalled, "the sum had grown larger, and the figures were appalling. There were

[22] *Revenue Act of 1916*, 39 Stat. 767 (1916); W. Elliot Brownlee, "Wilson and Financing the Modern State: The Revenue Act of 1916," *Proceedings of the American Philosophical Society* 129(2) (1985), 173–205; Roy G. Blakey and Gladys C. Blakey, *The Federal Income Tax* (New York: Longmans, Green, and Co., 1940), Chapter 4; *Brushaber v. Union Pacific Railroad Co.*, 240 U.S. 1 (1916). The munitions tax, in particular, was a rifle-shot provision aimed squarely at the E. I. du Pont de Nemours Company, also known as the "Powder Trust," because it was the leading maker of gun powder and military explosives. In 1916, roughly 90 percent of the revenues from the munitions tax came from the Du Pont Company. Stuart D. Brandes, *Warhogs: A History of War Profits in America* (Lexington: University of Kentucky Press, 1997), 135.

[23] "McAdoo Talks Over Loan at Lunch with Bankers," *Wall Street Journal*, May 5, 1917; William G. McAdoo, *Crowded Years: The Reminiscences of William G. McAdoo* (Boston: Houghton Mifflin, 1931), 389–90; Dale N. Shook, *William G. McAdoo and the Development of National Economic Policy, 1913–1918* (New York: Garland Publishing, 1987), 263–4; Gilbert, *American Financing of World War I*, 84.

so many uncertain factors in the problem that a definite conclusion was not possible."[24]

As Treasury confronted the mounting war costs, and American troops began sailing overseas, the social demands for confiscatory taxes on income, profits, and wealth transfers became more vociferous. Calls for the "conscription of wealth" to match the conscription of men began to fill the editorial pages of the country's leading publications. While Congress debated a new tax bill in the summer of 1917, newspapers like the *Los Angeles Times* rhetorically queried whether the minor financial sacrifices made by the Rockefellers and the Fords could compare "with that of the man who bares his breast to the bullets or the bayonets of the foe and risks his life for his country. What are the sacrifices of capitalists compared with the sacrifices of those whom the solider leaves behind?"[25]

With social pressures growing, lawmakers began to ratchet up the powers of the new tax regime. The 1917 Revenue Act dramatically raised the stakes, especially for the wealthy. The new law increased the top individual marginal tax rates to unprecedented heights, enacted several nominal excise taxes, and adopted a new controversial levy on excess profits. Whereas the 1916 munitions profits tax levied a flat 12.5 percent tax on the profits of all armament producers, the newly created excess-profits tax applied to profits "over a reasonable return on invested capital" and affected all businesses, not just those in the munitions industry.[26]

Other nations also used excess-profits taxes as a funding source, but the historically unprecedented turn to this levy by the United States signaled the Wilson administration's desire to alter the concept and meaning of business profits. Like the earlier levies on corporate earnings, the new wartime taxes reflected a profound change in the social meaning of business profits. The term "excess" profits implied that there was some reasonable level of earnings that a business was entitled to, but that any surplus amount above that level was "unreasonable" or "abnormal." Such surpluses generated by the war were windfall gains that exceeded

[24] McAdoo, *Crowded Years*, 372; Kennedy, *Over Here*, 107, 109.

[25] "Conscripting Capital," *Los Angeles Times*, June 4, 1917, II4; "Where the Burden Shall Fall," *Puck*, April 21, 1917, A7; "The Conscription of Wealth," *The Independent*, April 28, 1917, 193.

[26] Eight percent was established as the "reasonable rate of return," and all profits above that level were taxed at graduated rates ranging from 8 percent to a maximum of 60 percent on corporate profits that were in excess of 32 percent of invested capital. *Revenue Act of 1917*, 40 Stat. 300 (1917). For an elementary and useful example of how excess profits were calculated, see Rockoff, *America's Economic Way of War*, 116.

a legitimate amount of financial profit. A tax on these profits reflected the belief that the broader public, operating through the powers of the state, had a legitimate stake in collecting excess profits generated by war profiteering. Profits, in this sense, were no longer simply the gains earned by private effort. At a time when ordinary Americans were sacrificing life and limb, the enactment of an excess-profits tax expressed a growing social and political indignation with war profiteering; it also reflected a demand for shared sacrifice that was at the center of the Treasury Department's egalitarian sense of fiscal citizenship. The new valence of profits did not escape the notice of populist leaders, economic experts, and progressive lawmakers who strongly supported the new levy – as well as those conservatives who opposed it.[27]

Even before the 1917 tax law was enacted, New York lawyer Amos Pinchot boldly and presciently proclaimed: "If we ever get a big income tax on in war time, some if it – a lot of it – is going to stick."[28] To help make this new tax stick, the Treasury Department itself underwent a major reorganization. The formal, top-down, hierarchical structure of the Treasury Department expanded dramatically. Several new assistant secretary positions were created, and the number of rank-and-file personnel grew significantly. The Bureau of Internal Revenue (BIR), the unit responsible for interpreting, assessing, and collecting taxes, including the excess-profits levy, grew enormously under Daniel Roper's leadership. Between 1913 and 1920, the number of BIR personnel increased by nearly fourfold, rising from roughly 4,000 employees to almost 16,000. Though that figure declined slightly after the war, it soon reached a new plateau that remained at a multiple above the prewar amount, thus, giving credence

[27] "The Excess Profits Tax – Discussion," *American Economic Review* 10:1 (March 1920), 19–32; W. Elliot Brownlee, "Economists and the Formation of the Modern Tax System in the United States: The World War I Crisis," in *The State and Economic Knowledge*, ed. Mary O. Furner and Barry Supple, 401–34, 409–11; W. Elliot Brownlee, "Social Investigation and Political Learning in the Financing of World War I," in *The State and Social Investigation in Britain and the United States*, ed. Michael Lacey and Mary O. Furner (Cambridge: Cambridge University Press, 1993), 323–64, 328–32. The 1917 law also significantly raised taxes on alcohol, tobacco, and wealth transfers, in addition to enacting a variety of excise taxes on luxury items, sporting goods, and even chewing gum and movie tickets – all in the hopes of symbolically, if not substantively, spreading the burden of wartime fiscal sacrifice.

[28] *Revenue Act of 1917*, 40 Stat. 300 (1917); Pinchot quoted in John W. Hillje, "New York Progressivism and the War Revenue Act of 1917," *New York History* 53:4 (October 1972), 446.

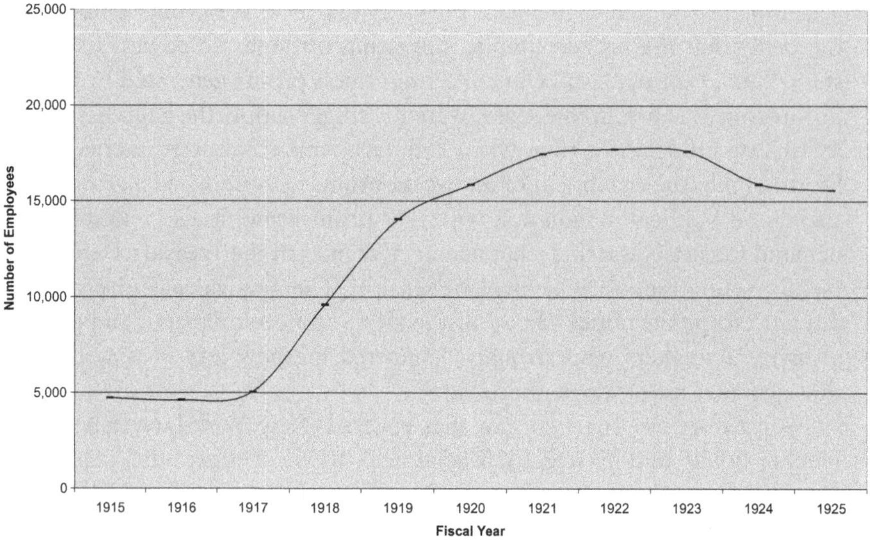

CHART 6.1. Growth of Bureau of Internal Revenue, 1915–1925.
Source: Blakey and Blakey, *Federal Income Tax*, 540, Table 32; *Annual Reports of the Treasury Department*, 1914–1926.

to the notion that the war had a ratchet effect on the BIR's administrative capacity (see Chart 6.1).[29]

Treasury Department spending during and after the war mirrored the increase in personnel. Not only did the Department's overall budget, in real terms (constant 1913 dollars), more than double, increasing from $86 million in 1915 to $187 million by 1919, such spending remained relatively consistent after the war. During the same period, the BIR's specific budget (in real terms) increased at an even greater pace, with spending rising from just under $7 million to over $19 million, nearly a threefold increase. These figures illustrate the financial commitments to administrative power demanded by the war.[30]

In sum, World War I triggered a sea change in the historical development of a powerful American nation-state. Unparalleled interconnections among economy, society, and polity were undergirded by fundamental transformations in public finance and federal bureaucratic capacity. After

29 Blakey and Blakey, *Federal Income Tax*, 540, Table 32; Alan T. Peacock and Jack Wiseman, *The Growth of Public Expenditure in the United Kingdom, 1890–1955* (London: George Allen & Irwin, 1967); Sparrow, *From the Outside In*.

30 *Annual Report of the Secretary of the Treasury*, 1914–1925; Sparrow, *From the Outside In*, 295–8. *Historical Statistics of the United States*, Table Cc1–2.

the war, the steeply progressive tax rates were scaled back, just as tariff revenues increased in response to the revival of international trade. But the national tax system did not return to either its prewar levels or even its prewar trajectory – the war was thus the pivot upon which the early-twentieth-century fiscal revolution turned. The conflict consolidated the powers of the new fiscal polity. It redistributed the financial obligations of funding a modern state. It gave new meaning to the idea of shared sacrifice and fiscal citizenship. And perhaps most importantly the Great War provided the context for the irreversible expansion of administrative capacity.

The Treasury Lawyers

It was amid the dramatic wartime changes in state power that the Treasury lawyers made their mark. McAdoo, who himself had been a New York City commercial lawyer before turning to other pursuits, filled key Treasury posts with leading members of the bar, often with individuals he knew personally. Roper and Love, for example, were longtime Southern Democrats. A former South Carolina lawyer and state legislator, Roper had been a staff member at numerous government commissions and agencies, and he was among the first group of modern state officials to assemble the revolving door between the public and private sectors.[31] Love, a former Texas legislator and insurance lawyer, was appointed to his Treasury post mainly because of his role as the head of Wilson's Texas reelection campaign. Throughout his career, including during his tenure in Treasury, Love seemed more interested in the partisanship of Democratic politics than the intricacies of insurance law or government service.[32]

[31] After working for the Interstate Commerce Commission in the 1890s, Roper leveraged his regulatory knowledge and experience and became the manager of a railway and public utilities financing firm. Daniel C. Roper, *Fifty Years of Public Life* (Durham: Duke University Press, 1941), 90–1. "The Public Service Record of Daniel C. Roper," Box 11: Honorary Bound Volume, March 31, 1920, Daniel C. Roper Papers, Rare Book, Manuscript & Special Collections Library, Duke University, Durham, N.C. [hereinafter DCRP].

[32] "New Treasury Assistant," *Washington Post,* December 11, 1917; Thomas B. Love to Newton Baker, Jan. 3, 1916; Love to J. Howard Ardery, Dec. 20, 1917, Box 6 (IU7D), Thomas B. Love Papers, Dallas Historical Society, Dallas Tax [hereinafter TBLP]. For more on Love, see Lewis L. Gould, *Progressives and Prohibitionists: Texas Democrats in the Wilson Era* (Austin: University of Texas Press, 1973), 61–2, 278–9; McAdoo, *Crowded Years*, 403; Sue E. Winton Moore, *Thomas B. Love, Texas Democrat, 1901–1949* (Master's thesis, University of Texas, 1971).

If Roper and Love reflected the Southern Democratic roots of the Wilson administration, Leffingwell and Ballantine were the epitome of Yankee aristocracy. Leffingwell was undoubtedly the central node in this network of government attorneys. A graduate of Yale College and Columbia Law School, and a former partner in the prestigious New York firm of Cravath & Henderson, Leffingwell was the de facto undersecretary of the Treasury during most of the war.[33] As a legal advisor for many of New York's leading financial institutions, he had supervised numerous complex corporate reorganizations before the war and had navigated the issuance of some of the most challenging corporate and municipal securities offerings.[34] Paul Cravath, his senior law partner, referred to Leffingwell as "one of the best lawyers at our Bar, with no superior as a contract lawyer."[35]

Like Leffingwell, Ballantine emerged from the ranks of the Northeastern legal elite. Educated at Harvard College and Law School, he became a leading Boston corporate lawyer, specializing in bankruptcy reorganizations and corporate finance. At the start of the war, he was a temporary consultant on the BIR's "committee of lawyers," but he soon became Solicitor of Internal Revenue, the Bureau's chief lawyer, where he played a central role in organizing the tax collection process and defending the constitutionality of the excess-profits tax.[36]

33 During his tenure in Treasury, Leffingwell was a capacious note-taker and correspondent who left behind an abundant collection of documents, as perhaps only a former Cravath partner could. Russell C. Leffingwell Papers, Library of Congress, Washington, D.C. [hereinafter RCLP].

34 Leffingwell was instrumental in assisting the investment house of Kuhn, Loeb & Co. to float $60 million worth of short-term debt for the Pennsylvania Railroad just as the Panic of 1907 hit. Robert T. Swaine, *The Cravath Firm and Its Predecessors, 1819–1947*, 3 vols. (New York: Ad Press, 1946), Vol. I, 716.

35 Stephen A. Schuker, "Leffingwell, Russell Cornell," in *Dictionary of American Biography, Supplement 6, 1956–1960*, ed. John A. Garraty (New York: Charles Scribner's Sons, 1990), 376–8; W. Elliot Brownlee, "Russell Cornell Leffingwell," in *Banking and Finance, 1913–1989*, in *Encyclopedia of American Business History and Biography*, ed. Larry Schweikart (New York: Facts on File, 1990), 216–39; *Selected Letters of R. C. Leffingwell*, ed. Edward Pulling (Oyster Bay, N.Y., 1979), 3–5; Paul Cravath to William G. McAdoo, May 4, 1917, Russell C. Leffingwell Papers, Series I, Correspondence, Box 6, Folder 119, Sterling Memorial Library, Yale University, New Haven, Conn.

36 "Arthur Ballantine, Lawyer, Dies," *New York Times*, October 12, 1960; "Hoover Aid in Treasury Dies in N.Y." *Washington Post*, October 12, 1960; Melvin I. Urofsky, "Ballantine, Arthur Atwood," in *Dictionary of American Biography, Supplement Six, 1956–1960*, ed. John A. Garraty (New York: Charles Scribner's Sons, 1990), pp. 3–4. "Named Legal Advisors on War Revenue Regulations," *Official Bulletin*, December 1, 1917; Arthur A. Ballantine to Daniel C. Roper, November 25, 1918, Box 1: IRS Solicitor

Daniel C. Roper (1967–1943)

Arthur A. Ballantine (1883–1960)

Russell C. Leffingwell (1878–1960)

FIGURE 6.1. The Treasury Lawyers. These three government officials were instrumental in helping develop the administrative capacity of the wartime fiscal state. Courtesy of the Library of Congress, Prints & Photographs Division, LC-USZ62-99049 (Roper), LC-DIG-hec-21468 (Leffingwell); and The New York Public Library (Ballantine).

These Treasury lawyers generally entered government service in predictable ways. Love and Roper, as longtime Wilson supporters, were rewarded with their high-level positions because of years of loyal service to the Democratic Party. Meanwhile, Leffingwell and Ballantine were appointed because of their practical expertise and experience. Yet, despite their similar backgrounds, Leffingwell and Ballantine became "dollar-a-year" men through different channels. The Leffingwell family had social ties to the McAdoos, but it was Paul Cravath who brought Leffingwell to McAdoo's attention.[37] By contrast, Ballantine entered the wartime corporatist state through a more conventional route. He likely came to the attention of administration officials because of his progressive stance on the use of insurance, rather than traditional tort suits, to compensate victims of railway injuries.[38]

Leffingwell and his colleagues wielded tremendous authority at a time when the American legal profession itself was undergoing dramatic change. The Great War began during the tail end of the transition from what legal historian Robert W. Gordon has dubbed "liberal legal science" to "progressive legal science." By the start of the war, elite lawyers were less concerned about policing the boundaries between public and private power than they were about using their professional contacts and technical expertise to develop efficient solutions to social conflicts. As the elite practice of law expanded beyond common-law courts and into the boardrooms and corridors of large corporations, lawyers become more than just zealous trial advocates of their clients' interests; they also became pivotal mediators and negotiators seeking to broker big deals and execute complex transactions that affected a variety of interests.[39]

1917–1919, Arthur A. Ballantine Papers, Herbert Hoover Presidential Library, West Branch, Iowa [hereinafter AABP]; Roper, *Fifty Years*, 174.

37 Brownlee, "Russell Cornell Leffingwell." According to Robert Swaine, when the United States officially entered the war Leffingwell demonstrated his patriotism – and perhaps his disillusionment with his successful legal career – by joining the Plattsburg Reserve Officers' Training Camp. Cravath was astonished to learn about his junior law partner's seemingly rash decision, and he intervened to ensure that Leffingwell's expertise in legal and financial matters would not be wasted on the battlefield. Swaine, *Cravath Firm*, 209. Cravath contended that Leffingwell with his age and experience could provide the country with greater service in Washington than by "toting a gun, doing K.P., or teaching American young men how to stick their bayonets through the bodies of imaginary Huns." Ibid.

38 Arthur A. Ballantine, "A Compensation Plan for Railway Accident Claims," *Harvard Law Review* 29:7 (May 1916); "Modernizing Railway Accident Law," *The Outlook*, November 15, 1916.

39 Robert W. Gordon, "The American Legal Profession, 1870–2000," in *The Cambridge History of Law in America, Vol. III: The Twentieth Century and After (1920–)*, ed.

The Treasury lawyers embodied the new vision of the highly skilled transactional attorney as essential intermediary. Though their individual personalities undoubtedly played a part in shaping their decisions and actions, their professional networks, legal skills, and practical experience reflected a historically specific professional mindset about the broad role of lawyers in building a modern, liberal polity. As Leffingwell observed toward the end of his career, the main role of his generation of lawyers was not to be merely a specialist in any one area of legal practice, but to be, as he put it, the "doctor who knew when to call in the specialist."[40]

In their role as legal doctors to the Treasury Department, Leffingwell and his colleagues used a particular type of legal analysis and problem-solving ability, one that provided systematic, forward-looking, long-term solutions. They used a broad and holistic perspective to build the Department's organizational capacity, to formulate fiscal policy options, to search for alternative sources of revenue, and to evaluate the distributional impact of the new tax laws and policies. To accomplish these tasks, these legal professionals understood that they needed to create a core institutional culture committed to gaining the public trust. Given the Department's historical lack of administrative capacity and inability to build public faith in its earlier use of monetary policy, World War I tax policy afforded the Department a new opportunity to gain the confidence and support of the populace.[41]

The Treasury lawyers seized this opportunity. They used the skills of cooperation and negotiation – developed as part of their prewar transactional practices – in their government service. As Roper recounted in his memoirs, his main goal in running the BIR was to cultivate a collaborative relationship between the BIR and taxpayers. "With the Government in partnership with business, it was increasingly important that the partners co-operate for their common good and not antagonize each other," he recalled. The exigencies of the war emergency, of course, forced American citizens to relax, at least temporarily, their long-held skepticism of centralized power, thus limiting antagonisms. But Roper and his

Michael Grossberg & Christopher Tomlins (New York: Cambridge University Press, 2008), 92–8; Hurst, *Growth of American Law*.

40 R. C. Leffingwell, "Comments on the Proposal," 4 *Journal of Public Law* 5 (1955), 5.

41 James Q. Wilson, *Bureaucracy: What Government Agencies Do and Why They Do It* (New York: Basic Books, 1989), 370–3. Gretchen Ritter, *Goldbugs and Greenbacks: The Antimonopoly Tradition and the Politics of Finance in America* (New York: Cambridge University Press, 1997), 175; Richard Bensel, *Yankee Leviathan, The Origins of Central State Authority in America 1859–1877* (New York: Cambridge University Press, 1990), Chapter 4; Carpenter, *Forging Bureaucratic Autonomy*, 60–3.

colleagues were well aware that they could not squander the tolerance provided by the crisis. Winning the war and making the world safe for democracy meant melding public power and private rights in unique ways. It meant creating confidence and legitimacy in the fairness and effectiveness of wartime fiscal policies.[42]

Recruiting, Training, and a Common Commitment to Building Public Trust

For the Treasury lawyers, one way to build public trust was by recruiting and hiring like-minded colleagues who embraced the Department's core mission of cooperating with citizens in raising revenue. Developing a homogeneous cadre of officials and staff was a challenge, especially given Treasury's growing size, the initial social divisions over the war, and the allure of a prosperous wartime economy. Nonetheless, administrators like Leffingwell and Roper tapped their social and professional contacts to hire assistants who shared their vision of – and their professional biases toward – corporatist state-building. Leffingwell naturally turned to the Cravath firm. He recruited several of his key lieutenants from the firm, including Hugh Satterlee and S. Parker Gilbert, a well-regarded corporate attorney who would succeed Leffingwell as undersecretary. He also "turned the tables" on Paul Cravath, volunteering the services of his senior partner to assist the U.S. representatives to the Inter-Allied Conference in Europe.[43]

Likewise, Roper assembled his "cabinet" of assistants by hiring friends and associates from his days in the Post Office Department, the Tariff Commission, and the Ways and Means Committee. With his experience shuttling between government and private service, Roper also anticipated the future benefits that could inure to those who were willing to help usher in a new fiscal order. As the leading tax lawyers E. Barrett Prettyman Sr. and Albert L. Hopkins later recalled, Roper recruited young, struggling attorneys, as well as some of Washington's first "lady lawyers," with appeals to patriotic duty, shared sacrifice, and remarks about how "this tax business is likely to develop into quite a thing for lawyers."[44]

42 Roper, *Fifty Years*, 177, 193.

43 Swaine, *Cravath Firm*, 210; Lawrence L. Murray, "Bureaucracy and Bipartisanship in Taxation: The Mellon Plan Revisited," *Business History Review* 52:2 (Summer 1978), 200–25.

44 Roper, *Fifty Years*, 174–5; "Robert Miller, U.S. Tax Lawyer under Woodrow Wilson, Is Dead" *New York Times*, January 2, 1968, 41; Albert L. Hopkins, *Autobiography of*

With their vast professional and social connections, the lawyers-turned-administrators quickly became pivotal intermediaries between the wartime fiscal state and the business community. Indeed, because they were central nodes in an elite network of bankers, attorneys, accountants, and business leaders, the Treasury lawyers could consult with a variety of interests and recruit like-minded legal professionals. Leffingwell regularly consulted former colleagues and clients to test ideas about fiscal policy, to gauge private perceptions of government actions, and to develop a dialogue about the ongoing relationship among taxpayers, bond investors, and the Treasury Department. Some of these contacts, in turn, did not hesitate in soliciting Leffingwell's influence in their own personal tax matters with the BIR.[45]

Meanwhile, Roper developed his own cooperative methods. At the start of the war, he created several advisory boards and a "committee of attorneys," which initially included Ballantine, to "review from time to time the decisions of the legal forces of the Bureau" and to "arouse a public consciousness of the partnership relation" formed by the new wartime tax laws. This "public consciousness" was necessary, Roper concluded, "if we were to achieve cooperation between the Government and the taxpayers in administering the law with justice and equity."[46] Like the progressive political economists who had been making the case

a Lawyer (Chicago, 1966), 106; E. Barrett Prettyman, "Autobiography of an Obscure Man at Forty," unpublished manuscript in Box 122, E. Barrett Prettyman Papers, Library of Congress, Washington, D.C. I am grateful to Dan Ernst for identifying the Prettyman manuscript and its relevance to my research. Many Treasury lawyers went on to have prosperous postwar tax law careers, including Prettyman, Hopkins, Robert N. Miller, and Annabel Matthews, one of the few female attorneys working in Ballantine's office. Matthews began her career as a clerk in the BIR in 1914, worked her way up to become a Senior Attorney, and then became the first female judge on the U.S. Board of Tax Appeals in 1930. "Miss Matthews, U.S. Tax Expert," *Washington Post*, March 25, 1960; see also the appointment and promotion letters contained in "Folder 11: Correspondence, 1914–1930," Annabel Matthews Papers, 1880–1960, Schlesinger Library, Radcliffe Institute, Harvard University, Cambridge, Mass.

45 Leffingwell to Thomas W. Lamont, Jr. (Officer of J. P. Morgan & Co.), February 21, 1918, Reel 3; Leffingwell to Otto Kahn (Member of Kahn, Loeb investment banking house), June 10, 1918, Reel 5; Leffingwell to Goldman, Sachs & Co., July 8, 1918, Reel 9; Leffingwell to George O. May (Senior Partner, Price Waterhouse & Co.), August 12, 1918, Reel 10, RCLP. Brownlee, "Russell Cornell Leffingwell," 217. On Leffingwell's assistance to friends and former colleagues see Leffingwell to W.M. Cutcheon (of Cravath), Dec. 1917, Reel 1; Leffingwell to Love, January 23, 1918, Reel 2 RCLP.

46 "D.C. Bank Merges Foreign Branches: Roper Names Advisors," *Washington Post*, April 3, 1918, 5; Roper, *Fifty Years*, 174; Roper, "The War Revenue Act and the Taxpayer," 2, December 13, 1917, Box 27: Addresses, DCRP. As a political insider, Roper was also consistently fielding requests for assistance in helping politicians land

that direct and graduated taxation could reinvigorate a modern notion of civic engagement, Roper and his colleagues similarly used taxation to bolster the new social contract between the public sector and private interests.

Professional loyalty, the promise of future riches, and patriotic appeals helped the Treasury lawyers recruit close confidantes, but the staffing of clerical personnel posed other challenges. Although the total number of personnel hired by Treasury increased sharply throughout the war, conscription and the lure of private sector jobs reduced the pool of available staff members and tarnished the image of government work. Maintaining the continuity of personnel and staff morale were critical issues for public confidence. When there was talk in the summer of 1918 that the draft age would be lowered, Leffingwell feared that the Department's personnel would be decimated. Revealing perhaps his own anxieties about his decision not to enlist in the military, Leffingwell warned McAdoo that "the efficiency of this Department and the Liberty Loan organization is in danger of being undermined as a result of the proposed extension of the draft age." Since Leffingwell himself "was on the way to being a soldier when [McAdoo] drafted him into the Treasury," he could empathize with those staffers who longed for more active participation in the war. "These men would gladly enough be fighting instead of figuring," wrote Leffingwell. "We are only keeping them on their present jobs because they feel they are doing the work they are best fitted for to help win the war."[47]

Roper went further in using patriotism to link "figuring" and "fighting." Addressing BIR field agents, the commissioner conveyed how their work was pivotal to the war effort. "While our soldiers and sailors pay the full price," Roper announced, "you will be giving your vigilant, unselfish and indefatigable service with quick understanding and keen enthusiasm to keeping open the life stream of revenue that finances the nation in both peace and war. And let no man lack the knowledge of just how the paying of his tax is a part of the winning of the war."[48]

government jobs for their friends and constituents. Breckinridge Long (Third Assistant Secretary of State) to Daniel C. Roper, February 28, 1920, Box 11, DCRP.

47 Leffingwell to McAdoo, August 17, 1918, Reel 10, RCLP; "1,500,000 for France," *Washington Post*, April 4, 1918, 2.

48 Roper, *Fifty Years*, 183; BIR field agents responded in kind to the confidence that Roper had instilled in them, and they understood that by following Roper their postwar careers "will be more remunerative and less exacting." A. S. Walker to Daniel C. Roper, March 27, 1920, Box 11, DCRP.

As the war progressed, the training of new Department hires became increasingly important to the mission of building a coherent and cohesive institutional culture. To be sure, the Treasury lawyers underwent their own learning by fire. Roper and Ballantine struggled to create a rational collection process that could make sense of the new profits taxes. Love, working closely with Leffingwell, learned first-hand about the exacting demands of the "Cravath system," as he became the junior partner in Leffingwell's own public finance practice, frequently enduring the stern rebukes of his professional superior.[49]

Developing the core commitment of building public trust also meant retaining and inculcating a group of highly trained staffers. For no sooner had new assistants and clerks been hired and trained, than the private sector frequently lured many away. "The complex character" of the new tax laws, Roper explained, unexpectedly led to a "drain upon our best men," with businesses "continually skimming the cream of our trained men from our organization" in order to comply with the new laws and regulations. "As man after man left to accept financial beguilement, the condition gave cause for alarm," Roper recalled. In response to this "exodus of trained personnel," Roper, ever the pragmatic institutional entrepreneur, consulted with his "Little Cabinet" to develop a "training school" for BIR personnel on the fundamentals of tax law and accounting. Although the new training program did not stem the tide of departures, it did maintain a high level of knowledge and competence among agents and staffers. Homer S. Pace, a well-known New York accountant, became the night school's supervisor, and the heads of the different BIR divisions became its "professors."[50]

The recruitment, retention, and training of highly skilled professionals appeared to pay dividends. Roper, for instance, nostalgically – and perhaps exaggeratedly – recounted how the BIR's advisory groups and committees had convinced disgruntled taxpayers of the accuracy and effectiveness of the tax assessment process. Other senior Treasury Department officials, similarly, focused on the importance of building public trust.

[49] Unsurprisingly, Love's patience for being the direct subordinate to a New York Republican and Cravath partner eventually wore thin, as he quickly returned to the comforts of Texas Democratic politics soon after the war. "Excess Tax Review Board," *Wall Street Journal*, April 3, 1918.

[50] Roper, *Fifty Years*, 181; Lillian Doris, *The American Way in Taxation: Internal Revenue, 1862–1963* (Englewood Cliffs, N.J.: Prentice-Hall, 1963). 218. Roper set up similar training for BIR field offices. Roper, "The War Revenue Act and the Taxpayer," 3, DCRP.

"The problem of statesmanship," McAdoo once explained, "is to establish a just relation between necessary taxation and the earning power of the Nation."[51] Leffingwell, likewise, admired how McAdoo had "managed to make himself an advocate of huge taxes without antagonizing" citizens, and how he had "on the contrary gained the confidence of the taxpayers," especially business interests. McAdoo accomplished all this, Leffingwell concluded, because the Treasury Department was careful to distance itself "from the ignorant or malicious corporation-baiting" that other federal agencies "habitually practiced."[52]

Administrative Capacity and the Image of a Rational Executive Agency

Developing a cooperative, corporatist relationship between state and society was crucial to the Treasury Department's institutional mission of building public trust. So too was the creation of administrative capacity. For if "figuring" rather than "fighting" was what Treasury personnel could do to help win the war, the lawyers wanted to make sure that the Department had all the administrative power that it needed. The Treasury Department therefore, first, needed to establish and guard its jurisdictional prerogatives, especially since war mobilization created numerous government organizations that frequently blurred the institutional lines of control. In the process, the Department needed to project the image, if not the reality, of an agency that was imposing rationality onto the fog of war financing.

To do this, the Treasury lawyers used their professional contacts and legal skills to protect the scope of their administrative powers. They defended their authority over fiscal policy by rebuking other, often newly created, federal entities such as the Capital Issues Committee (CIC) – the organization created as part of the War Finance Corporation to filter and supervise the flow of capital to private businesses. When the CIC attempted to regulate conventional bank loans, the Treasury lawyers relied on their skills of statutory interpretation to quash what they saw as

[51] McAdoo to Kitchin, June 5, 1918, Record Group 56 – General Records of the Office of the Secretary of the Treasury, Box 187, Folder "Tax – Excess Profits & War Profits. 1917–1920," National Archives and Record Administration, College Park, Md. [hereinafter NARA Excess Profits Tax Folder].

[52] "Excess Tax Review Board," *Wall Street Journal*, April 3, 1918; Roper, *Fifty Years*, 175; Leffingwell to George R. Cooksey (Assistant to the Secretary of the Treasury), August 23, 1918, Reel 11, RCLP.

an encroachment onto their powers. "I think it would be bad organization and contrary to the spirit, if not the letter of the Act under which the Capital Issues Committee was formed, for it to interfere in any way with bank loans," Leffingwell notified McAdoo.[53]

Similarly, Treasury officials also policed the boundaries of fiscal federalism, demarcating the limits of state government powers. In the summer of 1918 when some states attempted to tax the interest from federal debt instruments – contrary to the law – the Treasury Department unleashed its powers and those of the Justice Department and the Federal Reserve System to remind state tax officials to respect the bounds of fiscal federalism. Stern rebukes from federal officials quickly reminded state lawmakers of the supremacy of federal legislation in this area. Treasury's legal staff also drafted legislation, coaxed lawmakers, and considered new rules that would contain the autonomous powers of state governments within the structures of American federalism. In curbing the powers of other war agencies and state governments, Treasury consolidated its own powers by clearly delimiting the authority of competing organizations.[54]

The different bureaus within the Treasury Department themselves frequently clashed over the exercise of administrative power, particularly when it came to communicating with the taxpaying public. A fall 1918 correspondence between Ballantine and Leffingwell, for instance, revealed a potential conflict over who had proper jurisdiction to issue Treasury regulations related to tax collections. Leffingwell contended that it was Treasury Secretary McAdoo and not his subordinate, Commissioner of Internal Revenue Roper, who was ultimately responsible for accepting Treasury certificates as payment for income and profits taxes. He sternly informed Ballantine "the public debt and public monies are matters which do not concern the Commissioner; and investors ... will be reassured by

[53] Leffingwell to McAdoo, August 24, 1918, Reel 11, RCLP; Eisner, *From Warfare State to Welfare State*, 230–1. Leffingwell took similar steps to ensure that the War Finance Corporation did not also directly take part in financing the war effort. Leffingwell to Thomas V. Lamont (Partner, J. P. Morgan & Co.), February 21, 1918, Reel 3, RCLP.

[54] Leffingwell to Attorney General Thomas W. Gregory, March 23, 1918; Leffingwell to Gregory, October 14, 1918; Leffingwell to Gregory, December 1918; Leffingwell to Senator Robert L. Owen, March 26, 1918; Leffingwell to McAdoo, December 1917; Leffingwell to Congressman Carter Glass, January 16, 1918; Leffingwell to Richmond Weed, September 3, 1918, RCLP. For more on the importance of delimitation for bureaucratic power, see Weber, "Bureaucracy." On the importance of federalism to American political development during this period, see Kimberley S. Johnson, *Governing the American State: Congress and the New Federalism, 1877–1929* (Princeton: Princeton University Press, 2007).

reading that the regulations are to be prescribed by the same authority which issues them." In his typically self-assured style, Leffingwell even provided Ballantine with detailed legislative language backing his legal point.[55]

Maintaining jurisdictional control was not only an issue of power, however. It was also a matter of establishing the perceived legal transparency, stability, and legitimacy that were critical to broadcasting the impression of an organized and coherent executive agency. At times, this meant that the Treasury lawyers were willing to use their legal and financial expertise to help taxpayers execute unique and complex commercial transactions, such as when Henry Ford bought out the minority shareholders of the Ford Motor Company in 1919. This transaction, as Roper later recalled, proved to be "an exceptional opportunity" for the BIR to demonstrate its commitment to working with taxpayers. The Bureau provided tax guidance to Ford that helped effectuate the buyouts, yielded substantial tax revenue, and garnered the trust of the business community.[56]

Besides such special cases, the Treasury lawyers understood that to impose clarity onto the uncertainty of war financing they needed to control the flow of public information. After all, as the lawyers knew first hand, information was vital to the effective functioning of capital markets and the overall revenue-raising process. But in reality, controlling information to project a judicious image was frequently less about increased transparency than it was about carefully managing public perceptions. To this end, Leffingwell kept a tight personal grip over public access to government information. He was quick to admonish his bureau chiefs for press leaks. He often personally edited the official press releases issued by the Department. And he regularly read the New York and Washington papers to review how they were covering war financing, and to gauge how editors were responding to new policies.[57]

55 Leffingwell to Ballantine, October 25, 1918, Reel 16, RCLP.

56 "Fords Acquire Stock Control in their Company," *New York Times*, July 12, 1919, 1; Roper, *Fifty Years*, 181–2; Douglas Brinkley, *Wheels for the World: Henry Ford, His Company, and a Century of Progress, 1903–2003* (New York: Viking, 2003), 240–2.The Ford transaction was also the origins of a significant tax controversy that would have broad implications for the creation of the congressional joint committee on taxation. George K. Yin, "James Couzens, Andrew Mellon, the 'Greatest Suit in the History of the World,' and Creation of the Joint Committee on Taxation and Its Staff," *Tax Law Review* 66 (in press).

57 Leffingwell to McAdoo, September 11, 1918; Leffingwell to Thomas Love, July 19, 1918; Leffingwell to McAdoo, August 17, 1918; "For Morning Papers," (Leffingwell

The Treasury lawyers also shaped public perceptions in other ways. Thomas Love, at McAdoo's behest, tapped his Texas contacts and used his skills as a political operative to campaign for Liberty Loans. He stressed how buying war bonds was one way for citizens to demonstrate their patriotism. Roper, as we have seen, used the BIR's advisory boards and ad hoc committees to convince taxpayers of the effectiveness and fairness of tax assessments. In a rare moment of self-congratulation, even Leffingwell acknowledged how Treasury's proficient administration of war financing had enhanced public confidence in the Department. After learning, in the fall of 1918, that the press and investors had favorably received the fourth and largest Liberty Loan distribution, he wrote to McAdoo, we "have undertaken stupendous tasks and imposed heavy burdens but heretofore without arousing antagonism or controversy. Now more than ever we need to make the people feel that the great machine is running smoothly."[58]

If maintaining jurisdictional powers and controlling public information were indispensable to developing Treasury's claims of professional proficiency, managing revenue collections and coordinating them with the timing of debt payments stretched the limits of such organizational capacity. The extent of the Department's capacities was tested during the spring of 1918 when Treasury contemplated allowing taxpayers to defer the payment of the recently adopted income and profits taxes. Initially, the Treasury lawyers acquiesced to the plan, but upon further reflection they agreed that any deferment past the June 15, 1918, deadline for paying the income and profits taxes would upset the delicate timing of cash flows. As early as December 1917, Leffingwell warned McAdoo that "we could not safely" issue a new series of certificates "if deferred payments of taxes were permitted." Waiting for badly needed tax

approved press release regarding recent issuance of Treasury certificates), September 12, 1918; Leffingwell to John Burke (Treasurer of the United States), December 3, 1917; Leffingwell to McAdoo, January 16, 1918, Reel 1, RCLP.

58 George S. Adams to Love, Jan. 19, 1918, Box 7 (IU 7D-8A) TBLP; Leffingwell to McAdoo, September 11, 1918, Reel 12, RCLP. Schafer, *America in the Great War*, Chapter 1. Treasury officials also worked with George Creel's Committee on Public Information (CPI) to spotlight the fiscal obligations of buying Liberty Loans and to cajole Americans to do their Christmas shopping early to expedite the receipt of federal sales taxes. George Creel to Woodrow Wilson, August 6, 1918; Wilson to Creel, August 8, 1918, Container 2, George Creel Papers, Manuscript Division, Library of Congress, Washington, D.C. For more on the Committee on Public Information, see Stephen Vaughn, *Holding Fast the Inner Lines: Democracy, Nationalism, and the Committee on Public Information* (Chapel Hill: University of North Carolina Press, 1980).

revenue would compromise interest payments on outstanding government debt.[59]

Yet, although the Treasury Department opposed the idea of deferment, it also realized that forcing taxpayers to pay all their income and profits taxes at once could cause a dramatic shock to the economy. Bankers feared that tax payments by their large corporate clients could trigger a panic run on their reserves at a time when other clients might need to borrow to pay their taxes. Many in the business and financial communities thus urged lawmakers to allow for deferred installment payments of federal taxes. The Treasury lawyers carefully monitored revenue estimates, as they considered alternatives to tax deferment.[60]

Treasury proposed several recommendations to resolve this timing issue. In a widely circulated letter to lawmakers, bankers, and leading members of the business community, Leffingwell synthesized the work of his legal staff to illustrate how existing laws and regulations provided several possible solutions, including the opportunity for "the partial payment, in advance, of income and profits taxes," and the use of short-term certificates in lieu of cash to pay taxes. The recently enacted Liberty Bond Act, Leffingwell reminded policymakers, also permitted the Treasury Department to deposit the proceeds of tax payments into U.S. banks, thereby mitigating any potential short-term turnover in bank deposits. The law, moreover, provided an appropriately timed coupon payment to bondholders/taxpayers that would help them meet their tax liabilities. With these and other safeguards in place, Leffingwell confidently persuaded McAdoo and other officials that there was no need to concede to the demands for tax deferment.[61]

As the June tax deadline approached, Leffingwell and Love anxiously monitored the increasing news coverage of expected tax payments.[62] In the end, the federal government collected nearly $2.8 billion in profits and income taxes by the deadline, and an additional $855 million in

[59] Leffingwell to McAdoo, December 1917, Reel 1, RCLP; "May Accept Part Payment of Taxes," *Washington Post*, April 12, 1918, 3.

[60] "Banks Want Excess Tax Paid in Installments," *Wall Street Journal*, September 28, 1917, 2; "Want Only Revision in the War Tax Bill," *New York Times*, December 11, 1917, 14; "Installment Plan for Taxes Urged" *Washington Post*, March 14, 1918, 10; Leffingwell to Love, March 2, 1918; March 7, 1918; March 19, 1918, Reel 3, RCLP.

[61] Leffingwell to Daniel Roper, [n.d.]; Leffingwell to Hoxsey, April 22, 1918; Leffingwell to Frank E. Howe (President, Manufacturers National Bank); Leffingwell to Benjamin Strong, April 22, 1918, Reel 4, RCLP.

[62] Leffingwell to Love, April 12, 1918, Reel 4, RCLP; "Income Tax May Net $4,000,000," *New York Times*, April 12, 1918, 17.

other internal revenues.[63] More important, the BIR was able to perform the collection process without any difficulties for money markets or the economy as a whole. "The tax payments were made without a ruffle," one banker explained with surprise. "The immense financial transaction was consummated almost without being noticed. The transaction was put through with perfect balance and without the least disturbance to business or banking." McAdoo sent along his personal congratulations to Leffingwell for guiding the successful collection process.[64]

In administering wartime tax laws and policies, Treasury developed the bureaucratic capacity that undergirded the legal legitimacy of the wartime fiscal state. Even though, at times, they may have limited the transparency of their actions, Leffingwell and his colleagues attempted to build public trust by projecting the image of a rational executive agency. In the process, they also bolstered their own power, both within the executive branch and across the bounds of fiscal federalism. Yet gaining and maintaining the faith of taxpayers and citizens was only one of the early and ongoing challenges. When it came to formulating the broad principles of fiscal policy, Treasury officials faced an equally daunting task of assuring the public that the costs and sacrifices of waging a global conflict were being shared equitably by all citizens – not only those who went overseas to sacrifice life and limb, but also those who stayed home and reaped the financial benefits of a booming wartime economy.

Formulating Policy and the State Obligations of Fiscal Citizenship

Among the principal policy issues confronting Treasury officials, none was more salient than analyzing the war financing options. While nearly everyone agreed that a balance between taxes and public borrowing was necessary, economic experts, social commentators, and lawmakers vastly disagreed on the appropriate mix. Underpinning these policy debates was the fundamental issue of how one defined the relationship among patriotism, wartime sacrifice, and fiscal citizenship. What rights and obligations, in other words, did citizens and the state have toward each other during a war emergency?

[63] "U.S. Reaps Richest Harvest in Taxes," *Washington Post*, June 26, 1918; "War Taxes in Year Yield $3,694,703,000," *New York Times*, August 7, 1918, 15.

[64] "$3,000,000,000 Tax Paid with No Strain," *New York Times*, June 17, 1918, 10; "Banks Easily Meet Income Tax Drain," *Washington Post*, June 23, 1918. Leffingwell to McAdoo, June 28, 1918, Reel 8, RCLP.

For many social critics and policymakers, the answer was obvious. Fiscal citizenship meant that all members of the political community – as taxpayers, creditors, and consumers – had a moral and patriotic duty to make the necessary wartime sacrifices to support the state. "A new sense of the obligations of citizenship will transform the spirit of the nation," progressive journalist Fredrick Lewis Allen predicted at the start of the war. Progressive tax reformers had for decades been promoting direct and graduated taxation as a way to forge a new ethos of social solidarity and civic obligation. Graduated taxes were based on the notion that each citizen owed a debt to society in proportion to her ability to pay. By weaving direct and graduated taxes into the fabric of American legal institutions and culture, the Great War became a historic moment to further the progressive commitment to shared social responsibility.[65]

Yet, despite a growing sense of national allegiance, deep-seated regional conflicts persisted. On the eve of the war, Claude Kitchin (D-N.C.), the House majority leader and powerful chair of the Ways and Means Committee, did not hide his sectional bias. When wealthy New York citizens, he wrote "are thoroughly convinced that the income tax will have to pay for the increase in the army and navy, they will not be one-half so frightened over the future invasion of Germany and preparedness will not be so popular with them as it now is." Like William Jennings Bryan, Kitchin was both a strident supporter of the income tax and an opponent of the war. And, like Bryan, Kitchin was not afraid to exploit the fear and anxieties created by the new direct and graduated tax regime. Other political leaders went further in criticizing the moneyed classes. "The stock brokers would not, of course, go to war, because the very object they have in bringing on war is profit," declared the progressive Senator George W. Norris (R-Neb.). "They will be concealing in their palatial offices on Wall Street, sitting behind mahogany desks, covered with clipped coupons – coupons soiled with the sweat of mothers' tears, coupons dyed in the lifeblood of their fellow man."[66]

[65] Kennedy, *Over Here*, 43–4; Richard T. Ely, *Taxation in American States and Cities* (New York: Crowell & Co., 1888); Edwin R. A. Seligman, *The Income Tax: A Study of the History, Theory and Practice of Income Taxation at Home and Abroad* (New York: Macmillan, 1911).

[66] Arthur Link, *Wilson: Campaigns for Progressivism and Peace*, 62. For more on Kitchin, see Alex M. Arnett, *Claude Kitchin and the Wilson War Policies* (Boston: Little Brown, 1937); Homer Larry Ingle, *Pilgrimage To Reform: A Life of Claude Kitchin* (Ph.D. dissertation, University of Wisconsin, 1967); Norris quoted in Norman L. Zucker, *George W. Norris, Gentle Knight of American Democracy* (Urbana: University of Illinois Press, 1966), 128. The claims that New York's wealthy citizens were paying a significant

Despite the sectional and class tensions, several Treasury lawyers believed that the national crisis provided a unique opportunity to promote a new type of civic identity – a new social contract with progressive taxation as the binding force. The Treasury Department, working closely with George Creel's Committee on Public Information, engaged in a publicity campaign stressing the links between taxpaying and winning the war. Building on the promotional techniques used to sell Liberty Loans, the government sent out "Four-Minute Men," groups of volunteers who spoke at movie theaters, churches, lodges, and other social locations to preach the virtues of taxpaying. "Help Pershing take the flag to the front," announced one slogan, "by taking your income tax to the Collector of Internal Revenue."[67]

Similarly, Roper frequently instructed his BIR staff to emphasize appeals to patriotism, civic duty, and citizenship in the collection of taxes. He also enlisted the influence of the American clergy and the publicity powers of popular and business periodicals to spread the word about "The Glory of Paying the Income Tax." He informed business journalists that they had a professional obligation to remind "the man who pays his Liberty tax in full, without question or murmur, is no less a patriot than the man who invests in the Liberty bond or volunteers his services for military duty." And when opportunistic individuals sought to profit from turning in tax evaders, Roper personally rebuked such attempts at personal gain with nationalistic zeal, illustrating the mix of patriotism and coercion that was at the heart of the wartime state. "Certainly no good citizen," he instructed one potential informant, "would think of profiting on the understated taxes of his neighbors – people unfamiliar with the intricacies of this complicated tax law, not if he were a good citizen and had the right attitude toward his own people – and the right attitude toward defending his country in this war."[68]

In the process of formulating broad fiscal policy, however, Treasury lawyers stretched the meaning of fiscal citizenship beyond the conventional, singular focus on the obligations and duties of *citizens*. Like the prewar tax theorists and political activists who supported progressive

portion of the income tax were supported by contemporary statistics: in 1916 alone New York was responsible for 35 percent of the total proceeds of the income tax. U.S. Internal Revenue, *Statistics of Income: Compiled from the Returns for 1916* (Washington, D.C.: Government Printing Office, 1918), 12–13.

67 Schaffer, *America in the Great War*, 4–7; Bank, *War and Taxes*, 68.

68 "An Urgent Duty and a Glorious Privilege," *Literary Digest*, January 12, 1918, 32; Roper, *Fifty Years*, 176, 180. Roper, "The War Revenue Act and the Taxpayer," 5, DCRP. On the significance of coercion to the World War I culture of citizenship, see Capozzola, *Uncle Sam Wants You*.

taxation, the wartime Treasury lawyers believed that fiscal citizenship meant that the state had a reciprocal social obligation and democratic responsibility to its citizens, a duty not only to protect them during war, but to ensure that the responsibilities of wartime fiscal sacrifice were equitably distributed among all community members.

In this way, fiscal citizenship was not solely a unidirectional force, requiring the allegiance only of individual citizens to the activist state. Fiscal citizenship, instead, entailed a set of mutual responsibilities on state actors to spread more evenly the costs and sacrifices of underwriting a modern global war. Because the new tax laws had made the "government a partner with business," as Roper had explained, the scale and scope of the new fiscal policies made it "increasingly important that the partners co-operate for their common good." Simply put, the new social contract based on steeply progressive taxes required both the state and citizens to fulfill their respective duties.[69]

The dynamics of patriotism, wartime sacrifice, and fiscal citizenship were perhaps best expressed in the policy debates over the proper mix of wartime funding sources. On one side, there was a fragile congressional coalition led by populist and progressive lawmakers like Kitchin and Robert M. La Follette Sr. (R-Wis.) who wanted to use the newly created taxing powers and the war emergency to redistribute wealth – not just tax burdens – in a more radical direction. Like their populist predecessors in Congress, who led the constitutional battle over the Sixteenth Amendment and the 1913 income tax, these wartime legislators sought to use the tax system to address the massive inequalities of the time. La Follette acknowledged that there was a limit to how far the new tax laws could go: "We should not tax high enough to cripple industry or impede production." Still, it was incumbent upon progressive leaders, he informed his fellow lawmakers, to ensure that "the wealth of this country will be taken as mercilessly through the power of taxation as men are taken by force of the draft."[70]

Aligned against this political coalition was a business community that favored consumption taxes and a more general use of income taxes aimed at all classes of society. Led by members of the Northeastern commercial elite, this group was cognizant of the regional ramifications of shifting

[69] Roper, *Fifty Years*; Roper, "The War Revenue Act and the Taxpayer," DCRP.

[70] Robert M. La Follette, "War Taxes and Profiteering," in *The Political Philosophy of Robert M. La Follette*, ed. Ellen Torelle et al. (Madison, Wis.: Robert M. La Follette Co., 1920), 222.

from a system of indirect consumption taxes to a regime of direct and graduated levies. Even before the Revenue Act of 1917 was introduced, the New York Chamber of Commerce issued a statement urging "the advisability of a more nearly universal participation of the country's population in bearing the burdens of taxation; that the indirect sources of revenue should not be abandoned or unduly minimized, and that direct sources should not be overworked to the extent of arresting the financial ability of the country to develop enterprise at home and abroad." The business community, of course, did not speak with one voice. Many companies understood that the war required economic sacrifice, and more than a few firms did their part to hold the line on prices and profits as part of their patriotic service. But when it came to taxes, especially the new profits levies, American companies used a variety of maneuvers to ensure that wartime profits were not always returned to the Treasury.[71]

If the disagreements between Southern and Western lawmakers and Northeastern business elites echoed the tensions of the past, professional economic experts did little to placate such opposition. Economists, in fact, were similarly divided over the issue of war financing. Some like O. M. W. Sprague of Harvard and Irving Fisher of Yale favored a "pay-as-you-go" method, using progressive income taxes and broad-based consumption taxes to curb inflation and finance the war. The "conscription of men," wrote Sprague, "should logically and equitably be accompanied by something in the nature of conscription of current income above that which is absolutely necessary."[72] Other leading experts such as Edwin R. A. Seligman, Henry Carter Adams, and Charles J. Bullock feared that a resort to excessive taxation would blunt the incentives for economic productivity. Although these political economists, as we have seen, had been longtime supporters of progressive taxation, the war context blunted some of their enthusiasm. While they conceded that taxes ought to be an important part of war financing, they recommended a more balanced approach,

[71] "New York Chamber of Commerce and the Excess Profits Tax," *Commercial and Financial Chronicle,* February 3, 1917, 421; "Opposition to the Excess Profits Tax By Business Men," *Commercial and Financial Chronicle,* February 10, 1917, 517; "The Injustice of the Excess Profits Tax," *Commercial and Financial Chronicle,* May 19, 1917, 1957; Braneds, *Warhogs*, 174–5, 172.

[72] O. M. W. Sprague, "The Conscription of Income a Sound Basis for War Finance," *Economic Journal* 27:105 (1917), 1–15, 5; "Loans and Taxes in War Finance," *American Economic Review* (Suppl., March 1917), 199–223; Irving Fisher, "How the Public Should Pay for the War," *Annals of the American Academy of Political and Social Science* 78 (July 1918), 112–17.

forecasting that increased borrowing would soon become necessary, especially if the conflict became protracted.[73]

In their role as moderators, Treasury lawyers had to confront the dueling views of war financing. In doing so, Leffingwell and his colleagues underscored how fiscal citizenship entailed a reciprocal social and democratic obligation on the state to distribute fairly the burdens of wartime sacrifices. As policymakers were considering a third round of Liberty Loans in the spring and summer of 1918, Leffingwell the "Wall Street Republican" remained committed to the importance of steeply graduated taxes. "The sound rule to stick to," Leffingwell reminded McAdoo, "is that taxes should be as heavy as they can safely be levied."[74] Although McAdoo had initially agreed, he soon became enamored with the ease of issuing low-interest, tax-favored government debt.[75] In his attempt to capitalize patriotism, McAdoo embarked on a nationwide speaking tour and enlisted the services of several of his Treasury lawyers, including Thomas Love, and some of the country's leading artists and celebrities to publicize the sale of government bonds.[76]

Leffingwell agreed that "there is no substitute for the appeal to patriotism," but he held a broader understanding of patriotism, sacrifice, and fiscal citizenship. Patriotism for McAdoo meant that the state could rely on the obligations and responsibilities of its citizens to participate directly in funding the war through loans and taxes. For Leffingwell and his legal colleagues an unreflective resort to more borrowing without a greater reliance on taxation was an abdication of the state's social responsibility

[73] E. R. A. Seligman, "Borrowing Must Supplement Taxes in War Finance," *New York Times*, April 15, 1917, E3; Seligman, "Loans versus Taxes in War Finance," *Annals of the American Academy of Political and Social Science* 75 (January 1918), 52–82; Henry Carter Adams, "Borrowing as a Phase of War Financing," *Annals of the American Academy of Political and Social Science* 75 (January 1918), 23–30; Charles J. Bullock, "Financing the War," *Quarterly Journal of Economics* 31:3. (May 1917), 357–79; Bullock, "Conscription of Income," *North American Review* 205:739 (June 1917), 895–904.

[74] Leffingwell to McAdoo, March 1, 1918, Reel 3, RCLP.

[75] Reflecting back on the war, McAdoo boasted in his memoirs about how he, unlike his Civil War predecessor Treasury Secretary Salmon Chase, was able to appeal directly to the patriotic fervor of the people through several successful and oversubscribed bond drives. "Any great war must necessarily be a popular movement," wrote McAdoo. "It is a kind of crusade; and like all crusades, it sweeps along on a powerful stream of romanticism." To harness such powerful emotions, McAdoo recalled, "we went direct to the people and that means to everybody – to businessmen, workers, farmers, bankers, millionaires, school teachers, laborers. We capitalized the profound impulse called patriotism." McAdoo, *Crowded Years*, 374.

[76] McAdoo, *Crowded Years*, 374; Kennedy, *Over Here*, 105–6; "McAdoo Calls Bankers," *Washington Post*, March 22, 1918, 5.

to its citizens. It was a breach of the new social contract undergirded by direct and progressive taxation. To be sure, the Treasury lawyers did not agree with Sprague and the political activists who wanted to rely mainly on taxes; nor did they agree with those who were issuing dire warnings about excessive taxation.

Rather, as arbiters of social forces, the lawyers sought to pave a more moderate path. Leffingwell reminded McAdoo that reliance on a variety of taxes could raise revenue, curtail consumption, and equitably spread the costs of the war. With their experiences in the capital markets, the lawyers understood that the trade-off between taxes and bonds was fundamentally about timing – whether current or future taxpayers were responsible for the war costs. A war financing policy that "forced people to take bonds" was, in Leffingwell's estimation, a double penalty against future taxpayers who would have to contend with paying back the war loans and financing the postwar recovery. A resort to more borrowing posed other problems as well. Flooding the credit market with government loans was, Leffingwell assured McAdoo, a sure step toward financial ruin; it "simply means an enormous amount of undigested securities chocking the market, depreciation in bond prices and ruin to the credit of the United States and inflation of the currency." As the war progressed, Leffingwell seemed to forget the significance of his comments, but his remarks concerning inflation would prove to be quite prophetic.[77]

Besides analyzing the mix of financing options, the Treasury lawyers also used their networks, skills, and experience in other more mundane, though equally important, policymaking functions. Leffingwell and his legal staff drew on their specific legal and business knowledge to channel Treasury efforts in particular directions – to act, in other words, as gatekeepers of state power. When McAdoo, for instance, wanted to explore the "federal taxation of real estate" it was the Treasury lawyers working with the Attorney General's office who reminded the secretary that a national property tax required "a Constitutional amendment to permit the United States to levy direct taxes without apportionment." The Sixteenth Amendment, as the lawyers knew, only authorized an income tax without apportionment. A direct, national tax on real property would require further constitutional modifications.[78]

[77] Leffingwell to McAdoo, March 1, 1918, Reel 3, RCLP.

[78] Leffingwell to Richmond Weed (Treasury legal staff), February 5, 1918; Leffingwell to McAdoo, March 1918, Reel 2, RCLP; Brownlee, "Social Investigation and Political Learning," 338.

In monitoring state power Treasury lawyers did not act only as constraints, however. Just as all good gatekeepers are aware of alternative routes, Treasury lawyers often used their technical legal knowledge and access to expertise to navigate around legal challenges to policy proposals. In the fall of 1918, with German troops in retreat, the Wilson administration was contemplating the creation of a War Trade Export Corporation to raise revenue by taxing exports. Leffingwell and his legal staff reminded McAdoo that such a levy was "prohibited by express provision of the Constitution." But the Treasury lawyers did not stop there. They also went on to make a plausible alternative recommendation.[79]

The recommendation illustrated how the Treasury lawyers used their professional network and legal skills to craft long-run, forward-looking, corporatist solutions. After consulting with members of the War Trade Board – the existing agency supervising all import and export activity – and his former Cravath partner, E. C. Henderson, whom Leffingwell described as "the best lawyer I know, bar none," Leffingwell suggested that the administration forsake the short-term – and constitutionally futile – step of trying to tax exports and focus instead on how the government could look ahead toward establishing the country's postwar trade position and long-term geopolitical power.

To that end, he suggested that a new corporatist agency be established along the lines of the War Industries Board to organize and license exporters. This plan, Leffingwell explained, "would have the great advantage... of tending to bring the export houses in a position where they would be able after the war to develop our foreign trade, instead of practically putting them out of business during the period of the war and leaving them disorganized and disheartened to deal with after-the-war problems." To assuage the administration's desire to tax the growing profits of exporters, Leffingwell assured McAdoo that the robust wartime profits tax "can be trusted to take into the Treasury excessive profits which may result from the adoption of this plan."[80] The imminent end of the war less than a month later precluded McAdoo from pursuing an export tax or creating a new export licensing agency, but Leffingwell's

79 Leffingwell to McAdoo, October 16, 1918, Reel 15, RCLP.

80 Ibid. Efforts to bolster American postwar trade policy would, of course, also benefit the corporate bar, as leading Treasury lawyers like Leffingwell and Roper embarked upon postwar careers with a growing international focus. Ron Chernow, *The House of Morgan: An American Banking Dynasty and the Rise of Modern Finance* (New York: Atlantic Monthly Press, 1990), 251, 312–14; Roper, *Fifty Years*, 207–8.

suggestion vividly illustrated how Treasury lawyers had become attracted to the corporatist model of state-building.

The search for new sources of tax revenues and the appeals to patriotism and fiscal citizenship were examples of how the Treasury Department attempted to spread the costs of the war across a broad swath of socioeconomic classes, regions, and even generations. But, ultimately, the war financing policies had complex and often contradictory consequences. McAdoo seemed to be aware of how the interest rate on bonds could have far reaching implications. In deliberately setting an initially low rate of interest, McAdoo contended that "we should be reducing the cost of war, not only today for ourselves, but, in the future for ourselves and for our brave men who are fighting in France and will have little or no opportunity to accumulate and invest in Liberty Bonds though they must upon their return join the army of taxpayers who must pay this interest."[81]

Yet, McAdoo's rhetoric about helping the quotidian "army of taxpayers" did not match his actions, or wartime reality. The so-called "army" of ordinary taxpayers was potentially rather slim. Though the sundry consumption taxes affected a broad swath of citizens, and generated some colorful protests, the vast bulk of federal tax revenue came from the income and profits taxes on wealthy individuals and prosperous businesses. Preoccupied with allaying the social concerns over war profiteering, policymakers seemed to give little consideration to taxing the mass of middle-class wage earners – an option that would be effectively exercised in World War II.[82]

The initially low, tax-exempt interest rates set on government debt, furthermore, did not extract the type of wartime financial sacrifice that the Treasury Department claimed. The tax exemption disproportionately benefited wealthy individuals because they were the primary investors in the largest bond offerings, and because they were also the ones subject to the highest progressive marginal rates.[83] Though the consistent

[81] McAdoo to Kitchin and Simmons, September 5, 1918, Reel 12, RCLP; Gilbert, *American Financing*, 126.

[82] Brandes, *Warhogs*, 129–31. For more on how World War II policymakers helped institutionalize a mass income taxpaying culture, see David M. Kennedy, *Freedom From Fear: The American People in Depression and War* (New York: Oxford University Press, 1999), 624–5; Carolyn Jones, "Class Tax to Mass Tax: The Role of Propaganda in the Expansion of the Income Tax during World War II," 37 *Buffalo Law Review* 685 (1989); Sparrow, *Warfare State*, Chapter 4.

[83] In fact, as the economic historian Hugh Rockoff has shown, investors in Liberty Loans received an after-tax rate of return that matched the yield on other assets of equal risk,

oversubscription of Liberty Loans was a clear political victory, the bonds did not have the economic impact that Treasury envisioned. The tax-exempt interest proved to be a large revenue give-away. With their knowledge of the interactions of taxes and market forces, the Treasury lawyers were undoubtedly aware of these contradictory actions but they seemed ineffective in altering policy.[84]

Another way in which financing policies undermined economic goals was the inadvertent increase in the price level. In its enthusiasm to issue debt, Treasury fostered a "borrow and buy" mentality among bond investors. Rather than redirecting monies away from current consumption, Treasury created new money and fueled inflation. In theory, bond sales to the nonbanking public could restrain inflation by absorbing consumer spending, while transferring real economic resources from private consumption to war production. But because the Treasury Department encouraged individual investors to use borrowed funds to purchase government debt, and because much of the below-market, short-term debt issued by the Treasury was bought directly by banks, the massive wartime borrowing, in the end, fueled rather than contained inflation.[85]

Changes to the nascent Federal Reserve System further exacerbated inflationary pressures. Legal modifications to reserve requirements, the centralization of reserves in district banks, and the expansion of banks eligible to be federal depositories were just some of the subtle changes to monetary policy that led to an incredibly elastic money supply. Indeed, the combination of increased bank borrowing and permissive monetary policies led to an explosive growth in the money supply and a concomitant mushrooming of the price level.[86] Although he claimed to have learned from the errors of the past, McAdoo's resort to easy money, in the end, had a striking resemblance to the Civil War printing of greenbacks.

suggesting that, in spite of McAdoo's ambitions, the bond drives did little to capitalize on patriotism. Rockoff, "Until It's Over," 322–7.

84 Studenski and Krooss, *Financial History*, 288–92. The attractiveness of government securities continued to be a thorny issue well after the war. On the postwar effects of tax-favored government securities, see Murray, "Bureaucracy and Bipartisanship;" M. Susan Murnane, "Selling Scientific Taxation: The Treasury Department's Campaign for Tax Reform in the 1920s," *Law & Social Inquiry* 29:4 (2004), 819–58.

85 Friedman and Schwartz, *Monetary History*; Studenski and Kroos, *Financial History*, 288–9; Rockoff, "Until It's Over," 317–19.

86 From June 1916 to June 1919, the money supply expanded by over $11 billion and consumer prices increased nearly 66 percent, while the cost of living rose over 70 percent. Friedman and Schwartz, *Monetary History*, 216. As economic historians have explained, "The Federal Reserve became to all intents and purposes the bond-selling window of the Treasury, using its monetary policy almost exclusively to that end." Ibid.

The Treasury lawyers unwittingly contributed to the increased bank borrowing and the resulting inflation. From his perch as undersecretary, Leffingwell endorsed McAdoo's contradictory ideas and actions. Despite his earlier warnings about the adverse impact of excessive borrowing, Leffingwell seemed to suspend his financial judgment. Not only did Leffingwell encourage financial institutions, including Federal Reserve member banks, to accept U.S. bonds as collateral for loans,[87] he also supported McAdoo's attempts to use moral suasion and appeals to patriotism, rather than legal restrictions, to prevent investors from selling their bonds for further spending. Leffingwell believed, like McAdoo, that a liberal democracy, even during wartime – perhaps especially during wartime – could not restrict the economic decisions of its citizens by prohibiting them from selling their financial assets. "It is of course important to avoid making people think that if they subscribe they will not be permitted to sell," Leffingwell remarked in an April 1918 telegram to McAdoo. "We realize that subscribers might have to sell their bonds and should be protected as far as possible against losses."[88]

Like McAdoo, Leffingwell preferred to contain inflation with appeals to patriotism and the fiscal responsibilities of investors, rather than more forceful actions. "It should be the object of the Secretary of the Treasury, and of all public men," Leffingwell sternly informed lawmakers, "not to encourage people to lend their money to the Government one day and to take it back the next, nor to make it easy for them to do so, but to teach the people to save and lend their money to the Government for a period of years. Liberty loans are an investment – the best on earth. They are not currency and are not meant to be."[89]

Leffingwell went even further in relying on civic duty to restrain private spending. He reminded McAdoo with words from the secretary's own annual report that wealthy Americans had additional wartime financial and civic responsibilities. "The men and women of large and moderate means owe a greater duty, because they have a larger margin of income, to cut off self-indulgences, to deny themselves useless and needless luxuries, to make sacrifices of comforts, pleasures, and conveniences that will effect genuine economies and set an example to the Nation."[90]

[87] See, e.g., Leffingwell to McAdoo, December 8, 1917; Leffingwell to F. H. Meeker, Esq. (President, Unadilla National Bank), December 1917, Reel 1, RCLP.

[88] Leffingwell to McAdoo, April 6, 1918, Reel 4, RCLP.

[89] Leffingwell to Kitchin, December 1917; Leffingwell to Rep. Richard Olney, December 1917, Reel 1, RCLP.

[90] Leffingwell to McAdoo, April 6, 1918, Reel 4, RCLP; *U.S. Treasury Department, Annual Report, 1917*, 3.

The fiscal sacrifices of citizens at home were inextricably linked to the physical sacrifices made by soldiers at the frontlines. As Leffingwell reminded McAdoo, quoting again from the secretary's annual report:

> It is a sacred duty of every citizen and it should be regarded as a glorious privilege of every patriot to uphold the Government's credit with the same kind of self sacrifice and nobility of soul that our gallant sons exhibit when they die for us on the battle fields of Europe. It is as imperative to sustain the Government's credit as it is to sustain our armies because our armies cannot be sustained unless the Government's credit is always above reproach.[91]

Not all citizens, of course, embraced this "sacred duty" or "glorious privilege," and some lawmakers may have viewed the Treasury Department's words as hollow rhetoric. But Leffingwell and McAdoo certainly believed they could mobilize patriotism to their advantage, even though their actions were, in the end, obfuscating the true costs of the war.[92]

Although the dynamics of the war frequently overwhelmed policymakers' intentions, the Treasury lawyers did moderate the formation of broad fiscal policies. Leffingwell's admonishments in spring 1918 to balance taxes and borrowing expressed a broader social desire to spread equally the costs of wartime sacrifices. The subsequent legislation, which was not enacted until the winter of 1919, after the armistice and after Republicans took control of Congress, was not nearly as progressive as some populist lawmakers had anticipated; nor was it as reactionary as some business leaders and conservative legislators had hoped. Instead, the new tax law was a compromise – one that revealed the Wilson administration's attempts to maintain its social and ethical obligations of fiscal citizenship.

In their role as policymakers, the Treasury lawyers were not simply passive scientific or legal engineers; they were also policy and political entrepreneurs, seeking to convince lawmakers of the legitimacy and usefulness of their expertise and knowledge. They were not simply builders of organizational capacity; they occasionally used their increased power to exercise a new-found bureaucratic autonomy.[93] Simply put, they were

91 Ibid.

92 Gilbert, *American Financing*, 232–36; Rockoff, "Until It's Over," 332–8; Kennedy, *Over Here*, 137–43.

93 For more on how "mezzo-level" government officials used their networks and reputations to create policies that were independent of lawmakers, see Carpenter, *Forging Bureaucratic Autonomy*.

TABLE 6.2. *Increases in Corporate Profits of Select U.S. Corporations, 1914–1916 (nominal dollar amounts)*

Corporation	1914	1916	Amount of Increase	% Increase
American Locomotive Co.	$2,076,127	$10,769,429	$8,693,302	419%
Bethlehem Steel Corp.	5,590,020	43,593,968	38,003,948	680%
U.S. Steel Corp.	23,496,768	271,531,730	248,034,962	1056%
Du Pont (E. I.) Nemours & Co.	4,831,793	82,013,020	77,181,227	1597%
General Motors Co.	7,249,733	28,789,560	21,539,827	297%

Source: "Helping the War Pay for Itself," *The Outlook*, June 27, 1917, 319–20. A similar yet more extensive table was printed in the *Congressional Record* as part of the House discussion of the excess-profits tax. *Congressional Record*, 65th Cong., 1st sess. (1917), 55, part 3:2541.

not just interest takers, but interest makers who engaged the legislative process with their insights about the consequences of the laws and policies they were asked to implement. Thus, in advancing the administrative framework of the new fiscal polity, the Treasury lawyers both effectively executed the democratic will of Congress and at times challenged lawmakers when the implications of new statutes seemed to become unhinged from the original aims. One of the most forceful challenges of existing law came in the spring and summer of 1918 when the Treasury Department questioned the efficacy of the excess-profits tax.

Between Justice and Revenue: Evaluating and Defending the Excess-Profits Tax

From the start, the initial 1916 profits tax on munitions makers and the subsequent excess-profits tax on all businesses were rooted in social concerns over war profiteering. As early as 1917, the popular journal *The Outlook* documented "the extraordinary increase in profits" among the leading industrial concerns. Comparing the profits of over one hundred companies from 1914 to 1916, the editors calculated that the aggregate profits of these corporations "exceed the profits of the year in which the war began by over a billion dollars." (see Table 6.2). With these soaring profits came bloated dividends and rising returns on equity, at a time when stock markets as a whole were witnessing substantial drops in real value. From this statistical evidence, *The Outlook* joined other leading popular periodicals in supporting an excess-profits tax to make "the war-brides pay up."[94]

The social protest against war profiteering helped propel the adoption of the 1917 excess-profits tax. Unlike the earlier *war* profits tax, the newly adopted *excess-profits* tax was intended to apply to a broader base of business income by measuring "excess" profits against a statutory level of reasonable or "normal" profits.[95] Many economic and legal experts, however, questioned the efficiency, administrability, and even constitutionality of a tax on all "excess" profits beyond a "normal level." The main point of contention seemed to rest with the idea of using "invested capital" as a baseline from which excess profits could be determined. Seligman summarized the hostility toward the notion of "invested capital" when he wrote that "what constitutes capital is so elusive as to be virtually impossible of precise calculation."[96]

Members of the business and legal communities echoed Seligman's concerns. *The Commercial and Financial Chronicle* – that bastion of orthodox business thinking – attacked the "Excessive Taxation of 'Excess' Profits" as "governmental confiscation of wealth." Favoring the British version of a war profits tax, the editors of *The Wall Street Journal* similarly disparaged the excess-profits tax as "hasty and ill-advised legislation . . . rushed through Washington by politicians desiring political favor with the many by taxing the capital of the few." Lawyers representing financial interests added their voice. Harping on the alleged unconstitutionality of the excess-profits tax, Robert R. Reed, the counsel for the Investment Bankers' Association, assailed the law as a "confiscatory tax on businesses."[97]

94 "Helping the War Pay for Itself" *The Outlook*, July 27, 1917, 319–20; "To Tax 'Excess Profits,'" *Literary Digest*, January 27, 1917, 176; "The Excess Profits Tax" *New Republic*, September 15, 1917, 174–5; Brandes, *Warhogs*, 135–7. Hugh Rockoff has estimated that the profits taxes accounted for roughly 40 percent of total wartime taxes, making it the leading source of tax revenue. Rockoff, *America's Economic Way of War*, 117–18.

95 War Revenue Act of 1917, 40 Stat. 300. The new excess-profits tax also applied to partnerships and individuals, as well as corporations.

96 Despite his longtime support of graduated income taxes as the proper method of taxing according to the principle of faculty, Seligman opposed the excess-profits tax because "the choice of capital not only constitutes a clumsy attempt to reach taxable ability, but introduces a gross inequality in principle and a deplorable uncertainty in administration." Edwin R. A. Seligman, "The Excess-Profits Tax," *The Nation*, March 28, 1918, 365–6.

97 "Excessive Taxation of 'Excess' Profits," *Commercial and Financial Chronicle*, September 1, 1917; "The Mysteries of the 8% Excess Profits Tax," *Commercial and Financial*

Soon after it was enacted, business opponents of the excess-profits tax commissioned a group of economists to conduct a comparative investigation of U.S. and British war financing. To counter this study, the Treasury Department organized its own team of experts to examine the consequences of the different types of profits taxes. The Treasury study was led by Thomas S. Adams, the Wisconsin economist who as we have seen was instrumental in the Badger state's adoption of the first effective state-level income tax. Adams's study supported what many in the financial and academic communities had predicted from the start, namely that the excess-profits tax appeared to have pernicious unintended consequences. The existing levy, with its use of "invested capital" as the baseline for determining "excess profits," was adversely affecting small businesses more than the large corporations it was designed to attack.

Larger corporations were able to manipulate the law to reduce their tax liability. By increasing their invested capital, either by issuing more equity or by increasing their investments in intangible assets or through other accounting maneuvers, they could inflate the base from which their rates of return and profits were calculated, thereby placing their net profits in a lower tax bracket. By contrast, smaller enterprises, especially those that relied mainly on personal services such as family businesses, did not have high levels of capital to begin with, nor did they have the slack or flexibility to adjust their capital levels or annual investments. Thus, they were hardest hit by the excess-profits tax.[98]

Even before the Treasury Department completed its study, McAdoo was encouraging lawmakers to consider supplementing the excess-profits tax with a new British-style profits tax that levied a high flat rate on all profits above prewar average earnings. Since Claude Kitchin remained the key congressional supporter of the excess-profits tax, McAdoo took his recommendation directly to the powerful Southern congressman. In a carefully drafted letter, McAdoo explained how "the existing excess profits tax does not always reach *war* profits." McAdoo argued that "a

Chronicle, April 28, 1917,; "Assails the Profits Tax; Counsel of Bankers' Association Warns against Hasty Legislation," *New York Times*, December 6, 1918.

[98] "Memorandum on the Differences between a War Profits and an Excess Profits Tax," July 27, 1918, NARA Excess Profits Tax Folder; Leffingwell to Adams, July 27, 1918, Reel 10, RCLP; Brownlee, "Economists and the Modern Tax System," 415–17. George O. May, "Methods of English War Profits Tax," *New York Times*, September 4, 1917.

flat rate of 80% on all *war* profits," those measured against a prewar average of profits, was a better method for attacking war profiteering.[99]

Kitchin remained unconvinced. From the beginning, populist lawmakers like him wanted to make the excess-profits tax a permanent part of the national tax system. Some Treasury officials concurred. "The manifest advantage" of the excess-profits tax, one Treasury lawyer wrote during the war, is that it could become "a permanent part of the Government's revenue system, and can be used, if need be, as a check upon monopolies or trusts earning exorbitant profits." Enacting a tax that relied on prewar earnings as its baseline would mean conceding that the levy was a temporary measure – one that could be discarded easily at the end of the conflict.[100]

The Treasury lawyers rallied behind McAdoo. After the initial investigation of the excess-profits tax was completed, Treasury lawyers eagerly used the Department's study to build the necessary support to replace an excess-profits levy with a war profits tax. Because Leffingwell had long suspected the inequities of using invested capital as a measure of excess profits, he enthusiastically marshaled the resources of the Department to lobby Kitchin.[101] Adams's study, together with numerous petitions from small businesses, confirmed Leffingwell' s intuition that the excess-profits tax did not accurately capture the profits created by the war, and that it was permitting the growth of corporate capitalism rather than curbing or taming it.[102]

Although Adams's report carefully critiqued both the rate structure and the base of the new levy, Leffingwell did not hesitate in using the study selectively to call for a revision of the excess-profits tax. Like many of his

[99] McAdoo to Kitchin, June 5, 1918, (emphasis in the original) NARA Excess Profits Tax Folder.

[100] Arnett, *Claude Kitchin*, 260; Blakey and Blakey, *Federal Income Tax*, 133. Perry S. Talbert (Head of Law Division, Commissioner of Internal Revenue) to George R. Cooksey (Assistant to Secretary McAdoo), August 8, 1917, quoted in Brownlee, "Economists and the Modern Tax System," 408. Talbert was a member of the BIR throughout the war and leveraged his position to become a Washington, D.C., tax consultant after the war. Roper, *Fifty Years*, 181–2; P.S. Talbert, "Relief Provisions and Treasury Procedure on Appeal," in *The Federal Income Tax*, ed. Robert M. Haig (New York: Columbia University Press, 1921), 250–61.

[101] Leffingwell to McAdoo, July 31, 1918, Reel 10, RCLP.

[102] Brownlee, "Social Investigation and Political Learning," 357–9. For a sample of some of the complaints from small businesses against the excess profits tax see Leffingwell to Love, August 24, 1918; Leffingwell to Tunstall, September 4, 1918; J. MacFarlane (President, Red River Iron Works) to Leffingwell, August 21, 1918, NARA Excess Profits Tax File.

colleagues from the private sector, Leffingwell seemed particularly uneasy about using newly created state capacity to regulate corporate profits. In a confidential memo to the president's secretary, George Tumulty, Leffingwell identified what he thought were the fundamental differences between the war profits and the excess-profits taxes:

> A war profits tax finds its sanction in the conviction of all patriotic men of whatever economic school, that no one should profit largely by the war. The excess profits tax must rest upon the wholly indefensible notion that it is a function of taxation to bring all profits down to one level with relation to the amount of capital invested, and to deprive industry, foresight and sagacity of their fruits. The excess profits tax exempts capital and burdens brains, ability and energy.[103]

The Department's study did not explicitly criticize the excess-profits tax in such sharp terms. Indeed, some economic experts believed that the existing levy might not be excessive, or that it would not hinder economic productivity. Some, like the economists David Friday and Robert Murray Haig, even believed that it might be a useful way to combat monopolies.[104] But, for Leffingwell, the excess-profits tax was "wholly indefensible" because it challenged the profit motive and the fundamental precepts of modern American capitalism. The former corporate lawyer was willing to attack war profiteering, but he was not willing to undermine the long-term incentives that he believed were the driving force of the nation's economic growth and productivity.

In his private memo to Tumulty, Leffingwell went even further in criticizing the general theory of taxing corporations at progressive rates. "Any graduated tax upon corporations is indefensible in theory for corporations are only aggregations of individuals and by such a tax the numerous small stockholders of a great corporation may be taxed at a higher rate than the very wealthy large stockholders of a relatively smaller corporation." In echoing this common critique, Leffingwell emphasized the report's conclusion about the unintended consequences of the existing excess-profits tax. "The object of a graduated tax should be to make taxes fall upon the rich who are best able to pay them," Leffingwell explained. "The graduated excess profits tax disregards this, and often produces the

103 "Confidential Memorandum Concerning War Profits Taxes and Excess Profits Taxes," July 31, 1918, NARA Excess Profits Tax Folder.

104 David Friday et al., "The Excess Profits Tax – Discussion," *American Economic Review* 10:1 (Suppl.; March 1920), 19–32; Blakey and Blakey, *Federal Income Tax*, Chapter 8.

reverse result."[105] In criticizing progressive corporate tax rates, Leffingwell was seeking indirectly to support the move to a higher flat rate on all war – as opposed to excess – profits. At the same time, by stressing the importance of taxing according to the ability to pay, Leffingwell was maintaining his progressive commitment to using the state's new fiscal capacity in a just and effective manner.

Leffingwell's confidential memo appeared to achieve its intended objective. "The course of the Administration is plain," Tumulty responded the following day. "We must stand for the War Profits Tax to the end." He hastened to add that "the 'staging' of the whole business" of presenting the administration's position to Congress and the public, was "most important." Bureaucratic autonomy rested heavily on how the ideas of unelected administrators were framed for democratically accountable lawmakers. That same day President Wilson wrote Kitchin to inform him of the importance of "a war profits tax as distinguished from a mere excess profits tax." The former, the president claimed, was "manifestly equitable." Acknowledging the difficulty of enacting a tax increase during an election year, Wilson optimistically assured Kitchin that a new profits tax would be well received by the business community. "I do not believe that the manufacturers of the country who are now making profits directly from war work would object" to the new tax, wrote Wilson. "On the contrary, I think that they would feel a certain pride in sharing the burdens of the war directly with the men who are giving their lives for the safety of America and the freedom of the world."[106]

Wilson's confidence in the business community may have been misplaced, but his ultimate goal was to persuade Kitchin and others of the political viability of the war profits tax. It was a difficult argument to make. The existing excess-profits levy still had strong political and social support. In addition to Kitchin, there were others who maintained that the excess-profits tax, even with its flaws, was, as one agrarian group described it, a potent symbol of "justice over revenue." In a letter to McAdoo, the Farmers' National Committee contended that not enough of the war was being financed through taxation. Its members proposed

105 "Confidential Memorandum Concerning War Profits Taxes and Excess Profits Taxes."

106 Tumulty to Leffingwell, August 1, 1918; Wilson to Kitchin, August 2, 1918, NARA Excess Profits Tax Folder. Leffingwell bolstered his case by directly contacting President Wilson to notify him that the difference between the two levies was not merely semantic. "It is sufficient to say that the difference is not one of words but one of substance and goes to the very root of the social and economic problem." Leffingwell to Wilson, August 2, 1918, quoted in Ingle, *Pilgrimage to Reform*, 150.

a "Liberty Tax Bill" as a corollary to the Liberty Loan drives. Speaking on behalf of numerous farmer and labor groups, the Farmers' National Committee called for a fiscal policy in which "one-half of the cost of the war shall be raised by current taxation upon excess and war profits, upon incomes, and upon the unearned increment of land values." McAdoo passed along this correspondence to Leffingwell, who responded with a letter of his own optimistically stating how taxation had made up "almost one-third of our total expenditures in the fiscal year 1918."[107]

To reinforce its support for a war profits tax, the Treasury Department commissioned T. S. Adams to conduct yet another systematic comparison of profits taxes. Before taking responsibility for a new wartime tax measure – during an election year no less – the Treasury Department wanted to be certain that the war profits tax could promote egalitarian ideals without harming revenue. Adams's second report confirmed that an 80 percent flat tax on profits above a prewar average would extract more revenue from big businesses as compared to smaller enterprises, with only a small decline in revenue. The second study, however, explicitly recommended maintaining the excess-profits tax, as a supplement to a new war profits tax. An excess-profits levy would reach those corporations, such as the Ford Motor Company, "which earned an unusually high rate of profits in the prewar period... but would pay no war-profits tax." The study's emphasis on the virtues of the excess-profits tax may have disappointed Leffingwell, who was eager to replace the excess-profits tax with a war profits levy. Nonetheless, he set aside his personal views and redoubled his efforts to support the Department's position to maintain the excess-profits tax as a supplement to a new British-style war profits tax.[108]

Eventually, Treasury officials were able to persuade Congress to accept the proposal of levying both a war profits and excess-profits tax. By

107 Arthur Capper (Chairman of the Farmers' National Committee for War Finance) to McAdoo, August 10, 1918; Leffingwell to Capper, August 27, 1918, NARA Excess Profits Tax Folder. Agrarian associations echoed these demands in a more formal proposal before lawmakers, which called for the "democratic financing of war costs by the retention of the income and excess profits taxes." "Farmers Outline Their Program for Legislation," *New York Times*, December 15, 1919, 1. Some newspaper editors, and even some officials within the Wilson administration, seemed to agree with the farmers. "Dodging the War-Profits Issue," *New York World*, July 30, 1918, 7; "An Example of War Profits," *New York World*, August 1, 1918, clippings in NARA Excess Profits Tax Folder.

108 "Corporations Paying War-Profits and Excess-Profits Taxes," October 18, 1918, NARA Excess Profits Tax Folder.

September 1918, the House drafted and passed a comprehensive revenue bill that included a dizzyingly complex law containing both an excess-profits and war profits tax. The mobilization of the Department's economic and legal expertise helped broker a compromise that convinced Kitchin and other lawmakers that a hybrid or dual profits tax was the appropriate solution to war profiteering. Consequently, Treasury officials were able to reframe the new profits tax as a temporary measure, one that was linked to prewar average profits and that, therefore, could be easily dismantled after the conflict. Leffingwell and his colleagues thus were able to reorient the demands of activist social groups like the Farmers' National Committee and populist lawmakers like Kitchin.[109]

At the same time that lawmakers and Treasury officials were evaluating the merits of the excess-profits tax, BIR lawyers were considering the constitutionality of the levy. These attorneys knew early on that one of the greatest challenges in administering the excess-profits tax was "clarifying what invested capital means." In tackling this task, Ballantine, the lead BIR lawyer, acknowledged that the excess-profits levy might face some constitutional challenges. Opponents of the law, such as Robert Reed, the legal representative of investment banking interests, had been suggesting in no uncertain terms that the vagueness of invested capital made the excess-profits tax an unconstitutional form of government confiscation. With these comments in mind, Ballantine used his technical legal skills and his wartime experience to lay out a detailed doctrinal defense of the excess-profits tax in a 1919 article in the *Yale Law Journal*.[110]

There were primarily two parts of the excess-profits tax law that Ballantine believed might pose some constitutional issues. The first was, as Reed suggested, a Fifth Amendment due process challenge to the use of "invested capital" as the tax base for measuring excess profits. The second potential issue was whether the "relief clauses" of the law, which allowed the BIR to use comparative statistics to impute invested capital for those businesses that did not have any invested capital, was an

109 Corporations were required to pay the higher of either a graduated excess profits tax, ranging from 35 to 70 percent, measured with reference to invested capital, or a war profits tax of 80 percent on net income in excess of a specific credit and the average net income for the prewar years of 1911–13. Blakey and Blakey, *Federal Income Tax*, 167–9; Bank, *War and Taxes*, 74–6.

110 "Boston Man Named for Job; Ballantine Chosen by President for Solicitor of Internal Revenue," press clipping, Box 1: IRS Solicitor 1917–19, AABP; "Excess Tax Review Board," *Wall Street Journal*, April 3, 1918; Ballantine, "Some Constitutional Aspects of the Excess Profits Tax," *Yale Law Journal* 29:6 (1919), 625–42, 625.

unconstitutional delegation of congressional authority. On both counts, Ballantine concluded, "the decided cases appear to disclose little probability that the statute will be upset on either ground."[111]

Ballantine agreed that the due process clause of the Fifth Amendment theoretically could be a legitimate restraint on the arbitrary exercise of Congress's taxing powers. But in his analysis of the case law, a tax based on the ratio of profits to invested capital was wholly permissible and well within Congress's taxing powers. "As to a method of taxation, like any 'classification,' the question is whether there is any reasonable ground for it or whether it is simply arbitrary," wrote Ballantine. Analyzing a litany of cases, Ballantine contended that any judicial challenge to the congressional taxing power on the grounds of due process was likely to fail. "So vigorous has been the Court in its support of federal taxing power," Ballantine reasoned, "that all the attacks upon taxing statutes under the Fifth Amendment, upon the ground of their unequal operation, have so far failed."[112]

The second aspect of the excess-profits tax that Ballantine addressed was the constitutionality of the "relief sections" that gave the BIR discretion in imputing invested capital to a business. In determining whether these provisions were an unconstitutional delegation of legislative authority, Ballantine contended that providing "relief" through these provisions was simply a function of administering the law, and was not therefore an exercise in legislative authority. "So long as it can be said that all that is left by Congress to administrative officers is the determination of how a taxing provision applies to a particular state of facts," Ballantine reasoned, "no delegation is involved." Ballantine, moreover, maintained that the congressional use of "invested capital" to measure excess profits was part of the practical, institutional deference that the Court had long granted to Congress in the making of tax laws. In words that echoed Justice Thomas Cooley's writings from nearly a half century earlier, Ballantine reiterated how: "The decided cases show that the presumption that each act of Congress is valid, is applied with special readiness to revenue acts and that the Court, even without the persuasive effect of the imperative need for war revenue, would not be likely to declare invalid a taxing act framed with anything like reasonable regard to its just incidence."[113]

[111] "Urges A Sound Basis for Wartime Taxes," *New York Times*, June 18, 1918, 17; Ballantine, "Some Constitutional Aspects of the Excess Profits Tax," 627.

[112] Ballantine, "Some Constitutional Aspects of the Excess Profits Tax," 630.

[113] Ibid., 639.

Ballantine bolstered his defense by appealing to changing historical conditions. Like the new school political economists who had justified the adoption of direct and graduated taxes as necessary to meet the changing needs of American industrial society, Ballantine similarly pointed to the broader social and political context to defend the discretionary powers of executive agencies. He admitted that in an earlier age one could claim that legislatures should maintain the responsibility of creating and administer revenue laws. But in a modern, industrial society where a complex array of laws and regulations were increasingly needed to provide stability and consistency, effective administration of these new laws and regulations required the creation of new government agencies and organizations. "Recognizing the increasing variety of the subject matter upon which statutes operate, and the increasing complexity of the result sought to be achieved by statutes," Ballantine wrote, "the courts have gone much farther than under the simpler conditions of an earlier period in supporting the extensive use by the legislative arm of the more flexible executive instrumentality."[114] Ballantine's legal defense of the excess-profits tax was not just an academic exercise. His views provided stability for an uncertain legal environment, and in time his legal analysis would be vindicated when the Court upheld the excess-profits tax soon after the war.[115]

Yet, lest one confuse Ballantine's constitutional defense of the excess-profits tax as an unequivocal endorsement, the former corporate lawyer judiciously balanced his support of the levy with some biting criticism of it on nonlegal grounds. Like many others, Ballantine thought the tax had several significant drawbacks. It did not curb inflation, it angered taxpayers with its inquisitorial requirements, and it could promote a great deal of uncertainty and delay in generating revenue. Together, these concerns would ultimately lead to the repeal of the excess-profits tax after the war, but as far as its constitutionality was concerned, Ballantine was convinced that "there is little likelihood that the court will conclude that the discrimination involved in the excess profits tax is hostile or arbitrary." If business owners and taxpayers believed that the excess-profits tax was unwise, there were other methods to address the problem beyond judicial challenges. Ballantine, ever the moderate, concluded, "It is to Congress rather than to the courts that the taxpayer must look for a fairer and wiser distribution of the revenue burden."[116]

[114] Ibid., 641.

[115] *LaBelle Iron Works v. United States*, 256 U.S. 377 (1921), 393.

[116] Ballantine, "Some Constitutional Aspects of the Excess Profits Tax," 635, 642.

Ballantine's words were prescient. Soon after the war, it was to Congress that opponents of the excess-profits tax successfully turned in repealing the measure – to the immense disappointment of some populist lawmakers, economic experts, and social groups who had hoped to make the excess-profits tax a permanent part of the American tax and regulatory regime.

Postwar Visions of a New Fiscal Order

After the war ended in November 1918, many of the Treasury lawyers gradually returned to the private sector. Roper led many of his BIR colleagues into a burgeoning Washington, D.C., consulting and tax law practice, only to return to public life as Franklin D. Roosevelt's Secretary of Commerce.[117] Love was equally eager to return to the private sector and Texas politics, as he leveraged his Washington contacts to develop a lucrative postwar legal practice.[118] Ballantine also returned to private practice after the war, eventually joining the New York law firm that would become Dewey, Ballantine. Throughout the 1920s, he led the firm's tax practice and became a leading voice of the elite tax bar. The war experience, as we shall see, transformed Ballantine from a conventional corporate lawyer into an active income tax advocate. In 1931, he returned to Washington to serve as his Harvard classmate Ogden L. Mills's Treasury undersecretary, and to defend the use of an excess-profits tax during wartime.[119]

Leffingwell, by contrast, remained at Treasury to ensure a smooth postwar transition. He served McAdoo and his immediate successor, Carter Glass, admirably, gaining the respect of both men.[120] Leffingwell came

[117] Roper, *Fifty Years of Public Life*, 170–1, 211, 269–70.

[118] Thomas B. Love to Kermit Roosevelt, January 26, 1916; Love to Kermit Roosevelt, September 23, 1919, Kermit Roosevelt Papers, Library of Congress, Manuscript Division, Washington, D.C.; George S. Adams to Love, Jan. 19, 1918, TBLP.

[119] Urofsky, "Ballantine, Arthur Atwood." Arthur A. Ballantine, "War Policies in Taxation, Statement before the War Policies Commission," May 20, 1931, Record Group 56 – General Records of the Office of the Secretary of the Treasury, Box 187, Folder "Tax – Excess Profits & War Profits. 1923–32." NARA II.

[120] After the war, Glass commended Leffingwell as being "an indispensable factor in the most important activities of the Department." Similarly, McAdoo recalled that he valued how Leffingwell, the "Wall Street Republican," challenged his ideas without being disloyal. "While [Leffingwell's] point of view and mine were frequently at variance, nevertheless these differences were brought out in argument and enabled me to reach decisions with greater confidence and satisfaction to myself than if he had agreed with me about everything," wrote McAdoo. "Whenever I made a final decision Leffingwell acquiesced and carried it out with loyalty and energy." Carter Glass to Leffingwell,

to relish his role as a government official, and he did not hide his disappointment when Wilson selected David F. Houston, the Secretary of Agriculture, as Glass's successor ahead of Leffingwell. In 1920, Leffingwell rejoined the Cravath firm, but soon left to take a senior position at the investment house of J. P. Morgan.[121]

It did not take long for the Treasury lawyers to realize the historic significance of their government service. In a series of correspondence in the fall of 1919, Roper and Leffingwell assessed their contributions and shared their respective visions of a postwar fiscal order. Having weathered the war crisis, the seasoned administrators reflected on how the past three years had dramatically changed the everyday operations of the federal fiscal system. Building upon their experiences, Roper and Leffingwell discussed how they could make the tax system even more effective after the war. In his letters to Leffingwell, Roper made two principal policy proposals. First, he recommended the creation of a "Court of Internal Revenue Tax Appeals" to adjudicate appeals directly from the district courts. Second, and perhaps more important, he suggested that the Treasury Department consider fundamentally restructuring the tax regime to focus on "revenue sources" that might be collected "with the least inconvenience to taxpayers."[122]

Roper's recommendations elicited a mixed response from Leffingwell. On the one hand, Leffingwell was "quite taken with the idea of a Court of Internal Revenue Tax Appeals."[123] Both Roper and Leffingwell understood how the complexity of wartime tax laws raised numerous legal questions and burdened the judicial system. It was essential, Roper observed, revealing his unquestioned faith in expertise, to have these

February 2, 1920, quoted in Pulling, ed., *Selected Letters of R. C. Leffingwell*, 9; McAdoo, *Crowded Years*, 430; Murray, "Bureaucracy and Bipartisanship in Taxation."

121 Writing to a friend in 1952, Leffingwell recounted that he was disappointed but not surprised to learn that Wilson had appointed Houston ahead of him. After all, Leffingwell was neither a Democrat nor a close friend of Wilson's. "Under all the circumstances," Leffingwell wrote, "it was most natural and proper for the President to appoint a long-time friend and Democrat and trusted Cabinet minister to this high office, instead of a stranger whom he knows only by reputation." Quoted in Pulling, ed., *Selected Letters of R. C. Leffingwell*, 7. Leffingwell's postwar status as a partner in J. P. Morgan probably also cost him an appointment in Franklin Roosevelt's administration. Schuker, "Leffingwell, Russell Cornell" in *Dictionary of American Biography*, 377; Swaine, *Cravath Firm*, Vol. II, 315.

122 Daniel C. Roper to Russell C. Leffingwell, October 17, 1919, NARA Excess Profits Tax Folder.

123 Leffingwell to Roper, October 20, 1919, NARA Excess Profits Tax Folder.

complex legal issues "considered by men especially trained in Internal Revenue Taxation," so that "a sound basis of internal revenue court decisions may be assured for both the benefit of the Government and the taxpayer."[124]

Leffingwell agreed. Providing taxpayers with a stable and predictable set of tax laws had been one of the hallmarks of the wartime Treasury Department. And having a quasi-independent judiciary of professionally trained tax experts was certainly one way to institutionalize the consistent resolution of tax controversies, and thus provide the type of formal rationality that state-builders craved. Such a court could also carve out an autonomous institutional sphere for the nascent tax bar. Although Leffingwell did not elaborate on this self-serving possibility, a specialized court of tax appeals could protect the legal profession's monopoly on the provision of scarce services and thereby enhance the collective power of lawyers within the new polity. It could also further the stratification of the bar, setting tax law experts apart from other corporate and business lawyers.[125]

Though Leffingwell supported the idea of a specialized tax appeals court, he was less enthusiastic about Roper's suggestion to alter revenue sources. Similar calls to return to a more "convenient" system of broad-based tariffs and excise taxes would soon be made by Senator Reed Smoot (R-Utah) and other congressional opponents of progressive income and wealth-transfer taxes. To Leffingwell, this recommendation seemed to hearken back to the prewar regime of regressive indirect taxation – a system that Leffingwell believed was rendered obsolete by the successful administration of the wartime tax policies. Leffingwell informed Roper that his suggestion "if pressed to the limit... would mean that we should have nothing but indirect taxes such as the protective tariff, the excess profits tax, and the consumption tax."[126]

124 Roper to Leffingwell, October 17, 1919, NARA Excess Profits Tax Folder.

125 A Court of Internal Revenue Tax Appeals did not come into being, but this idea may have been the kernel that led to the creation of specialized federal trial courts for tax issues, the U.S. Board of Tax Appeals, which was a forerunner of today's U.S. Tax Courts. Harold Dubroff, *The United States Tax Court: An Historical Analysis* (Chicago: Commerce Clearing House, 1979). Tax scholars have analyzed the case for a specialized court of tax appeals, see William D. Popkin, "Why a Court of Tax Appeals Is So Elusive," *Tax Notes* May 28, 1990, 1101–10; Griswold, "The Need for a Court of Tax Appeals," 57 *Harvard Law Review* 1153 (1944).

126 Leffingwell to Roper, October 20, 1919, NARA Excess Profits Tax Folder. "Three Plans for Tax Revision" *New York Times*, December 21, 1919, 38.

A return to the old fiscal regime meant a return to a regressive, opaque, and ultimately undemocratic system of public finance. "In the case of indirect taxes the whole community pays through increased cost of living, and there is a minimum of inconvenience to the taxpayers," Leffingwell conceded. "Indeed, most of them know nothing about it." This invisible form of taxation violated the principles of democracy and modern economics by favoring convenience of collections over the transparency of direct taxation. "I take it that it is good democratic doctrine – certainly it is good economics," wrote Leffingwell, "that a direct tax, such as the income tax, which inevitably involves a certain amount of inconvenience to the taxpayer, is to be preferred to the indirect tax which involves none at all."[127]

Although Leffingwell did not elaborate on what he meant by "good democratic doctrine," his ideas and actions during his tenure in the Treasury Department suggest that he had in mind the inextricable link that existed between direct taxes, democracy, and fiscal citizenship. Since the late nineteenth century, as we have seen, tax reformers and new school political economists had been claiming that the "inconvenience" of direct levies on incomes, profits, and inheritances made citizens more attuned to the workings of the state, that paying taxes directly to the federal government gave citizens a greater stake in how public funds were raised and used, and that direct taxation ultimately helped forge a renewed sense of civic identity. Indeed, Richard Ely and the other progressive public finance economists had supported directed and graduated taxation precisely on these grounds, that a more visible and salient tax system could raise civic consciousness.[128]

Leffingwell and the other Treasury lawyers endorsed these views with their actions, if not their words. In the process of building the Treasury Department's administrative capacity during the war, they sought to assure taxpayers that revenues were collected in a consistent and equitable manner. By clarifying the operations of complex new rules and by evaluating and reevaluating the income and profits taxes, the lawyers helped build the trust between citizens and their government that was essential to the success of a liberal democracy engaged in global war.

But they also did much more. Their vision for a postwar fiscal order, reflected in Leffingwell's remarks to Roper, went beyond simply using direct taxes to imbue citizens as stakeholders with a sense of belonging to

[127] Leffingwell to Roper, Oct. 20, 1919, NARA Excess Profits Tax Folder.
[128] See, e.g., Ely, *Taxation in American States and Cities*; Seligman, *The Income Tax*.

a new national community. The Treasury lawyers knew all too well that even the robust wartime tax laws affected only a fraction of American citizens. In rebuking Roper's suggestion to alter revenue sources, Leffingwell focused, once again, on the state's fiscal obligations to its citizens, on the responsibility that government officials had toward the larger body politic – the duty to distribute equitably and effectively the fiscal burdens of financing a modern industrial democracy. This was one way of striking the balance between justice and revenue.

The Great War fundamentally transformed the national system of public finance. The conceptual transformation underpinning the rise of a new fiscal order had its roots in the turmoil of the late nineteenth and early twentieth centuries and the rise of transatlantic ideas about social belonging and fiscal citizenship. Likewise, the efforts of theorists, reformers, and jurists helped embed these new ideas into the fabric of American legal and political culture. But it was the war that eventually fortified the federal government's use of direct and progressive taxes. It was the war that triggered the unprecedented interdependence of state and society, and the attendant explosive growth in federal spending and administrative capacity. And it was the war that ushered in a new fiscal state and all that the new polity stood for.

Yet, while the global conflict provided the historical conditions for a fiscal and administrative revolution, a particular group of government lawyers exploited this opportunity to shape the emerging fiscal polity into their particular vision of a robust and fair legal Leviathan. Their vision did not always correspond with the public interest. The legal professionals who worked in the Wilson administration's Treasury Department were by no means purely valiant tribunes of the people. In helping to formulate policy, they privileged their administrative expertise over the popular will of social groups and elected lawmakers. In recruiting and staffing their offices, they assisted personal friends and former colleagues, while they developed the potential for a lucrative area of postwar practice.

Indeed, the Treasury lawyers were among the post–World War I government officials who helped grease the revolving door between the public and private sectors and thus set the mold for future generations of "Washington lawyers." Despite their allegiance to the wartime state, these elite lawyers could not in the end divorce themselves from their intractable professional faith in corporate capitalism as the source of economic growth and productivity. Even when they intended to spread the war costs more evenly across regions, classes, and generations, the unpredictable dynamics of war often overwhelmed their intentions and aims.

Still, the Treasury lawyers used their professional networks, legal skills, and practical experience to navigate the wartime fiscal system between the extremes of radical change and conservative inertia. From creating an executive agency committed to building public trust and enhancing its own administrative capacity, to formulating broad policies that spotlighted the reciprocal rights and obligations of fiscal citizenship, to evaluating and defending the novel excess-profits tax, to developing the parameters of the postwar fiscal order, the Treasury lawyers helped underwrite the Allied victories in Europe. In the process, they also strengthened the revenue-generating powers of the burgeoning modern American liberal state.

The fiscal regime forged during the Great War did not simply wither away after the conflict. Although some opponents of direct and progressive taxation attempted to return the American system of public finance back to the regressive prewar regime of tariffs and excise taxes, the new fiscal polity proved remarkably resilient. The war-related budget deficits, to be sure, provided a short-term structural floor on the ability of lawmakers to eviscerate the new and robust taxing powers, even as the scale and scope of federal taxing powers were retrenched. But the durability of the new fiscal polity owed just as much to the intellectual and legal foundations laid by previous thinkers and political reformers, as well as to the patterns of financing established by the wartime Treasury Department. The modern American fiscal state, in sum, went through a formative period of institutional development during the Great War. For it was during this national emergency that Treasury Department lawyers exercised their new-found taxing powers to build the administrative foundations of a new fiscal order.

7

The Paradox of Retrenchment

Postwar Republican Ascendancy and the Resiliency of the Modern Fiscal State

> It is true that not every instrumentality brought into the war for the purpose of maintaining the public interest will last. Many of them will melt away when the war comes to an end. But it must be borne in mind that the war did not create that interdependence of interests which has given enterprises once private and limited in scope social significance.... In this sense, no matter how many among the special agencies for public control decay with the disappearance of war stress, the movement will never go backward.
>
> – John Dewey

In the late summer of 1921, little more than two years after the Peace of Versailles marked the official end of the Great War, Congress was in the midst of drafting a new tax bill. As a result of the previous national elections, Republicans were nominally in control of national policymaking. They held significant, though unstable, majorities in both houses of Congress, and one of their Old Guard stalwarts, Ohio Senator Warren G. Harding, had swept into the White House on campaign promises to return the country to "normalcy." A swift dismantling of the "soak-the-rich" wartime tax regime seemed imminent. Without the war emergency as an impetus for a steeply progressive tax system, many contemporary observers anticipated that the existing fiscal structure would be one of the early and consistent targets of postwar Republican retrenchment. The tax bill did not disappoint. As part of the larger effort toward a "return to normalcy," the pending revenue law promised to slash top marginal rates on individual incomes, eliminate the controversial excess and war profits taxes on businesses, and provide generous tax benefits to owners of capital.[1]

Yet, some pro-business Republicans wanted even more. Postmaster William H. Hays, the former chairman of the National Republican Party

[1] 67th Congress, 1st sess., House Report 350 (1921); Roy G. Blakey and Gladys C. Blakey, *The Federal Income Tax* (London: Longmans, Green and Co., 1940), 189–222.

during its recent ascent to power, complained bitterly about what he saw as the limited scope of the bill's tax benefits for investors. Hays was representative of his party's dominant postwar strand of anti-statism. Just as Congress was concluding its final discussions of the revenue bill, Hays wrote to the newly appointed Treasury Secretary Andrew W. Mellon to encourage him to intensify and accelerate the process of rolling back the wartime tax regime.

Mellon was quick to respond. He informed Hays that nonpartisan economic experts within the Treasury Department "deemed it unwise to endeavor to have [the bill] broadened." With the economy struggling through a postwar recession, the Pittsburgh banker turned Treasury Secretary believed that to provide a stable and predictable environment for economic growth he needed to curb the tax-cutting exuberance of some of his Republican colleagues. Immediate and dramatic changes to the fiscal system seemed hasty and ill-informed, not to mention politically impetuous, especially given the fragile Republican majority in Congress. "I think you will agree," Mellon informed Hays, "that it was advisable to take what we could get rather than to risk losing the whole [bill] by asking for more."[2]

Mellon's caution revealed the broader postwar tensions over political and economic retrenchment. The business community, to be sure, was eager to loosen the state's grip over the economy, to remove the federal government's control over transportation industries and capital markets, to cut tax rates and perhaps even replace the income tax with a national sales tax, and ultimately to transport American society back to a mythical golden age of laissez-faire political economy. Yet, at the same time, some economic elites wanted to maintain and even bolster certain aspects of wartime corporatism. Just as they had during the war, business leaders after the conflict continued to dictate how the federal government itself could become more effective, efficient, and businesslike. They also solicited the assistance of national agencies in making their own pursuit of profits more rational and routinized – assistance that Herbert Hoover's Commerce Department was happy to provide. Industrialists, moreover, turned to the state in the early 1920s to help discipline labor. And, together with certain agricultural interests, many business

[2] Mellon to Hays, November 17, 1921, Record Group 56, General Records of the Department of the Treasury, Correspondence of the Office of the Secretary of the Treasury, Central Files of the Office of the Secretary of the Treasury, 1917–32, Box 187, Folder "Tax – Exchanges of Property, 1921–1932," National Archives and Record Administration, College Park, Md. [hereinafter NARA II].

leaders attempted to revive the protective tariff to limit foreign competition.[3]

The dissonance between the rhetoric of formal retrenchment and the reality of institutional continuity was particularly pronounced in the realm of fiscal policy. Throughout the postwar decade, under the leadership of Republican lawmakers, the federal government incrementally rolled back the highly progressive, "soak-the-rich" tax regime. Against the backdrop of calls for a national sales tax, policymakers enacted a number of important changes to the new tax system. They repealed the excess-profits tax. They dramatically reduced the reach of the estate tax by increasing exemption levels and decreasing rates. And, perhaps most important, through the Mellon Plan of "scientific tax reform," they whittled down top marginal income tax rates on individuals from wartime highs of 77 to 25 percent by the end of the 1920s. Accordingly, effective income tax rates on the wealthiest American households (those making more than $50,000) declined precipitously from a 1920 high of 22 to roughly 9 percent by 1930.[4]

Still, despite the pleas of some reactionary lawmakers, the federal system of direct and progressive taxes endured. It did not revert to the prewar regime of regressive import duties and excise taxes, or adopt a new sales tax base. Nor did the tax regime even return to the prewar historical trajectory of relying on direct and graduated taxes for only a small portion of government revenues. The 1926 top marginal rate of 25 percent on individual income, for instance, remained far above the prewar figure of 7 percent, as did the effective tax rate on the richest Americans. The

[3] Marc Allen Eisner, *From Warfare State to Welfare States: World War I, Compensatory State Building, and the Limits of the Modern Order* (University Park: Pennsylvania State University Press, 2000); David J. Goldberg, *Discontented America: The United States in the 1920s* (Baltimore: Johns Hopkins Press, 1999); Joseph A. McCartin, *Labor's Great War: The Struggle for Industrial Democracy and the Origins of Modern American Labor Relations, 1912–1921* (Chapel Hill: University of North Carolina Press, 1997); Ellis Hawley, *The Great War and the Search for a Modern Order: A History of the American People and their Institutions, 1917–1933* (New York: St. Martin's Press, 1979); John D. Hicks, *Republican Ascendancy, 1921–1933* (New York: Harper & Row, 1960); William E. Leuchtenburg, *The Perils of Prosperity, 1914–1932* (Chicago: University of Chicago Press, 1958).

[4] Revenue Act of 1921, 42 Stat. 227, 233 (1921); Revenue Act of 1924, 43 Stat. 253 (1924); Revenue Act of 1926, 44 Stat. 9 (1926); Revenue Act of 1928, 45 Stat. 791 (1928); *Historical Statistics of the United States, Millennial Edition*, ed. Susan B. Carter et al. (New York: Cambridge University Press, 2006), Table Ea758–772. Paul Studenski and Herman E. Kroos, *Financial History of the United States* (New York: McGraw Hill, 1963), 312–15.

TABLE 7.1. *Top Personal Income Tax Rates, and Sources of Tax Revenue, 1916–1929*

	1916	1919	1922	1925	1927	1929
Top Marginal Tax Rate	15%	73%	58%	25%	25%	24%
Effective Tax Rate on Richest Households	3.0%	13.1%	9.8%	7.5%	7.8%	8.1%
Income and Profits Tax Revenue (as % of Total Federal Revenue)	16.4%	67.2%	51.8%	48.4%	55.3%	60.4%
Customs and Excise Tax Revenue (as % of Total Federal Revenue)	72.1%	17.0%	16.7%	25.2%	25.0%	27.2%

Sources: Roy G. Blakey and Gladys C. Blakey, *The Federal Income Tax* (New York: Longmans, Green & Co., 1940), Tables 20 and 21, 512–15; W. Elliot Brownlee, "Historical Perspectives on U.S. Tax Policy toward the Rich," in *Does Atlas Shrug? The Economic Consequences of Taxing the Rich*, ed. Joel Slemrod (New York: Russell Sage Foundation, 2000), Table 2.3, 45; U.S. Treasury Department, Bureau of Internal Revenue, *Statistics of Income for 1930* (Washington, D.C.: GPO, 1932); *Historical Statistics of the United States*, ed. Susan B. Carter et al. (New York: Cambridge University Press, 2006), Series Ea588–593, Series Ea594–608.

federal estate tax, likewise, endured as a highly salient symbol of the progressive legacy, and the continued commitment to a new notion of fiscal citizenship based on the principle of "ability to pay." Revenue from corporate income taxes, moreover, increased steadily during most of the decade from approximately $207 million in 1917 to about $1.3 billion by 1928. In fact, throughout the 1920s, individual and corporate income tax revenues alone accounted for roughly 50 percent of total federal receipts, exceeding the prewar level of approximately 8 percent (see Table 7.1).[5]

Similarly, the commitment to a depoliticized Treasury Department – one free of purely political appointments and focused mainly on bureaucratic efficiency – became one of the hallmarks of Mellon's tenure as secretary. Thus, notwithstanding the continued calls for cutbacks and a return to the old way of doing things, a professionally administered, direct and graduated tax system remained the central component of the new fiscal order. As John Dewey had correctly predicted, the progressive movement and all it stood for would not be replaced after the war.

[5] Carter, *Historical Statistics of the United States*, Table Ea594–608; W. Elliot Brownlee, "Historical Perspective on U.S. Tax Policy toward the Rich," in *Does Atlas Shrug? The Economic Consequences of Taxing the Rich*, ed. Joel Slemrod (New York: Russell Sage Foundation, 2000), 29–73. According to Brownlee, the effective tax rate on the top 1 percent of American households skyrocketed from 3 percent before U.S. entry in the Great War to nearly 16 percent at the height of the conflict, but then remained at roughly 8 percent throughout most of the 1920s. Ibid., 45, Table 2.3.

A Decade of Political Uncertainty and Conservative Disillusionment

The 1920s were a politically charged period of contestation and contingency. Though the Roaring Twenties and the Jazz Age are often remembered today as a period of social and culture liberation, for contemporaries it was also a time of great tension. It was a time when the country's political and economic future was constantly challenged and highly unsettled. This was evident in the disparity between the political rhetoric of retrenchment and the systematic persistency of the new fiscal regime. Influential business and civic leaders, who may have tempered their anti-tax sentiments during the war, soon unleashed a barrage of anti-tax campaigns in an effort to return the nation to a period of fiscal "normalcy." Numerous politically conservative organizations, from the American Tax League to the Business Men's National Tax Committee, attempted to convince lawmakers to eliminate many of the existing "obnoxious" taxes, and even adopt a national sales tax.[6] These demands were met head-on by working-class social groups, activist intellectuals, government advisors, and progressive politicians. These supporters of the new fiscal state sternly challenged the calls for a return to the old order. In the early 1920s, it was uncertain which side in this battle would eventually triumph.

By the end of the decade, however, the social and political assumptions underpinning the new tax system had become an accepted part of American law and political economy. Conservatives were forced to come to grips with their "failure of policy crafting." The 1920s became, for them, "a decade of disillusionment."[7] Though anti-tax activists were able to erode portions of the new fiscal order, they were unable to mobilize a full-fledged social movement to overturn the direct and progressive tax system. In short, the postwar decade demonstrated the resiliency of the modern American fiscal state.

Not everyone, of course, was pleased with the specific contours of the new fiscal order. The partial victories disappointed some populist and progressive activists, and reinforced the narrow commitment to a particular type of tax reform. The elimination of the excess-profits tax, for example, dashed the hopes of lawmakers like Claude Kitchin and Robert

6 Isaac William Martin, *Rich People's Movements* (New York: Oxford University Press, 2013); Romain D. Huret, *Taxed: American Resisters to Taxation from the Early Republic to the Present* (Cambridge, Mass.: Harvard University Press, forthcoming).

7 Martin, *Rich People's Movements*, Chapter 2; Huret, *Taxed*, Chapter 4.

La Follette, as well as economic experts like David Friday and Robert Murray Haig, who had hoped to make this levy a potent tool for attacking monopoly profits. More significantly, the progressive preoccupation with consolidating a direct and graduated tax regime, and the specific resistance to the proposals for a national sales tax, had far-reaching, though unintended, consequences for the development of the new fiscal regime. The consistent stigmatization of consumption taxes and the intellectual and emotional obsession with stabilizing a fiscal system based almost exclusively on taxpaying ability, ironically, foreclosed the possibility of using the full powers of the new fiscal polity to address the many ills of modern industrial capitalism. The historical legacy of regressive and politicized consumption taxes, in the form of import duties and excise taxes, blinded reformers from envisioning how a more holistic tax-and-transfer system could be used to counter the possible regressive incidence of consumption taxes. Simply put, progressive fiscal consolidation came at a steep price. The resiliency of the fiscal state fortified a fiscal myopia that would come to afflict subsequent generations of American thinkers, legislators, and activists.

How was all this possible? Given the steady postwar assaults on the graduated rate structure, how can we explain the remarkable persistence and resiliency of the nascent fiscal state and the continued narrowing of liberal fiscal visions? With Republicans controlling the key institutions of national political power, and with Andrew Mellon at the helm of the Treasury Department, how and why was the growing fiscal polity, initially envisioned by progressive reformers, able to survive and prosper during the 1920s?

Part of the answer to this historical puzzle rests with the theoretical distinction between "programmatic" and "systemic" retrenchment. As historically minded social scientists have shown, retrenchment outcomes are conditioned by the "lock-in effects" and "policy feedback" of previous political choices. These historically constituted forces frequently permit the programmatic dismantling of particular laws and rules, while constraining the systemic roll back of an entire structure of statecraft.[8] In this sense, the Great War was a pivotal juncture in this path-dependent process. It locked in a pattern of public financing and prompted a series

[8] Paul Pierson, *Dismantling the Welfare State? Reagan, Thatcher and the Politics of Retrenchment* (New York: Cambridge University Press, 1994); Pierson, *Politics in Time: History, Institutions, and Social Analysis* (Princeton: Princeton University Press, 2004), Chapter 3.

of policy feedback mechanisms in the 1920s that allowed for the formal weakening of the steeply graduated rate structure, without completely undermining the substantive intellectual and legal foundations, administrative capacities, and popular social support for the new progressive tax system.

In this sense, the Twenties were neither an abrupt end to Progressivism, nor a simple continuation of the wartime tax regime.[9] The durability of the new fiscal era was rooted, instead, in a much broader and deeper lineage of reform – a lineage that could be traced back to growing social antagonism toward the late-nineteenth-century tax regime, to the intellectual revolution advanced by an earlier generation of progressive political economists, and to the lawmakers who absorbed these new economic ideas to create the legal foundations of the emerging fiscal polity. To be sure, wartime government lawyers extended the ideas of tax theorists by building an administrative framework onto the prewar legal foundations. That administrative framework not only helped underwrite a global war; it also secured a pattern of public financing that endured beyond the immediate crisis of the international conflict.

But even these bureaucratic achievements were the culmination of decades of social unrest, intellectual agitation, and political activism. The war, as John Dewey noted, simply accelerated the "interdependence

[9] Conventional historical periodization continues to characterize World War I as the end of Progressivism. See, e.g., *The American Promise: A Compact History*, ed. James L. Roark et al. (Boston: Bedford/St. Martin's Press, 2010), 565; Alan Brinkley, *American History: A Survey* (New York: McGraw-Hill, 2007), 704–5. Other scholars have identified the limits of fiscal retrenchment during the 1920s by focusing on structural forces like the unprecedented postwar federal deficit, bipartisan politics, and bureaucratic continuity. John F. Witte, *The Politics and Development of the Federal Income Tax* (Madison: University of Wisconsin Press, 1985); Jacob Metzer, "How New Was the New Era? The Public Sector in the 1920s," *Journal of Economic History* 45:1 (1985), 119–26; Lawrence L. Murray, "Bureaucracy and Bi-Partisanship in Taxation: The Mellon Plan Revisited, *Business History Review* 52:2 (summer 1978), 200–25; Benjamin Rader, "Federal Taxation in the 1920s: A Reexamination," *The Historian* 33:3 (1971), 415–35; Sidney Ratner, *Taxation and Democracy in America* (New York: John Wiley & Sons, 1947). Other scholars have emphasized how Mellon and his staff of professional experts were much less hostile to direct and graduated taxes than was once imagined, and how the social movement for veteran's benefits created significant bipartisan political pressure to maintain progressive income and profits taxes. W. Elliot Brownlee, *Federal Taxation in America: A Short History* (New York: Cambridge University Press, 1996); Joseph Thorndike, "The Republican Roots of New Deal Tax Policy," *Tax Notes*, August 28, 2003; M. Susan Murnane, "Selling Scientific Taxation: The Treasury Department's Campaign for Tax Reform in the 1920s," *Law & Social Inquiry* 29:4 (2004), 819–56; Anne Alstott and Benjamin Novick, "War, Taxes, and Income Redistribution in the Twenties: The 1924 Veterans' Bonus and the Defeat of the Mellon Plan," *Tax Law Review* 59 (2005), 373–438.

of interests" that had undergirded the broader progressive movement. If the process of regime building and state formation entails "rearranging institutional relationships to stabilize and routinize governmental operations around a new set of political assumptions,"[10] the 1920s was a period when organizational links and government routines reflected how lawyers, jurists, legislators, economists, journalists, and ordinary Americans came to embrace and secure the previous era's commitment to social democratic tax reform.

The acceptance of new political and social assumptions about fiscal relations between state and society was, indeed, pervasive throughout the postwar decade. From the elite discourse of legal professionals, to the juridical acquiescence of a new administrative framework, to the writings of a new generation of economists, and to the voices of legislators and quotidian citizens, there was an abundance of evidence that a changed mindset about the basis of modern American public finance had taken hold. Although the new tax system remained a "rich man's tax" aimed at the wealthiest Americans, by the end of the decade the intellectual, legal, and administrative foundations of a new fiscal order were firmly set.

There were, to be sure, more than a few pockets of resistance. For the most part, though, a wide cross section of Americans welcomed the transformation from an antiquated system of disaggregated, hidden, politicized, indirect, and regressive taxes to a centralized, transparent, professionally administered regime dedicated to direct and progressive taxation. Even though the income tax only touched a fraction of American households, affluent taxpayers regularly lined up to pay their taxes (see Figure 7.1). The bold new ideas about the modern fiscal state articulated by reformers well before World War I had by the end of the 1920s become an accepted part of the vocabulary of mainstream social, political, and economic discourse, as well as the institutions of American life.

Elite Discourse and the Ascent to a New Fiscal Order

Even before the end of the Great War, as we have seen, national policymakers were debating competing visions of the postwar fiscal regime. The October 1919 correspondence between Daniel Roper and Russell Leffingwell illustrated how the war experience had convinced even some "Wall

[10] Karen Orren and Stephen Skowronek, "Regimes and Regime Building in American Government: A Review of the Literature on the 1940s," *Political Science Quarterly* 113:4 (winter 1998–9), 689–702, 693; Orren and Skowronek, *The Search for American Political Development* (New York: Cambridge University Press, 2004), Chapter 3.

FIGURE 7.1. 1920 Taxpayers Lined Up to Pay Their Income Taxes. This circa 1920 photograph depicts individual taxpayers lined up at a local Bureau of Internal Revenue office to pay their income taxes. Courtesy of the Library of Congress, Prints & Photographs Division, LC-DIG-npcc-20560.

Street Republicans" of the administrative advantages and democratic promise of a tax system based on the principle of "ability to pay."[11] Other former Treasury attorneys also did their part to bolster the new fiscal regime. Following the war, many of these legal professionals returned to the private sector and capitalized on their new-found expertise and access to political power. Yet, the influence of their wartime service persisted.

After the war, Thomas B. Love leveraged his Washington contacts to build a lucrative Dallas-based law practice, to admonish local citizens for not paying their taxes, and to reengage with Texas politics, especially with regard to Prohibition.[12] But Love did not forget the lessons he learned from running the Bureau of War Risk Insurance about the "great social

[11] Daniel C. Roper to Russell C. Leffingwell, October 17, 1919; Leffingwell to Roper, October 20, 1919; Roper to Leffingwell, October 17, 1919, Record Group 56, Excess Profits Folder, NARA II. Even after he left the Treasury, Leffingwell continued to consult with his handpicked successor, S. Parker Gilbert Jr., about the development of tax policy. Murray, "Bureaucracy and Bi-partisanship in Taxation," 217–19.

[12] Thomas B. Love to Kermit Roosevelt, September 23, 1919, Kermit Roosevelt Papers, Library of Congress, Washington, D.C.; Thomas B. Love to Daniel Roper, December 13, 1918, Thomas B. Love Papers, Dallas Historical Society, Dallas, Tex.

principle of mutuality and cooperation." In fact, his successful tenure in the Treasury Department convinced him of the need to extend government insurance to a wider swath of industrial workers beyond public employees. Toward the end of the conflict, Love thus began pushing for increased government regulation of industrial relations, arguing that the new fiscal polity could use tax laws to manage how private employers provided disability insurance. Love's advocacy did not directly address the conceptual, juridical, or bureaucratic aspects of taxation; he was arguing, instead, that tax policy could be used instrumentally to promote other social goals. Still, his support for an expanded system of government-mandated insurance illustrated how the war experience had opened new perspectives on the growing and robust role of the positive state.[13]

While Love was endorsing government-mandated workers' insurance, Daniel Roper was reaching out to the business community to convince them of the necessity of making permanent the dramatic changes wrought by the war. Even as he was planning his exit from the Bureau of Internal Revenue (BIR), Roper was meeting regularly with business groups to explain how the war had precipitated a sea change in American public finance. In an address before the Business Man's Club of Cincinnati, the BIR Commissioner proudly proclaimed that "the income and excess profits taxes constitute our main sources of revenue and typify the transformation that has been wrought by the last decade." Roper may have been troubled in his private correspondence with Leffingwell about retaining the "inconvenience" of an income tax, but in his public appearances he celebrated the monumental shift occasioned by the war. As he plainly put it, the new-found significance of graduated taxes on incomes, profits, and wealth transfers meant that "We have thus crossed the threshold of a new era in internal revenue taxation."[14]

[13] Thomas B. Love, "The Social Significance of War Risk Insurance," *Annals of the American Academy of Political and Social Science* 79 (1918), 46–51; "The Government's Responsibility for Disabled Industrial Workers," *Proceedings of the Academy of Political Science in the City of New York* 8:2 (February 1919), 152–6. For more on Love, see Lewis L. Gould, *Progressives and Prohibitionists: Texas Democrats in the Wilson Era* (Austin: University of Texas Press, 1973), 60–3; Sue E. Winton Moore, *Thomas B. Love, Texas Democrat, 1901–1949* (Master's thesis, University of Texas, 1971).

[14] Daniel C. Roper to Bernard Baruch, August 26, 1920, Box 1, Alphabetical Correspondence, Folder Ba-Bf, 1918–43; "Business Taxation in the Period of Reconstruction, Address of Daniel C. Roper before Business Man's Club of Cincinnati, Ohio," November 20, 1918, Box 27, Folder: Addresses, 1913–1930, Daniel C. Roper Papers, David M. Rubenstein Rare Book & Manuscript Library, Duke University, Durham, N.C. [hereinafter DCRP].

Roper took great pride in having helped usher the nation across this historic threshold. His speech reminded businessmen and wealthy taxpayers that it was the "open minded and even handed administration of tax laws" that had been integral to building public confidence in the wartime fiscal state. Such mutual trust between private interests and the public sector would need to continue if the graduated tax system was to survive the postwar reconstruction. "The citizens must be made to respect the law," declared Roper, "and, in turn, the Government must manifest confidence in its citizens." Taxpayers and government officials alike would need to acknowledge the reciprocal benefits and duties that accompanied the new fiscal citizenship. "The intelligent unity that has been prompted by necessity and patriotism will be perpetuated by recognition and understanding of the obligations of citizenship and by appreciation of the fact that the results secured are of the utmost advantage to both the Government and the people," Roper announced.[15]

The taxpayer's civic duties and obligations were, for Roper, obvious. Any citizen who failed to fulfill his or her portion of this new social contract by evading taxes was not only violating a legal duty, but also a moral one. In language that echoed the teachings of the progressive public finance economists, Roper explained the ramifications of tax evasion:

> Only from a narrow and essentially selfish and shortsighted viewpoint, can the individual propose to himself the evasion of tax liability as a desirable course of action. The damage to those who follow this course may be intangible but it is none the less real. It breaks down moral fiber and impedes the highest degree of intellectual development. The same unfortunate defect is produced in the individual who employs in dealing with his fellowmen the methods and practices which do not accord with the ethics of modern business.[16]

By linking tax evasion with unethical commercial behavior, Roper attempted to animate a theme that would resonate with his business audiences.

Roper also stressed more pragmatic concerns. Speaking before businessmen familiar with the importance of balance sheets and revenue statements, Roper identified the structural pressures on the federal budget – pressures that would require the continued maintenance of a robust, revenue-generating administrative machinery. In an April 1919 address to the Illinois Manufacturers' Association, aptly titled "What Shall We

[15] Roper, "Business Taxation in the Period of Reconstruction;" Roper, "Personality in Service," April 18, 1925, Box 27, "Folder: Address, 1913–30," DCRP.

[16] Roper, "Business Taxation in the Period of Reconstruction."

Do with the Income Tax?" Roper explained how recent economic and social conditions placed a floor on the efforts of either political party to dismantle the existing tax regime. In addition to servicing the war debt and providing for veterans' benefits, the national government, Roper reminded his listeners, also had to deal with a new "social development:" Prohibition. The ratification of the Eighteenth Amendment and the enactment of the Volstead Act toward the end of the war marked the beginning of Prohibition, and the end of a significant source of internal revenue. As we have seen, the relationship between temperance and tax reform was complex. But for income tax advocates like Roper, one thing was clear: Prohibition meant that a principal source of taxation was "completely removed."[17]

Besides identifying these new structural constraints, Roper explained why a seemingly complex system of taxing incomes, profits, and estates was still necessary even after the conflict. In contrast to Republican officials, like Will Hays, who were clamoring for a swift dispatching of the wartime regime under the banner of "tax simplification," Roper emphasized how legal complexity was inherent in any modern tax system, especially one premised on taxing individuals and businesses based on their ability to pay. "The theory of the income tax requires that the ability of every taxpayer be accurately determined," Roper announced. "The law is intricate because provisions have been written into it with the express purpose of making the incidence of the tax fair and impartial."[18]

Roper did not elaborate on why taxpaying ability was the proper conceptual foundation for the new tax system, perhaps because by this time it had become an accepted part of the everyday vocabulary. Yet, it was clear that taxes were not merely the price for government services; there was no reference to how taxation might correspond with the benefits provided by government. Rather, Roper took it for granted that taxpaying faculty had become the touchstone for modern taxation. "Having ascertained with care and approximate accuracy the amount necessary to maintain the Government," Roper informed one business group in 1925, "the taxes to meet this budget should be levied and collected in accordance with that ability of the citizens to pay." A phrase and idea that was

[17] Daniel C. Roper, "What Should We Do with the Income Tax?" Box 27, Folder: Addresses, 1913–30, DCRP.

[18] Ibid.

once fraught with highly charged political meaning had by the 1920s become a well-accepted proposition.[19]

Just as ability to pay was premised on notions of fairness, the administrative complexity of the new tax laws was similarly grounded in the process of accurately determining "net income" in a just and equitable manner. From the start, revenue reformers believed that taxpayers were entitled to deduct the costs related to the production of income. Following this principle frequently meant designing complex rules and regulations that could ensure that similarly situated taxpayers were treated similarly. Yet, as rates climbed during the war and new levies were established, the laws and regulations governing deductions and the determination of net income and excess or war profits became increasingly complex. Calculating these important figures accurately and fairly became more challenging. Roper believed that maintaining administrative attention on accurate and fair assessments would have long-term beneficial repercussions by fortifying public trust in government. "It must be remembered also that we are establishing a basis of taxation which may be expected to endure for many years," he declared. "The problem will not be difficult in the future, if a sound basis is established now."[20]

Roper may have been overly optimistic about the future challenges of administering an income tax system, but he certainly believed that inculcating a taxpaying culture was critical to the continued success of the new tax regime. Although he assured business leaders that the BIR was doing its part to hire and train the best field agents, the income tax rested at bottom on the quasi-voluntary compliance of citizens. "The income tax came from the people and it must be supported by the people," declared Roper.

> The most important function of the Bureau of Internal Revenue is going to be not so much to enforce compliance with the law, but rather to intelligently direct the voluntary action of the people. It is a great and serious test of our citizenship. Every good citizen who desires the perpetuation of Government institutions and the peace and security of our people should regard it as his duty to set the best possible example in meeting the requirement of this law.[21]

19 Roper, "Personality in Service," 2.

20 Roper, "What Should We Do with the Income Tax?" 2, 5.

21 Ibid., 5. For more on the theoretical importance of "quasi-voluntary compliance" to tax collections, see Margaret Levi, *Of Rule and Revenue* (Berkeley: University of California Press, 1988), 52–5.

Since the postwar income tax remained principally a "rich man's tax," Roper was underscoring how the wealthy elite had an important civic obligation to pay their taxes, and thus to serve as leaders of the commonwealth.

Meeting these civic obligations was no easy task. Roper understood that the complexity of the tax code compelled taxpayers "to secure competent advice." Because of such growing demand, "thousands of consulting services have been established throughout the country." Roper feared, however, that many of these new services were "not competent to advise taxpayers and frequently exact fees that are exorbitant." Though he was careful not to discourage the use of "competent lawyers and accountants" – Roper himself would soon embark on a lucrative position in the private sector advising corporate taxpayers – he contended that businessmen needed to be careful in selecting their tax counsel. In a less than subtle attempt to further the growing stratification of the tax professions, Roper recommended that businessmen trust "those individuals and firms who are well known to be substantial and reliable and whose membership adheres to the high ethics of the American professions."[22]

Regardless of the type of tax counsel they hired, Roper believed that all taxpayers needed to follow their own conscience when it came to meeting their fiscal obligations. To further that aim, the commissioner did not hesitate in linking sacrifices on the home front with those made on the battlefield. With the ravages of the war still fresh in the minds of his listeners, Roper frequently concluded his speeches to business associations with a reference to how an honest, taxpaying citizen could identify with the battle-worn soldier – both, after all, had done their part. "When it is all over," Roper concluded, the civic-minded taxpayer could share "the comforting thought with the soldier who risked his life, 'I, too, have done my full duty.'"[23]

If Roper became one of the key intermediaries between the fiscal state and the business community, Arthur Ballantine served a similar mediating function between the state and legal professionals. After tendering his resignation to Roper just two weeks after the armistice, Ballantine began turning his attention back to his career as a corporate lawyer. Having enhanced his reputation during the war as a tax technician and having

22 Roper, "What Should We Do with the Income Tax?" 5.

23 Ibid., 6–7, 8. Policymakers and political activists would make similar pleas during World War II. James Sparrow, *Warfare State: World War II Americans and the Age of Big Government* (New York: Oxford University Press, 2011), Chapter 4.

developed numerous contacts in the business and legal communities, Ballantine was looking ahead to his return to the private sector. His goal was to extend his legal practice beyond general corporate law into taxation. Rather than return to Boston, though, he relocated to New York City where he joined some Harvard Law School classmates in starting the Wall Street law firm of Root, Clark, Buckner and Ballantine.[24]

In the process of reinvigorating his private career, Ballantine became a leading speaker throughout the country. As an esteemed member of the Massachusetts and New York State bars, he was frequently invited to share his experiences and his tax law knowledge with other attorneys and elite citizens. Indeed, Ballantine became a popular speaker at numerous well-attended bar association meetings across the nation. On several of these speaking occasions, Ballantine used the opportunity to convince his listeners that, despite the political rhetoric of retrenchment, direct and progressive taxation had become a permanent part of American law and political economy. "While Congress may modify the rates and make the tax simpler and more just in its application," Ballantine announced, direct and progressive taxation "will undoubtedly be retained as a principal source of revenue."[25]

Like Roper, Ballantine had come to this conclusion through his war experience. The war years demonstrated, to Ballantine and many other ambivalent state-builders, the flexibility and effectiveness of taxing incomes, profits, and estates. The postwar budget deficit, likewise, placed structural pressure on the need to maintain a productive source of federal revenues. More importantly, however, Ballantine believed that "the income tax is unquestionably here to stay" because it had become a part of popular notions of social justice and civic responsibility. It had become woven into the fabric of mainstream American legal, political, and social discourse and culture. "A large part of the tax burden is going to be placed on income and profits taxes," Ballantine informed his brethren at the bar, "because, whatever we may think about it, there is a conviction

[24] Arthur A. Ballantine to Daniel C. Roper, November 25, 1918; Roper to Ballantine, November 29, 1918, Box 1 Alphabetical Correspondence, "Folder Ba-Bf, 1918–1943," DCRP; Melvin I. Urofsky, "Ballantine, Arthur Atwood," John A. Garraty, ed., *Dictionary of American Biography, Supplement Six, 1956–1960* (New York: Charles Scribner's Sons, 1990), 33–4; Ajay K. Mehrotra, "Ballantine, Arthur Atwood," Roger K. Newman, ed. *Yale Biographical Dictionary of American Law* (New Haven: Yale University Press, 2009), 27–8.

[25] Arthur A. Ballantine, "The Lawyer and the Income Tax," December 10, 1920 (Annual Meeting of the Massachusetts Bar Association), Box 24, Arthur A. Ballantine Papers, Herbert Hoover Presidential Library, West Branch, Iowa [hereinafter AABP].

on the part of the average voter that this system of taxation, based on ability to pay, is a fair system, fairer perhaps than any other." Like Roper, Ballantine did not elaborate on the popular assent to the "ability-to-pay" principle, perhaps because he too believed that after decades of prewar agitation and a global conflict in which income and profits tax revenues sustained the fighting forces and creditworthiness of the national government, it was a foregone conclusion that most Americans supported a direct and graduated tax system based on taxpaying ability. By the early1920s, Ballantine also understood that the nation had entered a new era of taxation.[26]

Yet not everyone was convinced that the postwar decade was the dawn of a new fiscal epoch. There was still a great deal of social and political resistance, especially among the main targets of the new progressive tax regime: the wealthy elite. One of the central aims of the speaking engagements that Ballantine and Roper took on was to persuade lawyers, jurists, businessmen, and other elite citizens to support the new tax regime. This frequently meant appealing indirectly to individual and associational self-interests. In the process of educating elite professionals, Ballantine and Roper did not explicitly refer to the personal and professional benefits for the bar and bench that accompanied the advent of new era of taxation. They did not emphasize how the new tax laws also created tremendous demand for what Roper referred to as "competent lawyers and accountants." Crass appeals to material and social benefits remained in the subtext of such formal addresses.

The pecuniary rewards of the new fiscal regime, however, were never far from the minds of these former policymakers. Like many of the other lawyers who joined the Treasury Department during the war, Ballantine had been lured to Washington by a mix of civic duty, patriotic pride, and the promise of postwar riches – by calls for everyone to share in wartime sacrifice and by claims similar to Roper's that "this tax business is likely to develop into quite a thing for lawyers."[27] Yet "this tax business" could

[26] Arthur A. Ballantine, "Practical Aspects of the Income Tax," June 4, 1921 (Before Louisiana Bar Association), Box 24, AABP. Ballantine also testified in the early 1930s, when he was an Assistant Treasury Secretary in the Hoover administration, about the efficacy of the World War I excess-profits tax. Arthur A. Ballantine, "War Policies in Taxation, Statement Before the War Policies Commission," May 20, 1931, RG 56 – General Records of the Office of the Secretary of the Treasury, Box 187, Folder "Tax – Excess Profits & War Profits. 1923–32," NARA II.

[27] Daniel C. Roper, "What Should We Do with the Income Tax?"; E. Barrett Prettyman, "Autobiography of a an Obscure Man at Forty," unpublished manuscript, Box 122, E. Barrett Prettyman Papers, Library of Congress, Washington, D.C.

develop into "quite a thing for lawyers," and other tax professionals, only if these experts and their elite clientele could be convinced that direct and graduated taxes had become a permanent part of the new legal order. Since there was still some pressure for a return to the previous regime of consumption taxes based on the tariff, as well as new calls for a national sales tax, Ballantine and Roper knew that they needed to do their part to convince elite lawyers and businessmen of the popular support and private benefits of the new direct and progressive tax system.

Juridical Acquiescence and the Practical Framework for an Income Tax

The former Treasury lawyers were not alone in their attempts to influence elite taxpayers and their tax counsel. Indeed, in many ways, their remarks reflected how the courts themselves had begun the process of accepting the legal legitimacy of the new tax regime. After the war, the U.S. Supreme Court followed its 1916 validation of the national income tax with a series of decisions demonstrating its increasing concern about the functional framework of the new income tax system. Ironically, even as the Court was seemingly limiting the scope of the Sixteenth Amendment, it was addressing more pragmatic concerns related to the proper definition of income and the fair and effective administration of the new tax regime.

Practicing lawyers and the legal academy quickly took notice. By the mid-1920s, a new series of legal treatises focusing on federal income taxation began to supplement, and in many cases replace, the late-nineteenth-century texts on subnational taxation written by Thomas M. Cooley, W. H. Burroughs, and Francis Hilliard. Leading law schools, in turn, refocused their pedagogy accordingly by integrating the analysis of federal cases, U.S. Treasury regulations, and the provisions of new national revenue acts into their tax law classes. As a result, subsequent generations of lawyers, jurists, and policymakers came of age firmly believing that graduated taxes on incomes, profits, and wealth transfers were a central and relatively uncontested part of a modern life. In fact, by the end of the 1920s, the juridical acquiescence to direct and progressive taxation revealed the extent to which elite, legal discourse had come to embrace the conceptual revolution in tax policy that had begun in the late nineteenth century.

Before such acceptance was cemented, the Supreme Court itself had to work through the constitutional implications of the Sixteenth Amendment and the wartime revenue laws. That process began in 1916 when the Court, in *Brushaber v. Union Pacific Railroad Co.*, upheld the 1913 income tax against a taxpayer challenge that progressive income taxes violated the specific language of the Sixteenth Amendment and the Due Process Clause. The taxpayer in this case was a stockholder of the Union Pacific Railroad who was attempting to prevent the corporation from withholding taxes on his behalf in compliance with the administrative aspects of the 1913 law. Justice Edward White, who had been one of the dissenters in *Pollock* and who was Chief Justice at the time, wrote for a unanimous Court in *Brushaber*.[28]

White argued that the Sixteenth Amendment was not meant to be a new limitation on the national government's plenary taxing powers. Rather, the amendment was a direct repudiation of *Pollock*. Referring back to *Veazie Bank v. Fenno*, the 1869 case upholding a federal tax on state bank notes, White declared that the Constitution's original apportionment and uniformity requirements were "not so much a limitation upon the complete and all-embracing authority to tax, but in their essence were simply regulations concerning the mode in which the plenary power was to be exerted." Having reduced apportionment to a mere regulation "concerning the mode" of taxation, White went on to declare that the Sixteenth Amendment did not "purport to confer power to levy income taxes in a generic sense." Article I, Section 8 of the original Constitution had already empowered Congress with such plenary taxing authority. Rather, wrote White, "the whole purpose of the Amendment was to relieve all income taxes when imposed from apportionment from a consideration of the source whence the income was derived." Simply put, the Sixteenth Amendment eviscerated the claim in *Pollock* that a tax on income derived from property was a direct tax that needed to be apportioned. Lastly, White summarily dismissed the Due Process claim as a baseless attempt to find a new way to limit Congress's plenary taxing powers.[29] For many contemporary observers, the Court's decision had

[28] 240 U.S. 1 (1916). In recent years, *Brushaber* has attracted new found attention as part of a debate among legal scholars about the meaning of the direct tax clause. Erik M. Jensen, "The Apportionment of 'Direct Taxes': Are Consumption Taxes Constitutional?" *Columbia Law Review* 91 (1997), 2334–2419; Bruce Ackerman, "Taxation and the Constitution," *Columbia Law Review* 99 (1999), 1–58; Leo P. Martinez, "'To Lay and Collect Taxes': The Constitutional Case for Progressive Taxation," *Yale Law & Policy Review* 18 (1999), 111–54.

[29] 240 U.S. 1 (1916), 13, 17–18, 24. More specifically, the Court held that there was no basis for reliance on the Due Process Clause "since it is equally well settled that such clause is not a limitation upon the taxing power conferred upon Congress by the Constitution; in other words, that the Constitution does not conflict with itself by

"settled" the constitutionality of an income tax; the case was even hailed as "the final triumph" of congressional attempts "to bring within the taxing power of the United States the productive field of private incomes."[30]

If *Brushaber* had "settled" the constitutionality of an income tax, the Court still needed to clarify more practical and seemingly mundane legal issues about the new tax system – issues such as what precisely constituted taxable income and when such income was attributable to a taxpayer. By resolving such questions in subsequent rulings, the Supreme Court not only helped define the specific legal parameters of the new tax regime, it also solidified the judicial commitment to the progressive taxation of income. Indeed, even when the Court attempted to limit the reach of the Sixteenth Amendment, as it did in the landmark case of *Eisner v. Macomber* (1920), the Court indirectly and perhaps unwittingly set the foundation for a more workable income tax system.[31]

In *Macomber*, the Court was asked to determine whether receipt of a common stock dividend constituted taxable income. Myrtle H. Macomber, the taxpayer in the suit, was a stockholder in the Standard Oil Company of California. In 1916, Standard Oil issued a pro rata 2-for-1 stock dividend to all shareholders. Although the Treasury Department had previously equivocated on the taxability of stock dividends, the Revenue Act of 1916 expressly treated stock dividends as taxable income.[32] Macomber challenged the statute. Justice Mahlon Pitney, writing for a 5–4 majority, agreed with the taxpayer, holding that stock dividends were not taxable because they were not "income" within the specific

conferring, upon the one hand, a taxing power, and taking the same power away, on the other, by the limitations of the due process clause." Ibid., 24.

30 "The Income Tax and the Sixteenth Amendment," *Harvard Law Review* 29:5 (1916), 536–8; "B.M.K.", "Constitutional Law: The Constitutionality of the Federal Income Tax of 1913," *University of Pennsylvania Law Review* 64:5 (1916), 498–502, 498. Present-day constitutional scholars have been more forthright in celebrating *Brushaber*. With this case, constitutional law scholar Bruce Ackerman has written, "the Chief Justice triumphantly led his Court into a brave new world where Congress had wide discretion to pursue distributive justice through progressive taxation." Ackerman, "Taxation and the Constitution," 40.

31 252 U.S. 189 (1920). For more on the historical context and continued significance of *Macomber*, see Marjorie E. Kornhauser, "The Story of *Macomber*: The Continuing Legacy of Realization," in Paul Caron, ed., *Tax Stories* (New York: Foundation Press, 2009), 93–135; Charlotte Crane, "*Pollock*, *Macomber*, and the Role of the Federal Courts in the Development of the Income Tax in the United States," *Law & Contemporary Problems* 73:1 (2010), 1–23.

32 T.D. 2163, 17 Treas. Dec. Int. Rev. 114, rev'd, T.D. 2274, 17 Treas. Dec. Int. Rev. 279 (1915); Revenue Act of 1916, 39 Stat. 756.

meaning of the Sixteenth Amendment. Reading the amendment narrowly, the majority defined income "as the gain derived from labor, from capital, or from both combined." The Sixteenth Amendment had expressly removed the apportionment requirement for "taxes on income, from whatever source derived." Instead of reading this language as a capacious definition of income, the Court focused on the literal meaning of the sources of income. Since the stock dividends had not been separated or "derived" from the taxpayer's original capital investment or from her labor, Pitney ruled that they were not income within the precise meaning of the amendment.[33]

Even though the majority's constitutional argument was controversial, and ultimately undermined by subsequent decisions, Pitney's economic logic and practical reasoning was sound. The issuance of stock dividends, by themselves, did not provide Macomber with an accretion to wealth, as Edwin Seligman explained in a significant article included in the taxpayer's legal briefs.[34] Macomber was no richer after the dividends than before. Although the value of her capital investment had increased over time, the issuance of dividends was not the appropriate time to tax such earlier appreciation. Moreover, since the dividends were in the form of stock, rather than cash, they may not have accurately represented "the antecedent accumulation of profits," nor did they provide the cash or liquidity necessary to pay a tax.[35]

The stock dividends may have reflected long-term appreciation in the value of the corporation, but until such appreciation was separated from the original capital investment, the majority reasoned, a taxpayer did not realize such gain as taxable income. As Justice Pitney put it:

> The essential and controlling fact is that the stockholder has received nothing out of the company's assets for his separate use and benefit; on the contrary, every dollar of his original investment, together with whatever accretions and accumulations have resulted from employment of his money and that of the other stockholders in the business of the company, still remains the property of the company, and subject to business risks which may result in wiping out the entire investment. Having regard to the very truth of the matter, to substance and not to form, he has received nothing

[33] 252 U.S. 189 (1920), 207; Sixteenth Amendment, U.S. Constitution. For more on the spread of stock ownership during this period, see Julia C. Ott, *When Wall Street Met Main Street: The Quest for an Investors' Democracy* (Cambridge, Mass.: Harvard University Press, 2011); Lawrence E. Mitchell, *The Speculation Economy: How Finance Triumphed over Industry* (San Francisco: Berrett-Koehler Publishers, 2007).

[34] Edwin R. A. Seligman, "Are Stock Dividends Income?" *American Economic Review* 9:3 (1919), 517–36; Kornhauser, "The Story of *Macomber*," 60.

[35] 252 U.S. 189 (1920), 212.

> that answers the definition of income within the meaning of the Sixteenth Amendment.[36]

Pitney's analysis of the economic substance of the transaction was correct, but his constitutional claim seemed more than a bit attenuated. In receiving a stock – rather than cash – dividend, Macomber clearly maintained her investment in Standard Oil, "subject to business risks." But did that mean constitutionally that income could only be realized, and hence taxed, if it was "derived from labor, from capital, or from both combined," as the majority ruled? Did the Sixteenth Amendment stand for the proposition that the *sources* of income could determine taxability?

Justice Oliver Wendell Holmes Jr. thought not. In a characteristically curt dissent, Holmes contended that the majority seemed to have strained the popular understanding of the new amendment. "I think the word 'income' in the Sixteenth Amendment," wrote Holmes, "should be read in a sense most obvious to the common understanding at the time of its adoption." For Holmes, that meant eliminating fine, granular distinctions about the constitutional meaning of a direct tax, such as whether income was "derived" from a particular source. "The known purpose of this Amendment was to get rid of nice questions as to what might be direct taxes," wrote Holmes, "and I cannot doubt that most people not lawyers would suppose when they voted for it that they put a question like the present to rest."[37]

Many well-known legal commentators concurred with Justice Holmes. Columbia University constitutional law professor Thomas Reed Powell, who had been consulting with Arthur Ballantine about the *Macomber* decision, agreed with Holmes's common-sense understanding of the Sixteenth Amendment. In an article in the *Columbia Law Review*, Powell declared that the amendment was "widely regarded as in effect a 'recall' of the *Pollock* case."[38] To the chagrin of Powell and many other legal experts, the dead hand of *Pollock* still seemed to govern from the grave. For later generations of scholars, the Court's slim majority in *Macomber* was reminiscent of a laissez-faire constitutionalism that had come to be

36 Ibid., 211.

37 Ibid., 220 (Holmes, J. dissenting). Justice Louis Brandeis also dissented in this case, with a much lengthier and more muddled opinion questioning the majority's economic logic. Ibid., 220–38.

38 Thomas Reed Powell, "Stock Dividends, Direct Taxes, and the Sixteenth Amendment," *Columbia Law Review* 20:536–49 (1920), 538. Thomas Reed Powell to Arthur A. Ballantine, Dec. 30, 1920, Folder D1, Memo in consultant work, 1918–19, Thomas Reed Powell Papers, Harvard Law School Library, Cambridge, Mass. [hereinafter HLSL].

identified with the Court's 1905 decision in *Lochner v. New York* – a constitutionalism that seemed to privilege individual property rights over the growing powers of the positive state.[39] Anti-statist Republicans like Will Hays no doubt welcomed the Court's decision to read the Sixteenth Amendment narrowly.

Macomber was hardly the last word on the constitutional definition of income, however. Although in the following years the Court issued several decisions supporting *Macomber's* constitutional reasoning, namely that taxable income had to be *derived* from either labor or capital, or both,[40] in subsequent decades the Court gradually began to erode the constitutional importance of the sources of income. By 1940, the Court had effectively ruled that taxable gain could be determined without regard to the source of income and without segregating or separating such gain from capital. Within two decades, the principle that income had to be realized before it was taxable had been whittled down from a constitutional requirement to a simple rule "founded on administrative convenience."[41]

Still, the practical aspects of *Macomber* endured, illustrating the deep irony and lasting legacy of the Court's holding. Tax authorities agreed with the majority's argument that mere accretions in wealth would be difficult to tax. First, there were the administrative problems. Because of the uncertainty surrounding the changing value of investments and because increases in so-called "paper profits" did not provide cash with which to pay taxes, taxing stock dividends seemed patently unfair. Second, because simple appreciation in an investment without some kind of intervening disposition event still left the taxpayer "subject to business risk," taxing a shareholder when they received stock dividends appeared to be an inopportune time. In sum, the Court's contention that general accretions in wealth should not be taxed became embedded in modern

[39] 198 U.S. 45 (1905). Present-day scholars continue to link *Macomber* with *Lochner*. Jed Handelsman Shugerman, *The People's Courts: Pursuing Judicial Independence in America* (Cambridge, Mass.: Harvard University Press, 2012), 161. Kirk Stark has even referred to *Macomber* as the "*Lochner* of federal income taxation." Kirk J. Stark, "The Unfulfilled Tax Legacy of Justice Robert H. Jackson, *Tax Law Review* 54:171 (2001), 198, 214.

[40] See, e.g., *Merchants' Loan & Trust Co. v. Smietanka*, 255 U.S. 509 (1921); *Bowers v. Kerbaugh-Empire Co.*, 271 U.S. 170 (1926).

[41] *Helvering v. Bruun*, 309 U.S. 461 (1940); *Helvering v. Horst*, 311 U.S. 112 (1940), 116. By the mid-1950s, with the case of *Commissioner v. Glenshaw Glass Co.*, the constitutional logic of *Macomber* had been eviscerated. *Commissioner v. Glenshaw Glass Co.*, 348 U.S. 426 (1955). For more on *Glenshaw Glass*, see Joseph M. Dodge, "The Story of *Glenshaw Glass*: Towards a Modern Concept of Gross Income," in *Tax Stories*, ed. Caron, 15–51.

American tax law. It became identified as the "realization requirement." While realization as a concept was not new, *Macomber* imbued it with great constitutional significance.[42] Even though that constitutional meaning incrementally dissipated, *Macomber* came to stand for the practical rule that economic appreciation in capital investments was not generally taxable until there was a realization event, some sort of "sale or other disposition of property."[43]

It is highly unlikely that Justice Pitney and the majority could have envisioned that, in the process of curtailing the scope of the Sixteenth Amendment, they were also unwittingly establishing one of the defining aspects of the modern, realization-based income tax system. The short-term holding of the case did not match its far-reaching implications. The realization requirement not only clarified what was taxable income; it also helped resolve the issue of *when* income ought to be attributed to taxpayer-investors. The Court, in short, was helping to give some constitutional meaning to the definition of income. By providing one of the pivotal practical rules for the administration of an income tax, the Court inadvertently helped to ensure the continued vitality of the new tax system.[44]

Following the Court's lead, tax professionals were doing their part to further the juridical acceptance of the new tax regime. Just as Roper and Ballantine were publicly addressing trade groups and bar associations, and just as the Supreme Court was providing the practical framework for a workable income tax system, leading tax lawyers and academics were writing new federal tax treatises, which summarized the leading cases, Treasury rulings, and new statutory provisions regarding federal income, profits, and wealth-transfer taxes.[45] Earlier tax treatises had frequently combined national and state law coverage. After the war, however, the

42 The Treasury Department and IRS regularly referred to the need to "realize" income before it could be taxed. The Supreme Court's elevation of this idea "gave added weight to this concept of income and ensured that realization played a large role in the development of the tax laws." Kornhauser, "The Story of *Macomber*," 97.

43 This concept remains part of current tax law. U.S. Internal Revenue Code, §1001(a). See also Edward J. McCaffery, *The Oxford Introductions to U.S. Law – Income Tax Law* (New York: Oxford University Press, 2012), 12–15, 36–40.

44 Crane, "*Pollock*, *Macomber*, and the Role of the Federal Courts." As the legal scholar Paul Caron has explained, though *Macomber* did not invent the realization concept, "it embedded it so early and so deeply into the fabric of our tax system that any attempt to eliminate it now would face insurmountable political and institutional obstacles." Paul L. Caron, "Tax Archaeology," in *Tax Stories*, 4.

45 George E. Holmes, *Federal Income Tax* (Indianapolis: Bobbs-Merrill Co., 1920); Herbert C. Fooks, *Leading Cases, Federal Taxation* (Federalsburg, Md., 1926). At the same

explosive growth in federal case law and Treasury rulings led to a great demand among tax professionals for a synthesis of the changing aspects of the new tax system and for a guide to lead them through the labyrinth of new tax rules and procedures.[46]

George E. Holmes was a New York City tax lawyer and one of the first to capitalize on this new demand. A former tax newsletter editor at the Corporation Trust Company, Holmes established his own legal practice soon before the war. His firm prospered, attracting affluent clients and sharp young lawyers like Randolph E. Paul, who would go on to became a leading New Deal tax expert and a founding member of the New York law firm of Paul, Weiss. When the Revenue Act of 1916 broadened the scale and scope of the new tax system, Holmes began his prolific publishing career as a tax treatise writer.[47] As one of the first attorneys to specialize in federal income tax matters, Holmes quickly became an authority on the topic. During the war, he assisted Thomas S. Adams and the U.S. Treasury Department, as well as the American Economic Association, with the regular reevaluations of the excess-profits tax, including the global comparative analysis of the levy. Throughout the 1920s, moreover, Holmes continuously updated his tax treatises and served as a leading member of professional organizations like the National Tax Association.[48]

In the 1925 edition of his *Federal Income Tax* treatise, Holmes reflected back on the tremendous legal transformation that had occurred within the decade. From his perspective, "some knowledge of the income tax" had become "an essential part . . . of the equipment of the practicing attorney." Any legal professional "who does not to some degree familiarize himself with the intricacies of the [income tax] law runs serious risks,"

time that Holmes and Fooks were educating lawyers, the accountants Robert H. Montgomery and George O. May were performing the same function for their professional brethren. Robert H. Montgomery, *Income Tax Procedure* (New York: Ronald Press, 1921); George O. May, *Twenty-five Years of Accounting Responsibility, 1911–1936; Essays and Discussions* (Lawrence, Kans.: Scholars Book Co., 1936).

46 See, e.g., Henry C. Black, *Treatise on the Law of Income Taxation under Federal and State Laws* (Kansas City, Mo.: Vernon Law Book Co., 1916).

47 George E. Holmes, *Federal Income Tax: Including Tax on Undistributed Net Income, Capital Stock Tax, and War Excess Profits Tax* (Chicago: Callaghan, 1917). For more on the significance of the 1916 Revenue Act, see W. Elliot Brownlee, "Wilson and Financing the Modern State: The Revenue Act of 1916," *Proceedings of the American Philosophical Society* 129 (1985), 173–210.

48 "Seventh Session: Federal Taxes," in *Proceedings of the Fourteenth Annual Conference on Taxation under the Auspices of the National Tax Association* (New York: National Tax Association, 1922), 301–26; "Blackmer Lawyer Killed in Subway," *New York Times,* June 3, 1932, 42.

wrote Holmes. "It is realized now that taxation is one of the most important branches of the law." Holmes's celebration of the new-found salience of the income tax was no doubt partly self-serving. Just as Ballantine and Roper were aware that their public speeches could redound to the benefit of tax professionals like themselves, Holmes surely understood that he had a personal stake in ensuring the long-term durability of the new tax system.[49]

Still, Holmes's primary mission in updating his latest version of the treatise was to demonstrate that by the mid-1920s the U.S. fiscal regime had "witnessed a complete change." The high-level plateauing of rates and the proliferation of state-level income taxes, Holmes reasoned, "have made the subject too important to be any longer disregarded." Despite all the political rhetoric about tax cuts and fiscal retrenchment, any sensible lawyer who took stock of the recent changes understood, as Roper had put it, that the country and the legal profession had "crossed the threshold of a new era" in taxation.[50]

Among the many signs that the income tax had become firmly embedded in American law, one of the most telling, as Holmes pointed out, was the legal academy's growing interest in the topic. Holmes was only exaggerating slightly when he claimed that by 1925 "courses on taxation are given by nearly all the leading law schools."[51] To be sure, state and local tax courses, focusing mainly on property taxes and jurisdictional issues, had always been a staple of many law schools. The earlier writings of Judge Cooley and Frank J. Goodnow made sure of that. But by the mid-1920s, courses and casebooks on the federal taxation of incomes, profits, and wealth transfers began to appear more regularly. In 1922, Harvard Law Professor Joseph H. Beale penned what was arguably the first student-focused casebook on the leading federal tax law cases. Although Beale was best known for his work on conflicts of laws, he had earlier also authored a treatise on the state taxation of corporations. This early interest led to his 1922 casebook, which went through several editions and soon became one of the leading law school texts in the field.[52]

[49] George E. Holmes, *Federal Income Tax*, 6th ed. (Indianapolis: Bobbs-Merrill Co., 1925), iii.

[50] Ibid.

[51] Ibid.

[52] Joseph Henry Beale, *A Treatise on the Conflict of Laws*, 3 vols. (New York: Baker, Voorhis, 1935); Beale, *The Law of Foreign Corporations: And Taxation of Corporations*

Without discounting the importance of subnational taxation and jurisdictional conflicts, Beale's *Cases on Taxation* provided a comprehensive digest of nearly all the leading federal income, inheritance, and profits tax cases.[53] Nearly a quarter of the entire first edition was dedicated to the issue of "Federal Income Taxation." These pages analyzed the evolving judicial definition of income since *Macomber*, the computation of income, the allowance of permissible deductions, and several other issues related to statutory interpretation and annual accounting. Revised throughout the 1920s and into the 1930s, during the early heyday of American legal realism, Beale's subsequent editions reflected the shifting views of the legal academy, and the growing acceptance of the new tax regime. The 1924 edition, for example, included an appendix containing suggested "collateral readings," as well as problems to help familiarize the student with "the application of principles."[54]

Although Beale was frequently ridiculed by legal realists like Walter Wheeler Cook, as an old guard representative of an antiquated formalism, his overall scholarship and intellectual vision was far more wide ranging and interdisciplinary. His tax casebook, with its supplemental materials and problems, was evidence of Beale's forward thinking. Like his junior colleague Roscoe Pound, Beale proved to be a pivotal transitional figure in the development of American jurisprudence. While much of his early work, especially in conflicts of laws, stressed the formalism of mechanical rules, his larger body of scholarship, including his tax law casebook, and his institution-building suggested that he was hardly the anti-modernist that some of his critics caricatured. Indeed, in his 1914 address before the American Association of Law Schools, Beale proclaimed that the current cohort of law professors was called upon not only to continue the work of previous generations to study "the separate branches of our science," but also to take on "a more modern task: to bring the law into closer relation with the needs of contemporary life." His tax law casebook was one way in which Beale sought to bridge the gap between the law and modern life.[55]

Both Foreign and Domestic (Boston: W. J. Nagel, 1904); Beale, *Cases on Taxation* (Cambridge, Mass.: Harvard University Press, 1922).

53 Beale, *Cases on Taxation*, 368–511. The focus on jurisdictional issues was a seminal part of Harvard Law School's taxation courses. See John Leo Carten Jr. "Notes Taken for Course Work at HLS," Box V, c24, Taxation, HLSL.

54 Beale, *Cases in Taxation* (1924 ed.), "Preface," 369–77.

55 Beale quoted in John Henry Schlegel, *American Legal Realism and Empirical Social Science* (Chapel Hill: University of North Carolina Press, 1995), 45. On Beale as foil for

Like some of the other early legal realists, Beale sought to study "law in action" from a more "scientific" vantage point so as to reform the "law on the books." As Thomas Reed Powell noted in his glowing review of *Cases in Taxation*, Beale's focus on the functional aspects of tax law revealed how law on the ground was contingent upon a broader social context. "One who knows what goes on in lawyers' offices," wrote Powell, "when a problem of taxation is presented is keenly aware of the dependence of the law upon understanding of many things which traditionally lie outside the law." In later editions of the tax casebook, Beale and his junior collaborator, Columbia law professor and future New Dealer Roswell Magill, expanded the chapters on federal taxation to keep up with the proliferation of administrative regulations, formal statutory revisions, and the growing social acceptance of the new tax regime. By 1926, the casebook had gone through several editions and had become one of the dominant texts in its field. J. M. Maguire, one of Beale's junior colleagues, used the casebook regularly in his Harvard tax law classes, praising it for recognizing early on that a new tax system "held the zenith of our fiscal heavens, and for years to come will continue in that position."[56]

The Unsuccessful 1921 Sales Tax, Economic Experts, and Fiscal Myopia

The growing interest in taxation exhibited by the practicing bar and the legal academy was certainly one strong indication of just how deeply the new tax system had become embedded in the juridical order. Yet, in many ways, this legal acquiescence reflected a trend that was already occurring throughout the postwar decade at the national level of high politics. For in the corridors of Congress and the Treasury Department there was a similar, though at times halting, acknowledgment – even among Republican leaders otherwise eager to dismantle the robust revenue regime – that

the early legal realists, see Neil Duxbury, *Patterns of American Jurisprudence* (Oxford: Oxford University Press, 1995), 22–4. For a more nuanced view of Beale, see Perry Dane, "Joseph Henry Beale, Jr." in *Yale Biographical Dictionary of American Law*, 31–2.

56 Thomas Reed Powell, "Review of Cases on Taxation," *Harvard Law Review* 36:4 (1923), 499; Joseph Henry Beale and Roswell Magill, *Cases on Federal Taxation* (New York: Prentice Hall, 1926); "Memo to Professor Campbell April 1, 1933," Folder 31–1: Evaluation of Tax Problems Class, John MacArthur Maguire Papers, HLSL; J.M. Maguire, "Review of Cases on Taxation," *Harvard Law Review* 39:6 (1926), 791. Magill would continue editing the tax law casebook well into the 1930s when he became an advisor to Henry Morgenthau's Treasury Department. "Roswell Magill, Lawyer, 68, Dead," *New York Times*, December 18, 1963; Joseph J. Thorndike, "Profiles in Tax History: Roswell Magill," *Tax Notes*, January 25, 2008.

the fiscal success of the war had sealed the future fate of the direct and progressive tax system.

The early decade's historical plasticity and progressive resolve was perhaps most visible during the political debates over the 1921 Revenue Act – the same legislation that led Treasury Secretary Mellon to rebuff Will Hays for his tax-cutting exuberance. The 1921 Revenue Act was historically significant for several reasons. First, it was during the debates over this tax bill that Congress first seriously considered proposals to establish a national sales tax. Second, the social and political discussion leading up to this law provided tax experts with a critical context within which they could fortify the intellectual commitment to the new fiscal polity. Finally, the early 1920 debates were pivotal because they helped launch what would come to be known as the "Mellon Plan" for "scientific tax reform." The ultimate defeat of the sales tax proposals and the gradual curtailment of the Mellon Plan's main tenets demonstrated how the 1920s marked not an end to progressive reform, but rather a vindication of the tax reform movement's social democratic aims.

The Road Not Taken: Rejecting the 1921 Sales Tax

Even before the Treaty of Versailles was signed, opponents of progressive taxation began demanding an end to the robust wartime tax regime. Their first and central target was the excess-profits tax. As we have seen, business leaders and academic experts had convinced Treasury lawyers and Congress during the war that a hybrid war profits tax was superior to an excess-profits tax levied on all business profits beyond a "normal" rate of return. After the conflict, the next step of completely eliminating the profits tax did not seem far off. Indeed, in its last months in power, the Wilson administration opened the door to a postwar Republican onslaught against the excess-profits tax.

In 1920, Wilson appointed David F. Houston as Treasury Secretary. Echoing his predecessor Carter Glass, Houston called for an end to the excess-profits tax. He argued that the levy discriminated "against conservatively financed corporations," that its administration was "exceedingly complex," and that it was "rapidly losing its productivity." The newly appointed Treasury Secretary recommended replacing the excess-profits tax with a new corporation profits tax to ensure adequate revenue "upon grounds of equality and justice."[57]

[57] *Annual Report of the Secretary of the Treasury on the State of the Finances, for the Fiscal Year Ended June 30 1920* (Washington, D.C.: Government Printing Office, 1921), 38–9; Ratner, *Taxation and Democracy in America*, 403.

Business leaders and conservative lawmakers seized upon Houston's remarks. By the summer of 1921, with Republicans in control, the Treasury Department and the White House were inundated with demands for an end to the excess-profits tax and an overall reduction in tax rates. As one banker reminded President Harding and his Treasury colleagues, the future success of the Republican Party rested on "effectively dealing with our tax laws, ... perhaps particularly with regard to two points: first, the necessity for the repeal of the excess profits tax and second, the very considerable reduction of the high surtaxes."[58] The Boston Chamber of Commerce similarly communicated to Congress the results of a survey showing that businesses overwhelmingly favored the abolition of the excess-profits tax and a reduction of the high marginal rates.[59]

The business community may have been united in its opposition to the excess-profits tax, but there was much less consensus about the optimal substitute for this levy. Investment banker Otto Kahn, who had always been apprehensive about the robust wartime tax regime, criticized the excess-profits tax for laying "a heavy and clumsy hand on business." Rather than support a substitute corporate tax, however, Kahn advocated a progressive sales tax as a replacement. His projections were rather optimistic. Kahn believed that a graduated sales tax, beginning with a 1 percent rate on all sales above two dollars, could replace the lost revenue from the excess-profits tax and permit the "drastic reduction" of the steeply progressive personal income taxes.[60]

Modified versions of sales tax recommendations soon spread to the halls of Congress. In 1921, Representative Isaac Bacharach (R-N.J.) and Senator Reed Smoot (R-Utah) introduced companion bills that sought

[58] James G. Cutler, President, Lincoln-Alliance Bank, Rochester, N.Y., to President Harding (July 30, 1921); Andrew Mellon to Cutler (August 6, 1921), contained in Record Group 56, General Records of the Dept. of the Treasury, Correspondence of the Office of the Sec. of the Treasury, Central Files of the Office of the Sec. of the Treas, 1917–1932, Folder, "Tax – Corporations, 1917–1926," Box No. 178, Entry 191, NARA II. Surtaxes referred to the top marginal rates.

[59] James A. McKibben, Secretary, Boston Chamber of Commerce, to Hon. James A. Gallivan (April 7, 1921), Brooklyn Chamber of Commerce to Hon. John Kissel (November 1, 1921), Record Group 233, Records of the U.S. House of Representatives, 67th Congress, Petitions & Memorials, Committee on Ways & Means (HR67A–H23.5) Internal Revenue, Box 504. NARA D.C.

[60] "O. H. Kahn Criticizes Excess Profits Tax," *New York Times*, January 22, 1920. Kahn was not the only person advocating a sales tax to replace the excess-profits tax. The tax expert Morris F. Frey made a similar plea just two months earlier. "Would Eliminate Excess Profits Tax," *New York Times*, November 9, 1919, 23. For a summary of the groups and individuals for and against the 1921 sales tax, see K. M. Williamson, "The Literature on the Sales Tax," *Quarterly Journal of Economics* 35:4 (August 1921), 618–33.

to replace the excess-profits tax with a flat sales tax. Later, in the same session, the recently elected Congressman Ogden L. Mills (R-N.Y.), who would eventually succeed Mellon as Treasury Secretary, proposed a progressive sales tax along the lines suggested by Kahn.[61]

The political and social debates over the sales tax – both within and outside of Congress – vividly illustrated the deep class and regional cleavages that continued to riddle tax reform. In addition to Kahn, many other business elites came out in support of a sales tax substitute. In fact, several Northeastern organizations, such as the Business Men's National Tax Committee and the Tax League of America, were created by elite businessmen mainly to advocate for the sales tax. The American Tax League, founded by the conservative organizer J. A. Arnold, quickly became a prolific, if unoriginal, font of anti-tax literature. And Arnold, who opposed nearly every progressive reform – but especially the income tax – soon became a well-known and politically connected lobbyist who helped spearhead the grass-roots conservative support for the Mellon Plan.[62]

Sales tax proponents had no trouble finding like-minded Republican lawmakers to back their proposals. Besides Smoot, Bacharach, and Mills, numerous legislators came out in support of using a sales tax as a replacement for high individual income taxes and the excess-profits taxes. Smoot's proposal for a flat sales tax gained particular traction among those lawmakers who were seeking both to revert back to a consumption-based tax regime and eliminate the progressive rate structure. For Senator George H. Moses (R-N.H.), Smoot's proposal was a welcomed opportunity to "strike down the vicious principle of graduated taxation which appears in the pending tax bill, and which is but a modern legislative adaptation of the Communistic doctrine of Karl Marx." Less vitriolic legislators recommended that the United States join the global trend toward sales taxes. While Senator Smoot was using the successful experience of the Philippines as a model for his bill, other lawmakers

[61] S. 202 "The Sales Tax Act of 1921," *Congressional Record*, 67th Cong., 1st sess. (1921) 61:151; Blakey and Blakey, *Federal Income Tax*, Chapter VIII. During the war, Smoot had also proposed using a general sales tax to replace the sundry assortment of excise taxes. Blakey and Blakey, *Federal Income Tax*, 179. In supporting his graduated "spendings tax," Mill illustrated how the concept of progressivity had become accepted among moderate conservative lawmakers. *Congressional Record*, 67th Cong., 1st sess. (1921), 61, part 5:5138.

[62] Williamson, "Literature on the Sales Tax," 618–19. For more on Arnold, see Susan Murnane, "Selling Scientific Taxation," 843–51; Martin, *Rich People's Movements*, Chapter 2; Huret, *Taxed*, Chapter 4.

pointed to the recent adoption of sales taxes in France and Canada as achievements worth emulating. Even as they formally rejected the League of Nations and notions of American internationalism, political leaders appeared willing to look abroad for novel ideas about tax policy.[63]

Nonetheless, there were still Republican lawmakers concerned about moving to a sales tax. For many, the levy appeared to be an untried and possibly dangerous experiment.[64] This political caution mirrored the anxiety that sales tax proposals ignited among certain sectors of the business community, which certainly did not speak with one voice when it came to postwar tax reform. Although the vast majority of businessmen opposed the excess-profits tax, there was tremendous division over the sales tax substitute. Organizations like the National Industrial Conference Board (NICB), the National Association of Credit Men, and the National Association of Retail Grocers all came out against the sales tax proposals for a variety of reasons. For some, the allegedly "minor" concerns of accurately defining "sales," administering a new and untried levy, and creating equitable exceptions were strong enough issues to end support for the sales tax proposals. For others, the progressivity of Mills's "spending tax" did not go far enough in rolling back the existing tax regime.[65]

The most common rationale for rejecting the sales tax, however, was its uncertain incidence. Even before the differing sales tax proposals gained currency in Washington, businessmen throughout the country were meeting to discuss the merits of a new form of consumption tax. One of the largest and most influential of these business associations was the NICB, which carefully considered the incidence of a sales tax before categorically rejecting Smoot's proposal. As the Board's special tax committee explained, a sales tax was "indefensible," no matter who ultimately paid it. If businesses were able to pass the full amount of the levy onto consumers, the distributional impact, as well the social perception, was unconscionable. "We haven't the nerve, as good citizens of the

[63] Moses quoted in Ratner, *Taxation and Democracy in America*, 410. For references to global trends, see *Congressional Record*, 67th Cong., 1st sess. (1921), 61, part 7:7238–7340.

[64] *Congressional Record*, 67th Cong., 1st sess. (1921), 61, part 7:7236. Business leaders and lawmakers also considered other corporate taxes including an undistributed profits tax. Steven Bank, *Anglo-American Corporate Taxation: Tracing the Common Roots and Divergent Approaches* (New York: Cambridge University Press, 2011), Chapter 3.

[65] "The Sales or Turn-Over Tax; Its Unfairness to Business and to the Consumer," *Credit Monthly* (May 1921), 19–21; Williamson, "The Literature on the Sales Tax," 622. For more on Mills's proposal, see Steven A. Bank, "The Progressive Consumption Tax Revisited," *Michigan Law Review* 101 (May 2003), 2238–60, 2243–45.

country – which we are, and are trying to be – to say to a body of business men in this country, who are suggesting that business be relieved from a billion dollars of excess profits tax, that we propose a tax which will cause the billion to be paid by the ultimate consumer," the committee explained. "That is such a violent divergence from the principle of payment upon the basis of ability to pay, that we cannot ask this body of business men to get behind that sort of a tax."

Even though the war emergency had passed, fiscal citizenship and adherence to a tax system based on taxpaying capacity appeared to endure, even among the economic elite. The NICB could not in good conscience demand that Congress replace the excess-profits tax with a sales tax. "We don't think that is good citizenship; and we don't think that is good economics. That is the real reason that we disposed of or rejected the sales tax, upon the assumption that the tax is paid by the ultimate consumer."[66]

The NICB may not have thought that it was "good citizenship" to support a seemingly regressive sales tax as a replacement for the steeply graduated income and excess-profits taxes. But that did not mean that it was motivated solely by civic duty or fiscal citizenship. Echoing comments made by other business groups, the Board's tax committee contended that it was against businesses' own interests to back a levy that operated in their view as a "gross receipts tax." If businesses were unable to shift the sales tax to consumers, if they had to absorb the levy as an operating cost, there was tremendous potential for the tax to have an uneven and unequal impact on similarly situated businesses. "A tax on gross receipts which leaves out of the equation all the difference in cost of the conduct of your business as compared to mine," the committee noted, "is an unjustifiable tax."[67]

For businessmen who had become accustomed to focusing on "net income" as the proper definition of the tax base, moving to a new regime seemed ill-advised. Enacting a sales tax that effectively operated as a "gross receipts tax," the NICB explained, would "produce such inequalities that our dissatisfaction with the excess profits tax would be as nothing, and we would find ourselves in the face of inequalities vastly greater than heretofore." Thus, while the NICB initially framed its opposition to the sales tax in terms of fiscal citizenship and distributional equity,

[66] *Proceedings of the Second National Industrial Tax Conference, No. 17* (New York: National Industrial Conference Board, 1920), 40–1.

[67] Ibid., 41.

ultimately it was the pecuniary interests of their members that prevailed. "We do not think," the committee concluded, "that the business men of this country ought, for their own best interests and for the interests of equality among all classes of taxpayers, to father a scheme which will cause the most profound differences in terms of net income, from which taxes are to be paid, as between different concerns whose costs of doing business, one with other, vary so much."[68]

The business community's fragmented views provided the opening that opponents of the sales tax needed to defeat the congressional proposals. These opponents consisted of the usual Southern and Western lawmakers and their constituents. They relied upon the ability-to-pay logic to defeat the sales tax proposals. Just as they had during the war, organized agricultural and labor associations once again supported maintaining the excess-profits tax as way to regulate corporate monopolies and promote "justice over revenue."[69] Petitions from labor unions and farm federations poured into congressional offices. They reminded lawmakers that ordinary farmers and workers, who decades earlier were among the first groups to protest the unfairness of indirect and regressive taxes, were firmly against any backsliding to the old fiscal order. The social significance of the tectonic turn in American public finance triggered by the war was not lost on those everyday citizens who had a great stake in sustaining the new fiscal state.[70]

Many labor and agrarian associations, therefore, wanted to maintain the excess-profits tax in the process of defeating the sales tax. As H. S. McKenzie of the American Farm Bureau Federation explained to Congress, one reason that businessmen were eager to scrap the excess-profits tax was because they feared that "if it is put into an efficient form" businesses "will have to pay it forever." Speaking on behalf of the two million members of the American Farm Bureau, McKenzie stressed the distributional consequences of shifting to a sales tax. "I believe that if the

[68] Ibid., 41–2. The National Association of Credit Men leveled nearly identical critiques against the sales tax. "The Sales or Turn-Over Tax," 19–20.

[69] Arthur Capper (Chairman of the Farmers' National Committee for War Finance) to McAdoo, August 10, 1918; Leffingwell to Capper, August 27, 1918, NARA Excess Profits Tax Folder, NARA II.

[70] See, e.g., John J. Quinlivan, Toledo Central Labor Union, to Congressman William W. Chalmers (April 29, 1921); J. R. Howard, American Farm Bureau Federation, to House Ways & Means Committee (August 16, 1921), Record Group 233, Records of the U.S. House of Representatives, 67th Congress, Petitions & Memorials, Committee on Ways & Means (HR67A–H23.5) Internal Revenue, Box 503, National Archives and Record Administration I, Washington, D.C.

general sales tax... were substituted for the higher surtax brackets and the excess profits tax," he informed lawmakers, "you would be putting an undue burden on the people who are already heavily burdened under the present tax rate."[71]

This reminder of how graduated taxes on incomes and profits were seen as an equitable and necessary counterbalance to the already existing regressive import duties and excise taxes was not lost on legislators. But in case any listeners were unsure of where ordinary workers and farmers like McKenzie stood on the vital issue of the proper tax base, the New York dairy farmer reiterated what he believed to be the "four general principles" that ought to govern any type of tax reform:

> (1) That a man's net income is the true measure of ability to pay taxes in support of National Government; (2) that the rates should be progressive; that is, that the larger the man's income the higher the rate; (3) that as this is the country of all the people everybody should have some part in supporting the Government, and that a certain portion of the taxes can, therefore, justly be raised through the tariff and other consumption taxes; and (4) while recognizing that the raising of revenue is the first consideration in any tax scheme, the taxes should be so laid as to tend, as far as possible, to the distribution of wealth in the hands of the many and not to its concentration in the hands of the few.[72]

With these four maxims, McKenzie succinctly summarized the main objectives of the progressive tax movement.

Congressional opponents of the sales tax heeded the words of McKenzie and other representatives of organized workers and farmers. Populist lawmakers like Claude Kitchin may have been relatively reticent during the debates, still staggering from their electoral losses. But there were plenty of insurgent Republicans willing to challenge the sales tax proposals. Progressive Republican James Frear (R-Wis.) reminded his colleagues that the unprecedented, war-induced deficit alone meant Congress needed to raise the existing taxes on income and profits, rather than replace them with an experimental sales tax, and an uncertain revenue yield. A sales tax, Frear noted, would also have adverse distributional consequences

[71] *Internal-Revenue Hearings on the Proposed Revenue Act of 1921 Before the Senate Committee on Finance*, 67th Congress, 45 (1921), 310, 320.

[72] Ibid., 307–8. These sentiments were shared throughout the Western and Southern states by similarly minded farmers and workers. See, e.g., "Farm v. White House," *Idaho Statesman*, August 24, 1921; "Farm Bureau Resolutions," *Grand Forks Herald*, December 17, 1921; "Farmers Favor Lot of Changes," *Charlotte Observer*, November 18, 1921.

falling "on everything that we eat and wear, whereby every man, woman, and child in this country would be taxed." Frear's words were meant to harken back to an earlier era when other indirect taxes had a similarly regressive effect on the distribution of national tax burdens.[73]

The Continued Autonomy and Influence of Tax Experts

If lawmakers were expressing the conflicting wishes of their constituents, at least one powerful and influential group within the bourgeoning positive state was relatively clear and steadfast in its position on postwar tax reform. With their newfound authority and power, Treasury Department tax experts illustrated the growing bureaucratic and legal autonomy of the new fiscal polity. Through the uncertainty of the war crisis, these professionals established a reputation as nonpartisan bureaucrats. Although they often came from the private sector and the academy where they represented a varied of interests, the lawyers and economists in the Treasury Department leveraged their contacts, skills, and knowledge to help build the fiscal state's administrative autonomy. Unhinged from the usual political pressures that legislators faced, these professional experts had demonstrated during the war that they could be trusted to shape the contours of the new fiscal order.[74]

One of the leading representatives of this new administrative authority was Thomas S. Adams, who stayed on at the Treasury Department briefly after the war to help manage the postwar transition. Regarded by many at the time as the "dean of tax experts," Adams had made a name for himself during his government service as an astute and objective expert who could play the pivotal role of honest broker between competing political groups. Educated at Johns Hopkins under the German "seminary" style of historicist graduate study, Adams spent much of his early academic career at the University of Wisconsin, where he was Richard Ely's first external hire and subsequently a co-author with Ely on a popular economics textbook. As we have seen, Adams also served on the Wisconsin Tax Commission and was a reform-minded academic throughout his life. By the end of his career, he came to be known as a "shining example"

[73] *Congressional Record*, 67th Cong. 1st sess. (1921), 61, part 5:5141.

[74] W. Elliot Brownlee, "Economists and the Foundation of the Modern Tax System in the United States," in *The State and Economic Knowledge: The American & British Experiences*, ed. Mary O. Furner and Barry Supple (New York: Cambridge University Press, 1990), 425–9.

of a "scholar in politics" and as "a liaison officer between the world of thought and the world of action."[75]

After the war, Adams's remarks before congressional hearings, business organizations, and concerned civic associations had a significant impact not only on public opinion, but also on how lawmakers approached postwar tax reform. As a second, generation new school economist, Adams had worked assiduously to provide the administrative framework for Wisconsin's first effective income tax. During the war, he played a similar role in the Treasury Department. But his practical wartime experience left him disenchanted, especially about the future promise of the excess-profits tax. Unlike other progressive political economists, such as Robert Murray Haig and David Friday, who supported the excess-profits tax after the conflict, Adams believed that the levy's bureaucratic complexity was crushing the fiscal state's still fledgling administrative machinery.[76]

Yet, rather than concur with conservative businessmen and lawmakers who wanted to turn back the clock on progressive fiscal reforms, Adams contended that the excess-profits tax had to be eliminated in order to save the income tax. "I find the deepest reason for the repeal of the excess profits tax in the conviction that its continuance would endanger the life of the income tax itself," wrote Adams in 1921. "No Federal administration, in my opinion, is capable during the next five or six years of carrying with even moderate success two such burdens as the income tax and the excess profits tax."[77]

[75] "Tommy Adams," *Saturday Evening Post*, June 3, 1933, 20; "Thomas Sewall Adams (1873–1933)" *Bulletin of the National Tax Association* 18 (April 1933), 194–201; Roy G. Elliot, "Dean of Tax Experts," *Credit Monthly* (March 1921), 21; Thomas Earl Geu, "Professor T. S. Adams (1873–1933) on Federal Taxation: Déjà vu All Over Again," *Akron Tax Journal* 10 (1993), 29–46; Michael J. Graetz and Michael M. O'Hear, "The 'Original Intent' of U.S. International Taxation," *Duke Law Journal* 46:5 (March 1997), 1020–1109.

[76] Robert Murray Haig (assisted by George E. Holmes), *The Taxation of Excess Profits in Great Britain* (Princeton, N.J.: American Economic Association, 1920). Robert M. Haig et al., "The Excess Profits Tax," *American Economic Review* 10 (Suppl.; March 1920), 1–32. Although Haig, like nearly all tax experts, was critical of the administrative burdens of the excess-profits tax, he supported the levy in principle as a way of "seizing some of the promised advantages of socialized industry without incurring the risks and disadvantages of socialism." Haig, *The Taxation of Excess Profits in Great Britain*, 174–5.

[77] Thomas S. Adams, "Should the Excess Profits Tax be Repealed?" *Quarterly Journal of Economics* 35:3 (May 1921), 363–93, 370. See also *Hearings before the Committee on Finance U.S. Senate, 67th Congress, 1st session on H.R. 8245* (Washington, D.C.: Government Printing Office, 1921).

Adams's primary objective was to preserve the income tax. "A successfully administered income tax," he argued, was "an essential part of financial democracy." The breakdown of the new tax regime would be, for him, "something in the nature of political tragedy." Revealing his historicist leanings, Adams emphasized that his opposition to the excess-profits tax and other substitutes was premised mainly on the existing limits of American administrative capacity. He favored the income tax because he believed the recent wartime experience demonstrated that it was a flexible, effective, and equitable source of revenue – and one that could be feasibly collected given the limits of American administrative capacity.

Like the former Treasury lawyers, Adams believed that the income tax was unquestionably here to stay. "Looking at the matter impersonally and historically, it seems inevitable that the income tax shall fill an important, if not the primary, part of our system of federal finance," Adams boldly predicted. "We must succeed with it." Succeeding, for Adams, meant refraining from recklessly trying new fiscal experiments, at least until the country had come to grips with the management of a still infant income tax. Adams feared that future generations "would be lost in trying out substitutes." To diminish the appeal of such substitutes it was vital to make sure that the income tax was not "discredited and discarded." To do that, Adams concluded, "it is essential that we learn the rudiments of the game – the proper application of the ordinary graduated income tax – before we attempt its more difficult applications."[78]

Learning the "rudiments of the game" did not preclude Adams and other experts from supporting improvements to the existing tax structure and recommending certain types of sales taxes. Indeed, just as Adams believed repealing the excess-profits tax could help safeguard the income tax, he also contended that adopting a modified business sales tax could further ease administrative burdens and thus complement the existing taxation of incomes, profits, and wealth transfers. Lost revenue from the repeal of the excess-profits tax could be replaced by taxing manufacturers and retailers on, what Adams referred to as, their "modified gross income," by which he meant the value that these businesses added to the process of making and selling certain goods. "In the case of producers and sellers of 'goods, wares and merchandise' further simplicity could be achieved," explained Adams, "by giving the tax the form of a sales tax with a credit or refund for taxes paid by the producer or dealer (as

[78] Adams, "Should the Excess Profits Tax Be Repealed?" 370–1.

purchaser) on goods bought for resale or for necessary use in the production of goods for sale." This particular aspect of Adams's normative vision was arguably one of the first conceptual articulations of a modern "credit invoice" type of value-added tax (VAT).[79] At bottom, Adams privileged administrative simplicity. As a thoroughgoing progressive, he favored rounding "out the tax system toward greater justice," just as Seligman had advocated. But in the tradeoff between administrative ease and distributional equity, Adams seemed to prefer the former.

Writing at the height of the 1921 sales tax debate, Adams had hoped to influence policymakers with his recommendations. His criticism of the excess-profits tax, in fact, had a significant effect on the ultimate repeal of that levy.[80] Yet, at the same time, Adams understood the political futility of certain parts of his bold and ambitious recommendations, particularly his "modified gross income" tax. After more than two decades of public service at the state and national level, Adams had come to realize that economic ideas did not exist in a vacuum, that broader social and political factors frequently determined the fate of fiscal policies. "The plan has little chance of adoption," Adams presciently noted about his modified business sales tax or proto-VAT.[81]

Still, for Adams, there was much to be learned from the possible rejection of a simplified sales tax. In words that would resonate for decades as future U.S. policymakers and analysts considered other forms of consumption taxes, Adams eloquently explained how and why the democratic desire for fairness appeared to trump the logic of administrative ease. Adams conceded that the failure to adopt a sales tax served "the useful purpose of illustrating the futility of basing one's principles on one's personal experience":

> It demonstrates the supreme necessity of subordinating administrative logic and personal predilections to the great political and social forces which

79 Thomas S. Adams, "Fundamental Problems of Federal Income Taxation," *Quarterly Journal of Economics* 35:4 (August 1921), 527–56, 553. Adams has been credited by some tax scholars as being one of the first thinkers to support a value-added tax. Kathryn James, "Exploring the Origins and Global Rise of VAT," in *The VAT Reader: What a Federal Consumption Tax Would Mean for America* (Falls Church, Va.: Tax Analysts, 2011), 15–16; Clara K. Sullivan, *The Tax on Value Added* (New York: Columbia University Press, 1965), 17. For more on the current "credit-invoice" VAT, see generally Alan Schenk and Olivier Oldham, *The Value Added Tax: A Comparative Approach* (New York: Cambridge University Press, 2007), 34–9.

80 Ratner, *Taxation and Democracy in America*, 403–10; Randolph E. Paul, *Taxation in the United States* (Boston: Little, Brown, 1954), 764–6.

81 Adams, "Fundamental Problems of Federal Income Taxation," 554.

> control the evolution of tax systems. These forces must be accepted as facts. The historical fact is that modern states prefer equity and complexity to simplicity and inequality. The cry for equality and justice is louder and more unanswerable than the demand for certainty and convenience. You may think it sentimental and stupid, but that does not alter the fact.[82]

Adams, in fact, did not believe that the democratic clamor for equality and justice in fiscal relations was either sentimental or stupid.

Indeed, for Adams and other fiscal reformers, the income tax seemed to have its own internal dynamic and inertia. "The income tax, whose complexity is not exaggerated by its critics, spreads and grows;" wrote Adams, "it has a deeper and wider following with the passing generations." Evoking both Tocqueville and the recent history of the income tax, Adams identified how the levy seemed to have a special appeal in liberal democracies like the United States. "It seems to be particularly irresistible in a democratic state in which customs, excise or sales taxes (whose burden is or is believed to be regressive) constitute the backbone of the tax system," wrote Adams. "Replace the complexities of the income tax with the simplicities of the sales tax tomorrow, and within ten years the income tax would be back. In the light of financial history 'simplicity' is a lesser gold."[83] Adams's remarks accurately foreshadowed the American experience with the income tax for many decades to come.

Implicit in Adams's notion about the income tax replacing the old system of indirect and regressive taxes was his historical sensibility about the importance of context and sequence. Adams seemed to recognize more than any of his fellow progressive revenue reformers that the peculiar historical chronology of events and forces that lead to the adoption of direct and graduated taxation had a profound effect on the American fiscal system. Because Americans had been revolting against an *ancien régime* that they perceived to be regressive and unfair, consumption taxes as a whole were perceived as antiquated and retrograde. Even though the income tax was still in its infancy in 1921, it was seen as the equitable counterweight – the fair and effective levy – to an earlier and "backward" tax regime.[84] A graduated tax system based on incomes, profits, and wealth transfers became identified with modern progress and enlightened

[82] Ibid.

[83] Ibid., 555.

[84] Robert Murray Haig and his student would later describe the move to sales taxes by the states as "an unnecessary and backward step in taxation." Robert Murray Haig and Carl Shoup, *The Sales Tax in the American States* (New York: Columbia University Press, 1934), 108.

innovation. Meanwhile, consumption taxes like the tariff and excise levies, which were seen as sales taxes, were characterized as part of an old and decrepit fiscal order, one linked to party politics, apathetic citizenship, elite concentrations of wealth, and a traditional night watchman state.

In many ways, T. S. Adams was simply following in the footsteps of his intellectual mentors. When Henry Carter Adams, Edwin R. A Seligman, Richard Ely, and other progressive public finance economists set out to advance the income tax movement in the late 1880s and 1890s by touting the intellectual superiority of a tax based on the principle of economic "faculty" or "ability to pay," they were deliberately trying to tar consumption taxes like the tariff and excise levies as pernicious fiscal instruments. These reform-minded economists used the principle of taxpaying capacity and the key words "ability to pay" to challenge the "benefits theory" of taxation that was loosely identified with the late-nineteenth-century consumption tax regime, and the laissez-faire view of the state of which the benefits theory was an instrumental part.

In the process, these progressive political economists may have unwittingly set U.S. fiscal history on a highly ironic path. By undermining the "benefits" rationale supporting consumption taxes, these thinkers severed the link between government spending and taxation. A revenue system based primarily on ability to pay ignored how the modern fiscal state spent its tax revenue. This elision may have created a fiscal myopia among U.S. tax experts and their followers. By narrowly focusing only on the revenue extraction process, supporters of the faculty theory neglected to see how distributional justice could be achieved through the tax-*and-transfer* process as a whole. They failed to realize how potentially regressive but highly efficient and productive taxes could generate tremendous revenue that could be used, in turn, for progressive social-welfare spending – spending that could counter the possibly regressive incidence of consumption taxes. In other words, the new school of American political economists may have foreclosed the possibility of the United States adopting a consumption tax like the VAT in subsequent years.

Unlike his mentors, T. S. Adams seemed to understand how the nation had become blinded by this fiscal myopia. Perhaps his longtime government service, or his travels back and forth between academic duties and fiscal state-building, provided Adams with the broad vision and pragmatic skills to reconsider even the most "backward" and pernicious of fiscal measures. Regardless, Adams's ideas in many ways proved to be well ahead of his time, at least for the United States. For while other Western industrialized nations soon began experimenting with turnover taxes and other precursors to the VAT during the 1920s, the United States – at least at the national level – firmly rejected the path toward a consumption-based tax system. Despite Adams's support, each of the 1921 sales tax proposals was rejected, either within congressional committees or on the legislative floor. The business community's ambivalence and the resistance from organized workers and farmers and their political representatives were ultimately too difficult to overcome.

The Economic Definition of Income and the Ossification of Fiscal Myopia

While Adams's vision for a simplified sales tax may have reflected an alternative road not taken, other fiscal experts, following in the footsteps of the new school political economists, were cementing the path toward a progressive income tax regime – and, in the process, exacerbating the fiscal myopia. One of Seligman's leading students, Robert Murray Haig, was carrying the mantle of his mentor into a new era of fiscal relations. After earning his doctorate in economics at Columbia in 1914, Haig embarked, at Seligman's behest, on an empirical study of land-value taxation in Canada.[85] Having completed a doctoral thesis on the Illinois property tax, Haig traveled to Canada to strengthen his understanding of property levies and to learn more about the single-tax experiments conducted in that country. Afterward, he assisted the Treasury Department in its comparative analysis of war profits taxation. With Seligman's help, Haig began teaching, first, in Columbia's School of Journalism, then later the recently created School of Business.[86]

In 1931, when Seligman retired, Haig replaced his mentor as the McVickar Professor of Political Economy. Like Seligman, Haig was completely committed to Columbia University, the study of public finance,

[85] "The Teacher, An Address by Robert Murray Haig," in *Edwin Robert Anderson Seligman, 1861–1939* (Stamford, Conn.: Overlook Press, 1942), 16–17. Contemporaries described Haig as Seligman's "intellectual heir" and as a person that Seligman "loved like a son." H. S. Bloch to Robert M. Haig, July 23, 1939; Eustace Seligman to Haig, July 28, 1939, Carl S. Shoup Papers, Yokohama National University Library, Yokohama, Japan.

[86] Robert M. Haig, *A History of the General Property Tax in Illinois* (Urbana: University of Illinois Studies in the Social Sciences, 1914); Robert M. Haig to E. R. A. Seligman, July 22, 1914, Edwin R. A. Seligman Papers, Butler Library Rare Book and Manuscript Collections, Columbia University, New York; Robert Murray Haig, *The Exemption of Improvements from Taxation in Canada and the United States: A Report Prepared for the Committee on Taxation of the City of New York* (New York: M. B. Brown Printing & Co., 1915).

and progressive reform movements. Throughout his career, he not only helped maintain the university's tradition as a leading center for the study of public finance, Haig also remained a staunch supporter of progressive taxes on incomes, profits, and wealth transfers.[87]

In December 1920, Haig and Seligman gathered together some of the country's leading tax experts at a conference held at Columbia to discuss the future promise and practical challenges of the federal income tax. This seminal event helped mark Columbia as a leading center for the study of public finance; it also produced an edited volume that advanced the conceptual commitment to an income-based tax system. The conference's goal, as Seligman explained, was "to elucidate the basic principles of importance to the framer, the administrator, and the payer of the modern income tax."[88] Speakers included T. S. Adams, Thomas Reed Powell, George E. Holmes, Arthur A. Ballantine, and several other former Treasury officials.[89] Each of the addresses helped fortify an understanding of the practical framework of the new tax regime.

But one paper in particular had a profound and far-reaching impact on the theoretical development of the meaning of income. In his essay, Robert Murray Haig set out to contrast the differences between economic and legal definitions of income, with the goal of assisting tax experts and lawmakers in their efforts to bring "the statutory" meaning of income closer to the economist's "conceptual" definition. Like the economic thinkers who preceded him, Haig began with a utilitarian premise, namely that "fundamentally, income is a flow of satisfactions, of intangible psychological experiences." Haig conceded that measuring such "psychic satisfactions" was "diaphanous and elusive." Yet, the goal for the economist was not to give up on this ideal view of income, but rather to find suitable proxies that could provide closer approximations

[87] Edwin R. A. Seligman to A. E. Chandler, Aug. 22, 1915; Seligman to Robert M. Haig, April 13, 1911; Aug. 18, 1915; Oct. 29, 1917, Correspondence: Seligman, 1908–1922, Robert M. Haig Papers, Butler Library Rare Book and Manuscript Collections, Columbia University, New York, N.Y. [hereinafter RMHP]. "Robert Murray Haig," *Political Science Quarterly* 68:3 (September 1953), 479–80; W. Elliot Brownlee, "Shoup Mission to Japan: Two Political Economies Intersect," in *The New Fiscal Sociology: Taxation in Comparative and Historical Perspective*, ed. Isaac William Martin et al. (New York: Cambridge University Press, 2009).

[88] Edwin R. A. Seligman, "Introduction – The Problem in General," in *The Federal Income Tax*, ed. Robert Murray Haig (New York: Columbia University Press, 1921), x.

[89] Thomas S. Adams, "When Is Income Realized?"; Thomas Reed Powell, "Constitutional Aspects of Federal Income Taxation," 51, 90; George E. Holmes, "Loss as a Factor in the Determination of Income," 138; Arthur A. Ballantine, "Inventories," 160, in *Federal Income Tax*, ed. Haig.

to this ideal. Haig, thus, arrived at what he believed to be a provisional starting point. "The definition of income which the economist offers," wrote Haig, "is this: income is *the money value of the net accretion to one's economic power between two points of time*."[90]

With this succinct yet comprehensive conceptual definition, Haig not only summarized the views of previous generations of economic thinkers, including Ely and Seligman; he also provided a normative baseline that would guide future tax reformers. Haig readily admitted that he was building upon the work of other scholars in generating his concise definition. As we have seen, nearly forty years earlier, Francis Walker, Seligman, and other American thinkers first began considering how economic power could be used as a metric for determining taxpaying ability. By his own account, Haig was simply synthesizing these earlier theories to come up with a usable touchstone for further tax reform. To the existing theories about economic power, Haig added the important elements of relying on monetary values, net increases, and a defined period of time. These were not small considerations; they provided much needed clarity and precision to the more amorphous definition based on "psychic satisfactions." Haig's goal, in short, was to provide an intellectual reference point for the future development of taxable income.[91]

Although Haig may not have predicted the implications of his essay, it did not take long for other scholars, including Haig's leading students Carl S. Shoup and William S. Vickrey, to understand the significance of his clear and concise definition of income. Indeed, Haig initially planned to follow up his brief essay with a comprehensive monograph, cowritten with Shoup, on the origins and consequences of the conceptual definition of income. That project was not completed, despite Shoup's persistent efforts, mainly because a junior University of Chicago economist, Henry Simons, soon took up the task where Haig's essay had left off. Simon's monograph, along with Haig's essay, soon became a canonical text in the inchoate fields of public economics and tax law. By the late 1930s, when tax experts spoke about the economic meaning of income, they had in mind the Haig-Simons definition.[92]

90 Robert Murray Haig, "The Concept of Income – Economic and Legal Aspects," in *Federal Income Tax*, ed. Haig, 2, 7 (emphasis in the original).

91 Francis A. Walker, "The Bases of Taxation," *Political Science Quarterly* 3:1 (March 1888), 1–16; Edwin R. A. Seligman, *Progressive Taxation in Theory and Practice*, 2nd ed. (Princeton: American Economic Association, 1908); Haig, "Concept of Income," 3.

92 Henry Simons to Robert M. Haig, October 22, 1936, Henry C. Simons Papers, Box 3, Folder 22, Special Collections Research Center, University of Chicago Regenstein

One reason why Haig's definition gained such traction was because it attended to some of the practical limitations that could constrain an ideal tax base. Like his economic colleagues in Europe, who at the time were advancing the study of public finance by examining how the state could use tax policy to correct market failures and optimize the taxation of commodities, Haig was concerned about how his comprehensive definition of income could operate under real-world conditions.[93] In his essay, Haig conceded that any definition based on "money-value" was inherently vulnerable to the pressures of inflation, or what he referred to as "the imperfections of the economic standard of value." If the economic definition of income failed to account for an increase in the price level, unjust results would ensue. Likewise, any ideal characterization of income was limited, in practice, by the accounting methods used to determine net income and by the administrative capacity of the taxing authorities. Legal or "taxable income," therefore, had to be narrower than the concept of "economic income."[94]

Haig identified these limitations to demonstrate that the "statutory definition of income" ought to be an evolving doctrine, reflecting the ambient economy and society. "The concept of taxable income," noted Haig illustrating his historicist leanings, "is a living, mutable concept which has varied widely from time to time and from country to country with the conditions under which it has had to operate." As a result, lawmakers and policy analysts needed to approach the income tax "in a mobile, flexible state," so as to "permit the statutory definition of income to become progressively more precise and accurate with the improvement of the technique of our economic environment."[95]

In acknowledging the provisional nature of taxable income, Haig appeared to be open to alternative methods of taxing economic power

Library, Chicago, Ill. On the many drafts of the project written by Shoup, see, e.g., Box 29, Folder 4: "Carl's Outlines – Research Project," RMHP; Henry Simons, *Personal Income Taxation: The Definition of Income as a Problem of Fiscal Policy* (Chicago: University of Chicago Press, 1938). Present-day textbooks in tax law, accounting, and public economics generally refer to the Haig-Simons definition of income as a conventional standard. See, e.g., Joseph Bankman et al., *Federal Income Taxation* (New York: Walter Kluwer, 2012), 12–14; Harvey Rosen and Ted Gayer, *Public Finance* (McGraw-Hill, 2008), 382–3.

93 Agnar Sandmo, *Economics Evolving: A History of Economic Thought* (Princeton: Princeton University Press, 2011), 261–3. This was the period, of course, when the formal subfield of public economics was first taken shape in Europe with the path-breaking work of Arthur C. Pigou and Frank Ramsey. Ibid.

94 Haig, "Concept of Income," 19–20.

95 Ibid., 28.

or taxpaying ability. His historical and comparative methods of analysis suggested that "economic income" might not always and everywhere be the best way to measure "the net accretion to economic power between two points in time," and that the United States might not be the vanguard in pragmatically defining "taxable income." Yet, like his mentor, Haig appeared wedded to a linear view of historical progress, with the United States leading the way. Just as Seligman maintained a seemingly Whiggish perspective on American economic and political development, despite his German historicist training, Haig likewise appeared to embrace a provincial view of the United States as a fiscal beacon for other nation-states.[96]

Though he admitted that U.S. administrative capacities were comparatively inferior to other industrialized nations, such as Britain and its "splendid civil service," Haig exalted the American fiscal state's capacious legal definition of income. The U.S. statutory definition, he proudly proclaimed, "is by all odds the most theoretically perfect income tax law extant, from the point of view of its general scope." Haig's nationalistic zeal resonated with the historical and geopolitical dominance of the United States at the time. With other countries seeking to reconstruct their fiscal regimes in the wake of the war, it was not hard for Haig and other intellectuals to believe that the U.S. legal system could be a model for others to follow.[97]

Haig's admiration for the American legal definition of income went well beyond nationalistic pride. As a staunch supporter of the income tax, he celebrated the existing legal meaning of taxable income as a way to foreclose alternative fiscal reforms. Writing at the apex of the sales tax debates, Haig appeared to stress the theoretical perfection of the U.S. income tax law for a particular purpose: to deter American lawmakers and economic experts from entertaining alternative tax bases. The Columbia professor was willing to accept modifications to the definition of income, as long as such changes did not open the possibility of other tax systems. "Certainly such changes in the abstract definition of income as are necessary to make the statute practical and workable must be

[96] Edwin R. A. Seligman, *The Economic Interpretation of History* (New York: Columbia University Press, 1907). For more on Seligman's liberal bourgeois version of the economic interpretation of history, see Richard Hofstadter, *The Progressive Historians: Turner, Beard, Parrington* (London: Jonathan Cape, 1969), Chapter 5.

[97] Haig, "Concept of Income," 19. On the post–World War I rise of American geopolitical hegemony, see generally Emily S. Rosenberg, *Spreading the American Dream: American Economic and Cultural Expansion, 1890–1945* (New York: Hill & Wang, 1982), Chs. 7 and 8.

accepted," wrote Haig, "provided the cost in terms of equity is not so great as to make some available alternative tax a more attractive method of raising the revenue." Though he did not explicitly explain what the "available alternative tax" might be, there was no doubt that he had the sales tax in mind. In fact, in subsequent studies, Haig, along with his co-author Shoup, was highly critical of consumption taxes, including the postwar French turn-over tax and the sales taxes adopted by many U.S. subnational governments. Even as he was bolstering the conceptual commitment to the American income tax, Haig was foreclosing the road to alternative revenue regimes.[98]

The Mellon Plan and the Fortification of the Fiscal State

The 1921 rejection of "available alternative tax" proposals was ultimately part of a compromise revenue act, just as Mellon had suggested to Hays. The new law, as Daniel Roper aptly put it, was "merely a collection of patches on the old act." Many business leaders and wealthy taxpayers, nonetheless, were quite pleased with some of the "patches," including the elimination of the excess-profits tax, the decrease in the top surtax rate from 65 to 50 percent, the exclusion of stock dividends from income, codifying the holding in *Macomber*, and the adoption of a reduced tax rate for long-term capital gains.[99] For Democratic leaders like Roper and Cordell Hull, the new law similarly provided some solace by rejecting the sales tax, raising exemption levels for the individual income tax, and increasing corporate income tax rates. The law did not provide the "simplified structure" that reformers of all political perspectives had hoped for, but it did sustain, what Hull termed, the "fundamental principles" of the new direct tax regime; it did not "wipe out all graduated income taxation," as Hull had feared. In the process, the new law helped vindicate the progressive reform impulse that could be traced back to the

[98] Haig, "Concept of Income," 19; Robert Murray Haig (with the assistance of Carl S. Shoup, Alexander Werth and Nathalie Molodovsky), *The Public Finances of Post-war France* (New York, Columbia University Press, 1929); Haig and Shoup, *Sales Tax in the American States*.

[99] Revenue Act of 1921, 42 Stat. 227 (1921). On the origins of capital gains taxation during this period, see Marjorie Kornhauser, "The Origins of Capital Gains Taxation: What's Law Got to Do with It?" *Southwestern Law Journal* 39:4 (1985), 869–928.

late-nineteenth-century conceptual revolution in economic thinking and the fiscal state-building efforts that followed in its wake.[100]

The 1921 act, however, was only the beginning of the contested consolidation of the fiscal state. In the following year, proponents of protectionism were able to solidify an earlier emergency tariff measure with the Fordney-McCumber Tariff, which once again raised import duties to an all-time high.[101] Providing protection to Northeastern industries as well as Midwestern farmers suffering from a postwar decline in commodity prices proved irresistible to Republican lawmakers. Old political habits did not die easily. Though this limited return to protectionism was a sure sign of the resiliency of the old order, it turned out to be a vain effort to restore the *ancien régime*. Throughout the rest of the decade, Congress stridently debated and eventually adopted three other compromise revenue measures. Enacted under the auspices of the Mellon Plan for "scientific tax reform," these new tax laws illustrated the puzzling, contradictory nature of 1920s tax reform.[102]

Indeed, while the Mellon Plan eroded the graduated rate structure, it also fortified the nation's commitment to the new fiscal polity. By the end of the decade, top marginal tax rates, to be sure, had been dramatically reduced. But the central elements of the new fiscal state endured. Wealthy Americans continued to bear a greater share of the overall federal tax burden, far greater than they had during the late nineteenth century or even before the war, as evidenced by the relative stability of top effective rates of taxation on the wealthiest Americans. Notwithstanding the conservative onslaught against wealth-transfer taxes, the federal estate tax also persisted as a significant symbol of "soak-the-rich" taxation – as did the relatively high level of corporate tax rates and revenues. The civic obligations of modern fiscal citizenship did not dissolve away with the erosion of the graduated rate structure.

Even the bureaucratic structure of the new fiscal system grew stronger during this period of alleged public sector austerity. Not only did Mellon reinforce the "scientific" or unbiased and professional administration of tax laws by blocking Republican efforts to politicize the Treasury

100 Daniel C. Roper, "Administrative Problems in United States Internal Taxation," *South Atlantic Quarterly* 21 (April 1922), 97–108; Blakey and Blakey, *Federal Income Tax*, 217–22.

101 Fordney-McCumber Tariff Act of 1922, 42 U.S. Stat. 858 (1922).

102 Revenue Act of 1924, 43 Stat. 253 (1924); Revenue Act of 1926, 44 Stat. 9 (1926); Revenue Act of 1928, 45 Stat. 791 (1928).

Department, he also helped usher through Congress several critical institutional changes to the tax machinery, including the creation of the Board of Tax Appeals – the forerunner to the federal tax court – and the Congressional Joint Committee on Taxation. The postwar reconversion, thus, appeared to be a contradictory mix of rollbacks and institution building.

Mellon's Enlightened Capitalism and the Assault on Graduated Rates

In many ways, Mellon himself embodied the paradox that was at the heart of the so-called retrenchment process. Hailed by elites as a new "Moses leading sorely burdened businessmen out of the desert of high taxation," the former financier quickly became the savior for a class of taxpayers that had grown increasingly weary of the potential persistence of the wartime tax regime.[103] Mellon took his responsibilities, both to the U.S. Treasury and his class, seriously. He was, of course, vilified by populists like Williams Jennings Bryan, who characterized him as a "party dictator." But Mellon was no reactionary.

Like Roper and Ballantine, the financier turned statesman understood that the Great War marked a seismic shift in American law and society. Mellon saw his role as providing stability during a tumultuous period of reconversion. His decade-long tenure as secretary, in fact, proved to be a ballast during a highly uncertain era. Contemporaries often quipped that "three presidents served under him." Mellon, moreover, was not a dogmatic tax cutter, looking to return the country to some mythical golden age. Rather, he was a fiscal conservative, a banker who believed in balanced budgets. As an enlightened capitalist, he realized that a moderately active federal government, one that provided a stable and predictable political and social environment but little else, could do much more for commercial interests than any laissez-faire state. This, after all, was the implicit message that he had sent to overly exuberant Republican tax cutters like Will Hays.[104]

Mellon had sent a similar message to Congress in his 1921 annual report, where he first intimated the vital elements of his eponymous plan. Urging lawmakers to restrain their "shocking rate" of spending, the

[103] Paul, *Federal Taxation*, 133.

[104] William Jennings Bryan, "Bryan Calls Mellon 'A Party Dictator,'" *New York Times*. May 11, 1924, 3; David Cannadine, *Mellon: An American Life* (New York: Knopf, 2006); Mellon to Hays, November 17, 1921, NARA II.

secretary recommended several changes to the tax code, including replacing the excess-profits tax with an increased corporate income tax rate, maintaining the assortment of miscellaneous wartime sales and excise taxes, and adopting new levies on financial transactions and automobile licenses. Yet, the most controversial of Mellon's proposals and the one that would soon become the centerpiece of his plan was the recommendation to slash the top marginal tax rates on individual income. Echoing what Treasury officials in the Wilson administration had been saying since the end of the war, Mellon claimed that steeply progressive surtaxes had become counterproductive. They "put constant pressure on taxpayers to reduce their taxable income," wrote Mellon, and "interfere with the transaction of business and the free flow of capital into productive enterprise." High rates were inducing wealthy citizens to avoid taxes by investing in tax-exempt securities, namely state and local bonds, rather than more "productive" private investments.[105]

Although Congress rebuked many of the Treasury Department's recommendations in 1921, Mellon remained undeterred. Sure enough, it was not long before changing economic and political circumstances provided the ideal conditions for Mellon's tax cutting agenda. By 1922, the economy began to rebound rapidly from the immediate postwar recession; at the same time, the belated transition to peace helped reduce public spending. Consequently, significant annual surpluses soon provided Treasury with new opportunities to make the case for cutting tax rates. Meanwhile, the political transition in 1923 from a scandal-ridden Harding administration to the stability of Calvin Coolidge, in whom Mellon placed great personal confidence, also gave Republican tax cutters an added boost, as did new congressional victories the following year.[106]

To ensure popular support for Treasury's agenda, Mellon and his staff took their message directly to the American people. In April 1924, Mellon published a popular, trade book titled *Taxation: The People's Business.* Written with the assistance of his key assistants, including the Wilson administration holdover and former Cravath attorney S. Parker Gilbert, the book synthesized several of Mellon's earlier writings and popular press interviews to make the case for how and why tax cuts and reduced

[105] U.S. Treasury Department, *Annual Report of the Secretary of the Treasury on the State of the Finances for the Fiscal Year Ended June 30, 1920* (Washington, D.C.: Government Printing Office, 1921), 352–3.

[106] Leuchtenburg, *The Perils of Prosperity*; Cannadine, *Mellon*, 313–15.

government spending could benefit the entire nation. It quickly became a bestseller.[107]

The book reiterated Mellon's earlier claims about the unproductive nature of steeply progressive personal income taxes. Written for a broad audience, *Taxation* explained how the prevailing high rates led wealthy taxpayers to avoid their fair share of the tax burden by funneling resources to less productive, tax-exempt securities. "The history of taxation shows that taxes which are inherently excessive are not paid," wrote Mellon.

> The high rates inevitably put pressure upon the taxpayer to withdraw his capital from productive business and invest it in tax-exempt securities or to find other lawful methods of avoiding the realization of taxable income. The result is that the sources of taxation are drying up; wealth is failing to carry its share of the tax burden; and capital is being diverted into channels which yield neither revenue to the Government nor profit to the people.[108]

The solution, Mellon maintained, was to lower tax rates and decrease spending. This meant slashing all individual income tax rates and opposing social-welfare spending such as the World War I soldiers' bonus. Unsurprisingly, the book found a receptive audience among elite taxpayers and business organizations, which soon initiated an unprecedented national publicity campaign to back the Mellon Plan.[109]

The popular campaigns for the Mellon Plan, however, took some time to shape public opinion and influence political leaders. The 1924 Revenue Act, like its predecessor, did little to further Mellon's agenda. Pivotal progressive lawmakers, led by La Follette, Hull, and John Nance Garner (D-Tex.), successfully opposed dramatic tax cuts; they also prevailed in increasing wealth-transfer taxes and in authorizing the veteran's bonus over President Coolidge's initial veto.[110] Yet, the 1924 law was a short-lived political achievement. Just months after Coolidge grudgingly signed the new tax law, the Republican Party celebrated a new set of electoral victories on the heels of ever expanding economic prosperity. The Roaring Twenties were well on their way, and Mellon got much of the credit. He

107 Ratner, *Taxation and Democracy in America*; Andrew W. Mellon, *Taxation: The People's Business* (New York: Macmillan Co., 1924); Murray, "Bureaucracy and Bi-Partisanship in Taxation."

108 Mellon, *Taxation*, 13.

109 Murnane, "Selling Scientific Taxation," 834–6.

110 Revenue Act of 1924, 43 Stat. 253 (1924); Alstott and Novick, "War, Taxes, and Income Redistribution in the Twenties."

was even hailed by some as "the greatest Secretary of the Treasury since Alexander Hamilton."[111]

With the economy booming steadily, if unevenly, the grass-roots movement for the Mellon Plan began to gain momentum in 1925. Throughout the South and Midwest, tax clubs supporting the plan began lobbying Congress to adopt Mellon's central proposal of lowering personal income tax rates. J. A. Arnold of the American Tax League helped organize many of these tax clubs. Composed mainly of farmers, merchants, and rural mortgage bankers, the tax clubs targeted key congressional opponents of the Mellon Plan as part of their demands for tax cuts.[112] William R. Green (R-Wis.), the Ways and Means Committee Chair and progressive opponent of the Mellon Plan, characterized the tax clubs as "the most extraordinary, highly financed propaganda for a selfish purpose ... that has ever been known in the history of this country." Behind this seemingly popular uprising, Congress enacted two revenue acts, one in 1926 and another in 1928, that adopted several of Mellon's key recommendations, including an across-the-board tax cut that lowered the top individual surtax rate to 20 percent, an increase in personal income tax exemption levels, and a reduction in wealth-transfer taxes. At long last, Mellon could bask in the glory of his relentless efforts. "The income tax in this country," he proudly proclaimed, "has become a class rather than a national tax."[113]

Of course, the income tax had, from its origins, always been a class tax. What the Mellon Plan did, in essence, was concentrate the new direct tax regime on the truly affluent. As exemption levels climbed and miscellaneous excise taxes were repealed, it was mainly America's richest households that were underwriting federal government expenses. To be sure, many of the changes instituted by the Mellon Treasury diminished the scale and scope of the new tax system, especially the progressive rate structure. But other reforms also strengthened the new fiscal order and its commitment to maintaining an equitable distribution of the tax burden. The richest Americans, for instance, continued to pay nearly

[111] Leuchtenburg, *The Perils of Prosperity*, 98.

[112] Martin, *Rich People's Movement*, Chapter 2; Murnane, "Selling Scientific Taxation," 845–7.

[113] Ratner, *Taxation and Democracy in America*, 432; Revenue Act of 1926, 44 Stat. 9 (1926); Revenue Act of 1928, 45 Stat. 791 (1928); Cannadine, *Mellon*, 338; U.S. Treasury Department, *Annual Report of the Secretary of the Treasury on the State of the Finances for the year 1926* (Washington, D.C.: Government Printing Office, 1926), 12.

all federal personal taxes. Even though top marginal rates on individual income declined precipitously over the course of the decade, the growing economic prosperity meant that the richest households continued to face relatively stable effective rates that were well above prewar averages. As a result, the vast majority of income tax revenues came from the wealthiest Americans.[114]

Similarly, corporate tax rates reflected a concern for distributional justice. From the start, Mellon believed that the rich had a civic responsibility to contribute their fair share to the national Treasury. In his first annual report, he labeled the excess-profits tax and high personal rates as "clogs upon productive business," but he also stressed that these levies "should be replaced by other more equitable taxes upon incomes and profits." Given the prevailing assumption that corporate taxes were paid mainly by shareholders, Mellon specifically proposed using higher corporate income tax rates as a substitute for the excess-profits tax – a substitute that could sustain the distributional equilibrium of the new fiscal order. Consequently, general corporate income tax rates and revenues remained relatively high throughout the decade. It was not until the 1928 Revenue Act that the general corporate income tax rate was cut for the first time, and even then it was a negligible decline that kept the rate close to its wartime high of 12 percent.[115]

The distributional consequences of tax policy also continued to implicate concerns about fiscal citizenship. With the 1922 Fordney-McCumber Tariff reestablishing relatively high import duties, policymakers were well aware that a graduated income tax aimed mainly at the wealthiest citizens was a necessary counterbalance to the regressive consumption taxes paid by most ordinary Americans. The income tax, after all, was originally pushed as a way to restore the fiscal "equilibrium," as Edwin Seligman and Senator William Borah had put it.[116]

Like the government officials who preceded him, Mellon understood that the Treasury Department had a reciprocal obligation under the terms

[114] Marginal rates ranged from 11 to 73 percent in 1920, and declined to a range of 5 to 25 percent by 1929, but effective rates hovered around 9 percent throughout the decade, well above the prewar level of 3 percent. Brownlee, "Historical Perspective on U.S. Tax Policy," Table 2.3. Thomas Picketty and Emmanuel Saez, "Income Inequality in the United States, 1913–1998," *Quarterly Journal of Economics* 118:1 (2003), 1–39.

[115] U.S. Treasury Department, *Annual Report of the Secretary of the Treasury on the State of the Finances for the Fiscal Year Ended 1921* (Washington, D.C.: Government Printing Office, 1921), 352–3; Revenue Act of 1928, 45 Stat. 791 (1928).

[116] Edwin R. A. Seligman, *The Income Tax: A Study of the History, Theory, and Practice of Income Taxation at Home and Abroad* (New York: Macmillan Co., 1914), 640; *Congressional Record*, 63rd Cong., 1st sess. (1913) 50, part 4: 3838–40.

of fiscal citizenship to ensure that tax burdens were fairly distributed. This meant maintaining exemption levels that included even moderately affluent Americans. In 1925, when there was growing bipartisan support to raise income tax exemption levels, Mellon quickly quashed the idea. Not only would higher exemption levels compromise revenues. More importantly, they would permit well-off Americans to disengage from their civic and political duties. "As a matter of policy, it is advisable to have every citizen with a stake in his country," wrote Mellon. "Nothing brings home to a man the feeling that he personally has an interest in seeing that government revenues are not squandered, but intelligently expended, as the fact that he contributes individually a direct tax, no matter how small, to his government."[117] If ordinary Americans were expected to bear the incidence of import duties and miscellaneous excise taxes, Treasury had a responsibility to make sure that a class-based income tax touched those who had the greatest ability to pay.

In fact, Mellon backed the notion of securing a tax system based on the progressive principle of faculty or taxpaying ability, though he did so indirectly and with significant caveats. In the opening pages of *Taxation*, Mellon emphasized that "sound tax policy... must lessen, so far as possible, the burden of taxation on those least able to bear it." This clever inversion of the logic of "ability to pay" permitted Mellon to simultaneously back tax cuts and higher corporate taxes. Citing no less an authority than Adam Smith, Mellon further elaborated on how sound tax policies based on taxpaying ability needed to be judged in the broader context of economic conditions. "The principle that a man should pay taxes in accordance with his 'ability to pay' is sound," wrote Mellon, "but, like all other general statements, has its practical limitations and qualifications." When "it becomes evident that the sources of taxation is drying up and wealth is being diverted into unproductive channels, yielding neither revenue to the Government nor profit to the people, then it is time to readjust our basis of taxation upon sound principles." The readjustment that Mellon had in mind was, of course, to lower tax rates.[118]

The inherent self-interest of tax cuts proposed by one of the richest men in America was not lost on Mellon's detractors. Throughout the decade,

[117] U.S. Treasury Department, *Annual Report of the Secretary of the Treasury on the State of the Finances for the Fiscal Year Ended 1926* (Washington, D.C.: Government Printing Office, 1926), 6; Philip H. Love, *Andrew W. Mellon: The Man and His Work* (Baltimore: F. Heath Coggins and Co., 1929), 148–9.

[118] Mellon, *Taxation*, 9, 14–16.

congressional critics contended that the Mellon Plan was simply a self-serving attempt to benefit fellow millionaires, and to shift the burden of taxation back onto ordinary Americans. But the details of the Mellon Plan suggested otherwise.

The main goal was to maximize revenue while maintaining a relatively equitable distribution of the tax burden. After all, the tax cuts were intended to encourage the wealthy to generate *more* taxable income, not less. This fiscal pragmatism was also at the heart of Mellon's recommendation to tax income from labor at a lower rate than income from capital – a recommendation that was adopted as part of the 1924 Revenue Act. As we have seen, progressive political economists, most notably Henry C. Adams, had been making a similar case since at least the 1890s. Mellon agreed that equity required a tax preference for "earned" income. "The fairness of taxing more lightly incomes from wages, salaries and professional services than the incomes from business or from investments is beyond question," he wrote in *Taxation*. Labor income "is uncertain and limited in duration; sickness or death destroys it and old age diminishes it." By contrast, for the capitalist, "the source of income continues; the income may be disposed of during a man's life, and it descends to his heirs." Because the tax code had already provided a lower rate for capital gains, it was only fair that a larger benefit also be granted to labor income.[119]

Mellon backed a lower rate for "earned" income not because he had any sympathy for the laboring classes. He certainly had no solicitude for organized labor. Rather, as a fiscal conservative dedicated to balanced budgets, Mellon sought a specific tax preference for labor income for the same reason he endorsed tax cuts: to increase government revenue. Indeed, because nearly all ordinary workers were already exempt from the income tax, the labor income tax preference was really a benefit for upper-income professionals – the doctors, lawyers, merchants, and business managers whose salaries placed them within the lower rungs of the graduated tax ladder. Indeed, salaries were a significant portion of total individual income throughout the decade (see Table 7.2). Just as reduced top marginal rates could encourage wealthy citizens to invest in taxable securities, a tax benefit for "earned" income was intended to provide an added incentive for salaried professionals. Together, these tax changes were designed to encourage economic growth and provide the fiscal state with the additional revenue necessary to decrease war debts and balance annual budgets. From this perspective, the Mellon

[119] Ibid., 56–7.

TABLE 7.2. *Sources of Individual Income, 1916–1930 (nominal dollars in thousands and as percentage of total individual income)*

	1916		1920		1925		1930	
Salaries	$1,851,276	22%	$15,270,373	57%	$9,742,159	39%	$9,921,952	44%
Business*	$2,637,474	32%	$5,927,327	22%	$3,688,804	15%	$2,628,056	12%
Dividends	$2,136,468	26%	$2,735,845	10%	$3,464,624	14%	$4,197,303	19%
Interest	$667,566	8%	$1,709,299	6%	$1,814,402	7%	$1,940,437	9%
Rents	$601,919	7%	$1,047,423	4%	$1,471,332	6%	$974,325	4%
Other Personal Income**	$455,196	5%	–		$5,090,711	20%	$2,750,369	12%
Total Income	$8,349,901	100%	$26,690,269	100%	$25,272,034	100%	$22,412,445	100%

* Business income includes business, trade and commerce gains and profits.

** Other personal income includes partnership earnings and miscellaneous sources such as royalties.

Sources: U.S. Treasury Department, U.S. Internal Revenue, *Statistics of Income Compiled from the Returns for 1916, 1918, 1920, 1925, 1930* (Washington, D.C.: Government Printing Office, 1918, 1921, 1922, 1927, 1932).

Plan was arguably one of the first American attempts at what policy analysts decades later would refer to as "supply-side economics."[120]

Progressive Resolve and the Strengthening of Impartial Administrative Expertise

If the signature features of the Mellon Plan illustrated the paradoxical durability of the fiscal state, there were other parts of 1920s tax policy that displayed the progressive resolve of a minority of lawmakers. The legislative battles over wealth-transfer taxes, for instance, showed how a highly significant symbol of "soak-the-rich" taxation persisted well beyond the supposed rollback of the robust fiscal polity. Although the federal estate tax did not generate more than 4 percent of total national revenues, it remained a central part of tax law throughout the decade. In fact, as part of the initial congressional rebuke of the Mellon Plan, the 1924 Revenue Act even dramatically increased the top estate tax rate from 25 to 40 percent. This measure also introduced the first federal gift tax to prevent wealthy citizens from avoiding the estate tax. These progressive feats, like much of the congressional rebuff of Mellon, were ephemeral. Two years later, the gift tax was repealed, and estate tax rates were slashed and exemption levels were increased. By the end of the Twenties, only a tiny minority of the wealthiest American households paid these death duties.[121]

The stubborn persistence of the federal estate tax, however, demonstrated the extent of the modern fiscal order's new found stability. By nearly all accounts, there were few reasons to keep the estate tax. The levy raised little revenue at a time when lawmakers were seeking to pay down wartime debts. It was loathed by powerful citizens and government officials alike, particularly Mellon who sought to abolish the tax throughout his tenure as Treasury Secretary. And the federal estate tax competed

120 Veronique de Rugy, "Tax Rates and Tax Revenue, The Mellon Income Tax Cuts of the 1920s," *Cato Institute, Tax & Budget Bulletin*, 13 (February 2003); Gene Smiley and Richard H. Keehn, "Federal Personal Income Tax Policy in the 1920s" *Journal of Economic History* 55 (June 1995), 285–303; Bruce R. Bartlett, *Reaganomics: Supply Side Economics in Action* (New York: Quil, 1982); William Greider, *Secrets of the Temple: How the Federal Reserve Runs the Country* (New York: Simon & Schuster, 1989), 353.

121 Revenue Act of 1924, 43 Stat. 253 (1924); Revenue Act of 1926, 44 Stat. 9 (1926); Revenue Act of 1928, 45 Stat. 791 (1928). The 1924 Act had a graduated rate for the estate tax that began at 1 percent for estates in excess of $50,000 and reached a maximum of 40 percent for estates above $10 million. Blakey and Blakey, *Federal Income Tax*, 249–50.

with state-level inheritance taxes and thus triggered political pressures within the structures of American fiscal federalism – pressures that J. A. Arnold and the American Tax League attempted to exploit. Still, despite these strains, a determined group of progressive lawmakers led by Green and Garner were able to preserve the national estate tax in exchange for concessions to Mellon's relentless demands for lower individual rates.[122]

The preservation of the estate tax may have been a triumph of progressive politics. But a far more significant sign of the durability of the new fiscal state could be seen in the way the Treasury Department guarded the neutrality and professional nature of tax administration. Indeed, this is what Mellon meant by "scientific" tax reform. "Tax revision should never be made the football either of partisan or class politics," insisted Mellon, "but should be worked out by those who have made a careful study of the subject in its larger aspects and are prepared to recommend the course which, in the end, will prove for the country's best interest." These were not just platitudes for the Treasury Secretary. His words matched his actions. From the start, Mellon was committed to sustaining an unbiased and professionally administered fiscal bureaucracy. He had little faith, for instance, in the party politics surrounding protectionism. Though he did his part to make sure his companies were not left out of the tariff trough, he abhorred how congressional politics surrounding the duty list frequently trumped the expert knowledge of Treasury officials and in the process hindered fundamental tax reform.[123]

Given his background in banking and industry, it is no surprise that Mellon privileged professional ability over party affiliation. Though he was not above using his influence to help friends and family land positions within the federal government, just as McAdoo and the wartime Treasury lawyers had done, Mellon, like those wartime fiscal state-builders, drew the line at the overt politicization of the Treasury Department. This was a line that Mellon frequently policed vigilantly. When President Harding in 1921 attempted to install his friend James F. McConnochie as the internal revenue agent in charge of the District of New York, a crucial post responsible for overseeing hundreds of field agents, Mellon quashed the appointment on the grounds that McConnochie was a wholly unqualified,

122 Blakey and Blakey, *Federal Income Tax*, Chapter 10. The pressures of fiscal federalism led to the adoption of a federal tax credit for state inheritance taxes paid by citizens, which effectively provided state governments with an incentive to raise their own inheritance taxes. Martin, *Rich People's Movement*, Chapter 2.

123 Mellon, *Taxation*, 11.

political hack. In his place, the Secretary promoted from within, elevating a longtime staffer to the position.[124]

Mellon also defended the rights of qualified civil servants to retain their administrative posts regardless of their party politics. In the spring of 1922, the press was reporting that a recent Harding Treasury appointee and old friend, Elmer Dover, was in the process of orchestrating a "reorganization" of the BIR. Weeks earlier, Dover, who had been appointed by Harding without Mellon's knowledge, had conducted a similar "reorganization" of the Bureau of Engraving that was nothing short of a political purge, dismissing numerous career civil servants and replacing them with loyal Republicans. Dover proudly proclaimed that he and the president were seeking to "Hardingize the Government."[125]

Mellon quickly intervened to prevent the further politicization of the Treasury. "The affairs of the Treasury are of too great importance to allow of interference to its proper conduct through the introduction of petty politics," he wrote in an official press release. "This department particularly the collection of revenue and the handling of the public debt must be conducted on business principles and kept free at all times from detrimental influences." Though he acknowledged that Republicans had earned the right through their electoral victories to guide the Treasury according to Republican policies, he explained that "those Democrats who hold positions in the Treasury have been retained because of their qualifications for the office they hold, and I have no evidence of partisan activity on their part." The battle between Dover and Mellon came to a swift resolution, when the Treasury Secretary threatened to resign. In response, Harding announced in July 1922 that Dover would no longer be serving in the Treasury Department.[126]

The authority of impartial bureaucratic expertise was also enhanced through the institutions that were created during the 1920s. As part of the 1924 Act, Congress established the Board of Tax Appeals (BTA), an independent, quasi-judicial body charged with adjudicating disputes between taxpayers and the Treasury. The BTA had its origins in the many special committees that had been created during the war, including the Excess Profits Tax Advisory Committee, which first brought T. S. Adams and Arthur Ballantine to Washington. Daniel Roper had also suggested

124 Cannadine, *Mellon*, 283–5.

125 "Mellon Allays Fears of Revenue Employees: Tells Them Drastic Changes Are Not Planned – Clash with Dover Indicated," *New York Times*, April 5, 1922, 8.

126 "Mellon Refuses to Oust Democrats: Replies to Republican Petition That He Will Keep Efficient Treasury Officeholders," *New York Times*, June 16, 1922, 1. Cannadine, *Mellon*, 284–5.

a similar court to Russell Leffingwell as part of his postwar vision for the fiscal state. Yet unlike the earlier ad hoc administrative bodies, which were housed within and managed by the Treasury, the BTA had expert members that were appointed by the president with senatorial advice and consent. This provided a layer of neutrality in resolving the many tax controversies that were increasingly clogging the country's trial court dockets.[127]

A similar institutional innovation came with the creation of the Joint Committee on Internal Revenue Taxation. Designed to bring together key legislators from both the House Ways and Means Committee and the Senate Finance Committee, the joint committee was initially charged with simplifying the tax code and improving administration. Guided by its technical staff of fiscal experts, the joint committee soon took on the tasks of studying ways to reform the tax laws, drafting legislation, and acting as a general liaison between Treasury and both houses of Congress. As the tax code became increasingly complex, the joint committee's responsibilities and authority grew. By the end of the decade, lawmakers were commending "the splendid staff of experts employed by the committee," which included "many noted political economists," for their efforts in drafting legislation and rationalizing administrative provisions. "The work this committee has been doing," noted one legislator, "is on a much larger and more comprehensive scale than few if any of us realized when the committee was created."[128]

The 1920s congressional coalition of liberal Democrats and progressive Republicans that challenged many aspects of the Mellon Plan played a pivotal role in shaping the details of the decade's tax laws. Yet, they did so from a defensive posture. Given their limited numbers, progressive reformers and politicians found themselves parrying against conservative attacks rather than thrusting forward with their own fiscal agenda. As the economist and political commentator Henry R. Mussey noted at the time, this fragile coalition of reform leaders had "no apparent purpose to use the tax machinery to accomplish any well-defined social end."

[127] Blakey and Blakey, 543–5; Daniel C. Roper to Russell C. Leffingwell, October 17, 1919; Leffingwell to Roper, October 20, 1919; Roper to Leffingwell, Oct. 17, 1919, Record Group 56, Excess Profits Folder, NARA II. Harold Dubroff, *The United States Tax Court: An Historical Analysis* (Chicago: Commerce Clearing House, 1979).

[128] Blakey and Blakey, *Federal Income Tax*, 546–7; *Congressional Record*, 70th Cong., 2nd sess. (1929), 70, part 2:1198. For more on the historical origins of the Joint-Committee, see George K. Yin, "James Couzens, Andrew Mellon, the 'Greatest Suit in the History of the World,' and Creation of the Joint Committee on Taxation and Its Staff," *Tax Law Review* 66 (forthcoming).

Massey predicted that these activists and lawmakers "may embarrass the Old Guard, but their victories will be empty."[129]

Mussey was only partially correct. The new liberals in Congress, like their counterparts in the academy and the juridical realm, did much more than just embarrass the Old Guard. And their victories were hardly hollow. As a whole, progressive tax reformers in the 1920s were able to sacrifice the formal, programmatic retrenchment of the graduated rate structure in exchange for securing the systemic base of the new fiscal polity. Former Treasury lawyers, federal judges, treatise writers, and even law professors successfully participated in the gradual juridical acceptance of a new fiscal order that was, as Ballantine observed, "unquestionably here to stay."

Ordinary Americans and their congressional representatives, likewise, spoke up on behalf of the new tax regime. Though more dissenting voices were unsuccessful in making excess-profits taxation a permanent part of postwar American law and political economy, their opposition to the sales tax helped foreclose – for better or worse – the possibility of an alternative national revenue source. Meanwhile, public finance theorists within the academy did their part to buttress the conceptual commitment to the direct and graduated tax regime, even if, in the process, they may have unwittingly colored the fiscal imagination of future revenue reformers.

Even when key elements of the Mellon Plan were implemented successfully in the second half of the decade, the formal erosion of graduated rates belied how the underlying structural features of Mellon's proposals sustained crucial aspects of the new fiscal state. Though the excess-profits tax was quickly repealed, the corporate income tax remained vibrant. Despite the demands to abolish the estate tax, it too remained a stable, if merely symbolic, part of the tax system. And Mellon's protection of the professional autonomy of the BIR also solidified the administrative aspects of the new fiscal polity. Republicans themselves seemed to understand the irreversible, path-dependent development of the fiscal state. After all, this was part of Mellon's point in containing the exuberance of tax-cutting colleagues like Will Hays. As John Dewey had intimated, no matter how much of the graduated rate structure withered away, the overall progressive tax movement would never go backward.

[129] Henry Raymond Mussey, "The Fiscal Ponus Asinorum," *The Nation* (October 26, 1921), 469. Rader, "Federal Taxation in the 1920s," 432–3.

Conclusion

By the end of the 1920s, the central foundations of a new fiscal order were securely in place. What had begun decades earlier as a series of social movements against the prevailing system of regressive, hidden, politicized, and ineffectual taxes gradually crystalized over the course of three generations into an intellectual, legal, and administrative revolution – one that dramatically changed the distribution of fiscal burdens, the meaning of fiscal citizenship, the regime of American governance, and the opportunities for an activist state. Writing in 1927, toward the end of a long and illustrious academic career that paralleled the span of the progressive tax reform movement, Edwin R. A. Seligman reflected on how changing economic conditions had provided the crucial context for the profound turn-of-the-century transformation. Resorting to his well-known economic determinism, the Columbia professor explained how all levels of American government could now enjoy the fruits of a highly productive, equitable, and efficient revenue regime. Seligman singled out how the federal government had "come to rely principally upon direct taxes – the income tax and the estate tax."[1]

But there was a downside, Seligman warned, to the consolidation of the new fiscal order. Because state governments had also come to rely on income and inheritance taxes along with taxes on transactions and gasoline, there was some conflict over "largely identical, or at least equivalent, sources of revenue." Vertical competition between states and the federal government, to be sure, had always been a latent tension within the modern tax reform movement. After all, the conceptual, juridical, and bureaucratic shift at the heart of the new fiscal polity was meant to encapsulate all levels of American statecraft. But, as we have seen, the modern forces of centralization often compelled policymakers to defer

[1] Edwin R. A. Seligman, "Need for Readjusting the Fiscal System of the United States," *Annals of the American Academy of Political and Social Science*, 129 (1927), 1–8, 6.

to the authority of higher levels of governance. Just as state tax commissions sought to pull power away from politically appointed, local property assessors in the name of greater administrative efficiency, the U.S. Treasury exercised a similar prerogative over states and commonwealths. The national inheritance and estate taxes adopted during the Spanish-American War and World War I, and secured during the 1920s, Seligman noted, were examples of this centralizing tendency.[2]

Still, the centralization of fiscal authority was met with continued resistance. Seligman directed his 1927 essay at those who stood in the way. Such opposition, for him, was futile. The nation's long fiscal history revealed how changing economic circumstances had determined the shape of the new tax regime. Now, there was no turning back. "Let us no longer be guided by the lawyers who so often look backwards, and whose hands are tied by effete constitutional traditions," Seligman advised. "Let us no longer listen to the politicians who weary us with their old slogans and out-worn shibboleths. Let us study the actual economic conditions, and especially the ownership and distribution of wealth as among individuals and classes; for these are the things of fundamental importance."[3]

Seligman surely exaggerated the role of economic conditions and underestimated the efficacy of law and politics. "Actual economic conditions" provided a pivotal context for fiscal reform. But it was populist social activists, progressive political economists, powerful insurgent lawmakers, and astute government bureaucrats who responded to the disparity in "the ownership and distribution of wealth," and who in the end seized the opportunities provided by changing material circumstances to build the intellectual, legal, and administrative foundations of the modern American fiscal state.

The contested and contingent process of fiscal state-building began with the growing social antagonism toward the *ancien* tax regime. Gradually, populist groups and independent political parties were able to overcome their initially fragmented and halting views on taxation to support the progressive tax reform movement. Reacting to this social unrest and to the growing inequalities of the time, a new school of American political economists began to challenge the prevailing assumptions about the so-called "natural" relations among state, society, and economy. In so doing, these progressive theorists helped lead a conceptual revolution in American public finance by touting the superiority of a tax system

[2] Ibid., 6.
[3] Ibid., 8.

based on the principle of "ability to pay." Although the privileging of ability-to-pay logic would in the long run have some unanticipated and perverse implications for the stunted development of the American fiscal state, these reform-minded economists and activists had little choice but to react to the institutional context and the sequence of historical events that they inherited. "Men make their own history," Karl Marx famously noted, "but they do not make it just as they please; they do not make it under circumstances chosen by themselves, but under circumstances directly found, given and transmitted from the past."[4]

Meanwhile, fiscal reformers at the state and local levels were similarly confronting the legacies of the past as they engaged in a parallel battle to improve the subnational tax system. Loath to give up on the property tax, these activists first attempted to save this traditional levy on wealth through a number of administrative reforms. These organizational experiments, in turn, opened up new possibilities for industrial states and commonwealths to try novel sources of revenue, including direct taxes on individual incomes, business profits, and wealth transfers – all levies based on the notion of ability to pay. Thus, once again, the ideas and arguments of the progressive public finance economists came into play. In due time, the innovative fiscal ideas and the reimagined sense of civic obligations that these new concepts entailed gained traction among influential policymakers at all levels of government, at least until the Great Depression forced many states to reconsider their commitment to an income tax base.

The historical process of reforming the fiscal system faced numerous obstacles, to be sure. None was more formidable than the U.S. Supreme Court's 1895 invalidation of the first peacetime federal income tax. Yet, rather than spelling the end of the progressive tax reform movement, the Court's decision became a renewed rallying cry that empowered and galvanized revenue reformers. Led once again by the reform-minded economists, activists prodded populist and progressive lawmakers to redouble their efforts in response to the Supreme Court. Reformers and lawmakers pointed to the growing powers of Big Business and the attendant rising social anxiety toward corporate capitalism to push for a constitutional amendment along with a new corporate excise tax. Eventually, the ratification of the Sixteenth Amendment and the subsequent enactment of the 1913 income tax law solidified the legal basis of the emerging fiscal polity.

4 Karl Marx, "The Eighteenth Brumaire of Louis Bonparte," in *The Marx-Engels Reader*, 2nd ed., ed. Robert C. Tucker (New York: W. W. Norton & Co., 1978), 594–617, 595.

Once the legal foundations were set, U.S. entry into the Great War provided government officials with a renewed context in which to build the bureaucratic capacity necessary to maintain and consolidate the powers of the nascent fiscal state. It was during the war emergency that an entrepreneurial group of Treasury Department lawyers helped create, manage, and defend the substantive laws and administrative machinery of the nascent tax regime. The corporatism of the war certainly provided the "actual economic conditions" for a major change in American public finance, yet the ultimate shape of this change was determined by the actions of key historical figures and by the momentum of decades of social protest and intellectual agitation.

During the postwar decade, resistance to the fiscal polity took on new strength. The political ascendancy of conservative lawmakers marked a new era of retrenchment. Even so, by the 1920s the foundations of the modern fiscal state were well established. Though opponents of the new tax system were able to diminish the graduated rate structure, the rhetorical demands for a "return to normalcy" contradicted the intellectual and institutional continuity that existed between the earlier periods of revolt and the new postwar era. Not only did economic conditions and progressive resolve prevent the new fiscal polity from withering away, certain aspects of the new tax regime, such as the taxation of corporate income and the commitment to taxing wealth transfers, persisted in the face of other political and economic rollbacks. An incremental and contested process that had begun in the 1880s as a direct reaction to what Seligman referred to as the unequal "ownership and distribution of wealth" culminated in the 1920s with the paradoxical achievements of a new fiscal order.

The development of the modern American fiscal state did not, of course, end in the 1920s. Although the turn-of-the-century transformation provided the foundations for a fiscal regime that has remained with us today, there were two subsequent periods in the twentieth century when the fiscal polity underwent similarly dramatic changes. The first came during the height of the Second World War when the "class tax" that Treasury Secretary Andrew Mellon celebrated and helped preserve in the 1920s was transformed into a "mass tax" that touched tens of millions of American households. Initially, Franklin D. Roosevelt's New Deal attempted to continue the existing policy of requiring those with the greatest tax-paying ability to finance the bulk of federal spending. Yet, over time, as New Deal structural critiques of modern industrial capitalism gave way to a more accommodating approach toward political economy, tax policy appeared to follow suit. As New Deal liberalism shifted toward a focus on Keynesianism and leveraging the powers of mass consumption, the tax system similarly shifted from a "class tax" to a "mass tax."[5] The depths of the Great Depression – which itself was initially triggered in part by a return to a high-tariff regime – and the revenue demands of a second global conflict were too cataclysmic for the narrow, "soak-the-rich" tax laws and policies to continue. Governments at all levels across the United States were pressed.

The Second World War, a much longer and more expensive conflict than the Great War, thus precipitated an expansion of the direct and graduated tax system. This marked the second great transformation in American fiscal history. Income tax exemption levels dropped and top marginal rates once again soared to historic highs. The excess-profits tax reemerged, and wealth-transfer taxes were strengthened. These changes, particularly the drop in exemption levels, forced more and more American households onto federal tax rolls. Consequently, the new mass income tax system hastened the social legitimacy and cultural acceptance of the American warfare state.[6]

Nevertheless, the roots of the World War II tax regime could be traced back to the intellectual, legal, and administrative foundations created earlier in the century. The mass income tax, after all, was still premised on the notion of taxpaying capacity. The exigencies of war and the demands of Big Government simply meant that a larger number of Americans had an increased civic duty to take on a shared sense of national sacrifice and the more general obligations of fiscal citizenship. Franklin Roosevelt's relentless commitment to the principle of ability to pay translated into a staunch opposition to the sales tax, which was considered again as a source of federal revenue during the 1940s.[7] The continued rejection of a national sales tax demonstrated how the blinkered visions of an earlier

[5] Alan Brinkley, *The End of Reform: New Deal Liberalism in Recession and War* (New York: Vintage Books, 1995); W. Elliot Brownlee, *Federal Taxation in America: A Short History* (New York: Cambridge University Press, 2004); 107–19; Joseph J. Thorndike, *Their Fair Share: Taxing the Rich in the Age of FDR* (Washington, D.C.: Urban Institute Press, 2012).

[6] Bartholomew H. Sparrow, *From the Outside In: World War II and the American State* (Princeton: Princeton University Press, 1996); James T. Sparrow, *Warfare State: World War II Americans and the Age of Big Government* (New York: Oxford University Press, 2011), 122–33.

[7] Mark Leff, *The Limits of Symbolic Reform: The New Deal and Taxation, 1933–1939* (New York: Cambridge University Press, 1984); Lawrence Zelenak, *Learning to Love*

generation of theorists and policymakers persisted, how the fiscal myopia of previous years continued to limit the vision of later generations.

Similarly, the World War II fiscal regime was in many ways a rearticulation of the legal and policy principles that guided World War I lawmakers. Even before the United States officially entered the Second World War, former World War I Treasury officials like Arthur A. Ballantine were touting the effectiveness of levies such as the excess-profits tax, which reemerged during World War II as a dominant source of national revenues.[8] In the end, neither wartime regime required a fundamental change to the juridical system – that change had already been established with the Sixteenth Amendment and the first set of peacetime direct and graduated taxes. Finally, although the bureaucratic capacity of the Treasury Department increased at an explosive rate during World War II, even these changes were merely extensions, albeit on a grand scale, of the patterns first exhibited during the Great War. In short, though the latter war dramatically altered the relationship between state and society, that transformation was an expansion not a departure from the earlier, formative period of development.

If the Second World War tax regime was built on the earlier foundations, the third great transformation in American public finance came as a direct assault on that fundamental framework. In the last quarter of the twentieth century, a new fiscal paradigm began to take hold. As part of what historian Daniel T. Rodgers has called an "Age of Fracture," the tax laws and policies of this period expressed a deteriorating sense of social responsibility and democratic obligation. During this era "strong metaphors of society," writes Rodgers, "were supplanted by weaker ones. Imagined collectivities shrank; notions of structure and power thinned out." The greater sense of belonging that had helped create and nurture the new fiscal order began to wane.[9]

The dissolution of society as a national community was expressed in the anti-tax policies and anti-statist ideology that came to rule the times.

Form 1040: Two Cheers for the Return-Based Mass Income Tax (Chicago: University of Chicago Press, 2013), Ch. 5.

[8] Arthur A. Ballantine, "War Policies in Taxation, Statement before the War Policies Commission," May 20, 1931, Record Group 56 – General Records of the Office of the Secretary of the Treasury, Box 187, Folder "Tax – Excess Profits & War Profits. 1923–32." National Archives and Record Administration II, College Park, Md.; Stuart D. Brandes, *Warhogs: A History of War Profits in America* (Lexington: University Press of Kentucky, 1997).

[9] Daniel T. Rodgers, *The Age of Fracture* (Cambridge, Mass.: Harvard University Press, 2011), 3.

Beginning in the 1970s, the structural emergence of stagflation signaled the end to an "era of easy finance" – the end of a prolonged postwar period of robust economic growth that had permitted increased discretionary spending without increased taxes.[10] The economic slowdown, in turn, fueled popular resentments that led to new institutional constraints on state-level property tax rates, constraints that began with California's Proposition 13 and soon swept through states across the country. A concomitant revival of free market ideology on an epic scale also meant that tax cuts and "supply-side" economic theories became the dominant objectives and rationales of national fiscal policymaking. As a result, appeals to taxing citizens based on their "ability to pay" became increasingly rare. When they were articulated, they generally fell on deaf ears. Even after the crisis of 9/11 and the subsequent conflicts in Afghanistan and Iraq heralded the potential for a revival of patriotic duties and concern for the common good, the disintegration of the social continued apace. "Nothing is more important in the face of war," announced one key Republican lawmaker, "than tax cuts."[11]

There is no denying that times have changed, and that ideas and beliefs about our fiscal polity have changed with them. Still, even the recent conservative, anti-statist revolts against taxation – whether they are seen as grass-roots limitations on state property taxes or as more amorphous and at times contradictory anti-tax claims made by the "Tea Party" movement – share a link with the roots of our modern fiscal polity.[12] That link

[10] C. Eugene Steuerle, "Financing the American State at the Turn of the Century," in *Funding the Modern American State, 1941–1995: The Rise and Fall of the Era of Easy Finance*, ed. W. Elliot Brownlee (Washington, D.C.: Woodrow Wilson Center Press, 1996), 409–44. This period was also marked by the dominance of Keynesian thinking, which relied on tax policy to help manage the macro economy and the business cycle. Brinkley, *End of Reform*; Herbert Stein, *The Fiscal Revolution in America* (Washington, D.C.: AEI Press, 1990).

[11] Rodgers, *The Age of Fracture*, Chapter 1; Isaac William Martin, *The Permanent Tax Revolt: How the Property Tax Transformed American Politics* (Stanford: Stanford University Press, 2008); "The Budge Fight Is Now," *New York Times*, April 3, 2003, A20. On the importance of elite rhetoric to the rise of a tax-cutting political culture, see Andrea Louise Campbell, "What Americans Think of Taxes," in *The New Fiscal Sociology: Taxation in Comparative and Historical Perspective*, ed. Isaac William Martin, et al. (New York: Cambridge University Press, 2009), 48–67.

[12] Jacob S. Hacker and Paul Pierson, "Tax Politics and the Struggle over Activist Government," in *The Transformation of American Politics: Activist Government and the Rise of Conservatism*, ed. Paul Pierson and Theda Skocpol (Princeton: Princeton University Press, 2006), 256–80; Theda Skocpol and Vanessa Williamson, *The Tea Party and the Remaking of Republican Conservatism* (New York: Oxford University Press, 2012).

may be tenuous, but it is no less real. The recent revolts are a reaction to the turn-of-the-century fiscal transformation. The intellectual, legal, and administrative origins of our fiscal polity continue to set the agenda for today's conservative uprisings.

The early-twentieth-century foundations also continue to shape current debates about tax policy and the relationship between citizens and the state. The rise of the New Right, like the formal fiscal retrenchment of the 1920s, is a belated response to the social democratic victories of an earlier era. And just as Andrew Mellon had to come to grips with his institutional context and the sequence of historical events he inherited, so too have the heirs of the Reagan Revolution acknowledged the limits of their achievements. For all the talk about tax cuts, a commitment to the notion of ability to pay continues to resonate among many Americans. Popular opinion polls continue to show that most Americans support increased taxation on the rich. Despite all the claims to "starve the beast," the modern fiscal polity has endured.[13] The long history of the making of the modern fiscal state, chronicled in the previous pages, continues to press upon the thinking of today.

Yet one could still claim today that the story told in this book about law, politics, and the making of the American fiscal state is a tale of lost opportunities – that the early intentions of progressive tax reformers have been marginalized, and that our current tax system is simply a muddle of incoherent, special interest giveaways and loopholes. There is certainly some truth to that popular perception. But such a perspective is remarkably ahistorical. Judging the American fiscal state based solely on what it does not do today obscures what it did do during its early years. The effective displacement of a regressive, hidden, and highly politicized tax system was in and of itself a tremendous achievement. That accomplishment may have lost some luster over the years, but it can still remind us of what was, and is, possible.

Roughly a century after the establishment of the modern fiscal state, many scholars have concluded today that our current income-based tax system is an economically inefficient means of raising public revenue. In

[13] C. Eugene Steuerle, *Contemporary Tax Policy* (Washington, D.C.: Urban Institute Press, 2008), 3; Bruce Bartlett, *The Benefit and the Burden: Tax Reform – Why We Need It and What It Will Take* (New York: Simon & Schuster, 2012), 226–9; Greg M. Shaw and Laura Gaffey, "American Public Opinion on Economic Inequality, Taxes, and Mobility: 1900–2011," *Public Opinion Quarterly* 76:3 (2012), 576–96; William A. Niskanen, "Limiting Government: The Failure of 'Starve the Beast,'" *Cato Journal* (fall 2006), 553–8.

calling for a shift to a progressive consumption tax, these economic evaluations illustrate the sharp analytical logic that often drives most current academic and policy debates.[14] Yet, these models elide the complex historical and incremental development of the political, economic, and social ideas and institutions within which current policymakers must operate. In their ahistorical assessments, these current studies frequently overlook how earlier conceptions of fiscal citizenship, social belonging, and collective responsibility drove Progressive-Era tax reformers to stress the significance of a robust public sphere.[15] Clouded by the anti-statist rhetoric and anti-tax ideology that appears to dominate present debate, most ordinary Americans, likewise, have lost sight of how and why activists from earlier generations searched for a stronger source of financing for the positive state.

As the current income tax system marks its centennial, lawmakers and politicians have taken every opportunity to decry the failings of the present system. In the name of "tax reform," political leaders have vowed to rectify these defects with fundamental changes to the progressive income tax regime. Recent calls for a "flat tax," for instance, exemplify the current assault against the principles of direct and progressive taxation.[16] Meanwhile, the turn of the twenty-first century has brought with it a new era of rising inequality.[17] As the United States enters a second Gilded Age,

[14] See, e.g., Daniel S. Goldberg, *The Death of the Income Tax: A Progressive Consumption Tax and a Path to Fiscal Reform* (New York: Oxford University Press, 2013); Alan D. Viard and Robert Carroll, *Progressive Consumption Taxation: The X-tax Revisited* (Lanham, Md.: Rowman & Littlefield, 2012); Joseph Bankman and David A. Weisbach, "The Superiority of an Ideal Consumption Tax over an Ideal Income Tax," *Stanford Law Review* 58:5 (2006), 1413–56; Laurence S. Seidman, *The USA Tax: A Progressive Consumption Tax* (Cambridge, Mass.: MIT Press, 1997). By contrast, other public finance experts have recently come out in support of higher marginal income tax rates, while acknowledging the political and social constraints that accompany present-day policymaking. Peter Diamond and Emmanuel Saez, "The Case for a Progressive Tax: From Basic Research to Policy Recommendations," *Journal of Economic Perspectives* 25:4 (2011), 165–90.

[15] One recent tax reform proposal, calling for an income tax on wealthy Americans supplemented by a value-added tax, echoes what the U.S. tax system might have looked like in the 1920s if a national sales tax was adopted to supplement the income tax. Michael J. Graetz, *100 Million Unnecessary Returns: A Simple, Fair, and Competitive Tax Plan for the United States* (New Haven: Yale University Press, 2008).

[16] Neal Boortz and John Linder, *The Fair Tax Book: Saying Goodbye to the Income Tax and the IRS* (New York: Regan Books, 2005); Steve Forbes, *Flat Tax Revolution: Using a Postcard to Abolish the IRS* (Washington, D.C.: Regnery Publishers, 2005).

[17] For more on rising inequality and its causes, see Thomas Piketty and Emmanuel Saez, "Income Inequality in the United States, 1913–1998," *Quarterly Journal of Economics* 118:1 (2003), 1–39; "How Progressive Is the U.S. Federal Tax System? A Historical and

new social movements – representing the "99 percent" – have once again emerged to challenge the growing concentrations of wealth and opportunity. As these new movements search for ways to combat the seemingly inexorable forces of our post-industrial condition, it may be instructive to look back at the first Gilded Age, and how an earlier generation of progressive activists responded to changing circumstances by envisioning and implementing dramatic reforms.[18]

By turning to an earlier period in American history, when serious comprehensive tax reform was not only conceived but also achieved, we can recall the emotional and imaginative energies, the social and economic conditions, and the political will necessary for fundamental fiscal reform. In the process, we can appreciate the hard-fought roots of our current tax system and the social and economic justice ideals that it represents, as well as the unintended and paradoxical consequences of an earlier generation of thinkers and policymakers. In this sense, this study about the making of the modern American fiscal state is about much more than just the intellectual, legal, and administrative foundations of a new form of governance. It is ultimately a tale about American democracy – about the winners and losers of a process seeking to change the structures of wealth and opportunity in the United States.

International Perspective," *Journal of Economic Perspectives* 21:1 (2007), 3–24; Paul Pierson and Jacob S. Hacker, *Winner-Take-All Politics: How Washington Made the Rich Richer – and Turned Its Back on the Middle Class* (New York: Simon & Schuster, 2010).

[18] Larry M. Bartels, *Unequal Democracy: The Political Economy of the New Gilded Age* (Princeton: Princeton University Press, 2008); Sarah Van Gelder, *This Changes Everything: Occupy Wall Street and the 99% Movement* (San Francisco: Berrett-Koehler, 2011).

Index